A Book Of

PHARMACEUTICAL ORGANIC CHEMISTRY

SIMPLIFIED

For

F. Y. B. Pharm [Semester I and II]
As Per New Revised Syllabus of Pune University

Dr. K. S. Jain
M. Pharm., Ph.D., FIC
Principal and Professor
Jain Vidya Prasarak Mandal's
Rasiklal M. Dhariwal Institute of Pharmaceutical Education and Research (RMDIPER)
Chinchwad Station, Pune 411 019

Dr. P. B. Miniyar
M. Pharm., Ph.D., FAGE
Professor and Vice-Principal
Sinhgad Technical Education Society's
Sinhgad Institute of Pharmacy, Narhe, Pune - 411 041

Dr. A. R. Shaikh
M. Pharm., Ph.D., FIC
Associate Professor
MET Bujbal Knowledge City
Institute of Pharmacy, Nashik - 422 003

N1672

PHARMACEUTICAL ORGANIC CHEMISTRY-SIMPLIFIED (Sem. I & II)   ISBN 978-93-5164-003-5

Second Edition : August, 2015
© : Authors

The text of this publication, or any part thereof, should not be reproduced or transmitted in any form or stored in any computer storage system or device for distribution including photocopy, recording, taping or information retrieval system or reproduced on any disc, tape, perforated media or other information storage device etc., without the written permission of Authors with whom the rights are reserved. Breach of this condition is liable for legal action.

Every effort has been made to avoid errors or omissions in this publication. In spite of this, errors may have crept in. Any mistake, error or discrepancy so noted and shall be brought to our notice shall be taken care of in the next edition. It is notified that neither the publisher nor the authors or seller shall be responsible for any damage or loss of action to any one, of any kind, in any manner, therefrom.

Published By :
NIRALI PRAKASHAN
Abhyudaya Pragati, 1312, Shivaji Nagar
Off J.M. Road, Pune – 411005
Tel - (020) 25512336/37/39, Fax - (020) 25511379
Email : niralipune@pragationline.com

Printed By :
Repro Knowledgecast Limited
Thane

♦ DISTRIBUTION CENTRES

PUNE
Nirali Prakashan : 119, Budhwar Peth, Jogeshwari Mandir Lane, Pune 411002, Maharashtra
Tel : (020) 2445 2044, 66022708, Fax : (020) 2445 1538
Email : bookorder@pragationline.com, niralilocal@pragationline.com
Nirali Prakashan : S. No. 28/27, Dhyari, Near Pari Company, Pune 411041
Tel : (020) 24690204 Fax : (020) 24690316
Email : dhyari@pragationline.com, bookorder@pragationline.com

MUMBAI
Nirali Prakashan : 385, S.V.P. Road, Rasdhara Co-op. Hsg. Society Ltd.,
Girgaum, Mumbai 400004, Maharashtra
Tel : (022) 2385 6339 / 2386 9976, Fax : (022) 2386 9976
Email : niralimumbai@pragationline.com

♦ DISTRIBUTION BRANCHES

JALGAON
Nirali Prakashan : 34, V. V. Golani Market, Navi Peth, Jalgaon 425001,
Maharashtra, Tel : (0257) 222 0395, Mob : 94234 91860

KOLHAPUR
Nirali Prakashan : New Mahadvar Road, Kedar Plaza, 1st Floor Opp. IDBI Bank
Kolhapur 416 012, Maharashtra. Mob : 9850046155

NAGPUR
Pratibha Book Distributors : Above Maratha Mandir, Shop No. 3, First Floor,
Rani Jhanshi Square, Sitabuldi, Nagpur 440012, Maharashtra
Tel : (0712) 254 7129

DELHI
Nirali Prakashan : 4593/21, Basement, Aggarwal Lane 15, Ansari Road, Daryaganj
Near Times of India Building, New Delhi 110002
Mob : 08505972553

BENGALURU
Pragati Book House : House No. 1, Sanjeevappa Lane, Avenue Road Cross,
Opp. Rice Church, Bengaluru – 560002.
Tel : (080) 64513344, 64513355, Mob : 9880582331, 9845021552
Email: bharatsavla@yahoo.com

CHENNAI
Pragati Books : 9/1, Montieth Road, Behind Taas Mahal, Egmore,
Chennai 600008 Tamil Nadu, Tel : (044) 6518 3535,
Mob : 94440 01782 / 98450 21552 / 98805 82331,
Email : bharatsavla@yahoo.com

niralipune@pragationline.com | www.pragationline.com
Also find us on www.facebook.com/niralibooks

Foreword ...

I have read the book "Pharmaceutical Organic Chemistry - Simplified (Sem. I and II)" written by Dr. K. S. Jain, Dr. P. B. Miniyar and Dr. A. R. Shaikh, for Nirali publication, Pune. Each of the authors has rich experience in teaching the subject with a few books already to their credit. This book has been written for the students of first year B. Pharm. and consists of 18 chapters following the revised syllabus of the first year B. Pharmacy course implemented by University of Pune, with effect from the academic year 2013-14.

The style of presentation of this book is such that, it will not only give a deeper understanding of the subject, but also overcome the fright of the beginners for the subject. Keeping in mind the importance of the subject-organic chemistry, the authors have indeed made the contents of the chapters very simple, lucid and easy to understand with numerous figures, examples and illustrations. I feel the book shall be liked by both the students, as well as, the subject teachers for its unique quality and style of presentation, lucid explanatory language, as well as, complete coverage of the syllabus. There are question banks provided at the end of each of the chapters, solving which shall help the students to face the exams with much confidence.

I congratulate the authors for bringing out this book and wish them the very best of the success in this endeavour.

Dr. C. J. Shishoo, B.Pharm., M.S.(IOWA), Ph.D.
Former Principal, L. M. College of Pharmacy, Ahmedabad
Former Director NIPER, Ahmedabad
Former Director, B. V. Patel PERD Centre Ahmedabad
Trustee, CERC, Ahmedabad

Preface ...

It is with great gratitude towards all students and teachers for such a great response and acceptance to the first edition of this book.

Organic chemistry is one such subject in the Pharmacy curriculum which, if grasped and digested systematically and sincerely, not only prepares the student for just the exams, but expands his/her thinking horizons and abilities, effectively to inculcate unique sense of confidence in him/her to face practical challenges of future career. This subject lays a foundation for many other subjects like, medicinal chemistry, drug synthesis, drug design, biochemistry, phytochemistry, pharmaceutical analysis, as well as, gives better understanding of some other subjects of pharmacy, directly or indirectly. If approached in a sincere way, it can be a friendly subject to score or else can give nightmares during exams. It is often criticized and commented particularly, in the industry that pharmacy students are weak in this subject.

These above facts laid the foundation and conceptualization of this book Pharmaceutical Organic Chemistry Simplified (Sem. I and II) to be written by us. Though, there are a plethora of books by many Indian and a foreign author on this subject, this book is unique in its style and presentation. We have indeed made the contents of the chapters very simple, easy to understand with numerous figures, examples and illustrations and adhered to 18 chapters and their contents in same order, as per, the revised syllabus of the First year B. Pharmacy course implemented by University of Pune, w.e.f. the academic year 2013-14.

We expect good and positive response for this book by both the students, as well as, the subject teachers for its quality and style of presentation, contents and lucid explanatory language. The coverage of syllabus is complete and sincere reading and solving of questions provided in the question banks, can assure the students of a good grasp of the basics, as well as, gaining confidence to appear for any viva voce or exam.

Special thanks to Ms Neeta Shinde for help in revision of this edition.

We wish enjoyable learning for the students and satisfactory teaching for the teachers of the subject- Organic chemistry.

Authors

Date : 15th August 2015 (Independence Day)

Contents ...

Semester I

1. **Basic Principles and Concepts of Organic Chemistry** — 1.1 – 1.30
2. **Classification of Organic Compounds** — 2.1 – 2.30
3. **Structure Property Relationship** — 3.1 – 3.18
4. **Classes of Reactions and Classes of Reagents** — 4.1 – 4.14
5. **Reaction Intermediates** — 5.1 – 5.18
6. **Acidity and Basicity** — 6.1 – 6.16
7. **Alkanes** — 7.1 – 7.10
8. **Alkenes and Alkynes** — 8.1 – 8.22
9. **Benzene and Aromaticity** — 9.1 – 9.28

Semester II

1. **Aldehydes and Ketones** — 1.1 – 1.28
2. **Phenols** — 2.1 – 2.14
3. **Sulfonic Acids** — 3.1 – 3.6
4. **Alcohols and Ethers** — 4.1 – 4.14
5. **Amines** — 5.1 – 5.14
6. **Cyanides and Isocyanides** — 6.1 – 6.4
7. **Esters and Amides** — 7.1 – 7.10
8. **Alkyl Halides** — 8.1 – 8.22
9. **Carboxylic acids (Aromatic and Aliphatic)** — 9.1 – 9.32
   Index — I.1 – I.2

SEMESTER - I

SEMESTER - II

Chapter 1 ...

BASIC PRINCIPLES AND CONCEPTS OF ORGANIC CHEMISTRY

CONTENTS

Atomic and molecular orbitals, Hybridization of atomic orbitals of carbon, Nitrogen and oxygen to form molecular orbitals, Covalent bond, Electronegativity, Bond fission, Hydrogen bonding, Theory of reaction mechanism, Bond energy, Inductive effect, Steric effect, Electromeric effect, Mesomeric effect and resonance effect, Hyperconjugation, Concept of tautomerism and types.

ATOMIC ORBITALS

The precise location and the moment of an electron cannot be simultaneously determined. This means that we can never say exactly where an electron is at a given moment. We can only describe its probable location; as an **atomic orbital**

An **atomic orbital** is a 3-dimensional region or space around the atomic nucleus where probability of finding the electron is more i.e., the region where the electron spends more time. Also called as *"electron cloud of negative charge"* or simply as *"electron density"*. The shape of electron cloud is the shape of the orbital.

Different orbitals of various sub-shells have different shapes. e.g., **s-orbital** is spherical, **p-orbital** is dumb-bell shaped, while **d** and **f orbitals** are with more complicated geometrical shapes.

1. **The s-orbitals (s-subshell):**

    Subtypes 1s, 2s, 3s, 4s and so on. For each energy level or shell there is one s-orbital. A s orbital has the shape of a sphere. Being spherical in shape the s-orbital is non-directional. In this, orbital there is an equal probability of finding the electrons in any direction away from the nucleus. The difference between an electron in a 1s and 2s orbital is that, the electron in the 2s orbital is further away from the nucleus and has greater energy. Thus, the 2s orbital is larger in size and spread at larger distance from the nucleus as compared to the 1s orbital (Fig. 1.1).

    There is a region between two adjacent s-orbitals where the probability of finding electron is zero and this is called as node.

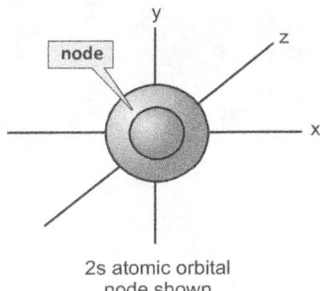

2s atomic orbital
node shown

Fig. 1.1: The s orbitals

2. **The p orbitals:**

   Subtypes: $2p_x$, $2p_y$, $2p_z$, $3p_x$, $3p_y$, $3p_z$ and so on.

   These are present in second and higher energy levels or p-sub shells. There are no p-orbitals in first energy levels.

   A 2p-orbital is a set of three orbitals of same energy. ($2p_x$, $2p_y$, $2p_z$, where x, y, z indicate axes perpendicular to each other.)

   A p-orbital is dumb-bell shaped. There are two lobes associated with this orbital. They are located on opposite sides of the nucleus and directed along a particular axis. In contrast to the s sub-shell for which there is only one orbital, in the p sub-shell there are three orbitals of equal energy. The three p-orbitals are directed along the three co-ordinate axes (Fig. 1.2).

   The p-orbitals have directional character.

3. **The d and f orbitals:**

   Subtypes of d-orbitals: From the 3rd orbit onwards there are five different d-orbitals (d_{xy}, d_{xz}, d_{yz}, d_z^2 and $d_{x^2-y^2}$) (Fig. 1.2).

   Of these the first three have their lobes between the co-ordinate axes and the remaining two have their lobes along the co-ordinate axes. These orbitals have very complex shapes and are higher in energy than the s and p orbitals.

   Subtypes of f orbitals: From the 4th orbit onwards, there are seven different f orbitals (f_z3, $f_{zx}2$, $f_{yz}2$, f_{xyz}, $f_z(x^2-y2)$, $f_x(x2-3_y2)$, $f_y(3_x2-y2)$) with much more complicated geometrical shapes. (Fig. 1.3)

   The subshells s, p d, f contain 1 s-orbital, 3 p-orbitals, 5 d-orbitals and 7f-orbitals and each orbital can have maximum 2 electrons with opposite spins.

   In organic chemistry, we are mainly concerned with the s and p orbitals.

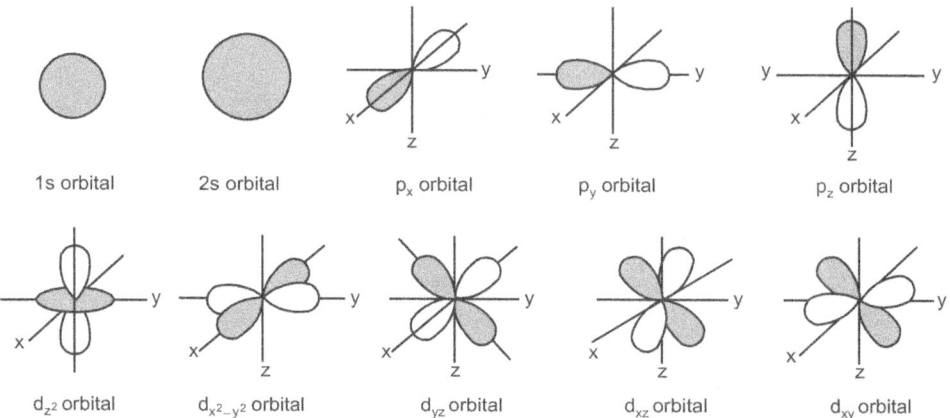

Fig. 1.2: Shapes of the s, p and d orbitals

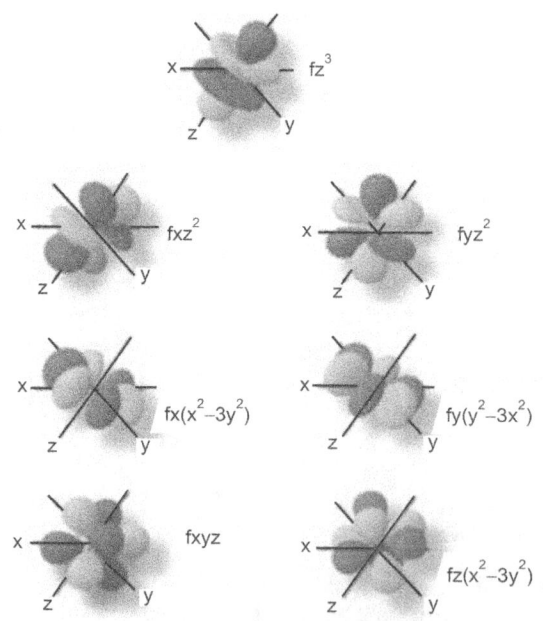

Fig. 1.3: Shapes of the f orbitals

The following two terminologies though different, are often confused.

Electronic Orbit	Electronic Orbital
1. Fixed circular path defined by a moving electron around the nucleus.	1. Space around the nucleus where there is maximum probability of finding an electron
2. Designated by K, L, M, N, etc.	2. Designated by s, p, d, f etc.
3. Number of orbits (energy levels) from nucleus are n = 1, 2, 3, 4, 5 etc.	3. Number of orbitals relative to orbits are n^2 = 1, 4, 9, 16, etc.
4. Two dimensional.	4. Three dimensional.
5. Maximum number of electrons in an orbit is given by $2n^2$ rule.	5. Maximum number of electrons present in any orbital is always 2 with opposite spins.
6. Circular or elliptical in shapes	6. Spherical or dumb-bell shaped.

Orbital electronic configuration is the manner and order in which the arrangement (filling up) of electrons in the orbitals takes place and is guided by Hund's rule and Aufbau's principle.

(a) Hund's rule of maximum multiplicity:

When several orbitals of same type (energy) are available the electrons first fill all the orbitals with parallel spins before, pairing in any other orbital. Thus, if 3 eletrons available then they to be filled in three p orbitals first, as per Hund's rule;

↑	↑↓		Not allowed	↑	↑	↑	Allowed
p_x	p_y	p_z		p_x	p_y	p_z	

(b) Aufbau's principle:

The electrons enter in the orbitals in order of increasing energy. i.e., orbital of lower energy occupied first and after that is filled, electrons enter in next higher energy orbitals. i.e., the electrons occupy the 1s orbital before occupying 2s orbital. The energy of various sub-shells follows sequence given bellow 1s < 2s < 2p < 3s < 3p < 4s < 3d < 4p < 5s.

MOLECULAR ORBITALS

Orbital Mixing: When atoms share electrons to form a bond, their atomic orbitals mix to form Molecular Orbitals (Fig. 1.4). In order for atomic orbitals to mix, they must:
- Have similar energy levels.
- Overlap well.
- Be close together.

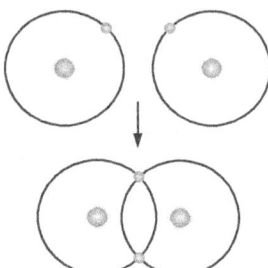

Fig. 1.4: This is an example of orbital mixing. The two atoms share one electron each from their outer shell. In this case both 1s orbitals overlap and share their valence electrons

Atomic *versus* molecular orbitals:

In atoms, electrons occupy **atomic orbitals**, but in molecules they occupy similar **molecular orbitals** which surround the molecule.

The two 1s atomic orbitals combine to form two molecular orbitals, of which one is bonding (s) and one is anti-bonding (s*).

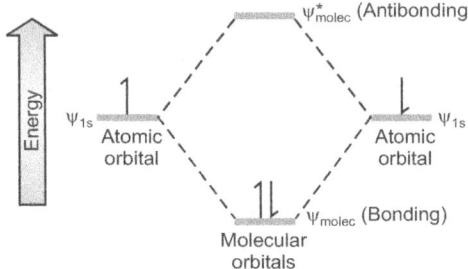

Fig. 1.5: Illustration of molecular orbital diagram of H_2. Notice that one electron from each atom is being "shared" to form a covalent bond. This is an example of orbital mixing.

The molecular orbital theory:

- The molecular orbital volume encompasses the whole molecule.
- The electrons fill the molecular orbitals of molecules like electrons fill atomic orbitals in atoms.
- Electrons go into the lowest energy orbital available to form lowest potential energy for the molecule.
- The maximum number of electrons in each molecular orbital is two. (Pauli's exclusion principle)
- The available electrons first fill all the orbitals, with parallel spin, before they begin to pair up. (Hund's Rule.)

Below are the representative molecular orbital diagrams of a few commonly occurring molecules

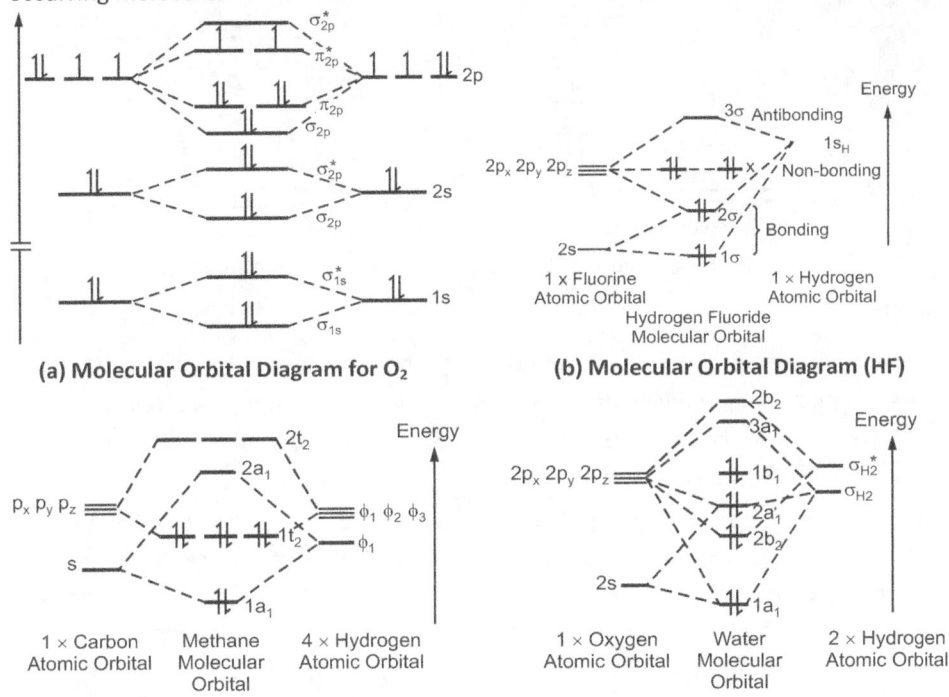

Fig. 1.6

HYBRIDIZATION OF ATOMIC ORBITALS

The process of mixing of pure orbitals to give a set of new equivalent orbitals is termed as hybridization of orbitals and any atom undergoing such a process for example, like carbon atom in organic compounds, is said to be in hybridised state.

The sp³ hybridization of carbon:

Electronic configuration of carbon atom in ground state is $1s^2, 2s^2, 2p_x^1, 2p_y^1, 2p_z^0$, while in excited state the configuration is $1s^2, 2s^1, 2p_x^1, 2p_y^1, 2p_z^1$. Carbon atom on sp³ hybridization (mixing) of one 2s and three 2p orbitals leads to 4 sp³ hybrid orbitals for bonding and acquires a configuration as $1s^2\ 2(sp^3)^1\ 2(sp^3)^1\ 2\ (sp^3)^1\ 2(sp^3)^1$. For example, methane (CH₄) (Fig. 1.7).

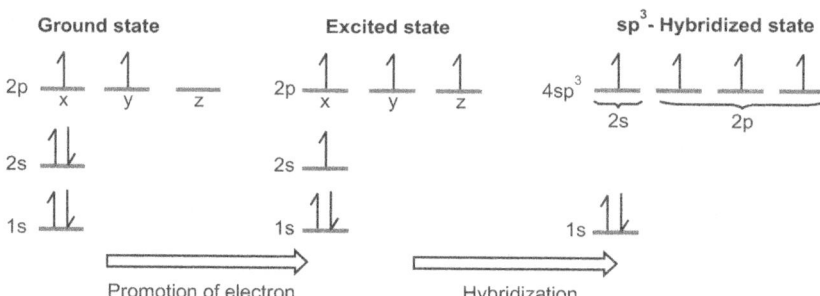

Fig. 1.7: The sp³ hybridization of carbon-electronic configuration

Example:

The concept of mixing of one 2s and three p orbitals is rather like mixing of 1 gallon of pure red paint and 3 gallons of white paint to give 4 gallons of pink paint. In case of orbital mixing newly shaped 4 orbitals are formed, while in case of paints newly colored (pink) 4 gallon paint is formed.

The four sp³ orbitals are arranged in such a way that their axes are directed towards the corners of a regular tetrahedron with carbon located at the center. The angle between any two orbitals is 109° 29'. The smaller lobes are not indicated because they do not extend sufficiently far from nucleus to participate in bond formation.

The tetrahedral arrangement is favored because it allows the *sp³* orbitals to stay as far away from each other as possible and thereby reducing the electron-electron repulsion (Fig. 1.8). e.g., bonding seen in molecules like methane, as well as ethane (Fig. 1.9).

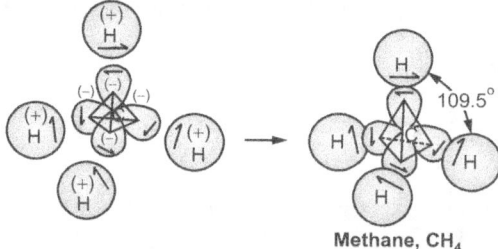

Methane, CH₄

Fig. 1.8: The sp³ hybridization of carbon-orientation and shape of new hybrid orbitals. Since each sp³ orbital is obtained from one s and three p orbitals, it has 25% s-character and 75% p-character.

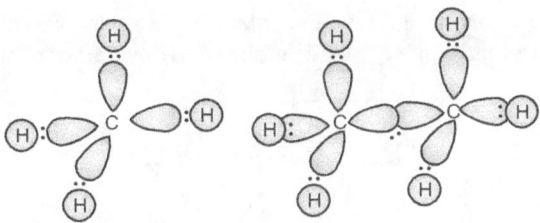

Fig. 1.9: *Bonding in methane and ethane molecules are due to sp³ hybridization*

Other compounds involving sp^3 hybrid orbitals: CF_4, CH_4,: NH_3, H_2O::, SiO_4^{4-}, SO_4^{2-}, ClO_4^-, etc.

The sp² hybridization of carbon:

The interaction of one *s* and two *p* orbitals are referred to as sp² hybridization. Carbon atom always uses sp² hybridized orbitals whenever it is bonded to three other atoms or groups of atoms to form the bonds. *For example,* ethylene (ethene). Carbon atom on sp² hybridization acquires a configuration as $1s^2\ 2(sp^2)^1\ 2(sp^2)^1\ 2(sp^2)^1\ 2p_z^1$. (Fig. 1.10).

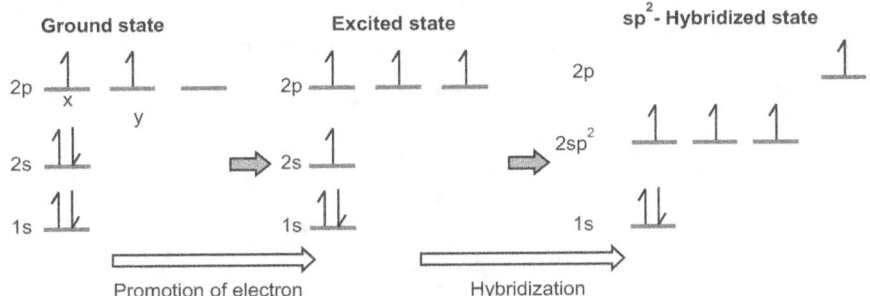

Fig. 1.10: sp² Hybridization of carbon - electronic configuration

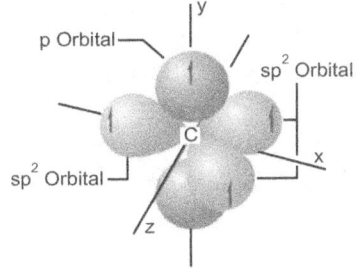

Fig. 1.11: The sp² hybridization of carbon - orientation and shape of new hybrid orbitals. Since each sp² orbital is obtained from one s and two p orbitals, it has ~33.33% s-character and ~66.33% p-character.

The three sp² orbitals lie in the same plane with their axes directed towards the corners of an equilateral triangle. The angle between any pair of orbitals is thus 120°.

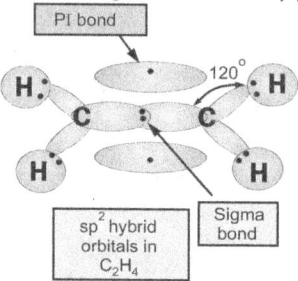

Fig. 1.12: Bonding in ethylene (ethene)

The sp hybridization of carbon:

The interaction of one s and just one of the three 2p orbitals to get new equivalent orbitals is referred as sp hybridization. Whenever carbon is bonded to only two other atoms or groups (as in acetylene), it always uses sp hybrid orbitals and two 2p (p_y and p_z) orbitals to form its bonds. Carbon atom on sp hybridization acquires a configuration as $1s^2$, 2(sp), 2(sp), $2p_y$, $2p_z$.

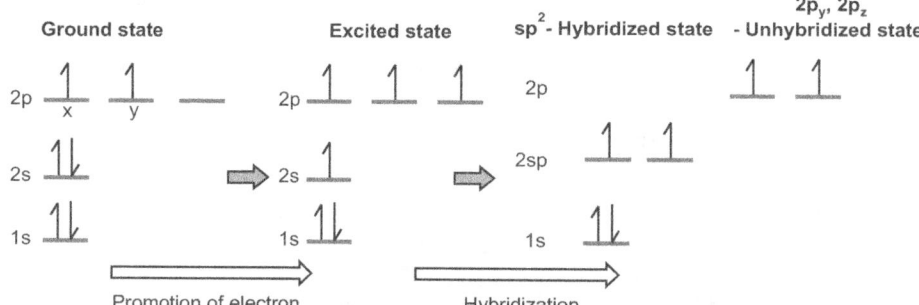

Fig. 1.13: The sp hybridization of carbon - electronic configuration

The sp orbitals obtained above are identical but differ only in their orientation in space with respect to each other. They lie in straight line. The angle between the two *sp* orbitals is thus 180°.

Fig. 1.14: The sp Hybridization of carbon - orientation and shape of new hybrid orbitals. Since each sp orbital is obtained from one s and one p orbital, it has 50% s-character and 50% p-character.

Each carbon atom in acetylene (H-C ≡ C-H) is attached to one hydrogen atom by a single covalent bond and to another carbon atom by a triple bond. Since each carbon is attached to two other atoms, it uses sp hybrid orbitals and two unhybridized 2p orbitals (p_y and p_z) to form its bonds.

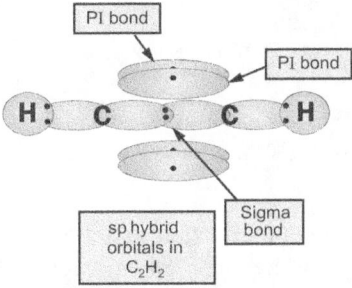

Fig. 1.15: Bonding in acetylene (ethyne)

Hybridization of the atomic orbitals takes place for other elements also. Examples of sp^3 hybridization of oxygen (water (H_2O)) and nitrogen (ammonia (NH_3)) are discussed below.

The sp^3 hybridization of oxygen: Bonding in water:

The oxygen atom in water (H_2O) forms two covalent bonds. Because oxygen has two unpaired electrons in its ground-state electronic configuration, it does not need to promote an electron to form the number (two) of covalent bonds required to achieve an outer shell of eight electrons (i.e., to complete its octet). If we assume that oxygen uses p orbitals to form the two O-H bonds, as predicted by oxygen's ground-state electronic configuration, we would expect a bond angle of about 90° because the two *p* orbitals are at right angles to each other. However, the experimentally observed bond angle is 104.5°. How can we explain the observed bond angle? Oxygen must use hybrid orbitals to form covalent bonds just as carbon does. The *s* orbital and the three *p* orbitals must hybridize to produce four sp^3 orbitals (Figs. 1.16 and 1.17).

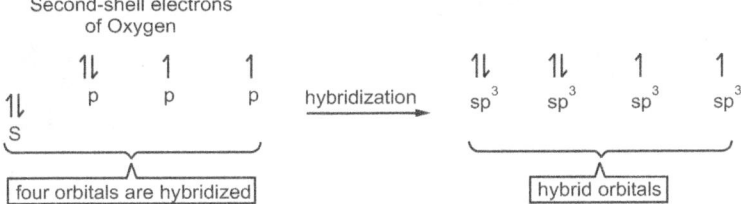

Fig. 1.16: The sp^3 hybridization of oxygen in water

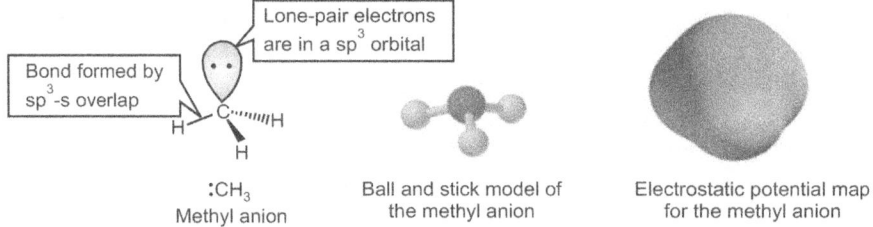

:CH₃
Methyl anion

Ball and stick model of the methyl anion

Electrostatic potential map for the methyl anion

Fig. 1.17: Bonding in water explaining its polar nature

sp³ hybridization of nitrogen:
Bonding in ammonia:

The experimentally observed bond angles in ammonia are 107.3°. The bond angles indicate that nitrogen also uses hybrid orbitals when it forms covalent bonds. Like carbon and oxygen, one s and three p orbitals of the second shell of nitrogen hybridize to form four degenerate orbitals. (Fig. 1.18)

Fig. 1.18: the sp³ hybridization of nitrogen in ammonia

The N-H bonds in ammonia are formed from the overlap of an orbital of nitrogen with the s orbital of a hydrogen. The single lone pair occupies an orbital. The bond angle (107.3°) is smaller than the tetrahedral bond angle (109.5°) because the electron sp³. (Fig. 1.19).

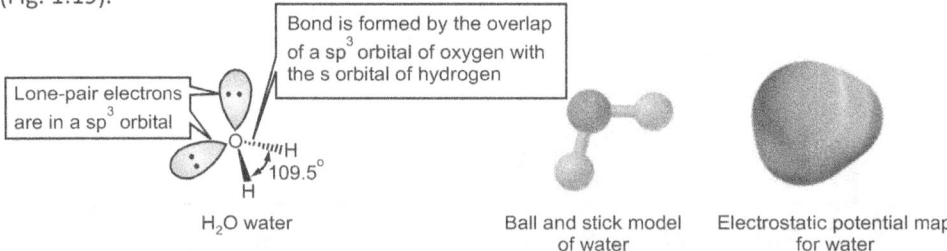

Fig. 1.19: Bonding in ammonia explaining its polar nature

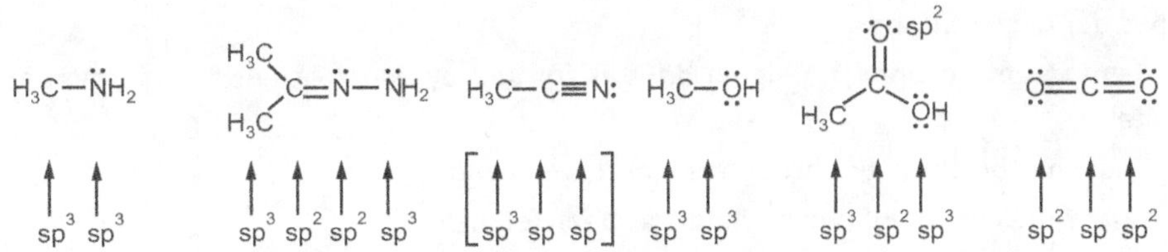

Fig. 1.20: Summary of orbital hybridization in different molecules

COVALENT BOND

Chemical Bonding:

Forming a Bond:
- Molecules can form bonds by sharing electrons.
  - Two shared electrons form a single bond.
- Atoms can share one, two or three pairs of electrons
  - Forming single, double and triple bonds.
- Other types of bonds are formed by charged atoms (ionic) and metal atoms (metallic).

Types of bonds:

Thus, there are three basic ways in which chemical combination occurs (*Though there are others!*):

1. Ionic or electrovalent bond
2. Covalent bond
3. Co-ordinate bond

In organic chemistry, we more often deal with covalent bonding so we need to understand this type in better details.

A covalent bond is a bond in which a pair of electrons is shared between two atoms. Depending on the atoms electronegativity the bond is either polar or non-polar.

A pair of atoms with the same electronegativity would form a **non-polar covalent bond**, such as:

$$H\cdot + H\cdot \longrightarrow H:H$$

A polar **covalent bond** is one in which the atoms have different electronegativities, such as:

$$H\cdot + \cdot\ddot{C}l: \longrightarrow H-\overline{\underline{Cl}}|$$

These bonds are commonly formed in organic compounds. In organic chemistry, covalent bonds of two types are encountered *viz.,* σ bond (sigma bond) and π bond (Pi bond).

Types of Covalent Bonds:

Sigma bond (σ bond): A sigma bond is formed by linear or end to end overlap of orbitals.

They may be obtained through any of the following;

(a) by the overlap of two s orbitals as depicted below.

(b) by the overlap of p and s orbital as shown in the figure.

(c) by the overlap of two p orbitals as illustrated below.

Sigma bond is common terminology applied to all those bonds in which overlap of orbitals produces a circularly symmetrical bond when viewed along bond axis. The bond axis is an imaginary line connecting the two nuclei. The electrons that occupy sigma bond are called sigma electrons.

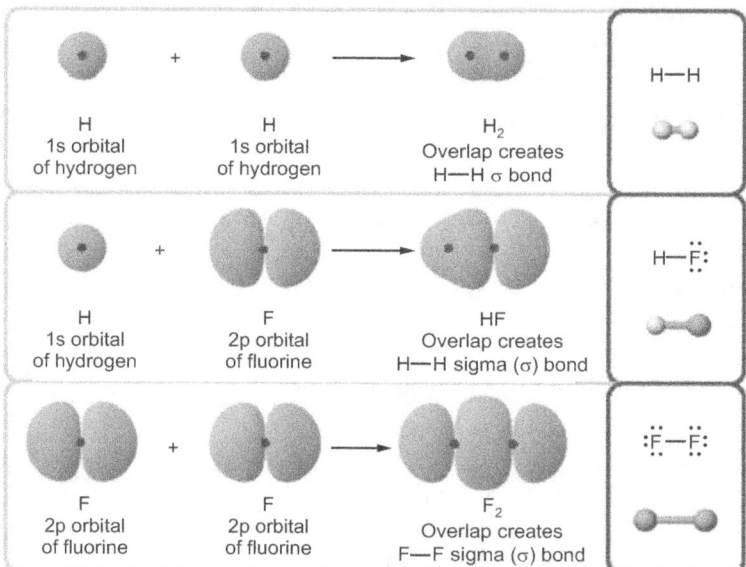

Fig. 1.21: Examples of sigma bond formation

Pi bond (π bond): A pi bond is formed by parallel or side to side overlap of p orbitals as shown in the Fig. 1.22. In other words, it is a bond where the overlapping regions exist above and below the internuclear axis (with a nodal plane along the internuclear axis). A π bond has two lobes, with one half of the π bond lying above the plane containing two nuclei and the other half below. The electrons that occupy the π bond are known as π electrons are lossely held compared to the pair of electrons in sigma bonds. π bonds are easily broken and more reactive than sigma bonds. Rotation about π bond is not possible and this restriction in rotation around the π bond is responsible for cis and trans isomerism in alkenes.

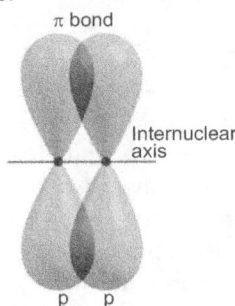

Fig. 1.22: Pi bond (π bond)

Comparison of covalent bonds:

σ Bond	π Bond
Axial overlap of atomic orbitals	Lateral or sideways overlap of orbitals
Strong in nature	Relatively weaker in nature
Overlap of s-s, s-p, p-p orbitals	Overlap of p or d orbitals
Present in single, double and triple bonds	Present in only double and triple bonds
Free rotation around bond possible	Free rotation around bond not possible
Sigma electrons involved and are near to atomic nuclei	Pi electrons involved and are away from atomic nuclei
No delocalization of electrons	Delocalization of electrons
For example, Ethane	For example, Ethene, ethyne

ELECTRONEGATIVITY

Electronegativity: What happens when the two atoms (elements) are different during formation of bonds. First of all, how do the atomic orbitals of different elements differ? They have the same types of orbitals 1s, 2s, 2p, etc., of the same shapes. Still the orbitals will have different energies. For example, removing an electron completely from atoms of carbon, oxygen, or fluorine (that is, ionizing the atoms) requires different amounts of energy. Fluorine requires most energy, carbon least, even though in each case we are removing an electron from the same 2p atomic orbital.

The energies of the 2p orbitals must be lowest in fluorine, low in oxygen and highest in carbon.

The more electronegative an atom is, the more it attracts electrons. This can be understood in terms of energies of the AOs (atomic orbitals). The more electronegative an atom is, the lower in energy are its AOs and so any electrons in them are held more tightly. This is a consequence of the increasing nuclear charge going from left to right across the periodic table. As we go from Li across to C and on to N, O, and F, the elements steadily become more electronegative and the AOs lower in energy.

The AOs combine to form new MOs (molecular orbitals), but they do so unsymmetrically. The more electronegative atom, (e.g., O or F) contributes more to the bonding orbital and the less electronegative element (carbon is the one we shall usually be interested in) contributes more to the anti-bonding orbital. This applies both to σ bonds and π bonds, so here is an idealized case. We can expect a covalent bond to be polar if it joins atoms that differ in their tendency to attract electrons, that is, atoms that differ in electronegativity. Furthermore, the greater the difference in electronegativity, the more polar the bond will be.

The most electronegative elements are those located in the upper right-hand corner of the periodic table. Of the elements we are likely to encounter in organic chemistry, fluorine has the highest electronegativity, than oxygen, than nitrogen and chlorine, than bromine, and finally carbon. Hydrogen does not differ very much from carbon in electronegativity; it is not certain whether it is more or less electronegative.

The Electronegativity Rank Order: F > O > Cl , N > Br > C, H

Bond polarities are intimately concerned with both physical and chemical properties. The polarity of bonds can lead to polarity of molecules and thus profoundly affect melting point, boiling point, and solubility. The polarity of a bond determines the kind of reaction that can take place at a bond and even affects reactivity at nearby bonds.

HYDROGEN BONDING

Covalent Intermolecular Forces - Hydrogen Bonding Force:

When hydrogen atom is covalently linked to the strong electronegative element, the molecule formed is a dipole. Thus, H-F is a dipole. In an aggregate of H-F molecules, dipole-dipole interaction takes place. When they come very close to each other, the obvious result is the orientation of poles and a weak bond is established between two unlike poles ($H^{\delta+}$ and $F^{\delta-}$). So, a hydrogen bond is a result of dipole-dipole interaction.

Hydrogen atom, covalently bonded to a strong electronegative atom, has relatively high positive charge density and minimal co-ordination number (only two) because it has very small volume which makes hydrogen bonding possible. Other electropositive atoms have neither high positive charge nor minimal co-ordination number because of their large volume and hence no such dipole-dipole interaction is possible.

The hydrogen bond dissociation energy varies from 21 to 42 kJ/Mole. Hence, it is stronger than usual dipole-dipole interaction. The strength of the bond depends upon the electronegativity of atom bonded to the hydrogen atom and it decreases with the decreasing electronegativity within the series, F > O > N > Cl > S.

Hydrogen bonds are two types:
1. Intermolecular Hydrogen bond (between two molecules).
2. Intramolecular Hydrogen bond (Internal; within the molecule).

Hydrogen bonding between two or more molecules; is known as **intermolecular hydrogen bonding**; while hydrogen bond formed between two atoms within a molecule, is called an **internal** or **intra molecular hydrogen bond**. The result of intra molecular hydrogen bond is the formation of cyclic structure known as chelate.

Intermolecular hydrogen bonding can also form cyclic structure. In such cases, dimeric molecules are obtained instead of a polymer.

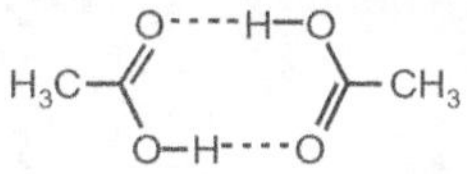

Intermolecular H-bonding 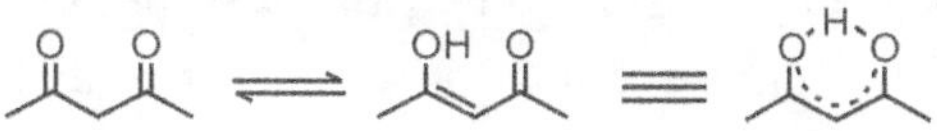   **Intramolecular H-bonding**

Effects of Hydrogen Bonding:

The intermolecular hydrogen bonding results in increase in **melting** and **boiling points.** This is due to an extra amount of energy that is required to break the hydrogen bond. Compounds with intermolecular hydrogen bond have greater *melting and boiling points* than compounds with intramolecular hydrogen bond. Methane, hydrogen fluoride and water molecules have comparable molecular weights. Methane cannot form hydrogen bond because carbon atoms has low electronegativity and hydrogen fluoride can utilize its lone pair to form hydrogen bond while water molecule forms hydrogen bond with both the hydrogen atoms. This is reflected in their *melting and boiling points* as indicated in the table.

Property	Water	Hydrogen fluoride	Methane
Melting point	0°C	– 110°C	– 190°C
Boiling point	100°C	19.5°C	– 161.5°C

Hydrogen bonding in a compound makes it soluble in water and in other solvents possessing hydrogen bonding. Hydrogen bond in solvent molecule and that in solute molecule breaks on dissolution.

Intra molecular hydrogen bonding brings stability to a compound. For example, Tautomeric forms of acetyl acetone.

Similarly, hydrogen bonding has an effect on acidity and basicity of compounds.

For example: Salicylic acid is a stronger acid than p-hydroxy benzoic acid as the conjugate base of salicylic acid gets stabilised by intramolecular hydrogen bonding, but p-hydroxybenzoate ion, the conjugate base of the *p*-hydroxybenzoic acid, does not stabilize by such hydrogen bonding.

Hence, it can be easily concluded that salicylate ion is a weaker base than the p-hydroxy benzoate ion, meaning that salicylic acid is a stronger acid than p-hydroxy benzoic acid. Dimethylamine is a stronger base than trimethylamine in aqueous medium, due to hydrogen bonding.

This is because of greater hydration effect on dimethylammonium ion than that of trimethylammonium ion.

Both inter and intra molecular hydrogen bondings play important roles in biological systems. The long helical structures of protein molecules and double helical structure of DNA molecules are stabilized by the existence of hydrogen bonding.

The hydrogen bonding force in proteins and cellulose makes them able to absorb dyes.

Strength of hydrogen bonding force is greater than dipole-dipole interaction which in turn is greater than London force and magnitude of these forces is as follows.

	Intermolecular force	Strength of intermolecular force
1.	Hydrogen bonding	~21.42 kJ/mole
2.	Dipole-dipole interaction	~8 kJ/mole
3.	London force	~4 kJ/mole

BOND FISSION OR BREAKING

The polarity of bonds due to the difference in electronegativities of the two atoms which are joined by them, play an important role in bond fission or breaking. Ofcourse, there are other factors involved. As a rule polar bonds are easier to break than non-polar bonds.

When bonds break in many cases, the leaving group takes both the electrons from the old σ bond. This type of decomposition is sometimes called **heterolytic fission** or simply **heterolysis** and is the most common in organic chemistry. One of the fragment is positively charged (lost electrons), while the other is negatively charged (taken or received both the electrons).

$$H-Br \longrightarrow H^{\oplus} + Br^{\ominus}$$

Heterolytic fission

There is another way that a σ bond can break. Rather than a pair of electrons moving to one of the atoms, one electron can go in either direction. This is known as **homolytic fission** as two species of the same charge (neutral) will be formed. It normally occurs when similar or indeed identical atoms are at each end of the σ bond to be broken. Both fragments have an unpaired electron and are known as radicals. This type of reaction occurs when bromine gas is subjected to sunlight. The weak Br–Br bond breaks to form two bromine radicals.

$$Br\!-\!Br \longrightarrow Br^\bullet + {}^\bullet Br$$
Homolytic fission

Bond Energy:

When a chemical reaction occurs, molecular bonds are broken and other bonds are formed to make different molecules. For example, the bonds of two water molecules are broken to form hydrogen and oxygen.

$$2H_2O \longrightarrow 2H_2 + O_2$$

Bonds do not break and form spontaneously for this an energy change is required. The energy input required to break a bond is known as **bond energy**. In a reverse case when bonds are formed energy is released. For exmaple: Bond formation between oxygen and hydrogen (O–H) atoms.

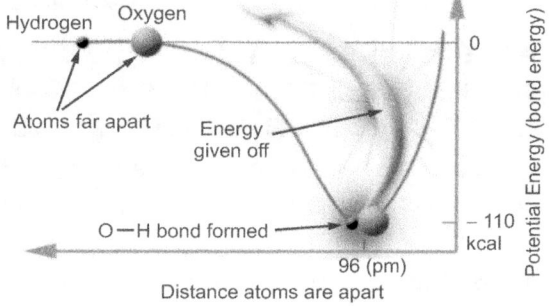

Fig. 1.23: Energies of bond formation

Bond energy serves a very important purpose in describing the structure and characteristics of a molecule. When a bond is strong, there is a higher bond energy because it takes more energy to break a strong bond. This correlates with **Bond Order** and **Bond Length**. When the bond order is higher, bond length is shorter, and the shorter the bond length means a greater the Bond Energy because of increased electric attraction.

Theory of Reaction Mechanism:

A **chemical reaction** is a process that leads to the transformation of one set of chemical substances (reactants) to another (products). Simply a chemical reaction involves changes in the positions of electrons in forming and breaking of chemical bonds between atoms, with no change to the nuclei. A chemical reaction is often described by a chemical equation.

Most of the organic reactions involve conversion of one functional group into another by the attack of a "**reagent**". Such organic compounds which are attacked by the reagent are known as "**substrates**" or "**reactants**". On the other hand, a simple organic or inorganic compound which is used to create a desired transformation in the compound is known as a "**reagent**". Thus, an organic reaction may be represented as below:

Example:

Substrate + Attacking Reagent → Intermediate → End product → Product

In simple words, a chemical reaction is a cascade of various events involving breaking of older bonds and formation of newer bond.

Whereas; "The steps of an organic reaction showing the breaking and making of new bonds of carbon atoms in the substrate leading to the formation of a final product through transitory intermediates" are referred as the **mechanism of reaction.**

FACTORS AFFECTING REACTIVITY: INDUCTIVE EFFECT; ELECTROMERIC EFFECT; RESONANCE OR MESORMERIC EFFECT; STERIC EFFECT; HYPERCONJUGATION; TAUTOMERISM

Electron withdrawal and release in a molecular system (or reaction) result from the operation of two factors; the **inductive effect** and the **resonance effect**.

Inductive Effect:

Definition: *Inductive Effect* is an experimentally observable effect of the transmission of charge through a chain of atoms in a molecule. The permanent dipole induced in one bond by another is called inductive effect. The electron cloud in a σ-bond between two unlike atoms is not uniform and is slightly displaced towards the more electronegative of the two atoms. This causes a permanent state of bond polarization, where the more electronegative atom has a slight negative charge (δ−) and the other atom has a slight positive charge (δ+).

$$H_3C - \overset{\delta-}{\ddot{\underset{..}{O}}} - \overset{\delta+}{H} \longrightarrow H_3C - \overset{\delta+}{\underset{..}{\overset{\delta-}{\ddot{Cl}}}}:$$

Salient features of inductive effect:
- It arises due to electronegativity difference between two atoms forming a sigma bond.
- It is transmitted through the **sigma bonds**.
- The magnitude of inductive effect decreases while moving away from the groups causing it.
- It is a **permanent** effect.
- It influences the chemical and physical properties of compounds.

Example:

Illustration of inductive effect:

The C-Cl bond in the butyl chloride, CH_3-CH_2-CH_2-CH_2-Cl is polarized due to electronegativity difference. The electrons are withdrawn by the chlorine atom. Thus, the first carbon atom gets partial positive charge. In turn, this carbon atom drags electron density partially from the next carbon, which also gets partial positive charge. Thus, the inductive effect is transmitted through the carbon chain.

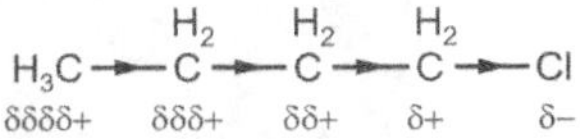

$$H_3C \rightarrow \underset{\delta\delta\delta\delta+}{\overset{H_2}{C}} \rightarrow \underset{\delta\delta\delta+}{\overset{H_2}{C}} \rightarrow \underset{\delta\delta+}{\overset{H_2}{C}} \rightarrow \underset{\delta+}{C} \rightarrow \underset{\delta-}{Cl}$$

If the electronegative atom is then joined to a chain of atoms, usually carbon, the positive charge is relayed to the other atoms in the chain. This is the electron-withdrawing inductive effect, also known as the **– I effect**.

Some groups, such as the alkyl group are less electron withdrawing than hydrogen and are therefore considered as electron releasing. This is electron releasing character and is indicated by the **+I effect**. In short, alkyl groups are tending to give electrons leading to induction effect.

The inductive effect may be caused by some molecules also. Relative inductive effects have been experimentally measured with reference to hydrogen:

Electron - releasing groups (showing +I effect)

$NO_2 > COOH > Cl > Br > I > OH > OR > C_6H_5 > H > CH_3 > MeCH_2- > Me_3C-$

Electron - withdrawing (–I effect)

Also, the inductive effect is dependent on the distance between the substituent group and the main group (functional group) that reacts. That is, as the distance of the substituent group increases the inductive effect weakens or decreases.

Electromeric Effect:

This is a temporary effect and takes place between two atoms joined by a multiple bond, i.e., a double or triple bond. It occurs at the requirements of the attacking reagent and involves instantaneous transfer of a shared pair of electrons of the multiple bond to one of the linked atoms. It is temporary in nature because the molecule acquires its original electronic condition upon removal of the attacking reagent. **Electromeric effect** refers to a molecular polarizability effect occurring by an intramolecular electron displacement (sometimes called the 'conjugative mechanism' and previously, the 'tautomeric mechanism') characterized by the substitution of one electron pair for another within the same atomic octet of electrons. However, this term is now considered and this effect is considered along with the inductive effect.

+E and –E groups: Electromeric effect can be classified into +E and –E effects based on the direction of transfer of the electron pair.

When the electron pair moves towards the attacking reagent, it is termed as the +E effect. The addition of acids to alkenes is an example of the +E effect. After the transfer takes place, the reagent gets attached to the atom where the electrons have been transferred to.

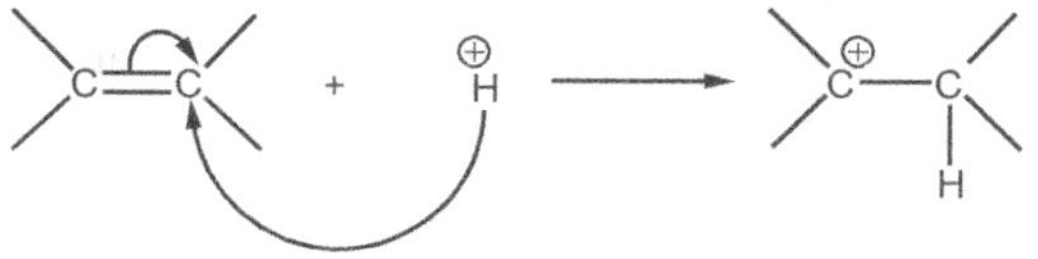

The –E effect can be found in reactions such as addition of cyanide ion to carbonyl compounds. In these reactions, the electron pair moves away from the attacking reagent.

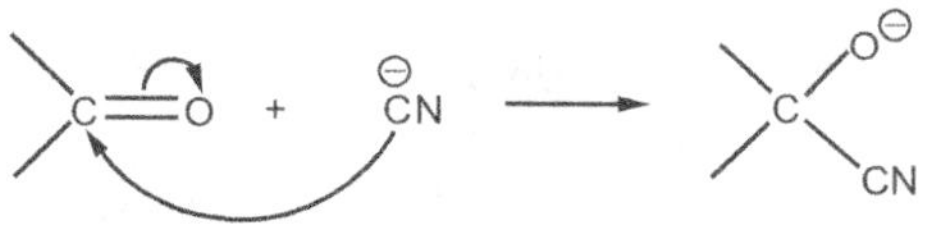

Resonance or Mesomeric Effect:

The electron withdrawing or releasing effect attributed to a substituent through delocalization of p or π electrons, which can be visualized by drawing various canonical forms, is known as mesomeric effect or resonance effect. It depends upon the overlap of certain orbitals and therefore, can operate only when the substituent is located in certain special ways relative to the charge center. It amounts to electron withdrawal from a negatively charged center, and electron release to a positively charged center. It is symbolized by M or R.

Negative resonance or mesomeric effect (–M or –R): It is shown by substituents or groups that withdraw electrons by delocalization mechanism from rest of the molecule and are denoted by –M or –R. The electron density on rest of the molecular entity is decreased due to this effect. For example, $-NO_2$, Carbonyl groups (C=O), $-C\equiv N$, –COOH, $-SO_3H$ etc.

Positive resonance or mesomeric effect (+M or +R): The groups show positive mesomeric effect when they release electrons to the rest of the molecule by delocalization. These groups are denoted by +M or +R. Due to this effect, the electron density on rest of the molecular entity is increased. E.g., –OH, –OR, –SH, –SR, –NH$_2$, –NR$_2$ etc.

Example:

Illustrations and applications of resonance effect or mesomeric effect

1. The negative resonance effect (–R or –M) of carbonyl group is shown below. It withdraws electrons by delocalization of π electrons and reduces the electron density particularly on third carbon.

    $$H_2C=CH-\overset{O}{\underset{}{C}}-CH_3 \longleftrightarrow \overset{\oplus}{H_2C}-CH=\overset{O^{\ominus}}{\underset{}{C}}-CH_3$$

2. The nitro group, -NO$_2$, in nitrobenzene shows –M effect due to delocalization of conjugated π electrons as shown below. Note that the electron density on benzene ring is decreased particularly on *ortho* and *para* positions.

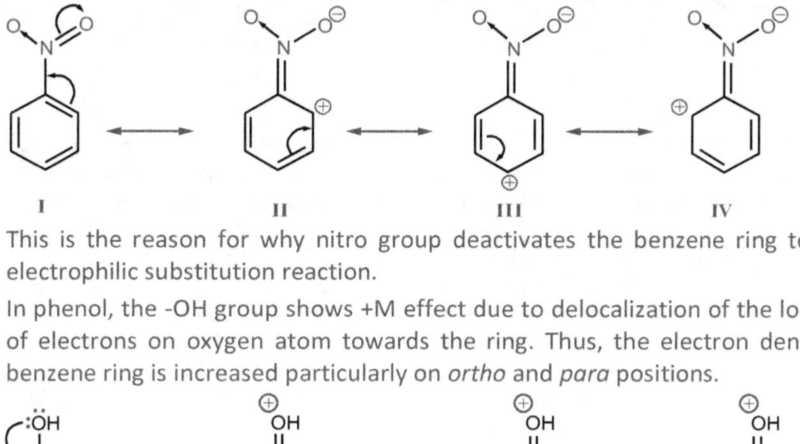

    I   II   III   IV

    This is the reason for why nitro group deactivates the benzene ring towards electrophilic substitution reaction.

3. In phenol, the -OH group shows +M effect due to delocalization of the lone pair of electrons on oxygen atom towards the ring. Thus, the electron density on benzene ring is increased particularly on *ortho* and *para* positions.

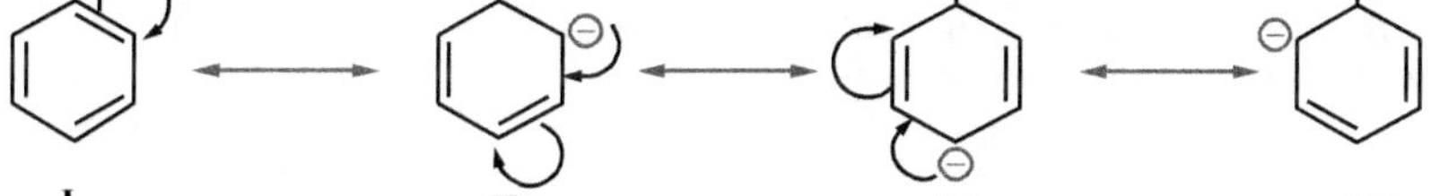

    I   II   III   IV

    Hence, phenol is more reactive towards electrophilic substitution reactions. The substitution is favored more at *ortho* and *para* positions.

Steric Effects:

Steric effects arise from the fact that each atom within a molecule occupies a certain amount of space. If atoms are brought too close together, there is an associated cost in energy due to overlapping electron clouds (Pauli or Born repulsion) and this may affect the molecule's preferred shape (conformation) and reactivity.

Types of steric effects:

1. **Steric hindrance** occurs when the large size of groups within a molecule prevents chemical reactions that are observed in related molecules with smaller groups. Although steric hindrance is sometimes a problem (it prevents), it can also be a very useful tool, and is often exploited by chemists to change the reactivity pattern of a molecule by stopping unwanted side-reactions (**steric protection**) or by leading to a preference for one stereochemical reaction course as in **stereoselectivity**.

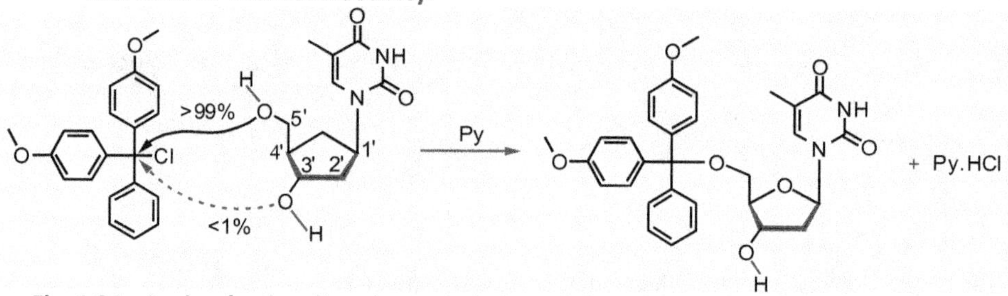

Fig. 1.24: Regioselective dimethoxytritylation of the primary 5'-hydroxyl group of thymidine in the presence of a free secondary 3'-hydroxy group as a result of steric hindrance due to the dimethoxytrityl group and the ribose ring (Py = pyridine).

2. **Steric shielding** occurs when a charged group on a molecule is seemingly weakened or spatially shielded by less charged (or oppositely charged) atoms, including counter ions in solution (Debye shielding). In some cases, for an atom to interact with sterically shielded atoms, it would have to approach from a vicinity where there is less shielding, thus, controlling where and from what direction a molecular interaction can take place.

3. **Steric attraction** occurs when molecules have shapes or geometries that are optimized for interaction with one another. In these cases, molecules will react with each other most often in specific arrangements.

4. **Chain crossing:** A chain, ring, or a set of rings cannot change from one conformation to another if it would require a chain (or ring - a ring is a cyclic chain) to pass through itself or another chain. This is responsible for the shape of catenanes and molecular knots.

5. **Steric repulsions** between different parts of molecular system are found to be of key importance to govern the direction of transition metal mediated transformations and catalysis. Steric effect can even induce a mechanism switch in the catalytic reaction.

HYPERCONJUGATION OR NO BOND RESONANCE OR BAKER-NATHAN EFFECT

The delocalization of σ-electrons or lone pair of electrons into adjacent π-orbital or p-orbital is called **hyperconjugation**. It occurs due to overlapping of σ-bonding orbital or the orbital containing a lone pair with adjacent π-orbital or p-orbital. It is also known as "no bond resonance" or "Baker-Nathan effect".

Conditions for Hyperconjugation:

There must be an α-CH group or a lone pair on atom adjacent to sp^2 hybrid carbon or other atoms like nitrogen, oxygen etc.

E.g., Alkenes, alkyl carbocations, alkyl free radicals, nitro compounds with α-hydrogen.

Illustration of Hyperconjugation:

The displacement of σ-electrons towards the multiple bond occurs when there are hydrogens on the α-carbon (which is adjacent to the multiple bond). This results in the polarization of the multiple bond.

E.g., In propene, the σ-electrons of C-H bond of methyl group can be delocalized into the π-orbital of doubly bonded carbon as represented below;

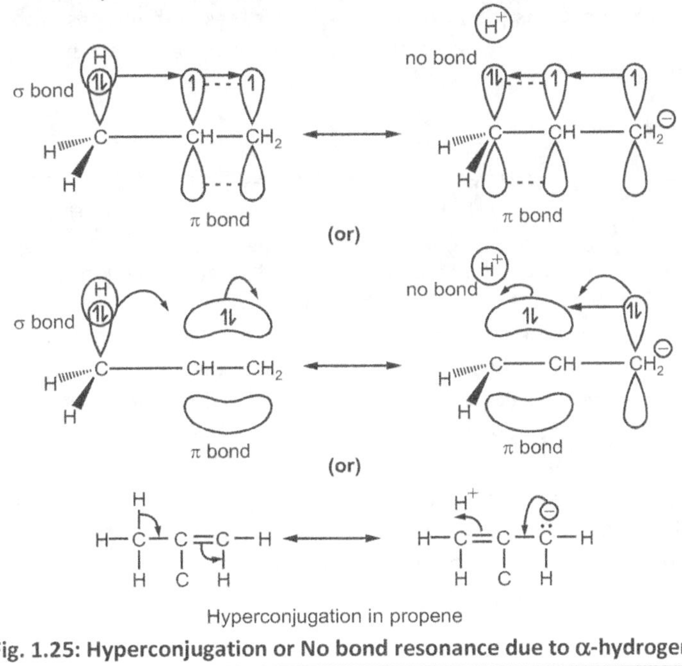

Hyperconjugation in propene

Fig. 1.25: Hyperconjugation or No bond resonance due to α-hydrogens

In same way, the other hydrogens on the methyl group also participate in hyperconjugation. Thus, the propene molecule can show the following resonance structures, which confer stability to it.

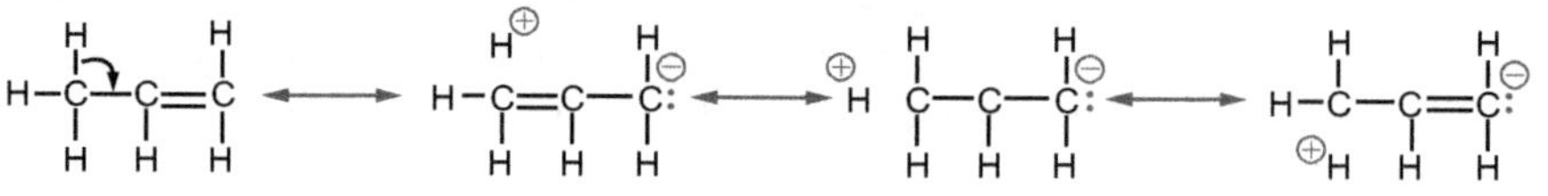

Fig. 1.26: No bond resonance structures shown by propene due to hyperconjugation

In the contributing structures; (II), (III) and (IV) of propene, there is no bond between an α-carbon and one of the hydrogen atom. Hence, the hyperconjugation is also known as "no bond resonance".

Consequences or Applications of Hyperconjugation

Stability of alkenes: Stability of alkenes increases with increase in the number of alkyl groups (containing hydrogens) on the double bond. It is due to increase in the number of contributing no bond resonance structures

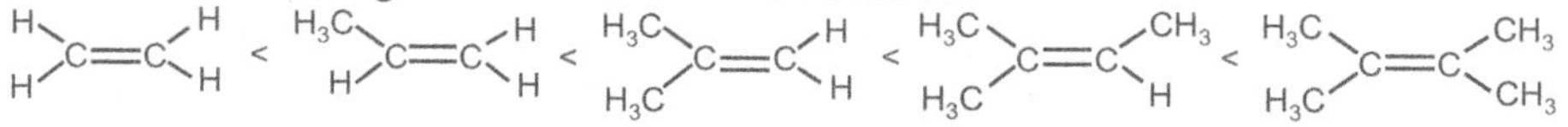

Stability of carbocations (carbonium ions): Increases with increase in the number of alkyl groups (containing hydrogen) attached to the positively charged carbon.

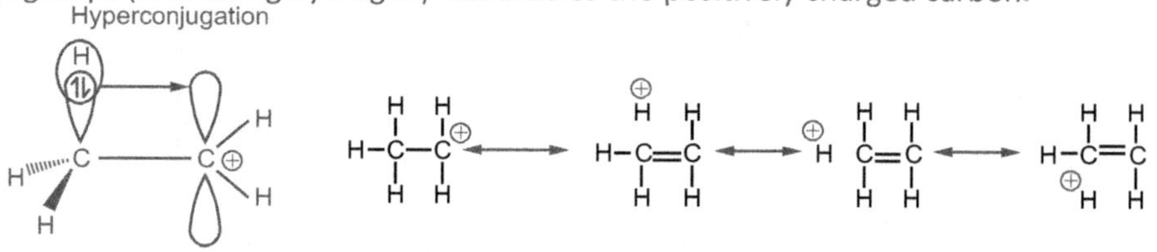

Fig. 1.27: Hyperconjugation in ethyl carbonium ion

Stability of free radicals: The stability of free radicals is influenced by hyperconjugation as in case of carbonium ions. The σ-electrons of the α-C-H bond can be delocalized into the p-orbital of carbon containing an odd electron. Due to hyperconjugation, the stability of free radicals also follow the same order as that of carbonium ions *i.e.,* methyl < primary < secondary < tertiary.

Dipole moment and bond length:
- The dipole moment of the molecules is greatly affected due to hyperconjugation since the contributing structures show considerable polarity.
- The bond lengths are also altered due to change in the bond order during hyperconjugation. The single bond may get partial double bond character and vice versa.

E.g., The observed dipole moment of nitro methane is greater than the calculated value due to hyperconjugation. The observed C–N bond length is also less than the expected value due to same reason.

Fig. 1.28: Hyperconjugation in nitromethane

TAUTOMERISM

A special case of structural isomerism. Tautomers are isomers (constitutional isomers) of organic compounds that readily interconvert into each other through **tautomerization**. This reaction commonly results in the formal migration of a hydrogen atom or proton, accompanied by a switch of a single bond and adjacent double bond. Because of the rapid interconversion, tautomers are generally considered to be the same chemical compound.

It is very important to note that the tautomers are not the resonance structures of same compound

Common tautomeric pairs are:
- ketone - enol, e.g., for acetone (see: keto-enol tautomerism)
- amide - imidic acid, e.g., during nitrile hydrolysis reactions
- lactam - lactim, an amide - imidic acid tautomerism in heterocyclic rings.
- enamine - imine

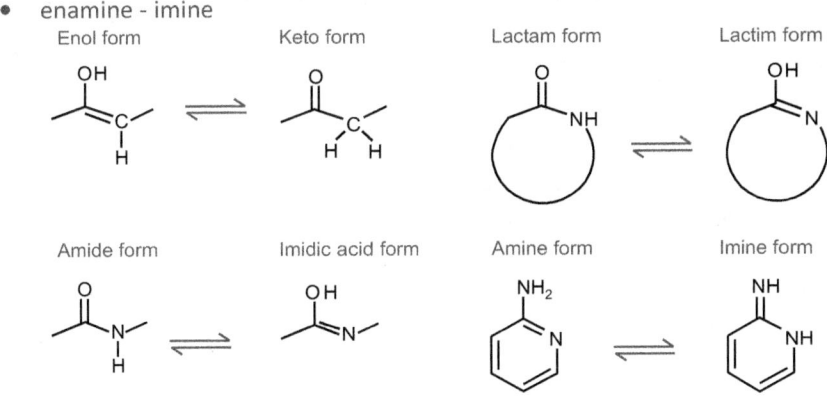

Fig. 1.29: Common tautomeric pairs

Types of tautomerism:
1. **Prototropy** is the most common type of tautomerism and refers to the relocation of a proton. Prototropic tautomerism may be considered as a subset of acid-base behavior. Prototropic tautomers are sets of isomeric protonation states with the same empirical formula and total charge. Two subtypes;
   (a) **Annular tautomerism:** A type of prototropic tautomerism wherein, a proton can occupy two or more positions of a heterocyclic system, for example, 1H- and 3H-imidazole; 1H-, 2H- and 4H- 1, 2, 4-triazole; 1H- and 2H-isoindole.
   (b) **Ring-chain tautomerism:** Occurring when the movement of the proton is accompanied by a change from an open structure to a ring, such as the open chain and pyran forms of glucose and furan form of fructose.
2. **Valence tautomerism** is a type of tautomerism in which single and/or double bonds are rapidly formed and ruptured, without migration of atoms or groups. It is distinct from prototropic tautomerism and involves processes with rapid reorganisation of bonding electrons. An example of this type of tautomerism can be found in the open and closed forms of certain heterocycles, such as azide - tetrazole. Valence tautomerism requires a change in molecular geometry and should not be confused with canonical resonance structures or mesomers.

QUESTION BANK

1. What are atomic orbitals? What are their different types and shapes?
2. Discuss the different types of orbitals and their shapes.
3. There is often confusion between the terms electronic orbits and electronic orbitals. What is the difference between an electronic orbit and electronic orbital?
4. Discuss the rules that govern the filling of electrons in the atomic orbitals.
5. What is a molecular orbital. Discuss how is it different from an atomic orbital?
6. What is meant by hybridization of atomic orbitals? Discuss various hybridizations of the atomic orbitals of carbon.
7. Is hybridization also observed for the atomic orbitals of elements other than carbon? If so, then discuss with a few examples.
8. What is chemical bonding? What are the main types of chemical bonds? Elaborate on Covalent Bond and its main types.
9. What is the concept of electronegativity? Explain with examples.
10. Discuss the types and effects of hydrogen bonding.

11. Discuss the breaking of bond and its major types. What is meant by bond energy?
12. Define the terms "chemical reaction" and "reaction mechanism"
13. Discuss the concepts of "Inductive effect", "Electromeric effect", "Resonance effect and Mesormeric effect" and "Steric effects" and their influence on the reactivity of molecules, with pertinent examples.
14. Explain with suitable examples the concept of hyperconjugation and how does it influence the reactivity of molecules.
15. Define the concept of tautomerism, its types with suitable examples.
16. Compare Sigma (σ) and Pi (π) bonds.
17. Write down the designation of *3p* and *sp* hybridized orbitals. Draw these orbitals. What are their orientations in space? Why are they oriented in such ways?
18. How do *3p* orbitals differ from *2p*?
19. Write down the order of stability and energy content of *s*, *p* and *s-p* hybridized orbitals. Give reasons.
20. What sort of bonds can be formed between *s* orbital and *p* orbital?
21. Which will provide better overlap *1s-2p* or *1s-3p*?
22. Which bonds will be stronger? Arrange in rank order and explain:
    (i)   H and C
    (ii) H and N
    (iii) H and O
    (iv) H and F
    (v)   H and S
    (vi) H and Cl
23. Construct MO diagram for the molecule H_2O, as well as, CS_2 and suggest what type of bonds each of these molecules may have.
24. Construct MOs for acetylene and discuss the hybridization involved.
25. You may be surprised to know that the molecule CH_2 which is a divalent carbon, can exist. It is of course very unstable but it is known and it can have two different structures. One has H-C-H bond angle of 180° and the other has 120°. Suggest the structures for these species and say which orbitals will be occupied by all bonding and non-bonding electrons? Which structures are likely to be more stable?

26. Describe briefly the *3s* orbital.
27. Why are the three *p* orbitals oriented at right angles to each other?
28. Write short notes on the following;
    (i) Hybridization
    (ii) Sigma and pi bonds
    (iii) Wave and particle nature of electrons
    (iv) Electronegativity
    (v) Resonance and mesomeric effects
    (vi) Hyperconjugation
    (vii) Steric and electromeric effects
    (viii) Tautomerism
    (ix) Reaction mechanism
    (x) Covalent bond
    (xi) Hydrogen bonding
    (xii) Bond fission
29. Arrange in the order of increased acidity based on inductive effect
    (i) $ClCH_2CH_2CH_2COOH$
    (ii) $ClCH_2CH_2COOH$
    (iii) $ClCH_2CH_2CH_2CH_2COOH$
    (iv) $ClCH_2COOH$
30. Name the effect that makes each of these following compounds acidic in nature and explain
    (i) FCH_2COOH
    (ii) C_6H_5COOH
    (iii) Acetylene
31. Write the various canonical or resonance structures for the following compounds
    (i) Nitrobenzene
    (ii) Aniline
    (iii) Phenol
32. What is meant by negative and positive Resonance. Explain with examples.
33. Show by various hyperconjugation contributing structures how *t*-Butyl carbonium ion is stabilized.

34. Explain with suitable examples how hydrogen bonding affects the m.p., b.p., as well as solubility of compounds.
35. Explain the terms: Steric hinderance, Steric shielding, steric attraction and steric repulsion.
36. What is bond energy? Explain.

Chapter 2 ...

CLASSIFICATION OF ORGANIC COMPOUNDS

CONTENTS

Classification of organic compounds on the basis of functional group and elemental composition:

1. Compounds containing carbon and hydrogen atoms only: Hydrocarbons (Alkanes, Alkenes, Alkynes, Aromatic Hydrocarbons, Arylalkyl Hydrocarbons, Alicyclic Hydrocarbons).
2. Compounds containing carbon, hydrogen and oxygen atoms only: Alcohols, Phenols, Ethers, Epoxides, Carbonyl compounds, Aldehydes and Ketones, Carboxylic acids, Esters, Anhydrides.
3. Compounds containing Carbon, Hydrogen and Nitrogen atoms only: Amines and Imines, Nitriles, Hydrazines.
4. Compounds containing Carbon, Hydrogen and Halogens with Oxygen: Alkyl Halides, Aryl Halides, Acyl Halides.
5. Compounds containing Carbon, Hydrogen, Oxygen and Nitrogen atoms only: Amides, Imides, Aldoximes, Ketoximes, Nitro compounds.
6. Compounds containing Carbon, Hydrogen and Sulphur with/without Nitrogen, Oxygen and Halogen: Sulphonic acids, Sulphonylhalides, Sulphonamides.
   At least five Mono-functional compound examples of each class including aromatic and aliphatic compounds should be covered with their common names.
7. IUPAC nomenclature of all classes of compounds; Nomenclature of Mono-substituted and Poly-substituted compounds. (Recent rules of IUPAC referred).

1. COMPOUNDS CONTAINING CARBON AND HYDROGEN ONLY

(A) Alkanes: C_nH_{2n+2}

Where n = 1, 2, 3, 4 etc., as number of carbon atom.

CH_4	H_3C-CH_3	$H_3C-H_2C-CH_3$	$H_3C-H_2C-H_2C-CH_3$	$H_3C-\underset{H}{\overset{CH_3}{C}}-CH_3$
1. Methane	2. Ethane	3. Propane	4. n-Butane	5. Isobutane

Prefix **n**- used for those alkanes, where all carbons are in continuous chain. Prefix **iso**- used for those alkane, where methyl group is attached to second last carbon atom of continuous chain.

Types of carbon atoms:
There are four types as follows:
1. **1° Primary carbon:** A carbon atom attached to only one (or to all 4 hydrogens) carbon.
2. **2° secondary carbon:** A carbon atom attached to two other carbon atoms.
3. **3° Tertiary carbon:** A carbon atom attached to three other carbon atoms.
4. **4° Quaternary carbon:** A carbon atom attached to four other carbon atoms.

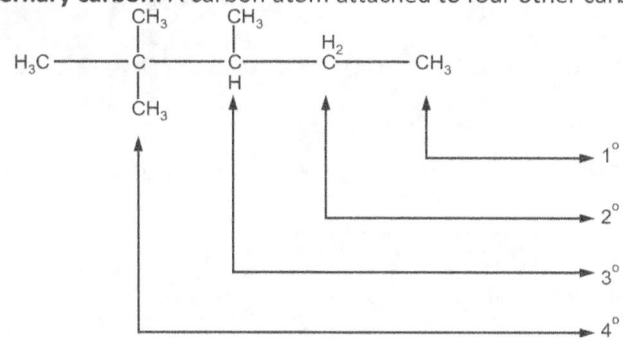

(B) Cycloalkanes:

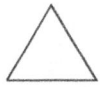

1. Cyclopropane   2. Cyclobutane   3. Cyclopentane   4. Cyclohexane

(C) Alkenes: (C_nH_{2n})

$CH_2=CH_2$ $CH_2=CH-CH_3$ $CH_2=CH-CH_2-CH_3$ $CH_3-CH=CH-CH_3$ 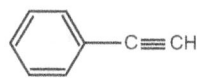

1. Ethylene   2. Propylene   3. 1-Butene   4. 2-Butene   5. Isobutene

(D) Alkynes: (C_nH_{2n-2})

$CH\equiv CH$ $H_3C-C\equiv C-CH_3$ 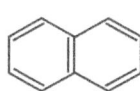   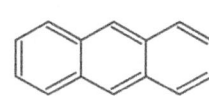

1. Acetylene   2. Dimethyacetylene   3. Isopropylacetylene   4. Phenylacetylene

(E) Aromatic Hydrocarbons:

       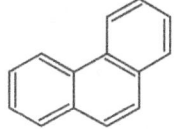

1. Benzene   2. Napthalene   3. Anthracene   4. Phenanthrene

(F) Arylalkyl Hydrocarbons:

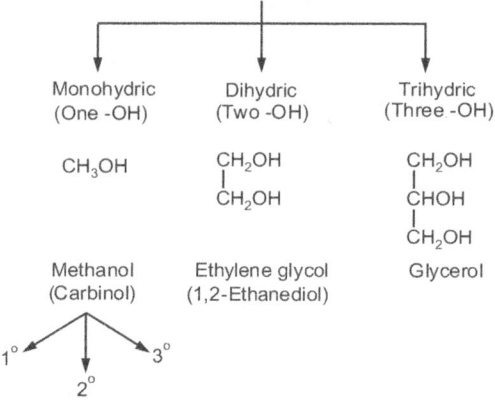

2. COMPOUNDS CONTAINING CARBON, HYDROGEN AND OXYGEN ONLY

(A) Alcohols: R-OH; (R= Alkyl or aryl) or R-OH; where, R = alkyl or aryl or aralkyl

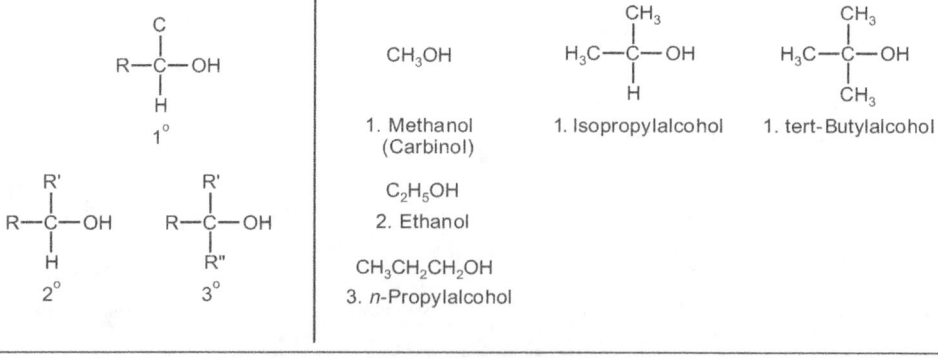

Monohydric alcohols are classified as primary (1°), secondary (2°), or tertiary (3°) depending upon –OH group attached to primary, secondary or tertiary carbon atom.

(B) Phenols: R = Aryl

1. Phenol   2. Catechol   3. Resorcinol   4. Quinol   5. o-Cresol

(C) Ethers: R-O-R'; where, R and R' = alkyl, acyl or aralkyl

```
        Symmetrical        Unsymmetrical
          R—O—R              R—O—R'
                              (R≠R')
```

CH_3-O-CH_3 $CH_3-CH_2-O-CH_3$ $CH_3-CH_2-O-CH_2-CH_3$
1. Dimethylether   2. Ethyl methylether   3. Diethylether

(D) Epoxides: (cyclic ethers)

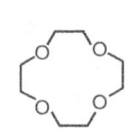 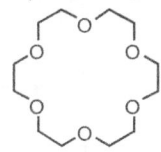 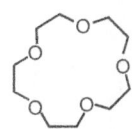

1. Ethyleneoxide (Epoxide)   2. Propyleneoxide   3. 1,4-Dioxane   4. Tetrahydrofuran

(E) Crown Ethers:
These are symmetrical cyclic polyalkyl ethers. Here 18 represents number of atoms in the cycle while, 6 refers to number of oxygen atoms.

1. [12] Crown-4   2. [18] Crown-6   3. [15] Crown-5

(F) Carbonyl Compounds:

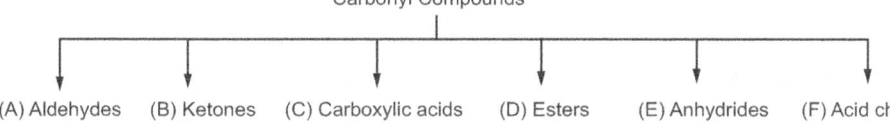

(A) Aldehydes   (B) Ketones   (C) Carboxylic acids   (D) Esters   (E) Anhydrides   (F) Acid chlorides

R—CHO   R—C(=O)—R'   R—C(=O)—OH   R—C(=O)—OR'   R—C(=O)—O—C(=O)—R'   R—C(=O)—Cl

(A) Aldehydes: R-CHO; where, R = Alkyl or aryl

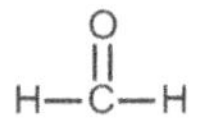

1. Formaldehyde: H—CHO

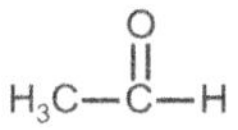

2. Acetaldehyde: H_3C—CHO

3. Propionaldehyde: H_3C—H_2C—CHO

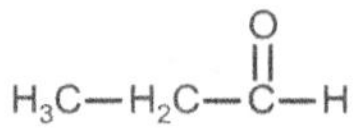

4. Butyraldehyde: H_3C—H_2C—H_2C—CHO

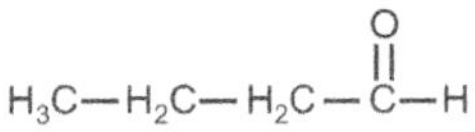

5. Benzaldehyde: C₆H₅—CHO

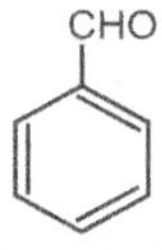

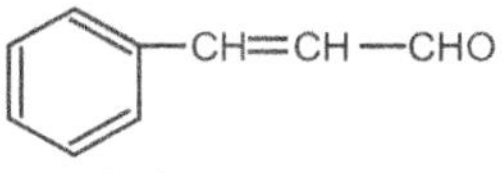

6. Cinnamaldehyde: C₆H₅—CH=CH—CHO

The carbon atom adjacent to carbonyl group in an aldehyde is called as α-carbon, the next one is β and so on.

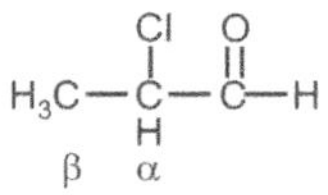

H_3C—$\underset{\beta}{C}H$—$\underset{\alpha}{C}(Cl)$—CHO   α-Chloropropionaldehyde

(B) Ketones: R—CO—R' where R = Alkyl or aryl

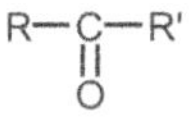

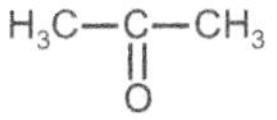

1. Acetone: H_3C—CO—CH_3

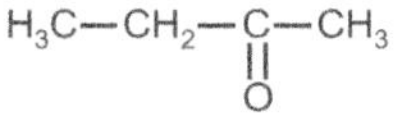

2. Ethyl methylketone: H_3C—CH_2—CO—CH_3

3. Diethylketone: H_3C—H_2C—CO—CH_2—CH_3

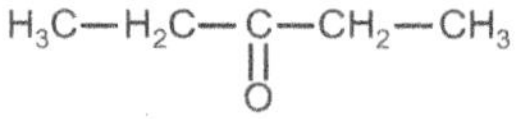

4. Acetophenone: C₆H₅—CO—CH_3

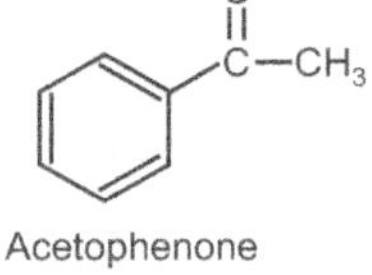

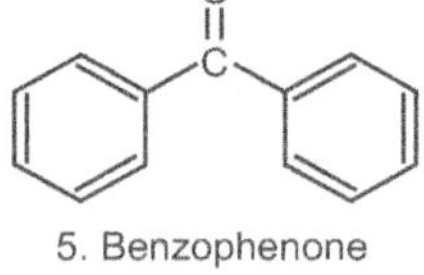

5. Benzophenone: C₆H₅—CO—C₆H₅

(C) Carboxylic Acids: R-COOH; R = Alkyl or aryl

Carboxylic acids
→ Mono-Carboxylic acids: R—COOH
→ Di-Carboxylic acids: HOOC—(CH$_2$)n—COOH

Mono-Carboxylic acids:

1. Formic acid: H—COOH
2. Acetic acid: H$_3$C—COOH
3. Propionic acid: H$_3$C—CH$_2$COOH
4. Butyric acid: H$_3$C—CH$_2$—CH$_2$COOH
5. Benzoic acid: C$_6$H$_5$—COOH

Di-Carboxylic acids:

1. Oxalic acid: COOH–COOH
2. Malonic acid: COOH–CH$_2$–COOH
3. Succinic acid: COOH–(CH$_2$)$_2$–COOH
4. Glutaric acid: COOH–(CH$_2$)$_3$–COOH
5. Phthalic acid: benzene-1,2-dicarboxylic acid

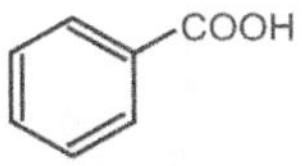

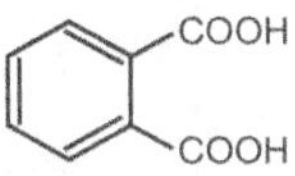

(D) Esters: R—C(=O)—OR' where, R = Alkyl

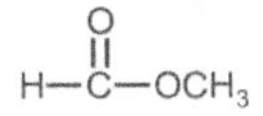

1. Methyl formate: H—C(=O)—OCH$_3$
2. Ethyl acetate: H$_3$C—C(=O)—O—CH$_2$—CH$_3$
3. Diethyl acetate: H$_3$C—CH$_2$—CH$_2$—C(=O)—O—CH$_2$—CH$_3$
4. Methyl butyrate: H$_3$C—H$_2$C—H$_2$C—C(=O)—OCH$_3$
5. Ethyl acetoacetate: H$_3$C—C(=O)—H$_2$C—C(=O)—OC$_2$H$_5$

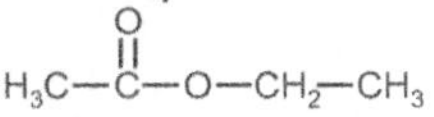

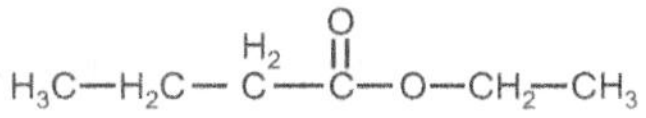

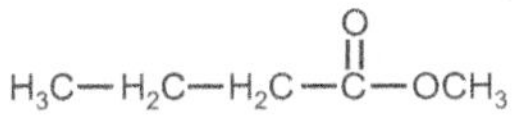

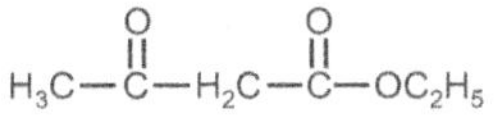

(E) Anhydrides: R-(CO)$_2$O-R'; where, R, R' = akyl, arylalcyl, aryl.

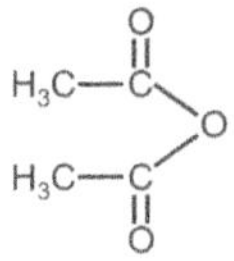

1. Acetic anhydride
2. Propionic anhydride 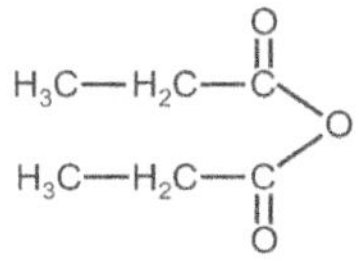
3. Succinic anhydride 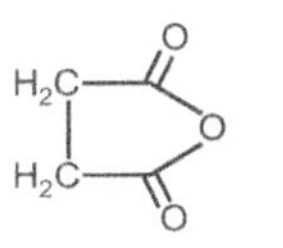
4. Malonic anhydride

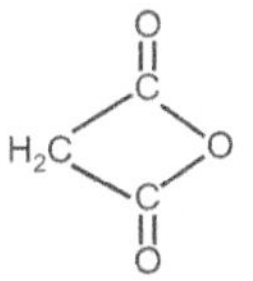

(F) Acid chlorides: R—C(=O)—Cl

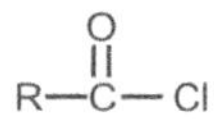

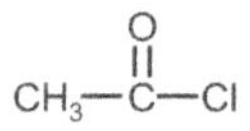

CH_3—C(=O)—Cl
1. Acetyl chloride

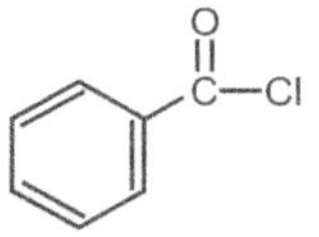

Ph—C(=O)—Cl
2. Benzoyl chloride

3. COMPOUNDS CONTAINING CARBON, HYDROGEN AND NITROGEN ONLY

(A) Amines: R-NH-R'; R = H, alkyl or aryl

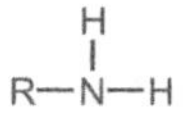

R—NH—H (with H on N) — Primary
R—N(R')—H — Secondary
R—N(R')—R" — Tertiary

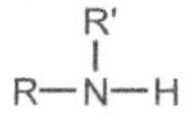

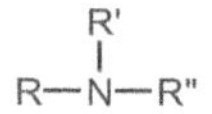

H_3C—NH_2
1. Methylamine

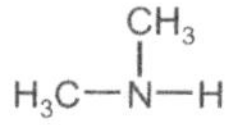

H_3C—N(CH$_3$)—H
1. Dimethyl amine

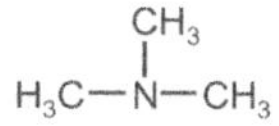

H_3C—N(CH$_3$)—CH_3
1. Trimethyl amine

H_3C—H_2C—NH_2
2. Ethylamine

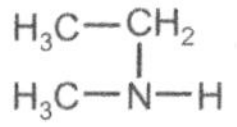

H_3C—N(CH$_2$CH$_3$)—H
2. Ethylmethylamine

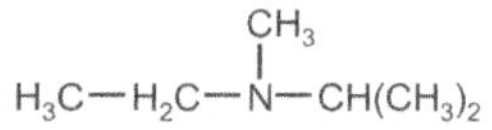

H_3C—H_2C—N(CH$_3$)—CH(CH$_3$)$_2$
2. Ethyl isopropylmethylamine

H_3C—H_2C—H_2C—NH_2
3. n-Propylamine

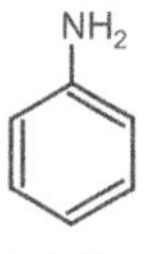

Ph—NH_2
4. Aniline

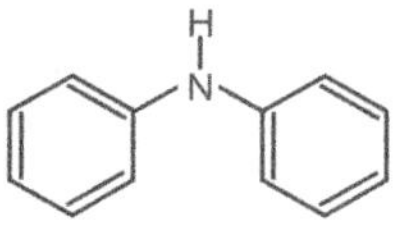

Ph—NH—Ph
3. Diphenylamine

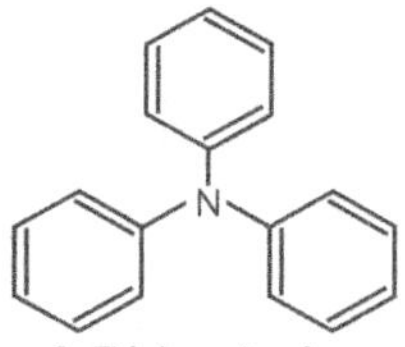

N(Ph)$_3$
3. Triphenylamine

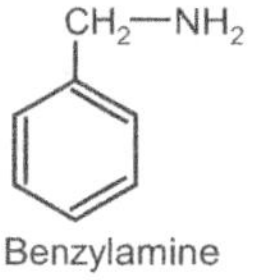

Ph—CH_2—NH_2
5. Benzylamine

(B) Imines: R—C(=NH)—R' (Shiff's base); where, R, R' = alkyl, arylalcyl, aryl.

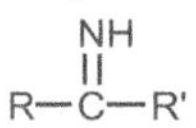

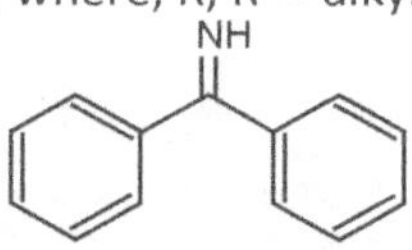

Ph—C(=NH)—Ph
1. Diphenylamine

(C) Nitriles: R – C ≡ N; where, R = alkyl, aryl, aryl alkyl.
(D) Isonitriles: (Isocyanates) R – N ≡ C; where, R = alkyl, aryl, aryl alkyl.
H₃C—C≡N
Methyl isocyanide

(E) Hydrazines: R – N(H) – NH₂; where, R = alkyl, aryl.

H₂N—NH₂—H₂O   H₃C—NH—NH₂   HN—NH₂ (phenyl)   (phenyl)-N(H)—NH-(phenyl)
1. Hydrazine hydrate   2. Methylhydrazine   3. Phenylhydrazine   4. Hydrazobenzene

4. COMPOUNDS CONTAINING CARBON, HYDROGEN, OXYGEN AND HALOGENS ONLY

(A) Alkyl-halides: R –X where, X = F/Cl/Br/I

Primary: R—CH₂—X   Secondary: R—CHR'—X   Tertiary: R—CR'R''—X

(a) Monohalogen compounds:

H₃C—Cl   H₃C—H₂C—Br   H₃C—CH(CH₃)—Cl   H₃C—C(CH₃)₂—Cl
1. Methyl chloride   2. Ethyl bromide   3. iso Propyl chloride   4. tert Butyl chloride

(b) Dihalogen compounds:

H—CHCl—Cl   H—CHCl—CHCl—H   H—CCl₂—CH₃
1. Dichloromethane   2. 1,2-dichloroethane   3. 1,1-dichloromethane
(Methylene dichloride) (Ethylene dichloride) (Ethylenedichloride)

If two halogen atoms are attached to same carbon atoms then it is called as *germinal* halide.
If two halogen atoms are attached to adjacent carbon atoms then it is called as *vicinal* halide.

(c) Trihalogen compounds:

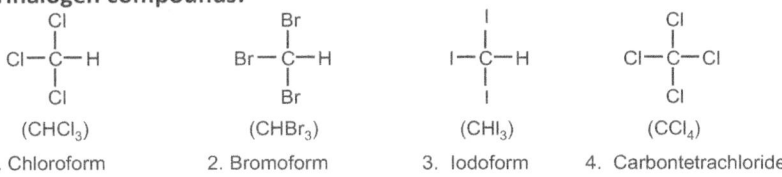

(CHCl₃)   (CHBr₃)   (CHI₃)   (CCl₄)
1. Chloroform   2. Bromoform   3. Iodoform   4. Carbontetrachloride

(d) Unsaturated Halides:

H₂C=CH—Cl
1. Vinyl chloride

H₂C=CH—Br
2. Vinyl bromide

H₂C=CH—I
3. Vinyl iodide

H₂C=CH—CH₂—Cl
4. Allyl chloride

H₂C=CH—CH₂—Br
5. Allyl bromide

H₂C=CH—CH₂I
6. Allyl iodide

(B) Aryl halides: (Ar – X)

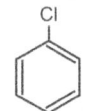
1. Chlorobenzene

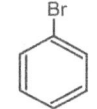
2. Bromobenzene

3. Iodobenzene

4. Benzyl chloride

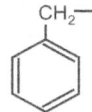
5. Benzyl bromide

6. Benzyl iodide

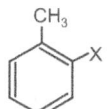
7. Halotoluene

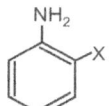
8. Haloamines

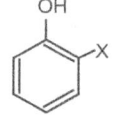
9. Halophenol

(C) Acyl halides:

CH₃COCl
1. Acetyl chloride

CH₃CH₂COCl
2. Propionyl chloride

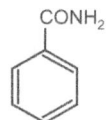
3. Benzoyl chloride

5. COMPOUNDS CONTAINING CARBON, HYDROGEN, OXYGEN, NITROGEN AND HALOGENS ONLY

(A) Amides:

R—C(=O)—NH₂

H—C(=O)—NH₂
1. Formamide

H₃C—C(=O)—NH₂
2. Acetamide

Ph—CONH₂
3. Benzamide

H₂N—C(=O)—NH₂
4. Urea

PHARMACEUTICAL ORGANIC CHEMISTRY - I CLASSIFICATION OF ORGANIC COMPOUNDS

(B) Imides:

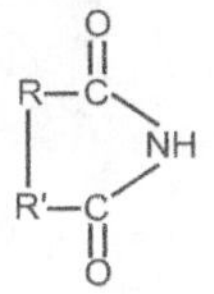

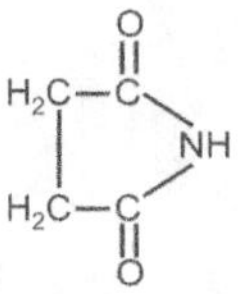

1. Succinimide
2. Phthalimide 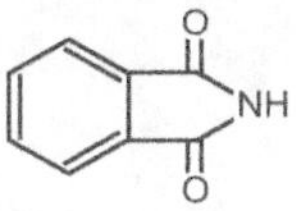

(C) Aldoximes:

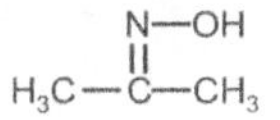

1. Acetone oxime
2. Ethylmethylacetoxime 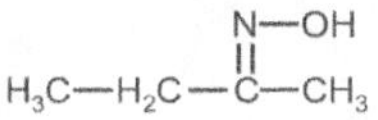
3. Acetophenoxime 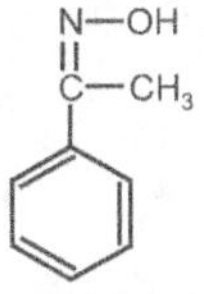

(D) Ketoxime:

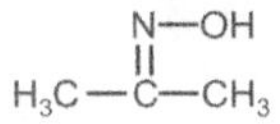

1. Acetone oxime
2. Ethylmethylacetoxime 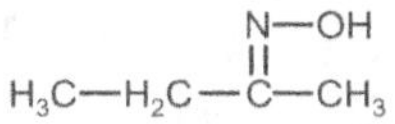
3. Acetophenoxime 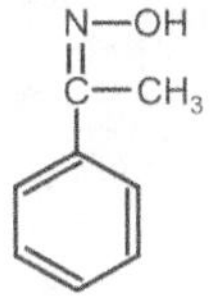

(E) Nitro Compounds:

1. Nitromethane
2. Nitroethane 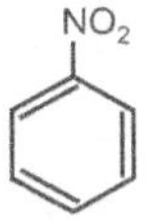
3. Nitrobenzene 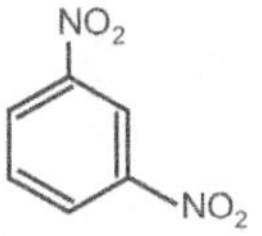
4. *m*-Dinitrobenzene (1,3-Dinitrobenzene) 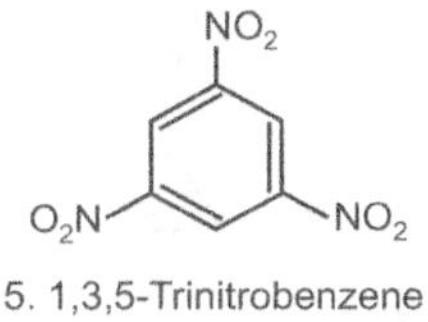
5. 1,3,5-Trinitrobenzene 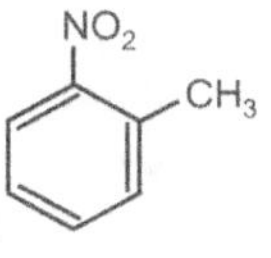
6. *o*-Nitrotoluene 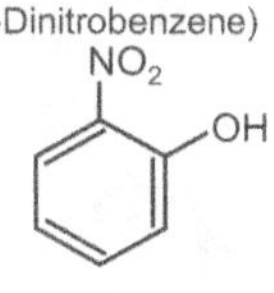
7. *o*-Nitrophenol

6. COMPOUNDS CONTAINING CARBON, HYDROGEN, OXYGEN, NITROGEN, SULPHUR AND HALOGENS ONLY

(A) Sulphonic acids: $R - SO_3OH$

1. Methane sulphonic acid
2. Ethane sulphonic acid 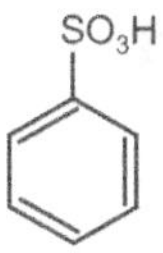
3. Benzene sulphonic acid

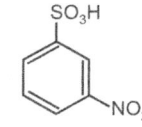
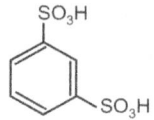

4. *m*-Bromobenzene sulphonic acid
5. *m*-Nitrobenzene sulphonic acid
6. Benzene, 1,3-disulphonic acid

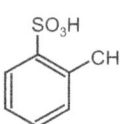
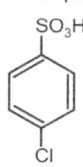
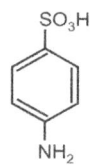
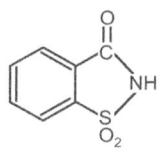

7. *o*-Toluene sulphonic acid (o - methyl benzene sulphonic acid)
8. *p*-Chlorobenzene sulphonic acid
9. Sulphanilic acid
10. Saccharin

(B) Sulphonyl halides:

1. Benzene sulphonyl chloride
2. Chloramine -T

(C) Sulphonamides:

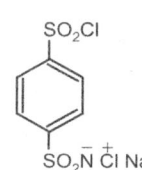

1. Sulphanilamide
2. Sulphacetamide

3. Sulphapyridine
4. Sulphadiazine

GENERAL RULES AND IUPAC NOMENCLATURE SYSTEM FOR ORGANIC COMPOUNDS

Millions of organic compounds are discovered till date. It is very difficult to remember every compound by a particular name. Hence, as seen above in this chapter, the organic compounds are classified on the basis of their chemical structures and properties. To be more precise the compounds are classified on the basis of their functional groups. Thus, each compound has an unique identity and it is imperative should have an unique name throughout the world. Thus, IUPAC (International Union of Pune and Applied Chemistry, Geneva) came with a harmonized system of naming the organic compounds, which is acceptable, followed and understood all across the world. This is called as the "IUPAC Nomenclature System".

General rules for writing IUPAC name:

- Locate the longest chain containing the principal functional group and as many of the secondary functional groups and multiple bonds as possible.
- Select the root word corresponding to the length of the chain e.g., pent for 5 carbon chain.
- Number the longest chain selected from the end nearer to the principal functional group or substituents or the side chain, if there is no functional group.
- Depending upon the nature of the carbon-carbon bond attach the suffix **'ane'** for –C-C-, **'ene'** for –C=C- and **'yne'** for – C ≡ C – to the root word.
- Add suitable prefixes and suffixes to indicate the number and position of each side chain, substituent or functional group.

Example:

$$\underset{\text{HO}}{}\overset{5}{C}H_3 \quad \overset{4}{C}H \quad \overset{3}{C}H_2 \quad \overset{2}{C}=O \quad \overset{1}{C}H_3$$

4-hydroxy-2-pentanone
or
4-hydroxypentan-2-one

IUPAC system of nomenclature is highly systematic. For a given IUPAC name only one structure can be written. This helps in translation of a structure to compound and *vice-versa*. The IUPAC name consists of a *base name* (a prefix may or may not be present). The base name may comprise of a root name and prefix.

Example:

H₃C—CH₃
Ethane

Here ethane is the base name without prefix.

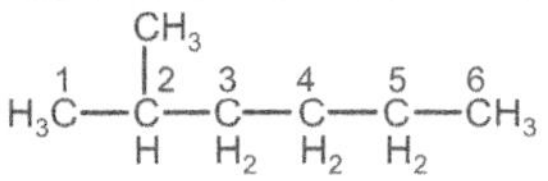

```
        CH₃
        |2  3    4    5   6
H₃C—C—C—C—C—CH₃
    1  H  H₂  H₂  H₂
```
2-Methylhexane

Here pentane is the base name and 2-chloro is the prefix.

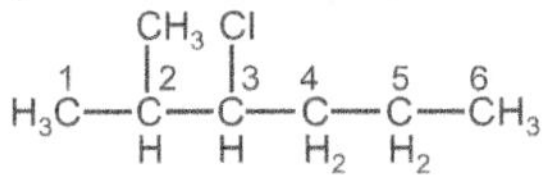

```
        CH₃  Cl
        |2   |3   4    5   6
H₃C—C—C—C—C—CH₃
    1  H   H   H₂  H₂
```
2-Methyl-3-chlorohexane

Here chlorohexane is the base name which consists of hexane (root name) and chloro (prefix).

IUPAC rules:

1. If the base name of a compound is the name of an actual compound, the prefix is joined to the base name to give one word name but, if the base name is not the actual compound the prefix stands alone and a space is left between the prefix and base name. For example, in 2-methyl-3-chlorohexane the *base name* is 'chlorohexane'. But chlorohexane itself is a compound. Hence, it is given a one word name. But for compounds such as sodium ethanoate the two words are written separately since, there is no compound of the name ethanoate. Thus, salts and esters do not have one word name.

2. To choose the base name of the compound one should choose the parent part of the molecule *i.e.* the most substituted largest part and important part bearing the functional group. For example in the following structure the labeled carbon chain is the longest chain, it has the most number of substituents and the important functional group. Hence, it is the parent chain.

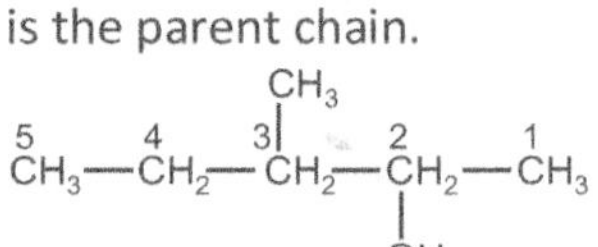

```
                    CH₃
        5    4    3|    2     1
    CH₃—CH₂—CH₂—CH₂—CH₃
                    |
                    OH
```

3. The nature of the base chain, the number of carbon atoms present and the functional group attached to it provide the root for the base name.

4. The most important functional group determines the suffix or prefix to the root for constructing the base name. If more than one functional group is present then the more important functional group gets the priority over other.

The order of precedence is:

Ammonium > Sulphonium > Hydroperoxyl > Carboxylic acid > Sulphonic acid > Ester > Carbonyl halide > Amido > Carbonitrile > Isonitrile > Formyl (Aldehyde) > Ketone > Hydroxyl > Mercapto > Amino > Ether > Alkyl sulphonyl > Double bond > Triple bond > Cl > Br > I > Azo > Nitro > Nitroso.

Example:

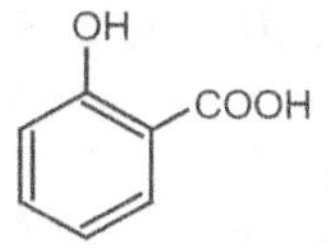

2-Hydroxybenzoic acid

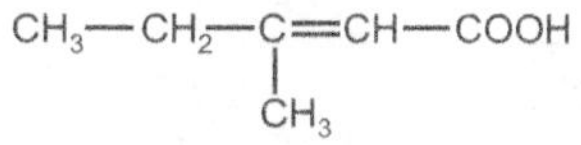

3-Methyl-2-pentenoic acid
3-Methylpent-2-enoic acid

5. Each of the carbon atoms in the base carbon chain is numbered sequentially; the positions of the functional groups and hydrocarbon groups are indicated by these numbers. The assigned number to a carbon atom which bears a substituent is called the location number or the locant of the substituents.

Example:

In 2-Hydroxybenzoic acid, –OH group is attached to the carbon number 2. Hence '2' is the locant.

6. The method of numbering base chain:
   - **Open chain compounds:** The numbering of the carbon atoms of the base chain is done from the end carbon that will give the lowest number to the primary function. If the primary functional group is equidistant from both ends, the numbering should be done from that end carbon which gives the lowest sum of the numbers for the carbons carrying the substituents.

     Example:

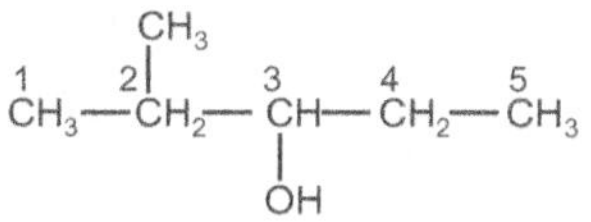

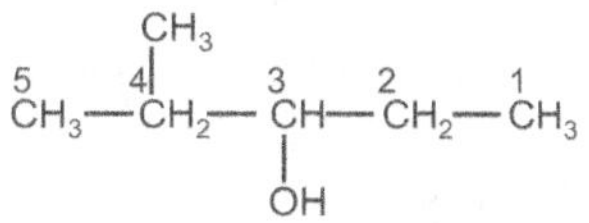

     The first method is the correct way of numbering the carbon chain since the sum of the locants in first case is (2 + 3 = 5) lower than in second case (3 + 4 = 7)

   - **Alicyclic compounds:** The numbering of the carbon atoms starts from that carbon atom which carries the primary substituents and in the direction which gives the lowest sum of the locants.

Example:

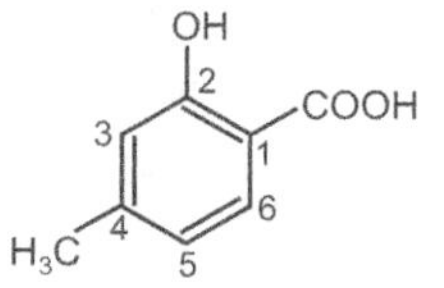

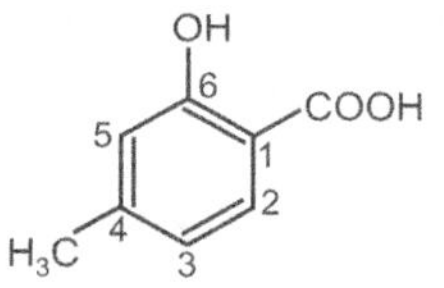

Here also first method is correct and not second.

- **Polynuclear aromatic and alicyclic compounds:** They have a special numbering system. Naphthalene can be numbered in four different ways.

  Example:

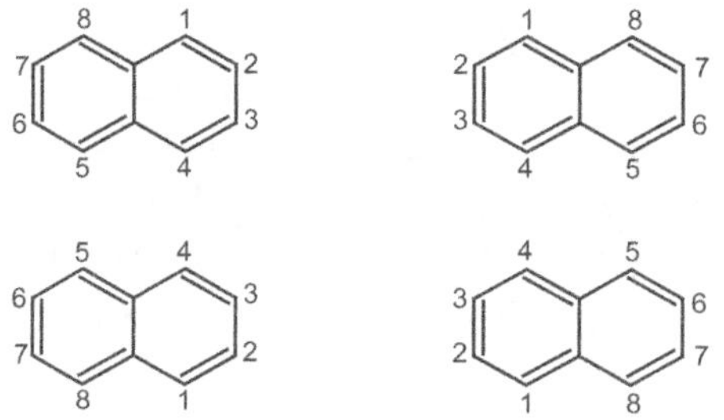

  The numbering starts from that position which will give smallest locant to highest important group.

  Example:

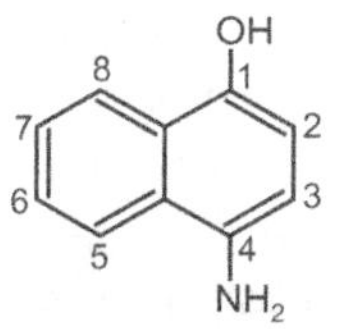

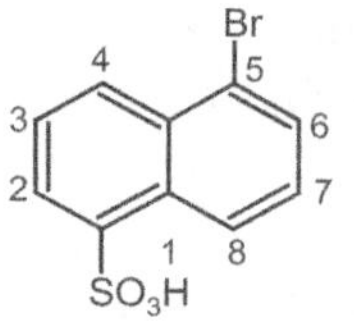

  Lowest sum of the locant rule should be followed.

- **Heterocyclic compounds:** Those compounds containing the heteroatom are usually numbered from that hetero atom. The more important functional group gets the lower number and the lowest sum rule is followed for numbering of substituents.

  Example:

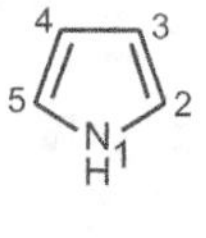

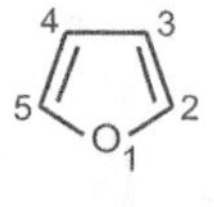

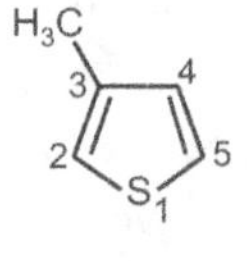

7. The locant of the primary function is joined to the base name by a hyphen (-) e.g. 2-hydroxybenzoic acid.
   - If the position of the primary functional group is unique its locant is not indicated e.g., butanone, propanal, propene etc.
   - If the primary function is apart of the base carbon chain then the carbon atom of the functional group is numbered one. All compounds containing the functional groups such as acid, aldehyde, ester, amide, carbonyl halide etc. For example, butanoic acid.
   - The locant of the nuclear substituents, the primary function of an alicyclic compound and benzene derivatives are always 1.
8. The names of the functional groups other than primary and those of branches are denoted by prefixes to the base name of a compound.

   Example:

   $$CH_3-CH(OH)-CH(CH_3)-CHO$$

   2-methyl-butanal

9. Branches are always indicated by prefixes. The locant is prefixed to its name by a hyphen and the combined part is joined to the base name.

   Example:

   $$CH_3-CH_2-CH(CH_3)-CH_2OH$$

   2-Methyl-1-butanol

10. If the base name bears the locant of primary function the prefix is joined to the base name by hyphen.

    Example:

    $$CH_3-CH(CH_3)-CH(CH_3)-CH_2OH$$

    2,3-Dimethyl-1-butanol

11. If there are two or more substituents, branches or functions each of them is combined with its locant and then the combined parts are arranged either alphabetically or in order of increasing complexity and joined to each other by hyphens. The last combined part is joined to the base name without hyphen if the base name does not have any locant; but if there is a locant then hyphen is put.

Example:

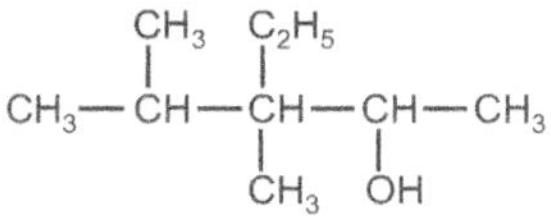

$$CH_3-\underset{\underset{CH_3}{|}}{CH}-\underset{\underset{CH_3}{|}}{\overset{\overset{CH_3}{|}}{C}}-\underset{\underset{OH}{|}}{\overset{\overset{C_2H_5}{|}}{C}}-CH-CH_3$$

3-Ethyl-3,4-dimethyl-2-pentanol

12. If there are two or more identical substituents the number of such a group is indicated by a prefix to its name di = two, tri = three, tetra = four, penta = five, hexa = six etc. the locants of such substituents are all retained and written in an increasing order, separated by commas and the last number is separated from the name of the substituents by hyphen. The first letters of di, tri, tetra get no importance in considering the alphabetical order for assembling prefixes.

Example:

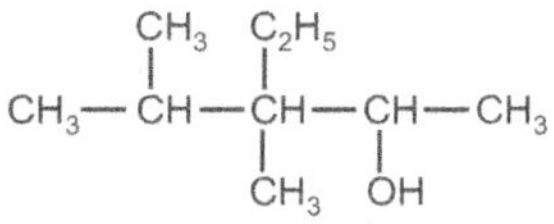

$$CH_3-\underset{\underset{CH_3}{|}}{CH}-\underset{\underset{CH_3}{|}}{\overset{\overset{CH_3}{|}}{C}}-\underset{\underset{OH}{|}}{\overset{\overset{C_2H_5}{|}}{C}}-CH-CH_3$$

3,3,4 - Trimethyl 2 - pentanol

If a substituents on a base chain contains substituent group, the substituents is called compound substituent.

Example:

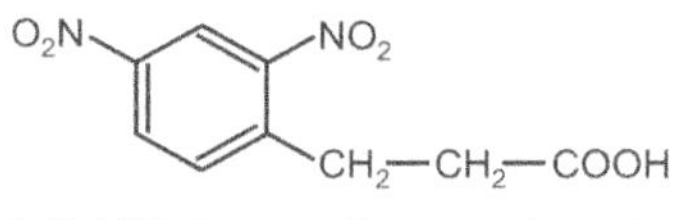

3-(2,4-Dinitrophenyl) propanoic acid

1. **Alkanes and Cycloalkanes:**

   Alkanes and cycloalkanes have the name ending with **ane**. For nomenclature of alkanes the longest chain is selected as the parent chain and given the corresponding name. For example, 2 carbon chain is ethane, 3 carbon chain is propane etc. Then numbering of this chain is done in a fashion so as to give the lowest number to the substituents. The locant and the respective substituents is then prefixed with the base name.

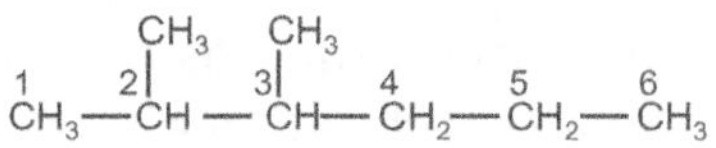

   2,3-Dimethylhexane 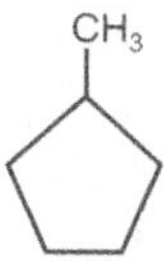   1-Methylcyclopentane

2. Alkenes and Cycloalkenes:

Alkenes and cycloalkenes have the name ending with **ene**. For nomenclature of alkenes the longest chain is selected as the parent chain and given the name of the corresponding alkane. The ending **ane of the alkane** is replaced by **ene**. For example, 2 carbon chain is ethane derived from ethane, 3 carbon chain is propene derived from propane etc. Then numbering of this chain is done from that end of the chain which gives the lowest number to the double bond. The name of the substituents and their respective locants are then prefixed with the base name.

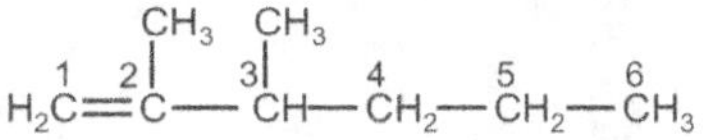

2,3-Dimethyl-1-hexene

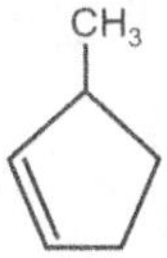

3-Methylcyclo-2-hexene

3. Alkynes:

- The suffix is **yne.**
- For nomenclature of alkenes the longest chain is selected as the parent chain and given the name of the corresponding alkane. The ending **ane of the alkane** is replaced by **yne.**
- The numbering of this chain is done from the end which gives the lowest number to the triple bond.
- The name of the substituents and their respective locants are then prefixed with the base name.

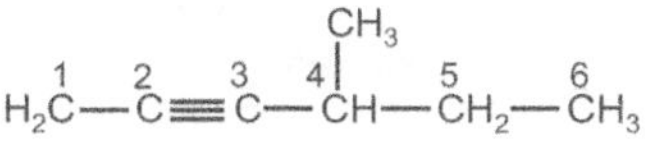

4-Methyl-2-hexyne

4. Carboxylic acids:

- The "suffix" is **oic acid.**
- For nomenclature of carboxylic acids the longest chain is selected as the parent chain and given the name of the corresponding alkane. The ending **ane** of the alkane is replaced by **oic acid.**
- The numbering of this chain is done from the carboxyl carbon.
- The name of the substituents and their respective locants are then prefixed with the base name.

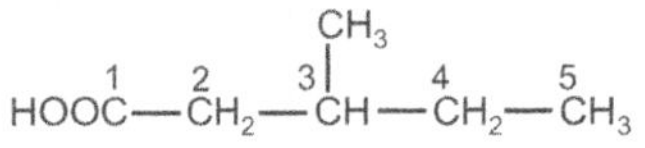

3-Methylpentanoic acid

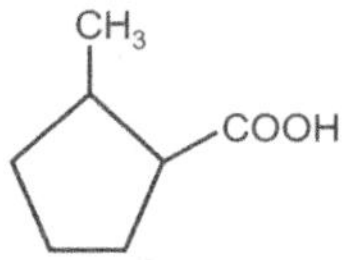

$$\overset{1}{HOOC}-\overset{2}{CH_2}-\overset{3}{CH}(CH_3)-\overset{4}{CH_2}-\overset{5}{CH_3}$$

2-Methylcyclopentanoic acid

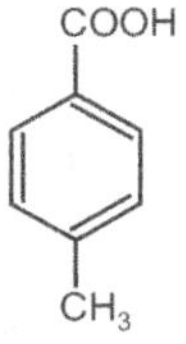

4-Methylbenzoic acid

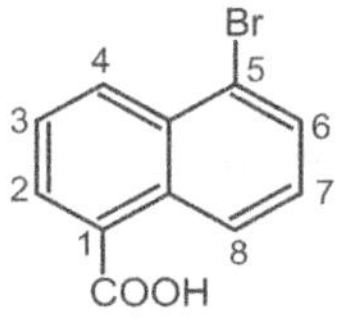

5-Bromonaphthoic acid

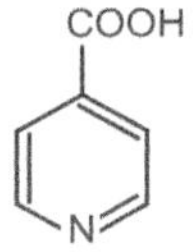

Pyridine-4-carboxylic acid

5. Acid halides, Amides, Acid anhydrides, Esters, Acid salts:

Acid halides, Amides, Acid anhydrides, Esters, Acid salts are the derivatives of acids in which the H atom of –COOH is replaced by a halogen X, amino -NH_2, R-C=O, alkoxy –OR, or with a metal cation respectively. The general rules applicable to the nomenclature of acid derivatives are adopted for these compounds. The suffix is different for each class.

Formula of functional group	Suffix when part of base chain	Suffix when substituent
—C(=O)—X	-oyl halide	Carbonyl halide
—C(=O)—NH_2	-amide	Carboxamide
—C(=O)—O—C(=O)—	-oic anhydride	Carboxy anhydride
—C(=O)—OR	R –oate	Name of R carboxylate
—COO$^-$ M$^+$	Name of the cationoate	Name of the cation carboxylate

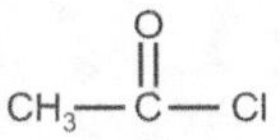

Ethanoyl chloride — CH₃—C(=O)—Cl

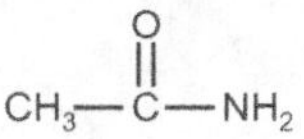

Ethanamide — CH₃—C(=O)—NH₂

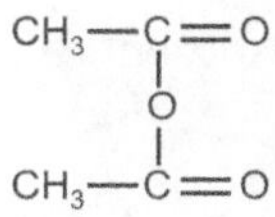

Ethanoic anhydride — CH₃—C(=O)—O—C(=O)—CH₃

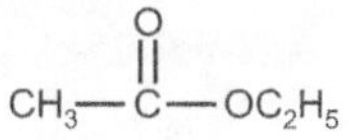

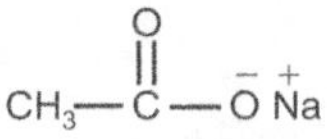

Ethyl ethanoate — CH₃—C(=O)—OC₂H₅

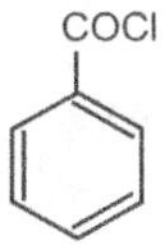

Sodium ethanoate — CH₃—C(=O)—O⁻ Na⁺

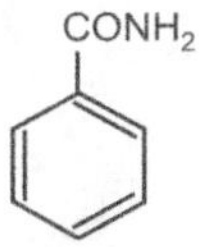

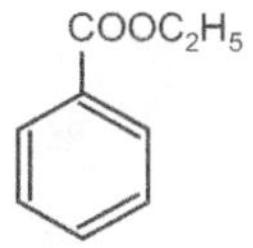

Benzoyl chloride — C₆H₅—COCl

Benzamide — C₆H₅—CONH₂

Ethyl benzoate — C₆H₅—COOC₂H₅

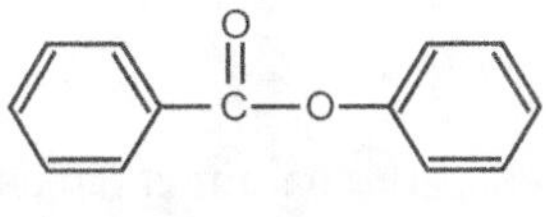

Phenyl benzoate

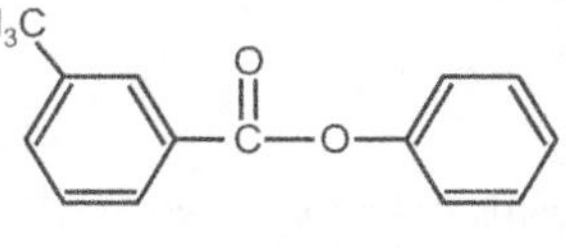

Phenyl 3-methylbenzoate

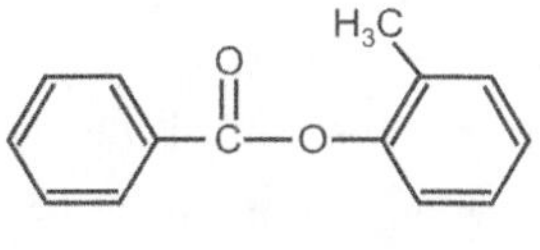

2-Methylphenyl benzoate

6. **Aldehydes:**

   The general rules of nomenclature are same.
   - The suffix is **al.**
   - For nomenclature of aldehydes the longest chain is selected as the parent chain and given the name of the corresponding alkane. The ending **ane** of the alkane is replaced by **al.**
   - The numbering of this chain is done from the carbonyl carbon.
   - The name of the substituents and their respective locants are then prefixed with the base name.

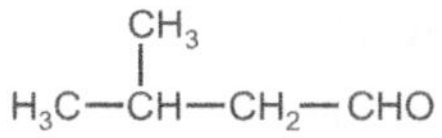

   H₃C—CH(CH₃)—CH₂—CHO
   3-Methylbutanal

7. **Ketones:**
   - The suffix is **one.**
   - For nomenclature of ketones the longest chain is selected as the parent chain and given the name of the corresponding alkane. The ending **e** of the alkane is replaced by **one.**
   - The numbering of this chain is done from the end carbon which gives least number to the carbonyl carbon.

- The name of the substituents and their respective locants are then prefixed with the base name.

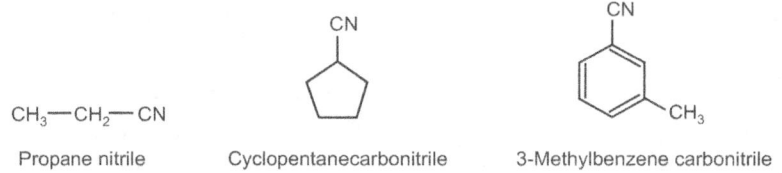

| Propanone | Acetophenone | Benzophenone |

4-Chlorobenzophenone   4-Chloro-3'-methylbenzophenone

8. **Nitriles:**
    - The suffix is **nitrile**.
    - For nomenclature of nitriles the longest chain is selected as the parent chain and given the name of the corresponding alkane. The suffix is added after the name of the alkane without a space.
    - The numbering of this chain is done from the nitrile carbon.
    - The name of the substituents and their respective locants are then prefixed with the base name.

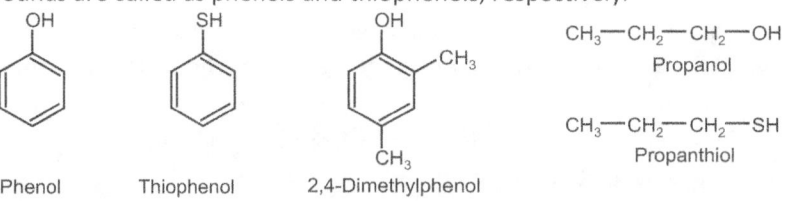

Propane nitrile   Cyclopentanecarbonitrile   3-Methylbenzene carbonitrile

9. **Hydroxy and Mercapto derivatives:**
    - Hydroxy and mercapto derivatives of acyclic and alicyclic compounds are called as alcohols and thiols, respectively. The suffixes for these compounds are **ol** and **thiol**, respectively. Nuclear substituted hydroxyl derivatives of aromatic compounds are called as phenols and thiophenols, respectively.

Phenol   Thiophenol   2,4-Dimethylphenol $CH_3-CH_2-CH_2-OH$ Propanol $CH_3-CH_2-CH_2-SH$ Propanthiol

PHARMACEUTICAL ORGANIC CHEMISTRY - I   CLASSIFICATION OF ORGANIC COMPOUNDS

10. Amines:
- The suffix is **amine**.
- For nomenclature of amines the longest chain is selected as the parent chain and given the name of the corresponding alkane. The ending **e** of the alkane is replaced by **amine**.
- The numbering of this chain is done from the end carbon which gives least number to the amino nitrogen.
- The name of the substituents and their respective locants are then prefixed with the base name.

$CH_3-CH_2-CH_2-NH_2$
Propanamine

Cyclopentanamine

2-Methylaniline

11. Ethers, halo, nitro and nitroso derivatives:
- In these compounds, the names of the functions are prefixed to the names of the parent carbon chain. Locants and branched groups are determined by the general rules.

$H_3C-O-CH_3$
Methoxymethane

$H_3C-O-C_2H_5$
Methoxyethane

Methoxybenzene

$CH_3-CH_2-CH_2-Cl$
1-Chloropropane

Chlorobenzene

$CH_3-CH_2-CH_2-NO_2$
1-Nitropropane

Nitrobenzene

2-Nitrosonaphthalene

12. Compounds containing two functional groups:
- For nomenclature purpose, the longest chain is selected as the parent chain and given the name of the corresponding alkane.
- The parent name is given according to the most important function as given in the priority list.
- Numbering of the carbon chain is done such that, the functional groups get the least numbers according to their priority order.

- The name of the substituents and their respective locants are then prefixed with the base name.

2-Nitrophenol   2-Hydroxyaniline   3-Chlorobutanoic acid

Writing the structural formula from the given IUPAC name is based on the following steps:

- Locate the parent alkane from the name and write the number of carbon atoms of this alkane in a straight chain and number them.
- Now locate suffix, which gives information about the name and the number of the functional groups along with their positions
- Lastly locate groups and/or substituents mentioned in the prefix and the carbon atoms to which these are attached as indicated by the locants.
- This gives the skeleton formula. Now add H atoms to satisfy the carbon bonds.

Example:

3-Ethyl-2,5-dimethyl-1,4-heptadiene

Below is provided a very novel and crisp, yet a very useful way of remembering the systematic IUPAC nomenclature of various organic compounds encountered in our syllabus. This can indeed serve as a very useful "ready-reckoner" for this purpose.

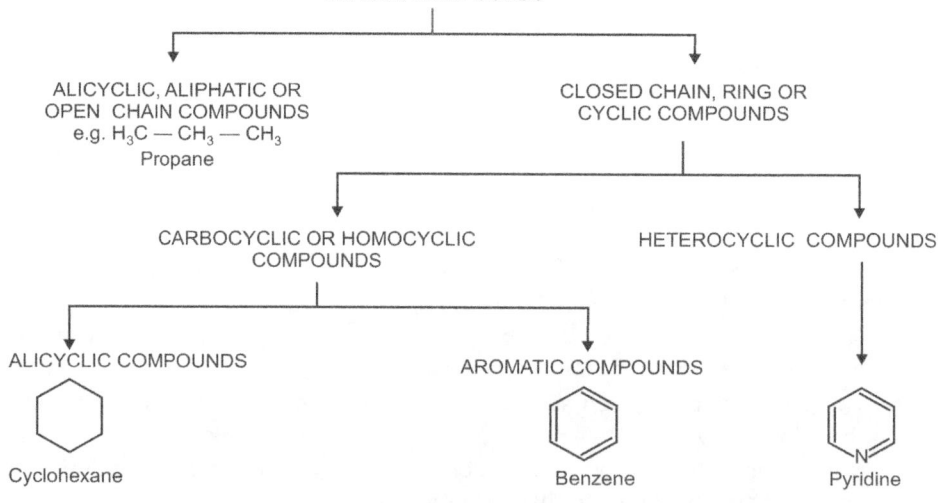

PHARMACEUTICAL ORGANIC CHEMISTRY - I — CLASSIFICATION OF ORGANIC COMPOUNDS

General Rules for writing IUPAC names:

(i) Locate the longest chain containing the principal functional group and as many of the secondary functional groups and multiple bonds as possible.

(ii) Select the root word corresponding to the length of the chain, e.g., pent for 5-C chain.

(iii) Number the longest chain selected from the end nearer to the principal functional group or substituents or the side chain if there is no functional group.

(iv) Depending on the nature of carbon carbon bonds (C–C, C=C, C≡C); attach the suffix -ane (for-C-C-); -ene (for -C=C-); -yne (for -C≡C-) to the root word.

(v) Add suitable prefixes and suffixes with numericals to indicate the number and position of each side chain, substituent or functional group.

```
Substituents ↘                    Functional Group ↗
              Prefix-Parent-Suffix
                       ↓
         Number of carbon atoms in parent chain
```

Priority of Groups:

– COOH > – COOR > – SO₃H > – COX > – CONH₂ > – CHO > – CN > ⟩C = O >
– OH > – SH > – NH₂ > – O – > – N = N > – NO₂ > – NO > alkenyl > alkyl > – X

Example:

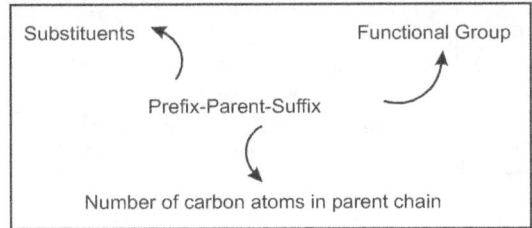

4-Hydroxy-2-pentanone   7-Hydroxy-3-methoxy-oct-5-ene-1-al

Writing the Structural Formula from the given IUPAC Name:

(i) Locate the parent alkane from the name and write the number of carbon atoms of this alkane in a straight chain and number them.

(ii) Now locate suffix, which gives information about the name and the number of the functional groups along with their positions.

(iii) Lastly locate groups or/and substituents mentioned in the prefix and the carbon atoms to which these are attached as indicated by the locants.

(iv) This gives the skeleton formula. Now add H atoms to satisfy the carbon bonds.

Example: Write the structural formula of 3-ethyl-2, 5-dimethyl-1, 4-heptadiene.

Step (i)

$\overset{7}{C}-\overset{6}{C}-\overset{5}{C}-\overset{4}{C}-\overset{3}{C}-\overset{2}{C}-\overset{1}{C}$

Step (ii)

$\overset{7}{C}-\overset{6}{C}-\overset{5}{C}=\overset{4}{C}-\overset{3}{C}-\overset{2}{C}-\overset{1}{C}$

Step (iii)

$\overset{7}{C}-\overset{6}{C}-\overset{5}{C}=\overset{4}{C}-\overset{3}{\underset{\underset{CH_3}{|}}{C}}-\overset{2}{\underset{\underset{CH_3}{|}}{\underset{H_5C_2}{C}}}-\overset{1}{C}$

Step (iv)

$H_3\overset{7}{C}-\overset{6}{CH_2}-\overset{5}{C}=\overset{4}{CH}-\overset{3}{\underset{\underset{CH_3}{|}}{CH}}-\overset{2}{\underset{\underset{CH_3}{|}}{\underset{H_5C_2}{C}}}=\overset{1}{CH_2}$

Name of the functional group	General formula	Example	IUPAC name (example)	Remark suffix	General/ Common name	Remark suffix/ prefix
Alkane (Carbon-Carbon Single bond)	$-\overset{|}{\underset{|}{C}}-\overset{|}{\underset{|}{C}}-$ C_nH_{2n+2}	CH_4	Alkene Methane	– ane	Paraffin	–ane e.g. Methane
Alkene (Carbon-Carbon Double bond)	$C=C$ C_nH_{2n}	$H_2C=CH_2$	Alkene Ethene	– ane to ene	Olefin	ane to –ylene e.g. Ethylene
Alkynes (Carbon-Carbon Triple bond)	$-C\equiv C-$ C_nH_{2n-2}	$H-C\equiv C-H$	Alkyne Ethyne	ane to yne	Acetylene	Prefix : alkyl acetylene e.g. Methyl acetylene
Halo alkanes	$R-X$ X = halide	H_3C-Cl	Haloalkane Chloro methane	Prefix : Halo Suffix : ane	Alkyl halide	ane to –yl halide e.g. Methyl chloride
Hydroxyl	$R-OH$	H_3C-OH	Alkanol Methanol	e to ol	Alkyl alcohol	ane to –yl alcohol e.g. Methyl alcohol
Ether	$R-O-R'$	$H_3C-O-CH_3$	Alkoxyalkane Methoxy-methane	ane to oxyalkane	Alkyl ether	ane to -ylether e.g. Dimethyl ether
Aldehyde	$R-\overset{O}{\underset{H}{\overset{\|\|}{C}}}$	$H-\overset{O}{\underset{H}{\overset{\|\|}{C}}}$	Alkanal Methanal	ane to al	Aldehyde	aldehyde e.g. Formaldehyde
Keto	$R-\overset{O}{\underset{R'}{\overset{\|\|}{C}}}$	$H_3C-\overset{O}{\underset{CH_3}{\overset{\|\|}{C}}}$	Alkanone Propanone	e to one	Ketone	ketone e.g. Acetone
Carboxyl	$R-\overset{O}{\underset{OH}{\overset{\|\|}{C}}}$	HCOOH CH_3CH_2COOH	Alkanoic acid Methanoic acid Propanoic acid	e to oic acid	Carboxylic acid	Many times as ic acid not always oic acid e.g. Formic acid Propionic acid
Carbonyl-halide	$R-\overset{O}{\underset{X}{\overset{\|\|}{C}}}$ X=halide	$H_3C-\overset{O}{\underset{Cl}{\overset{\|\|}{C}}}$	Alkanoyl halide Ethanoyl chloride	e to oyl halide	Acid halide	Suffix ic acid to -ylhalide e.g. Acetyl chloride

contd. ...

Class	Structure (R)	Structure (CH₃)	IUPAC name	Common name	IUPAC suffix/prefix	Example
Acid anhydride	R-C(=O)-O-C(=O)-R	CH₃-C(=O)-O-C(=O)-CH₃	Alkanoic anhydride / Ethanoic anhydride	e to oic anhydride	Acid anhyride	Acid to anhydride e.g. Acetic anhydride
Amido or Carboxamido	R-C(=O)-NH₂	H₃C-C(=O)-NH₂	Alkanamide / Ethanamide	e to amide	Acid amide	Suffix ic acid to amide e.g. Acetamide
Ester	R-C(=O)-OR'	H₃C-C(=O)-OC₂H₅	Alkyl alkanote / Ethyl ethanoate	e to oate	Alkyl ester	Prefix R' = alkyl ic acid to ate e.g. Ethyl acetate
Amino	R-NH₂	H₃C-NH₂	Alkanamine / Methamamine	e to amine	Alkyl amine	ane to -ylamine e.g. Methylamine
Nitro	R-NO₂	H₃C-NO₂	Nitro alkane / Nitromethane	Prefix Nitro	Nitroalkane	Prefix nitro Suffix alkane e.g. Nitromethane
Cyano	R-C≡N	H₃C-C≡N	Alkane nitrile / Methane nitrile	nitrile	Alkyl cyanide	ane to -ylcyanide e.g. Methyl cyanide
Sulfonic acid	R-SO₃H	H₃C-SO₃H	Alkane sulfonic acid / Methane sulfonic acid	sulfonic acid	Alkane sulphonic acid	suffix- sulphonic acid e.g. Methane sulphonic acid
Mercapto	R-SH	H₅C₂-SH	Alkane thiol / Ethane thiol	thiol	Alkyl mercaptan	ane to -ylmercaptan e.g. Ethyl mercaptan

QUESTION BANK

1. Classify hydrocarbons giving their chemical structures.
2. Classify alcohols giving their structural formulae.
3. Describe phenols and ethers giving their structures.
4. Classify carbonyl compounds giving their structures.
5. Classify carboxylic acids and their derivatives giving structures.
6. Classify amines giving structures of each class.
7. Classify alkyl halides, aryl halides and acyl ahalides giving structures.
8. Classify amides, imides, aldoximes and ketoximes giving their structures.
9. Classify sulphur containing compounds giving structures.
10. What is the IUPAC nomenclature system for organic compounds? What are its common rules?

11. Discuss in details the systematic IUPAC nomenclature rules for various classes of compounds classified as according to their functional groups giving suitable examples for each class.
12. Summarize the IUPAC nomenclature of organic compounds in a very simple and easy to understand way
13. Discuss how can a structural formula be written from the given IUPAC name
14. Write down the IUPAC names of the following compounds:
    1. $(CH_3)_3C \cdot COCl$
    2. $(CH_3)_2CHCH_2CH(Et)CONH_2$
    3. $(CH_3)_2CH-CH_3CHO$
    4. CH_3CH_2CN
    5. $CH_3-CH_2-CH(CH_3)-COOEt$
    6. Pyridine-2-carbonyl chloride structure
    7. 3-methylcyclohexyl-CH₂CONH₂
    8. 2-isopropylbenzaldehyde (CHO and CH(CH₃)₂ on benzene)
    9. Cyclopentane with CHO and C₂H₅
    10. Benzene with H₃C, CN, CH₃, CH₃ substituents
    11. Benzene with COCl, C(CH₃)₃, C₂H₅
    12. Pyrrole with CONH₂
    13. Benzene with COCH₃ and CH₃
    14. Pyridine with CH₂-C(=O)-CH-CH₃
    15. Cyclohexyl-C(=O)-CH₂-CH₂-CH₃
    16. Phenyl-CH₂-C(=O)-CH₂-cyclopentyl
    17. Benzene with CH₂CH₃ and SH
    18. 4-hydroxypyridine

19. 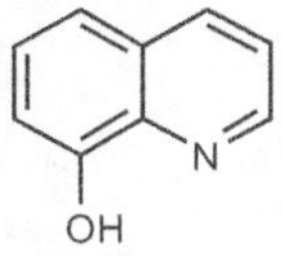 8-hydroxyquinoline structure (quinoline with OH at position 8)

20. 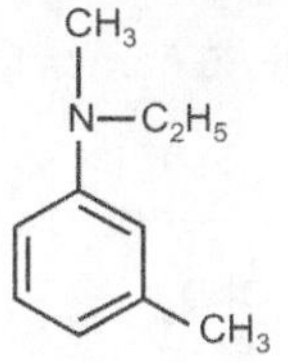 N,N-ethyl-methyl-3-methylaniline structure (benzene with N(CH₃)(C₂H₅) and CH₃ substituents)

21. 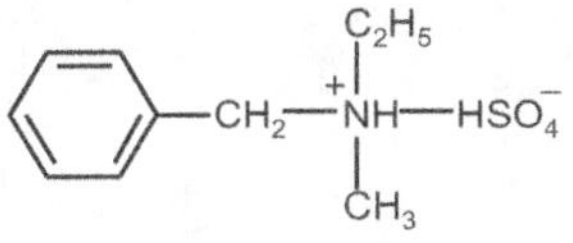 Benzyl-ethyl-methyl ammonium hydrogen sulfate: C₆H₅–CH₂–N⁺H(C₂H₅)(CH₃) HSO₄⁻

22. $CH_3-NH-CH_2-CH_3$

23. $CH_3-O-CH_2-CH_2-CH_3$

24. 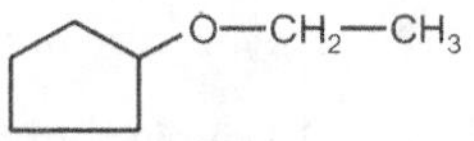 Cyclopentyl–O–CH₂–CH₃

25. 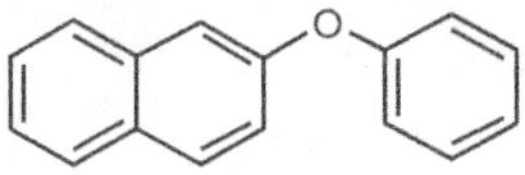 2-phenoxynaphthalene structure

26. 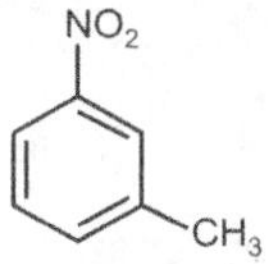 3-nitrotoluene (benzene with NO₂ and CH₃ in meta positions)

27. 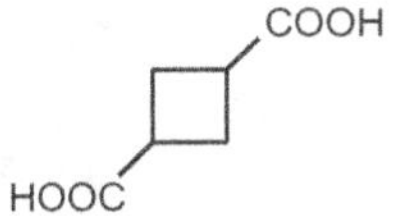 Cyclobutane-1,3-dicarboxylic acid (cyclobutane with COOH and HOOC)

28. 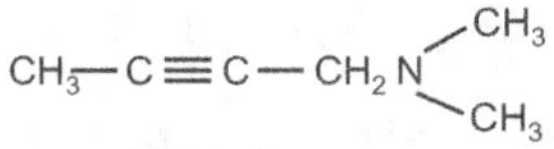 $CH_3-C \equiv C-CH_2-N(CH_3)_2$

29. 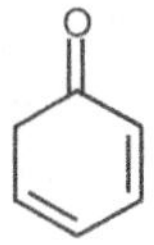 Cyclohexa-2,5-dien-1-one structure

30. 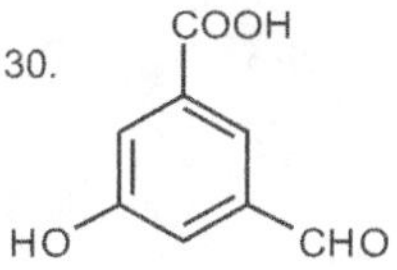 Benzene with COOH, OH, and CHO substituents (3,5-disubstituted benzoic acid)

31. (i) 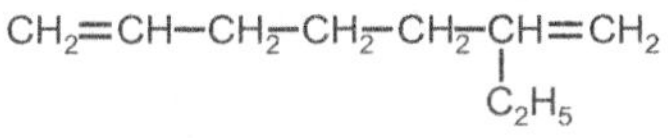 $CH_2=CH-CH_2-CH_2-CH_2-CH=CH_2$ with C_2H_5 branch

   (ii) 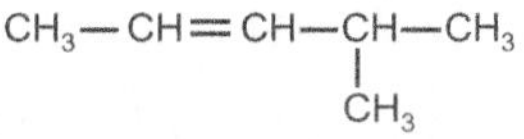 $CH_3-\underset{\underset{CH_3}{|}}{\overset{\overset{CH_3}{|}}{S}}-C-OH$ with CH_3

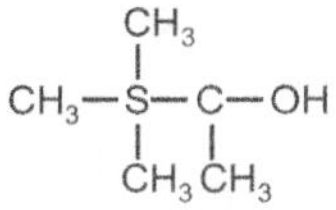

   (iii) 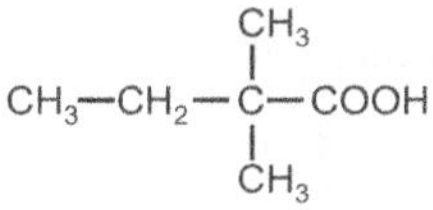 $CH_3-CH_2-\underset{\underset{CH_3}{|}}{\overset{\overset{CH_3}{|}}{C}}-COOH$

   (ii) $CH_3-CH=CH-\underset{\underset{CH_3}{|}}{CH}-CH_3$

32. (i) 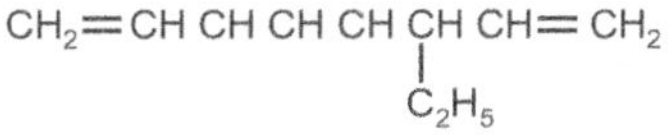 $CH_2=CH-CH-CH-CH-CH-CH=CH_2$ with C_2H_5 branch

   (ii) 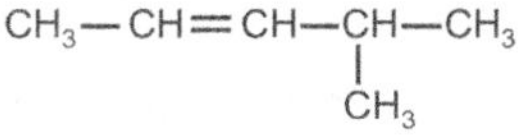 $CH_3-CH=CH-\underset{\underset{CH_3}{|}}{CH}-CH_3$

   (iii) 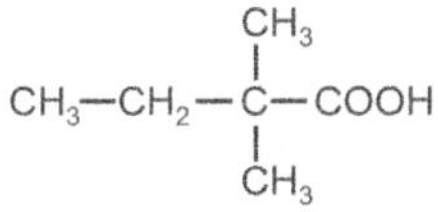 $CH_3-CH_2-\underset{\underset{CH_3}{|}}{\overset{\overset{CH_3}{|}}{C}}-COOH$

15. Write the IUPAC names for the following structures:

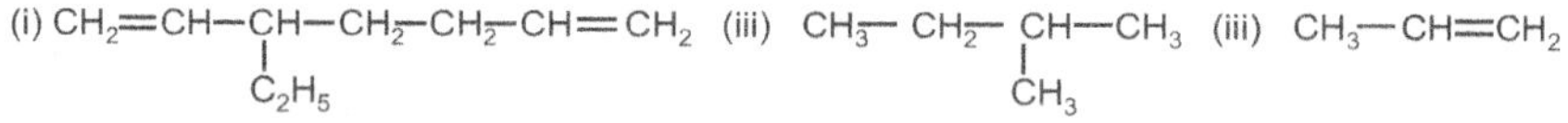

(i) CH$_2$=CH—CH—CH$_2$—CH$_2$—CH=CH$_2$
                |
                C$_2$H$_5$

(ii) CH$_3$—CH$_2$—CH—CH$_3$
              |
              CH$_3$

(iii) CH$_3$—CH=CH$_2$

16. Write down the structures of the following compounds:

(i) 5-Vinyl-2-naphthalenesulphonic acid

(ii) *m*-Nitrobenzamide

(iii) 2-Formyl-3-*tert*-butylpyrrole

(iv) 2-(2,4-Diaminophenyl) butandioic acid

(v) Vinyl allyl ketone

(vi) Ethyl 3,5-dimethylcyclohexanecarboxylate

(vii) Diethylmalonate

(viii) 2-Furoic acid

(ix) *m*-Bromobenzamide

(x) 2, 2, 4 – Trimethylpentane

(xi) Ethyl ethanoate

(xii) 2-Methyl-2-butene

(xiii) 4-Ethyl,2-4-dimethylpentane

(xiv) 2-Methyl-1-butene

(xv) 5-Oxohexanoic acid

(xvi) 3-Chloro-2-pentanone

(xvii) Tertiary butyl chloride

(xviii) Phthallic anhydride

(xix) 2,4-Dimethyl-3-hexanone

(xx) Prop-2-enol.

(xxi) 3-Chloro-1-butene.

17. Give an example for each of the 1°, 2° and 3° amines. Draw the structures.
18. Give an example for each of the 1°, 2° and 3° alcohols. Draw the structures.
19. Give the structures of 1-butyne and 2-butyne and explain which is acidic.

Chapter 3 ...

STRUCTURE PROPERTY RELATIONSHIP

CONTENTS

Dipole moment, Polarity of molecules, Intermolecular and Intramolecular forces of attraction (Hydrogen bonding, Van der Waal's) and effects of these on physical properties of molecules as Physical state, Physical constants (Melting point and Boiling point) and Solubility.

Isomerism: Introduction to principles of Stereochemistry: Enantiomerism and Distereomerism, *Meso*-compounds, Assigning configurations (*R* and *S*), Geometric isomerism (*Cis*, *Trans*, *Z* and *E*).

DIPOLE MOMENT

Dipole Moment = Charge × Distance

The dipole moment is the product of the magnitude of the charge and the distance between the charges. It is shown by μ. Polar compounds possess dipole moment. When a covalent bond is formed between two atoms with different electro negativities, an atom acquires small δ^- and small δ^+ charge. Such a bond is called as **Polar Bond**.

E.g., $\overset{\delta^+}{H}-\overset{\delta^-}{Cl}$

When a covalent bond is formed between two atoms with same electro negativities and there is no positive and negative end. Such a bond is called as **Non-polar Bond**.

E.g., H—H

POLARITY OF MOLECULES

Depending upon type of atoms joined together, a molecule is said to be polar or non-polar molecule.

If a molecule is said to be polar, it shall possess two characteristics:

1. Must contain one or two polar bonds.
2. Separate centers of positive and negative charges in the molecule.

E.g., $\overset{\delta^-}{O}=\overset{\delta^+}{C}=\overset{\delta^-}{O}$ $\overset{\delta^+}{H}-\overset{\delta^-}{O}-\overset{\delta^+}{H}$

Polar molecules have a great attraction for each other and have characteristic physical and chemical properties. Molecules without dipole moment are called non-polar molecules.

INTERMOLECULAR FORCES

The forces that hold molecules together may be called intermolecular forces. These forces arise from the attraction between negative and positive charges. Hence, intermolecular forces may be defined as dipole-interactions. These forces are classified as follows:

Dipole – dipole interaction

Induced – dipole interaction

Instantaneous dipole – induced dipole interaction *i.e.,* London force

Strongest dipole – dipole interaction *i.e.* Hydrogen bonding.

1. Dipole-dipole Interactions:

The attraction of positive end of a molecular dipole for the negative end of another dipole may be called dipole-dipole interaction. Dipole-dipole interactions may occur either head to tail or laterally as shown in figure.

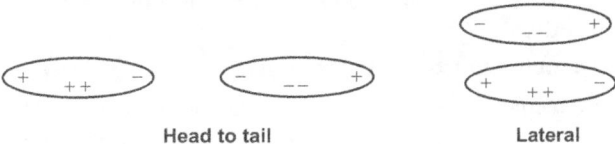

Head to tail   Lateral

Fig. 3.1: Dipole-Dipole Intraction

Dipole–dipole interactions are weaker than ion–dipole interactions:

Ions have strong but short range effect on dipoles. These are known as ion–dipole interactions. When an ion approaches a dipole, the end with charge opposite to that of the ion is directed toward the ion and other is directed away. Thus, an electrostatic force of attraction is established between the ion and the dipole. It is found to be inversely proportional to the square of the distance between the ion and the dipole (μ). Thus, the force acts at a short range though, it is strong.

Hydrogen chloride (HCl) is a polar molecule. There are dipole-dipole interactions amongst HCl molecules. Argon is non-polar entity and of the same molecular weight as that of HCl. Owing to the dipole-dipole interaction, HCl boils at a much higher temperature than Argon molecule. The difference in their B. P. is 101°C.

Hydration of protons: *Polar compound dissolves in polar solvent by dipole-dipole interaction.*

Hydration of proton forms a hydronium ion. The solvation of ion and dissolution of ionic lattices in polar solvents are the examples of ion–dipole interactions. Stabilization of ions by the attraction of solvent molecules is called solvation and hydration is a special case of solvation.

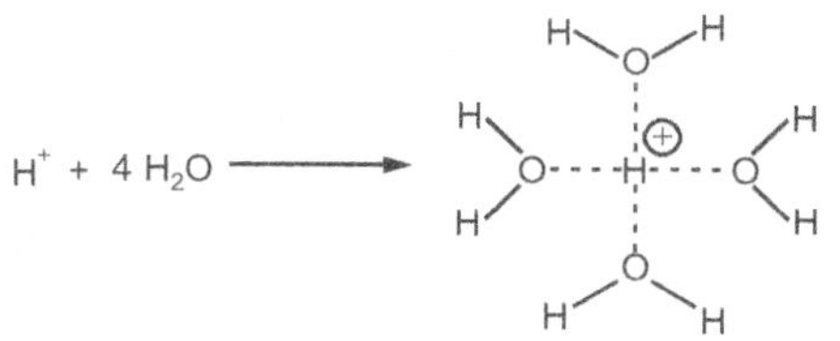

$H^+ + 4 H_2O \longrightarrow$ [hydrated proton structure]

Fig. 3.2: Hydration of Proton

2. **Induced–dipole interactions:**

If polar and non–polar molecules are present together then polar molecules i.e., dipoles can induce dipoles in non–polar molecules. i.e., bonding between the dipoles and the induced dipoles. This is called "dipole-induced dipole bond". It is effective over an extremely short range and very weak in nature.

Non-polar molecules dissolve in polar solvents by dipole-induced dipole interactions.

A charged particle, i.e., an ion can induce dipole in non-polar molecule when they came close to each other.

3. **Instantaneous dipole-induced dipole Interactions: London Force:**

A non–polar molecule is electrically neutral. Ofcourse, owing to the motion of the electrons within such a molecule, the centre of the negative charge density due to electrons does not always coincide with the centre of positive charge density of the protons. This disturbs momentarily the electrical symmetry of the molecule and an instantaneous dipole is formed. This instantaneous dipole, in its turn, induces dipole in another adjacent molecule. Thus, the instantaneous dipole and the induced dipole remain together by an attractive force or bonding known as Instantaneous dipole-induced dipole interaction.

It is true that the momentary dipole and induced dipoles keep on changing constantly to the neutral state, still the attractive force so generated is able to bind the molecules together and is known as *"London Force"*. (Van der Waal's force).

As the molecular volume and the number of electrons in a molecule increases, the molecular weight increases. Thus, the London forces increase rapidly with the increasing molecular weight. London forces are extremely short ranged in action. London forces are the weakest of all kinds of intermolecular forces. The bond dissociation energy is only of the order 4 kJ/mole; or something like that.

4. **Strongest dipole-dipole interaction: Hydrogen bonding:**

When a hydrogen atom is covalently linked to a strong electronegative element, the molecule formed is a dipole. Thus H – F is a dipole. In an aggregate of H – F molecules, dipole-dipole interactions take place. When they come very close to each other, the obvious result is the orientation of poles and a weak bond is established between two unlike poles ($H^{\delta+}$ and $F^{\delta-}$) so hydrogen bonding is a result of dipole-dipole interactions.

$$\overset{\delta+}{H}\text{---}\overset{\delta-}{F} \quad \overset{\delta+}{H}\text{---}\overset{\delta-}{F} \longrightarrow \overset{\delta+}{H}\text{---}\overset{\delta-}{F}\text{----}\overset{\delta+}{H}\text{---}\overset{\delta-}{F}$$

A hydrogen atom, covalently bonded to a strong electronegative atom, has relatively high positive charge density but minimal co-ordination number (only two) because it has a very small volume which makes hydrogen bonding possible. While, other electropositive atoms have neither high positive charge nor minimal co-ordination number because of their large volume.

The hydrogen bond dissociation energy varies from 21 to 42 kJ/mole. Hence, it is stronger than usual dipole–dipole interaction. The strength of the bond depends upon the electronegativity of the atom bonded to the hydrogen atom; it decreases with decreasing electronegativity within the series F, O, N, Cl, S.

Hydrogen bonds are of two types:
1. Intermolecular H–bonds.
2. Intramolecular (Internal) H–bond.

When hydrogen bonding happens or occurs between two or more molecules, it is known as *Intermolecular H – bond*.

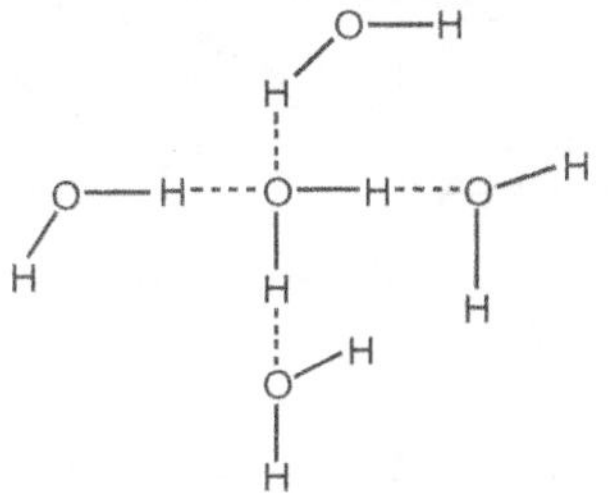

Fig. 3.3: Association of water molecules 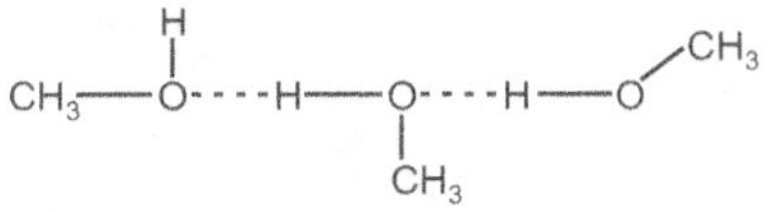   Fig. 3.4: Association of methanol molecules

In the beginning of H-bonding, it should be emphatically stated as "H-bonding phenomenon and is generally is observed between H-O, H-S, H-N and H-F and most of the examples deal with the combination only".

Intermolecular hydrogen bonding can also form ring. In this case, we get dimeric molecules instead of a polymer.

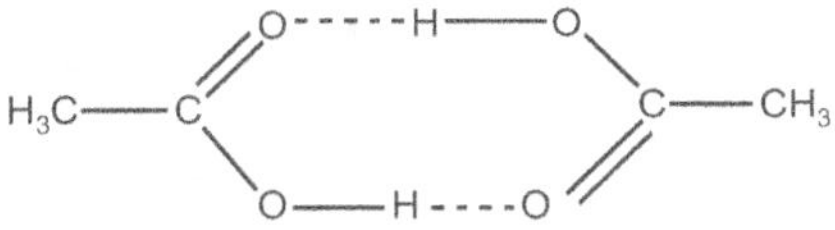

Fig. 3.5: Dimer of acetic acid

When hydrogen bond is formed between two atoms within the same molecule, it is called as an **internal** or **_intramolecular H–bond_**. The result is the formation of a ring known as chelate.

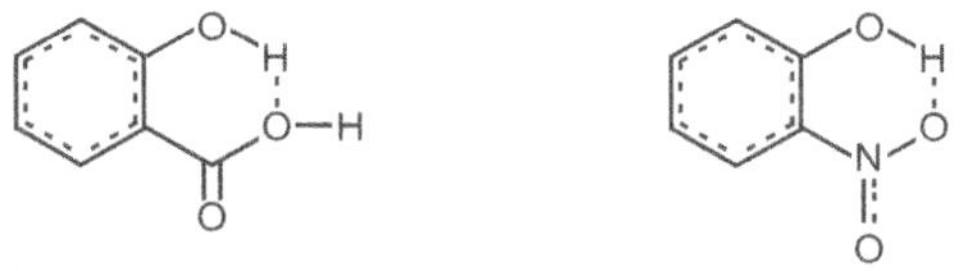

Salicylic acid   o-Nitrophenol

Fig. 3.6: Intramolecular H-bonding

EFFECT OF HYDROGEN BONDING

(a) Effect on M.P. and B.P.:

Compounds with intermolecular H–bonds have greater melting points and boiling points than that for compounds with intramolecular H–bond. The intermolecular hydrogen bonding increases melting points and boiling points. An extra amount of heat energy is required to break the intermolecular H–bond.

CH_4, HF and H_2O molecules have comparable molecular weights. CH_4 can not form H–bonds because C atoms has low electronegativity, HF can utilize its lone pair to form H–bond but water molecule forms H–bond with both the H–atoms.

	H_2O	HF	CH_4
M.P. Order	0°C	– 110°C	– 190°C
B.P. Order	100°C	19.5°C	– 161.5°C

(b) Effect on Solubility:

Hydrogen bonded molecules are soluble in another hydrogen bonded molecules. Alcohols are soluble in water but, alkanes are not, because alcohols are capable of forming H-bonds with water whereas non polar alkanes can not form the H-bond with water. The phenomenon **like dissolves like** or **polar dissolves polar** and **non-polar dissolves non-polar** is applicable in nature.

(c) Effect on stability of molecules:

Intramolecular H- bonding brings stability to a compound.

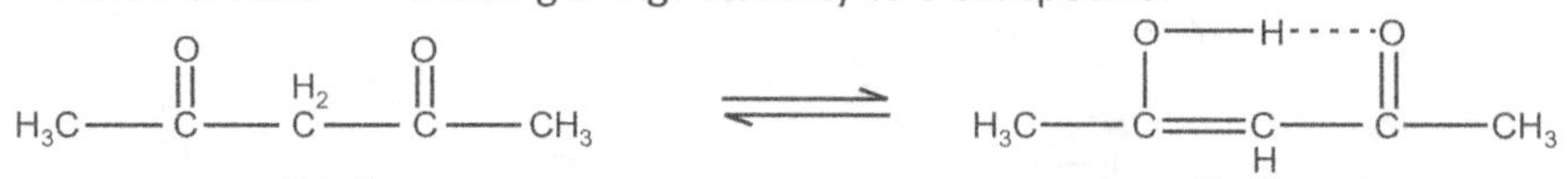

Keto form ⇌ Enol form
(More stable due to H bonding and Conjugation)

Fig. 3.7: Tautometric forms of acetyl acetone

(d) Effect on acidity and basicity:

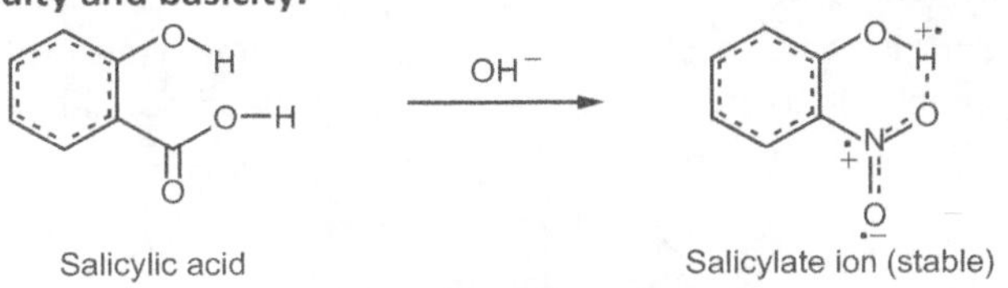

Salicylic acid → Salicylate ion (stable)

Fig. 3.8

The conjugate base of salicylic acid gets stabilized by the intramolecular H-binding, but the conjugate base of the *p*-hydroxybenzoic acid, does not stabilize by such a hydrogen bonding. We can easily conclude that salicylate ion is a weaker base than the *p*-hydroxybenzoate ion, this means salicylic acid is a stronger acid than *p*-hydroxybenzoic acid.

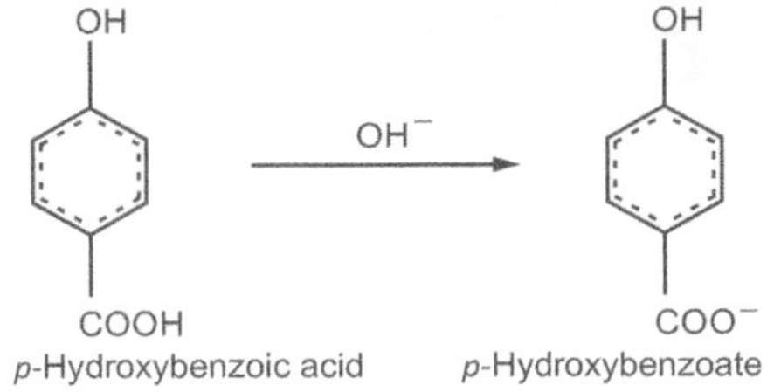

p-Hydroxybenzoic acid → *p*-Hydroxybenzoate

Fig. 3.9

Aqueous solution of dimethylamine is more basic than that of triethylamine.

This is because of greater hydration effect on dimethylammonium ion than that of trimethylammonium ion. So how does hydration enhances basicity. The answer is simple, it stabilises to an ionic species to greater extent, thus, dimethylamine tends faster or readily to get converted to its ammonium ion (hydrated) through donation of its electron pair and hydration.

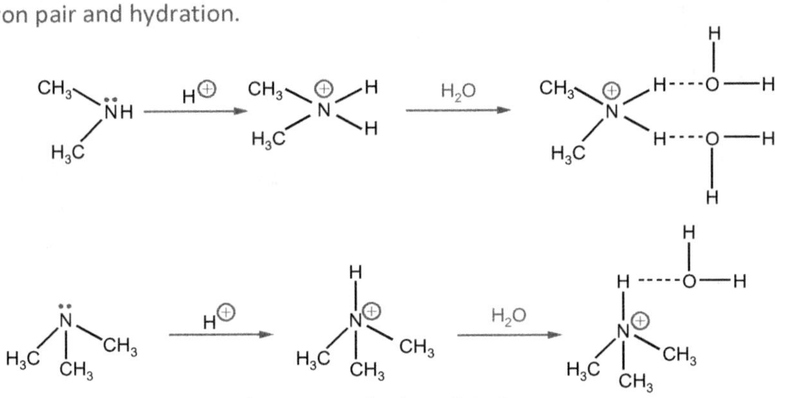

Fig. 3.10: Hydration of Amines

(e) Effect on biological systems:

Both inter and intra-molecular H–bondings play important roles in biological systems. The long helical structure of protein molecules and double helical structure of DNA molecules are stabilized by the existence of H–bonding.

$$\diagdown C=\overset{\delta-}{O}---\overset{\delta+}{H}-N\diagup$$

Fig. 3.11: H-Bonding in proteins

The H–bonding force in proteins and cellulose makes them able to absorb dyes.

Relative strengths of intermolecular forces:

| H-Bonding | > | Dipole-dipole interaction | > | London force |
| ~ 21-42 kJ/mole | | ~8 kJ/mole | | ~ 4 kJ/moles |

ISOMERISM

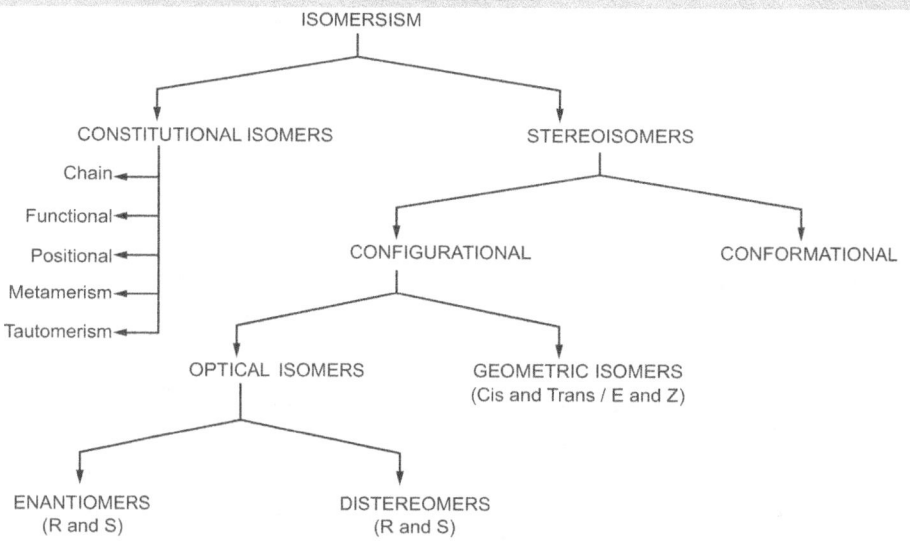

STEREOISOMERISM

Compounds with the same molecular formula and of identical constitution but, differing only in the spatial arrangement of the constituent atoms are called **"Stereoisomers"**.

E.g., Butenedioic acid [COOH – CH = CH – COOH]: Exists in two forms in nature

$$\underset{HOOC}{H}\diagdown C=C \diagup \underset{COOH}{H}$$

Cis Butenedioic acid
(Maleic Acid)

$$\underset{HOOC}{H}\diagdown C=C \diagup \overset{COOH}{H}$$

Trans Butenedioic acid
(Fumaric Acid)

They both differ in their physical and chemical properties. Their isomerism is caused by the different spatial arrangements of two –H atoms and two –COOH groups about the C=C, though their constitutions are identical. Hence, these are "stereoisomers".

The causes of different spatial arrangements in stereoisomerism are:
1. Conformational Isomerism: Restricted rotation of a part of the molecule about C – C single bond. (Dynamic stereoisomerism)
2. Configurational Isomerism: Restricted rotation of a part of the molecule about a C=C double bond or a ring and chirality. (Static stereoisomers)

The configurational isomers can be inter-converted only by breaking and making bonds.

These isomers may further be of two types: (1) Enantiomers and (2) Distereomers.

GEOMETRICAL ISOMERISM

Geometrical isomerism (also called *cis-trans* isomerism) results from a restriction in rotation about C=C double bonds, or about C-C single bonds in cyclic compounds. The geometrical isomers have different physical and chemical properties.

1. **Geometrical isomerism in alkenes:**

The carbon atoms of the C-C double bond are sp^2 hybridised. It consists of σ bond and π bond. The σ bond is formed by the overlap of sp^2 hybrid orbitals. The π bond is formed by the overlap of p orbitals. The presence of π bond locks the molecule in one portion. Rotation around the C = C bond is not possible because rotation will break the π bond. This restriction of rotation about the C = C is responsible for the geometrical isomerism in alkenes.

E.g., 2- butene exist in two spacial arrangements

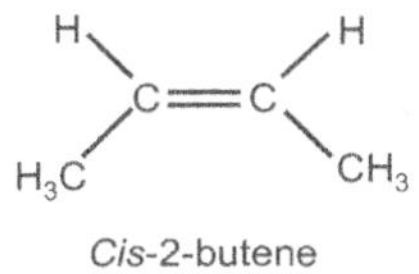

Cis-2-butene 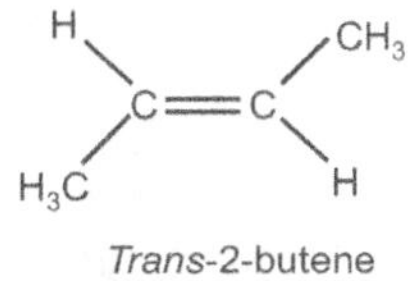   *Trans*-2-butene

In the *cis* isomer, the bulky groups are on the same side of the double bond. The steric repulsion of the groups makes the *cis* isomers less stable than the *trans* isomers in which the bulky groups are far apart.

In some cases, geometrical isomerism is not possible, because one of the double bonded carbons has two identical groups *i.e.*, H atoms.

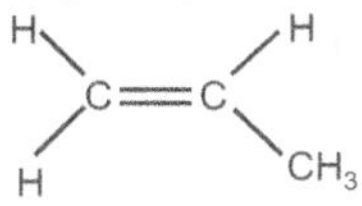

2. Geometrical Isomerism in Cyclic Compounds:

There can be no rotation about C-C single bonds forming a ring because rotation would break the ring.

E.g., 1,2-Dimethyl cyclopropane

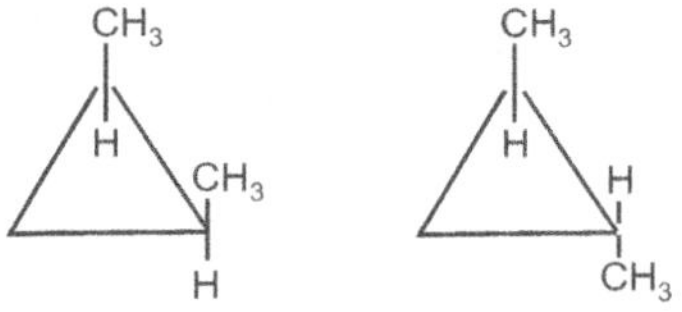

Cis   *Trans*

A requirement for geometrical isomerism in cyclic compound is that there must be at least two other groups besides hydrogen on the ring and these must be on different ring carbon atoms.

E.g., No geometrical isomers are possible for 1, 1–dimethyl cyclopropane.

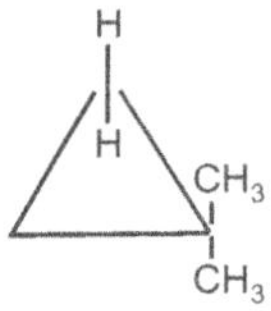

Requirement for geometrical isomers:
(i) C = C
(ii) C = N (oximes)
(iii) – N = N –
(iv) Cyclic compounds
(v) Compounds showing restricted rotation about a single bond.

ENANTIOMERS

When the two isomers are the non-superimposible mirror images of each other, they are known as *"Enantiomers"*.

E.g., Lactic acid

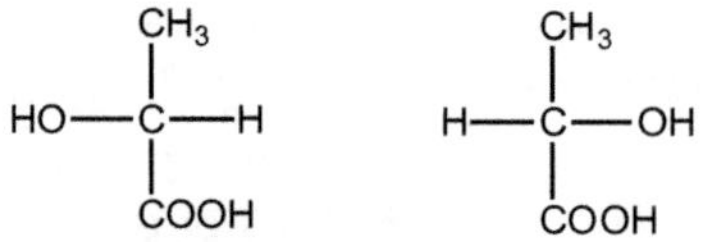

- Enantiomers are stable and optically active.
- They differ from one another in three-dimensional spatial arrangements of their substituent groups.

- They have same M.P., density, solubility, colour and reactivity towards acid and bases.
- Though both rotate plane of polarized light, one rotates to the right and is called as *'dextrorotatory'* while the other rotates the plane to the left and is called *'levorotatory'*.
- A mixture of two enantiomers in equal amount is called as *"Racemic Mixture"* and is optically inactive.

DIASTEREOMERS

When the configurational isomers are not the mirror images of each other, these are known as *"disatereomers"*.

Each asymmetric carbon atom in molecules doubles the number of theoretically possible isomers.

Hence, molecule within asymmetric carbon atoms should have 2n stereoisomers.

(A)	(B)	(C)	(D)
CH_3	CH_3	CH_3	CH_3
H—C—OH	OH—C—H	H—C—OH	OH—C—H
Br—C—H	H—C—Br	H—C—Br	Br—C—H
CH_3	CH_3	CH_3	CH_3

$2 \times 2 = 4$

2n (n = Chiral numbers of carbons)

(A) is the mirror image of (B)

(C) is the mirror image of (D)

Thus, the four isomers are two pairs of enantiomers.

So, (A) and (C) are distereomers.

Two distereomers will have different M. P., B.P. and solublities.

They will have different relativities toward most reagents.

MESO COMPOUNDS

A compound with two or more asymmetric carbon atoms but, also having a plane of symmetry (a mirror plane) is called as *"meso compound"*.

Both molecules are optically inactive, even though each has two asymmetric centers. Neither will rotate the plane polarized light.

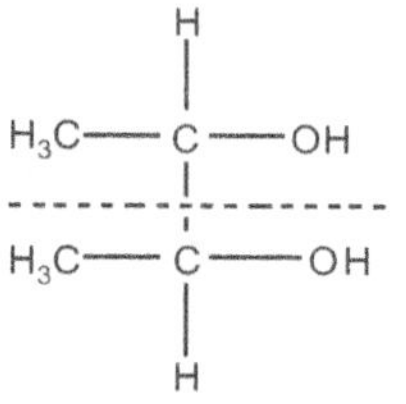

Meso-2,3-dihydroxybutane

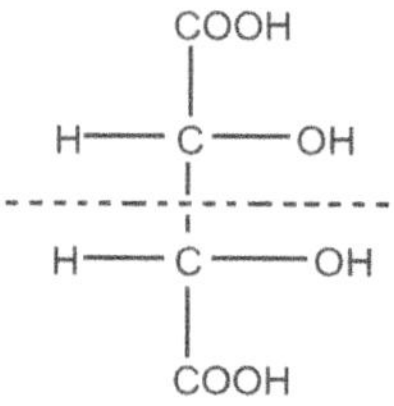

Meso-Tartaric acid

Nomenclature of Geometrical Isomerism:

1. *Cis* and *Trans*
2. *E* and *Z*

1. *Cis* and *Trans*:

***Cis* Isomers:** Two similar groups are on the same side of a double bond.

***Trans* Isomers:** Two similar groups are on the opposite side of the double bond.

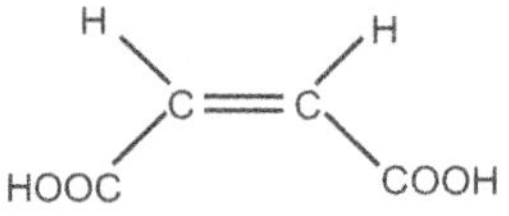

Cis Butenedioic acid
(Maleic Acid)

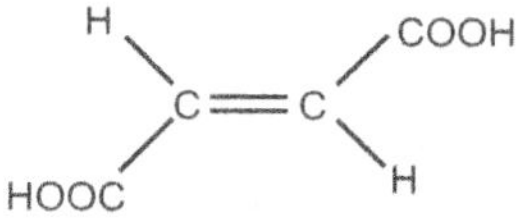

Trans Butenedioic acid
(Fumaric Acid)

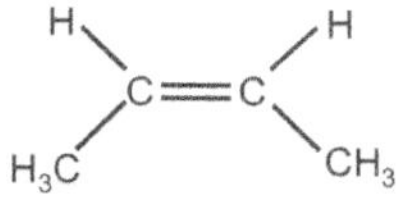

Cis-2-butene

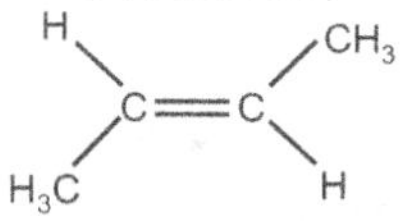

Trans-2-butene

Cumulenes possessing odd number of adjacent double bonds also exhibit geometrical isomerism.

E.g., Kuhn and Blum (1959) reported the following two forms of 1,4-di-*m*-nitrophenyl–1,4-diphenylbutatriene.

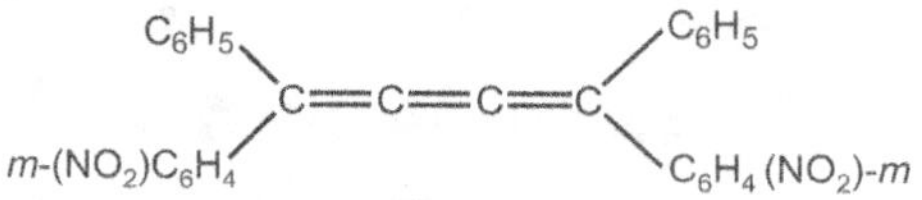

Cis

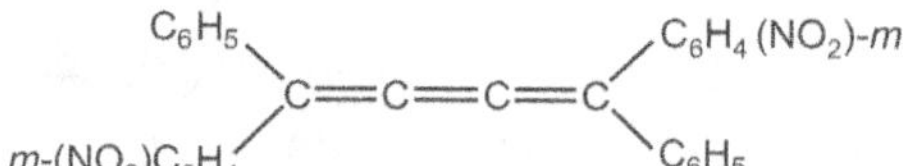

Trans

2. E and Z Systems:

Cis-trans nomenclature system is not applicable when there are four different substituent or (more than two different substitutes). **Cahn–In gold-Prelog (CIP)** in 1968 established E and Z system of nomenclature where all substitutes are different.

E = Entegegen (German word) → Opposite/ against
Z = Zusammen (German word) → Together

When two high priority groups are on the same side of double bond carbon → Z.

When two high priority group are on the opposite side of the double bond carbon → E.

1. Assign the priority order to the two groups attached to each other of the double bonded carbon in accordance with the sequence rule.

Sequence rule:
(a) Higher priority is assigned to atoms directly attached to the carbon atom of higher atomic number.

I > Br > Cl > F > O > N > C > H

(b) If isotopes of same element are attached, the isotope with higher mass number will have a higher priority.

(c) A doubly or triply bonded atom is considered equivalent to two or three such atoms.

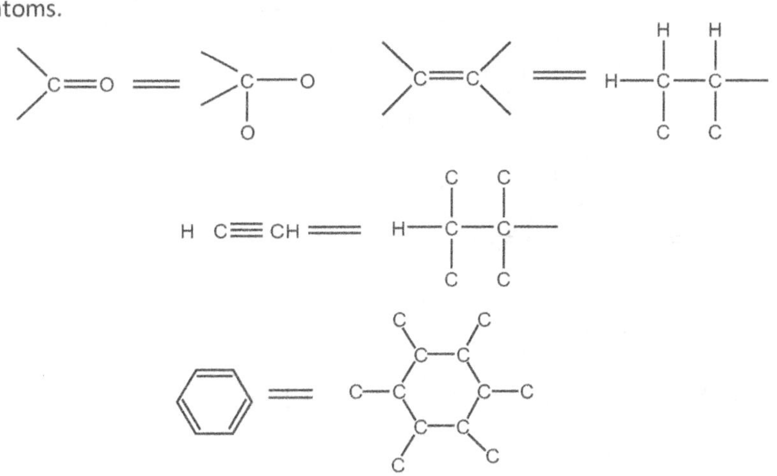

Ready Reference:

Highest Priority : I > Br > Cl > SH > F > O-CO⁻ > OR > OH > NO_2 > NH-CO-R > NR_2

> NHR > NH_2 > CCl_3 > CO-Cl > COOR > COOH > $CONH_2$ > COR > CHO > CN

> CH_2OH > C_6H_5 > CR_3 > CHR_2 > CH_2R > CH_3 > D > H : **Lowest Priority**

PHARMACEUTICAL ORGANIC CHEMISTRY - I — STUCTURE PROPERTY RELATIONSHIP

1. Select the atom or group with higher priority on each doubly bonded carbon.
2. Assign the higher number to higher priority. (atom of higher atomic number).
3. Assign the E and Z configuration.

E.g., **1-Bromo-2-chloro-2-fluoro-1-iodoethene**

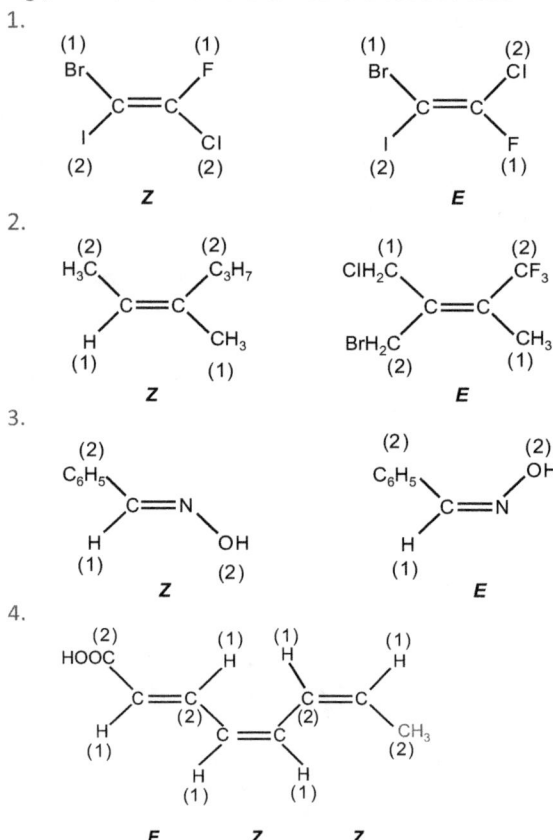

When an alkene has more than one double bond, the stereochemistry around each double bond must be specified.

E.g., 3-Bromo-(3Z, 5E)-octadiene

R and S System in Optical Isomerism:

The R and S nomenclature is used for optically active compounds to determine absolute configuration and applicable universally as described by **Cahn-Ingold-Prelog System (CIP)**.

R = Rectus (German word) → Clockwise
S = Sinister (German word) → Anti-clockwise

The following methodology is used to assign R and S designation to chiral carbon.

1. Each group on the chiral carbon is assigned a 'priority' in the sequence
$$1 > 2 > 3 > 4$$
2. Atoms with higher atomic numbers receive higher priorities

Highest Priority : $I > Br > Cl > SH > F > O\text{-}CO^- > OR > OH > NO_2 > NH\text{-}CO\text{-}R > NR_2$

$> NHR > NH_2 > CCl_3 > CO\text{-}Cl > COOR > COOH > CONH_2 > COR > CHO > CN$

$> CH_2OH > C_6H_5 > CR_3 > CHR_2 > CH_2R > CH_3 > D > H$: **Lowest Priority**

It is important to note that, one looks only at the atomic number of the atom directly attached to chiral carbon and not the entire group. In case there are ties, the next atom along the chain is used as the breaker. Thus, one would assign a higher priority to ethyl group ($-CH_2-CH_3$) than to methyl group ($-CH_3$). The carbon in methyl group is bonded with three hydrogen (H, H, H), while the first carbon in ethyl group is bonded to two hydrogen and one carbon (H, H, C) and hence, ethyl gets higher priority over methyl group.

E.g., Ordinarily you are given a Fischer Projection formula and asked to specify configuration by R and S notation.

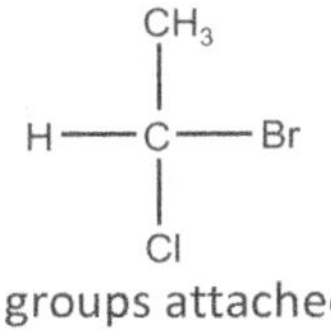

$$\begin{array}{c} CH_3 \\ | \\ H-C-Br \\ | \\ Cl \end{array}$$

Step 1: Determine the priority of groups attached to the asymmetric carbon atom.
Order of Priority:
$$Br > Cl > CH_3 > H$$

Step 2: Arrange the lowest priority group down *i.e.,* away from **observer (either on the top or bottom of the vertical line in the Fischer projection)**. This is done by interchanging groups bonded to the chiral carbon.

Remember: *The interchanging one pair of groups in the Fischer projection inverts the configuration but, interchanging two pairs of groups retains the configuration. Thus, interchange operation must always be done in pairs to avoid change in the configuration.*

Step 3: Specify the direction in decreasing order and ignore the lowest priority.

1 ⟶ 2 ⟶ 3

If groups occur in clockwise direction, the configuration is **'R'**.
If groups occur in anti-clockwise direction, the configuration is **'S'**.

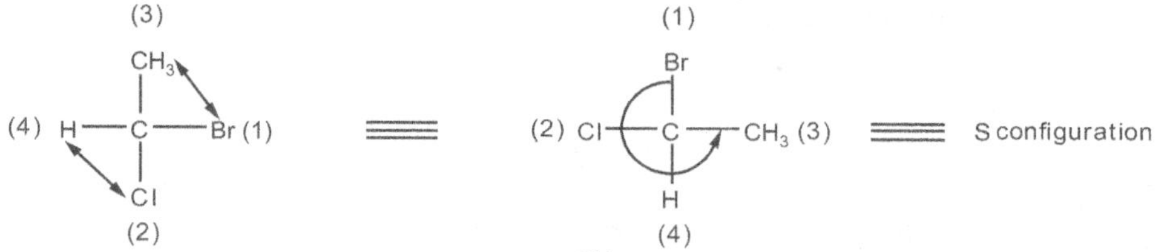

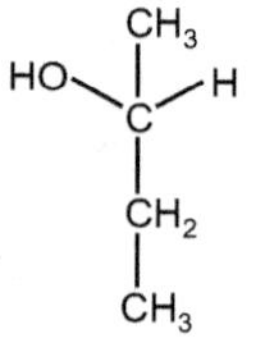

(4) H—C(CH₃(3), Br(1), Cl(2)) ≡ (2) Cl—C(Br(1), CH₃(3), H(4)) ≡ S configuration

2-Butanol (CH₃–CH(OH)–CH₂–CH₃)

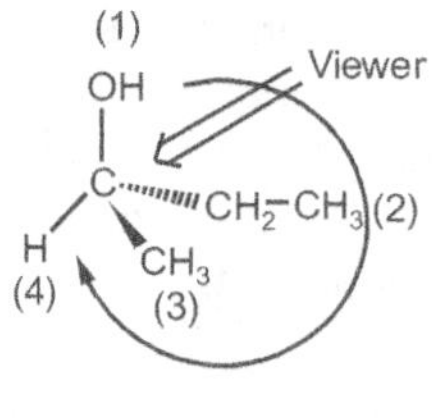

Clockwise
2-(R)-Butanol

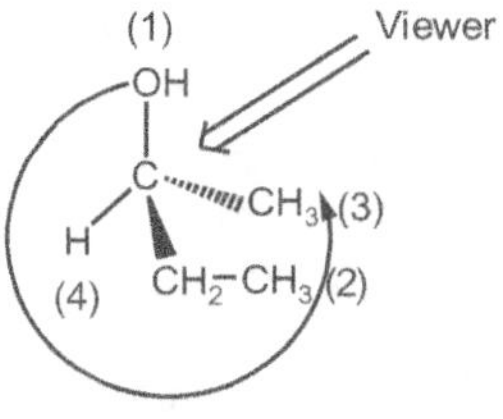

Anti-clockwise
2-(S)-Butanol

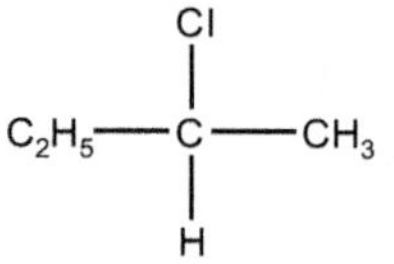

2-Chlorobutane (C₂H₅–C(Cl)(H)–CH₃)

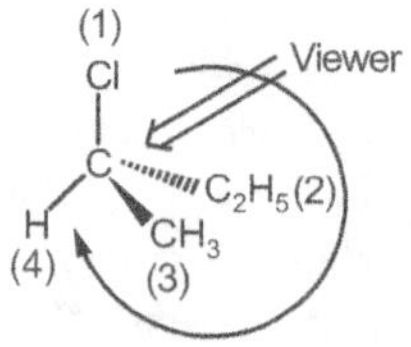

Clockwise
2-(R)-Chlorobutane

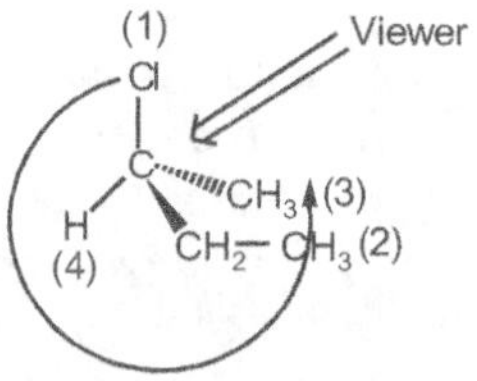

Anti-clockwise
2-(S)-Chlorobutane

PHARMACEUTICAL ORGANIC CHEMISTRY - I — STUCTURE PROPERTY RELATIONSHIP

```
      CH2OH                    CH2CH3
       |                         |
Br ——— C ——— Cl           H ——— C ——— Br
       |                         |
      CH3                       CH3
       (I)                       (II)
```

In the projection (I), the lowest priority substituent is at the bottom and interchanging of group is required and simply assigning the priority and rotating the groups in decreasing order to get the configuration.

```
             (3)
            CH2OH
             |
(1) Br ——— C ——— Cl (2)
             |
            CH3
            (4)
       Anti-clockwise
```

The configuration is **'S'**.

But in the projection (II), the lowest priority group is on the horizontal line and it is nearer to viewer, hence interchanging of groups is required to get the lowest priority group on the bottom of the vertical line and away from the viewer.

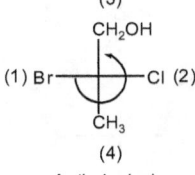

```
          (2)                              (1)
        CH2CH3                             Br
          |                                |
(4) H ——— C ——— Br (1)   ≡   (3) H3C ——— C ——— CH2CH3 (2)
          |                                |
         CH3                               H
         (3)                              (4)
                                       Clockwise
```

The configuration is **'R'**.

```
         1
        COOH
         |
    H —2— OH
         |
    OH —3— H
         |
        COOH
         4
     Tartaric acid
```

In the above structure, carbon number 2 and 3 are chiral.
First, we shall consider carbon number 2.

```
           (2)                              (1)
         COOH                              OH
           |                                |
(4) H ——— C ——— OH (1)   ≡   (3) (HOOC) HOHC ——— C ——— COOH (2)
           |                                |
        CHOH (COOH)                         H
          (3)                              (4)
                                    2-[R]-Tartaric acid
```

Chp 3 | 3.16

Now, we shall consider carbon number 3

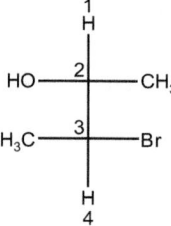

Hence, the given structure of tartaric acid is **2R, 3R-(+) Tartaric acid.**

3-Bromo-2-hydroxy-butane

QUESTION BANK

1. Define or explain dipole moment and polarity of molecules.
2. Describe different intermolecular forces with examples.
3. Why we don't get strong dipole–dipole interactions with atoms more electropositive than hydrogen?
4. Write a note on hydrogen bonding.
5. Explain effect of hydrogen bonding on physical properties of molecules?
6. Why salicylic acid is a stronger acid than *p*-hydroxybenzoic acid?
7. Why dimethylamine is a stronger base than trimethylamine in aqueous medium.
8. Explain concept of isomerism, its classification with suitable examples.
9. Define stereoisomerism and explain it with examples.
10. Define or explain geometrical isomerism with examples.
11. Why *trans* isomers are more stable than the corresponding *cis* isomers ?
12. Why all alkenes do not show geometrical isomerism?
13. Define or explain enantiomers, diastereomers and meso compounds with suitable examples.
14. Elaborate the different methods of nomenclature of geometrical isomers.
15. Assign R and S configurations to the isomers of 2-butanol.
16. Draw the enatiomers of 2-chlorobutane and assign R and S configurations to them.

17. Assign R or S configurations to tartaric acid (two chiral centers).
18. Establish R or S configurations to the 3-bromo, 2-hydroxybutane (two chiral centers).
19. Explain effect of hydrogen bonding on physical properties of molecules?
20. Define or explain following terms
    (a) Structural isomerism   (b) Stereoisomerism
    (c) Geometrical isomerism   (d) Enantiomers
    (e) Distereomers   (f) Meso compounds
    (g) Metamerism   (h) Structural isomerism
    (i) Geometrical isomerism   (j) Hydrogen bonding
    (k) Dipole-dipole interaction
21. State the necessary conditions for a compound to show geometrical isomerism. Illustrate your answer with examples.
22. Assign E & Z configuration to the following:
    (a)
    (b)
    (c)
    (d)
    (e)
    (f)
23. Draw a structure for 3-bromo-(3Z, 5E)-octadiene.
24. Discuss CIP rules for nomenclature of stereoisomers.
25. What is the necessary condition for the existence of enantiomers?
26. What do you understand from the designations R, S and E, Z?

Chapter 4 ...

CLASSES OF REACTIONS AND CLASSES OF REAGENTS

CONTENTS

Classes of Reactions, Classes of reagents, Electrophiles, Nucleophiles, and Radicals.

CLASSIFICATION OF REACTIONS

Chemical Reaction:

A **chemical reaction** is a process that leads to the transformation of one set of chemical substances (reactants) to another (products). Simply speaking, a chemical reaction involves changes in the positions of electrons in the forming and breaking of chemical bonds between atoms, with no change to the nuclei. A chemical reaction is often described by a chemical equation.

Most of the organic reactions involve conversion of one functional group into another by the attack of a "**reagent**". Such organic compounds which are attacked by the reagent are known as "**substrates**" or "**reactants**". One the other hand, a simple organic or organic compound which is used to create a desired transformation in the compound is known as a "**reagent**". Thus, an organic reaction may be represented as below:

Example:

$$\text{Substrate + Attacking Reagent} \rightarrow \text{Intermediate} \rightarrow \text{Product}$$

In simple word a chemical reaction is a cascade of various events involving breaking of older bonds and formation of newer bond.

Whereas, "The steps of an organic reaction showing the breaking and making of new bonds of carbon atoms in the substrate leading to the formation of a final product through transient intermediates" are collectively referred as the **mechanism of reaction.**

Bond Breaking:

Heterolytic bond fission and Homolytic bond fission:

Covalent bonds, which involve two electrons, can be broken in two ways, homolytically (homo = same, equally), when the electron is retained by each fragment or heterolytically (hetero = different, unequally), when both electrons (forming the bond) go with one of the fragments.

Electronegativity is a measure of the power of an atom or a group to attract electrons from other part of the same molecule (*e.g.,* Fluorine is the most electronegative element and cesium is most electropositive).

A **covalent bond** between two different elements is polarized in the direction of $^{\delta+}A-Y^{\delta-}$ where **Y** is the more electronegative element.

In a **Heterolytic breakdown** (also known as Heterolytic fission), the bond breaking takes place in the direction where the electrons move with more electronegative element. This results in the formation of a positively charge (cationic) fraction and a negatively charge (anionic) fragment.

Example:

$$H_3C-Cl \longrightarrow \overset{\oplus}{C}H_3 + \overset{\ominus}{Cl}$$

In a **Homolytic breakdown** (also known as Homolytic fission), the bond breaking takes place equally where both the electron move towards each element (forming a covalent bond). This results in the formation of a **radical** (species containing an unpaired electron).

Example:

$$H_3C-CH_3 \longrightarrow CH_3 + CH_3$$

Classification of reactions / Types of reactions:

Organic reactions can be classified based on:

(A) Net outcome or course of reaction
(B) Mechanism
(C) Oxidation state changes

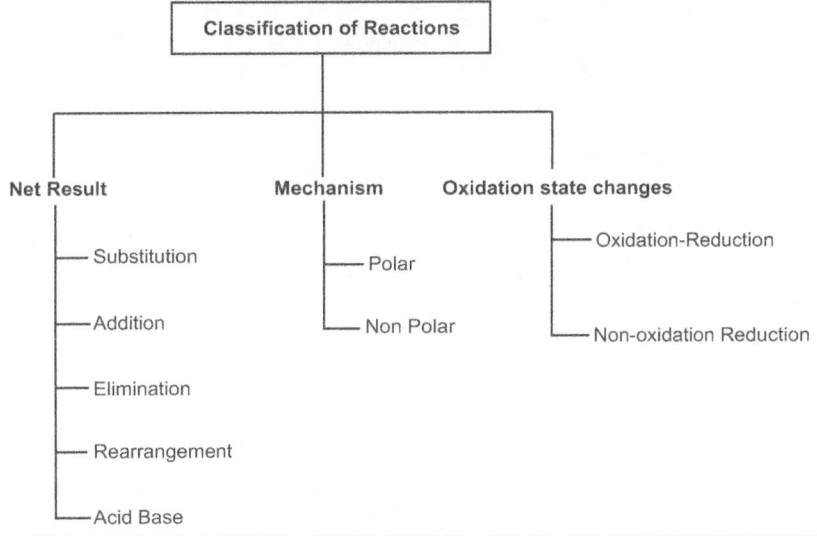

SUBSTITUTION, ADDITION, ELEMENTATION AND REARRANGEMENT REACTIONS

1. **Substitution reaction:**
   The replacement of an atom or a group from a molecule by a different atom or group is known as a **substitution** or **displacement reaction**.

   Example:

   1.
   $$H_3C\text{—}OH + H\text{—}Br \longrightarrow H_3C\text{—}Br + H\text{—}OH$$
   Reactants → Products
   Atoms or groups being displaced

   2.
   $$C_6H_5\text{—}H + NO_2^+ \longrightarrow C_6H_5\text{—}NO_2 + H^+$$
   Reactants → Products

   Depending upon the type of linkage to the carbon atom where actual reaction is taking place, substitution reaction can be of various types:

   (A) Substitution at saturated carbon atom or substitution at unsaturated carbon atom.
   (B) A substitution reaction may be initiated by an electrophile (Electrophilic substitution), nucleophile (Nucleophilic substitution) or Free radical.
   (C) Depending upon molecularity, these reactions are classified as, unimolecular substitution reaction and bimolecular substitution reaction.

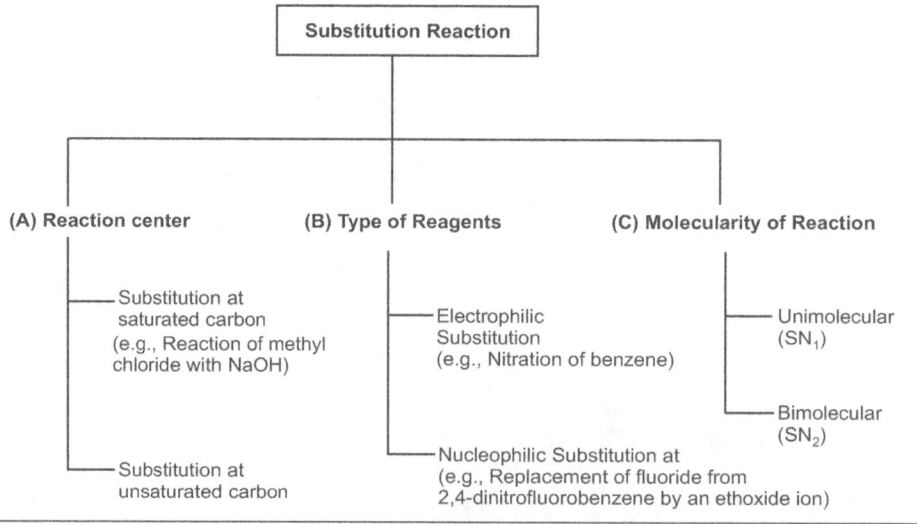

Substitution Unimolecular (SN₁) Reaction:

A nucleophilic substitution reaction in which one species is involved in the rate determining state. The slowest state is known as the rate determining state. (Rate of the reaction is "time taken to complete the reaction").

The reaction takes place in **two** steps:

Step 1: Slow ionisation of substrate to form a carbocation (or carbonium ion)

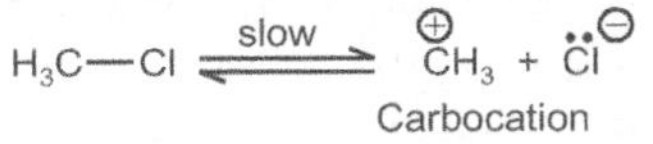

$$H_3C-Cl \xrightleftharpoons{slow} \overset{\oplus}{C}H_3 + \overset{\ominus}{Cl}$$
$$\text{Carbocation}$$

Step 1 (rate determining step) involves the substrate and not the attacking nucleophile, (i.e., Cl⁻), so the rate of the reaction depends on the concentration of substrate only. Therefore, it is known as a unimolecular substitution reaction **SN₁**.

Step 2: Attack of the incoming nucleophile (attacking group) on positively charged carbocation.

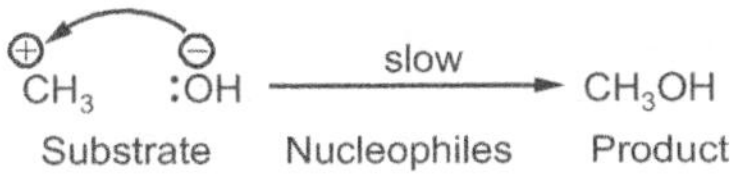

$$\underset{\text{Substrate}}{\overset{\oplus}{C}H_3} + \underset{\text{Nucleophiles}}{\overset{\ominus}{:}OH} \xrightarrow{slow} \underset{\text{Product}}{CH_3OH}$$

Substitution Bimolecular (SN₂) reaction:

When the rate determining transition state of a one step nucleophilic substitution reaction involves two species (substrate and nucleophile) it is said to be Substitution Nucleophilic Bimolecular and designated as **SN₂**.

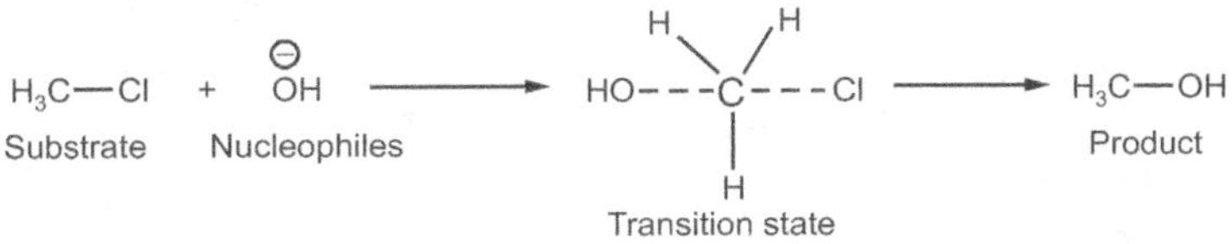

$$\underset{\text{Substrate}}{H_3C-Cl} + \underset{\text{Nucleophiles}}{\overset{\ominus}{O}H} \longrightarrow \underset{\text{Transition state}}{HO---\overset{H}{\underset{H}{C}}---Cl} \longrightarrow \underset{\text{Product}}{H_3C-OH}$$

Substitution, Nucleophilic, Internal (SNᵢ):

Aromatic alcohols when react with thionyl chloride, retains the configuration of hydroxyl-bearing carbon atom is known as SNᵢ reaction.

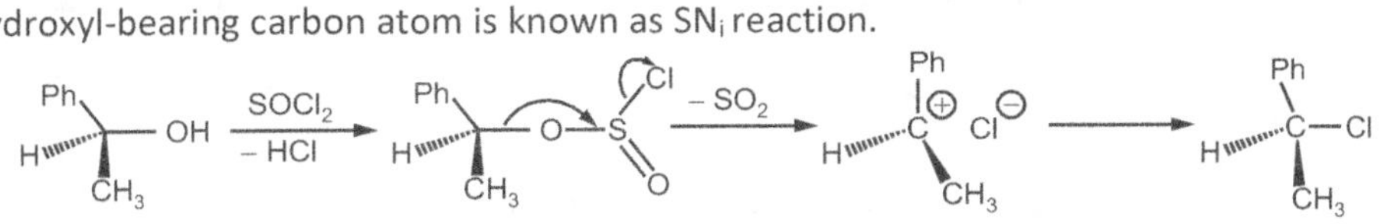

The role of aromatic substitutent is probably to stabilize the cationic part of the ion-pair by delocalising the positive charge.

2. Addition reactions:

Reactions in which atoms or group of atoms are added to a molecule, (i.e., there is simply a net gain of the reagent atoms in the product molecule) are known as addition reactions. This type of reactions occur only when there is a unsaturated centre in the molecule (substrate), which is generally due the presence of multiple bonds (double or triple) between atoms.

Example:

$$H_2C=CH_2 + HBr \longrightarrow H_3C-CH_2Br$$

Pi (π)-bond is responsible for addition reactions. For each Pi (π)-bond of the molecule two σ-bonds are formed and the hybridization state of carbon also changes. If the hybridization in reactant is sp it changes to sp^2 after addition similarly reactant with sp^2 after addition reaction becomes sp^3.

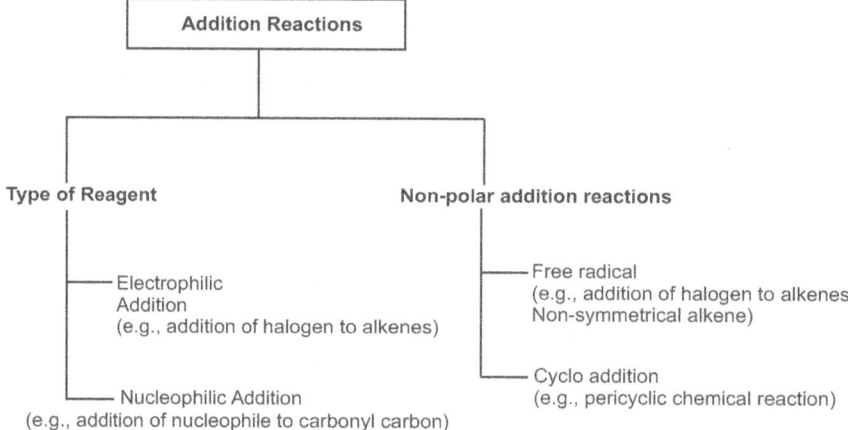

3. Elimination reactions:

These reactions are essentially the reversal of addition reactions and involve loss of atoms or groups from a molecule to form multiple bonds.

Most commonly, loss of atoms or groups occurs from adjacent carbon atoms to yield an olefin.

Example:

$$H_3C-\overset{H_2}{C}-Cl \longrightarrow CH_2=CH_2 + HCl$$

In elimination reactions, σ-bonds are converted to π-bond i.e the state of hybridization of carbon changes from sp^3 to sp^2 or sp^2 to sp.

Unlike substitution and addition, elimination reactions are not classified depending on nature of reagents (electrophile or nucleophile). Elimination reactions are only classified on the basis of *Molecularity of reactions*.

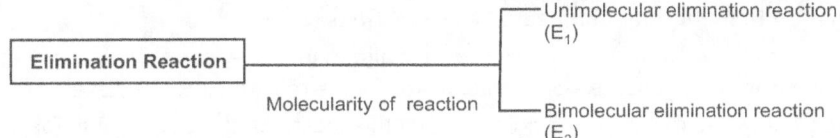

In elimination reactions, σ-bonds are converted to π-bond *i.e.*, the state of hybridization of carbon changes from sp^3 to sp^2 or sp^2 to sp.

Elimination Unimolecular Reactions (E_1):

It is a 1, 2-elimination reaction in which the transition state of the rate determining step involves only one species (substrate). It is known as Elimination Unimolecular or E_1 Elimination reaction.

Reaction takes place in two steps:

Step 1: Formation of carbocation

$$H-\underset{\underset{H}{|}}{\overset{\overset{H}{|}}{C}}-\underset{\underset{H}{|}}{\overset{\overset{H}{|}}{C}}-Cl \underset{}{\overset{Slow}{\rightleftharpoons}} H-\underset{\underset{H}{|}}{\overset{\overset{H}{|}}{C}}-\underset{\underset{H}{|}}{\overset{\overset{H}{|}}{C}}^{\oplus}$$

Step 2: This involves a rapid loss of a proton from the carbon atom adjacent to the carbon bearing the positive charge. This step is faster than step 1.

Base abstracts a hydrogen as proton

$$H-\underset{\underset{H}{|}}{\overset{\overset{H}{|}}{C}}-\underset{\underset{H}{|}}{\overset{\overset{H}{|}}{C}}^{\oplus} \xrightarrow{:B^{\ominus}} \underset{}{\overset{}{C}}=\underset{}{\overset{}{C}} + BH$$

Elimination Biomolecular Reactions (E_2):

E_2 reactions take place in a single concerted step in which two sigma bonds break and a π-bond forms simultaneously with the simultaneous departure of two groups, one of which is usually a proton. An E_2 reaction requires an added base which pulls out the proton.

$$-\underset{\underset{H}{|}}{\overset{\overset{H}{|}}{C}}-\underset{\underset{|}{|}}{\overset{\overset{G}{|}}{C}}- \longrightarrow \underset{}{\overset{}{C}}=\underset{}{\overset{}{C}} + G^{\ominus} + BH^{\oplus}$$

Since both the base and the substrate are involved in the T.S. of the single concerted rate-determining step of the E_2 reaction, it is kinetically second order-first order with respect to the substrate and first order also with respect to the base.

Elimination Unimolecular Conjugate Base Reactions (E_{1cB}):

This is a two-step base-catalysed 1,2-elimination reaction which involves a carbanion, the conjugate base of the substrate, as the reaction intermediate.

Step 1: Abstraction of most acidic BH from the substrate and a carbanion forms

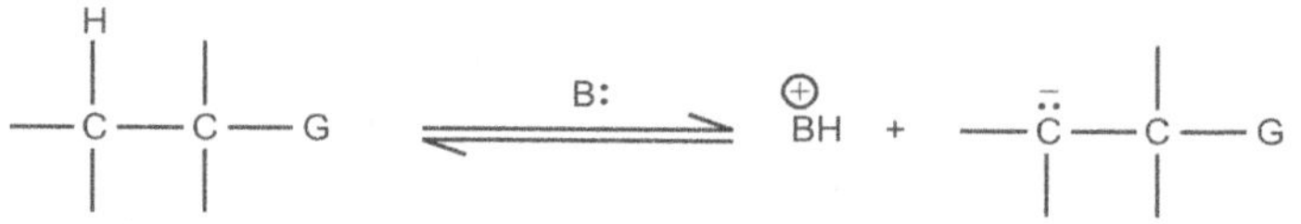

$$-\underset{|}{\overset{H}{\underset{|}{C}}}-\underset{|}{\overset{|}{C}}-G \;\; \underset{}{\overset{B:}{\rightleftharpoons}} \;\; \overset{\oplus}{BH} \;+\; -\underset{|}{\overset{..}{C}}-\underset{|}{\overset{|}{C}}-G$$

Step 2: This leaving group leaves the carbanion and a C-C double bond forms

$$-\underset{|}{\overset{..}{C}}-\underset{|}{\overset{|}{C}}\curvearrowright G \;\longrightarrow\; \diagup\!\!\!C=C\!\!\!\diagdown \;+\; G^{\ominus}$$

This sort of 1,2-elimination reaction is popularly called E_{1cB}-elimination unimolecular with respect to the conjugate base of the substrate.

The overall reaction is:

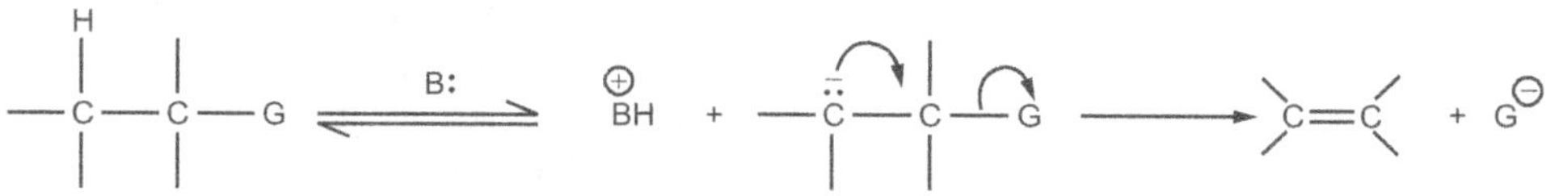

$$-\underset{|}{\overset{H}{\underset{|}{C}}}-\underset{|}{\overset{|}{C}}-G \;\; \underset{}{\overset{B:}{\rightleftharpoons}} \;\; \overset{\oplus}{BH} \;+\; -\underset{|}{\overset{..}{C}}-\underset{|}{\overset{|}{C}}\curvearrowright G \;\longrightarrow\; \diagup\!\!\!C=C\!\!\!\diagdown \;+\; G^{\ominus}$$

4. **Rearrangement reactions:**

   Rearrangement reactions involve;
   1. Migration of a functional group to another position in a molecule containing double bond.

   Example:

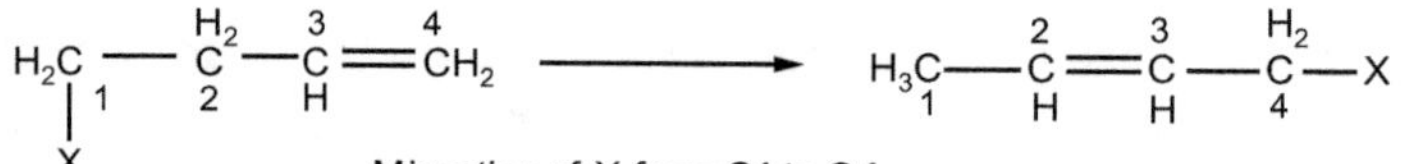

   $$H_2\underset{\underset{X}{|}}{\overset{}{C}}\!\!-\!\!\overset{H_2}{\underset{}{C}}\!\!-\!\!\overset{}{\underset{H}{C}}\!\!=\!\!CH_2 \;\longrightarrow\; H_3C\!\!-\!\!\overset{}{\underset{H}{C}}\!\!=\!\!\overset{}{\underset{H}{C}}\!\!-\!\!\overset{H_2}{\underset{}{C}}\!\!-\!\!X$$

   Migration of X from **C1** to **C4**

   2. Reshuffling of the sequence of atoms forming the basic carbon skeleton of the molecule to form a product with a new structure;

   Example:

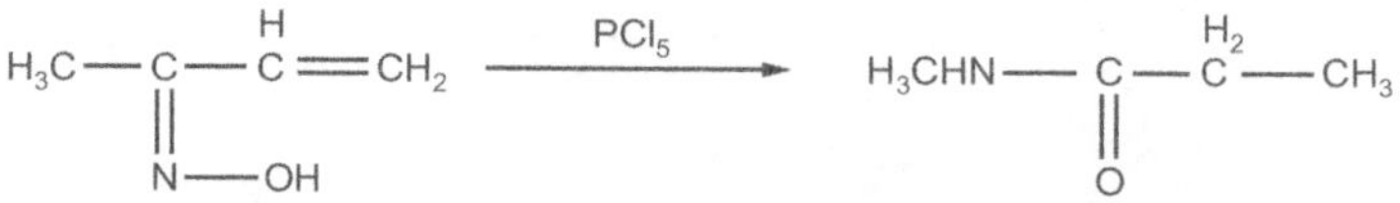

   $$H_3C-\underset{\underset{N-OH}{\|}}{C}-\overset{H}{C}=CH_2 \;\;\xrightarrow{PCl_5}\;\; H_3CHN-\underset{\underset{O}{\|}}{C}-\overset{H_2}{C}-CH_3$$

The rearrangement reactions vary in their types depending on the atom or group migrating in the molecule. The migrating groups may be anions or carbanions (negatively charged carbon centres), or cations or cabonium ions/carbocations (positively charged carbon centres).

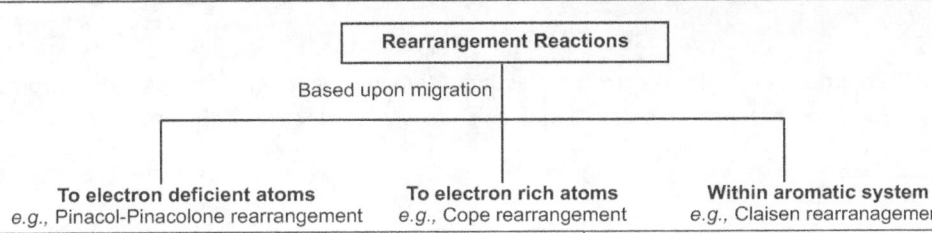

Reaction type	Subtype	Comment
Substitution Reactions	Nucleophilic aliphatic substitution	Follow SN$_1$, SN$_2$ and SN$_i$ pathways or reaction mechanism
	Nucleophilic aromatic substitution	
	Nucleophilic acyl substitution	
	Electrophilic aliphatic substitution	
	Electrophilic aromatic substitution	
	Radical substitution	
Addition Reactions	Electrophilic addition	Include reactions like halogenation, hydrohalogenation, hydration etc.
	Nucleophilic addition	
	Radical addition	
Elimination Reaction		Include reactions like dehydration following through E$_1$, E$_2$ or E$_{1CB}$ pathways
Addition Reaction	Nucleophilic addition	
	Radical addition	
Rearrangement Reaction	1,2-Rearrangements	
	Pericyclic reactions	
	Metathesis	
Organic Redox Reactions		redox reactions are specific to organic compounds and are very common.

CLASSES OF REAGENTS

The presence of electron-attracting (electronegative) groups or atoms (e.g., Halogens, NO_2 group etc.) in a molecule creates an **electron-deficient** centre in the molecule.

Example:

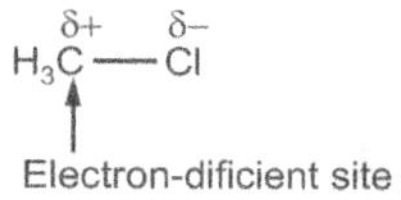

$$H_3\overset{\delta+}{C} - \overset{\delta-}{Cl}$$

Electron-dificient site

The presence of electron-donating (electropositive) groups (e.g., Alkyl groups, OH, NH_2) creates an **electron-rich** centre in the molecule.

Example:

(aniline with NH_2, Electron-rich site)

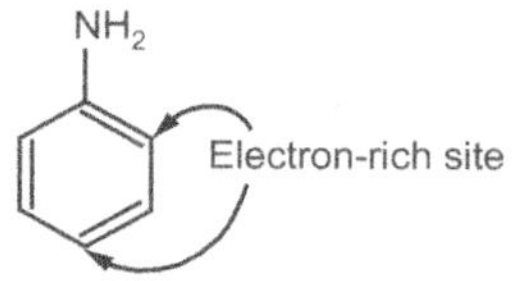

These facts help to predict the type of attacking reagents with which the molecule will most readily react.

An electron-deficient centre (such as carbon atom in methyl chloride) will tend to be most readily attacked by negatively charged ions (such as $-OH^-$, $-CN^-$ etc.). Similarly an electron-rich centre (such as *ortho* and *para* position in aniline) will tend to be most readily attacked by positively charged ions (such as NO_2^+, Cl^+ etc).

Thus, on the basis of the above facts, most of the reagents are classified into two types:

1. Electrophilic reagents (Electrophiles)
2. Nucleophilic reagents (Nucleophiles)

1. Electrophilic reagents (Electrophiles):

Electrophilic (*electro*-electron, *phile*-loving) reagents which are electron deficient and electron seeking and thus attack the substrate at its electron rich site (electron dense region or nucleophilic region). Thus, an electrophilic reagent or an electrophile is a species having electron-deficient atom or group.

Electrophilic reagents can be of two types, namely:

(A) Positive electrophilies and

(B) Neutral electrophiles

(A) Positive electrophiles:

The species, which carry a positive charge and include protons (H^+), cations and/or the carbon radicals (carbonium ions).

Example:

H^+, Br^+, Cl^+, NO_2^+, NH_4^+, NO^+, H_3O^+, R_3C^+

The positive electrophiles attack the substrate which is rich in electrons and accepts electron pair for sharing and form neutral molecule.

$$-\overset{|}{\underset{|}{C}}{:} \quad + \quad E^+ \quad \longrightarrow \quad -\overset{|}{\underset{|}{C}}-E$$

Substrate Electrophile (+ve charged) → Product (Neutral)

(B) Neutral electrophiles:

The electron deficient species, which do not carry positive charge are called as neutral electrophiles.

Example:

BF_3, $AlCl_3$, $ZnCl_2$ and carbon radicals having six electrons in the outermost orbit (carbenes). All these species have six electrons in the outermost orbit and are thus short of a pair of electrons to attain stable configuration and therefore behave as electron-seeking reagents.

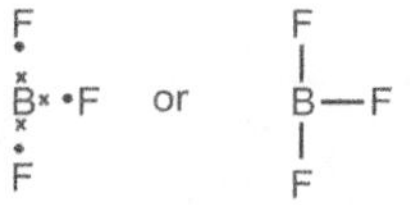

$$\underset{F}{\overset{F}{B}}{\cdot}F \quad \text{or} \quad \underset{F}{\overset{F}{B}}-F \qquad Cl{:}\ddot{C}{:}Cl \quad \text{Or} \quad Cl-\ddot{C}-Cl$$

Boron trifluoride 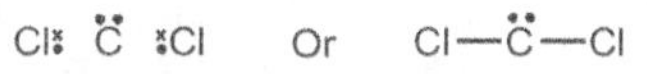   Dichlorocarbene

2. Nucleophilic reagents (Nucleophiles):

The reagents possessing at least one lone pair of electrons or negative charge are known as **nucleophiles** or **nulceophilic reagents** (*nucleo*-nucleus ; *phile*-loving). Since, they possess higher electron density, they attack the substrate at the point of minimum electron density.

Nucleophilic reagents can be of two types, namely

(A) Negative nucleophilies

(B) Neutral nucleophiles

(A) Negative nucleophiles:

The species, which carry an excess of electron pair and are negatively charged. These include, halide ions, alkoxy ions, hydroxyl ions and carbon radicals (carbanions).

Example:

$$Cl^-, Br^-, I^-, HO^-, RO^-, CN^-, R_3C^-$$

The negative nucleophiles attack the substrate which is deficient in electrons and donate electron pair for sharing and form neutral molecules.

$$-\overset{|}{\underset{|}{C^+}} \; + \; :Nu^- \longrightarrow -\overset{|}{\underset{|}{C}}-Nu$$

Substrate Nucleophile (–ve charged)   Product (Neutral)

(B) Neutral Nucleophiles:

The species which although electron rich (because of presence of unshared electron pair), yet are electrically neutral.

Example:

$$H-\ddot{\underset{..}{O}}-H, \; R-\ddot{\underset{..}{O}}-R, \; R-\ddot{\underset{..}{S}}-R, \; :NH_3, \; R-\ddot{N}H_2$$

Since, Nucleophiles are capable of donating electron pairs, they are considered as *Lewis bases*.

Nucleophile vs Electrophile:

Point	Nucleophiles	Electrophiles
1.	Electron rich	Electron deficient
2.	Donate an electron pair	Accept an electron pair
3.	Attack on electron-deficient atom	Attack on electron-rich atom
4.	Act as Lewis bases	Act as Lewis acids
5.	Possess an unshared pair of electrons which are not too strongly held to the atomic nucleus (usually atoms of group V and VI of periodic table)	Possess an empty orbital to receive the electrons pair from the nucleophile.
6.	Are able to increase their covalency by one unit.	Are able to form an extra or alternative bond with the nucleophile.

A nucleophile is species that has an **unshared electron** pair and can make use of this to react with an electron-deficient species or electrophile. This is similar to the definition of a base, as a base also has unshared electron pairs. Any species which is capable of acting as a base can also act as a nucleophile.

Both nucleophile and base work as donors of electrons to an electron deficient species. A nucleophile attacks an **electrophile**, whereas, the base attacks a **proton**. **Nucleophilicity** is the capacity of a nucleophile to combine with an electrophile, whereas, **basicity** is the ability to abstract a proton (H^+).

Nucleophilicity and basicity are very similar properties in a sense that species that are nucleophiles are usually also bases (*e.g.*, HO^-, RO^-). It shows that there is a close relationship between a group's capacity to act as a nucleophile *i.e.*, nucleophilicity and its ability to act as a base *i.e.*, basicity. *e.g.*, the hydroxide ion can act as a nucleophile or as base.

Hydroxide acting as nucleophile   Hydroxide acting as base

In a nucleophilic substitution reaction of a halide such as CH_3Br, the rate depends upon the nucleophilicity of the nucleophile. It shall attack the carbonium ion that gets formed in the course of reaction by slow ionization of C-Br bond in one step reaction.

(Acting as nucleophile)

(Acting as base)

The main difference between basicity and nucleophilicity is that basicity is a thermodynamic property, while nucleophilicity is kinetic property. Basicity affects the position of equilibria in a chemical reaction and nucleophilicity affects the rate of the reactions. In many cases nucleophilicity can be correlated with basicity.

Basicity is a measure of the position of equilibrium between a substrate and its conjugate acid, whereas nucleophilicity relates to a rate of reaction.

In the same row of periodic table, as atomic number increases, basicity decreases, but nucleophilicity increases. This is because the electrons associated with larger atoms become less localized, consequently forming weaker bonds with protons. On the other hand, electrons in the larger atoms are more easily polarizable, and it becomes easier for them to be donated to an electrophile. This leads to greater nucleophilicity.

QUESTION BANK

1. Define a chemical reaction? Explain types of bond breaking?
2. Classify chemical reactions with suitable examples. What are different types of reactions on the basis of (1) Reaction centre (2) Type of reagent (3) Molecularity.
3. What are electrophiles and nucleophiles? What are examples of positive electrophiles and neutral electrophiles? What are examples of negative nucleophiles and neutral nucleophiles?
4. Differentiate between nucleophiles and electrophiles.
5. Differentiate between nucleophilicity and electrophilicity, as well as, between nucleophilicity and basicity.
6. What is a chemical reaction. Explain different types of chemical reactions with one example of each.
7. Define and explain the following terms and concepts:
   (a) Homolytic bond fission
   (b) Heterolytic bond fission
   (c) Inductive effect
   (d) Mesomeric effect
   (e) Resonance
   (f) Electromeric effect
8. Classify following electrophiles and nucleophiles.
   (a) CN^-
   (b) H_2O
   (c) Br^+
   (d) NH_3
   (e) NO_2^+
   (f) ROH
9. Write notes on:
   (a) Inductive effect
   (b) Mesomeric effect
   (c) Hyperconjugation
   (d) Carbonium ions
   (e) Carbanions
   (f) Free radicals
   (g) Carbenes
   (h) Nitrenes

PHARMACEUTICAL ORGANIC CHEMISTRY - I   CLASSES OF REACTIONS AND CLASSES OF REAGENTS

10. Identify the type of reaction in the following:
    (a) $H_2C=CH_2 + HBr \longrightarrow H_3C-CH_2Br$
    (b) $H_3C-OH + H-Br \longrightarrow H_3C-Br + H-OH$
    (c) $H_3C-\underset{H_2}{C}-Cl \longrightarrow CH_2=CH_2 + HCl$
    (d) $\underset{\underset{X}{|}}{H_2C}\overset{}{\underset{1}{\,}}-\underset{2}{\overset{H_2}{C}}-\overset{3}{\underset{H}{C}}=\overset{4}{CH_2} \longrightarrow H_3\underset{1}{C}-\overset{2}{\underset{H}{C}}=\overset{3}{\underset{H}{C}}-\overset{H_2}{\underset{4}{C}}-X$

11. What are electrophiles and nucleophiles? Give two examples?

■■■

Chapter 5 ...

REACTION INTERMEDIATES

CONTENTS
Carbocations, Carbanions, Carbenes, Free radicals, Nitrene and Nitrenium ions.

REACTION INTERMEDIATES

Definition:
"A reaction intermediate is a molecular entity (atom, ion, molecule etc.) which is formed from the reactants (or preceding intermediates) and reacts further to give the products of a chemical reaction."

Most chemical reactions are stepwise, that is, they take more than one elementary step to complete. An intermediate is the reaction product of each of these steps, except for the last one, which forms the final product. Reactive intermediates are usually short lived and are very seldom isolated. Due to their short lifetime, they do not remain in the product mixture.

For example, consider this hypothetical stepwise reaction:

Example:

$$A + B \longrightarrow C + D$$

Above reaction is a multistep reaction which includes the following steps.

$$A + B \longrightarrow X^*$$

$$X^* \longrightarrow C + D$$

In above example, the chemical species **"X*"** is an intermediate or reaction intermediate.

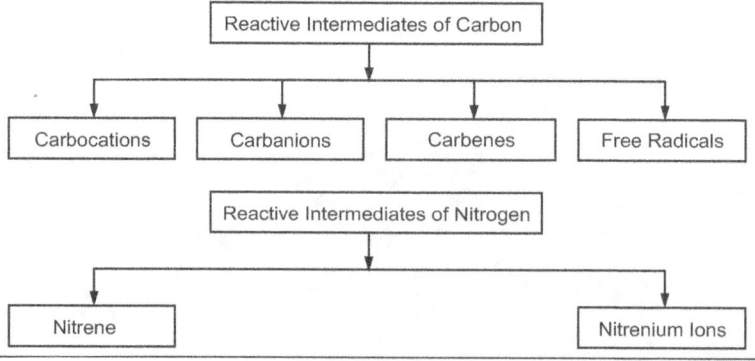

CARBOCATIONS

A carbon atom which is trivalent, contains an even number of electrons and carries a positive charge is called a *carbocation* or *cabonium ion*. The carbon atom of the carbocation is sp^2 hybridized and uses its three hybridized orbitals for bonding with atoms.

Example:

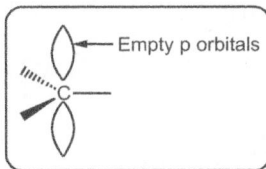

Chlorine is more electronegative than carbon

Structure and geometry:

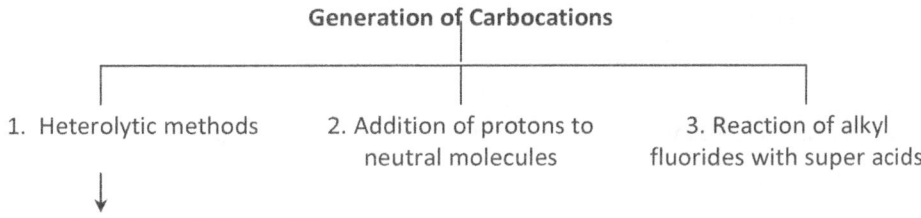

Fig. 5.1: Structure and geometry of carbon atom

The carbon atom is sp^2 hybridized and it uses its three hybridized orbitals for bonding with other atoms. The remaining $2p_z$ orbital is empty and is perpendicular to the plane of the other three bonds. Geometry is planar with bond angles of 120°.

Classification of carbocations:

Carbocations are classified as primary (1°), secondary (2°) and tertiary (3°).

A primary carbocation is one in which there is only one carbon group attached to the carbon bearing the positive charge. A secondary carbocation is one in which there are two carbons attached to the carbon bearing the positive charge. Likewise, a tertiary carbocation is one in which there are three carbons attached to the carbon bearing the positive charge.

Generation of Carbocations

1. Heterolytic methods
2. Addition of protons to neutral molecules
3. Reaction of alkyl fluorides with super acids

- Solvolysis of alkyl halides
- From diazonium Ions
- Protonation of alcohols
- Decarboxylation of acyl halides
- Decomposition of tetra-ammonium salts

Nomenclature of carbocations:

Depending on the number of carbon atoms:

Example:

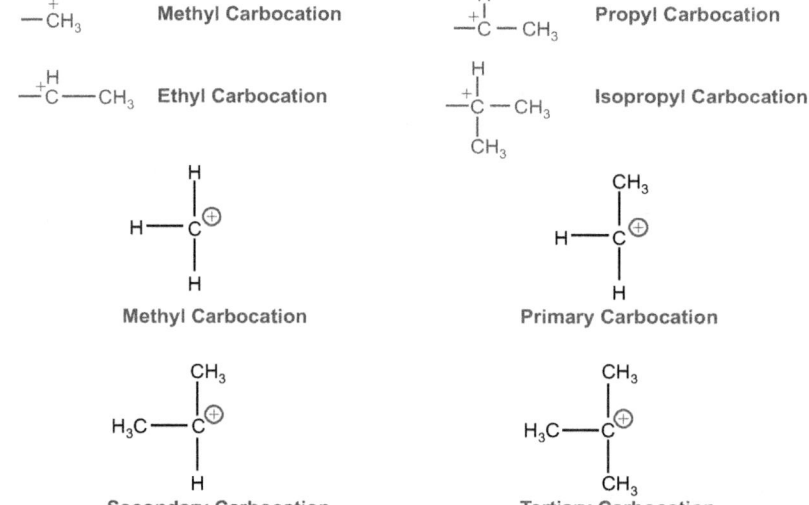

Carbocations are generated in a number of ways and occur as intermediates in chemical reactions. Generation of carbocations takes place as follows:

1. **Heterolytic Methods:**

   (a) **Solvolysis of alkyl halides**: Ionization of alkyl halides leads to the formation of carbocations. Here solvent plays a dual role of solvating medium as well as a reactant both.

   $$R-X \xrightarrow{\text{Solvent}} R^+ + X^-$$

   $$X = I, Br, Cl$$

   (b) **From diazonium Ions**: Alkyl diazonium ions being unstable, readily undergo decomposition at room temperature to give carbocations.

   Example:

   $$R-N\equiv N \longrightarrow R^+ + N_2\uparrow$$

   (c) **Protonation of alcohols**: Alcohols are easily protonated and lose a water molecule leading to the formation of carbocations. High acidity favors the process.

Example:

$$ROH + H^+ \longrightarrow R^+ + H_2O$$

(d) **Decarboxylation of acyl halides:** Acyl halides on treatment with aluminium chloride ($AlCl_3$) liberate carbon monoxide resulting in formation of carbocation.

Example:

$$R_3COCl \xrightarrow{AlCl_3} R_3C^+ + CO + AlCl_4^-$$

(e) **Decomposition of tetra-ammonium salts:** Carbocations are also formed on thermal decomposition of tetra-ammonium salts.

Example:

$$R_3\overset{+}{N}H-R \xrightarrow{Heat} R^+ + R_3N$$

2. **Addition of protons to neutral molecules:**

In acidic media, protonation of olefins (alkenes) leads to carbocations.

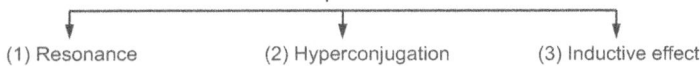

3. **Reaction of alkyl fluorides with super acids (FSO_3H or SbF_5):**

Greater reactivity of SbF_5 ensures quantitative conversion of alkyl fluoride to form a carbocation.

$$R-F + SbF_5 \longrightarrow R^+ + SbF_6^-$$

Reactions involving carbocations:

Carbocations are reaction intermediates in a large number of organic reactions:

Example:

1. Friedel Craft alkylation and acylation.
2. Organic reactions following SN_1 reaction mechanisms.
3. Name reactions involving electron deficient carbon centres e.g., Pinacol-Pinacolone rearrangement, Wagner-Meerwein rearrangement.

Stability of carbocations:

Stability of the carbocations can be explained on the basis of

(1) Resonance   (2) Hyperconjugation   (3) Inductive effect

1. **On the basis of resonance:** Resonance delocalizes the positive charge on a carbocation and creates additional bonding between adjacent atoms. Decreasing the electron deficiency increases the stability.

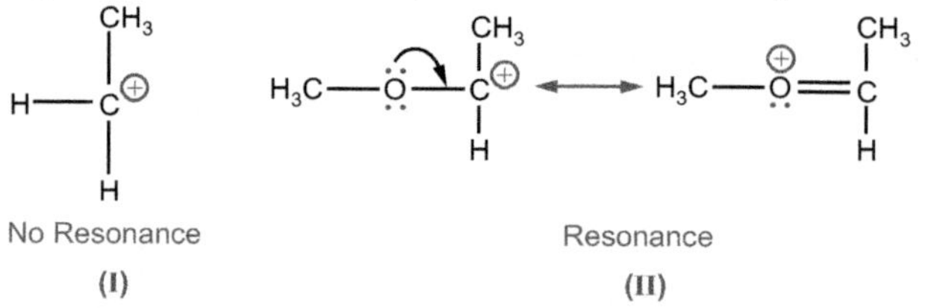

No Resonance (I)   Resonance (II)

The structure (I) does not have any resonance contributors in which electrons would be donated to the carbon with the open octet. Whereas the carbocation (II) that has resonance and a delocalized positive charge. Charge delocalization imparts stability, so the structure with resonance is lower in energy.

Stabilization of carbocations attached to aromatic and aliphatic systems:

Stabilization of carbocations attached to alkoxy groups

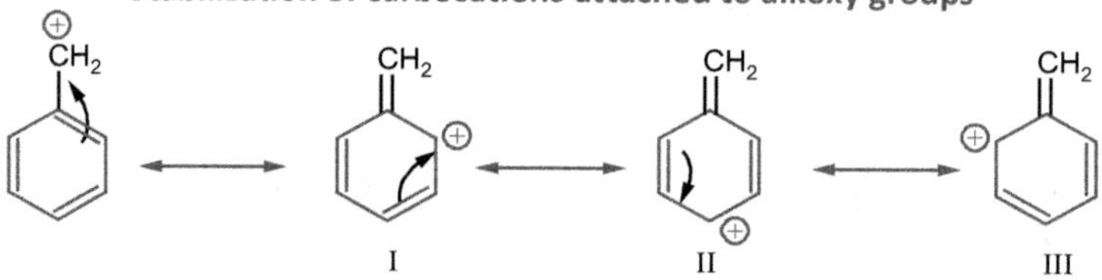

Stabilization of carbocations attached to aryl group/aromatic system

The electron deficient (positively charged) carbon attached to an alkoxy (e.g., methoxy) group is stabilized by only two canonical forms (resonating structures) whereas, the electron deficient carbon attached to an aromatic system is stabilized by more than two (in above example three) canonical forms. More the resonating structures for a compound, more will be the stability. Therefore, carbocations attached to an alkoxy/aliphatic system are less stable than those attached to an aromatic system.

2. **Hyperconjugation:** Increasing the number of hyperconjugative interactions increases carbocation stability. Therefore, increasing the number of bonds adjacent to the carbocations by increasing the number of alkyl groups attached

to the carbocation carbon results in an increase in carbocation stability. For example, a tertiary carbocation should be more stable than a secondary carbocation.

Primary Carbocation

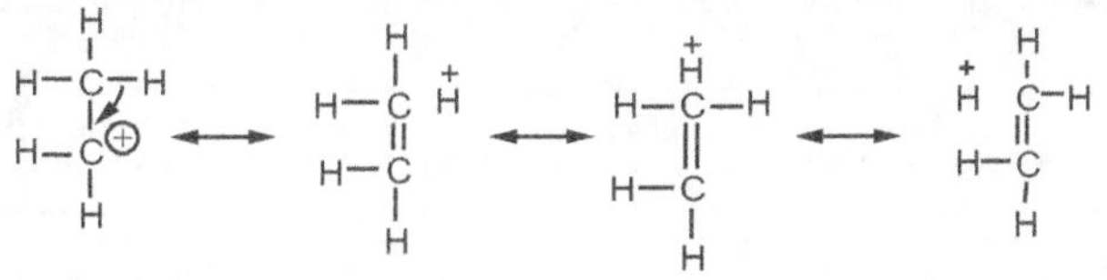

Three hyperconjugative structures possible with a primary carbocation

Secondary Carbocation

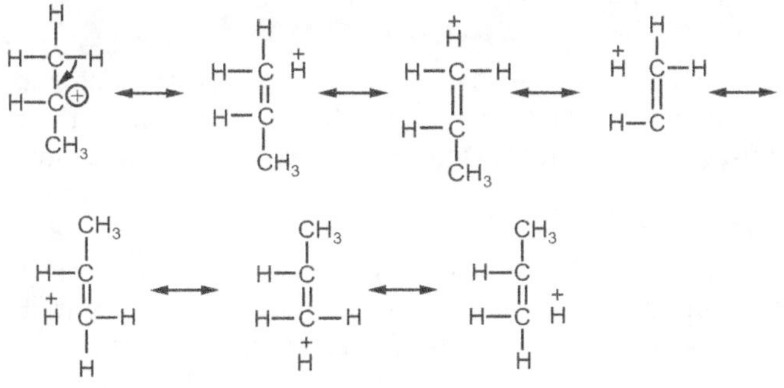

Six hyperconjugative structures possible with a secondary carbocation

More the hyperconjugative structures, higher will be stability. Hence, tertiary carbocation with nine (09) hyperconjugative structures, is more stable than secondary carbocation (six hyperconjugative structures), which more stable than primary (three hyperconjugative structures).

3. **Inductive effect:** As the carbocation contains a positively charged carbon (electron deficient), any substituent which has ability to donate electrons will increase the stability of carbocations due to positive indcutive effect. Therefore, electron donating substituents will increase the stability of the carbocation whereas, electron withdrawing substituents will decrease stability of the carbocations (–I effect).

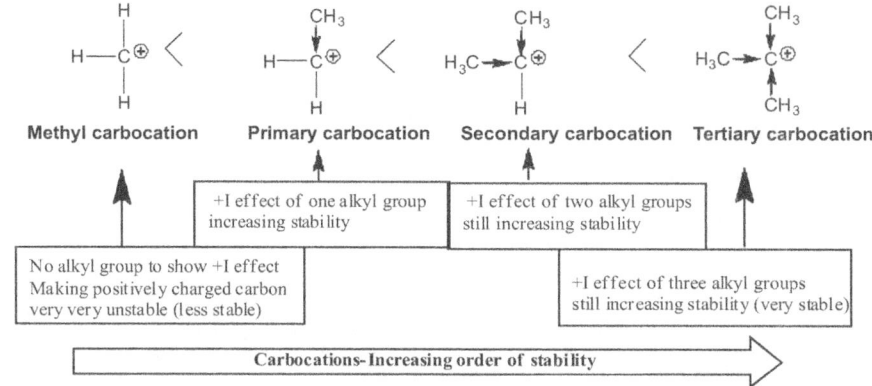

Carbocations- Increasing order of stability

CARBANIONS

A carbon atom which is trivalent i.e., contains an even number of electrons and carries a negative charge is called a *carbanion*. The carbon atom of the carbanions is sp^3 hybridized and uses its three hybridized orbitals for bonding with atoms. Geometry is tetrahedral.

Structure and geometry:

A carbanions contains a trivalent carbon with a lone-pair of electrons. There are eight electrons around the carbon atom so it is not electron deficient. It is iso-electronic i.e. contains the same number of electrons as with an amine.

Fig. 5.2: Structure and geometry of carbanions

Classification of Carbanions:

Methyl Carbanion

Primary Carbanion

Secondary Carbanion

Tertiary Carbanion

A primary carbanion is one in which there is one carbon group attached to the carbon bearing the negative charge. A secondary carbanion is one in which there are two carbons attached to the carbon bearing the negative charge. Likewise, a tertiary carbanion is one in which there are three carbons attached to the carbon bearing the negative charge.

Nomenclature of Carbanions:

Depending on the number of carbon atoms :

Example:

$^{\ominus}-CH_3$ Methyl Carbanion

$H-\overset{H}{\underset{\ominus}{C}}-CH_3$ Ethyl Carbanion

$H-\overset{H}{\underset{\ominus}{C}}-CH_3$ Propyl Carbanion
  (with extra H shown above)

$\overset{H}{\underset{CH_3}{\overset{\ominus}{C}}}-CH_3$ Isopropyl Carbanion

Generation of Carbanions:

Carbanions may be generated by the following methods:

1. H-Abstraction by a base
2. Metal halogen interchange
3. From alkyl halides
4. From unsaturated compounds

1. **Reaction by a base:** Deprotonation of an organic substrate (or H-abstraction by a base) also leads to the formation of a carbanion.

   Example:

   $H_3C-\overset{O}{\underset{}{C}}-H \xrightarrow{Base} H_2\overset{..-}{C}-\overset{O}{\underset{}{C}}-H$

2. **From Unsaturated Compounds:** In a number of organic reactions, a carbanion is generated by the addition of a nucleophiles to an unsaturated C-C or C-N bond.

   Example:

   (Michael Addition)

3. **From Alkyl Halides:** During the preparation of Grignard reagent, an alkyl halide is reacted with magnesium turnings in presence of ether.

   Example:

   $\overset{\delta+}{R}-\overset{\delta-}{X} + Mg \xrightarrow[Ether]{Anhydrous} \overset{\delta-}{R}-\overset{\delta+}{Mg}-X$

Stability of Carbanions:

Stability of the carbocations can be explained on the basis of

1. Resonance   2. Hybridization   3. Inductive effect

1. **Stability due to aromaticity, resonance:** An example of very high stability of carbanions is the cyclic unsaturated compound, cyclopentadienyl anion. It has six σ-electrons in the cyclic ring and according to Huckel rule, it offers stability due to aromatic character.

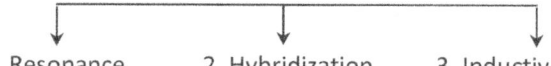

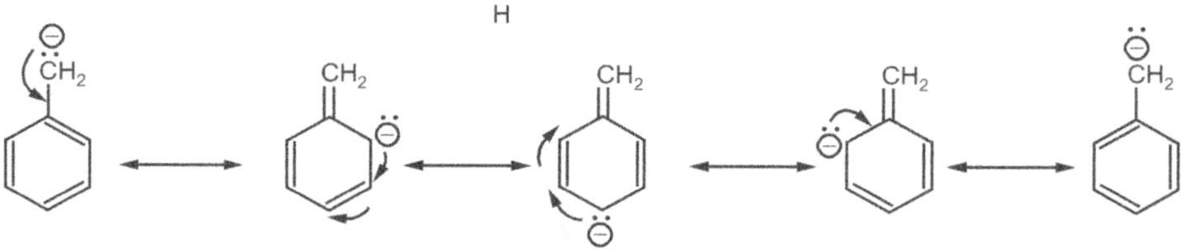

Stability of carbanion due to resonance

2. **Hybridization state and stability of carbanion:** It has been observed that greater the 's' character of the charge bearing the charge atom, greater is the stability due to larger surface area.

   (*e.g.*, triple bond (sp) > double bond (sp^2) > single bond (sp). Thus, allyl and benzyl carbonium ions are more stable than alkyl carbonium ions.

3. **Inductive Effect:**

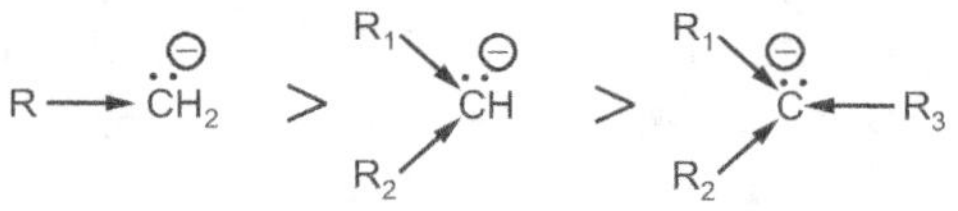

   $$R \rightarrow \overset{\ominus}{\ddot{C}H_2} \;>\; \underset{R_2}{\overset{R_1}{\diagdown}}\overset{\ominus}{\ddot{C}H} \;>\; \underset{R_2}{\overset{R_1}{\diagdown}}\overset{\ominus}{\ddot{C}} \leftarrow R_3$$

   Primary   Secondary   Tertiary

   Fig. 5.3: Types of carbanions

   (a) When 'R' is the alkyl group with +I effects, it will exert its influence on the stability of these carbanion. Stability will decrease due to pushing of electrons towards negative charge and localizing it. Tertiary carbanion with three alkyl substituents will be least stable as compared to primary carbanion with only one alkyl group.

   Therefore, stability order is,

   $$R=H- \;>\; -CH_3 \;>\; -C_2H_5 \;>\; -CH_2-CH_2-CH_3$$

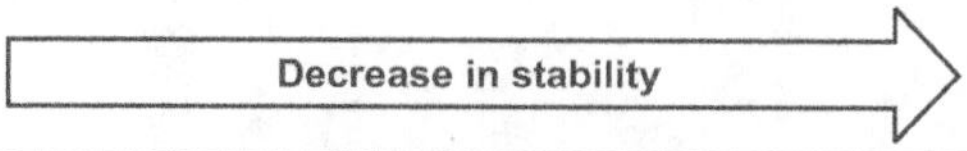

   Decrease in stability →

(b) If electron withdrawing group is attached - stability will increase. The increase in stability is due to decrease in electron density because of –I effects shown by electron withdrawing substituents, by delocalising it.

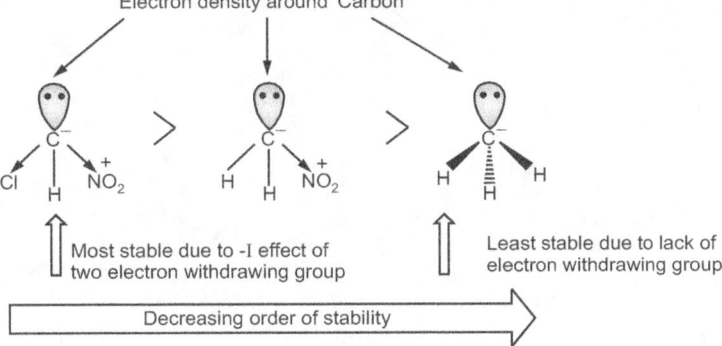

Fig. 5.4: Stability of carbanions

FREE RADICALS

Any species which is having an odd or unpaired electrons is called as a free radical. Free radicals are electrically neutral. Because of presence of odd electrons, free radicals are in constant search for another electron to pair up and hence these are highly reactive species.

Example:

Chloride Free Radical	Methyl Free Radical	Benzyl Free Radical	Allyl Radical
$:\overset{..}{\underset{..}{Cl}}\cdot$	$H-\overset{\cdot}{\underset{H}{C}}-H$	Ph–ĊH₂	$H_2C=\overset{\cdot}{\underset{H}{C}}-\dot{C}H_2$

Structure and Geometry:

Free-radicals are believed to possess planar or inverted pyramidal shape (depending on substituents attached to them).

The alkyl free-radicals have planar structure. The carbon atom of alkyl free radicals is sp^2 hybridized. The three sp^2 hybridized orbitals of carbon form bonds with the three alkyl groups, while the odd electron is situated in unused p orbital.

Free-radicals are electrically neutral and are formed as a result of homolytic bond fission.

Example:

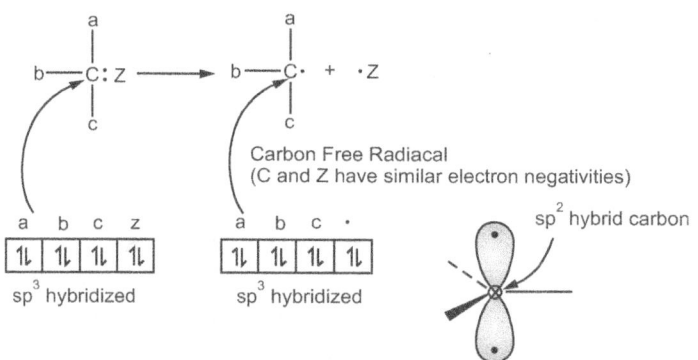

Fig. 5.5: Structure and geometry of free radical

The carbon atom in a carbon free radical uses sp^2 hybrid orbitals to form three σ-bonds. A half filled p orbital extends above and below the plane of σ-bonds. Thus carbon free radicals are electrically neutral and one unpaired (odd) electron.

They are extremely reactive because of the presence of one unpaired electron- which can be paired at the earliest opportunity. Free radicals can combine with other free radicals or with other molecules to produce larger free radicals.

Nomenclature of free radicals:

Free radicals are named after the parent alkyl group. A tertiary free radical is more stable than a secondary which is more stable than a primary free radical.

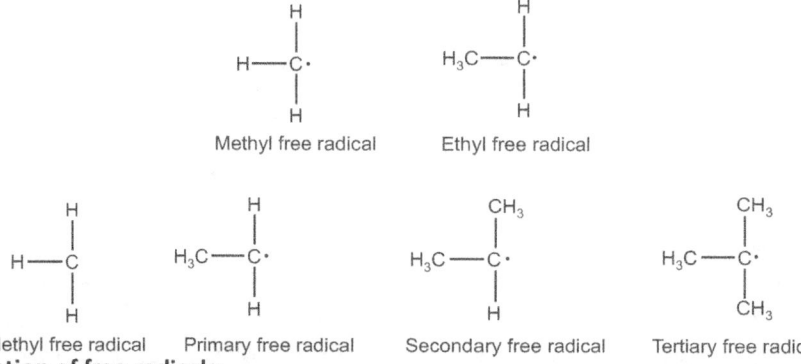

Generation of free radicals:

1. Photolytic and thermal breakdown:

Radicals are generally formed by heating a molecule, usually to a high temperature, or by irradiating it with UV light of proper wavelength. When molecule is heated, the bond that breaks first is usually the weakest bond. Bonds of type –O-O-, -N-N- and –X-X- (halogens) are weak and break homolytically by thermal or photochemical means.

Example:

$$C_6H_5-O-O-C_6H_5 \xrightarrow{70°C} C_6H_5-O\cdot + \cdot O-C_6H_5$$
Phenoxy redicals

$$Cl-Cl \xrightarrow{h\nu} Cl^\cdot + Cl^\cdot$$
Chloride redicals

2. Redox Reactions: Redox reactions are a convenient source of free radicals.

Example:

The combination of H_2O_2 with ferrous ion, produces hydroxyl radicals (Fenton's Reagent):

$$H_2O_2 + Fe^{2+} \xrightarrow{H^+} OH^\cdot + OH^- + Fe^{3+}$$

Stability of Free Radicals:

A tertiary free radical is more stable than a secondary one and secondary is more stable than the primary.

Stabilization by resonance: Free radical centres are stabilized by the replacement of one, two or three of the hydrogens of the methyl radical by alkyl groups.

Alkyl radical intermediates are stabilized by similar criteria as carbocations *i.e.*, the more substituted the radical will be more stable it will be as compared to the least substituted one.

Example:

The stability order of radicals: tertiary radical > secondary radical > primary radical.

Stability due to hyperconjugation:

Consider the stabilization in case of methyl, ethyl, *iso*-propyl and tert-butyl radicals:

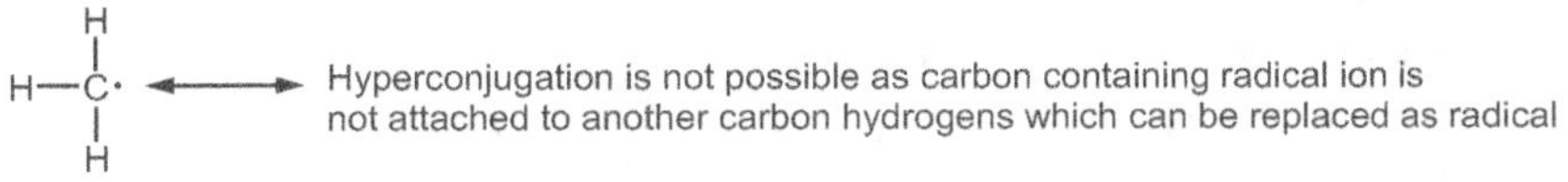

Methyl Radical — Hyperconjugation is not possible as carbon containing radical ion is not attached to another carbon hydrogens which can be replaced as radical

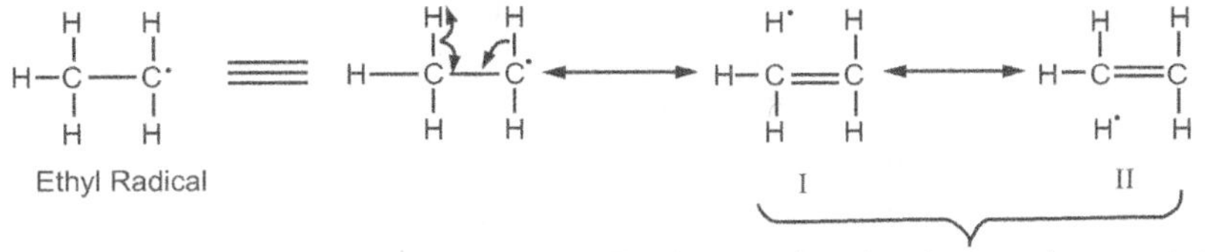

Ethyl Radical

I   II

Two hyperconjugating structures in case of ethyl radical

REACTION INTERMEDIATES

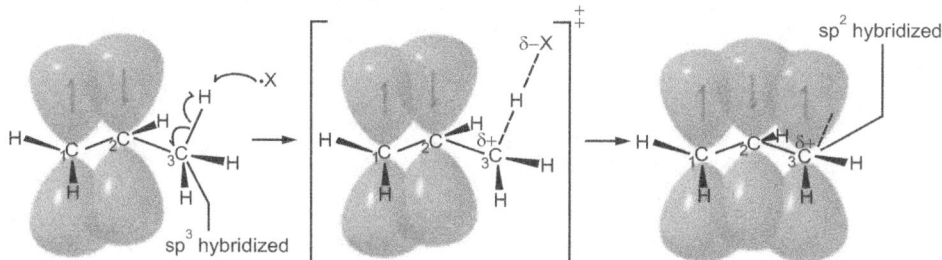

Five hyperconjugating structures in case of isopropyl radical

Nine hyperconjugating structures possible in case of butyl radical

Hyperconjugation (as resonance) contributes to the stability of structures. More the hyperconjugation (hyperconjugating structures), more will be the stability.

Stability of allyl and benzyl radicals can be explained on the basis of molecular orbital theory and resonance theory as below:

Fig. 5.6: Stability of allyl radical by hyperconjugation: orbital picture

Molecular orbital theory: When an allyl hydrogen is abstracted, the developing "p" orbital on the sp^2 carbon overlaps with "p" orbitals of alkene. Thus, the new "π" orbital is **conjugated** with the double bond "p" orbitals. The radical electron and the "π" electrons are delocalized over the entire conjugated system. Delocalization of charge and electron density leads to increased stability.

Resonance theory: The allyl radical has two contributing resonance forms, which are **interconvertible.** The resonance structures are equivalent and equivalent resonance structures lead to much greater stability of the molecule than either structure alone.

Fig. 5.7: Stabilization in benzyl radical

NITRENE

A **nitrene** (R-N:) is the nitrogen analogue of a carbene. Here the nitrogen atom has only "σ" electrons available and is therefore considered as an "electrophile". A nitrene is a reactive interemediate and is involved in many chemical reactions.

"Nitrenes are derivatives of molecule :NH in which nitrogen is monovalent. The nitrogen atom in a nitrene has sextet of electron (six electrons)."

Example:

R – N̈:

Structure and Geometry:

In the most simple nitrene, the linear imidogen (:N-H), two of the available "σ" electrons from a covalent bond with hydrogen, two other create a free electron pair and the two remaining electrons occupy two degenerate p orbitals. Consistent with Hund's rule the low energy form of imidogen is a triplet with one electron in each of the p orbitals and the high energy form is the singlet state with an electron pair filling one p orbital and the other one vacant.

Generation of nitrenes:

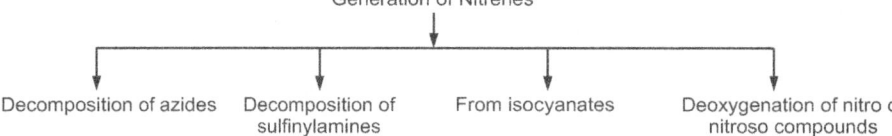

1. **Decomposition of azides:** Nitrenes are prepared by thermal or photochemical decomposition of azides ($-N_3$) resulting in the loss of nitrogen.

   Example:

   $$R-\ddot{\underset{..}{N}}-\overset{+}{N}\equiv N: \xrightarrow{\text{heat or h}\nu} R-\ddot{N} + N_2$$

2. **Decomposition of sulfinylamines:** Pyrolysis of sulfinylaniline forms phenylnitrene.

   Example:

   $$Ph-\ddot{N}=S=O \xrightarrow[\text{Gas phase}]{\Delta} Ph-\ddot{N} + SO_2$$

3. **From isocyanates with expulsion of CO:**

   Example:

   $$R-N=C=O \xrightarrow{-CO} R-\ddot{N}:$$

4. **Deoxygenation of nitro or nitroso compounds:** Deoxygenation of nitro and nitroso compounds may generate a nitrene. It can be achieved by using triethyl phosphate or metal ions (Fe^{2-}).

   $$\left.\begin{array}{c} C_2H_5NO_2 \\ \\ C_2H_5NO_2 \end{array}\right] \xrightarrow[\Delta]{Ph(OC_2H_5)_3} C_6H_5\ddot{N}$$

NITRENIUM IONS

Nitrenium ions are nitrogen-containing organic compounds in which the nitrogen atom has an incomplete (sextet) electron shell and a formal positive charge. Nitrenium ions can exist in two electronic states, the singlet state, where the electrons are paired and the triplet state where both non-bonding orbitals are singly occupied. As a rule these species are extremely electrophilic and their lifetimes in solution are in the picoseconds to microsecond range.

$$-\underset{\oplus}{\overset{|}{N}}: \qquad -\underset{\cdot}{\overset{|\oplus}{N}}\cdot$$

Singlet   Triplet

Generation of nitrenium ions:

Nitrenium ions are formed by heterolytic cleavage of a N-X bond.

$$-\ddot{N}-X \longrightarrow -\overset{\oplus}{\ddot{N}}: + X$$

$$-\ddot{N}-\overset{\oplus}{O}\overset{H}{\underset{H}{\diagdown}} \longrightarrow -\overset{\oplus}{\ddot{N}}: + H_2O$$

CARBENES

Carbenes: Carbene is a molecule containing a neutral carbon atom with a valence of two and two unshared valence electrons. The general formula is R-(C:)-R' or R=C: .

The term "carbene" may also refer to the specific compound $H_2C:$, also called methylene, the parent hydride from which all other carbene compounds are formally derived.

$$\underset{H}{\overset{H}{\diagdown}}C:$$

Classification: Carbenes are classified as either singlets or triplets depending upon their electronic structure. Most carbenes are very short lived, although persistent carbenes are known.

One well studied carbene is $Cl_2C:$, or dichlorocarbene, which can be generated *in situ* from chloroform and a strong base.

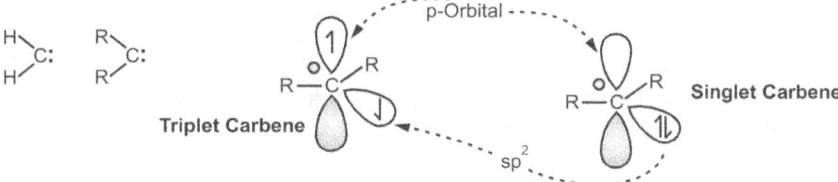

Fig. 5.8: Structure and geometry of carbene

Some facts about carbene:
- A carbene is a divalent carbon species linked to two adjacent groups by a covalent bond.
- It possesses two non-bonding electrons and six valence electrons.
- If the non-bonding electrons have **anti-parallel spins** then carbene is known as **singlet carbene.**
- If the non-bonding electrons have **parallel spins** in different orbitals then triplet carbine.
- Generally, carbenes are expected to be triplet carbenes (Hund's rule), but substituents can change this and in organic chemistry we normally use singlet carbenes.

- They are electron deficient like carbocations.
- They possess a non-bonding pair like carbanion.
- The nature of substituents R have profound effects on the electronics of the carbenes and their reactions.

Carbenes are highly reactive. They act as strong electrophiles because, they can accept a pair of electrons to completer their octet state.

Generation of carbenes:

Carbenes may be generated in a number of ways:

1. By reaction of chloroform in the presence of a strong alkali (*e.g.* Alkoxides).

$$CHCl_3 + RO^- \longrightarrow ROH + Cl_3C^-$$

2. By decomposition of diazomethane or ketene in the presence of uv light:

$$H_2C=N=N \xrightarrow{uv} H_2C: + N_2$$
Diazomethane

$$H_2C=C=O \xrightarrow{uv} H_2C + CO$$
ketene

Reaction of Carbenes:

An important reaction of carbene is their addition to a carbon-carbon double bond to form a cyclopropane derivative.

$$H_3C-\underset{H}{C}=CH_2 + CH_2N_2 \xrightarrow{uv} H_3C-\underset{H}{\overset{H_2}{C}}-CH_2$$

Propene   Diazomethane   Methyl cyclopropane

Ylide: A carbanion stabilized intramolecularly by a positively charged heteroatom directly connected to the negatively charged carbon is called as **"Ylide"**.

$$Ph-\underset{Ph}{\overset{Ph}{P^+}}-CH_2^- \qquad :S^+-CH_2^-$$

Phosphorous ylide   Sulfur ylide

Ylide is a strong nucleophile and takes part in the formation of alkene when condensed with aldehyde or ketone and the reaction is known as "Wittig reaction", phosphorous ylides are stable and lightly reactive.

QUESTION BANK

1. Define reaction intermediates. Classify them with examples.
2. Define carbocations? Classify them and explain their structure. How are they generated?
3. Write a short note on stability of carbocations. Arrange carbocations in increasing order of stability and give exlanation.
4. Carbocations attached to an alkoxy/aliphatic system are less stable than those attached to an aromatic system?
5. Define a Carbanion? Explain structure and geometry of carbanions.
6. What are free radicals? Explain their structure and geometry.
7. Write a short note on generation of free radicals.
8. Alkyl and benzyl radicals are more stable than alkyl radicals, why?
9. What are nitrenes? Explain their structure and geometry. Write an account on generation of nitrenes.
10. What are nitrenium ions? Explain their structure and geometry. Write an account on generation of nitrenium ions.
11. What are carbenes? How are they classified?
12. Write a note on generation of carbenes and discuss reactions of carbenes.
13. Define carbocations, carbanions, free radicals and carbenes.
14. Explain relative stability of primary, secondary and tertiary carbanions.
15. Explain why benzyl carbonium ion is more stable than ethyl carbonium ion.
16. What are carbonium ions? Arrange the following according to their increasing stability.

    (a) $H_3C - \overset{H_2}{C} - \overset{+}{C}H_2$

    (b) $(H_3C)_3 \overset{+}{C}$

    (c) $H_3C - \overset{H_2}{C} - \overset{H}{\overset{+}{C}} - CH_3$

17. Which one of following is correct order of stability of carbanions? Justify.

    (a) Primary > Secondary > Tertiary

    (b) Tertiary > Primary > Secondary

    (c) Secondary > Primary > Tertiary

    (d) Tertiary > Secondary > Primary

Chapter 6 ...

ACIDITY AND BASICITY

CONTENTS

Acidity and Basicity, Application of Inductive, Steric, Hyperconjugation and Resonance effects on Acidity and Basicity.

ACIDS AND BASES : BASIC CONCEPTS

Definitions:

Definition by	Acid	Base	Examples
Arrenhius	Ionises to give H^+ ion in water	Ionises to give OH^- ion in water	Acid: $HCl \xrightarrow{Water} H^+ + Cl^-$ Base: $NaOH \xrightarrow{Water} Na^+ + OH^-$
Bronsted-Lowry	A proton donor	A proton acceptor	$CH_3COOH + H_2O \rightleftharpoons CH_3COO^\ominus + H_3O^\oplus$ Acid (proton donar), Base (proton acceptor), Base (proton acceptor), Acid (proton donar)
Lewis	An electron pair acceptor	An electron pair donar	$HCl + \ddot{N}H_3 \longrightarrow \overset{\oplus}{N}H_4 Cl^-$ Acid, Base $CH_3Cl + AlCl_3 \longrightarrow AlCl_4^\ominus + \overset{\oplus}{C}H_3$ Base, Acid

Acidity:

Consider the simplified general equation of a simple acid base reaction:

$$H-A \rightleftharpoons H^+ + A^-$$

$$Ka = \frac{[H^+][A^-]}{[HA]} \quad pKa = -\log Ka$$

$$Ka = \text{Dissociation constant}$$

where A^- is a conjugate base of HA.

The more stable the conjugate base, **A⁻** is, the more equilibrium favours towards product side (Ka > 1), *i.e.*, more dissociation of **H-A**.
- More dissociation of **H-A**, the stronger acid is **H-A**.
- The more the equilibrium favours products, the more **H⁺** will be produced.
- If more **H⁺** is produced then the stronger acid is **H-A**.

So looking for factors that stabilise the conjugate base, A⁻.
- This gives us a "tool" for assessing acidity.
- The larger Ka implies more dissociation of **HA** and so the stronger the acid.
- The larger Ka is, the more negative pKa so the lower the pKa, the stronger the acid.

The acidity constant (or dissociation constant) tells us the extent of ionization and reactivity of the acid. The greater the value of Ka, the stronger the acid and the greater is its tendency to give up a proton. The acidity constant essentially expresses the relative ratio of the ionized product to the unionized reactants. For convenience purposes, the strength of the acid is generally denoted by its pKa value rather than its Ka value. The following equation can be used to interconvert between the two: pKa = − log Ka. This equation indicates that a more negative pKa value represents a stronger acid. Additionally a pKa change of one unit represents one order of magnitude in acidity. Generally, very strong acids have a pKa < 1, moderately strong acids fall between pKa's of 1 and 5, and weak acids have pKa > 5. It is important to distinguish between pKa and pH. While the pH scale is used to describe the acidity of a solution, the pKa is used to describe a particular compound.

Acidity:

Key factors that affect the stability of the conjugate base, A⁻:

1. **Electronegativity:** Electronegativity is a measure of an atom's attraction for electrons. The greater the electronegativity of an atom the greater is its desire to withhold its electrons. Electronegativity increases as we go across a period and up a column in the period table. Acids accept electrons to form new covalent bonds. Electronegativity is related to acidity. The greater the electronegativity of an atom in an acid molecule, the less it is willing to share its electrons. Electronegativity is an important consideration, when comparing atoms in the same row of the periodic table.

Example:

Which is the strongest acid H_2O, NH_3 or CH_4?

$H-O-H$ (pKa ~16) $\xrightarrow{Base}$ $H-\overset{..}{\underset{..}{O}}:^{\ominus}$

$H-NH-H$ (pKa ~38) $\xrightarrow{Base}$ $H-\overset{..}{N}^{\ominus}-H$

$H-CH_2-H$ with H above and below (pKa ~50) $\xrightarrow{Base}$ $H-\overset{H}{\underset{H}{C:^{\ominus}}}$

Increasing ion stability ↑

In comparing the strengths of acids we must analyze the structures of their conjugate bases. Each of their conjugate bases has one formal charge. In above example, none of the conjugate bases are stabilized by resonance. The negative charge lies on atoms in the same row (C, N, O) therefore, size is not a factor in determining basicity. Finally, we resort to use electronegativity differences between the atoms. The atoms are all in the same period and electronegativity increases as we move to the right. The more electronegative the atom the less likely it is to share electron density, and thus it is a weaker base. Oxygen is the most electronegative atom; this makes the hydroxide ion the weakest base. On the other hand, carbon is the least electronegative atom; therefore CH_3 – is the strongest base. We know that basicity and acidity are inversely related, therefore in order of acidity,

$$H_2O > NH_3 > CH_4$$

Decreasing acidity order →

Phenol (OH on benzene) > Cyclohexanol (OH on cyclohexane)

To determine the strength of the acids, we must analyze the strength of their conjugate bases. The strength of a base is proportional to charge density. The negative charge on the conjugate base of cyclohexanol cannot be delocalized because no significant resonance contributors. On the other hand, the conjugate base of phenol has four significant resonance contributors and this greatly delocalizes the electron density. As a result the conjugate base of phenol has less charge density which means more stability. Therefore, cyclohexanol is the weaker base and phenol is the stronger acid, between the two.

[Resonance structures of phenoxide ion]

2. Atomic Size: When comparing atoms of equal formal charge the larger atom provides more space for the charge. Therefore, in a larger atom the negative charge is more dispersed and the charge density decreases. As a result negative charges prefer to rest on large atoms rather than being localized on a small atom (due to increased stability). Therefore, smaller atoms have a greater driving force to share electron density because of increased charge concentration and are thereby stronger bases. It is important to understand that this principle applies when considering atoms in the same column of the period table (as size changes are significant). Because size does not greatly change across a period, this principle does not apply. When comparing atoms across a period, we consider electronegativity.

| Example: |

Across the period : Changes in atomic size are not significant factors in basicity

B	C	N	O	F
				Cl
				Br
				I

Down family:
Significant atomic radius effects on basicity, not acidity.

In determining the strongest acids, again we should look at the conjugate bases. In each conjugate base, resonance does not apply, so we can rule resonance out as an influence of charge density and hence basicity. Thus, we must look at the size of the atoms on which the negative (–1) formal charge lies. Since, each atom lies in the same column, we know that size increases as you move down. Therefore, charge density decreases as you move down the column. The –1 formal charge is most concentrated on the smaller atom, making it most willing to share its electrons. As a result, F^- is the strongest base, so it will have the weakest conjugate acid. On the other hand, I^- is the weakest base so its conjugate acid is strongest. The correct order of acid strength is:

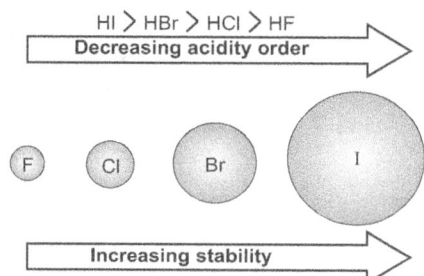

3. Effect of hybridization on acidity: Another important aspect to consider when determining acidity is the hybridization of the carbon. We know that s orbitals are closer to the nucleus than p orbitals. This tells us that the more s character a hybrid orbital has, the closer the electrons to the atom. Therefore, we see that there is a direct relationship between s character and electronegativity; the greater the s character of the hybrid orbital, the greater is the electronegativity of the atom. Such atoms are less willing to share their electron density and thereby have greater acidic character.

The greater the s character of the hybrid orbital, the greater the acidity of the acid.

Applications of inductive effect (Inductive effect and acidity):

Nearby atoms may add to or detract from the electron density of the atom sharing electrons with the proton. This in turn influences its driving force to share electron density and ultimately its basicity. In many cases, electronegative atoms near a molecule pull away the electron density and make it less basic because its driving force to share electron density is decreased. The inductive effect includes the effect of all the atoms other than the atom sharing electron density with the proton. This is the fourth most important factor influencing basicity and many times comes into play when the same functional groups are present on the molecules being compared. This is due to the fact that similar functional groups have similar resonance, atomic size and electronegativity.

(I) Chloroacetic acid   (II) Acetic acid

In order to analyze the acidity of the compounds we analyze the structures of their conjugate bases. Both compounds have the same functional group (carboxylic acid) and therefore, the resonance, atomic size, and electronegativity factors cannot be used to distinguish them. However, the atoms remote to each oxygen in the respective molecules differ. While, acetic acid has a remote methyl group, one hydrogen is substituted for a chlorine atom in the other molecule. Chlorine is far more electronegative in comparison to hydrogen and therefore, pulls away the electron density of the oxygen molecule. As a result, the base is weaker and its conjugate acid is thereby stronger.

Example:

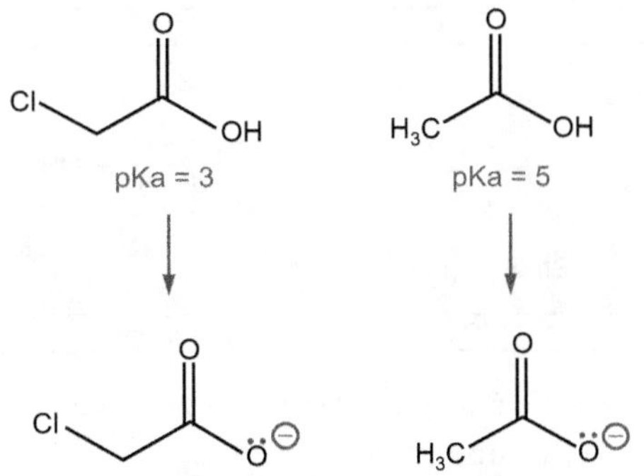

[Structures: ClCH₂COOH (pKa = 3) and CH₃COOH (pKa = 5), with arrows down to their conjugate bases ClCH₂CO₂⁻ and CH₃CO₂⁻]

This structural difference does not change the electronegativity or atomic radius of the oxygen atoms that share an electron pair with a proton, nor does it change the number of resonance contributors. A new explanation is in order. Recall that the role of a base is to share an electron pair with a proton to form a new covalent bond. The less electron density available (i.e., less negative charge), the harder it is for the atom to share this electron pair.

Chlorine is more electronegative than carbon, so the chlorine pulls electron density from the adjacent carbon atom. This carbon atom in turn borrows electron density from the neighboring carbonyl carbon, and so forth. The end effect is that the chlorine atom pulls electron density toward itself and away from the CO_2^- (carboxylate) group. The reduced electron density of the carboxylate group means lower basicity. Thus, we predict $ClCH_2CO_2^-$ to be a poorer base than $CH_3CO_2^-$, and by extension, $ClCH_2COOH$ to be a stronger acid than CH_3COOH. The actual pKa values are 2.86 for $ClCH_2COOH$ (stronger acid) and 4.76 for CH_3COOH (weaker acid). (You can read more about the inductive effect and the *pKa* of carboxylic acids in the text chapter on carboxylic acids.) The effect of one atom or group of atoms on the electron density on a remote portion of the molecule is called the inductive effect.

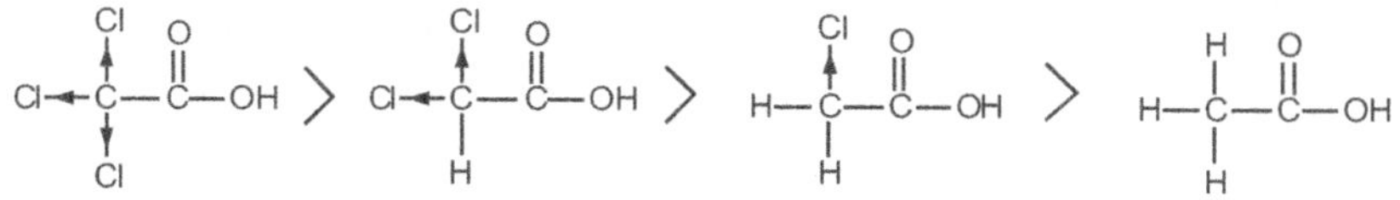

$$\underset{\substack{\text{Trichloroacetic acid}\\ \text{(–I effect of three chlorine atoms)}}}{\text{Cl}_3\text{C}-\text{COOH}} > \underset{\text{Dichloroacetic acid}}{\text{Cl}_2\text{CH}-\text{COOH}} > \underset{\substack{\text{Chloroacetic acid}\\ \text{(–I effect of one chlorine atom)}}}{\text{ClCH}_2-\text{COOH}} > \underset{\text{Acetic acid}}{\text{CH}_3-\text{COOH}}$$

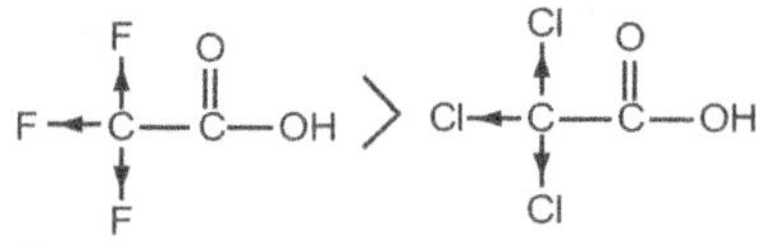

Strong acid ←——— Decreasing order of acidity ———→ Weak acid

$$\underset{\text{Strong acid}}{\text{F}_3\text{C}-\text{COOH}} > \text{Cl}_3\text{C}-\text{COOH}$$

Decreasing order of acidity

Fluorine being more electronegative than chlorine

Applications of Resonance (Resonance and acidity):

Resonance: A molecule is said to have resonance when its structure cannot be adequately described by a single Lewis structure. How does resonance influence the ability of a base to share electrons with a proton? Resonance may delocalize this the electron pair that the base might use to form the new bond with the proton. This delocalization increases the stability of the base. Greater stability results in lower reactivity. A base that has resonance delocalization of the electron pair that is shared with the proton will therefore be less basic than a base without this feature. Since a weaker base has a stronger conjugate acid, a compound whose conjugate base enjoys resonance stabilization will be more acidic.

Example:

In the carboxylate ion, RCO_2^- the negative charge is delocalised across 2 electronegative oxygen atoms which makes it more stable than being localised on a specific atom as in the alkoxide, RO^-.

$$RCO_2H > ROH$$

Decreasing acidity order

1. Which O-H proton is more acidic, ethanol (CH_3CH_2OH) or acetic acid (CH_3CO_2H)?

   Acidity can readily be analyzed by examining the corresponding conjugate bases:

PHARMACEUTICAL ORGANIC CHEMISTRY - I ACIDITY AND BASICITY

(Scheme I) $H_3C-CH_2-\ddot{O}H$ →(Remove Proton)→ $H_3C-CH_2-\ddot{O}:^{\ominus}$
Ethanol   Ethoxide ion: no resonance

(Scheme II) $H_3C-C(=\ddot{O})-\ddot{O}-H$ →(Remove Proton)→ [two resonance structures of acetate ion]
Acetic acid   Acetate ion: resonance possible
                                              two resonating structures

Deprotonation of ethanol affords ethoxide ion, which has no resonance (only one Lewis structure can be drawn). Deprotonation of acetic acid affords acetate ion that has resonance (two contributing Lewis structures can be drawn). Because acetate ion has resonance that delocalizes the electron pair to be shared with a proton and ethoxide ion does not, acetate ion is a weaker base than ethoxide ion. Recalling that weaker bases have stronger conjugate acids, we conclude that acetic acid is a stronger acid than ethanol. The actual pKa values agree with our prediction.

For acetic acid the pKa is 4.76 (stronger acid) and for ethanol the pKa is 15.9 (weaker acid). The resonance effect on pKa can be viewed in a variety of ways. For example, we can consider the magnitude of the charge on the atom(s) that would share an electron pair with a proton. An atom with greater charge has a higher incentive to stabilize this charge by sharing a pair of electrons with a proton. Thus, everything else being equal, an ion with more net charge per atom that shares an electron pair is a stronger base. Examination of the resonance hybrid structure for acetate ion suggests that the charge on each oxygen atom that would share an electron pair with a proton is −1/2. The charge on the oxygen of ethoxide ion is −1. Because each oxygen atom of acetate ion has a smaller charge, it has less incentive to stabilize this charge by sharing an electron pair. Less incentive to share an electron pair with a proton means lowers basicity.

$H_3C-CH_2-\ddot{O}:^{\ominus}$
Ethoxide ion: no resonance

[Acetate acid] →(Remove Proton)→ [Acetate ion] [Resonance hybrid structure]

Alternately, recall that stability tends to increase with an increasing number of significant resonance contributors. Protonation usually results in loss of one or more of these resonance contributors. A base with many resonance contributors stands to lose more resonance than a base with a lesser number of resonance contributors. Thus, a base with many resonance contributors will resist protonation (be a poorer base) than a similar structure with fewer resonance contributors. Acetate ion has two significant resonance contributors, and has more to lose upon protonation than ethoxide ion with a single resonance contributor. This analysis suggests acetate ion to be a poorer base than ethoxide ion and thus, acetic acid to be a stronger acid than ethanol.

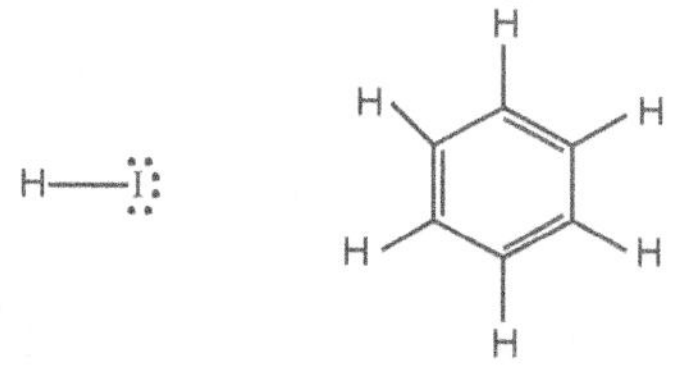

We know that stronger acids have greater Ka values and more negative pKa values. Therefore, we know that HI is the stronger acid in this case. This means that HI has a greater tendency to give up a proton. In a proton transfer equilibibrium essentially all of the HI will be deprotonated and the solution will be composed almost entirely of hydronium ion and conjugate base. The equilibrium will lie very far to the right in this reaction. HI can be classified as a strong acid because its pKa is less than 1. On the other hand, based on pKa we know that benzene is an extremely weak acid. Essentially, none of the benzene will deprotonate in a proton transfer reaction. The equilibrium will lie very far to the left in this reaction.

The s-Character and Acidity:

Hybridization: An important aspect to consider when determining acidity is the hybridization of the carbon. We know that "s orbitals" are closer to the nucleus than "p orbitals". This tells us that the more s character a hybrid orbital has the closer are the electrons to the atom. Therefore, we see that there is a direct relationship between s character and electronegativity; the greater the s character of the hybrid orbital, the greater is the electronegativity of the atom. Such atoms are less willing to share their electron density and thereby have greater acidic character.

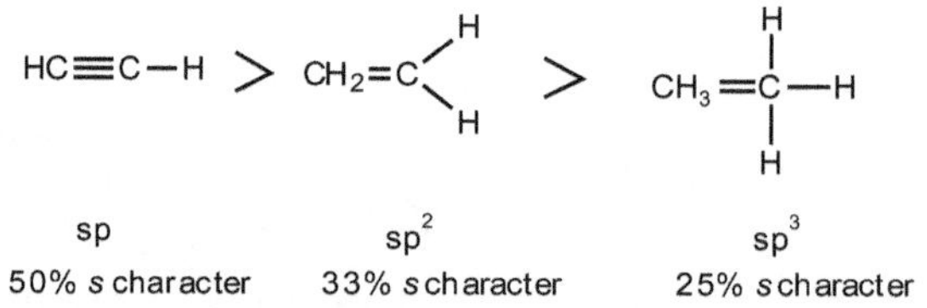

$$HC\equiv C-H \quad > \quad CH_2=CH_2 \quad > \quad CH_3-CH_3$$

$$sp \qquad\qquad sp^2 \qquad\qquad sp^3$$
$$50\% \text{ s character} \quad 33\% \text{ s character} \quad 25\% \text{ s character}$$

Basicity:

Basicity is based on electron pair availability. The more available the electrons, the more readily they can be donated to form a new bond to the proton and therefore the stronger base.

Key factors that affect electron pair availability in a **base, B** are:

1. Electronegativity: When comparing atoms within the same row of the periodic table, the more electronegative the atom donating the electrons is, the less willing it is to share those electrons with a proton, so the weaker the base.

$$CH_3^- > NH_2^- > HO^- > F^-$$

2. Size: When comparing atoms within the same group of the periodic table, the larger the atom the weaker the H-X bond and the lower the electron density making it a weaker base.

$$F^- > Cl^- > Br^- > I^-$$

3. Resonance: Anytime multiple Lewis structures can represent one compound it is said to have resonance. Resonance can either increase or decrease the electron density at the atom that will actually share electrons with the proton. Additionally, resonance delocalizes the electron density and thus leads to greater stabilization. Therefore, reactions which increase resonance are favored because of the gain in stabilization. Additionally, reactions which lead to a decrease in resonance are inhibited due to this loss. In most cases, the presence of resonance leads to less basicity although this does not always hold true.

$$RO^- > RCOO^-$$

General acidity trend of some **common organic bases**

Note that organic chemists tend to think about bases by looking at the pKas of their conjugate acids, i.e., think about B⁻ by looking at the acidity of BH. The implications are that the higher the pKa of the related conjugate acid, BH, the stronger the base B⁻.

Applications of inductive effect (Inductive effect and basicity):

The effect on electron density in one portion of a molecule due to electron withdrawing or electron donating groups elsewhere in the molecule.

Electron withdrawing groups:

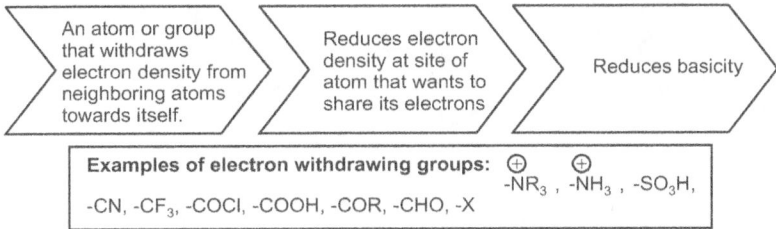

Electron donating groups:

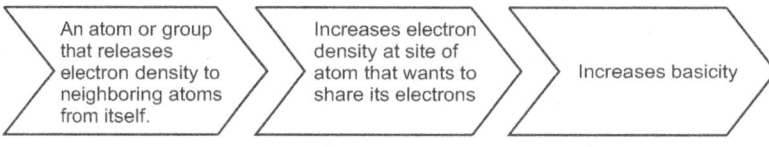

Examples of Electron donating groups: $-NR_2$, $-OH$, $-NH_2$, $-OR$, R

Inductive effect depends on the following:

1. **Electronegativity of the group:** Fluorine withdraws more electron density from neighboring atoms towards itself than hydrogen would = lower basicity (smaller pKa).

2. **Number of electron withdrawing or electron donating groups:** The greater the number of electron withdrawing groups/the smaller the number of electron donating groups = lower basicity (smaller pKa).

3. **Distance from the group:** The smaller the distance from the electron withdrawing group/the greater the distance from the electron donating group = lower basicity (smaller pKa).

Examples of Basicity:

(i) $-:\!\ddot{N}H_2$, $:\!NH_3$, $\overset{+}{N}H_4$

(ii) $CH_3CH_2NH_2$, CH_3CH_2OH, CH_3CH_2SH

(iii)

    $C_6H_4(NH_2)(OCH_3)$ $C_6H_4(NH_2)(Me)$ $C_6H_4(NH_2)(Cl)$ $C_6H_4(NH_2)(NO_2)$

(iv)

    piperidine   pyridine   aniline   pyrrole

1. $-:\!\ddot{N}H_2 > :\!NH_3 > \overset{+}{N}H_4$
   (I)   (II)   (III)

Revise the Lewis base definition and try to look at the lone pair availability (more available = stronger base). Concentrate on nitrogen (availability of electron pairs in each case).

The amide ion (I) is the strongest base since it has two pairs of non-bonding electrons (more electron-electron repulsion) compared to ammonia (II) which only has one. Ammonium (III) is not basic since it has no lone pair to donate as a base.

2. $CH_3CH_2\ddot{N}H_2 > CH_3CH_2\ddot{O}H > CH_3CH_2\ddot{S}H$

Amines are stronger bases than alcohols. Again we can use lone pair availability. 'N' is less electronegative than 'O' so it is a better electron donor. What about the alcohol and the thiol ? Acidity increases down a group, so the thiol is a worse base than the alcohol, larger atoms tend to form weaker bonds with the small proton.

3.

Since these are all substituted anilines, we need to look at the role of the substituent (after all, it is the only thing changing across the series). Substituents that are electron donors will make the N lone pair more available (electron donating ability -OCH_3 > -CH_3), whereas electron withdrawing groups will make the N lone pair less available (electron withdrawing ability -NO_2 > Cl)

4.

We can still use lone pair availability. Piperidine is the most basic (conjugate acid pKa = 11.2). The lone pair is in a sp^3 hybrid orbital and there is no resonance (no p system). In pyridine (II) (conjugate acid pKa = 5.2) the N lone pair is in a sp^2 hybrid orbital, but is not part of the σπ electron aromatic system nor is it involved in any resonance (perpendicular).

The sp² hybrid is smaller than the sp³ hybrid, so there is a stronger attraction to the nucleus, so less basic. In aniline (**III**) (conjugate acid pKa = 5.2), the N lone pair can interact with the p system of the aromatic ring which makes them less available for donation. In pyrrole (**IV**) is a very weak base (conjugate acid pKa = – 4). The N lone pair is involved in the σπ electron aromatic system. Protonation will destroy the aromaticity of the σπ electron aromatic system and this makes it an unfavourable process.

Applications of resonance (Resonance and basicity):

Resonance usually reduces basicity: Resonance delocalizes electron density from the atom that wants to share its electrons, which leads to the structure being a weaker base/stronger conjugate acid.

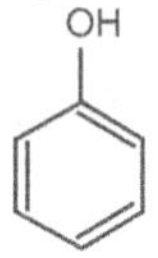

Due to resonance, phenol is weaker base (pKa = 10) than ethanol (pKa = 17)

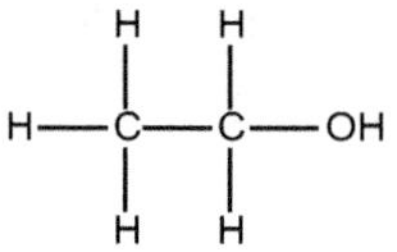

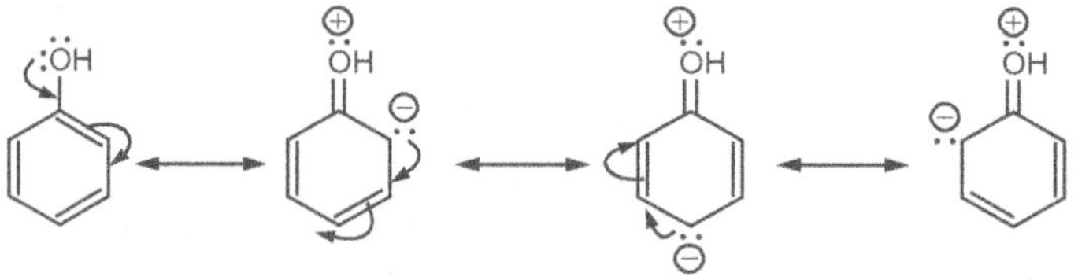

pKa = 10
Phenol

pKa = 17
Ethanol

Resonating (Canonical) forms of Phenol

Hyperconugation:

Hyperconjugation is the interaction of the electrons in a sigma bond (usually C–H or C–C) with an adjacent empty (or partially filled) non-bonding p-orbital, antibonding π orbital, or filled π orbital, to give an extended molecular orbital that increases the stability of the system. Only electrons in bonds that are β to the positively charged carbon can stabilize a carbocation by hyperconjugation.

Effect on chemical properties:

Hyperconjugation affects several properties.

Bond length: Hyperconjugation is suggested as a key factor in shortening of sigma bonds (σ bonds). For example, the single C–C bonds in 1,3-butadiene and methylacetylene are approximately 1.46 angstrom in length, much less than the value of around 1.54 Å found in saturated hydrocarbons. For butadiene, this can be explained as normal conjugation of the two alkenyl parts. But for methylacetylene, hyperconjugation between the alkyl and alkynyl parts.

Dipole moments: The large increase in dipole moment of 1,1,1-trichloroethane as compared with chloroform can be attributed to hyperconjugated structures.

The heat of formation of molecules with hyperconjugation are greater than sum of their bond energies and the heats of hydrogenation per double bond are less than the heat of hydrogenation of ethylene.

Stability of carbocations:

$$(CH_3)_3C^+ > (CH_3)_2CH^+ > (CH_3)CH_2^+ > CH_3^+$$

The C–C σ bond adjacent to the cation is free to rotate, and, as it does so, the three C–H σ bonds of the methyl group in turn undergoes the stabilization interaction. The more adjacent C-H bonds are present there, the larger hyperconjugation stabilization is.

Steric effects arise from the fact that each atom within a molecule occupies a certain amount of space. If atoms are brought too close together, there is an associated cost in energy due to overlapping electron clouds (Pauli or Born repulsion) and this may affect the molecule's preferred shape (conformation) and reactivity.

Steric inhibition of resonance and its effects on the acidity or basicity of compounds:

Steric inhibition may be used to explain the fact that 3,5-dimethyl-4-nitroaniline is a stronger base than the corresponding 2,6-dimethyl-4-nitroaniline. In 3,5-dimethyl-4-nitroaniline, the nitro group can not enter into resonance with the amino group, whereas, it enters in resonance with amino group in case of 2,6-dimethyl-4-nitroaniline.

3,5-Dimethyl-4-nitro aniline   2,6-Dimethyl-4-nitro aniline

Steric effect is operating between the amino group and the two *o*-methyl groups in 2,6-dimethyl-4-nitroaniline but, not in 3,5-dimethyl isomer, since only hydrogens (which are very small) are involved, the steric effect will be very much smaller.

N-alkylated anilines are stronger bases than aniline:

Alkyl groups have +I (inductive effect) that increases the resonance of lone pair (of nitrogen) with the aromatic ring (benzene). Also, since an N-ehtyl substituent increases the basic strength of aniline more than the N-methyl subsituent, this can be explained on the basis of steric effects of resonance. As the ethyl group is larger than the methyl group, the steric effect is greater for N-ethyl than N-methyl substituted aniline. Hence, there is greater steric inhibition in N-ethyl substituted aniline so the lone pair on nitrogen atom is more easily available for protonation and the basicity of N-ethylaniline is greater than N-methyl aniline.

```
     OH                    NH₂                       OH
     |                     |                         |
   [ring]               HeC—[ring]—CH₃           [ring with H₃C and CH₃ ortho]
     |                     |                         |
    NO₂                   NO₂                       NO₂
     A                     B                         C
                    Ka 700 × 10⁻¹⁰          Ka 60 × 10⁻¹⁰  Steric inhibition to resonance
```

From the Ka values of the above mentioned phenols, it is clear that (C) has the lowest acidity. The reduced acidity is due to steric effects. In order of resonance interaction to operate between substituent and the ring, the substitutent must lie in the plane of the ring. Such a geometry is not available for (C) because of presence of two *ortho* methyl groups. As a result the nitro group is pushed out of plane of the ring and effective delocalization of the resultant phenoxide ion does not take plane.

QUESTION BANK

1. Define acids and bases according to (1) Arrenius concept (2) Bronsted-Lowry theory (3) Lewis concept, with examples.
2. Explain the factors affecting stability of a conjugate base.
3. Which of the following acids is strongest, HF, HCl, HBr or HI?
4. What is the importance of inductive effect in assessing the acidity or basicity of compound?
5. Trichloroacetic acid is more stronger than chloroacetic acid, which in turn is more stronger than acetic acid. Why?
6. Explain the applications of resonance in explaining acidity or basicity of an organic compound with suitable examples?
7. HI is stronger acid than benzene? Explain?
8. What do you mean by "s-character". How is it important in explaining acidity?
9. Explain concept of basicity and factors affecting electron pair availability in a base?
10. Explain applications of inductive effect in defining the basicity of a base?
11. Explain the effect of resonance on basicity of organic compounds with suitable examples.
12. Define Hyperconjugation? Explain the effect of hyperconjugation on chemical properties?

13. Explain the steric inhibition of resonance and its effects on physical properties, acidity and reactivity of organic compounds.
14. Explain the steric inhibition of resonance and its effects on basicity and reactivity of organic compounds.
15. Explain the effect of hydrogen bonding on acidity and basicity of organic compounds.
16. Explain the effect of resonance and inductive effect on acidity and basicity of compounds.
17. N,N-Dimethyl aniline is a stronger base than aniline.
18. *p*-Nitrophenol is a stronger acid than phenol.
19. Arrange following acids in increasing order of acidity with justification.

    (a) H$_3$C—COOH (b) H$_2$C(Cl)—COOH (c) HC(Cl)(Cl)—COOH (d) H$_2$C(F)—COOH

20. Phenol is acidic. Explain.
21. Aromatic amines are more basic then aliphatic amines.
22. Arrange in order of increased acidity the phenols, alcohols, carboxylic acids. Explain the reasons for this order.
23. Which is more acidic; acetic acid or benzoic acid? Explain.
24. Which is more basic; anline or cyclohexylamine? Explain.
25. Phthalamide is neutral but Pthalimide is acidic. Why?
26. Guandine is a very strong base. Explain.
27. Which is more basic of the two; N, N-dimethylaniline or N, N, 2, 6-tetra-methyl-anline?

Chapter 7 ...

ALKANES

CONTENTS
Properties and Reactions of Alkanes, Mechanism and Kinetics of Halogenation.

ALKANES-PROPERTIES AND REACTIONS

Alkanes:

The simplest organic compounds are hydrocarbons. Hydrocarbons contain only two elements, hydrogen and carbon. A saturated hydrocarbon or alkane is a hydrocarbon in which all of the carbon-carbon bonds are single bonds. Each carbon atom forms four bonds and each hydrogen forms a single bond to a carbon. The bonding around each carbon atom is tetrahedral, so all bond angles are 109.5°. As a result, the carbon atoms in higher alkanes are arranged in zig-zag rather than linear patterns.

General formula:

Straight chain alkanes:

The general formula for an alkane is C_nH_{2n+2} where, n is the number of carbon atoms in the molecule. There are two ways of writing a condensed structural formula. For example, butane may be written as $CH_3CH_2CH_2CH_3$ or $CH_3(CH_2)_2CH_3$.

Branched alkanes:

Branched substituents are numbered starting from the carbon of the substituent attached to the parent chain. From this carbon, count the number of carbons in the longest chain of the substituent. The substituent is named as an alkyl group based on the number of carbons in this chain.

Numbering of the substituent chain starts from the carbon attached to the parent chain. The entire name of the branched substituent is placed in parentheses, preceded by a number indicating which parent-chain carbon it joins.

Substituents are listed in alphabetical order. To alphabetize, ignore numerical (di-, tri-, tetra-) prefixes (e.g., ethyl would come before dimethyl), but don't ignore positional prefixes such as *iso* and *tert* (e.g., triethyl comes before tertbutyl).

Cyclic Alkanes:

The parent name is determined by the number of carbons in the largest ring (e.g., cycloalkane such as cyclohexane).

In the case, where the ring is attached to a chain containing additional carbons, the ring is considered to be a substituent on the chain. A substituted ring that is a substituent on something else is named using the rules for branched alkanes.

When two rings are attached to each other, the larger ring is the parent and the smaller is a cycloalkyl or aryl substituent.

The carbons of the ring are numbered such that the substituents are given the lowest possible numbers.

Straight Chain Alkanes:

No. of Carbon (n)	Name	Molecular Formula C_nH_{2n+2}	Structural formula
1.	Methane	CH_4	CH_4
2.	Ethane	C_2H_6	$CH_3\text{-}CH_3$
3.	Propane	C_3H_8	$CH_3\text{-}CH_2\text{-}CH_3$
4.	Butane	C_4H_{10}	$CH_3\text{-}CH_2\text{-}CH_2\text{-}CH_3$
5.	Pentane	C_5H_{12}	$CH_3\text{-}CH_2\text{-}CH_2\text{-}CH_2\text{-}CH_3$
6.	Hexane	C_6H_{14}	$CH_3\text{-}CH_2\text{-}CH_2\text{-}CH_2\text{-}CH_2\text{-}CH_3$
7.	Heptane	C_7H_{16}	$CH_3\text{-}CH_2\text{-}CH_2\text{-}CH_2\text{-}CH_2\text{-}CH_2\text{-}CH_3$
8.	Octane	C_8H_{18}	$CH_3\text{-}CH_2\text{-}CH_2\text{-}CH_2\text{-}CH_2\text{-}CH_2\text{-}CH_2\text{-}CH_3$
9.	Nonane	C_9H_{20}	$CH_3\text{-}CH_2\text{-}CH_2\text{-}CH_2\text{-}CH_2\text{-}CH_2\text{-}CH_2\text{-}CH_2\text{-}CH_3$
10.	Decane	$C_{10}H_{22}$	$CH_3\text{-}CH_2\text{-}CH_2\text{-}CH_2\text{-}CH_2\text{-}CH_2\text{-}CH_2\text{-}CH_2\text{-}CH_2\text{-}CH_3$

Method Preparation of Alkane:

1. **Wurtz synthesis:**

When alkyl halides are heated with sodium metal in dry ether solution, higher alkanes are produced. This is known as Wurtz synthesis of alkanes.

$$2\,R-X + 2\,Na \xrightarrow{\text{ether}} R-R + 2\,NaX$$
Symmetrical alkane

$$2\,CH_3-Cl + 2\,Na \xrightarrow{\text{ether}} CH_3-CH_3 + 2\,NaCl$$
Methyl chloride   Ethane

Wurtz reaction has limitations towards the synthesis of unsymmetrical alkanes.

2. **Kolbe's synthesis:**

   The electrolysis of concentrated solution of sodium salt of carboxylic acid yields alkane at anode.

   $2RCOO^-Na^+ + 2H_2O \longrightarrow R-R + 2CO_2 + 2NaOH + H_2\uparrow$

   Sodium carboxylate   Alkane at anode   At cathode

   $2CH_3-COO^-Na^+ + 2H_2O \longrightarrow CH_3-CH_3 + 2CO_2 + 2NaOH + H_2\uparrow$

   Sodium acetate   Ethane

3. **Corey-House Alkane synthesis:**

   This method of synthesis is suitable for unsymmetrical alkane.

   Ethyl iodide treated with lithium dimethyl cuprate [Li(CH$_3$)$_2$Cu], Propane is formed.

   $CH_3CH_2I + Li(CH_3)_2Cu \longrightarrow CH_3-CH_2-CH_3 + CH_3Cu + LiI$

   Ethyl iodide   Propane

4. **Reduction of Alkyl halide:**

   Alkyl halides when reduced under nascent hydrogen gives alkanes.

   $R-X + 2[H] \longrightarrow R-H + HX$

   Alkyl   Nascent   Alkane
   halide   hydrogen

   $CH_3CH_2Br + 2[H] \longrightarrow CH_3-CH_3 + HBr$

   Ethyl bromide   Ethane

5. **Hydrolysis of Grignard Reagents:**

   The treatment of alkyl magnesium halides (Grignard reagent) with water yields alkane.

   $RMgX + H_2O \longrightarrow RH + MgX(OH)$

   $CH_3MgI + H_2O \longrightarrow CH_4 + MgI(OH)$

   Methyl   Methane
   Magnesium
   iodide

Properties of alkanes:

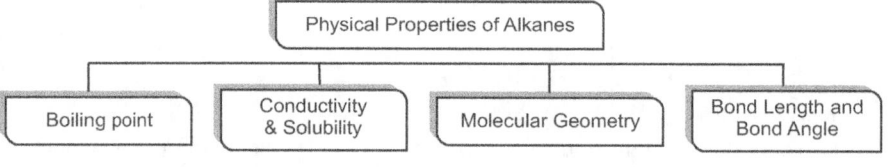

1. Boiling Point:

The boiling points shown are all for the "straight chain" isomers where there are more than one. Notice that the first four alkanes are gases at room temperature. Solids don't start to appear until about $C_{17}H_{36}$. One cannot be more precise than that, because each isomer has a different melting and boiling point. By the time one gets 17 carbons into an alkane, there are unbelievable numbers of isomers.

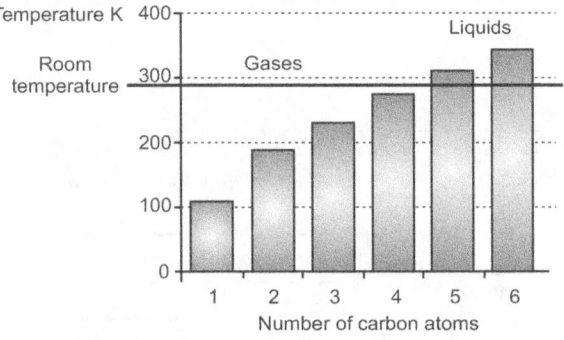

Fig. 7.1: Boiling points of the alkanes

Cycloalkanes have boiling points which are about 10–20°C higher than the corresponding straight chain alkanes.

Explanation:

There is not much electronegativity difference between carbon and hydrogen, so there is hardly any bond polarity. The molecules themselves also have very little polarity. A totally symmetrical molecule like methane is completely non-polar. This means that the only attractions between one molecule and its neighbours will be Van der Waal's dispersion forces. These will be very small for a molecule like methane, but will increase as the molecules get bigger. That is why the boiling points of the alkanes increase with molecular size.

Where you have isomers, the more branched the chain, the lower the boiling point tends to be. Van der Waal's dispersion forces are smaller for shorter molecules, and only operate over very short distances between one molecule and its neighbours. It is more difficult for short fat molecules (with lots of branching) to lie as close together as the longer thin ones.

For example, the boiling points of the three isomers of C_5H_{12} are:

Name of Alkane	Structure	Boiling point (K)
2-Methylbutane	CH$_3$ | CH$_3$ – CH – CH$_2$ – CH$_3$	309.2 K
2,2-Dimethylpropane	CH$_3$ | H$_3$C – C – CH$_3$ | CH$_3$	282.6 K

The slightly higher boiling points for the cycloalkanes are presumably because the molecules can get closer together as the ring structure makes them tidier and less "wriggly".

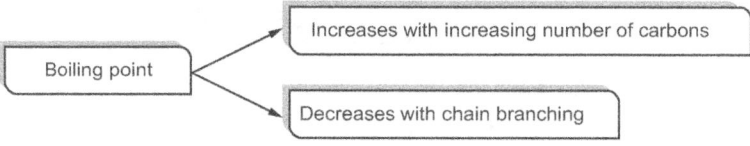

2. Melting Point:

The melting points of the alkanes follow a similar trend to boiling points for the same reason as outlined above. That is, (all other things being equal) the larger the molecule the higher the melting point. There is one significant difference between boiling points and melting points, solids have more rigid and fixed structure than liquids. This rigid structure requires energy to break down. Thus, the better put together solid structures will require more energy to break apart. The odd-numbered alkanes have a lower trend in melting points than even numbered alkanes. This is because even numbered alkanes pack well in the solid phase, forming a well-organized structure, which requires more energy to break apart. The odd-number alkanes pack less well and so the "looser" organized solid packing structure requires less energy to break apart.

The melting points of branched-chain alkanes can be either higher or lower than those of the corresponding straight-chain alkanes, again depending on the ability of the alkane in question to pack well in the solid phase. This is particularly true for isoalkanes (2-methyl isomers), which often have melting points higher than those of the linear analogues.

3. Conductivity and Solubility:

Alkanes do not conduct electricity, nor are they substantially polarized by an electric field. For this reason they do not form hydrogen bonds and are insoluble in polar solvents such as water. Since the hydrogen bonds between individual water molecules are aligned away from an alkane molecule, the coexistence of an alkane and water leads to an increase in molecular order (a reduction in entropy). As there is no significant bonding between water molecules and alkane molecules, the second law of thermodynamics suggests that this reduction in entropy should be minimized by minimizing the contact between alkane and water. Alkanes are said to be hydrophobic in that they repel water.

Their solubility in non-polar solvents is relatively good, a property that is called lipophilicity. Different alkanes are, for example, miscible in all proportions among themselves.

The density of the alkanes usually increases with increasing number of carbon atoms, but remains less than that of water. Hence, alkanes form the upper layer in an alkane-water mixture.

Molecular Geometry:

The molecular structure of the alkanes directly affects their physical and chemical characteristics. It is derived from the electron configuration of carbon, which has four valence electrons. The carbon atoms in alkanes are always sp^3 hybridized, that is to say that the valence electrons are said to be in four equivalent orbitals derived from the combination of the 2s orbital and the three 2p orbitals. These orbitals, which have identical energies, are arranged spatially in the form of a tetrahedron.

Bond lengths and Bond angles:

An alkane molecule has only C – H and C – C single bonds. The former result from the overlap of a sp^3-orbital of carbon with the 1s-orbital of a hydrogen; the latter by the overlap of two sp^3-orbitals on different carbon atoms. The bond lengths amount to 1.09 A° for a C – H bond and 1.54 A° for a C – C bond.

The spatial arrangement of the bonds is similar to that of the four sp^3-orbitals they are tetrahedrally arranged, with an angle of 109.47° between them. Structural formulae that represent the bonds as being at right angles to one another, while both common and useful, do not correspond with the reality.

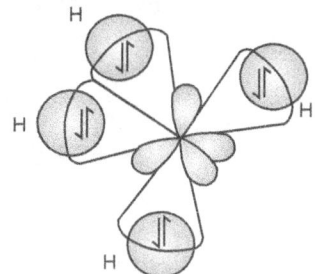

Fig. 7.2: sp^3 - hybridization in methane

Chemical properties and reactions of alkanes:
Chemical reactivity:

Alkanes contain strong carbon-carbon single bonds and strong carbon-hydrogen bonds. The carbon-hydrogen bonds are only very slightly polar and so there aren't any bits of the molecules which carry any significant amount of positive or negative charge which other things might be attracted to.

For example, many organic reactions start because an ion or a polar molecule is attracted to a part of an organic molecule which carries some positive or negative charge. This doesn't happen with alkanes, because alkane molecules don't have this separation of charge.

Cycloalkanes:

Cycloalkanes are very similar to the alkanes in reactivity, except for the very small ones - especially cyclopropane. Cyclopropane is much more reactive.

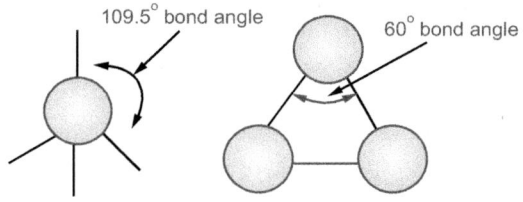

Fig. 7.3

The reason is due to the bond angles in the ring. Normally, when carbon forms four single bonds, the bond angles are about 109.5°. In cyclopropane, they are 60°. With the electron pairs this close together, there is a lot of repulsion between the bonding pairs joining the carbon atoms. That makes the bonds easier to break.

The net effect is that alkanes have a fairly restricted set of reactions.

Alkanes generally show low reactivity, because their C-C bonds are stable and cannot be easily broken. As they are inert against ionic or other polar substances, they are also called "paraffins" (Latin "para + affinis" = "lacking affinity").

Gaseous alkanes are explosive when mixed with air, the liquid alkanes are highly flammable. The most common reactions occuring with alkanes are reactions involving free radicals (combustion, substitution cracking and reformation).

REACTIONS OF ALKANES

1. **Reaction with halogens (Cl / I / Br / F):**

    The halogenation reactions of alkanes are quite different, depending on the halogen involved. While flourine reacts explosively with alkanes and the reaction can hardly be controlled, chlorine and bromine react satisfactorily (bromine much slower than chlorine), and iodine is unreactive. The calculated heats of reaction for the halogenation of hydrocarbons are (kcal/mol):

Halogen	Heat of Reaction (kcal/mol)
Fluorine (F)	– 116
Chlorine (Cl)	– 27
Bromine (Br)	– 10
Iodine (I)	+ 13

Free halogen radicals are the reactive species and usually lead to a mixture of products. For chlorine and bromine the free radicals have to be created by light and UV radiation, respectively. The fluorination is difficult to control; the only successful direct fluorination of liquid or solid alkanes is performed at low temperatures (on dry ice, –78°C) with highly diluted fluorine (in helium).

The chlorination of alkanes is a three step process which takes place *via* formation of free radical.

Step 1: Initiation: Splitting a chlorine molecule into two chlorine atoms with unpaired electrons (free radical). This step is initiated by ultraviolet radiation (thus chlorination of alkanes does not occur in the dark):

$$Cl:Cl \xrightarrow{uv\ light} Cl\cdot + Cl\cdot$$

Step 2: Propagation: A hydrogen atom is pulled off from methane resulting in a methyl radical. Then the methyl radical pulls a chlorine atom from the Cl_2 molecule, leaving chlorine radical.

$$CH_4 + Cl\cdot \rightarrow CH_3\cdot + HCl$$
$$CH_3\cdot + Cl_2 \rightarrow CH_3Cl + Cl\cdot$$

This results in the chlorinated product. This created radical will then go on to take part in another propagation reaction causing a chain reaction.

Step 3: Termination: The chain reaction stops if two free radicals recombine:

$$Cl\cdot + Cl\cdot \rightarrow Cl_2$$
$$CH_3\cdot + Cl\cdot \rightarrow CH_3Cl$$
$$CH_3\cdot + CH_3\cdot \rightarrow CH_3 - CH_3$$

2. **Cracking (Pyrrolysis);**

Cracking breaks larger molecules into smaller ones. This can be done with a thermal or catalytic method. The thermal cracking process follows a homolytic mechanism with formation of free-radicals. The catalytic cracking process involves the presence of acid catalysts (usually solid acids such as silica-alumina and zeolites), which promote a heterolytic (asymmetric) breakage of bonds yielding pairs of ions of opposite charges, usually a carbocation and the very unstable hydride anion. Carbon-localized free-radicals and cations are both highly unstable and undergo processes of chain rearrangement, C-C scission in position beta (i.e., cracking) and intra- and intermolecular hydrogen transfer or hydride transfer. In both types of processes, the corresponding reactive intermediates (radicals, ions) are permanently regenerated, and thus they proceed by a self-propagating chain mechanism. The chain of reactions is eventually terminated by radical or ion recombination.

$$C_{15}H_{32} \xrightarrow{500\text{-}800\,°C} 2C_2H_4 + C_3H_6 + C_8H_{18}$$
$$\phantom{C_{15}H_{32} \xrightarrow{500\text{-}800\,°C} 2\,} \text{Ethene} \quad \text{Propene} \quad \text{Octane}$$

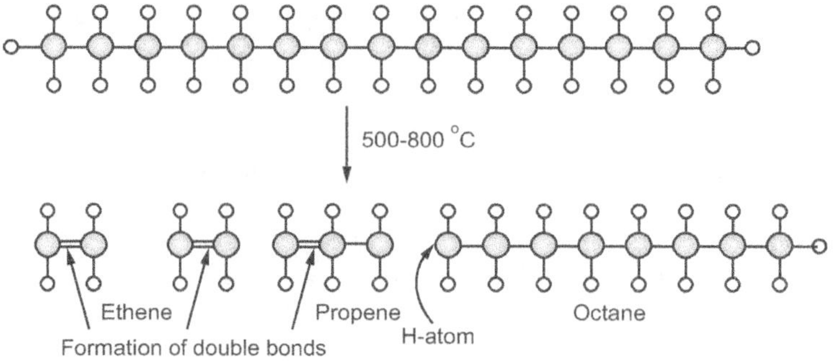

Fig. 7.4: Cracking of alkanes

3. **Oxidation (Combustion):**

   Higher alkanes are used as enegy source due to its important combustion property.

   When alkanes are burn in presence of excess oxygen form carbon dioxide and water.

   $$CH_4 + 2O_2 \longrightarrow CO_2 + 2H_2O + 212.8 \text{ kcal/mol}$$

   When burnt in insufficient supply of oxygen, alkanes form monoxide of carbon which is a hazardous pollutant.

   $$CH_4 + O_2 \xrightarrow{\text{flame}} CO + 2H_2O$$

   $$2CH_4 + 3O_2 \xrightarrow{\text{flame}} 2\,CO + 4H_2O$$

4. **Isomerization:**

   Alkanes are converted to their branched chain. Isomers in presence of aluminium chloride and HCl.

   $$CH_3-CH_2-CH_2-CH_3 \xrightarrow[\text{HCl}]{\text{AlCl}_3} CH_3-\underset{\underset{CH_3}{|}}{CH}-CH_3$$
   $$\text{n-butane} \qquad\qquad\qquad \text{Isobutane}$$

5. Aromatization:

Conversion of aliphatic compound (6 or more than 6 carbon atoms) to aromatic series is called as **aromatization reaction**.

Example:

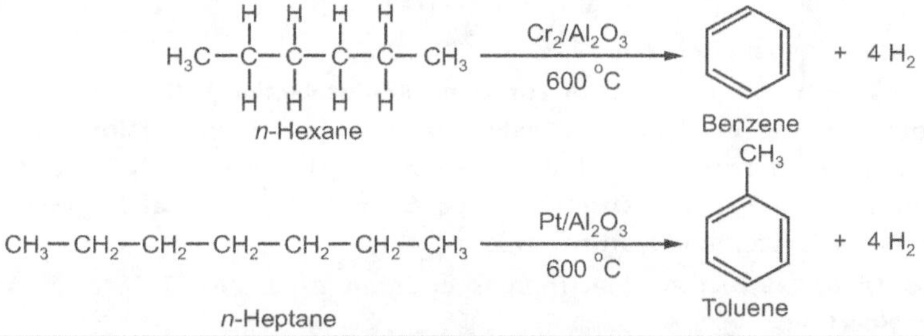

$$CH_3-CH_2-CH_2-CH_2-CH_3 \xrightarrow[600\,°C]{Cr_2/Al_2O_3} \text{Benzene} + 4H_2$$

n-Hexane

$$CH_3-CH_2-CH_2-CH_2-CH_2-CH_2-CH_3 \xrightarrow[600\,°C]{Pt/Al_2O_3} \text{Toluene} + 4H_2$$

n-Heptane

QUESTION BANK

1. What are alkanes? What are their general formulae? Classify with examples.
2. Write a note on physical and chemical properties of alkanes.
3. What are chemical properties of alkanes? Write a note on combustion of alkanes? Write down the mechanism of halogenation of alkanes with kinetics of halogenation? What do you mean by cracking of alkanes? Explain in details?
4. Write down the IUPAC names for the following:

    (a) 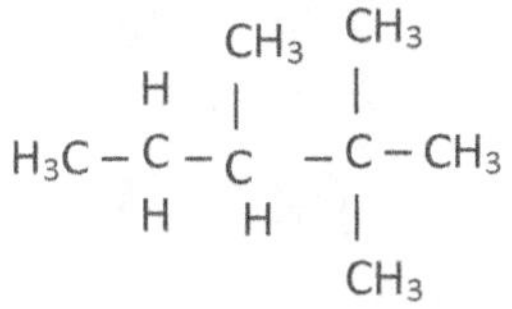 $H_3C-\underset{H}{\overset{H}{C}}-\underset{H}{\overset{CH_3}{C}}-\underset{CH_3}{\overset{CH_3}{C}}-C-CH_3$

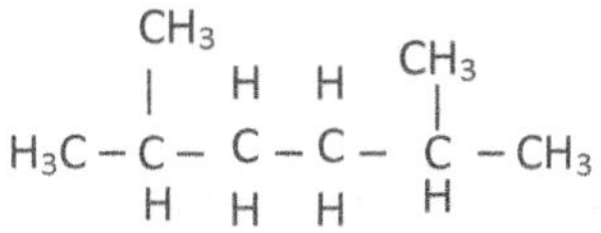

    (b) $H_3C-\underset{H}{\overset{CH_3}{C}}-\underset{H}{\overset{H}{C}}-\underset{H}{\overset{H}{C}}-\underset{H}{\overset{CH_3}{C}}-CH_3$

    (c) $H_3C-\underset{H}{\overset{H}{C}}-\underset{CH_3}{\overset{CH_3}{C}}-C-CH_3$

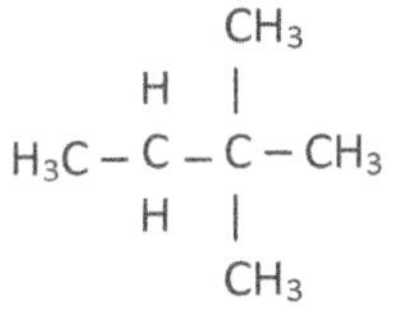

    (d) 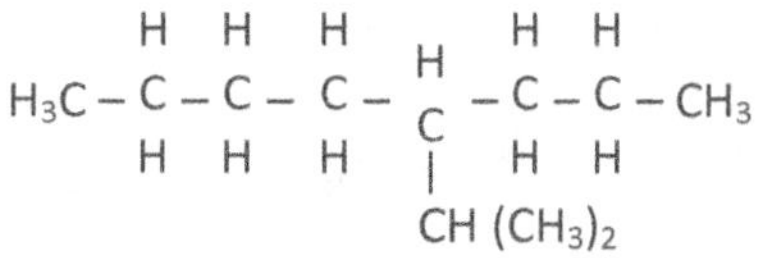 $H_3C-\underset{H}{\overset{H}{C}}-\underset{H}{\overset{H}{C}}-\underset{H}{\overset{H}{C}}-\underset{CH(CH_3)_2}{\overset{H}{C}}-\underset{H}{\overset{H}{C}}-\underset{H}{\overset{H}{C}}-CH_3$

5. Draw structures from IUPAC names of the following:
    (a) 2,2,4-Trimethylhexane
    (b) 2,5-Dimethylheptane
    (c) 4-Isopropyloctane
    (d) 4-Ethyl-2,2,3-trimethylhexane
    (e) 3,5 Dichloro hexane
6. What happens when ethane is heated at 500°C in the absence of air or oxygen.
7. Arrange the following isomeric alkanes in order of increasing boiling points:
    (1) Pentane (2) 2,2-Dimethylpropane (3) 2-Methylbutane
8. Discuss the mechanism of chlorination of methane.
9. Discuss the mechanism of cracking of alkanes.

Chapter 8 ...

ALKENES AND ALKYNES

CONTENTS

Alkenes: Preparation and Reactions.

Addition Reactions of Alkenes: Mechanism, Regioselectivity (Markonikov and Anti-Markonikov) Addition of Hydrogen, Halogen, Hydrogen Halide, Halohydrin Formation, Oxymercuration–Demercuration, Hydroboration – Oxidation, Hydroxylation, Allylic substitution (using NBS) and Ozonolysis. E_1, E_2 and E_{1cB} Elimination: Mechanism and Stereochemistry, Saytzeff and Hoffman rules.

Conjugated Dienes: Structure, Electrophilic addition of dienes: 1, 2 & 1, 4 additions, Diels–Alder Reaction.

Alkynes: General methods of preparation and reactions.

INTRODUCTION

Alkenes are hydrocarbons, commonly known as *Olefins*. They contain carbon-carbon double bond (C=C) with general formula C_nH_{2n}. Alkenes contain two hydrogen atom less than alkanes.

Examples:

Name	Structure	Name	Structure
Ethylene	$H_2C=CH_2$	2-Butylene	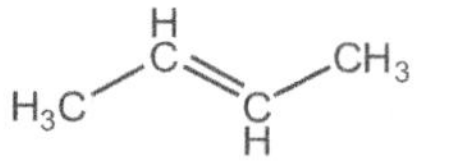 $H_3C-CH=CH-CH_3$
Propylene	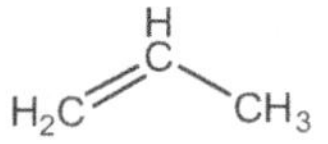 $H_2C=CH-CH_3$	1-Pentene	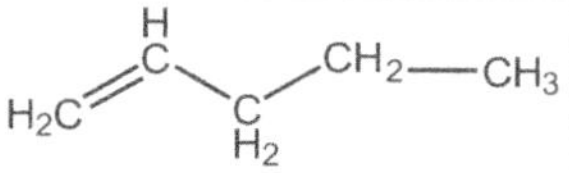 $H_2C=CH-CH_2-CH_2-CH_3$
1-Butylene	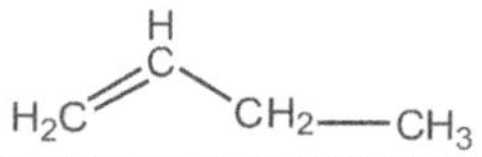 $H_2C=CH-CH_2-CH_3$	1-Hexene	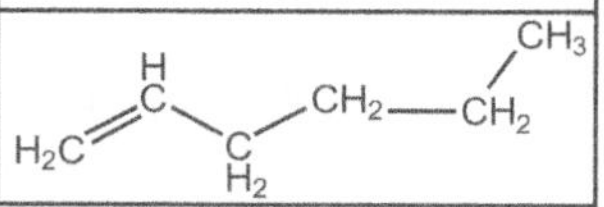 $H_2C=CH-CH_2-CH_2-CH_2-CH_3$

Methods of Preparation of Alkenes:

1. **Dehydration of alcohols:**

   Alkenes can be formed by heating an alcohol in presence of sulphuric acid. The order of dehydration of alcohols: $3° > 2° > 1°$.

Examples:

$$R\text{—}CH_2CH_2OH \xrightarrow{H_2SO_4, \Delta} R\text{—}HC\text{=}CH_2 + H_2O$$
Alcohol → Alkene
$R = CH_3, C_2H_5$ etc.

$$CH_3CH_2OH \xrightarrow{H_2SO_4, 170°C} H_2C\text{=}CH_2 + H_2O$$
Ethanol → Ethylene

$$CH_3CH_2CH_2OH \xrightarrow{H_2SO_4, 170°C} CH_3CH\text{=}CH_2 + H_2O$$
1-Propanol → Propylene

2. **Dehydrohalogenation of alkyl halides:**

   Alkene is formed by heating alkyl halide with alcoholic solution of sodium or potassium hydroxide.

   Example:

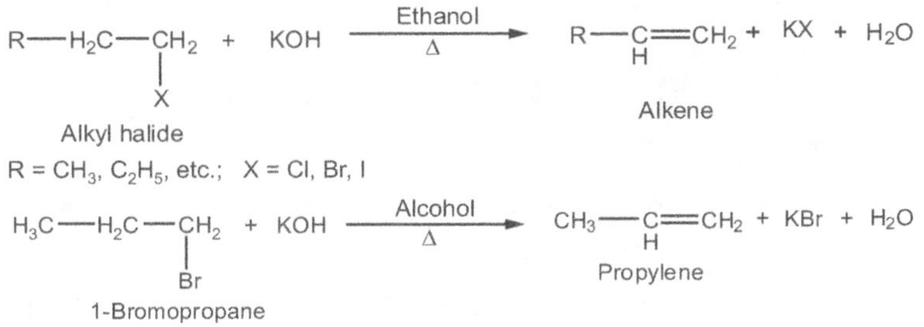

   $$R\text{—}H_2C\text{—}CH_2X + KOH \xrightarrow{Ethanol, \Delta} R\text{—}CH\text{=}CH_2 + KX + H_2O$$
   Alkyl halide → Alkene
   $R = CH_3, C_2H_5$, etc.; $X = Cl, Br, I$

   $$H_3C\text{—}H_2C\text{—}CH_2Br + KOH \xrightarrow{Alcohol, \Delta} CH_3\text{—}CH\text{=}CH_2 + KBr + H_2O$$
   1-Bromopropane → Propylene

3. **Dehydrohalogenation of vicinal dihalides:**

   Vicinal dihalides is a compound having two halogen atoms on adjacent carbon atoms. When these dihalides are heated in presence of zinc and alcohol they form alkene.

   Example:

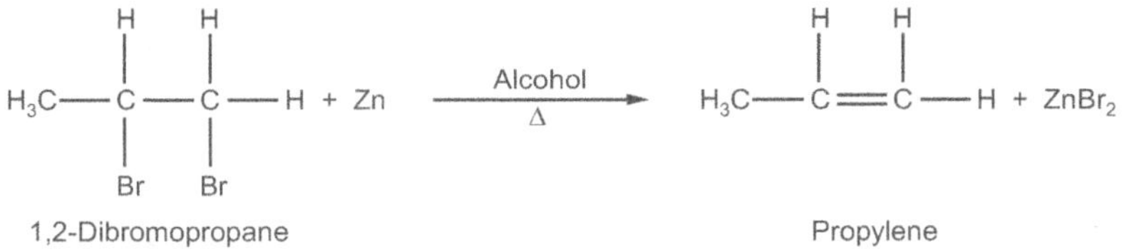

   $$H_3C\text{—}CHBr\text{—}CHBr\text{—}H + Zn \xrightarrow{Alcohol, \Delta} H_3C\text{—}CH\text{=}CH\text{—}H + ZnBr_2$$
   1,2-Dibromopropane → Propylene

4. Controlled hydrogenation of alkynes:

Alkynes react with hydrogen in the presence of **Lindlar's catalyst** to gives alkenes. Lindlar's catalyst is Pd with $CaCO_3$.

Example:

$$R-C\equiv C-H + H_2 \xrightarrow{Pd-CaCO_3} R-CH=CH_2$$
Alkyne → Alkene

$$H-C\equiv C-H + H_2 \xrightarrow{Pd-CaCO_3} H-CH=CH_2$$
Acetylene → Ethylene

5. Cracking of Alkanes:

Alkanes when heated at 500-800°C in the absence of air decompose to yield lower molecular weight alkenes and hydrogen.

Example:

$$CH_3-CH_3 \xrightarrow{600\,°C} H_2C=CH_2 + \ddot{C}H_4 + H_2$$

REACTIONS OF ALKENES

(A) Addition Reactions of Alkenes:

An atom or group of atoms are simply added to a double or triple bond without the elimination of any atom is called as **Addition Reactions**.

Carbon-carbon multiple bond is composed of a σ – bond and one or two π – bonds. Usually addition is the characteristic reaction of a π –bond. In the case of an ionic reaction, an Electrophile (E^+) or a Nucleophile (Nu^-) may initiate the process. When E^+ initiates the process, the reaction is termed as **electrophilic addition**; whereas a reaction initiated by Nu^- is termed as **nucleophilic addition**.

Example:

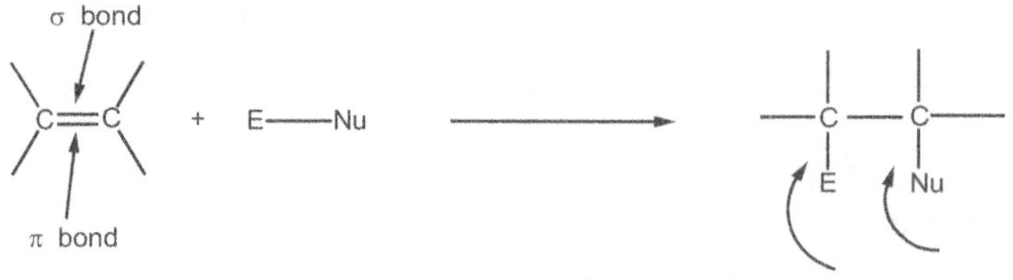

$$\underset{\pi\ bond}{\overset{\sigma\ bond}{C=C}} + E-Nu \longrightarrow \underset{E\ \ \ Nu}{-C-C-}$$

Mechanism:

Let us, now consider the addition of a reagent E-Nu to a carbon-carbon double bond. This involves the following three steps:

Step 1: The reagent E-Nu ionizes to give a positive ion and a negative ion

$$E—Nu \longrightarrow E^+ + :\bar{N}u$$

Step 2: Formation of a carbonium ion (Carbocation)

$$\text{Alkene} + E^+ \longrightarrow \text{Carbonium ion}$$

Step 3: Attack of nucleophile on carbonium ion to form the addition product

$$\text{Carbonium ion} + :\bar{N}u \longrightarrow \text{Addition Product}$$

Regioselectivity:

Addition of an unsymmetrical reagent to an unsymmetrical double bond proceeds in such a way as to involve the ***most stable carbocation***.

Or

"When an unsymmetrical alkene reacts with a hydrogen halide to give an alkyl halide, the hydrogen adds to the carbon of the alkene that has the greater number of hydrogen substituents and the halogen to the carbon of the alkene with the fewer number of hydrogen substituents."

Step 1: Ionisation of HBr

$$H—Br \longrightarrow H^{\oplus} + Br^{\ominus}$$

Step 2: Electrophile (H⁺) attaches the π – bond of propene to give more stable carbocation.

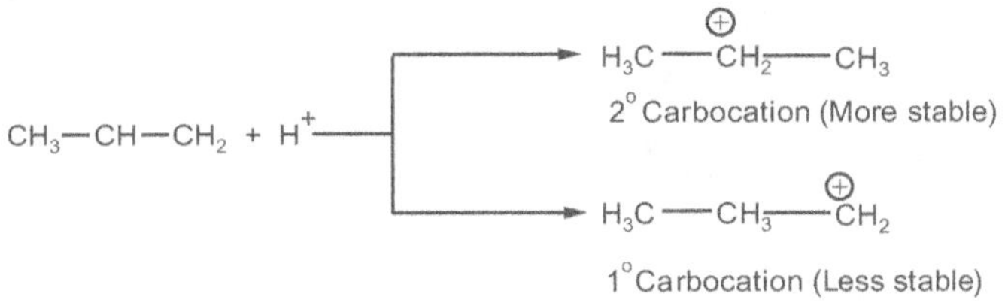

$$CH_3—CH—CH_2 + H^+ \longrightarrow H_3C—\overset{\oplus}{CH}—CH_3$$
2° Carbocation (More stable)

$$\longrightarrow H_3C—CH_2—\overset{\oplus}{CH_2}$$
1° Carbocation (Less stable)

Stability order of carbocation: 3° > 2° > 1°

Step 3: Nucleophile (Br⁻) combines with the more stable secondary carbocation to give major products.

$$CH_3-\overset{H}{\underset{\oplus}{C}}-CH_3 \;+\; \overset{\ominus}{Br} \longrightarrow CH_3-\underset{H}{\overset{Br}{C}}-CH_3$$

Isopropyl bromide

Markovnikov rule is quite general but not universal. In 1933, the American chemist M. S. Kharach discovered that the addition of HBr to unsymmetrical alkenes in the presence of organic peroxide (R – O – O – R) takes a cause opposite to that suggested by Markovnikov rule. This phenomenon of anti - Markovnikov addition of HBr in the presence of peroxide is known as *"Peroxide Effect"*.

$$CH_3-CH=CH_2 + HBr \begin{cases} \xrightarrow{\text{Peroxide}} H_3C-CH_2-\overset{H_2}{C}-Br \\ \text{n-Propyl bromide (anti-Markonikov product)} \\ \xrightarrow{\text{No Peroxide}} H_3C-\underset{Br}{CH}-CH_3 \\ \text{Isopropyl bromide (Markonikov product)} \end{cases}$$

Propylene

Mechanism: Propylene reacts with HBr in the presence of peroxide by a free radical mechanism.

Step 1: Peroxide dissociates to give alkoxy free radicals

$$R-O-O-R \xrightarrow{\Delta} 2\,R-\dot{O}$$

Step 2: Alkoxy free radical attaches HBr to form a bromine atom (free radical)

$$R-\dot{O} \;+\; H:Br \longrightarrow R-OH \;+\; Br^\bullet$$

Step 3: Bromine atom can attach propene to give a primary and secondary free radical

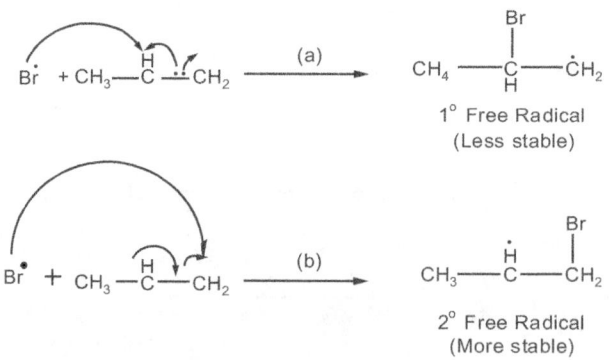

1° Free Radical (Less stable)

2° Free Radical (More stable)

Step 4: More stable 2° free radical attaches the H – Br to form anti-Markovnikov product and a bromine atom. The bromine atom goes back to step 3

$$CH_3\ CH-CH_2Br + H:Br \longrightarrow CH_3\ CH_2-CH_2Br + Br$$
n-Propyl bromide

Remember:

HCl and HI do not give anti–Markovnikov product in the presence of peroxide. This is because

(a) The H–Cl bond (103 kcal/mole) is stronger than H – Br bond (87 kcal/mole). It is not broken by the alkoxy free radicals obtained from peroxides.

(b) The H – I bond (71 kcal/mole) is weaker than the H – Br bond (87 kcal/mole). It is broken by the alkoxy free radicals obtained from peroxides. But the iodide ions formed readily combine with each other to yield iodine molecules rather than attack the double bond in alkenes.

Inhibitors: Hydroquinone, Diphenylamine.

If one carefully excludes peroxides from the reaction and adds above inhibitors i.e. hydroquinone or diphenylamine the addition of HBr to alkenes follows Markovnikov's rule.

1. Addition of hydrogen:

Alkenes and hydrogen under pressure and in the presence of Ni, Pt, or Pd catalyst to produce saturated hydrocarbons. A hydrogenation reaction carried in this manner is called **Catalytic hydrogenation**.

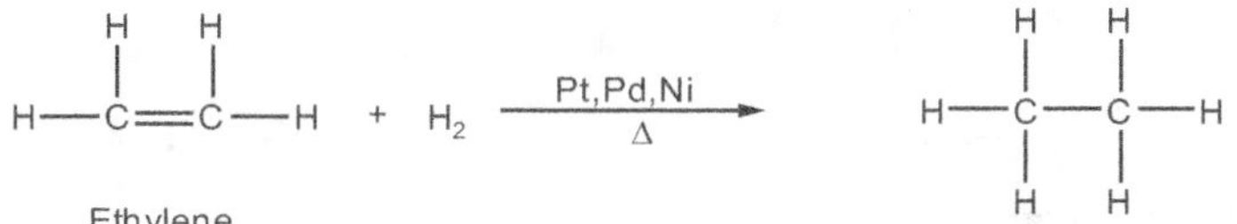

$$H_2C=CH_2 + H_2 \xrightarrow[\Delta]{Pt,Pd,Ni} H_3C-CH_3$$

Ethylene   Ethane

The above reaction does not occur through the ionic mechanism. The reaction depends on high affinity of hydrogen gas for certain metals –Ni, Pt, Pd. The hydrogen is absorbed on the metal surface along with alkene molecules. When a hydrogen molecule and an alkene molecule lie next to each other, their closeness and the weakening of their bonding permit a rearrangement of electrons to form new bonds. These hydrogenation reactions usually result in addition of two hydrogens to the same side of the carbon-carbon double bond. This is to be expected because the H_2 and alkene molecules lie side by side on the catalyst surface at the time of reaction.

2. Addition of halogens:

Halogen reacts with alkene in the presence of an inert solvent to form dihalogen derivatives.

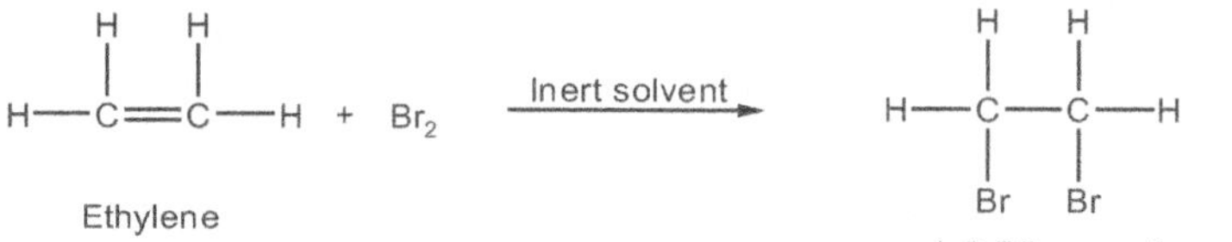

$$H_2C=CH_2 + Br_2 \xrightarrow{\text{Inert solvent}} \underset{\underset{Br}{|}}{H_2C}-\underset{\underset{Br}{|}}{CH_2}$$

Ethylene → 1,2-Dibromoethane

This reaction provides a useful "Test for Unsaturation", the red colour of the bromine being rapidly discharged as the colourless as a dibromo compound is formed.

Mechanism:

Step 1: The Br_2 molecule ionizes on interaction with π electron cloud to give the positive bromonium ion (electrophile) and a negative bromide ion (nucleophile).

$$Br_2 \longrightarrow Br^+ + :Br^-$$

Step 2: The positive bromonium ion, Br^+, attacks the double bond to form a carbonium ion.

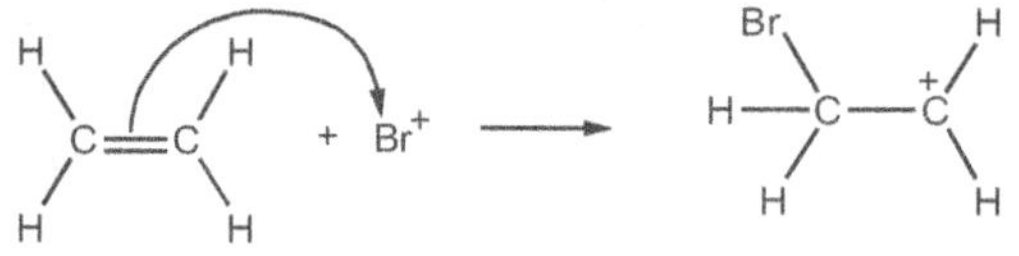

$$H_2C=CH_2 + Br^+ \longrightarrow H_2C-\overset{+}{C}H_2 \; (Br)$$

Ethylene → Carbonium ion

Step 3: The negative bromide ion :Br, attacks the carbonium ion to form the dibromo derivative.

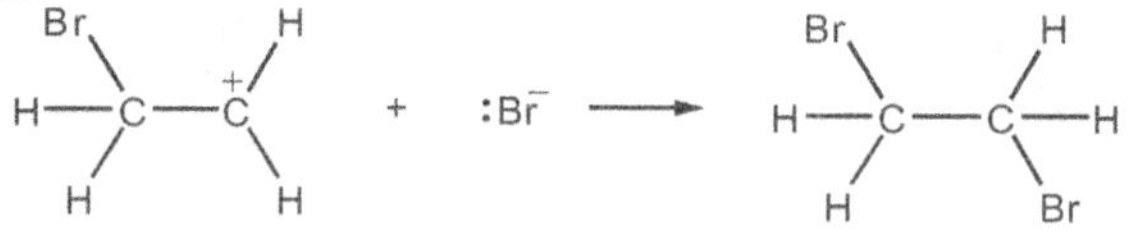

Carbonium ion + :Br⁻ → 1,2-Dibromomethane

3. Addition of a halogen halide:

Alkenes react with halogen acids (HCl, HBr, HI) to from alkyl halides.

Mechanism:

Step 1: HBr ionizes to give a proton (electrophile) and a bromide ion (nucleophile).

$$HBr \longrightarrow \overset{+}{H} + :Br^-$$

Proton   Bromide ion

Step 2: The proton attacks the double bond to form ethyl carbonium ion.

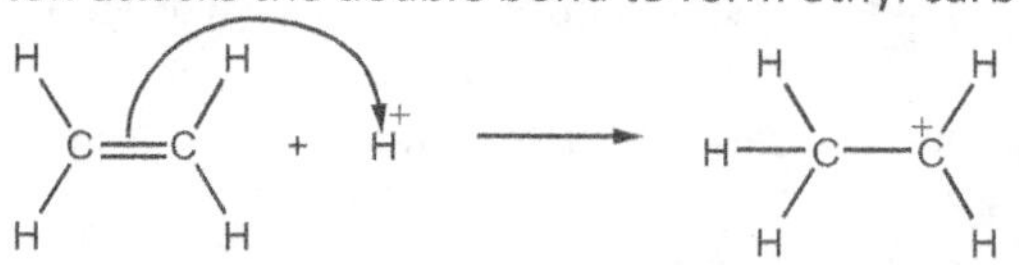

Ethylene + $\overset{+}{H}$ → Ethyl carbonium ion

Step 3: The negative bromide ion, :Br, attacks the carbonium ion to yield ethyl bomide.

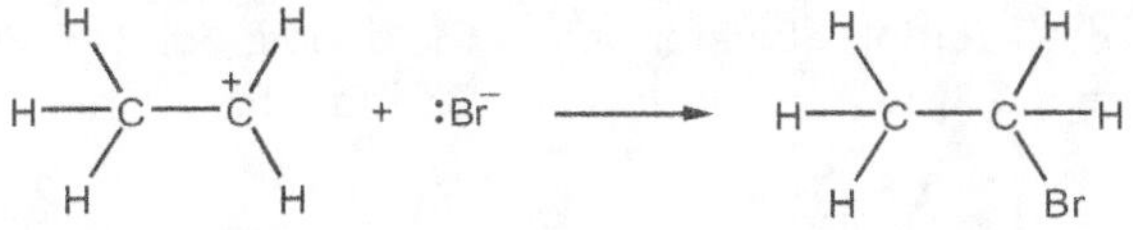

$$\text{Carbonium ion} + :Br^- \longrightarrow \text{Ethyl bromide}$$

When an alkene is symmetrical about the double bond as ethylene is; the product formed is the same, no matter which way H-Br becomes attached to the alkene.

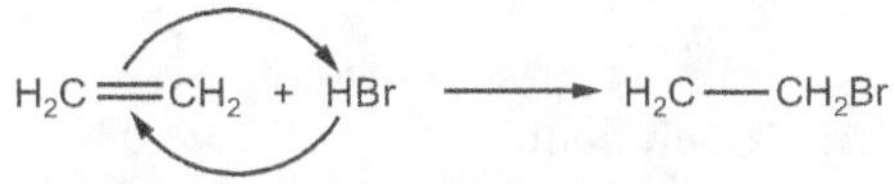

$$H_2C=CH_2 + HBr \longrightarrow H_2C-CH_2Br$$

4. Halohydrin formation (Addition of hypohalous acid):

Alkenes react with hypohalous acids (HOX) to give **halohydrins.** Markovnikov rule is followed in case of unsymmetrical alkenes. In these acids, halogen is the positive part and –OH group is the negative part.

$$H_2C=CH_2 + HO\overset{-}{C}\overset{+}{l} \longrightarrow \underset{\text{Ethylene chlorohydrin}}{H_2C(OH)-CH_2(Cl)}$$

5. Oxymercuration-demercuration:

The **oxymercuration reaction** is an electrophilic addition reaction that transforms alkenes into a neutral alcohol. Oxymercuration followed by demercuration is called an **oxymercuration– demercuration reaction**.

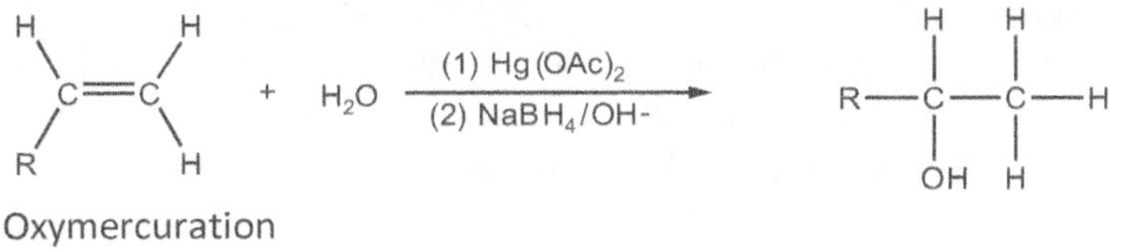

$$\underset{R}{\overset{H}{>}}C=C\underset{H}{\overset{H}{<}} + H_2O \xrightarrow[\text{(2) NaBH}_4/OH^-]{\text{(1) Hg(OAc)}_2} R-\underset{OH}{\overset{H}{C}}-\underset{H}{\overset{H}{C}}-H$$

Step 1: Oxymercuration

$$\underset{R}{\overset{H}{>}}C=C\underset{H}{\overset{H}{<}} + HO + Hg(OAC)_2 \longrightarrow R-\underset{OH}{\overset{H}{C}}-\underset{OAc}{\overset{H}{C}}-H + Hg(OAc) + CH_3COOH$$

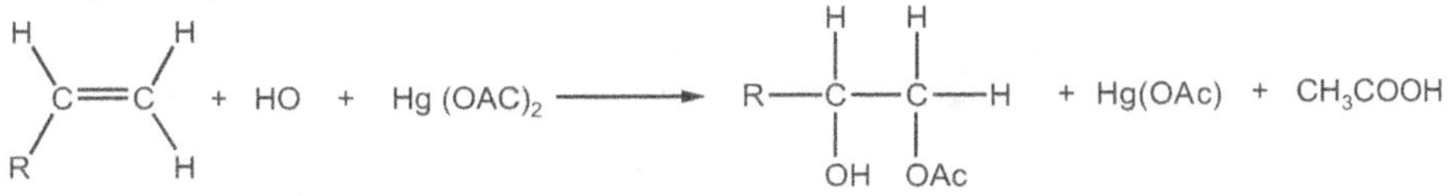

Step 2: Demercuration

$$R-\underset{OH}{\overset{H}{C}}-\underset{OAc}{\overset{H}{C}}-H + OH^- + NaBH_4 \longrightarrow R-\underset{OH}{\overset{H}{C}}-\underset{H}{\overset{H}{C}}-H + AcOH$$

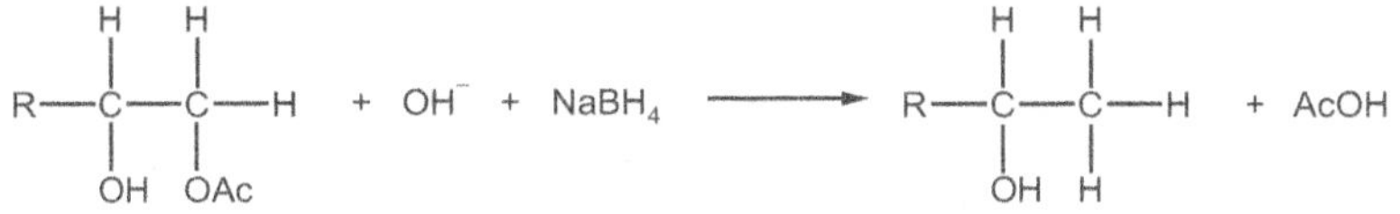

6. Hydroboration - Oxidation:

The hydroboration is a two-step organic reaction that converts an alkene into a neutral alcohol by the addition of water across the double bond. The reaction was first reported by Herbert C. Brown in the late 1950s and offered him the Nobel Prize in Chemistry in 1979.

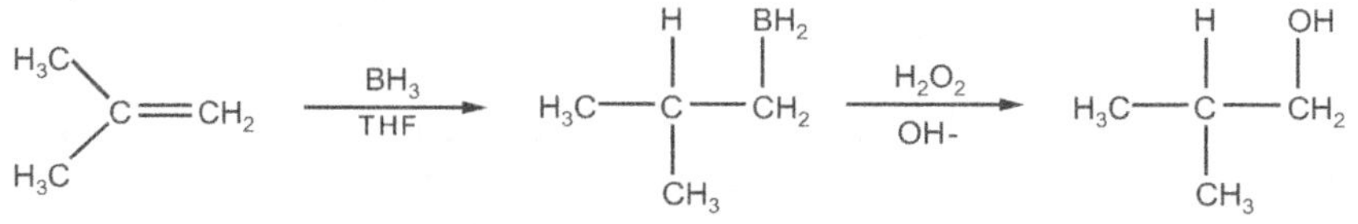

$$(CH_3)_2C=CH_2 \xrightarrow{BH_3, THF} H_3C-\underset{CH_3}{\underset{|}{C}}(H)-CH_2-BH_2 \xrightarrow{H_2O_2, OH^-} H_3C-\underset{CH_3}{\underset{|}{C}}(H)-CH_2-OH$$

Butylene   1-Dihydroisobutylborane   Isobutylalcohol

7. Oxidation with hot KMnO₄ Solution:

When treated with hot concentrated potassium permagnate solution, alkenes split at the double bond to form ketones or acids.

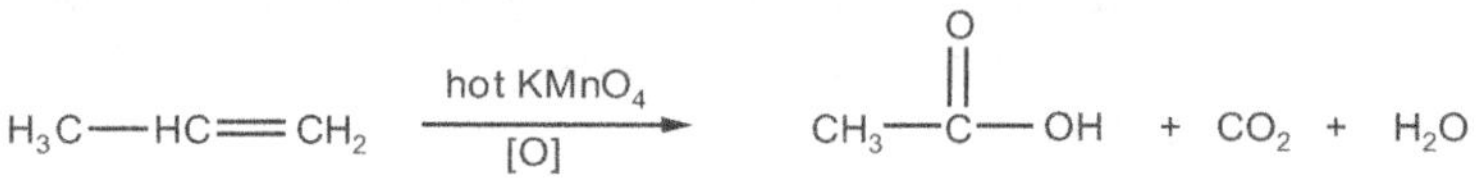

$$H_3C-HC=CH_2 \xrightarrow[\text{[O]}]{\text{hot KMnO}_4} CH_3-\underset{\underset{}{}}{\overset{O}{\overset{\|}{C}}}-OH + CO_2 + H_2O$$

Ethylene   Acetic acid

8. Catalytic Oxidation:

Alkenes react with oxygen in the presence of silver catalyst at 250-400°C to form epoxides.

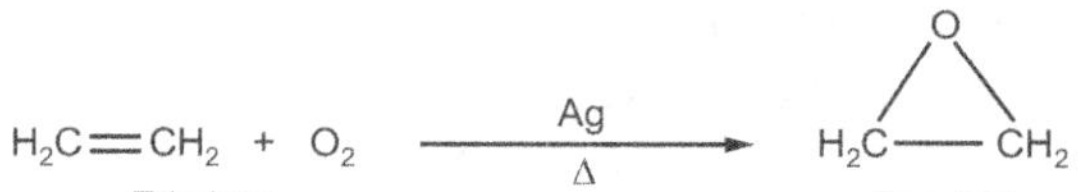

$$H_2C=CH_2 + O_2 \xrightarrow[\Delta]{Ag} H_2C\overset{O}{\underset{}{\triangle}}CH_2$$

Ethylene   Epoxide

9. Hydroxylation:

Alkenes react with cold dilute potassium permagnate solution to form glycols. Glycols are compounds whose molecules contain two –OH groups on adjacent carbons. The reaction looks like the addition of two –OH groups of hydrogen peroxide, HO-OH, to a double bond.

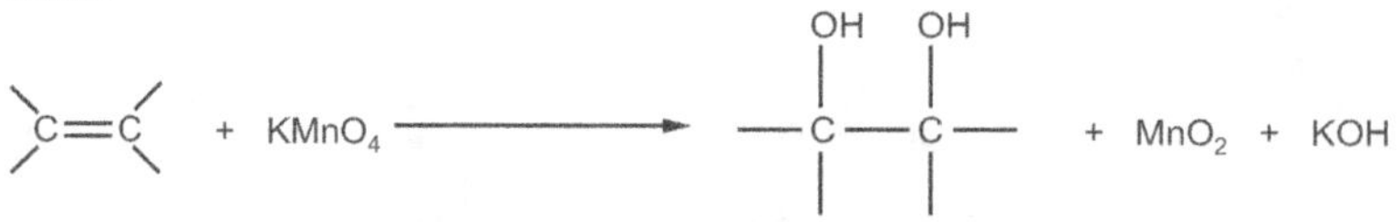

$$\underset{}{\overset{}{>}}C=C\underset{}{\overset{}{<}} + KMnO_4 \longrightarrow -\underset{}{\overset{OH}{\underset{|}{C}}}-\underset{}{\overset{OH}{\underset{|}{C}}}- + MnO_2 + KOH$$

Alkene   Glycol

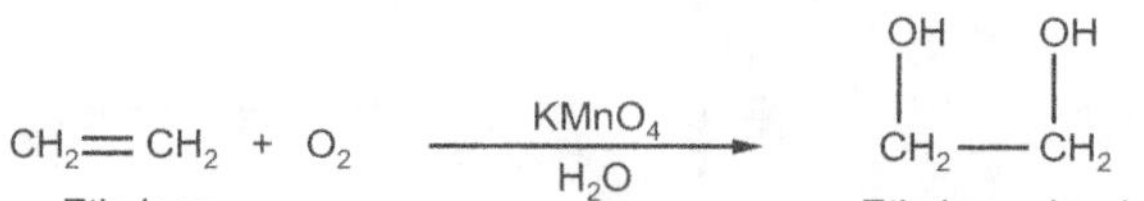

$$CH_2=CH_2 + O_2 \xrightarrow[H_2O]{KMnO_4} \underset{}{\overset{OH}{\underset{|}{CH_2}}}-\underset{}{\overset{OH}{\underset{|}{CH_2}}}$$

Ethylene   Ethylene glycol

10. Allylic substitution (using NBS):

The brominating reagent, N-bromosuccinimide (NBS), has proven useful for achieving allylic or benzylic substitution in CCl_4 solution at temperatures below its boiling point (77°C). The predominance of allylic substitution over addition in the NBS reaction is interesting. The N–Br bond is undoubtedly weak so bromine atom abstraction by radicals should be very favorable. The resulting succinimyl radical might then establish a chain reaction by removing an allylic hydrogen from the alkene.

11. Ozonolysis:

Ozonolysis is probably the best method for locating the position of the duble bonds in unknown alkenes. The oxygenated carbons in carbonyl compounds obtained by ozonolysis are the ones that were joined by a double bond in the original alkene.

When ozone is passed through an alkene in an inert solvent, it adds across the double bond to form an ozonide. Ozonides are explosive compounds. They are not isolated. On warming with zinc and water, ozonides cleave at the seat of the double bond. The products are aldehydes, ketones, or an aldehyde and a ketone, depending on the structure of the alkene.

The two steps process of preparing the ozonide and then decomposing it to get the carbonyl compounds is called Ozonolysis. Ozonolysis is a diagnostic reaction to detect the position of the double bond in alkenes.

(B) Elimination Reactions of Alkenes:

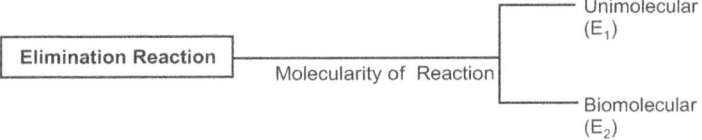

E_1 reaction:

1,2-Elimination reactions in which the T.S. of the rate determining step involves only one species is called E_1 reaction. The E_1 reaction usually follows the first order kinetics.

Step 1: Formation of carbonium ion

$$\overset{\underset{\mid}{H}}{-\underset{\mid}{C}}-\overset{\underset{\mid}{H}}{\underset{\mid}{C}}-G \xrightarrow{-G^-} \overset{\underset{\mid}{H}}{-\underset{\mid}{C}}-\overset{\underset{\mid}{H}}{\underset{\mid}{C}}^{\oplus}$$

This is the slow step and hence the rate-determining step.

Step 2: Loss of proton from the carbon atom adjacent to the C atom bearing the positive charge?

$$\overset{\underset{\mid}{H}}{-\underset{\mid}{C}}-\overset{\underset{\mid}{H}}{\underset{\mid}{C}}^{\oplus} \xrightarrow{-H^{\oplus}} \underset{}{\overset{}{>}}C=C\underset{}{\overset{}{<}}$$

Thus, the overall reaction is:

$$\overset{\underset{\mid}{H}}{-\underset{\mid}{C}}-\overset{\underset{\mid}{H}}{\underset{\mid}{C}}-G \xrightarrow{-G^-} \overset{\underset{\mid}{H}}{-\underset{\mid}{C}}-\overset{\underset{\mid}{H}}{\underset{\mid}{C}}^{\oplus} \xrightarrow{-H^{\oplus}} \underset{}{\overset{}{>}}C=C\underset{}{\overset{}{<}}$$

E₂ reaction:

E₂ reactions take place in a single concerted step in which two sigma bonds break and a π-bond forms simultaneously with the simultaneous departure of two groups, one of which is usually a proton. An E₂ reaction requires an added base which pulls out the proton.

$$\underset{B:}{\overset{H\ \ \ \ G}{-\underset{\mid}{\overset{\mid}{C}}-\underset{\mid}{\overset{\mid}{C}}-}} \longrightarrow \ \ >C=C< \ + \ G^{\ominus} \ + \ BH^{\oplus}$$

Since both the base and the substrate are involved in the T.S. of the single concerted rate determining step of the E₂ reaction, it is kinetically second order-first order with respect to the substrate and first order also with respect to the base.

E₁cB reaction:

This is a two-step base-catalysed 1,2-elimination reaction which involves a carbanion, the conjugate base of the substrate, as the reaction intermediate.

Step 1: Abstraction of most acidic B-H from the substrate and a carbanion forms

$$\overset{\underset{\mid}{H}}{-\underset{\mid}{C}}-\overset{\underset{\mid}{}}{\underset{\mid}{C}}-G \underset{}{\overset{B:}{\rightleftharpoons}} BH^{\oplus} + -\overset{\underset{\mid}{\ddot{}}}{\underset{\mid}{C}}-\overset{\underset{\mid}{}}{\underset{\mid}{C}}-G$$

Step 2: This leaving group leaves the carbanion and a C-C double bond forms

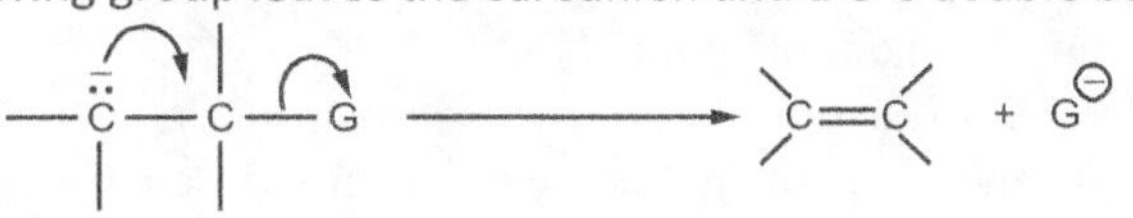

This sort of 1,2-elimination reaction is popularly called E_{1cB}-elimination unimolecular with respect to the conjugate base of the substrate.

The overall reaction is:

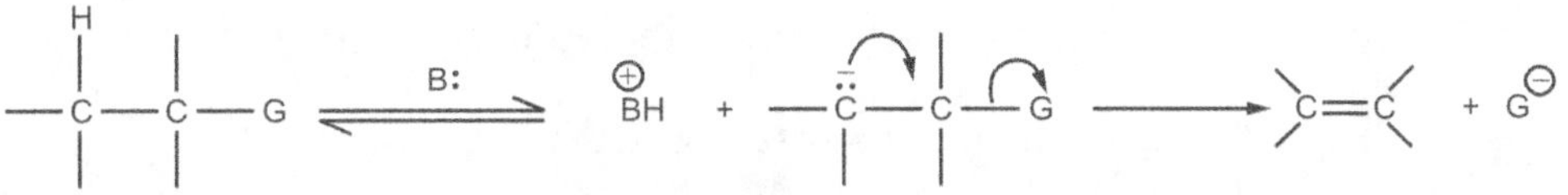

SAYTZEFF'S RULE

- Deals with the orientation of C-C double and triple bond in β-elimination reactions.
- Tells that the most substituted alkene will be formed predominantly in a β-elimination reaction.
- Thermodynamic stability of the product determines the formation of the double bond.
- Usually E_1 reactions follow the Saytzeff's rule.
- E_2 reactions involving neutral and small leaving groups also follow the Saytzeff's rule.
- As the bulk of the leaving group increases, the yield of the Saytzeff's product decreases.

E.g., Two alkenes are obtained when 2-bromobutane is heated with alcoholic KOH.

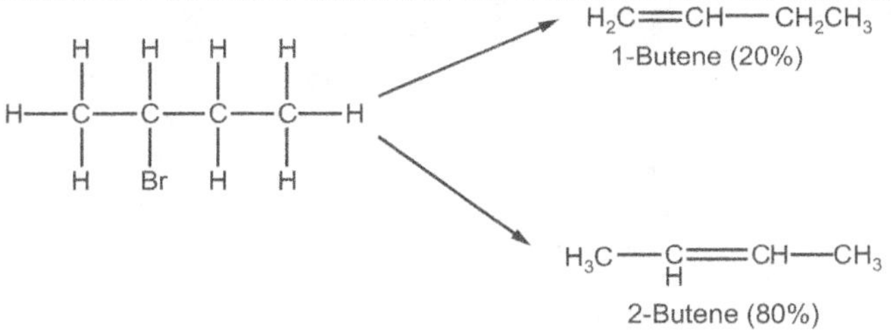

$H_2C=CH-CH_2CH_3$
1-Butene (20%)

$H_3C-CH=CH-CH_3$
2-Butene (80%)

According to Saytzeff rule, the main product is 2-butene, which is disubstituted.

HOFMANN'S RULE

- Deals with the orientation of C-C double and triple bond in β-elimination reactions.
- Tells that the least substituted alkene will be formed predominantly in a β-elimination reaction.

- The acidity of the β-H and the steric strain on the β-C determine the direction of the formation of the double bond.
- Usually E_2 and E_{1cB} reactions follow the Hofmann's rule.
- E_2 reactions involving bulky positively charged leaving groups follow the Hofmann's rule, e.g., $+NR_3$, $+SMe_2$.
- As the bulk of the leaving group increases, the yield of the Hofmann's product increases.
- With the increasing bulk of the bases the yield of the Hofmann's product increases.

E.g., In Hoffman elimination, the least substituted alkene is formed.

$$[H_3C-N(CH_3)_2-CH(CH_3)-CH_2-CH_2-H]^{\oplus} \xrightarrow[-H_2O]{OH^-, \Delta} H_2C=CH-CH_2CH_3 + (CH_3)_3N$$

1-Butene (Major product)

Mechanism:

The Hoffman elimination of quaternary ammonium hydroxides takes place by E_2 mechanism as follows:

$$R-CH_2-CH_2-N(CH_3)_3^+ \xrightarrow{OH^-} RCH=CH_2 + N(CH_3)_3 + H_2O$$

1-Alkene

DIENES

Alkenes containing two carbon-carbon double bonds are called dienes or alkadienes. If the double bonds are separated by more than one single bond (Isolated or Non-conjugated diene). If double bond are separated by one single bond (Conjugated Diene). If the double bonds are adjacent to each other (Cumulated diene). The most important class of dienes is that of conjugated dienes. Their chemical property are different from these of ordinary alkene.

Example:

Non-conjugated   Conjugated   Cumulated

Dienes are named by the IUPAC system in the same way as alkene except that ending –adiene is used. The position of the double bond are numbered to give the first carbon of each double bond a minimum number.

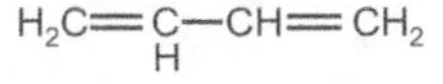

$$H_2C=\underset{H}{C}-CH=CH_2$$
1,3-Butadiene

1. Addition of halogen acids:

1,3-Butadiene reacts with halogen acids to yield a mixture of two compounds. They are 3-bromo-1-butene and 1-bromo-2-butene. The first product results from 1,2- addition to one of the double bond. The second product results from addition to terminal 1,4 position with the formation of a new double bond between C-2 and C-3. This latter process is known as 1,4- addition.

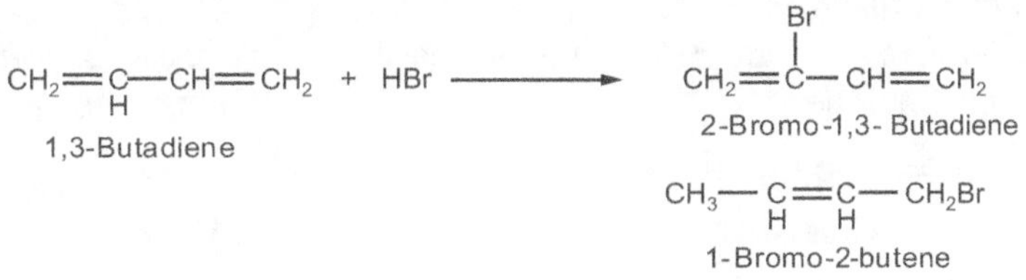

$$CH_2=\underset{H}{C}-CH=CH_2 + HBr \longrightarrow \underset{\underset{\text{2-Bromo-1,3- Butadiene}}{}}{CH_2=\underset{|}{\overset{Br}{C}}-CH=CH_2}$$

$$CH_3-\underset{H}{C}=\underset{H}{C}-CH_2Br$$
1-Bromo-2-butene

Mechanism:

Step 1: HBr ionizes to give a proton (electrophile) and a bromide ion (nucleophile)

$$HBR \longrightarrow \overset{+}{H} + :\overset{-}{Br}$$
Proton   Bromide ion

Step 2: Proton attacks a double bond according to Markovnikov rule to give a resonanace stabilized carbonium ion.

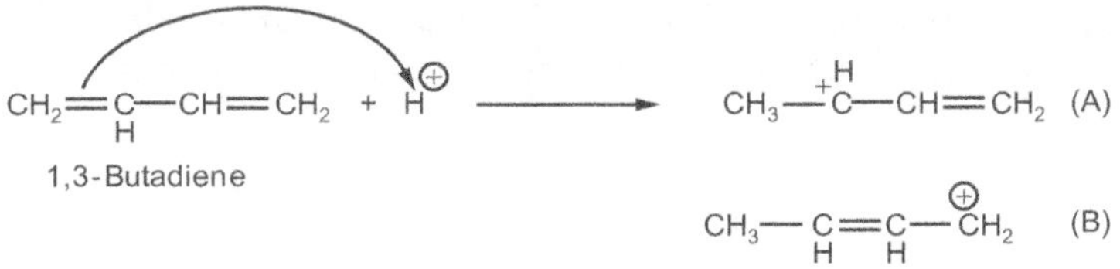

$$CH_2=\underset{H}{C}-CH=CH_2 + \overset{+}{H} \longrightarrow CH_3-\overset{+}{\underset{}{C}}\overset{H}{-}CH=CH_2 \quad (A)$$

$$CH_3-\underset{H}{C}=\underset{H}{C}-\overset{\oplus}{C}H_2 \quad (B)$$

Step 3: Bromide ion combines with (A) to give 3-bromo-1-butene (1,2 addition). If it combines with (B) it gives 1-bromo-2-butene

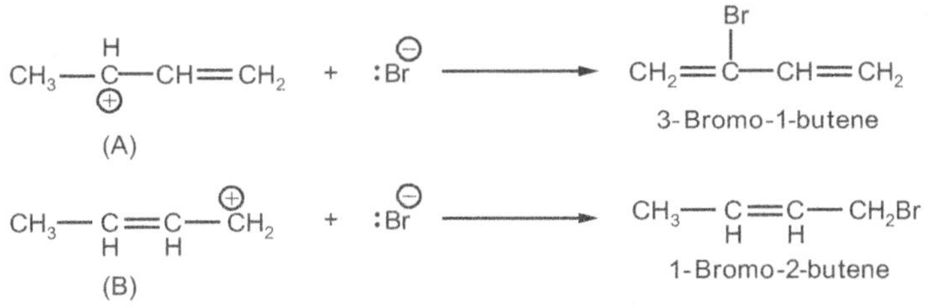

$$CH_3-\underset{\oplus}{\overset{H}{C}}-CH=CH_2 + :\overset{\ominus}{Br} \longrightarrow CH_2=\underset{|}{\overset{Br}{C}}-CH=CH_2$$
(A)   3-Bromo-1-butene

$$CH_3-\underset{H}{C}=\underset{H}{C}-\overset{\oplus}{C}H_2 + :\overset{\ominus}{Br} \longrightarrow CH_3-\underset{H}{C}=\underset{H}{C}-CH_2Br$$
(B)   1-Bromo-2-butene

2. Addition of halogens:

1,3- butadiene reacts with halogens (Br_2) in the presence of an inert solvent CCl_4 to give a mixture of two dibromo compounds.

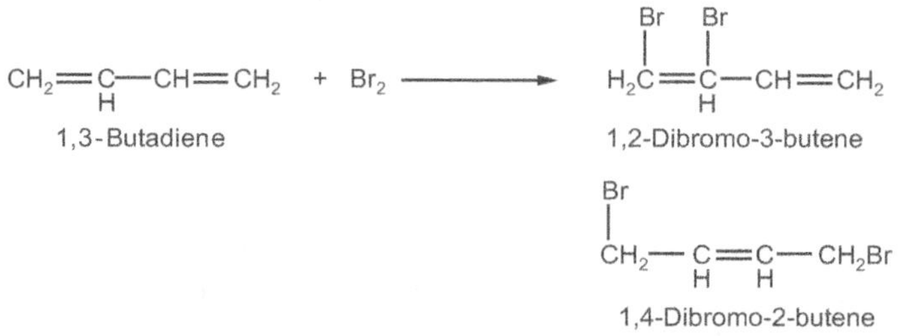

$$CH_2=\underset{H}{C}-CH=CH_2 + Br_2 \longrightarrow \underset{H}{H_2C}=\overset{Br}{\underset{|}{C}}-\overset{Br}{\underset{|}{CH}}-CH=CH_2$$

1,3-Butadiene → 1,2-Dibromo-3-butene

$$CH_2-\underset{H}{C}=\underset{H}{C}-CH_2Br$$
(with Br on first CH_2)

1,4-Dibromo-2-butene

3. Addition of hydrogen:

1,3-butadiene reacts with H_2 in the presence of a catalyst to give a mixture of 1-butene and 2-butene.

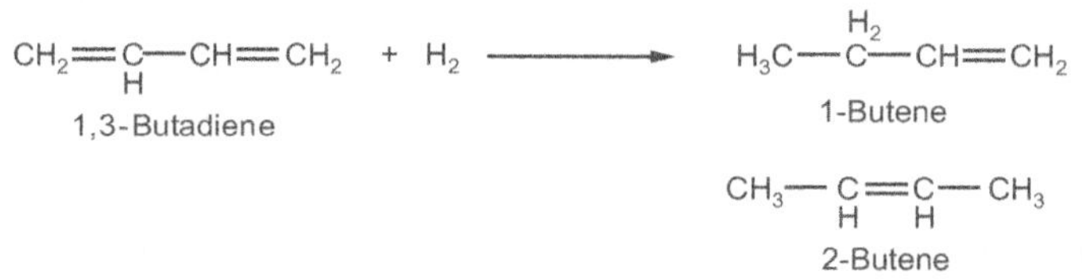

$$CH_2=\underset{H}{C}-CH=CH_2 + H_2 \longrightarrow H_3C-\overset{H_2}{\underset{}{C}}-CH=CH_2$$

1,3-Butadiene → 1-Butene

$$CH_3-\underset{H}{C}=\underset{H}{C}-CH_3$$

2-Butene

4. Diel's-Alder Reaction:

The alkene or alkyne used in Diel's alder reaction is referred to as dienophile (diene-lover). The product of Diel's alder reaction is called the adduct. The net result is the formation of two new σ bonds and one new π bond at the expense of three original π bonds.

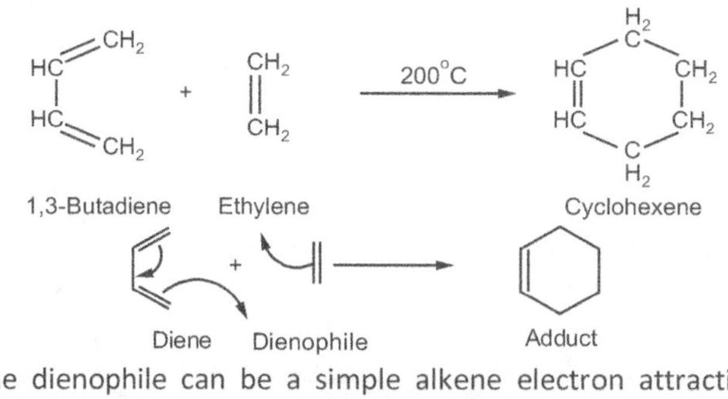

1,3-Butadiene + Ethylene → (200°C) → Cyclohexene

Diene + Dienophile → Adduct

Although the dienophile can be a simple alkene electron attracting groups such as –CN, -CHO, -COOH, -COOR) facilitate the reaction. The Diel's alder reaction is widely used in the synthesis of six membered ring compounds.

ALKYNES

Methods of Preparation:

1. **Dehydrohalogenation of vicinal dihalides:**

Compounds that contain halogen atoms on adjacent carbon atoms are called as vicinal dihalides or vic-dihalides. Alkynes are obtained by treatment of vicinal dihalides with alcoholic KOH followed by sodium amide (NaNH$_2$). This is a useful method since the vicinal dihalides are readily prepared from alkenes by the addition of halogens.

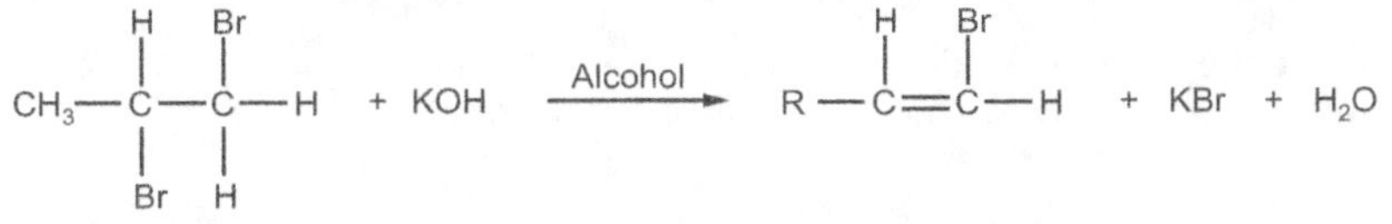

$$CH_3-CHBr-CHBr-H \xrightarrow{\text{Alcohol, KOH}} R-CH=CBr-H + KBr + H_2O$$
(vic-Dihalide) → (Vinyl halide)

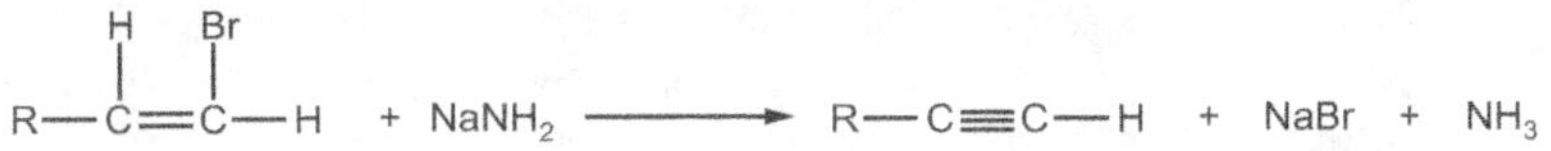

$$R-CH=CBr-H + NaNH_2 \longrightarrow R-C\equiv C-H + NaBr + NH_3$$
(Vinyl halide) → (Alkyne)

Notice that the product of the first HBr elimination is a substituted vinyl bromide. The vinyl halides are unreactive and a stronger base (NaNH$_2$) is used to remove the second HBr molecule. Acetylene and propyne can be prepared by this method as follows:

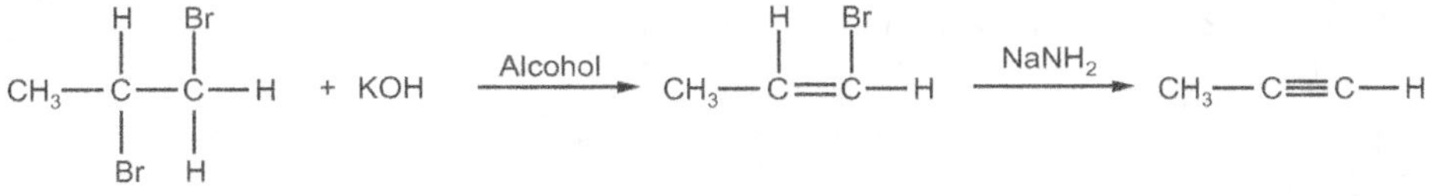

$$CH_3-CHBr-CHBr-H \xrightarrow{\text{Alcohol, KOH}} CH_3-CH=CBr-H \xrightarrow{NaNH_2} CH_3-C\equiv C-H$$
1,2-Dibromopropene → 1-Bromo-1-propene → Propyne

The vic-dihalides may be directly treated with NaNH$_2$ to give alkynes.

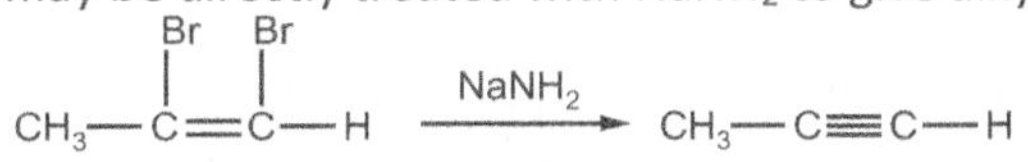

$$CH_3-CBr=CBr-H \xrightarrow{NaNH_2} CH_3-C\equiv C-H$$
1,2-Dibromopropene → Propyne

2. **Dehalogenation of tetrahalides:**

When 1,1,2,2-tetrahalides are heated with zinc dust in alcohol, alkynes are formed.

$$R-CX_2-CX_2-R + 2Zn \xrightarrow{\text{Alcohol}} R-C\equiv C-R + 2ZnX_2$$
(Tetrahalide) → (Alkyne)

This reaction is not of utility for preparing alkynes, because the tetrahalides are themselves generally made by addition of halogens to alkynes.

3. **Reaction of sodium acetylides and primary alkyl halides:**
   These sodium salts react with primary alkyl halides to form alkyl alkynes.

   Example:

   $$H-C\equiv C:Na + CH_3CH_2Br \xrightarrow{\text{Liquid } NH_3} HC\equiv C-CH_2CH_3 + NaBr$$

   Ethyl acetylide Ethyl bromide (1° halide) 1-Butyne

   The main advantage of this method is that it can be used to convert lower alkynes into higher alkynes.

4. **Reaction of calcium carbide with H_2O:**
   Calcium carbide reacts with water to yield acetylene.

   $$CaC_2 + H_2O \longrightarrow HC\equiv CH + Ca(OH)_2$$
   Calcium carbide   Acetylene

REACTIONS OF ALKYNES

Alkynes give the same kind of addition reactions as do alkenes. However, with alkynes the addition may take place in one step or two steps, depending upon the reaction conditions.

Step 1: Addition of one molecule of the reagent

$$-C\equiv C- + X-Y \longrightarrow -\underset{|}{\overset{X}{C}}=\underset{|}{\overset{Y}{C}}-$$

Step 2: Addition of two molecules of the reagent

$$-\underset{|}{\overset{X}{C}}=\underset{|}{\overset{Y}{C}}- + X-Y \longrightarrow -\underset{|}{\overset{X}{\underset{X}{C}}}-\underset{|}{\overset{Y}{\underset{Y}{C}}}- \text{ OR } -\underset{|}{\overset{X}{\underset{Y}{C}}}-\underset{|}{\overset{Y}{\underset{X}{C}}}-$$

Addition reactions occur with carbon-carbon triple bonds for the same reason that they occur with the carbon-carbon double bond, due to the availability of the loosely held π electrons.

1. **Addition of hydrogen:**
   In the presence of Ni, Pt, or Pd, alkynes add up two molecules of hydrogen first forming the corresponding alkenes and finally alkanes.

   $$R-C\equiv C-H + H_2 \xrightarrow{Ni} R-\underset{}{\overset{H}{C}}=CH_2 \xrightarrow{H_2} R-\underset{}{\overset{H}{C}}-CH_3$$
   Alkyne   Alkene   Alkane

   $$CH_3-C\equiv C-H + H_2 \xrightarrow{Ni} CH_3-\underset{}{\overset{H}{C}}=CH_2 \xrightarrow{H_2} CH_3-\underset{}{\overset{H}{C}}-CH_3$$
   Propylene   Propene   Propane

   The reduction can be stopped at the alkene stage by using Pd poisoned with $BaSO_4$ + quinoline (Lindlar catalyst).

2. Addition of halogens:

Halogens add to alkynes into two steps forming a dihalide and then a tetrahalide.

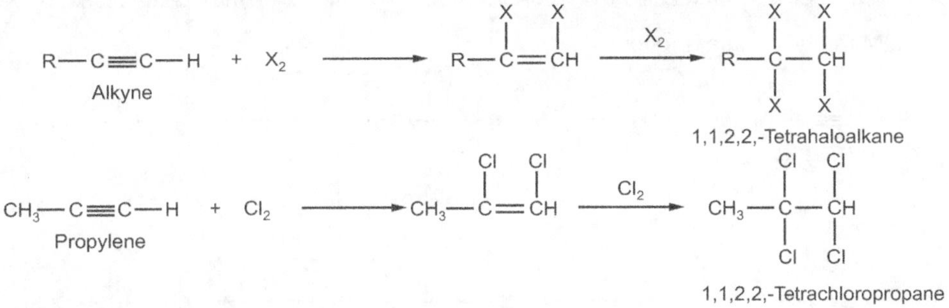

$$R-C\equiv C-H + X_2 \longrightarrow R-\underset{\underset{X}{|}}{\overset{\overset{X}{|}}{C}}=CH \xrightarrow{X_2} R-\underset{\underset{X}{|}}{\overset{\overset{X}{|}}{C}}-\underset{\underset{X}{|}}{\overset{\overset{X}{|}}{CH}}$$

Alkyne → 1,1,2,2,-Tetrahaloalkane

$$CH_3-C\equiv C-H + Cl_2 \longrightarrow CH_3-\underset{\underset{}{}}{\overset{\overset{Cl}{|}}{C}}=\overset{Cl}{CH} \xrightarrow{Cl_2} CH_3-\underset{\underset{Cl}{|}}{\overset{\overset{Cl}{|}}{C}}-\underset{\underset{Cl}{|}}{\overset{\overset{Cl}{|}}{CH}}$$

Propylene → 1,1,2,2,-Tetrachloropropane

3. Addition of halogen acids:

Halogen acids also add to symmetrical alkynes in two stages. After one molecule of the acid has been added to a symmetrical alkyne, the product is an unsymmetrical derivative of alkene so that the addition of a second molecule of the acid takes place in accordance with the Markonikov Rule. Thus, both the halogen becomes attached to the same carbon atom.

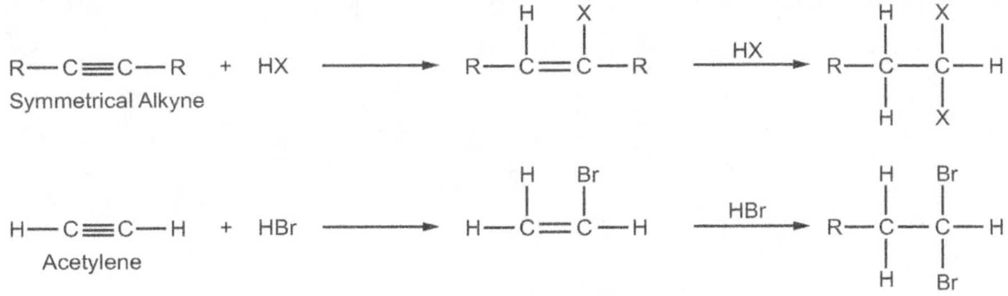

$$R-C\equiv C-R + HX \longrightarrow R-\overset{\overset{H}{|}}{C}=\overset{\overset{X}{|}}{C}-R \xrightarrow{HX} R-\underset{\underset{H}{|}}{\overset{\overset{H}{|}}{C}}-\underset{\underset{X}{|}}{\overset{\overset{X}{|}}{C}}-H$$

Symmetrical Alkyne

$$H-C\equiv C-H + HBr \longrightarrow H-\overset{\overset{H}{|}}{C}=\overset{\overset{Br}{|}}{C}-H \xrightarrow{HBr} R-\underset{\underset{H}{|}}{\overset{\overset{H}{|}}{C}}-\underset{\underset{Br}{|}}{\overset{\overset{Br}{|}}{C}}-H$$

Acetylene

The addition of halogen acid to unsymmetrical alkynes follows Markonikov rule in the first as well as the second step.

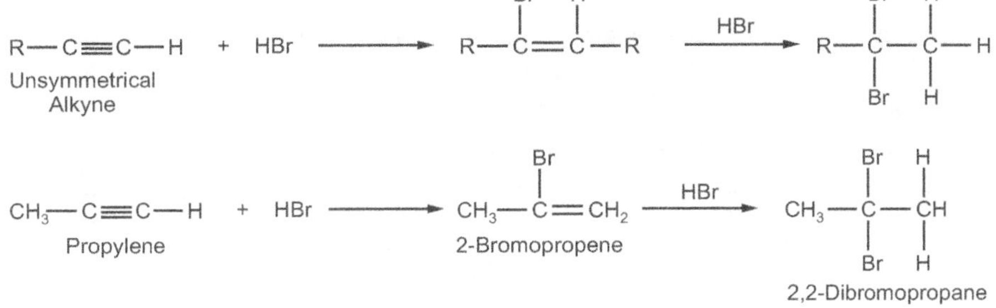

$$R-C\equiv C-H + HBr \longrightarrow R-\overset{\overset{Br}{|}}{C}=\overset{\overset{H}{|}}{C}-R \xrightarrow{HBr} R-\underset{\underset{Br}{|}}{\overset{\overset{Br}{|}}{C}}-\underset{\underset{H}{|}}{\overset{\overset{H}{|}}{C}}-H$$

Unsymmetrical Alkyne

$$CH_3-C\equiv C-H + HBr \longrightarrow CH_3-\overset{\overset{Br}{|}}{C}=CH_2 \xrightarrow{HBr} CH_3-\underset{\underset{Br}{|}}{\overset{\overset{Br}{|}}{C}}-\overset{\overset{H}{|}}{CH}$$

Propylene → 2-Bromopropene → 2,2-Dibromopropane

4. Halohydrin formation (Addition of hypohalous acid):

Addition of two molecules of hypohalous acids (HOX) to alkynes takes place in two steps. Markonikov rule is followed.

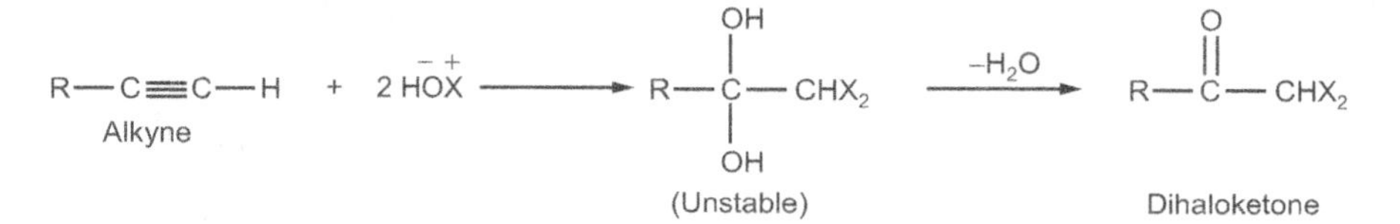

$$R-C\equiv C-H + 2\,HOX \longrightarrow R-\underset{OH}{\overset{OH}{\underset{|}{\overset{|}{C}}}}-CHX_2 \xrightarrow{-H_2O} R-\overset{O}{\overset{\|}{C}}-CHX_2$$

Alkyne → (Unstable) → Dihaloketone

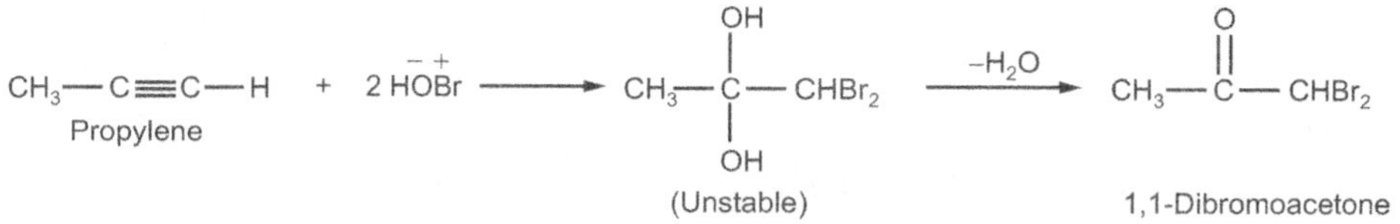

$$CH_3-C\equiv C-H + 2\,HOBr \longrightarrow CH_3-\underset{OH}{\overset{OH}{\underset{|}{\overset{|}{C}}}}-CHBr_2 \xrightarrow{-H_2O} CH_3-\overset{O}{\overset{\|}{C}}-CHBr_2$$

Propylene → (Unstable) → 1,1-Dibromoacetone

Acetylene under the same conditions gives dibromoacetaldehyde.

5. Hydration (Addition of water):

Alkynes react with water in the presence of mercuric sulphate and sulphuric acid to form an aldehyde or a ketone.

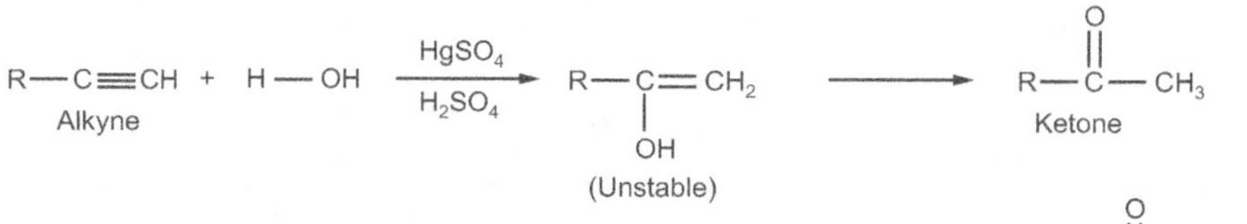

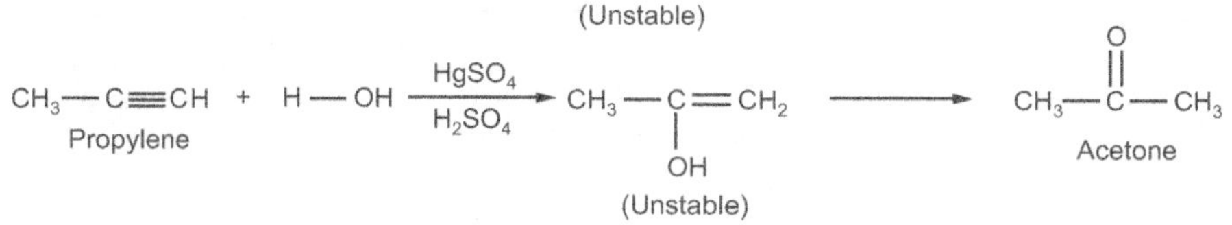

$$R-C\equiv CH + H-OH \xrightarrow[H_2SO_4]{HgSO_4} R-\underset{OH}{\overset{}{\underset{|}{C}}}=CH_2 \longrightarrow R-\overset{O}{\overset{\|}{C}}-CH_3$$

Alkyne → (Unstable) → Ketone

$$CH_3-C\equiv CH + H-OH \xrightarrow[H_2SO_4]{HgSO_4} CH_3-\underset{OH}{\overset{}{\underset{|}{C}}}=CH_2 \longrightarrow CH_3-\overset{O}{\overset{\|}{C}}-CH_3$$

Propylene → (Unstable) → Acetone

Acetylene under the same conditions gives acetaldehyde.

6. Addition of Hydrogen cyanide:

Alkynes react with HCN in presence of barium cyanide catalyst. Thus, acetylene yields vinyl cyanide or acrylonitrile from which the synthetic fiber 'orlon' is made.

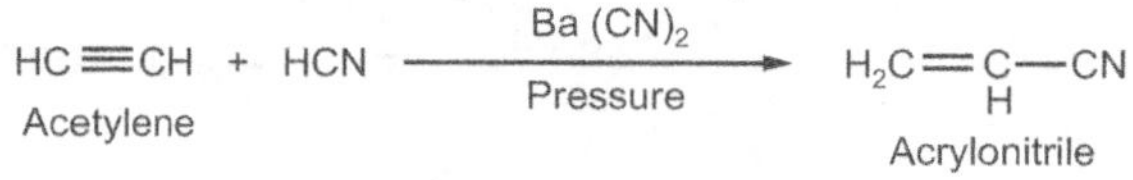

$$HC\equiv CH + HCN \xrightarrow[Pressure]{Ba(CN)_2} H_2C=\underset{H}{\overset{}{\underset{|}{C}}}-CN$$

Acetylene → Acrylonitrile

7. Oxidation with KMnO$_4$:

The oxidation of alkynes with alkaline potassium permangnate cleaves the molecule at the site of the triple bond to form carboxylic acids and CO$_2$.

$$R-C\equiv CH + 4[OH] \xrightarrow{NH_4OH} R-COOH + CO_2$$
Alkyne → Carboxylic acid

$$CH_3-C\equiv CH + 4[OH] \xrightarrow{NH_4OH} CH_3-COOH + CO_2$$
Propyne → Acetic acid

Acetylene under these conditions yields oxalic acid. This degradation reaction of alkynes is useful in determining the structure of alkynes.

8. Ozonolysis:

Alkynes react with ozone to give ozonides. These ozonides on decomposition with H$_2$O yield diketones, which are oxidised to acids by hydrogen peroxide produced in the reaction.

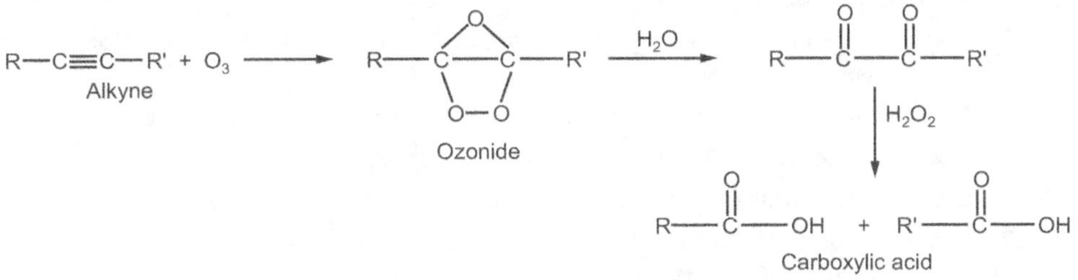

R—C≡C—R' + O$_3$ → Ozonide $\xrightarrow{H_2O}$ diketone $\xrightarrow{H_2O_2}$ R—COOH + R'—COOH (Carboxylic acid)

Propyne under these conditions gives a mixture of acetic acid and formic acid. Acetylene yields both glyoxal and formic acid. Use of ozonolysis and mechanism.

9. Polymerization:

Alkynes when passed through a red hot iron tube polymerize to form aromatic hydrocarbons. The reaction provides a method for passing from aliphatic to aromatic compounds.

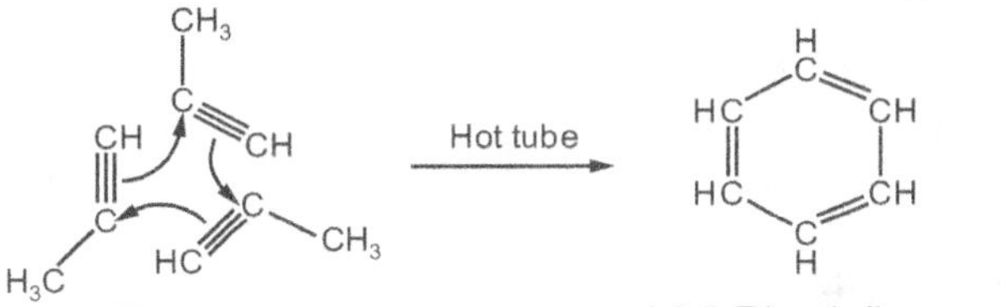

Propyne (3 molecules) $\xrightarrow{\text{Hot tube}}$ 1,3,5-Trimethylbenzene

Acetylene under these conditions yields benzene.

QUESTION BANK

1. How are alkenes prepared? Describe their important reactions.
2. Give two methods of preparation of propylene with reaction equations.
3. What do you mean by addition reactions of alkene? Give general mechanism of electrophilic addition reactions.
4. Write a note on Markonikov rule.
5. Write a note on Anti-Markonikov rule or Peroxide effect or Kharasch's effect.
6. Comment on catalaytic hydrogenation of alkenes.
7. Give mechanism of addition of bromine to ethylene.
8. Give mechanism of addition of HBr to ethylene.
9. What is oxymercuration-demercuration?
10. What is hydroboration-oxidation? Give an example.
11. Comment on allylic substitution using NBS.
12. Write a note on ozonolysis.
13. Classify elimination reactions. Describe E_1, E_2 and E_{1cB} reactions with mechanisms.
14. Explain Satzeff's and Hoffman's rules with examples.
15. How are alkenes prepared? Describe their important reactions.
16. Give two methods of preparation of propylene with reaction equations.
17. What do you mean by addition reactions of alkene? Give general mechanism of electrophilic addition reactions.
18. Comment on catalaytic hydrogenation of alkenes.
19. Give mechanism of addition of bromine to ethylene.
20. Give two methods for preparation of propene. What happens when propene is treated with
    (a) Br_2 / CCl_4
    (b) HBr / peroxide
    (c) HBr
    (d) HOCl
    (e) Cl_2 / 500°C
    (f) Cold dil. $KMnO_4$
21. Define dienes with suitable examples.
22. Give mechanism for the reaction of 1,3-butadiene with HBr.
23. Write a note on Diel's-Alder reaction.

24. How alkynes are prepared? Describe different methods of preparation of alkynes with reaction equations.
25. Give the general mechanism of electrophilic addition reactions.
26. Write notes on following:
    (a) Markonikov rule
    (b) Anti-Markonikov rule or Peroxide effect
    (c) Ozonolysis
    (d) Diel's-Alder reaction
27. Predict the product and complete the reactions:

    (a) $H-\underset{|}{\overset{H}{C}}=\underset{|}{\overset{H}{C}}-H + H_2 \xrightarrow[\Delta]{Pt, Pd, Ni}$

    (b) $H_2C=CH_2 + H\overset{-}{O}\overset{+}{Cl} \longrightarrow$

    (c) $H_3C-HC=CH_2 \xrightarrow[{[O]}]{hot\ KMnO_4}$

    (d) $CH_2=CH_2 + O_2 \xrightarrow{Ag}$

    (e) $CH_2=CH_2 \xrightarrow[H_2O]{KMnO_4}$

Chapter 9 ...

BENZENE AND AROMATICITY

CONTENTS

Hukel's Rule, Resonance in benzene and derivatives. Mechanism of electrophilic aromatic substitution: Halogenation, Nitration, Sulphonation and Friedel Crafts reaction, Orientation and reactivity in monosubstituted benzene. Mechanism of nueleophilic aromatic substitution. Addition – Elimination and Elimination – Addition (reactions involving benzyne intermediates)

INTRODUCTION

Structure of Benzene:

Benzene on which the study of aromatics began was discovered in 1825. However, it was not till 1866 that the Kekule's formula or structure I of benzene was known, till he proposed it. This structure of benzene is most accepted because the satisfactory answers it offers to various substitution products as compared with other four proposed structures II-V.

I Kekule formula   II Dewar formula   III

IV $H_3C-C\equiv C-C\equiv C-CH_3$

V $H_2C=\underset{H}{C}-C\equiv C-\underset{H}{C}=CH_2$

Fig. 9.1 (a): Different structures proposed for benzene

Great events in Chemistry ...

Fig. 9.1 (b):1865: Kekule, moments before his brilliant insight into the structure of benzene

Kekule proposed two structures (Fig. 9.2) having alternate single and double bonds in a ring of six carbon atoms, each having one hydrogen attached. Both these structures through a series of physical or chemical methods of structural elucidation, are proved to exist.

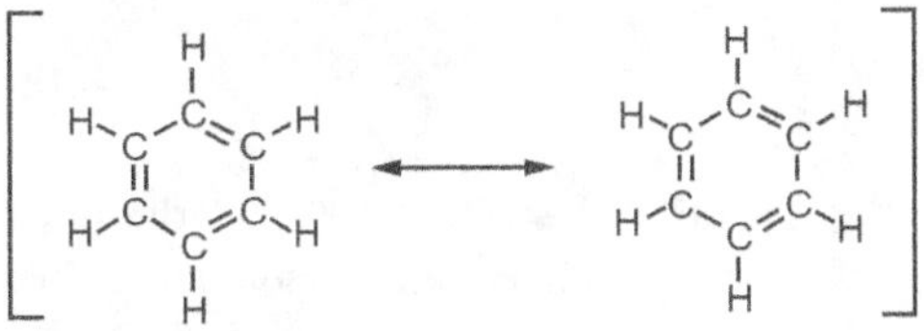

Fig. 9.2: Kekule's structures proposed for benzene

Further, since benzene has alternate single and double bonds, two different C-C bond distances are theoretically possible [(C-C) - 1.53 Å and (C=C) -1.33 Å]. But actually, the C-C bond length in benzene has been found to be 1.39 Å for all six C-C bonds. In short it can be said that- "Benzene is a regular hexagon with identical angles 120°C with molecular formula C_6H_6. All six C-C bonds have same length i.e., 1.395 Å, which is intermediate of $sp^2 - sp^2$ single bonds 1.46 Å and double bond length 1.33 Å ".

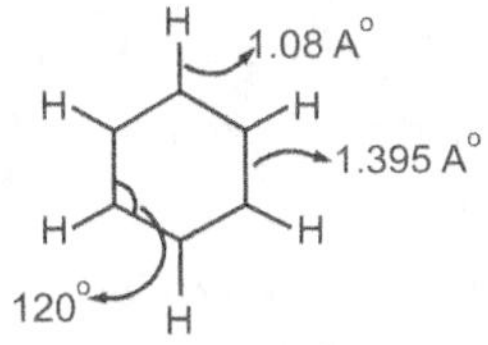

Fig. 9.3: Bond lengths and bond angles in benzene

Therefore, the structures of benzene can be shown as below;

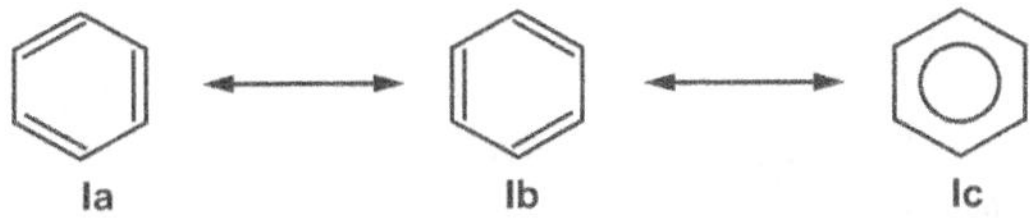

Ia   Ib   Ic

Fig. 9.4: Canonical forms of benzene

Benzene is an average of the first two structures. The C-C bond is neither a double nor a single bond, but is something in between.

Kekule's structure of benzene suggests that each carbon atom should be triagonal and therefore sp^2 hybridised. This means that each C atom has a 2p orbital and because the benzene molecule is planner and axes of all six 2p orbitals of benzene are parallel, these 2p orbitals can overlap the bonding π molecular orbitals of lowest energy as shown below.

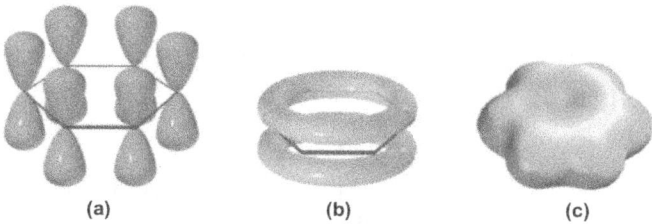

Fig. 9.5: Orbital overlap picture of benzene (a) Each carbon of benzene has a p orbital. (b) The overlap of the p-orbitals forms a cloud of electrons above and below the plane of the benzene ring. (c) The electrostatic potential map for benzene shows that all the carbon–carbon bonds have the same electron density

This molecular orbital shows that π electron density in benzene lies in a doughnut shaped region both above and below the plane of the ring. This overlap is symbolized by the resonance structures of benzene.

Stability of Benzene: Resonance Energy:

Chemical reactivity of any compound is measured in terms of its standard heats of formation ΔH_f^o.

The theoretically calculated ΔH_f^o of benzene is 82.93 kJ/mol or 19.82 k·cal/mol. of total six –CH groups of benzene [*per –CH group as 13.8 kJ/mol (or 3.3 k·cal/mo.)*]

Further, benzene is a cyclohexatriene (cyclic) and the ΔH_f^o for a double bond is 28-30 kcal, so it is expected to have 28.6 × 3 = 85.8 kcal/mole (theoretical) [As cyclohexene has ΔH_f = 28.6 kcal; cyclohexadiene has ΔH_f = 55.4 kcal].

However, in practical (reality) it is only 49.8 kcal. Therefore, benzene is stable by 36 kcal, or it contains 36 kcal, less energy.

This energy difference of 36 kcal/mol is called empirical resonance energy (RE) of benzene. RE is the energy by which benzene is stabilized and it is therefore, an energy that benzene doesn't have.

Let us understand more about what is resonance and aromaticity.

Concept of Resonance and Aromaticity:

Sometimes, multiple chemical structures in which electrons are shared between just two atoms can be used to represent a single molecule. In these cases no single such structure is correct, and the molecule exhibits special stability. This phenomenon imparts special chemical properties, especially, for certain cyclic systems. The reasons lie in the following two concepts.

Resonance:

Consider the following representations of an acetate anion:

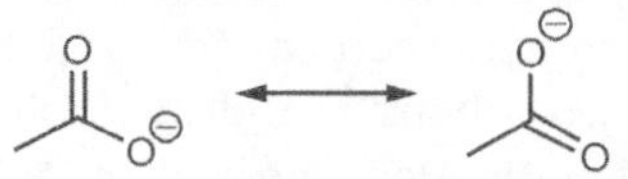

Fig. 9.6: Resonance structures of the acetate anion

The bonding in acetate may be described with a double bond made to the first oxygen atom and a negative charge placed on the second, or it may be represented with a negative charge on the first and a double bond to the second. **Which structure is correct?** Experimental evidence indicates that the bond lengths for the both carbon-oxygen bonds in acetate are actually in between the lengths of single and double bonds. When two chemical structures involving electrons shared between just two atoms may be drawn that represent a molecule, the molecule's true structure is intermediate between them. The contribution from multiple hypothetical structures to the true structure of a molecule is called **resonance**. The two structures are called **resonance structures** and the intermediate is called a **resonance hybrid**. Resonance often results in the presence of electrons which cannot be assigned to a single atom or bond; the electrons are said to be **delocalized**. A resonance hybrid is always more stable than the resonance structures (canonical forms) that contribute to it, a phenomenon known as **resonance stabilization**.

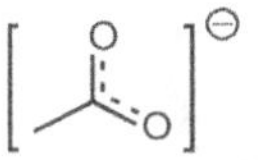

Fig. 9.7: Resonance hybrid of the acetate anion; the dashed line represents a delocalized electron

Aromaticity:

A **conjugated system** is a chemical system or structure bearing a series of alternating single and double bonds, meaning there is a p orbital on each atom. Owing to resonance, in a conjugated system of alternating bonds, the double and single bonds are able to switch places, producing an overall more stable structure. Conjugated systems can also exist in cyclic molecules. A conjugated cyclic system which is stabilized by resonance is called an **aromatic** system. The classic example of an aromatic system involves a six-membered ring.

RESONANCE IN BENZENE AND ITS DERIVATIVES

There are two possible chemical structures for a conjugated six-membered ring.

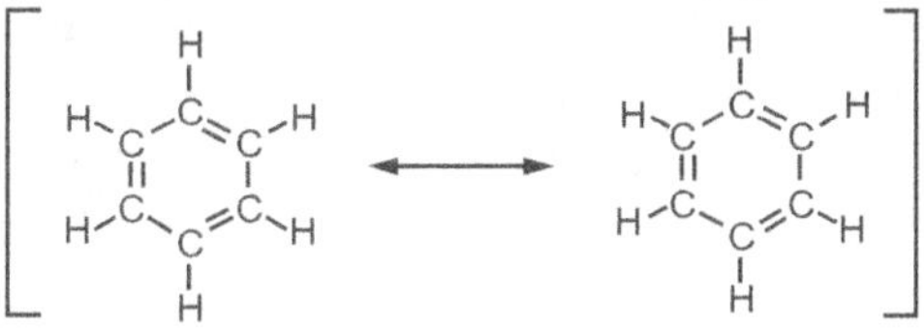

Fig. 9.8: Resonance structures of benzene

A conjugated six-membered ring is called **benzene**. In an aromatic system like benzene, each atom has a *p* orbital, the electrons of which are delocalized about the system. Benzene and other aromatic compounds exhibit a chemistry very different from ordinary, non-aromatic hydrocarbons. To distinguish between them, non-aromatic compounds are labelled **aliphatic**. Benzene and other aromatic compounds can have substituents. When benzene itself is a substituent, it is called a **phenyl group**. Benzene is typically drawn in such a way that the hybrid between the resonance structures is emphasized (Fig. 9.9).

Fig. 9.9: Benzene

AROMATICITY AND HÜCKEL'S (4n + 2) RULE

Benzene is unusually stable and this stability seems to be correlated with the overlap of its carbon 2p orbitals to form π molecular orbital. Ehrlich Hückel proposed criteria for this sort of stability, which are called aromaticity. He defined aromaticity (which had nothing to do with odour) with some rules or criteria.

A compound is said to be aromatic when it meets **all** the following criteria:

1. Aromatic compound consists of one or more rings that have a cyclic arrangement of p orbitals. Thus, aromaticity is a property of certain cyclic compounds.
2. Every atom of an aromatic ring has a p orbital.
3. Aromatic rings are planar.
4. Cyclic arrangement of p orbitals in an aromatic compounds must contain (4n + 2π) electrons, where n is any positive integer (0, 1, 2 ...) in other words an aromatic ring must contain 2, 6, 10, 14 ... π electrons.

These are collectively called Hückel 4n + 2 rule or simply 4n + 2 rule.

The basis of 4n + 2 rule lies in the molecular orbital theory of cyclic π electrons systems. The theory holds that aromaticity is observed only with continuous cycles of p orbital - *criteria 1 and 2*.

The theory also requires that p orbitals must overlap to form π molecular orbitals. This overlap requires that aromatic rings must be planner as the p orbitals cannot overlap in case of rings which are significantly distorted from planarity - *criterion 3*.

The last criterion has to do with the number of π molecular orbitals and number of electrons they contain for e.g., overlap 2p orbitals of of 6 carbon atoms in benzene results in 6π molecular orbitals. Three of these orbitals are bonding molecular orbitals and three are anti-bonding molecular orbitals. Quantum mechanics calculations show that bonding molecular orbitals of aromatic π electrons system have particularly low energies of the molecule. Thus, a compound has lowest energy when all its bonding molecular orbitals are filled because each molecular orbital accommodates two electrons which means six electrons are required to fill 3 bonding molecular orbitals of benzene i.e., 4n + 2 = 6 when n = 1 which shows that aromatic compound takes 4n + 2 electrons to fill exactly the bonding orbitals of π electrons system therefore criteria of 4. Each double bond contributes two π electrons.

Let's see some examples and understand, if they are aromatic, *e.g.* Benzene has 6 π electrons n = 1; naphthalene has 10 π electrons. n = 2; phenanthrene and anthracene have 14 π electrons …. n = 3.

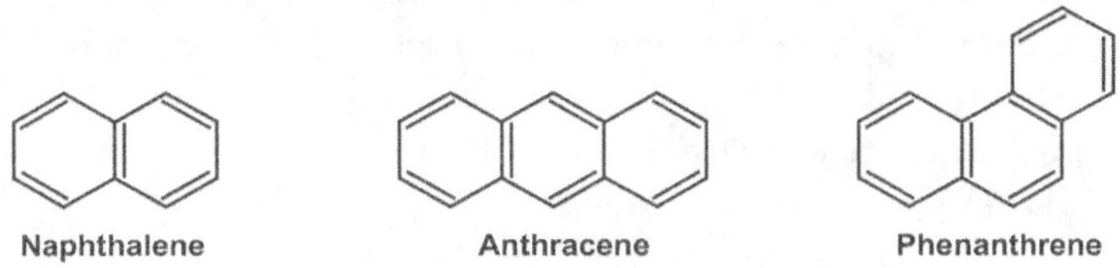

Naphthalene   Anthracene   Phenanthrene

Fig. 9.10: Aromatic benzene derivatives

Aromaticity is defined as ability to sustain induced ring current by a flat or nearly flat cyclic system with 4n + 2 π delocalized π electrons. (n = 0, 1, 2, 3 … n).

Some more examples:

1.

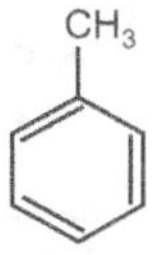

   The ring is toluene, like the ring in benzene it is a continuous planar cycle of 6π electrons. Hence, the ring in toluene is aromatic. The methyl group is a substituent on the ring and is not a part of ring system. Thus, as toluene contains an aromatic ring as the basic skeleton, it is considered to be an aromatic compound.

2. 1, 3, 5-Hexatriene
   $CH_2=CH-CH=CH-CH=CH_2$

   Although 1, 3, 5-hexatriene contains six π electrons, it is not aromatic, as it fails in the criterion 1 for aromaticity, as it is not cyclic. Aromatic species must be cyclic.

To summarize **Aromatic characteristics**:

The characteristic properties of aromatic compounds are:
- Low ΔH of hydrogenation.
- Undergo electrophilic substitution reactions.
- Resistant to addition reactions like alkenes/alkynes etc. are
- Flat molecules.
- They contain (4n + 2π) electrons - (Hückel's 4n + 2 rule).

Benzene can sustain in external magnetic field applied perpendicular to its plane, by circulating its delocalized electrons to form a ring in the opposite direction of the magnetic field.

Aromatic systems have special chemical and physical properties:
1. Though unsaturated, they undergo electrophilic substitution reactions rather than addition reactions.
2. They are resistant to $KMnO_4$ or HNO_3 oxidation
3. They exhibit unusual thermal stability
   - Low Δ H
   - Low Δ of combustion
4. Unique nuclear magnetic resonance properties.

Reactivity of Benzene:

Benzene is far less reactive than expected on the basis of its structural formula as a cyclohexatriene. As a matter of fact this compound could be expected to exhibit reactivity similar to any alkene. But benzene is rather inert and only sluggishly reactive to many substances that react readily with alkenes. This lower reactivity suggests high stability.

Sr. No.	Reagent	Cyclohexatriene gives	Benzene gives
1.	$KMnO_4$ (cold, dil, aq.)	Rapid oxidation	No reaction
2.	Br_2/CCl_4	Rapid addition	No reaction
3.	HI	Rapid addition	No reaction
4.	H_2/Ni	Rapid hydrogenation	Slow hydrogenation

In place of addition benzene readily undergoes a new set of reactions involving **electrophilic aromatic substitution.** e.g.,

Nitration:

$$C_6H_6 + HNO_3 \xrightarrow{H_2SO_4} C_6H_5NO_2 + H_2O$$

Halogenation:

$$C_6H_6 + Cl_2 \xrightarrow{Fe/FeCl_3} C_6H_5Cl + HCl$$

$$C_6H_6 + Br_2 \xrightarrow{Fe/FeBr_3} C_6H_5Br + HBr$$

Sulphonation:

$$C_6H_6 + H_2SO_4 \xrightarrow{SO_3^-} C_6H_5SO_3H + H_2O$$

Friedel Craft's Alkylation:

$$C_6H_6 + RCl \xrightarrow{AlCl_3} C_6H_5R + HCl$$

Friedel Craft's Acylation:

$$C_6H_6 - RCOCl \xrightarrow{AlCl_3} C_6H_5COR + HCl$$

In all the above reactions, it is evident that C_6H_6 resists additions in which benzene ring system is destroyed, whereas it readily undergoes substitution reactions in which ring system is preserved.

1. The halogenation reaction of benzene differs from halogenation reaction of alkenes in two ways:

Type of product involved: Alkenes react spontaneously with Br_2 or Cl_2 even in dilute solutions to give reactive addition products. Benzene however, gives a substitution product in which only the ring H is replaced by halogen.

Reaction conditions of benzene halogenation are much more severe than conditions for addition of halogens to alkenes.

ELECTROPHILIC AROMATIC SUBSTITUTION

Electron clouds below and above the aromatic ring shield it from the nucleophilic attack, but it is prone to electrophilic attack.

Because of the delocalised electrons exposed above and below the plane of the rest of the molecule, benzene is obviously going to be highly attractive to electrophiles - species which seek the electron rich areas in other molecules.

The electrophile will either be a positive ion, or the slightly positive end of a polar molecule.

General Mechanism:

It involves stepwise attack by an electrophile and liberation of a H^+.

First an electrophile, X^+ attacks benzene to form an intermediate C^+ ion (Benzonium ion or σ complex) alternatively a stable intermediate, which is stabilized by resonance as its positive charge is spread over all the C atoms of benzene. Its formation is the rate limiting step.

Step 1: Formation of C⁺ ion

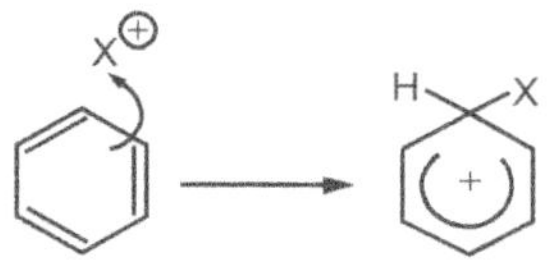

Step 2: Abstraction of H⁺

Y⁻ is simply the negative ion that was originally associated with X⁺. A lone pair of electrons on Y⁻ forms a bond with the hydrogen atom at the top of the ring. That means the pair of electrons joining the hydrogen onto the ring aren't needed any more. These then move down to plug the gap in the delocalised electrons, so restoring the delocalised ring of electrons which originally gave the benzene it's special stability.

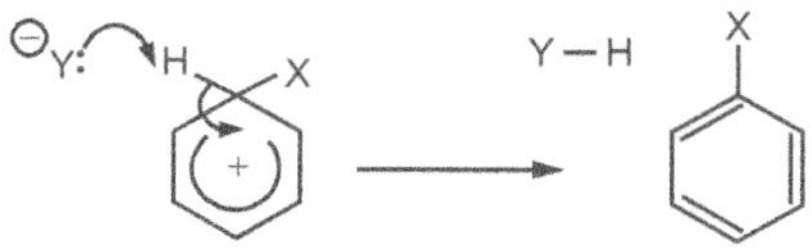

The energetics of the reaction:

The complete delocalisation is temporarily broken as X replaces H on the ring, and this costs energy. However, that energy is recovered when the delocalisation is re-established. This initial input of energy is simply the activation energy for the reaction. In this case, it is going to be high (something around 150 kJ mol^{-1}), and this means that benzene's reactions tend to be slow.

1. Nitration:

The electrophilic substitution reaction between benzene and nitric acid: The facts (Displacement of H (Ar-H) by NO_2^+ group.)

Benzene is treated with a mixture of concentrated nitric acid and concentrated sulphuric acid at a temperature not exceeding 50°C. As temperature increases there is a greater chance of getting more than one nitro group, -NO_2, substituted onto the ring. Concentrated sulphuric acid is acting as a catalyst. Nitrobenzene is formed.

Various Nitrating agents:
1. HNO_3
2. HNO_3/H_2SO_4
3. Fuming HNO_3 in conc. H_2SO_4
4. Fuming HNO_3 in fuming H_2SO_4
5. $RCOONO_2$ (Acyl Nitrates)
6. Nitronium salts

PHARMACEUTICAL ORGANIC CHEMISTRY - I   BENZENE AND AROMATICITY

7. N_2O_5 Nitronium pentoxide in CCl_4

$$C_6H_6 + HNO_3 \longrightarrow C_6H_5NO_2 + H_2O$$

or:

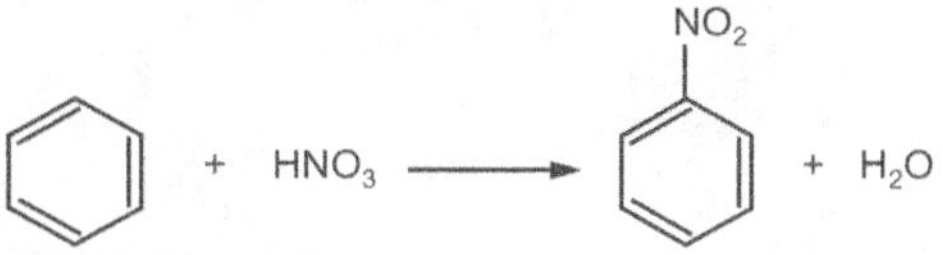

benzene + $HNO_3 \longrightarrow$ nitrobenzene + H_2O

The formation of the electrophile:

The electrophile is the "nitronium ion" or the "nitryl cation", NO_2^+. This is formed by reaction between the nitric acid and the sulphuric acid. (*The mixture of sulphuric acid with nitric acid is essential as sulphuric acid acts as a strong dehydrating agent to absorbs the water generated in-situ, else the reaction mixture gets diluted with this water and reaction becomes very sluggish*).

$$HNO_3 + 2H_2SO_4 \longrightarrow NO_2^+ + 2HSO_4^- + H_3O^+$$

Mechanism:

Step 1:

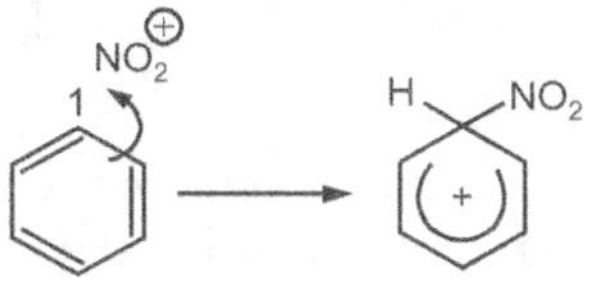

benzene + $NO_2^+ \longrightarrow$ arenium ion intermediate (H, NO_2)

Step 2:

arenium ion + $HSO_4^- \longrightarrow$ nitrobenzene + H_2SO_4

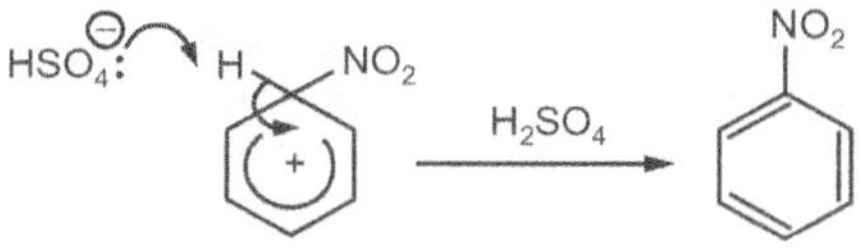

2. Halogenation:

The electrophilic substitution reaction between benzene and halogens (chlorine or bromine): The facts [Displacement of H (Ar-H) by X^+ (halonium ion)].

Benzene reacts with chlorine or bromine in an electrophilic substitution reaction, but only in the presence of a catalyst. The catalyst is either aluminium chloride (or aluminium bromide for reaction of benzene with bromine) or iron. Strictly speaking iron isn't a catalyst, because it gets permanently changed during the reaction. It reacts with some of the chlorine or bromine to form iron(III) chloride, $FeCl_3$, or iron(III) bromide, $FeBr_3$.

$$2Fe + 3Cl_2 \longrightarrow 2FeCl_3$$
$$2Fe + 3Br_2 \longrightarrow 2FeBr_3$$

These compounds act as the catalyst and behave exactly like aluminium chloride in these reactions.

The reaction with chlorine:

The reaction between benzene and chlorine in the presence of either aluminium chloride or iron gives chlorobenzene.

$$C_6H_6 + Cl_2 \longrightarrow C_6H_5Cl + HCl$$

Or

[benzene] + Cl_2 ⟶ [chlorobenzene] + HCl

The reaction with bromine:

The reaction between benzene and bromine in the presence of either aluminium bromide or iron gives bromobenzene. Iron is usually used because it is cheaper and more readily available.

$$C_6H_6 + Br_2 \longrightarrow C_6H_5Br + HBr$$

Or

[benzene] + Br_2 ⟶ [bromobenzene] + HBr

The formation of the electrophile:

We are going to explore the reaction using chlorine and aluminium chloride. If you want one of the other combinations, all you have to do is to replace each Cl by Br, or Al by Fe.

As a chlorine molecule approaches the benzene ring, the delocalised electrons in the ring repel electrons in the chlorine-chlorine bond.

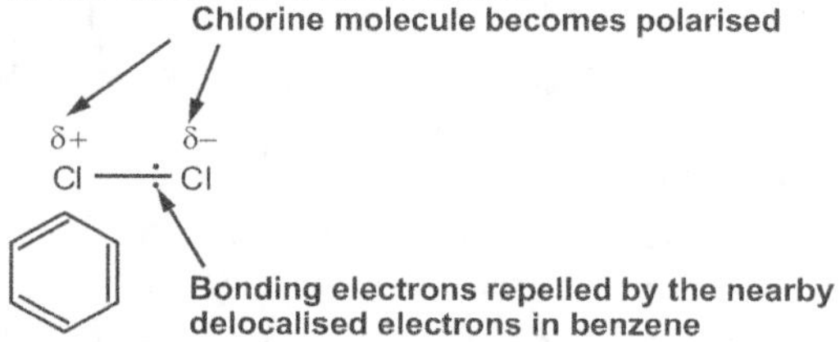

Chlorine molecule becomes polarised

$\overset{\delta+}{Cl} - \overset{\delta-}{Cl}$

Bonding electrons repelled by the nearby delocalised electrons in benzene

It is the slightly positive end of the chlorine molecule which acts as the electrophile. The presence of the aluminium chloride helps this polarisation.

Mechanism:

Step 1:

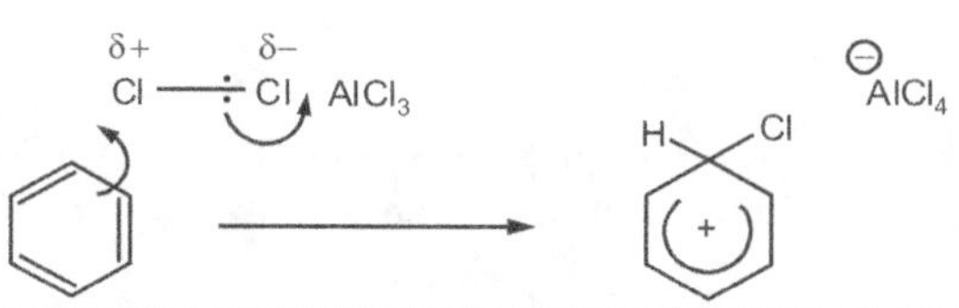

$\overset{\delta+}{Cl} - \overset{\delta-}{Cl}\ AlCl_3$ + [benzene] ⟶ [cyclohexadienyl cation with H and Cl] + $AlCl_4^{\ominus}$

Step 2:

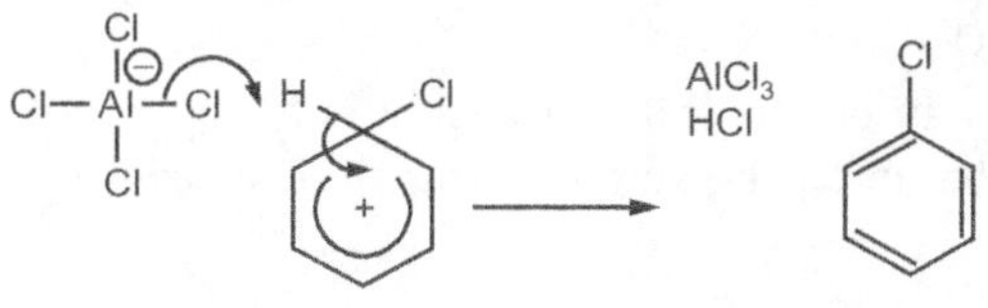

The hydrogen is removed by the $\overline{AlCl_4}$ ion which was formed in the first stage. The aluminium chloride catalyst is re-generated in this second stage.

3. Sulphonation:

The electrophilic substitution reaction between benzene and sulphuric acid: The facts [Displacement of H (Ar-H) by SO_3^+ (sulfuryl group)].

There are two equivalent ways of sulphonating benzene:
- Heat benzene under reflux with concentrated sulphuric acid for several hours or
- Warm benzene under reflux at 40°C with fuming sulphuric acid for 20 to 30 minutes.

$$C_6H_6 + H_2SO_4 \longrightarrow C_6H_5SO_3H + H_2O$$

Or:

$C_6H_6 + H_2SO_4 \longrightarrow C_6H_5SO_3H + H_2O$ ... equation (1)

The product is benzenesulphonic acid. The electrophile is actually sulphur trioxide, SO_3, and you may find the equation for the sulphonation reaction written as this also:

$C_6H_6 + SO_3 \longrightarrow C_6H_5SO_3H$ ... equation (2)

Note: Which version of this equation you use will depend on what question you are being asked. If the question refers to the reaction with sulphuric acid, then you must use equation (1). If the question refers to SO_3 as the electrophile, then you could use equation (2).

Often a mixture of $H_2SO_4 + SO_3$ is also employed (olem) for sulfonation.

The formation of the electrophile:

The sulphur trioxide electrophile arises in one of two ways depending on which sort of acid you are using. Concentrated sulphuric acid contains traces of SO_3 due to slight dissociation of the acid.

$$H_2SO_4 \rightleftharpoons H_2O + SO_3$$

Fuming sulphuric acid, $H_2S_2O_7$, as a solution of SO_3 in sulphuric acid and so is a much richer source of the SO_3.

Sulphur trioxide is an electrophile because it is a highly polar molecule with a fair amount of positive charge on the sulphur atom. It is species, which is attracted to the ring electrons.

Mechanism

Step 1:

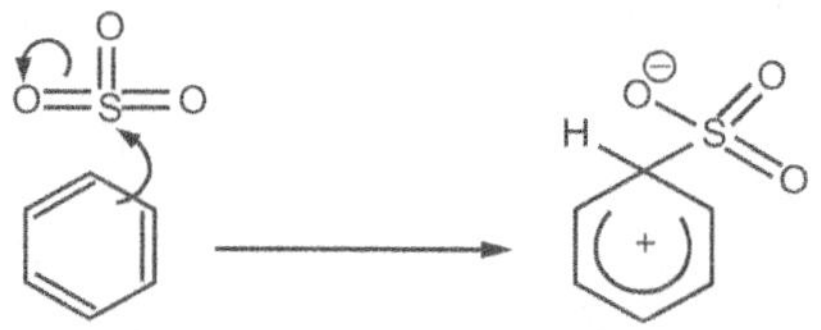

Step 2:

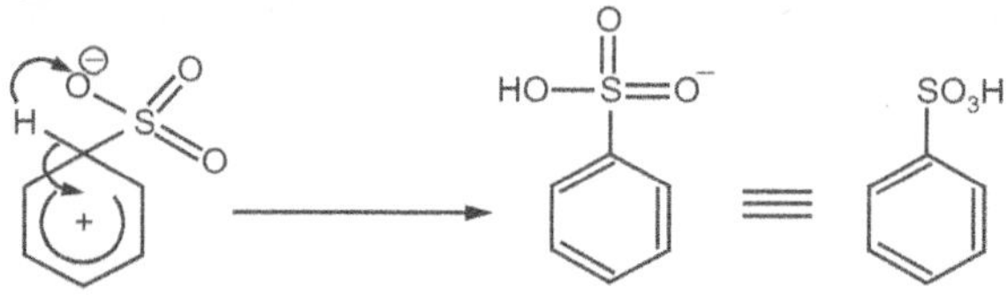

The second stage of the reaction involves a transfer of the hydrogen from the ring to the negative oxygen.

4. **Freidal Craft's Alkylation:**

The electrophilic substitution reaction between benzene and alkyl chloride: The facts (Displacement of H (Ar-H) by R^+ group.)

Benzene is treated with a chloroalkane (for example, chloromethane or chloroethane) in the presence of aluminium chloride as a catalyst. As an example, we will look at substituting a methyl group, but any other alkyl group could be used in the same way.

Substituting a methyl group gives methylbenzene - also commonly known as toluene.

$$C_6H_6 + CH_3Cl \longrightarrow C_6H_5CH_3 + HCl$$

or better:

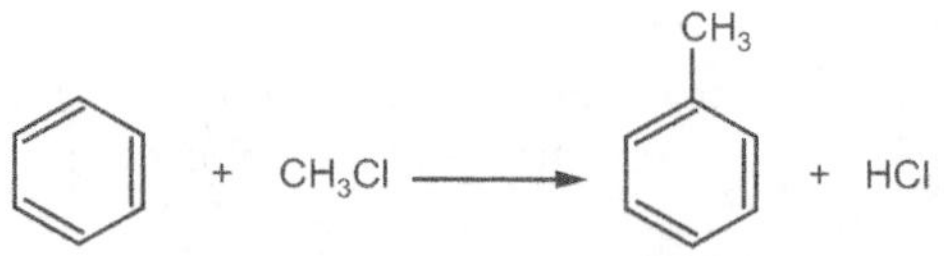

Aluminium chloride is acting as a catalyst. It is a Lewis acid.

The formation of the electrophile:

The electrophile is CH_3^+. It is formed by reaction between the chloromethane and the aluminium chloride catalyst.

$$CH_3Cl + AlCl_3 \longrightarrow \overset{\oplus}{C}H_3 + AlCl_4^{\ominus}$$

Mechanism:

Step 1:

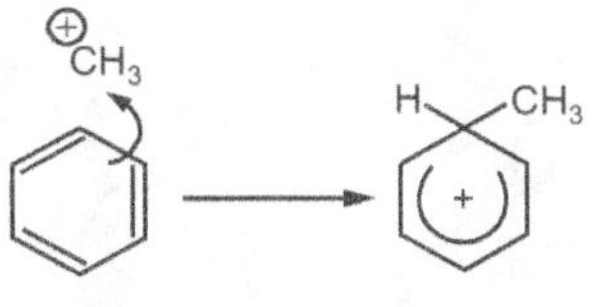

Step 2:

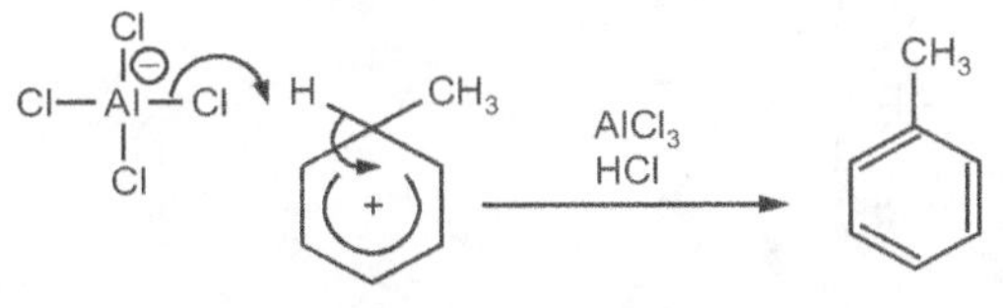

The hydrogen is removed by the $AlCl_4^-$ ion which was formed at the same time as the CH_3^+ electrophile. The aluminium chloride catalyst is re-generated in this second stage.

5. **Friedel Craft's Acylation:**

The electrophilic substitution reaction between benzene and an alkanoyl chloride:
The facts (Displacement of H (Ar-H) by RCO^+ group.) (RCO^+ = acylium ion)

The most reactive substance containing an acyl group is an acyl chloride (also known as an acid chloride). These have the general formula RCOCl.

Benzene is treated with a mixture of ethanoyl chloride, CH_3COCl, and aluminium chloride as the catalyst. A ketone called phenylethanone is formed.

$$C_6H_6 + CH_3COCl \longrightarrow C_6H_5COCH_3 + HCl$$

or better:

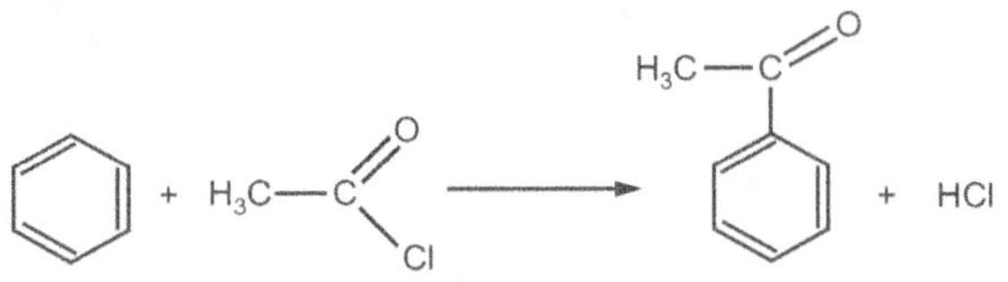

The aluminium chloride isn't written into these equations because it is acting as a catalyst. If you wanted to include it, you could write $AlCl_3$ over the top of the arrow.

The formation of the electrophile:

The electrophile is CH_3CO^+. It is formed by reaction between the ethanoyl chloride and the aluminium chloride catalyst.

$$CH_3COCl + AlCl_3 \longrightarrow CH_3CO_3^+ + AlCl_4^-$$

The electrophilic substitution mechanism:

Mechanism:

Step 1:

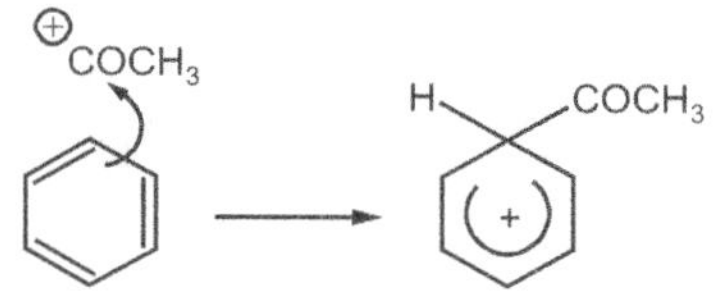

Step 2:

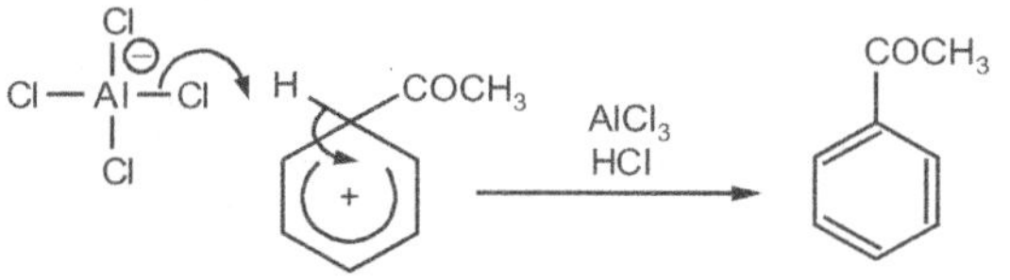

The hydrogen is removed by the $AlCl_4^-$ ion which was formed at the same time as the CH_3CO^+ electrophile. The aluminium chloride catalyst is re-generated in this second stage.

ORIENTATION AND REACTIVITY IN MONOSUBSTITUTED BENZENE

The Effect of substituents on orientation:

When a substituted benzene undergoes an electrophilic substitution reaction, where does the new substituent attach itself? Is the product of the reaction the *ortho* isomer, the *meta* isomer, or the *para* isomer?

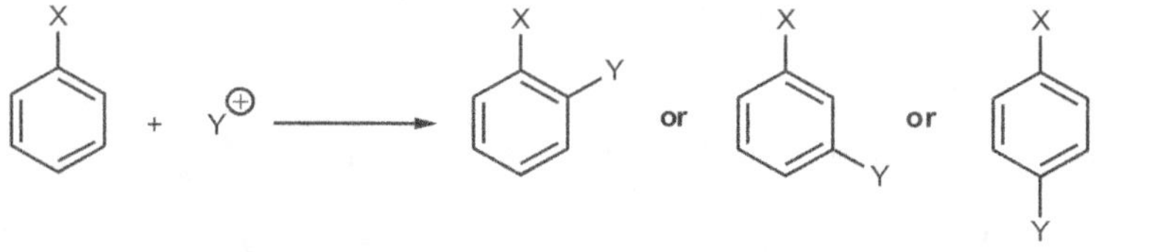

Ortho isomer   *Meta* isomer   *Para* isomer

The substituent already attached to the benzene ring determines the location of the new substituent. There are two possibilities: A substituent will direct an incoming substituent either to the *ortho and para* positions, or it will direct an incoming substituent to the meta position. All activating substituents and the weakly deactivating halogens are **ortho, para directors**, and all substituents that are more deactivating than the halogens are **meta directors**. Thus, the substituents can be divided into three groups:

1. All activating substituents direct an incoming electrophile to the *ortho* and *para* positions.

Toluene + Br$_2$ $\xrightarrow{FeBr_3}$ o-Bromotoluene + p-Bromotoluene

2. The weakly deactivating halogens also direct an incoming electrophile to the *ortho-* and *para-* positions.

Bromobenzene + Cl$_2$ $\xrightarrow{FeCl_3}$ o-Chlorobromobenzene + p-Chlorobromobenzene

3. All moderately deactivating and strongly deactivating substituents direct an incoming electrophile to the meta position.

Acetophenone + HNO$_3$ $\xrightarrow{H_2SO_4}$ m-Nitroacetophenone

Nitrobenzene + Br$_2$ $\xrightarrow{FeBr_3}$ m-Bromonitrobenzene

To understand why a substituent directs an incoming electrophile to a particular position, we must look at the stability of the carbocation intermediate that is formed in the rate-determining step. When a substituted benzene undergoes an electrophilic substitution reaction, three different carbocation intermediates can be formed: an *ortho*-substituted carbocation, a *meta*-substituted carbocation, and a *para*-substituted carbocation. The relative stabilities of the three carbocations enable us to determine the preferred pathway of the reaction because the more stable the carbocation, the less energy required to make it and the more likely it is that it will be formed.

If a substituent donates electrons inductively, e.g., a methyl group, then the indicated resonance contributors in Fig. 9.11. below are the most stable; the substituent is attached directly to the positively charged carbon, which the substituent can stabilize by inductive electron donation. These relatively stable resonance contributors are obtained only when the incoming group is directed to an *ortho* or *para* position. Therefore, the most stable carbocation is obtained by directing the incoming group to the *ortho* and *para* positions. Thus, any substituent that donates electrons inductively is an *ortho–para* director.

If a substituent donates electrons by *resonance*, the carbocations formed by putting the incoming electrophile on the *ortho* and *para* positions have a fourth resonance contributor (Fig. 9.11). This is an especially stable resonance contributor because it is the only one whose all atoms (except for hydrogen) have complete octets. Therefore, *all substituents that donate electrons by resonance are ortho–para directors.*

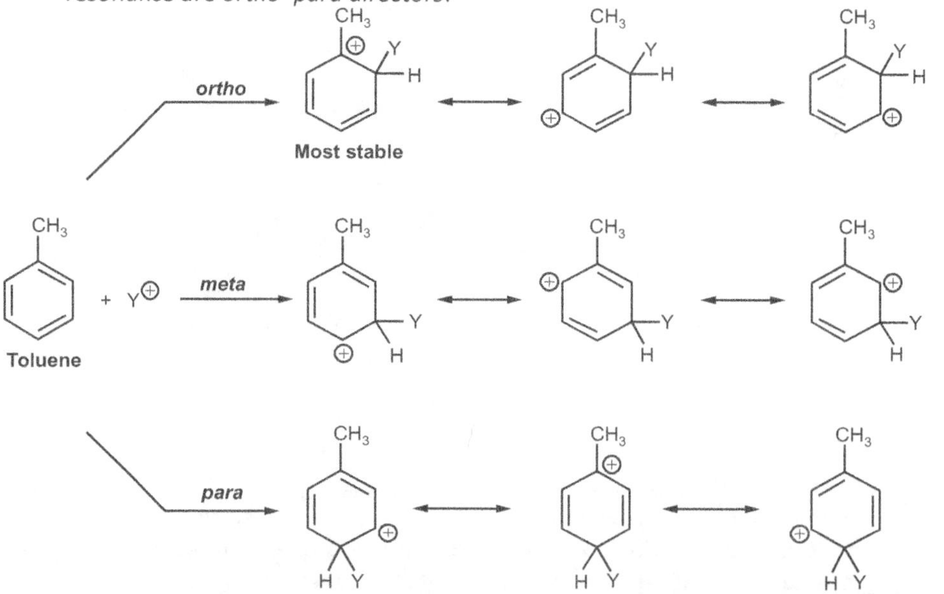

Fig. 9.11: The structures of the carbocation intermediates formed from the reaction of an electrophile with toluene at the *ortho*, *meta* and *para* positions

Table: Classification of substituents with respect to their directive effects on orientation of substitution *vis-a-vis* their activating or deactivating effects on benzene ring

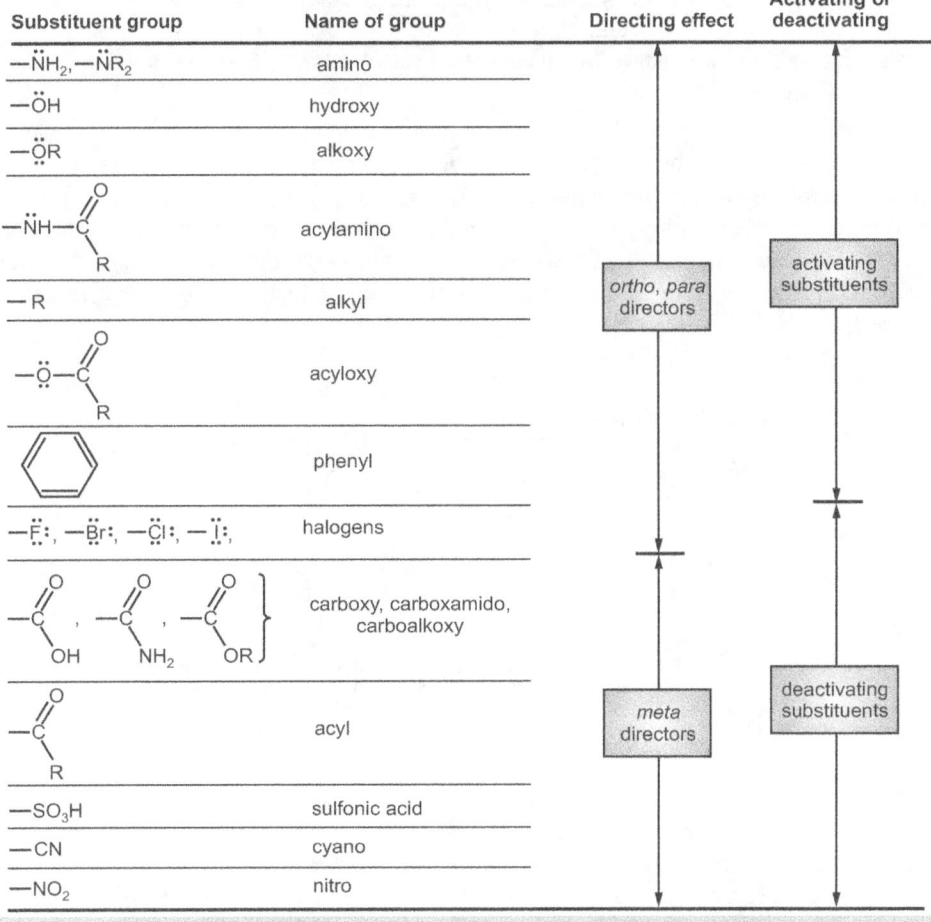

NUCLEOPHILIC AROMATIC SUBSTITUTION

Although most reactions of aromatic compounds occur by way of electrophilic aromatic substitution, aryl halides do not react with nucleophiles under standard reaction conditions. Aryl halides undergo only a limited number of substitution reactions that too with strong nucleophiles only. This is because the electron clouds repel the approach of a nucleophile towards the aromatic ring.

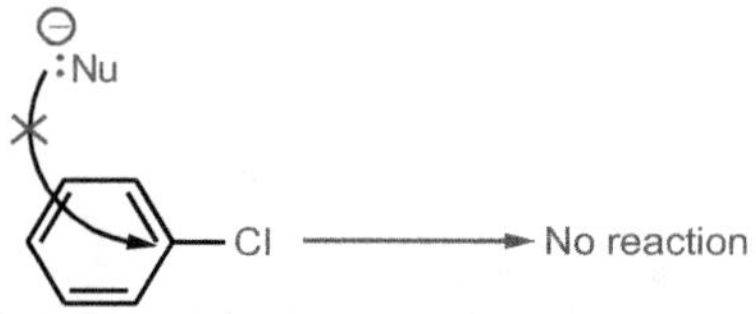

Fig. 9.12: Reason for disfavoured nucleophilic substitution by benzene derivatives under normal conditions

If, however, the aryl halide has one or more substituents that strongly withdraw electrons from the ring by resonance, **nucleophilic aromatic substitution** reactions can occur without using extreme conditions. The electron-withdrawing groups must be positioned *ortho* or *para* to the halogen. The greater the number of electron-withdrawing substituents, the easier it is to carry out the nucleophilic aromatic substitution reaction. The different conditions under which the following reactions occur:

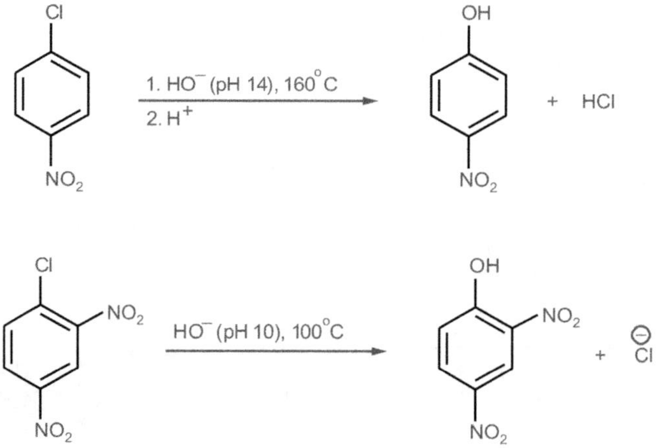

The strongly electron-withdrawing substituents that *activate* the benzene ring towards *nucleophilic aromatic substitution* reactions are the same substituents that *deactivate* the ring towards *electrophilic aromatic substitution*. In other words, making the ring less electron rich makes it easier for a nucleophile but more difficult for an electrophile to approach the ring. Thus, any substituent that deactivates the benzene ring towards electrophilic substitution activates it towards nucleophilic substitution and *vice versa*.

Nucleophilic aromatic substitution by addition-elimination:

Nucleophilic aromatic substitution takes place by a two-step reaction known as an **SNAr reaction** (substitution nucleophilic aromatic). In the first step, the nucleophile attacks the carbon bearing the leaving group from a trajectory that is nearly perpendicular to the aromatic ring. (The leaving groups cannot be displaced from sp² carbon atoms by back-side attack.) Nucleophilic attack forms a resonance-stabilized carbanion intermediate called a *Meisenheimer complex*. In the second step of the reaction, the leaving group departs, reestablishing the aromaticity of the ring.

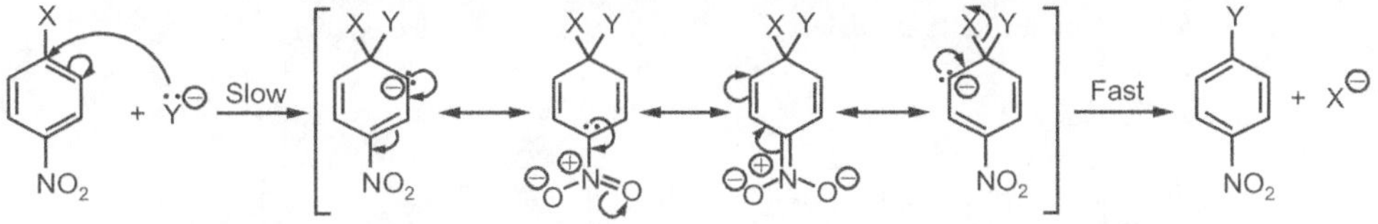

Fig. 9.13: General mechanism for nucleophilic aromatic substitution

In a nucleophilic aromatic substitution reaction, the incoming nucleophile must be a stronger base than the substituent that is being replaced, because the weaker of the two bases will be the one eliminated from the intermediate.

The electron-withdrawing substituent must be *ortho* or *para* to the site of nucleophilic attack because the electrons of the attacking nucleophile can be delocalized on to the substituent only if the substituent is in one of those positions.

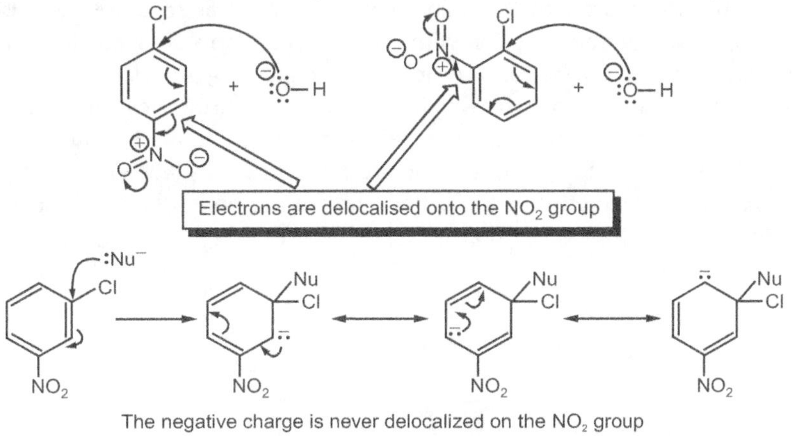

Electrons are delocalised onto the NO₂ group

The negative charge is never delocalized on the NO₂ group

Fig. 9.14: Mechanism of nucleophilic aromatic substitution: Nucleophilic aromatic substitution by an addition elimination mechanism occurs only with aryl halides that contain electron-withdrawing substituents at the *ortho* or *para* positions and not the meta position.

A variety of substituents can be placed on a benzene ring by means of nucleophilic aromatic substitution reactions. The only requirement is that the incoming group be a stronger base than the group that is being replaced.

p-Fluoronitrobenzene + CH_3O^- →Δ p-Nitroanisole + F^-

1-Bromo-2,4-dinitrobenzene + $CH_3CH_2NH_2$ →Δ [$\overset{+}{N}H_2CH_2CH_3$ intermediate, Br^-] →HO^- N-Ethyl-2,4-dinitroaniline + H_2O

REACTIONS INVOLVING BENZYNE INTERMEDIATE

An aryl halide such as chlorobenzene can undergo a nucleophilic substitution reaction in the presence of a very strong base such liquid ammonia, soda amide or sodium hydride. There are two surprising features about this reaction: The aryl halide does not have to contain an electron withdrawing group, and the incoming substituent does not always end up on the carbon vacated by the leaving group. For example, when chlorobenzene with the carbon to which the chlorine is attached isotopically labeled with is treated with amide ion in liquid ammonia, aniline is obtained as the product. Half of the product has the amino group attached to the isotopically labeled carbon (denoted by the asterisk) as expected, but the other half has the amino group attached to the carbon adjacent to the labeled carbon.

A: 2-chloronitrobenzene
B: 2-chloro-1,4-dinitro... (O$_2$N, Cl, NO$_2$)
C: 2-fluoro-1,4-dinitro... (O$_2$N, F, NO$_2$)

Increasing reactivity →

Nucleophilic aromatic substitution under strongly basic conditions: products proportionation

These are the only products formed. Anilines with the amino group two or three carbons removed from the labeled carbon are not formed.

The fact that the two products are formed in approximately equal amounts indicates that the reaction takes place by a mechanism that forms an intermediate in which the two carbons to which the amino group is attached in the product are equivalent. The mechanism that accounts for the experimental observations involves the formation of a **benzyne intermediate**. Benzyne has a triple bond between two adjacent carbon atoms of benzene. In the first step of the mechanism, the strong base removes a proton from the position *ortho* to the halogen. The resulting anion expels the halide ion, thereby forming benzyne.

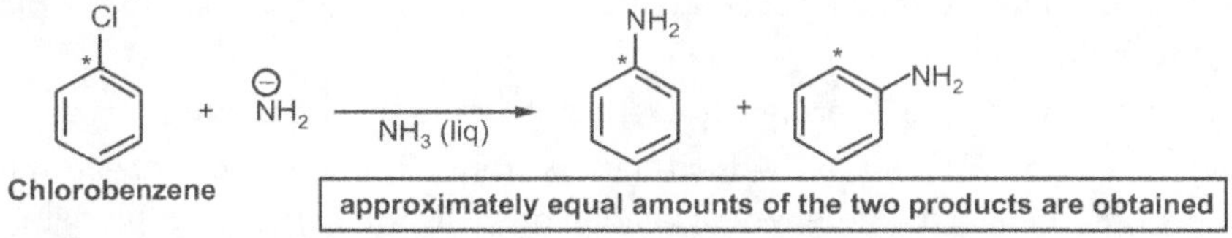

Fig. 9.15: The involvement of benzyne intermediate during nucleophilic aromatic substitution

Elimination and Addition:

The incoming nucleophile can attack either of the carbons of the "triple bond" of benzyne. Protonation of the resulting anion forms the substitution product. The overall reaction is an elimination–addition reaction: Benzene is formed in an elimination reaction and immediately undergoes an addition reaction.

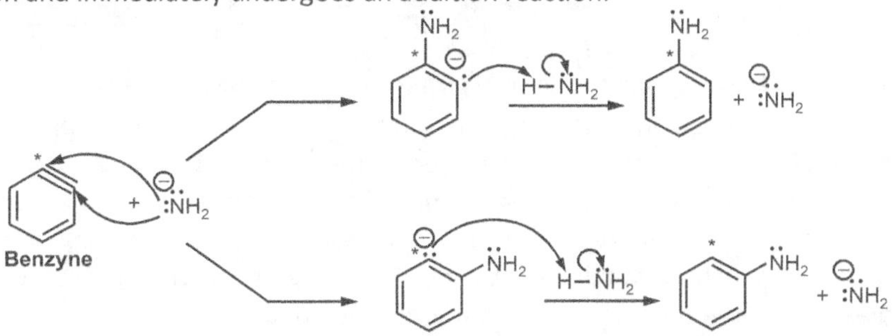

Fig. 9.16: The addition of the nucleophile (NH_2^-) to the benzyne intermediate at same (direct) or adjecant (cine) carbons

Substitution at the carbon that was attached to the leaving group is called **direct substitution**. Substitution at the adjacent carbon is called **cine substitution** (*cine* comes from *kinesis*, which is Greek word for "movement"). In the following reaction, *o*-toluidine is the direct-substitution product; *m*-toluidine is the *cine*-substitution product.

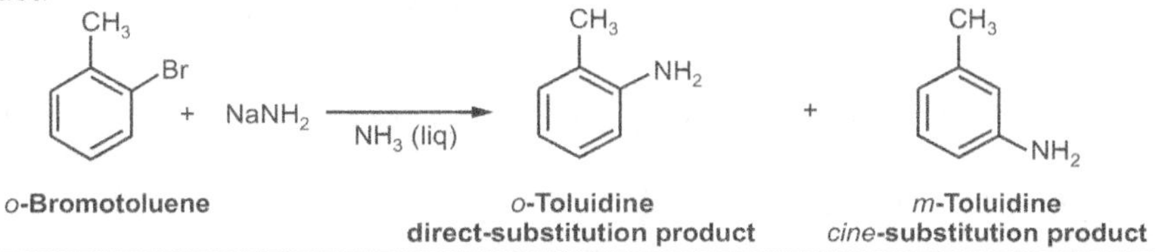

As you might expect, the triple bond in benzyne is unusual. Each carbon of the six-membered ring is sp² hybridized and as a result, the σ bond and two π bonds of the triple bond are formed with the following orbitals.

- The σ bond is formed by overlap of two sp² hybrid orbitals.
- One π bond is formed by overlap of two p orbitals perpendicular to the plane of the molecule.
- The second π bond is formed by overlap of two sp² hybrid orbitals.

Thus, the second π bond of benzene differs from all other π bonds seen thus far, because it is formed by the side-by-side overlap of sp² hybrid orbitals, not p orbitals. This π bond, located in the plane of the molecule, is extremely weak.

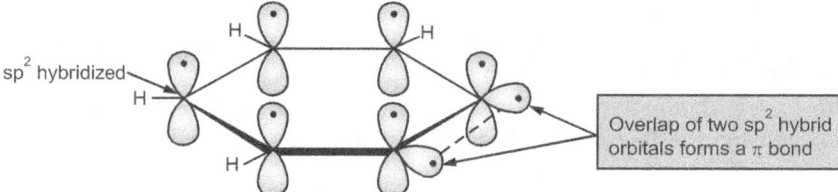

Fig. 9.17: The molecular orbital picture of the benzene intermediate

Benzyne is an extremely reactive species. In a molecule with a triple bond, the two *sp* hybridized carbons and the atoms attached to these carbons are linear because the bond angles are 180°. Four linear atoms cannot be incorporated into a six-membered ring, so the system in benzyne is distorted. The original bond is unchanged, but the orbitals that form the new bond are not parallel to one another. Therefore, they cannot overlap as well as the p orbitals that form a normal bond, resulting in a much weaker and much more reactive bond.

QUESTION BANK

1. Comment on the structure of benzene in details.
2. Comment on the stability of benzene. What is stabilization by resonance?
3. Discuss the concepts of resonance and aromaticity with suitable examples. What is meant by Hückel's (4n + 2) rule and what is the criteria for aromaticity? What is its basis? Explain with suitable examples.
4. Discuss the reactivity of benzene, the various electrophilic aromatic substitution reactions predominantly undergone by benzene with the reaction mechanism involved in each of them.

5. Discuss the orientation of electrophilic substitution in monosubstituted benzene, explaining the exact reasons for *ortho, para* and *meta* directing effects of various substituents.

6. Discuss the Nucleophilic Aromatic Substitution (SNAr) reactions of benzene derivatives and explain its mechanisms. Discuss the normal addition – elimination mechanism as well as the the elimination-addition mechanism involving the benzyne intermediate.

7. Complete the following:
   (a) Toluene $\xrightarrow{HNO_3, H_2SO_4}$

   (b) Toluene (CH$_3$) $\xrightarrow[D]{oxidation}$? $\xrightarrow{C_6H_5COCl}$

   (c) 3-bromoanisole (OCH$_3$, Br) $\xrightarrow[NH_3]{NH_2^- (NaNH_2)}$?

   (d) Benzene $\xrightarrow[H_2SO_4]{HNO_3}$?

   (e) Aniline (H$_2$N) $\xrightarrow[H_2SO_4]{HNO_3}$

8. Is benzene saturated or unsaturated? Explain properly. Comment on the bond character, bond strength and bond length of benzene.

9. Discuss the criteria for aromaticity. Are the following compounds aromatic? Explain why:
   (i) 1,3-Cyclopentadiene
   (ii) Pyrrole
   (iii) Cycloheptatrienyl cation
   (iv) Thiophene
   (v) Pyridine
   (vi) Benzene
   (vii) Naphthelene
   (viii) Anthracene
   (ix) Phenanthrene

10. Describe the mechanism of the nitration of benzene with conc. H_2SO_4 and conc. HNO_3. Enlist different nitrating reagents and add a note on effect of substituents on nitration of benzene.
11. Discuss the Friedal Craft's acylation reactions of benzene. Explain in detail the mechanism, reagents and reaction condtions.
12. Discuss the bromination of benzene and reason for the heterolytic fission of Br_2. Detail the mechanism, reagents and reaction condtions.
13. List out electron releasing groups and electron withdrawing groups. Discuss in details about the effect of substitution in electrophilic substitution of mono substituted benzenes.
14. Electrophilic aromatic substitution is more favourable than nucleophilic aromatic substitution. Comment
15. Explain the mechanism of Friedal Craft's alkylation. What is the role of nitrobenzene as well as a Lewis acid in the reaction? Why phenol and aniline do not undergo Friedal Craft's reactions.
16. Why halogens though electron withdrawing are *ortho* and *para* directors?
17. How will you prepare 4-nitrobenzophenone? Explain with proper reaction conditions.
18. Starting with simple benzene write equations and reactions conditions to prepare:
    (i) Phenol
    (ii) Benzoic acid
    (iii) Benzophenone
    (iv) Benzaldehyde
    (v) Acetophenone
    (vi) Aniline
    (vii) Toluene
    (viii) Iodobenzene
19. Explain what is diazotization and Sandmeyer's reaction. How shall you prepare aniline from the following:
    (i) Phenol
    (ii) Chorobenzene
    (iii) Iodobenzene

(iv) Bromobenzene
(v) Benzene
(vi) Benzonitrile.

Give the reaction equations, reagents and reaction conditions for each.

20. Predict the products of the following.

n-Butylbenzene reacted with hot $\xrightarrow{KMnO_4}$?

Nitrobenzene + Benzoyl chloride $\xrightarrow{AlCl_3}$

Phenol + Carbon dioxide $\xrightarrow{NaOH}$?

o-Nitrophenol + Dimethyl sulfate $\xrightarrow{NaOH}$?

21. Starting from benzene or toluene and suitable organic /inorganic regents how will you prepare the following.
    - m-Chlorobenzoic acid
    - m-Nitroanline
    - p-Toluidine
    - m-Bromotoluene
    - 2,4-Dinitrobenzoic acid
    - Sulfacetamide
    - Phenol
    - Benzaldehyde
    - N-N-Dimethylaniline
    - Salicylic acid
    - p-Bromoanline
    - Ethyl p-nitrobenzoate

22. Complete the following reactions.

(a) 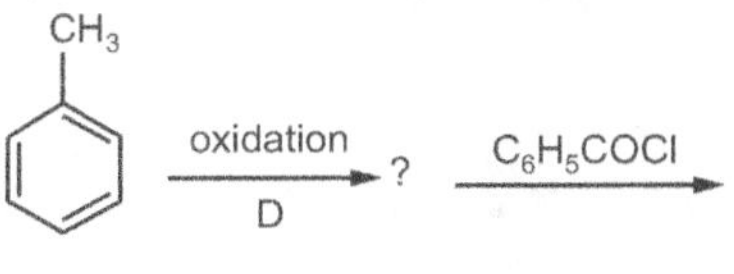 Toluene $\xrightarrow[D]{oxidation}$? $\xrightarrow{C_6H_5COCl}$

(b) 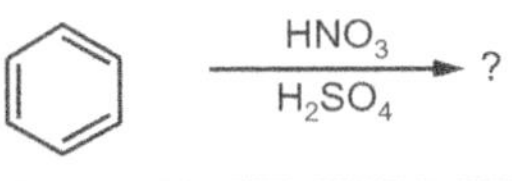 Benzene $\xrightarrow{HNO_3 / H_2SO_4}$?

(c) 3-Bromoanisole $\xrightarrow[NH_3]{NaNH_2}$?

(d) Aniline $\xrightarrow{HNO_3 / H_2SO_4}$?

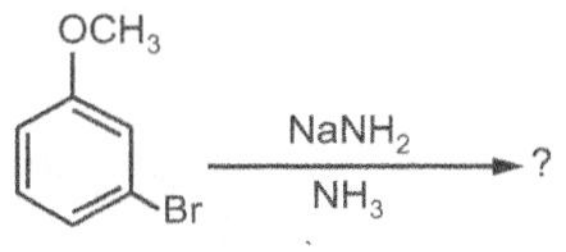

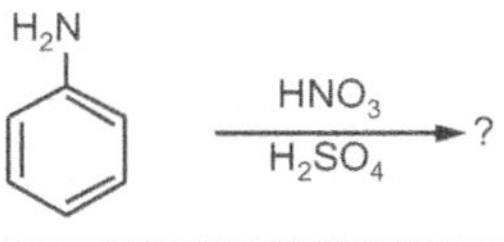

23. Draw the products of each of the reactions given below.
    (a) [F-C6H4-C(=O)-CH3 + ⁻OH →]
    (b) [2,4-dinitro-6-nitro-chlorobenzene + CH3NH2 →]

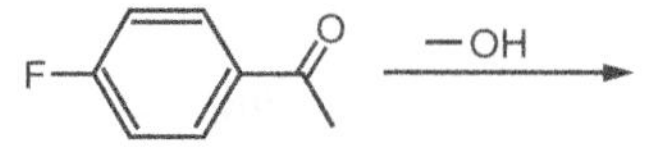

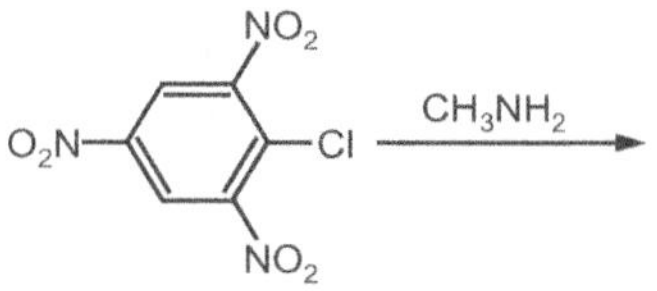

24. Rank the aryl halides in each group in order of increasing reactivity in nucleophilic aromatic substitution by an adition-elimination mechanism.
    (a) chlorobenzene, p-fluoronitrobenzene, m-fluoronitrobenzene
    (b) 1-fluoro-2, 4-dinitrobenzene, 1-fluoro-3, 5-dinitrobenzene, 1-fluoro-3, 4-dinitro-benzene.
    (c) 1-fluoro-2, 4-dinitrobenzene, 4-cholro-3-nitrotoluene, 4-fluoro-3-nitro-toluene.

25. Explain why a methoxy group (CH_3O) increases the rate of electrophilic aromatic substitution, but decreases the rate of nucleophilic aromatic substitution.

26. Draw a stepwise mechanism for the following reaction that forms ether D. This ether D can be converted to the antidepressant fluoxetine (trade name Prozac) in a single step.

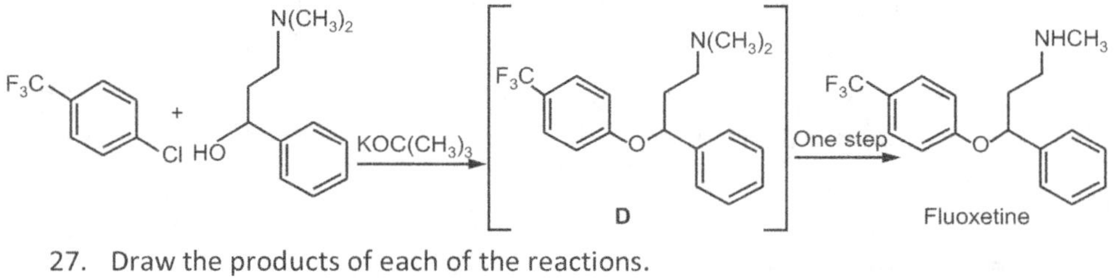

27. Draw the products of each of the reactions.
    a. [C6H5-Cl + NaNH2 / NH3 →]
    b. [CH3O-C6H4-Cl + NaOH, Δ H2O →]
    c. [o-CH3-C6H4-Cl + KNH2 / NH3 →]

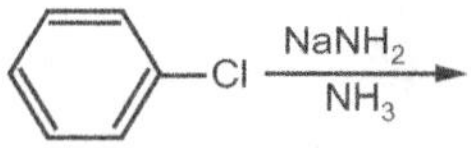

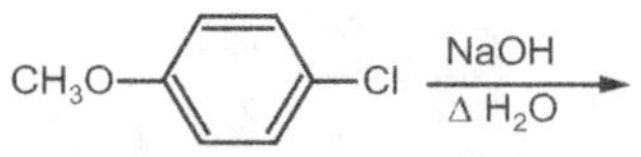

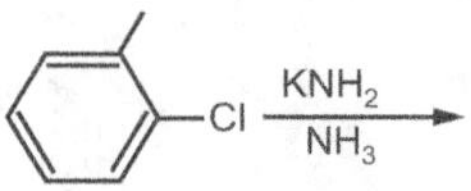

28. Draw all products formed when *m*-chlorotulene is treated with KNH$_2$ in NH$_3$.
29. Explain why 2-chloro-1,3-dimethylbenzene is inert to nucleophilic aromatic substitution by way of an elimination addition mechanism.
30. Draw a stepwise mechanism for the following reaction.

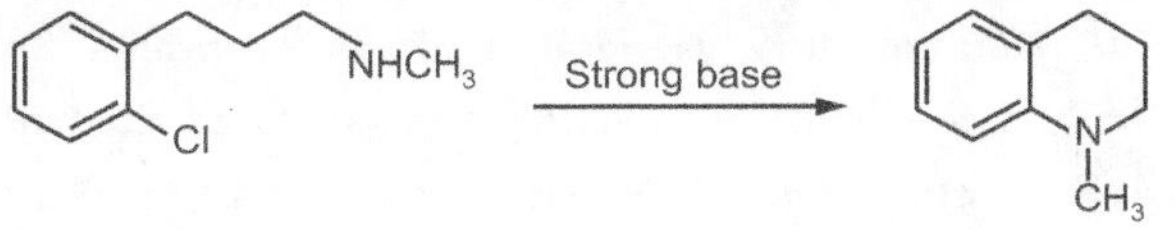

Chapter 1 ...

ALDEHYDES AND KETONES

CONTENTS

Common and IUPAC Nomenclature, General methods of preparation, Mechanism of nucleophilic addition and condensation reactions; Reactivity of aldehydes and ketones to nucleophilic addition, Acetal, Imine, Oximes, Hydrazones, Semicarbazones, Enamine preparation and uses. Addition of Grignard Reagents and hydrides, MPV reduction, Oppenaur oxidation, Aldol condensation, Cannizarro's reaction, Reformatsky reaction, Perkin reaction, Knoevenagel reaction, Haloform reaction and Mannich reaction.

IUPAC NOMENCLATURE

Introduction:

Aldehydes and ketones are organic compounds which incorporate a carbonyl functional group, C=O. The carbon atom of this group has two remaining bonds that may be occupied by hydrogen, alkyl or aryl substituents. If at least one of these substituents is hydrogen, the compound is an aldehyde. If neither is hydrogen, the compound is a ketone.

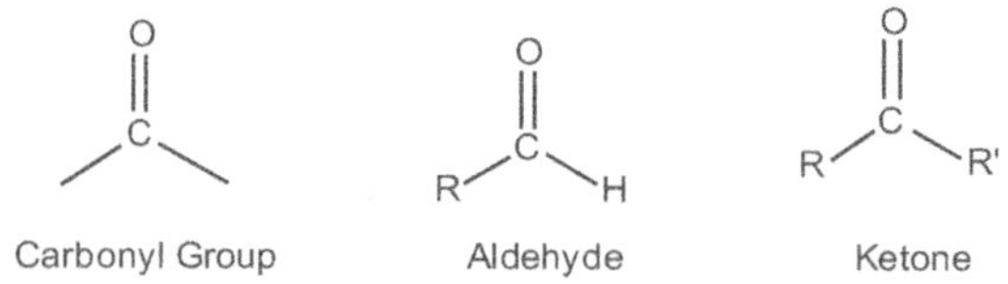

Carbonyl Group   Aldehyde   Ketone

Naming Aldehydes:

The IUPAC system of nomenclature assigns a characteristic suffix -al to aldehydes. For example, $H_2C=O$ is methanal, more commonly called formaldehyde. Since an aldehyde carbonyl group must always lie at the end of a carbon chain, it is always is given the number 1 (First) position in numbering and it is not necessary to include it in the name. There are several simple carbonyl group containing compounds which have common names, that are retained by IUPAC.

Also, there is a common method for naming aldehydes and ketones. For aldehydes common parent chain names, similar to those used for carboxylic acids, are used and the suffix aldehyde is added to the end. In common names of aldehydes, carbon atoms near the carbonyl group are often designated by greek letters. The atom adjacent to the carbonyl function is alpha, the next removed is beta and so on.

$$H_3C \overset{\delta}{-} \underset{\gamma}{\overset{H_2}{C}} - \underset{}{\overset{H_2}{C}} - \underset{\alpha}{\overset{H_2}{C}} - \overset{\beta}{\overset{O}{\underset{}{C}}} - H$$

If the aldehyde moiety R−C(=O)−H (-CHO) is attached to a ring the suffix **carbaldehyde** is added to the name of the ring. The carbon attached to this moiety will get the number 1 in naming the ring.

Summary of aldehyde nomenclature rules:
1. Aldehydes take their name from their parent alkane chains. The *-e* is removed from the end and is replaced with *-al*. The aldehyde funtional group is given the #1 numbering location and this number is not included in the name. e.g., propane → propanal.
2. For the common nomenclature of aldehydes, at starts with the common parent chain name and add the suffix *-aldehyde*. Substituent positions are shown with Greek letters. e.g., propane → propanaldehyde.
3. When the -CHO functional group is attached to a ring the suffix *-carbaldehyde* is added, and the carbon attached to that group is C_1.

The IUPAC system names are given on top while the common name is given on the bottom in parentheses.

Example:

Methanal
(Formaldehyde)

Ethanal
(Acetaldehyde)

Pentanal
(Valeraldehyde)

2-Chloropentanal

Butanal

3-Methyl butanal

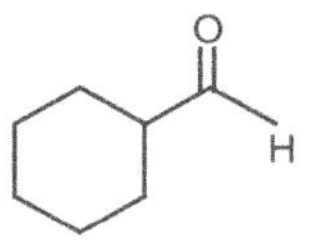

Cyclohexane carbaldehyde

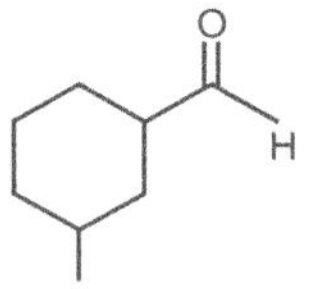

3-Methylcyclohexane carbaldehyde

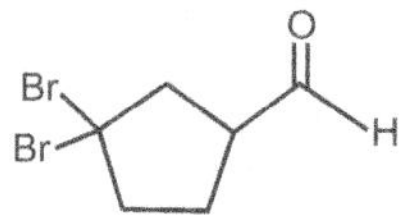

3,3-Dibromocyclopentane carbaldehyde

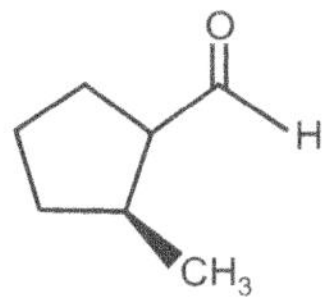

trans-2-Methylcyclopentane carbaldehyde

Naming ketones:

The IUPAC system of nomenclature assigns a characteristic suffix of -**one** to ketones. A ketone carbonyl function may be located anywhere within a chain or ring and its position is usually given by a location number. Chain numbering normally starts from the end nearest the carbonyl group. Very simple ketones, such as propanone and phenylethanone do not require a locator number, since there is only one possible site for a ketone carbonyl function.

The common names for ketones are formed by naming both alkyl groups attached to the carbonyl then adding the suffix -**ketone**. The attached alkyl groups are arranged in the name alphabetically.

Summary of ketone nomenclature rules:

1. Ketones take their name from their parent alkane chains. The ending -*e* is removed and replaced with -*one*. e.g., Butane → Butanone.

   Some applies for cyclic ketones, e.g., cyclohexane → cyclohexanone.

2. The common name for ketones are simply the **substituent groups listed alphabetically + *ketone*.** e.g., Butane → Butanone.

3. Some common ketones are known by their generic names. Such as the fact that *propanone* is commonly referred to as *acetone*, while butanone as ethylmethylketone.

Example:

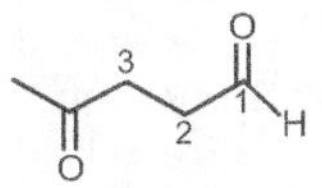

4-Oxopentanal
(3-Acetyl propionaldehyde)

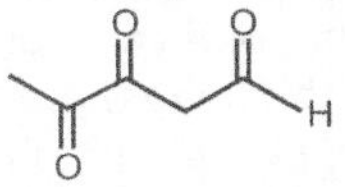

3,4-Dioxopentanal

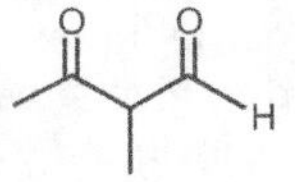

2-Methyl, 3-oxo-butanal
(2-Acetyl propionaldehyde)

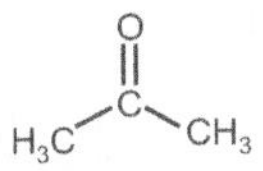

Propanone
(Acetone)

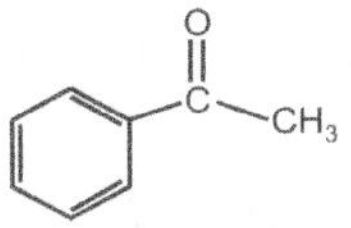

Acetophenone
(1-Phenylethanone)

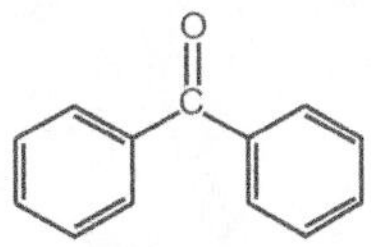

Benzophenone

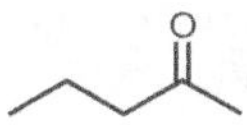

2-Pentanone
(Methyl propylketone)

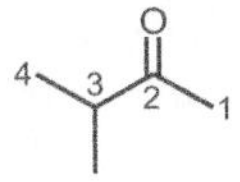

3-Methyl-2-butanone
(Methyl iso-Propylketone)

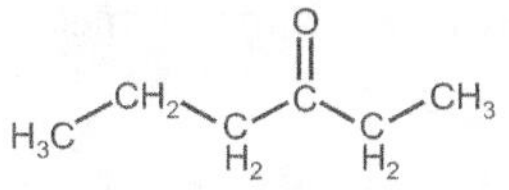

3-Hexanone
(Ethyl propylketone)

Naming aldehydes and ketones in the same molecule:

As with many molecules with two or more functional groups, one is given priority while the other is named as a substituent. Because aldehydes have a higher priority than ketones, molecules which contain both these functional groups together are named as aldehydes and the ketone is named as an **"oxo"** substituent. It is not necessary to give the aldehyde functional group a location number, however, it is usually necessary to give a location number to the ketone.

Example:

4-Oxopentanal.

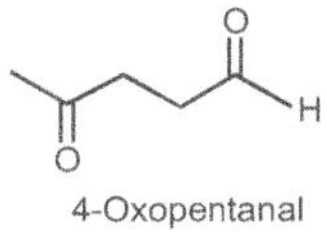

4-Oxopentanal

Example:

Naming dialdehydes and diketones:

For dialdehydes the location numbers for both carbonyls are omitted because the aldehyde functional groups are expected to occupy the ends of the parent chain. The ending –dial is added to the end of the parent chain name.

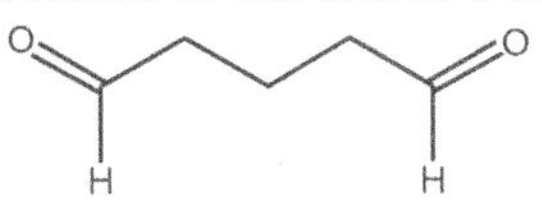

Pentanedial

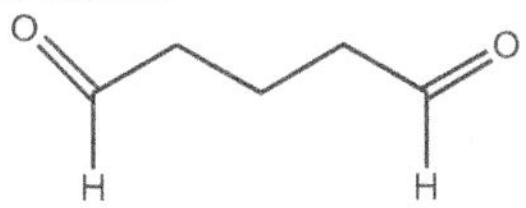

Butanedial

Naming cyclic ketones and diketones:

In cyclic ketones, the carbonyl group is assigned number 1 and this number is not included in the name, unless more than one carbonyl group is present. The rest of the ring is numbered to give substituents the lowest possible location numbers. Remember the prefix cyclo is included before the parent chain name to indicate that it is in a ring. As with other ketones the –e ending is replaced with the – one to indicate the presence of a ketone.

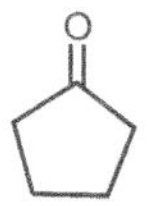

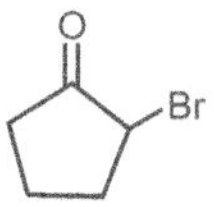

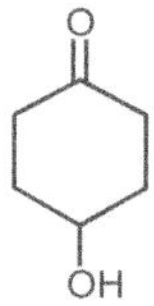

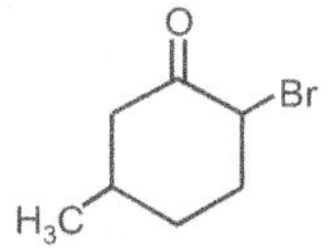

Cyclopentanone 2-Bromocyclopentanone 4-Hydroxycyclohexanone 2-Bromo-5-methylcyclopentahexanone

With cycloalkanes which contain two ketones both carbonyls need to be given a location numbers. Also, an –e is not removed from the end but the suffix –dione is added.

Additional examples of carbonyl nomenclature (IUPAC names the following compounds)

(A) 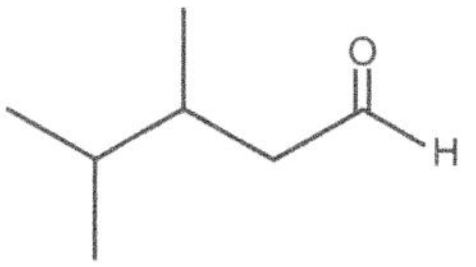 (B) 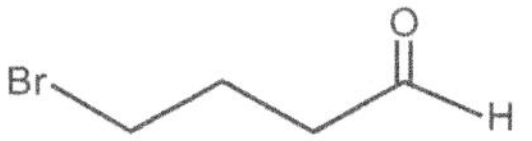 (C) 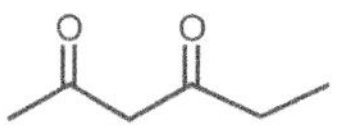 (D) 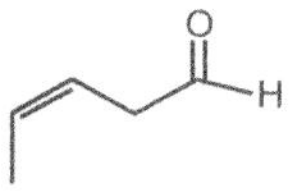 (E) 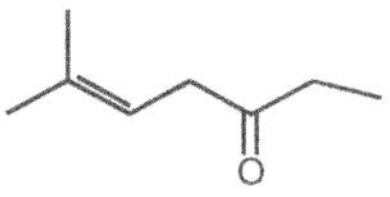 (F) 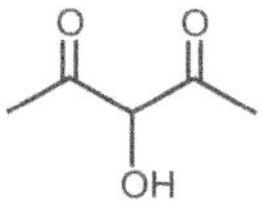 (G) 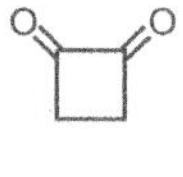 (H) 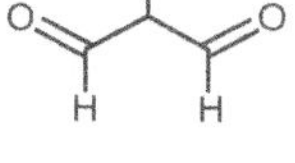 (I) 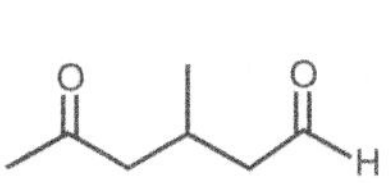 (J) 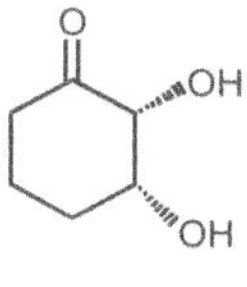 (K) 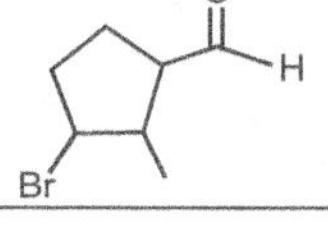 (L)

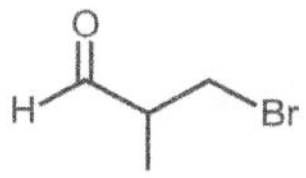

(A) 3,4-Dimethylhexanal (B) 5-Bromopentanal
(C) 2,4-Hexanedione (D) *cis*-3-Pentanal
(E) 6-Methyl-5-Hepten-3-one (F) 3-Hydroxy-2,4-Pentanedione
(G) 1,2-Cyclobutanedione (H) 2-Methyl-Propanedial
(I) 3-Methyl-5-oxo-Hexanal (J) *Cis*-2,3-Dihydroxycyclohexanone
(K) 3-Bromo-2-Methylcyclopentanecarbaldehyde
(L) 3-Bromo-2-methylpropanal

Give Structures from IUPAC names for following compounds:

(A) Butanal (B) 2-Hydroxycyclopentanone
(C) 2,3-Pentanedione (D) 1,3-Cyclohexanedione
(E) 3,4-Dihydoxy-2-butanone (F) 3-Methyl-2-hepten-4-one
(G) 3-Oxobutanal (H) *cis*-3-Bromocyclohexanecarbaldehyde
(I) Butanedial (J) 2-Methylhexanal

GENERAL METHDOS OF PREPARATION

ALDEHYDES

1. **Oxidation of 1° alcohols:**

   Oxidation of alcohols to be done under controlled condition using mild oxidizing agents, else strong oxidizing agents can convert them to carboxylic acids.

   Use of pyridinium chlorochomate ($C_6H_5 \overset{+}{N}H\ Cr\ \overset{-}{O_3}\ Cl$)

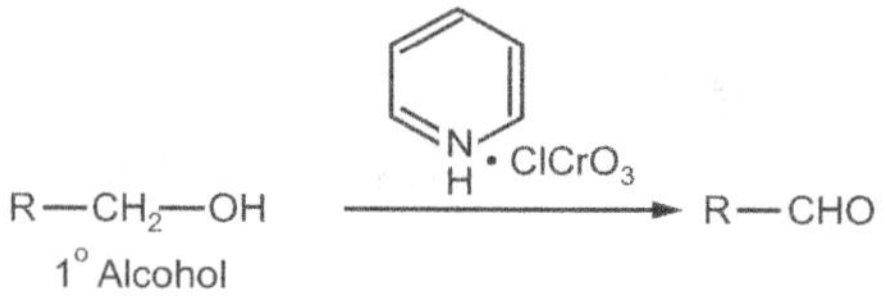

   $$R-CH_2-OH \xrightarrow{\text{ClCrO}_3 \cdot \text{pyridine}} R-CHO$$
   (1° Alcohol)

   Example:

   $$CH_3CH_2CH_2CH_2OH \xrightarrow{\text{Pyridinium chlorochromate}} CH_3CH_2CH_2CHO$$
   n-Butanol → n-Butanal

   In an inexpensive industrial method cobalt tetraoctoate is used as catalyst.

2. **Oxidation of methylbenzenes:**

   Alkyl benzenes, like toluene can be converted to benzaldehydes by use of various reagents, enlisted below:

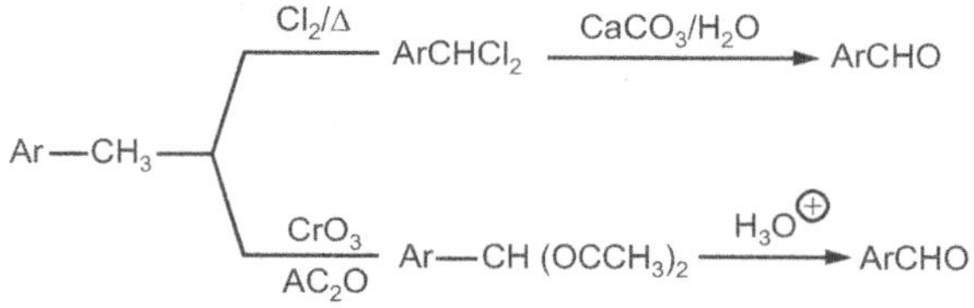

   $$Ar-CH_3 \xrightarrow{Cl_2/\Delta} ArCHCl_2 \xrightarrow{CaCO_3/H_2O} ArCHO$$

   $$Ar-CH_3 \xrightarrow[AC_2O]{CrO_3} Ar-CH(OCCH_3)_2 \xrightarrow{H_3O^{\oplus}} ArCHO$$

   The former method employs reaction with chlorine gas at high temperatures so alkyl chain chlorination occurs, the dichloromethane derivatives are hydrolysed with $CaCO_3/H_2O$ to the benzaldehyde.

   The later method uses a combination of cromic oxide-acetic anhydride, by the diacetylated derivative of the alkyl group is first formed which is hydrolysed to the benzaldehyde.

3. **Reduction of Acid chlorides:**

   $$\begin{array}{c} R-COCl \\ \text{or} \\ Ar-COCl \end{array} \xrightarrow{\text{Li AlH (t-BuO)}_3 \\ \text{(Lithium aluminium ortho ester)}} \begin{array}{c} RC-CHO \\ \text{or} \\ Ar-CHO \end{array}$$

The *tert*-butoxyorthoester of lithium aluminium hydride is a reagent which selectivity reduces alkyl or aryl acid chlorides to corresponding aldehydes.

Example:

O_2N—C$_6$H$_4$—COCl $\xrightarrow{\text{LiAlH (O}t\text{-Bu})_3}$ O_2N—C$_6$H$_4$—CHO

4. **Riemmer - Tiemann Reaction (Formylation of Phenol):**

Formylation of phenol at *ortho*-position with $CHCl_3$ in presence of strong aq. NaOH.

Phenol + $CHCl_3$ + aq NaOH $\xrightarrow[\text{70°C}]{\text{Reflux}}$ [o-O⁻-C$_6$H$_4$-CHCl$_2$ intermediate] → o-ONa-C$_6$H$_4$-CHO + p-ONa-C$_6$H$_4$-CHO (4 : 1)

$\xrightarrow{H_3O^+}$ o-hydroxybenzaldehyde + p-hydroxybenzaldehyde (4 : 1)

The *o*-isomer is more preferred as it is stabilized by intramolecular H-bonding.

(If CCl_4 instead of $CHCl_3$ is used, then salicylic acid is formed). The reaction proceeds *via* the formation of the electrophile $:CCl_2$.

$CHCl_3 + OH^- \rightleftharpoons H_2O + :\bar{C}Cl_3 \longrightarrow :CCl_2 + Cl^\ominus$

Dichlorocarbene

[Mechanism: phenoxide + :CCl$_2$ → intermediate → keto form with CCl$_2$ → $\xrightarrow{H_2O}$ salicylaldehyde (o-OH-C$_6$H$_4$-CHO)]

5. Vilsmeir Haack Formylation:

The combination of dimethylformamide / diphenylformamide with $POCl_3$ is called as Vilsmer Haack reagent, and serves as good formylating agent.

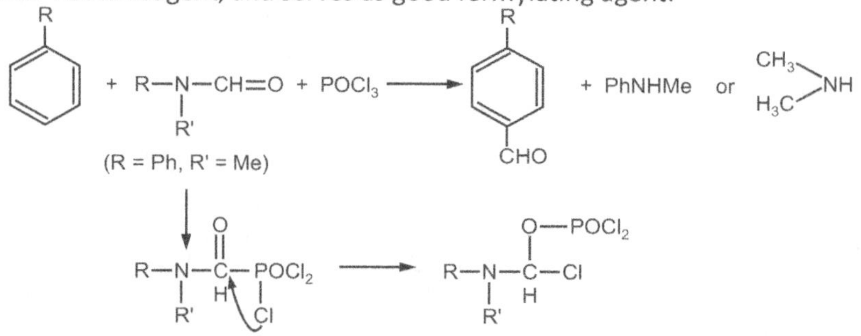

PhC$_6$H$_5$ + R—N(R')—CH=O + $POCl_3$ ⟶ R-C$_6$H$_4$-CHO + PhNHMe or $(CH_3)(H_3C)NH$

(R = Ph, R' = Me)

Intermediate: R—N(R')(H)—C(=O)—$POCl_2$ with Cl ⟶ R—N(R')(H)—C(—Cl)(O—$POCl_2$)

Vilsmeir haack reagent

KETONES

1. Oxidation of 2° alcohols:

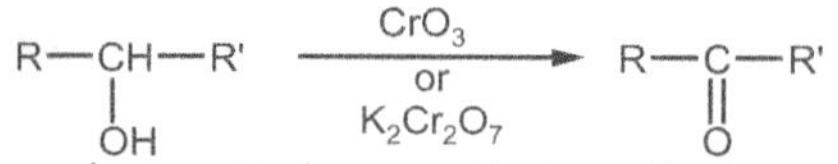

$$R\text{—CH(OH)—}R' \xrightarrow[\text{or } K_2Cr_2O_7]{CrO_3} R\text{—C(=O)—}R'$$

As 2° alcohols contain only 1 α-Hydrogen, their oxidation leads to ketone and stops there only. Carboxylic acids are not formed. This is fairly straight forward reactions.

2. Friedal-crafts Acylation (Use of Acylchlorides):

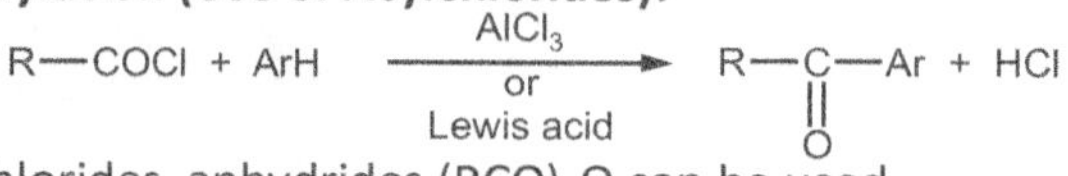

$$R\text{—COCl} + ArH \xrightarrow[\text{Lewis acid}]{AlCl_3 \text{ or}} R\text{—C(=O)—}Ar + HCl$$

Instead of acylchlorides, anhydrides $(RCO)_2O$ can be used

Mechanism:

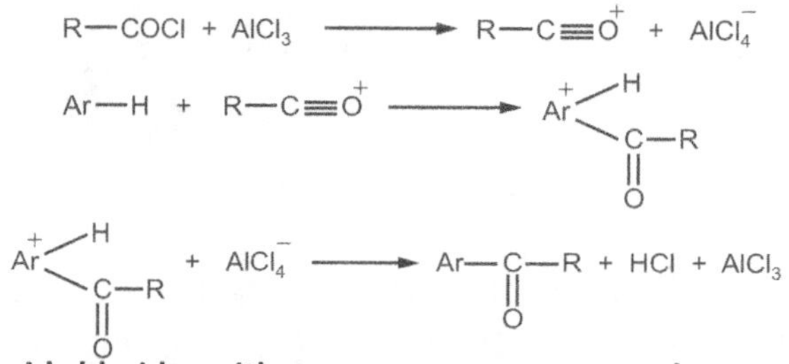

$$R\text{—COCl} + AlCl_3 \longrightarrow R\text{—C}\equiv\overset{+}{O} + AlCl_4^-$$

$$Ar\text{—H} + R\text{—C}\equiv\overset{+}{O} \longrightarrow Ar\overset{+}{\underset{C(=O)R}{\diagdown}}H$$

$$Ar\overset{+}{\underset{C(=O)R}{\diagdown}}H + AlCl_4^- \longrightarrow Ar\text{—C(=O)—}R + HCl + AlCl_3$$

3. Reduction of acid chlorides with organo copper compounds:

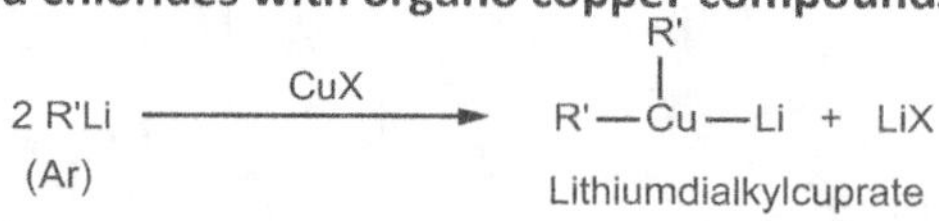

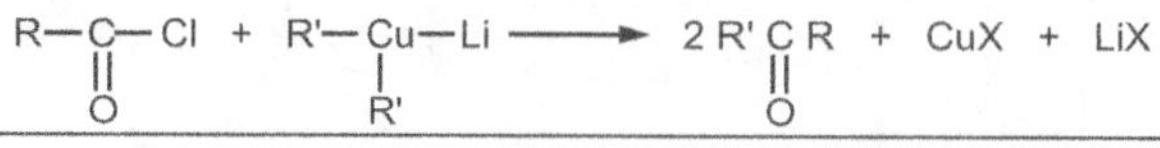

$$2\ R'Li\ (Ar) \xrightarrow{CuX} R'\text{—Cu(R')—Li} + LiX$$

Lithiumdialkylcuprate

$$R\text{—C(=O)—Cl} + R'\text{—Cu(R')—Li} \longrightarrow 2\ R'CR(=O) + CuX + LiX$$

Here, R' group is the nucleophile. Thus,

$$2\ R-\overset{\delta+}{\underset{O\delta-}{C}}\overset{Cl\delta-}{\diagdown} \quad R'-\underset{\delta-}{Cu}-\underset{\delta+}{Li} \longrightarrow 2\ \underset{O}{\overset{R\ \ \ R'}{Y}} + CuX + LiX$$

For example,

$$2\ NO_2-\underset{O}{\overset{}{\bigcirc}}-\overset{}{\underset{O}{C}}-Cl + CH_3-\overset{CH_3}{\underset{}{Cu}}-Li \longrightarrow 2\ NO_2-\bigcirc-\underset{O}{\overset{}{C}}-CH_3 + CuX + LiX$$

4. Acetoacetic ester synthesis of ketones (use of ethyl acetoacetate to ketones):

1. The acetoacetate ester is first converted to it Na salt by action to alkoxide

$$CH_3COCH_2-COOC_2H_5 + NaOC_2H_5 \longrightarrow CH_3\ CO-\overset{Na^+}{\underset{}{\overset{\ominus}{CH}}}-COOC_2H_5 + C_2H_5OH$$

2. This sodium salt is then treated with an alkyl halide.

$$CH_3\ CO\ \underset{Na^+}{\overset{\ominus}{CH}}\ COOC_2H_5 + RX \longrightarrow CH_3\ COCH-COOC_2H_5$$
$$\phantom{CH_3\ CO\ \overset{\ominus}{CH}\ COOC_2H_5 + RX \longrightarrow CH_3\ COCH-COOC_2H_5}|$$
$$\phantom{CH_3\ CO\ \overset{\ominus}{CH}\ COOC_2H_5 + RX \longrightarrow CH_3\ COCH-COOC_2H_5}R$$
Mono alkyl acetoacetate

3. Subsequent hydrolysis yields corresponding acid

$$CH_3\ COCH-COOC_2H_5 \xrightarrow[OH^-/H_2O]{H_3\overset{+}{O}\ or} CH_3COCH-COOH$$
$$|\phantom{CH_3\ COCH-COOC_2H_5 \xrightarrow[OH^-/H_2O]{H_3O\ or}}|$$
$$R\phantom{CH_3\ COCH-COOC_2H_5 \xrightarrow[OH^-/H_2O]{H_3O\ or}}R$$

4. The last step involves decarboxylation to the final ketone.

$$CH_3COCH-COOH \xrightarrow[-CO_2]{\Delta} CH_3COCH_2$$
$$|\phantom{CH_3COCH-COOH \xrightarrow[-CO_2]{\Delta}}|$$
$$R\phantom{CH_3COCH-COOH \xrightarrow[-CO_2]{\Delta}}R$$

Mechanism of nucleophilic addition and condensation reactions:

The general form of the nucleophilic addition to carbonyl group mechanism is as follows:

$$\underset{Nu:}{\overset{O}{\underset{}{\overset{\|}{\underset{\delta+}{C}}}}} \longrightarrow \underset{Nu}{\overset{\overset{..}{O}^-}{\underset{}{C}}} \xrightarrow{H^+} \underset{Nu}{\overset{\overset{..}{O}H}{\underset{}{C}}}$$

First step is the attack of the nucleophile on the partially positive carbon to make the tetrahedral intermediate with the full negatively charged oxygen. The oxygen then gets protonated to yield the alcohol.

Variety of nucleophiles:
- Grignard reagents
- Alcohols
- Amines
- Alkyl lithium reagents
- Acetylide ions

Example of nucleophilic addition to carbonyl groups:

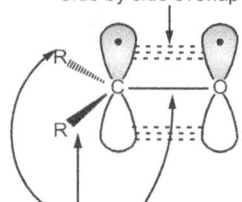

In this case, acetylide anion is acting as the nucleophile.

Reactivity of aldehydes and ketones to nucleophilic addition:

Before we consider in detail the reactivity of aldehydes and ketones, let us study the chemistry of carbonyl group. Carbonyl carbons are sp^2 hybridized, with the three sp^2 orbitals forming 's' overlaps with orbitals on the oxygen and on the two carbon or hydrogen atoms. These three bonds adopt trigonal planar geometry. The remaining unhybridized '2p' orbital on the central carbonyl carbon is perpendicular to this plane, and forms a 'side-by-side' pi-bond with a 2p orbital on the oxygen.

Side by side overlap 'pi' bond

's' overlaps with trigonal planar geometry

The carbon-oxygen double bond is polar: (Recall: Oxygen is more electronegative than carbon), so electron density is higher on the oxygen (more electronegative) side of the bond and lower on the carbon side. As the bond polarity can be represented with a dipole arrow, or by showing the oxygen as holding a partial negative charge and the carbonyl carbon a partial positive charge.

(A)   (B)   Major (I)   Minor (II)

Another way to illustrate the carbon-oxygen dipole is to consider the two main resonance contributors of a carbonyl group: the major form, which is typically drawn in Lewis structures (I), and a minor but very important contributor (II) in which both electrons in the 'pi' bond are localized on the oxygen, giving it a full negative charge where the carbon with an empty *2p* orbital represents a full positive charge.

This results into polarization of carbonyl bond (C=O). The carbon, because it is electron deficient, is an electrophilic and is a target for attack by an electron-rich nucleophilic group or nucleophile *(Recall: Nucleophiles are attaching at electron deficient or electrophilic nucleus)*. Because the oxygen end of the carbonyl double bond bears a partial negative charge (**A**), anything that can help to stabilize this charge by accepting some of the electron density will increase the bond's polarity and make the carbon more electrophilic. An acid group serves this purpose, donating a proton to the carbonyl oxygen. The same effect can also be achieved if a Lewis acid, such as a magnesium ion, is located near the carbonyl oxygen.

Carbon becomes more electrophilic

Unlike the situation in a nucleophilic substitution reaction, when a nucleophile attacks an aldehyde or ketone carbon there is no leaving group – the incoming nucleophile simply 'pushes' the electrons in the pi bond up to the oxygen.

Attack I

Similarly considering the minor resonance contributor (II), an attack by a nucleophile on a carbocation (Recall: carbon containing positive charge is known as carbocation).

Attack II

After the carbonyl carbon is attacked by the nucleophile (as in above **attack I** and **attack II**), the negatively charged oxygen has the capacity to act as a nucleophile. In most cases, this negatively charged oxygen acts as a base (Recall: base is a proton acceptor), abstracting a proton from an acid.

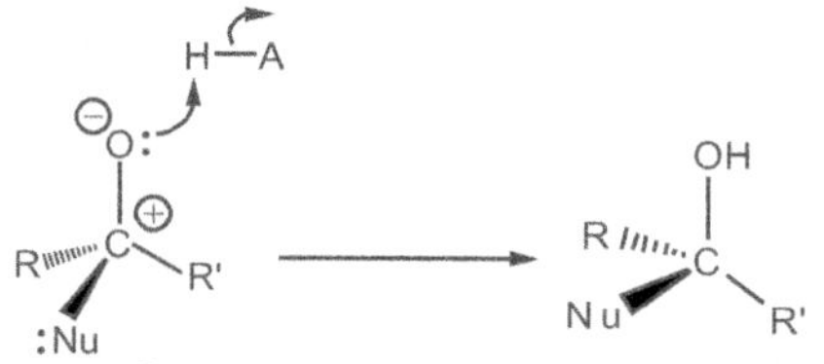

This is very common type of reaction is called a **nucleophilic addition** (a nucleophile is being added to carbonyl carbon, and a proton or electrophile to carbonyl oxygen). In many biologically relevant examples of nucleophilic addition to carbonyls or carbonyl carbon, the nucleophile is an alcohol oxygen or an amine nitrogen, or occasionally a thiol sulfur.

ACETAL-PREPARATION AND USES / ADDITION OF ALCOHOLS TO C=O

An acetal is a functional group with connectivity $R_2C(OR')_2$, where both R and R' are alkyl groups. The central carbon atom has four bonds to it, and is therefore saturated and has tetrahedral geometry. The two OR' groups may be equivalent to each other or not. If the two OR, groups are equivalent to each other (known as "symmetric acetal") or not (known a "mixed acetal"). The R groups can also be hydrogen atoms rather than organic fragments. Acetals are formed from carbonyl campounds (i.e., aldehydes and ketones) and also convertible to carbonyl compounds (aldehydes or ketones). The term ketal is used when both 'R' groups are alkyl, while it is acetal, when one of the R groups is a hydrogen.

Preparation of acetals:

Alcohols add to aldehydes and ketones in the presence of specific acid-catalysts to yield "acetals" *via* intermediate formation of "hemiacetals". Acetals are 1,1-diethers and hemiacetals are α-hydroxyethers (i.e., half acetals).

Example:

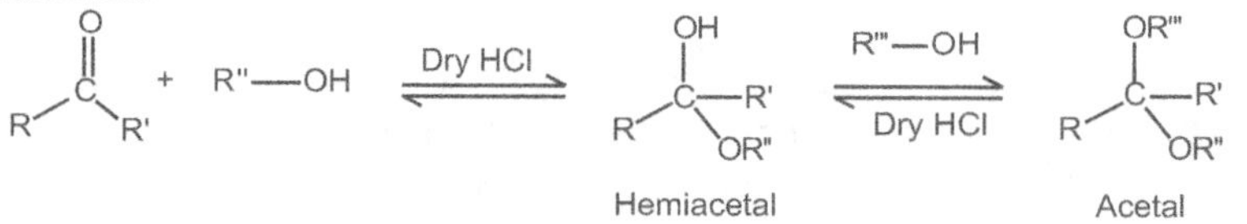

Hemiacetal Acetal

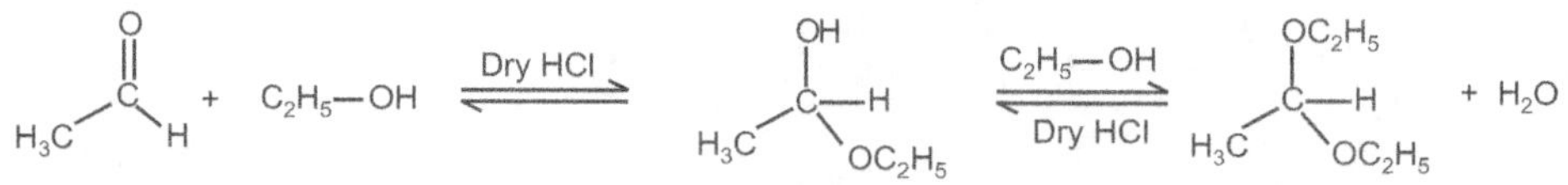

Acetaldehyde Acetaldehyde Hemiacetal Acetal

Usually aldehydes undergo the acetal formation reaction readily since, the equilibrium lies to right at room temperature.

Both aldehydes and ketones react with 1,2- and 1,3-diols to form cylic acetals.

Mechanism for acid catalyzed preparation of acetals:

- **Step 1:** Protonation of the carbonyl group to enhance the electrophilicity of the carbonyl carbon.
- **Step 2:** This is followed by the nucleophilic addition of alcohol to the carbonyl carbon.
- **Step 3:** An acid/base reaction. Deprotonation of the alcoholic oxonium ion neutralizes the charge giving the hemi-acetal. Now we need to substitute the -OH by -OEt. The unstable oxonium ion thus formed is deprotonated by the base and stabilized.
- **Step 4:** An acid/base reaction. In order for the -OH to leave we need to make it into a better leaving group by protonation. The alcoholic OH is again protonated.
- **Step 5:** Using the electrons from the other O, the leaving group departure is facilitated. The loss of water molecule is followed.
- **Step 6:** We now have what resembles a protonated ketone (compare with step 2). The nucleophilic O of the alcohol attacks the electrophilic C and the electrons of the pi bond move to neutralize the charge on the positive O.
- **Step 7:** An acid/base reaction. Deprotonation of the alcoholic oxonium neutralizes the charge and produces the acetal product and regenerates the acid catalyst.

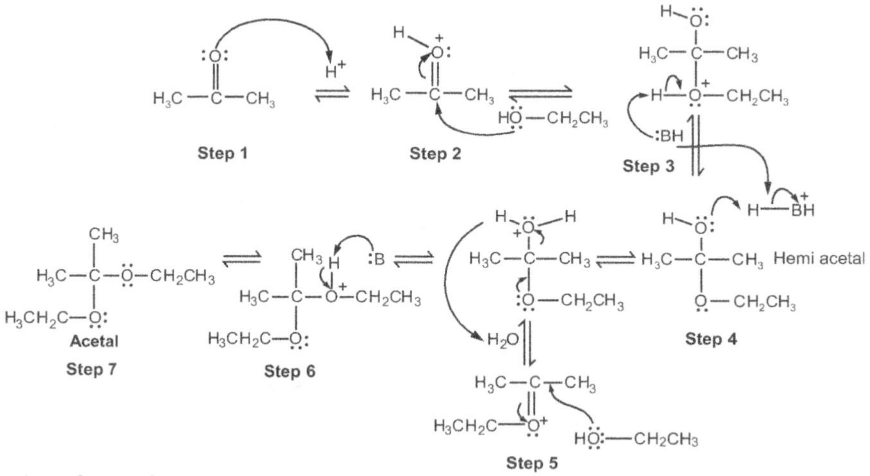

[Mechanism diagram showing Steps 1-7 for acetal formation from acetone and ethanol, proceeding through protonation, nucleophilic addition, proton transfer, loss of water, and second ethanol addition to give the acetal.]

Examples of Acetals:

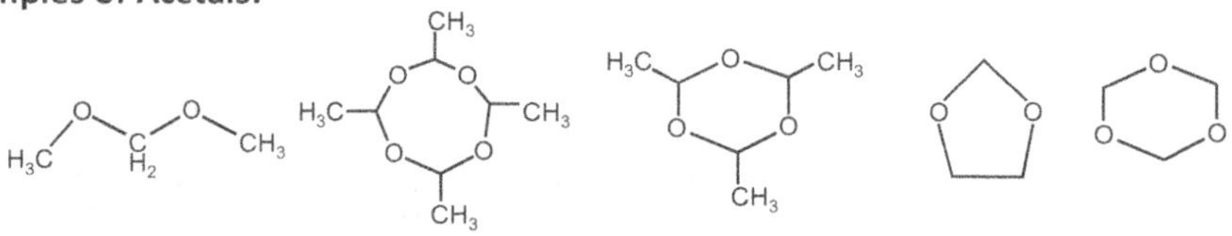

Dimethoxymethane   Metaldehyde   Paraldehyde   Dioxolane   1,3,5-Trioxane

Additions of derivatives of Ammonia:

General reaction: Certain ammonia derivatives form adducts with aldehydes/ketones under acidic conditions.

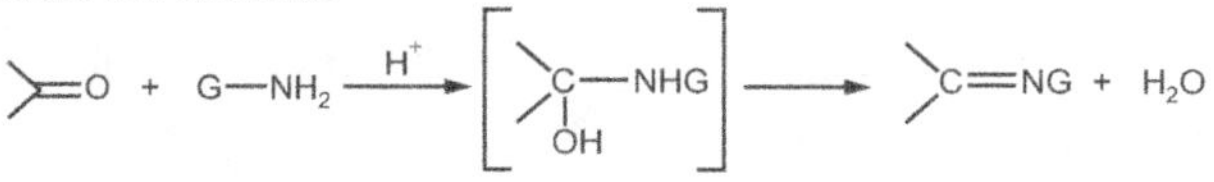

$$\text{>C=O} + \text{G—NH}_2 \xrightarrow{H^+} \left[\text{>C(OH)—NHG} \right] \longrightarrow \text{>C=NG} + H_2O$$

G-NH$_2$

1. If G = OH;   HO—NH$_2$—H   >C = N—OH
                Hydroxylamine   Oxime

     G = NH$_2$; NH$_2$—NH$_2$ >C = N—NH$_2$
                Hydrazine   Hydrazone

     G = NHPh;   PhNH—NH$_2$ >C = N—NHPh
                Phenyl hydrazine   Phenyl hydrazone

     G = NH CONH$_2$; NH$_2$CONHNH$_2$ >C = N—NH CONH$_2$
                        Semicarbazide   Semicarbazone

The adducts are crystalline solids with distinct melting points and are useful for characterization of aldehydes and ketones. All the products are basic in nature. They can be further stabilized to their HCl salts.

OXIMES-PREPARATION AND USES / ADDITION OF HYDROXYLAMINE TO C=O

An oxime is a chemical compound belonging to the imines, with the general formula $R_1R_2C=NOH$, where R_1 is an alkyl side chain and R_2 may be alkyl (ketoxime) or hydrogen (an aldoxime). Amidoximes are oximes of amides with general structure

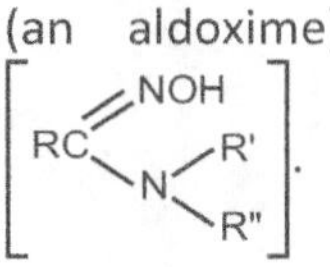

$$\left[RC\diagup^{NOH}_{\diagdown N\diagup^{R'}_{\diagdown R''}} \right].$$

Oximes are usually generated by the reaction of hydroxylamine and aldehydes or ketones. The term oxime dates back to the 19th century, a portmanteau of the words oxygen and imine.

Preparation of oximes:

Aldehydes and ketones react with hydroxylamine to yield oximes. The condensation of aldehydes with hydroxylamine gives aldoxime, similarly ketones and hydroxylamine gives ketoxime.

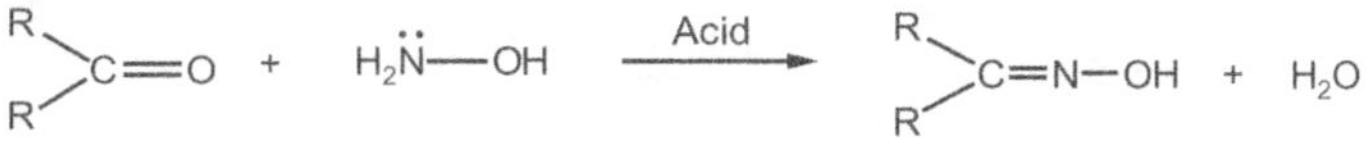

$$R_2C=O + H_2\ddot{N}-OH \xrightarrow{Acid} R_2C=N-OH + H_2O$$

An oxime

Oximes can also be obtained from reaction of nitrites such as isoamyl nitrite with compounds containing an acidic hydrogen atom. Examples are the reaction of ethyl acetoacetate and sodium nitrite in acetic acid, the reaction of methyl ethyl ketone with ethyl nitrite in hydrochloric acid and a similar reaction with propiophenone, the reaction of phenacyl chloride, the reaction of malononitrile with sodium nitrite in acetic acid.

The reaction begins with nucleophilic addition (by hydroxylamine-**II**) to the carbonyl group (**I**).

The addition product (**III**) is then protonated (**IV**) and dehydrated to give (**V**) which is then further depronated to give oxime (**VI**).

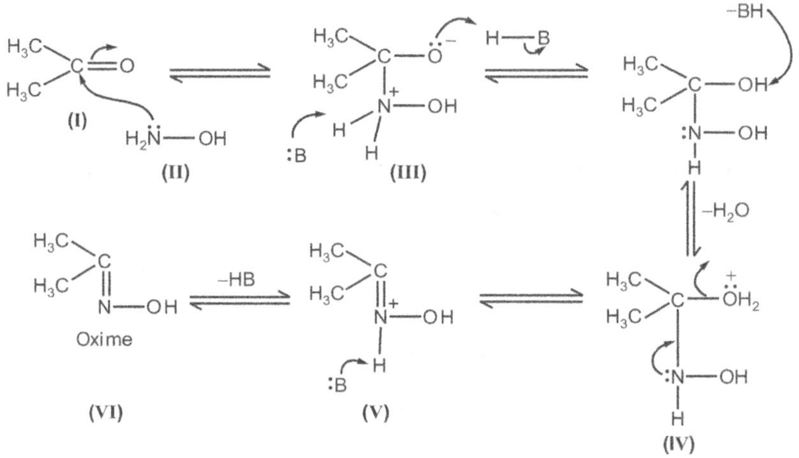

IMINE-FORMATION AND USES / ADDITION OF AMINE TO C=O

An imine is a functional group or chemical compound containing a carbon–nitrogen double bond, with the nitrogen attached to a hydrogen atom (H) or an organic group (R). If this group is not a hydrogen atom, then the compound can be referred to as a Schiff base. The carbon has two additional single bonds.

Formation of imine:

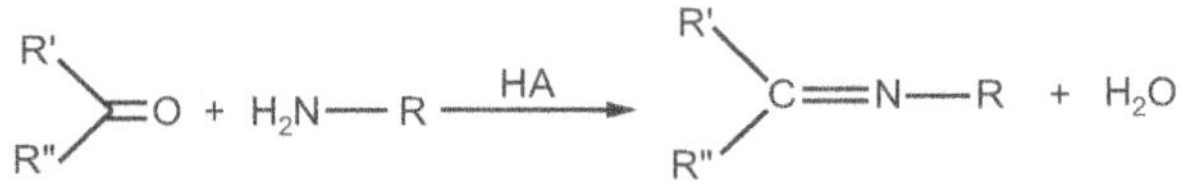

$$R'R''C=O + H_2N-R \xrightarrow{HA} R'R''C=N-R + H_2O$$

An Imine

Mechanism for formation of imine:

Formation of hydrazone is an acid catalyzed reaction and it involves the following steps:

Step I: Nucleophilic attack of amine (I) on carbonyl carbon (II) leading to formation of intermediate (III).

Step II: Protonation and further removal of water molecule (dehydration) of intermediate (III) by an acid (HA) gives (IV) containing a C=N.

Step III: Involves further deprotonation of (IV) by base (A:⁻ formed in step II) leading to the formation of Imine (V).

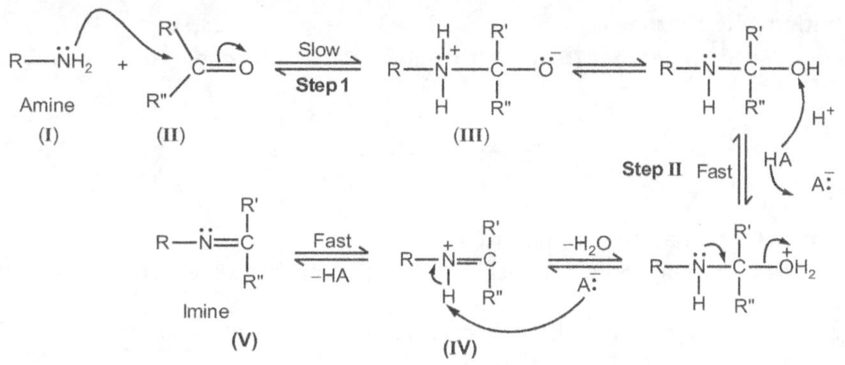

Uses of Imines:

Imines upon *hydrolysis* converts to the corresponding *amine* and *carbonyl* compound. Imines involved in the following reactions:

- An imine reacts with an *amine* to give an *aminal*, for example, the synthesis of *cucurbituril*.
- An imine reacts with *dienes* in the *Aza Diels-Alder reaction* to yield a tetrahydropyridine.
- An imine can be oxidized with *meta-chloroperoxybenzoic acid* (*m*-CPBA) to give an *oxaziridine*.
- An aromatic imine reacts with an *enol ether* to yield a *quinoline* in the *Povarov reaction*.
- A *tosylimine* reacts with an *α, β-unsaturated carbonyl compound* to yield an *allylic amine* in the *Aza-Baylis–Hillman reaction*.
- Imines are intermediates in the alkylation of amines with formic acid in the *Eschweiler-Clarke reaction*.
- A rearrangement in carbohydrate chemistry involving an imine is the *Amadori rearrangement*.
- A methylene transfer reaction of an imine by an unstabilised sulphonium *ylide* can give an *aziridine* system.
- An imine is an intermediate in *reductive amination*.

HYDRAZONES-FORMATION AND USES / ADDITION OF HYDRAZINES TO C=O

Hydrazones are a class of organic compounds with structure $R_1R_2C=NNNH_2$. They are related to ketones and aldehydes by the replacement of the oxygen with two functional groups.

Preparation of Hydrazones:

Aldehydes and ketones react with substituted hydrazines to yield substituted *hydrazones*.

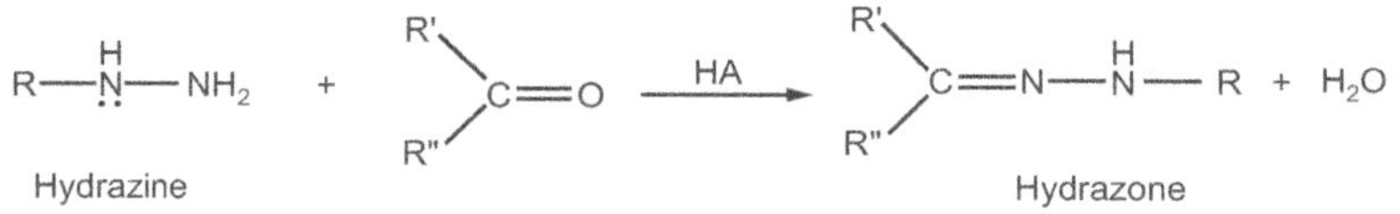

$$R-\overset{H}{\underset{..}{N}}-NH_2 + \underset{R''}{\overset{R'}{>}}C=O \xrightarrow{HA} \underset{R''}{\overset{R'}{>}}C=N-\overset{H}{\underset{}{N}}-R + H_2O$$

Hydrazine   Hydrazone

Mechanism for preparation of hydrazones:

Formation of hydrazone is an acid catalyzed reaction and it involves the following steps:

Step I: Nucleophilic attack of hydrazine (I) on carbonyl carbon (II) leading to formation of intermediate (III).

Step II: Protonation and further removal of water molecule (dehydration) of intermediate (III) by an acid (HA) gives (IV) containing a C=N system or bond.

Step III: Involves further deprotonation of (IV) by base (A:⁻ formed in step II) which leads to formation of hydrazone (V).

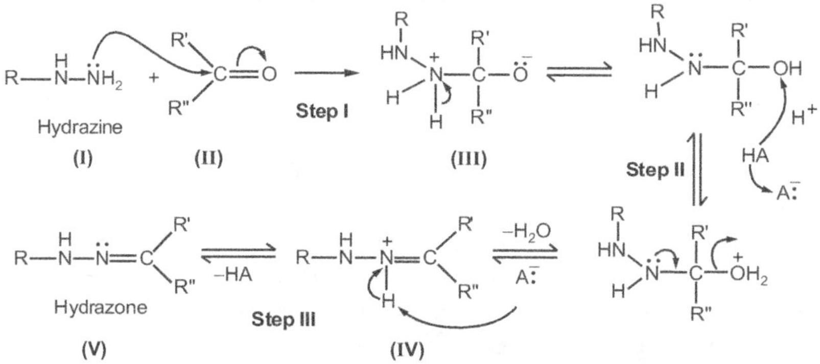

Uses of hydrazones:

Aromatic hydrozone derivatives are used to measure the concentration of low molecular weight aldehydes and ketones, e.g., in gas streams. For example: dinitrophenylhydrazine coated onto silica sorbent is the basis of adsorption of cartridge.

SEMICARBAZONES-PREPARATION AND USES / ADDITION OF SEMICARBAZIDES TO C=O

A semicarbazone is a derivative of imines formed by a condensation reaction between a ketone or aldehyde and semicarbazide. They are classified as imine derivatives because they are formed from the reaction of an aldehyde or ketone with the terminal -NH$_2$ group of semicarbazide, which behaves very similar to primary amines.

For example, the semicarbazone of acetone would have the structure $(CH_3)_2C=NNHC(=O)NH_2$.

A thiosemicarbazone is an analogue of a semicarbazone, which contains a sulfur atom in place of the oxygen atom.

Preparation of semicarbazone:

From ketones:

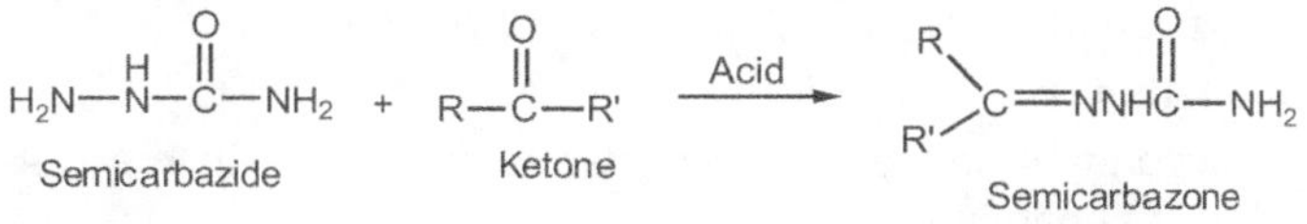

$$H_2N-NH-C(=O)-NH_2 + R-C(=O)-R' \xrightarrow{Acid} \underset{R'}{\overset{R}{>}}C=NNHC(=O)-NH_2$$

Semicarbazide + Ketone → Semicarbazone

From aldehydes:

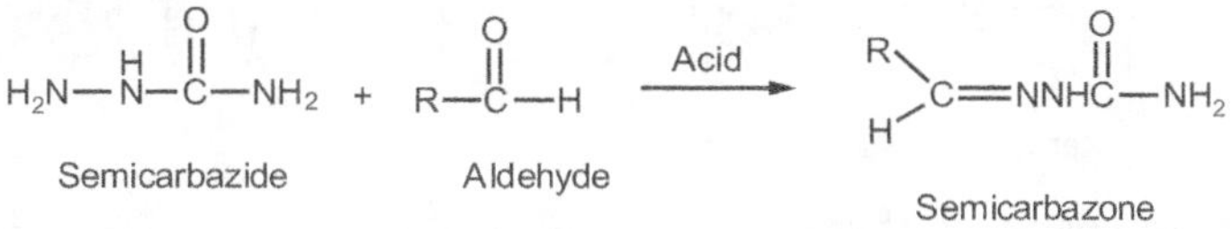

$$H_2N-NH-C(=O)-NH_2 + R-C(=O)-H \xrightarrow{Acid} \underset{H}{\overset{R}{>}}C=NNHC(=O)-NH_2$$

Semicarbazide + Aldehyde → Semicarbazone

Mechanism for preparation of semicarbazone:

Formation of semicarbazones is an acid catalyzed reaction which involves the following steps:

Step I: Nucleophilic attack of the semicarbazide (I) on carbonyl carbon of ketone (II) leading to formation of intermediate (III).

Step II: Protonation and further removal of water molecule (dehydration) of intermediate (III) by an acid (HA) to yield (IV) containing a C=N.

Step III: Involves further deprotonation of (IV) by base (A:⁻ formed in step II) leading to the formation of semicarbazone (V).

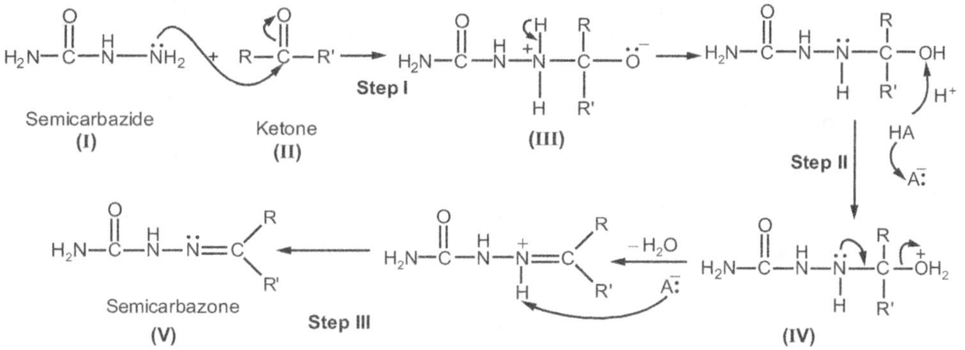

ENAMINES-PREPARATION AND USES / ADDITION OF SECONDARY AMINES TO C=O

Enamines are considered to be nitrogen analogs of enols. The word "enamine" is derived from "en-" (an alkene) and "amine" similar to "enol", which is a functional group containing both alkene (en-) and alcohol (-ol).

If one of the nitrogen substituents is a hydrogen atom, H, it is the tautomeric form of an imine. Enamines are both good nucleophiles and good bases.

Preparation of enamines:

Reaction of secondary amines with aldehydes or ketones in the presence of acid (acid catalyzed) yields enamines.

Mechanism for preparation of Enamine:

Formation of enamines is an acid catalyzed reaction which involves the following steps:

- **Step I:** Nucleophilic attack of secondary amine (I) on carbonyl carbon of (II), leading to formation of intermediate (III).
- **Step II:** Protonation and further removal of water molecule (dehydration) of intermediate (III) by an acid (HA) to give (IV), containing a C=N bond.
- **Step III:** Involves further deprotonation of IV, by base (A: formed in step II) leads to formation of semicarbazone (V).

REACTIONS OF ALDEHYDES AND KETONES

1. **Addition of Grignard Reagent:**

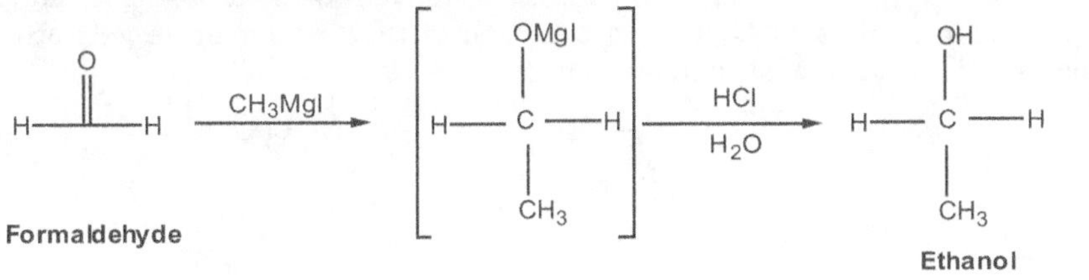

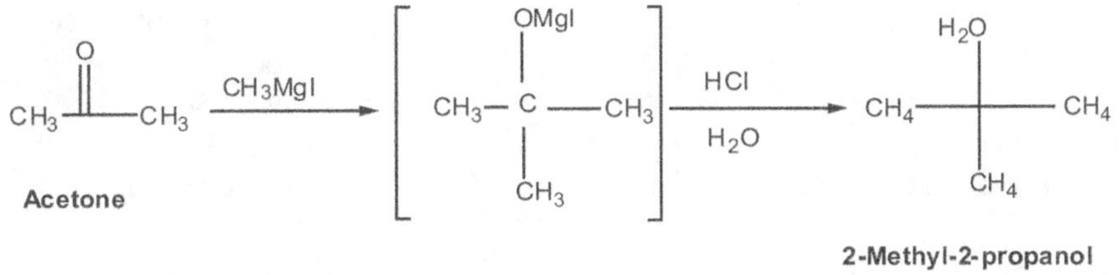

Formaldehyde + CH₃MgI → [intermediate with OMgI] → HCl/H₂O → Ethanol

$$H-CHO \xrightarrow{CH_3MgI} \left[H-\underset{CH_3}{\underset{|}{\overset{OMgI}{\overset{|}{C}}}}-H \right] \xrightarrow{HCl / H_2O} H-\underset{CH_3}{\underset{|}{\overset{OH}{\overset{|}{C}}}}-H$$

Formaldehyde → Ethanol

$$CH_3-CO-CH_3 \xrightarrow{CH_3MgI} \left[CH_3-\underset{CH_3}{\underset{|}{\overset{OMgI}{\overset{|}{C}}}}-CH_3 \right] \xrightarrow{HCl / H_2O} CH_4-\underset{CH_4}{\underset{|}{\overset{H_2O}{\overset{|}{}}}}-CH_4$$

Acetone → 2-Methyl-2-propanol

Alcohols are prepared from aldehyde and ketone by reacting with Grignard reagent.

2. **Reaction with hydride ion:**

Reduction by LiAlH₄ (Lithium Aluminium Hydride): LiAlH₄ may be prepared by reaction between LiH and AlCl₃ and is a good hydride ion donor and compounds containing >C=O moiety are good hydride ion acceptors.

$$4\,CH_3CHO \xrightarrow[Ether]{LiAlH_4} (CH_3CH_2O)_4\,Al^-Li^+ \xrightarrow{4\,H^+} 4\,CH_3CH_2OH + Li^+ + Al^{+++}$$

Acetaldehyde → Ethyl alcohol

$$4\,CH_3COCH_3 \xrightarrow[Ether]{LiAlH_4} (CH_3CHO)_4\,Al^-Li^+ \xrightarrow{4\,H^+} 4\,CH_3CH_2OH + Li^+ + Al^{+++}$$

Acetone → Ethyl alcohol

3. **M. P. V. Reduction (Meerwein-Pondrof-Verley):**

The conversion of a carbonyl compound into an alcohol by the action of aluminium isopropoxide in isopropyl alcohol medium is called as M.P.V. Reduction. The specific nature of the reagent and the mild reaction conditions give a wide scope for preparing unsaturated alcohols, nitro-alcohols, aldols etc.

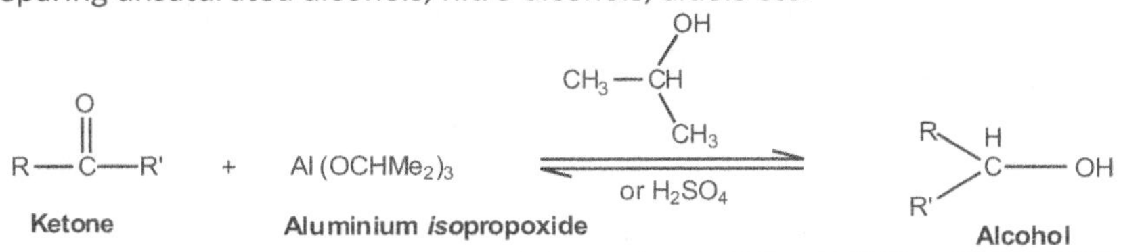

$$R-\overset{O}{\overset{\|}{C}}-R' + Al(OCHMe_2)_3 \underset{or\,H_2SO_4}{\overset{CH_3-CH(OH)CH_3}{\rightleftharpoons}} \underset{R'}{\overset{R}{>}}\!\!\overset{H}{\underset{}{C}}\!\!-OH$$

Ketone + Aluminium *isopropoxide* → Alcohol

4. Aldol Condensation:

In presence of a dilute acid or base 2 molecules of an aldehyde or ketone combine with each other to form a β-hydroxy aldehyde or ketone. "The addition or self-condensation is such that the α-carbon of the first molecule gets attached to the carbonyl carbon of second molecule".

$$R-CHO + -CH_2-CHO \longrightarrow R-CH(OH)-CH_2-CHO$$

Example:

$$CH_3-CHO + H-CH_2-CHO \xrightarrow{OH^-} CH_3-CH(OH)-CH_2CHO$$

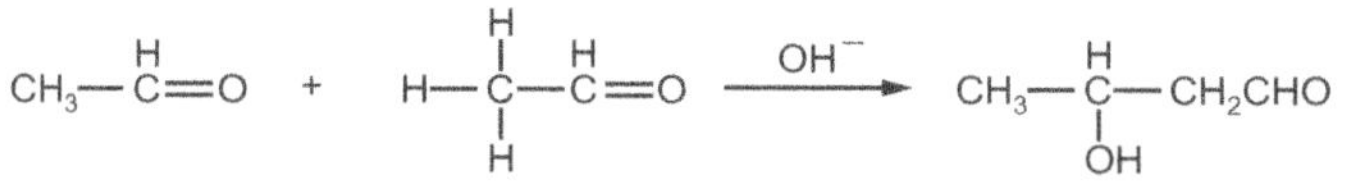

Acetaldehyde   Acetaldehyde   β-Hydroxybutyraldehyde

Mechanism:

Step 1: Base catalysed abstraction of proton of active methylene group.

$$CH_3CHO + OH^- \longrightarrow {}^-CH_2CHO + H_2O$$

Step 2: Nucleophilic attack of The carbinion on the carbonyl carbon of other molecule and condensation.

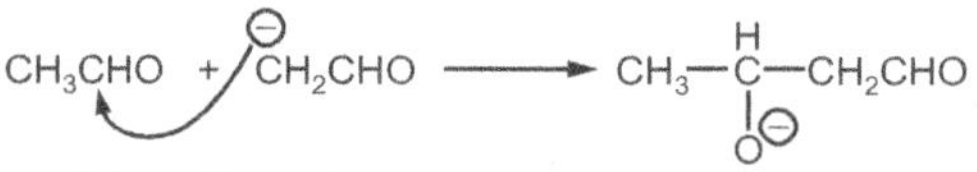

$$CH_3CHO + {}^-CH_2CHO \longrightarrow CH_3-CH(O^-)-CH_2CHO$$

Step 3: Protonation of the alkoxide.

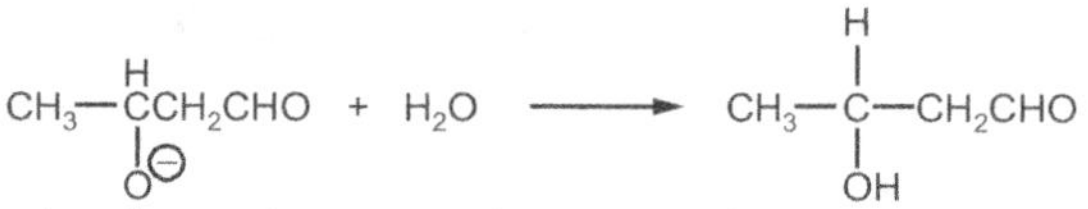

$$CH_3-CH(O^-)-CH_2CHO + H_2O \longrightarrow CH_3-CH(OH)-CH_2CHO$$

Crossed Aldol Condensation: Condensation between two different carbonyl compounds.

Example:

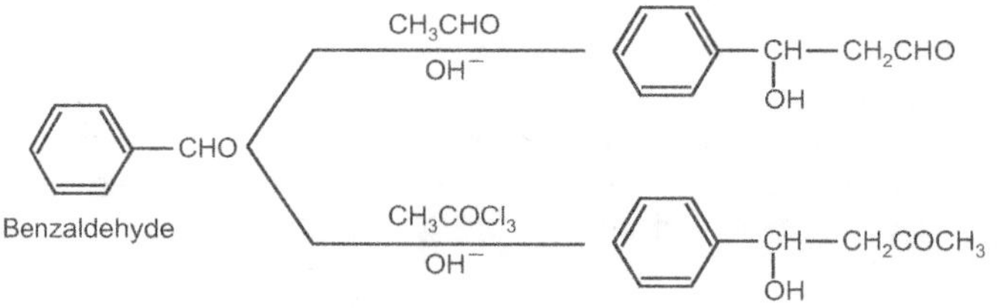

Benzaldehyde (C₆H₅—CHO)
- with CH₃CHO / OH⁻ → C₆H₅—CH(OH)—CH₂CHO
- with CH₃COCl₃ / OH⁻ → C₆H₅—CH(OH)—CH₂COCH₃

5. Cannizaro Reaction:

In presence of concentrated alkali two molecules of an aldehyde with no α-hydrogen undergo self oxidation and reduction to yield a molecule of corresponding alcohol and carboxylic acid salt. This reaction occurs by simply allowing such aldehyde to stand with aqueous alkali overnight.

PHARMACEUTICAL ORGANIC CHEMISTRY - I — ALDEHYDES AND KETONES

Example:

(i) $2HCHO \xrightarrow{OH^-} HCH_2OH + HCOO^-Na^+$
  Formaldehyde   Methanol   Sodium formate

(ii) $2\ Ph-CHO \xrightarrow{OH^-} Ph-CH_2OH + Ph-COO^-Na^+$
  Benzaldehyde   Benzylalcohol   Na-benzoate

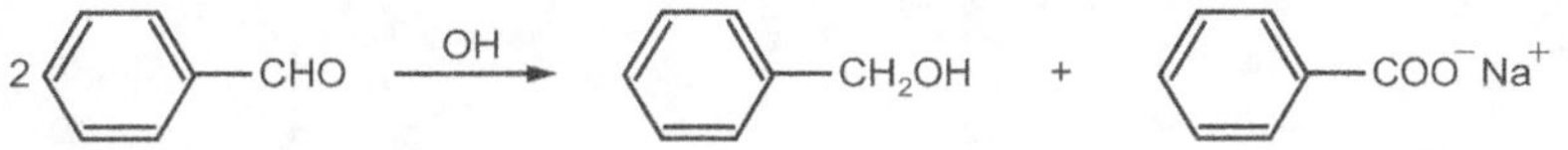

Mechanism:

Step 1: Nucleophilic addition of OH^- to carbonyl carbon

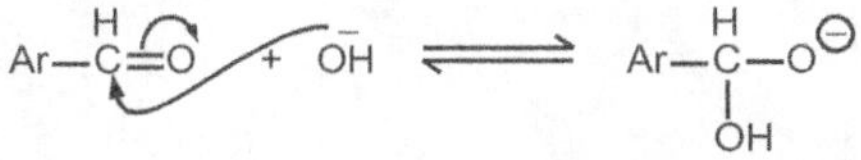

$$Ar-\underset{H}{\overset{H}{C}}=O + OH^- \rightleftharpoons Ar-\underset{OH}{\overset{H}{C}}-O^{\ominus}$$

Step 2: Abstraction of proton by another aldehyde molecule from the hydroxyl anion.

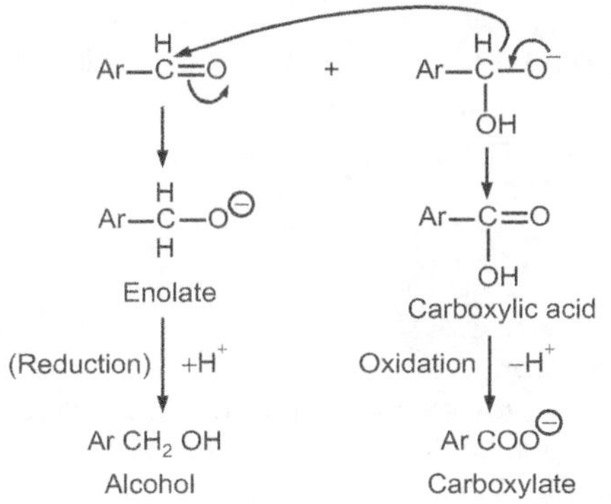

$$Ar-\overset{H}{C}=O \;+\; Ar-\underset{OH}{\overset{H}{C}}-O^-$$

$$\downarrow \qquad\qquad \downarrow$$

$$Ar-\underset{H}{\overset{H}{C}}-O^{\ominus} \qquad Ar-\underset{OH}{C}=O$$
Enolate   Carboxylic acid

(Reduction) $\downarrow +H^+$ Oxidation $\downarrow -H^+$

$Ar\ CH_2\ OH$ $Ar\ COO^{\ominus}$
Alcohol   Carboxylate

Crossed Cannizaro Reaction: Reaction between HCHO and ArCHO in presence of strong alkali formaldehyde always gets converted to the formate salt while the other aldehyde gets reduced to corresponding alcohol.

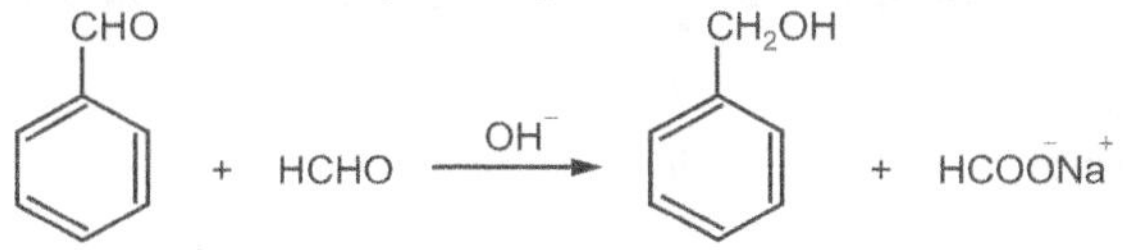

$Ph-CHO + HCHO \xrightarrow{OH^-} Ph-CH_2OH + HCOO^-Na^+$

6. Reformatsky Reaction:

Addition of an alpha halo ester to an aldehyde or ketone in the presence of metallic zinc to yield a beta hydroxyester is known as Reformatsky reaction.

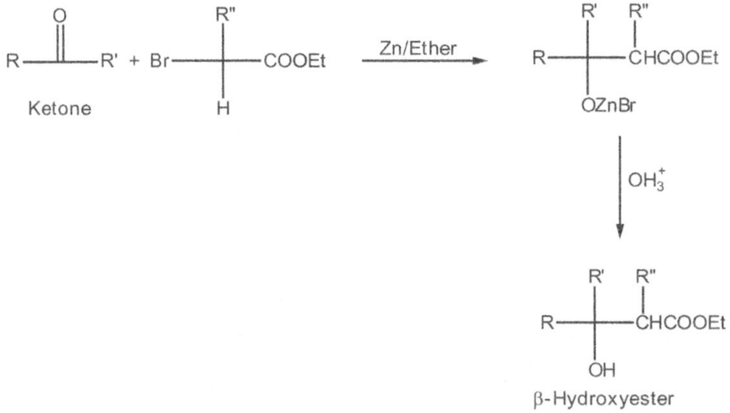

$$R-\underset{Ketone}{\overset{O}{\overset{\|}{C}}}-R' + Br-\underset{H}{\overset{R''}{\underset{|}{C}}}-COOEt \xrightarrow{Zn/Ether} R-\underset{OZnBr}{\overset{R'\ R''}{\underset{|}{C}}}-CHCOOEt$$

$$\xrightarrow{OH_3^+} R-\underset{OH}{\overset{R'\ R''}{\underset{|}{C}}}-CHCOOEt$$

β-Hydroxyester

R = R' = R'' = Alkyl or Aryl

7. Perkin Reaction:

The alpha, beta unsaturated acid is obtained from aromatic aldehyde reacts with anhydride.

E.g., Cinnamic acid is obtained upon treatment of acetic anhydride on benzaldehyde.

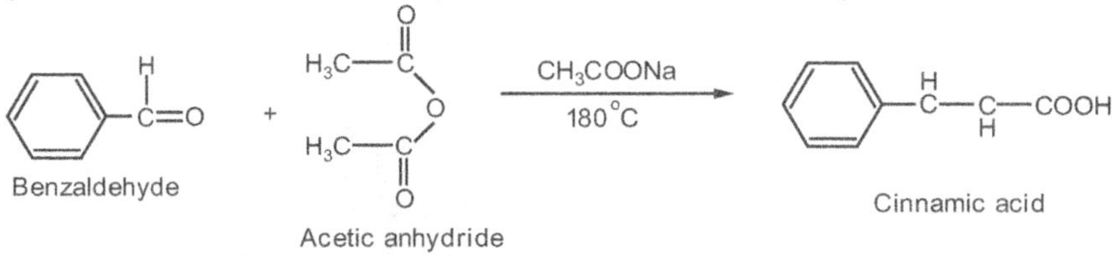

Benzaldehyde + Acetic anhydride $\xrightarrow[180°C]{CH_3COONa}$ Cinnamic acid

8. Knoevenagel Condensation:

The base-catalysed aldol type condensation reaction between a carbonyl compound, usually without any alpha hydrogen atom and a compound containing an active methylene group is called Knoevenagel condensation.

$$\underset{R'}{\overset{R}{>}}C=O + H_2C\underset{Y}{\overset{X}{<}} \xrightarrow{Base} \underset{R'}{\overset{R}{>}}C=C\underset{Y}{\overset{X}{<}}$$

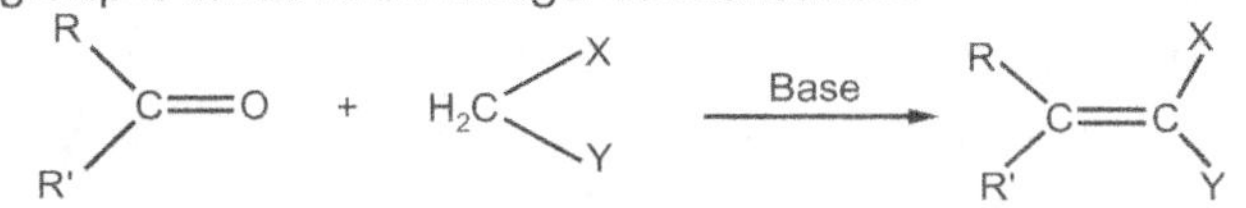

R = R' = R'' = Alkyl or Aryl; X & Y = –CHO, –COR, –COOR, –CN, –NO₂ (electron withdrawing group).

9. Haloform Reaction:

Aldehydes and ketone reacts rapidly with halogens (Cl₂, Br₂, I₂) in presence of alkali to form haloform. This reaction is used to distinguish methyl ketone from other ketones.

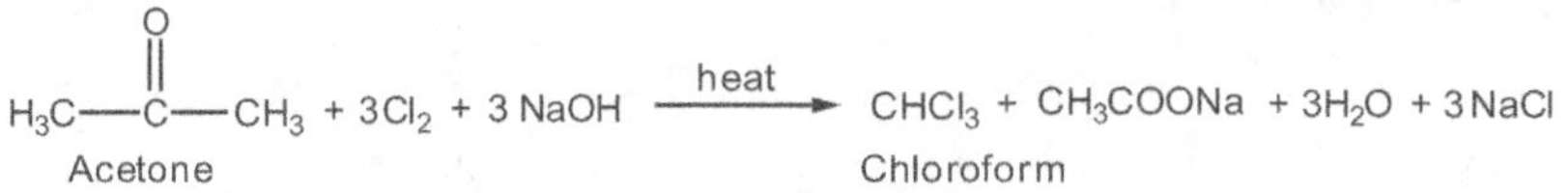

$$\underset{Acetone}{H_3C-\overset{O}{\overset{\|}{C}}-CH_3} + 3Cl_2 + 3\,NaOH \xrightarrow{heat} \underset{Chloroform}{CHCl_3} + CH_3COONa + 3H_2O + 3\,NaCl$$

10. Mannich Reaction:

Aromatic ketones containing alpha hydrogen undergoes mannich reaction, these are also known as mannich bases.

Acetophenone + Formaldehyde (HCHO) + Diethylamine $\xrightarrow{HCl}$ β-Aminoketone

E.g., Acetophenone reacts with formaldehyde in presence of primary or secondary amine to form beta aminoketone.

SUMMARY

Preparation of Aldehydes and Ketones:

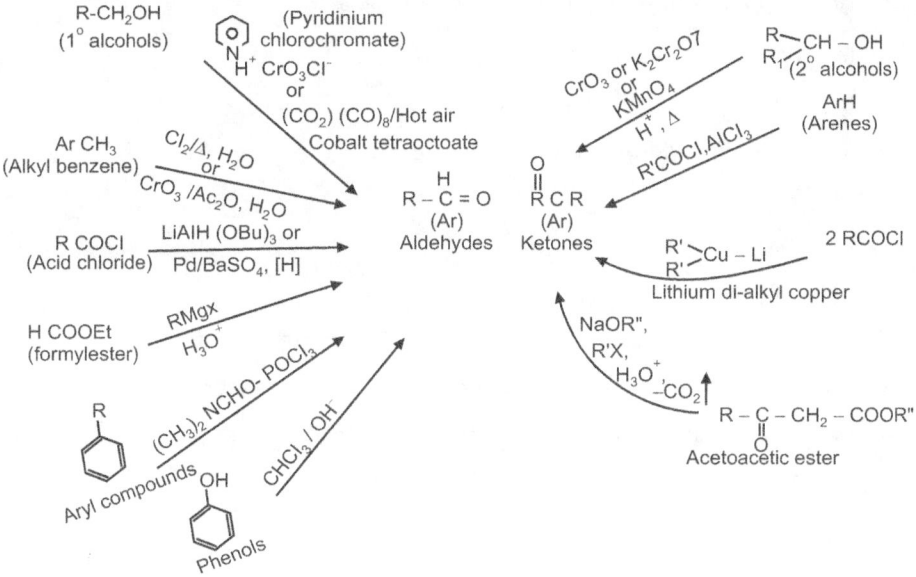

Reactions of Aldehydes and Ketones:

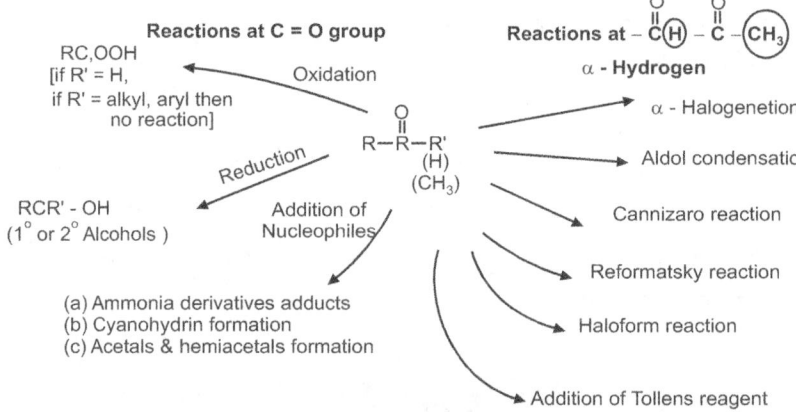

QUESTION BANK

1. Draw structures from IUPAC names of following:

   (a) Pentanal

   (b) 2-Methylbutanal

   (c) 2,2-Dimethylpropanal

   (d) 2-Pentanone

   (e) 3-Methyl-2-butanone

   (f) 3-Pentanone

2. How are aldehydes prepared? Describe their important reactions?

3. How are ketones prepared? Describe their important reactions?

4. Describe reactions of aldehydes/ketones with following reagents:

   (a) NH_3

   (b) HCN

   (c) CH_3MgI

   (d) NH_2OH

   (e) Hydroxylamine

5. Give an example and uses of the following and explain how each is prepared:
   (a) Hemiacetal
   (b) An imine
   (c) An enamine
   (d) An oxime
   (e) Hydrazone
6. Write down the reaction and mechanism of MPV reduction.
7. What is Oppenaur oxidation explain?
8. Write down the statement and mechanism of Cannizaro's reaction.
9. Write down the statement and mechanism of Mannich reaction.
10. Compare and discuss MPV reduction and Oppenaur oxidation.

Chapter 2 ...

PHENOLS

CONTENTS
Nomenclature, properties, methods of preparation and general reactions.

Introduction:
Compounds that have a hydroxy group attached to a benzene or arene ring are called **phenols**. Thus, phenols are chemically hydroxybenzenes. The phenyl ring can be substituted with various other groups to give substituted phenols. Phenols differ from alcohols in that they have –OH group attached to the aromatic ring while, alcohols have –OH group attached to an alkyl group. **Phenols = ArOH, Alcohol = R – OH**.

NOMENCLATURE OF PHENOLS

Phenols are named as derivatives of the simplest member of this class which, is also called as phenol. In many compounds 'phenol' is the base name. The methyl phenols are given the special name *cresol*. They are sometimes denoted as –*hydroxy* compounds.

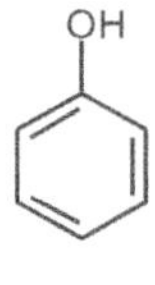

Phenol 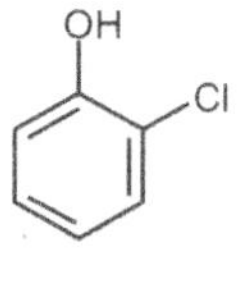   o-Chlorophenol 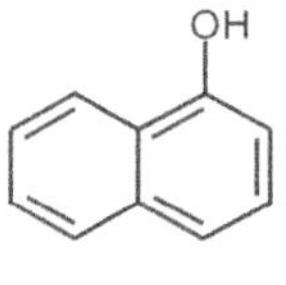   1-Naphthol   9-Phenanthrol 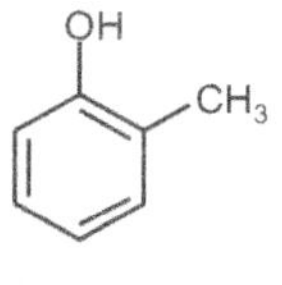   o-Cresol
                            (α-Naphthol)   (2-Methylphenol)

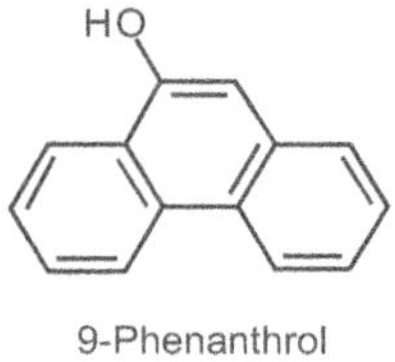

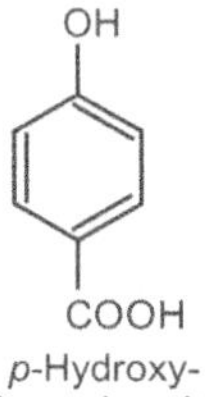

p-Hydroxy-   Hydroquinone   Resorcinol
benzoic acid (p-Dihydroxybenzene) (m-Dihydroxybenzene)

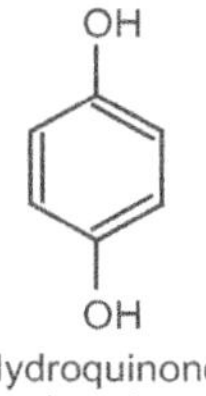

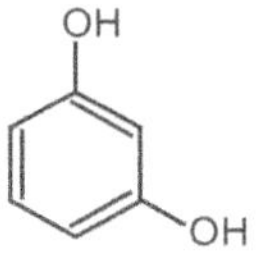

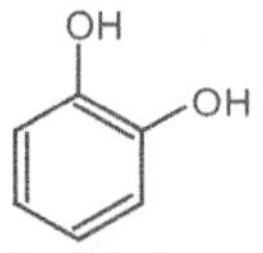

Catechol   Pyrogallol
(o-Dihydroxybenzene)   (Benzene-1,3,5-triol)

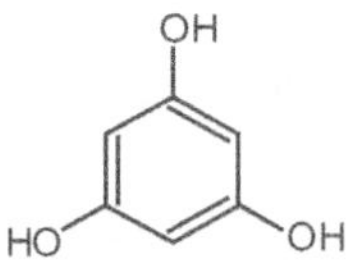

Physical Properties:

Simplest phenols are liquids or low-melting solids. They have high boiling points because of hydrogen bonding. They are somewhat soluble in water because of hydrogen bonding. They are colourless unless some group incorporating colour is present. They are easily oxidized. They can chelate metal ions. Most of the phenols bear a typical odour called as phenolic odour or termed as odour of carbolic acid (*e.g.*, smell of lifebuoy soap).

Acidity of Phenols:

In comparison to alcohols, phenols are strong acids. For example, phenol is a stronger acid than cyclohexanol. The benzene ring acts as electron withdrawing group (-*I* effect). As a result the oxygen of the –OH group becomes electropositive. Therefore, hydrogen is held less tightly and hence can be donated easily.

Also the carbon atom in phenol is sp^2 hybridized while in cyclohexane it is sp^3 hybridized. Hence, the percentage of *s* character in phenol (33%) is more than in cyclohexane (25%). Because of the greater *s* character sp^2 hybridized carbon atoms are more electronegative than sp^3 hybridized carbon atoms. But phenols are weak acids as compared to carboxylic acids. In phenol, the –OH oxygen is more electropositive.

As can be seen from the resonance of phenol, structures **ii-iv** have charge separation whereas, none of the resonating structures of phenoxide ion have charge separation. The negative charge on the phenoxide ion is distributed on the ring evenly, thus, making the species more stable. Hence, the greater stabilization of phenoxide ion makes phenol acidic in nature.

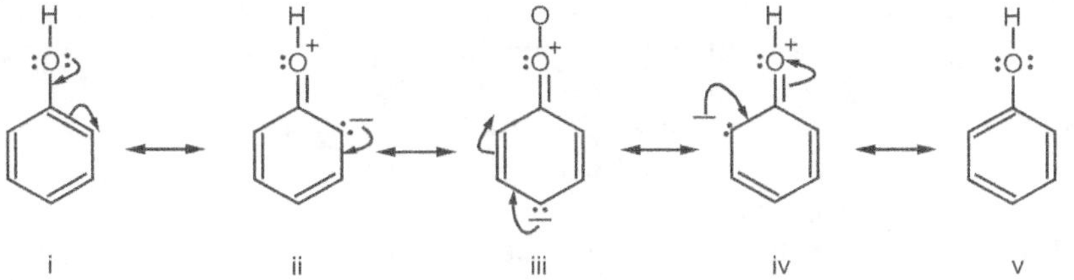

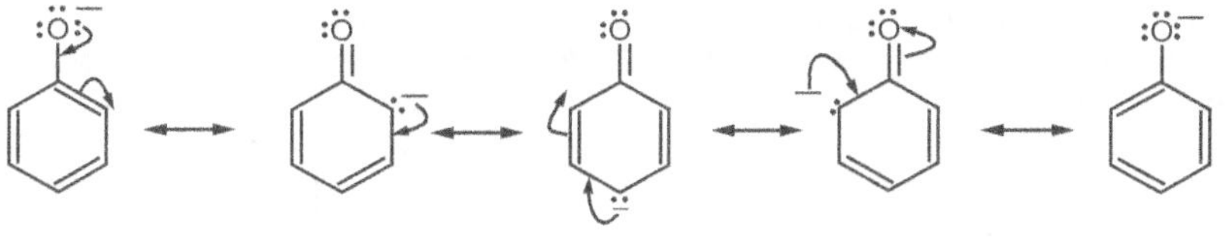

The presence of electron-withdrawing groups (*e.g.*, NO_2, CN, COOH etc.) on the phenol makes it more acidic because of the -*I* effect. While, the presence of electron-releasing groups like CH_3, NH_2, OCH_3 etc. decrease the acidity of phenol due to +*I* effect.

Methods of preparation:

Various synthetic methods for the preparation of phenols are discussed below under two headings, *viz;* I. Industrial (large scale) methods and II. Laboratory (small scale) methods.

(I) Industrial methods:

1. Hydrolysis of chlorobenzene (Dow Process):

In this process, chlorobenzene is heated at 350°C (under high pressure) with aqueous sodium hydroxide. This is a nucleophilic substitution reaction which is carried out at elevated temperature and pressure. Chlorobenzene reacts with sodium hydroxide to form sodium phenoxide, which on hydrolysis with hydrochloric acid liberates phenol.

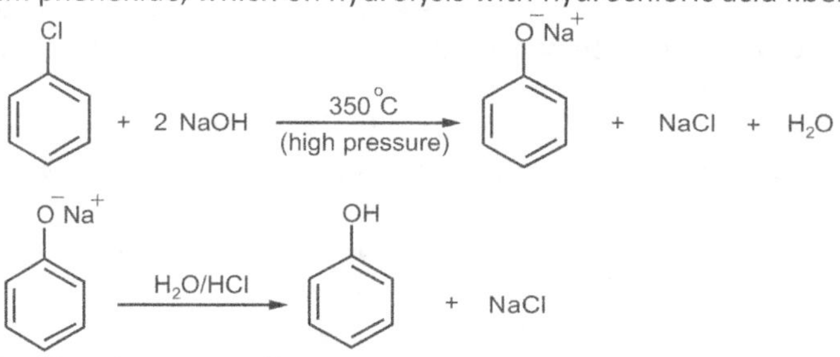

$$C_6H_5Cl + 2\,NaOH \xrightarrow[\text{(high pressure)}]{350\,°C} C_6H_5O^-Na^+ + NaCl + H_2O$$

$$C_6H_5O^-Na^+ \xrightarrow{H_2O/HCl} C_6H_5OH + NaCl$$

2. Fusion of sodium benzenesulfonate:

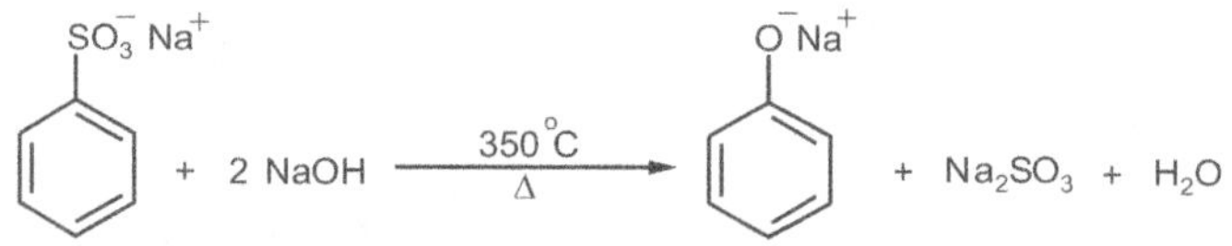

$$C_6H_5SO_3^-Na^+ + 2\,NaOH \xrightarrow[\Delta]{350\,°C} C_6H_5O^-Na^+ + Na_2SO_3 + H_2O$$

In this method, sodium benzenesulphonate is fused with sodium hydroxide to form sodium phenoxide which, on hydrolysis with acid gives phenol.

3. From cumene hydroperoxide:

In the first step cumene (isopropylbenzene) is synthesized by Friedel Craft's alkylation of benzene with propene. The isopropyl cation is generated by the reaction between propene and phosphoric acid. This alkylates the benzene ring as in any electrophilic aromatic substitution reaction. (Propyl bromide and $AlCl_3$ can also be used, but they are expensive).

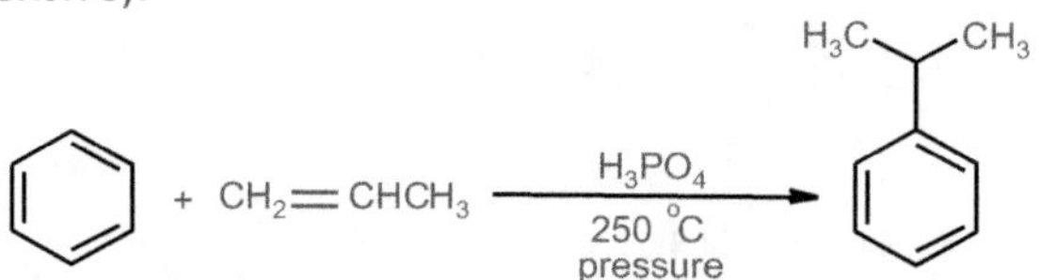

$$C_6H_6 + CH_2=CHCH_3 \xrightarrow[\text{pressure}]{H_3PO_4,\ 250\,°C} C_6H_5CH(CH_3)_2$$

Cumene (Isopropylbenzene)

In the next step, the cumene is oxidized to cumene hydroperoxide.

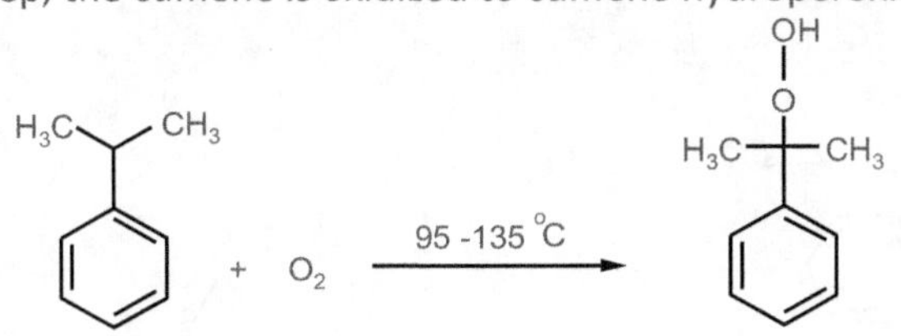

Cumene hydroperoxide

This is a free radical chain reaction. The initiator abstracts the benzylic hydrogen from cumene to form a tertiary benzylic radical. Then chain reaction propagates and continues with oxygen to form cumene hydroperoxide.

Chain initiation

Step 1

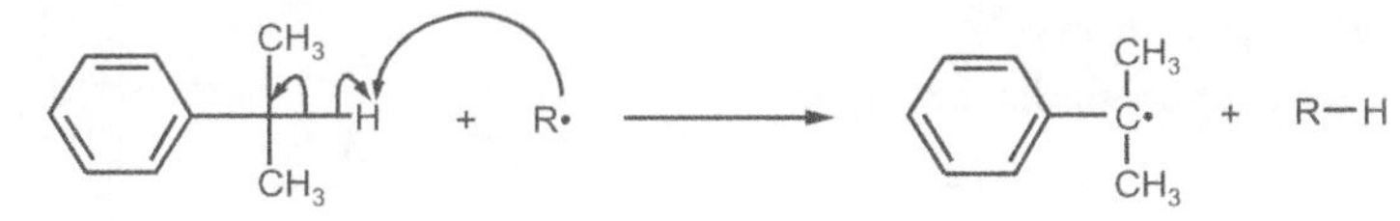

Chain propagation

Step 2

Step 3

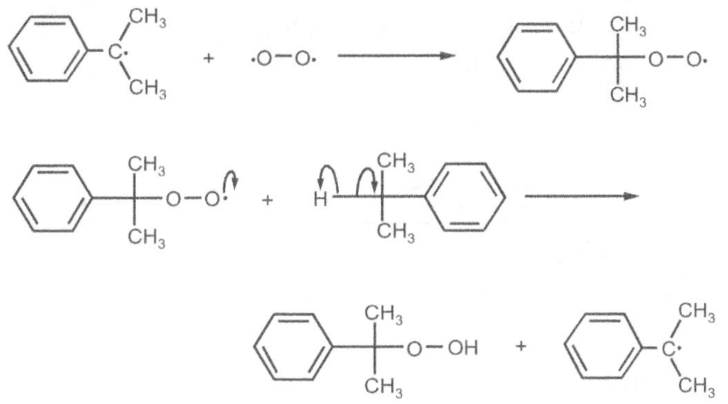

In the final step, the cumene hydroperoxide is treated with 10% sulphuric acid so it undergoes a hydrolytic rearrangement to form phenol and acetone.

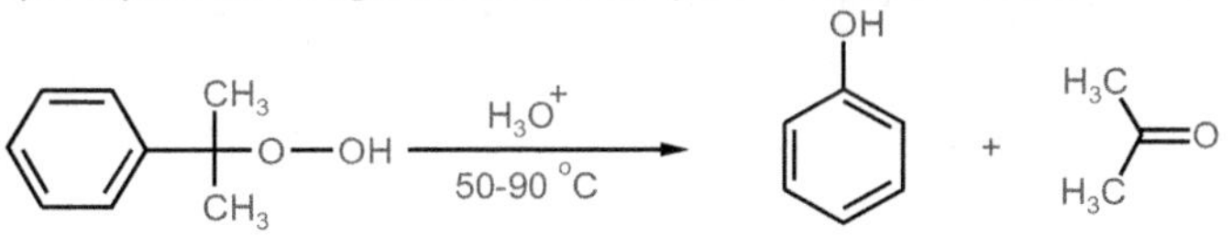

Phenol Acetone

This hydrolytic rearrangement involves migration of phenyl group to cationic oxygen atom to afford *iso*-propyloxybenzene. The last step involves acidic hydrolysis of the isopropyloxy group to acetone to give phenol.

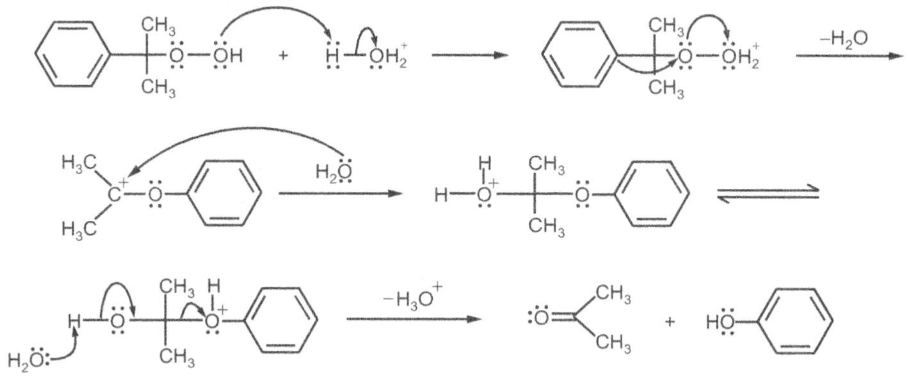

[Mechanism scheme showing acid-catalyzed cleavage with intermediates leading to acetone and phenol]

(II) Laboratory methods:
1. **Hydrolysis of arenediazonium salts:**

$$Ar-NH_2 \xrightarrow{HONO} ArN_2 \xrightarrow[Cu^{2+},\ H_2O]{Cu_2O} Ar-OH$$

Amines can be converted to phenols by diazotization reaction. The conditions required for the reaction are very mild and other groups present on the molecule are not affected. The initial step is diazotization, followed by Sandmeyer reaction.

Example:

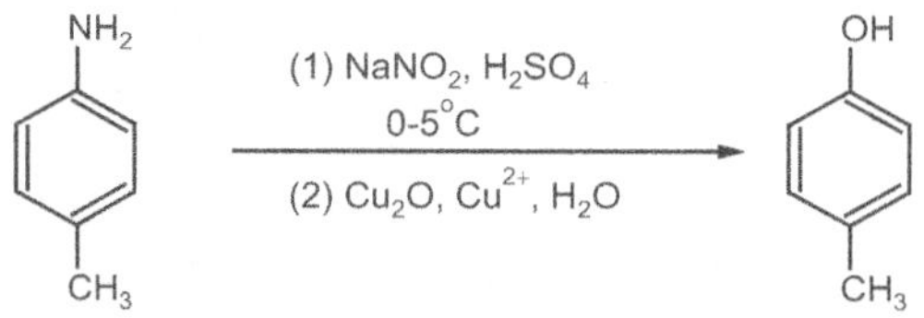

p-Toluidine $\xrightarrow[(2)\ Cu_2O,\ Cu^{2+},\ H_2O]{(1)\ NaNO_2,\ H_2SO_4\ \ 0\text{-}5°C}$ p-Cresol

Reactions of Phenols:

Various reactions undergone by phenols are due to the aryl- OH group as well as the aryl moiety and substituents attached to it.

1. **Acidity:**

Phenols are weakly acidic in nature. They react with various bases to form phenolate salts.

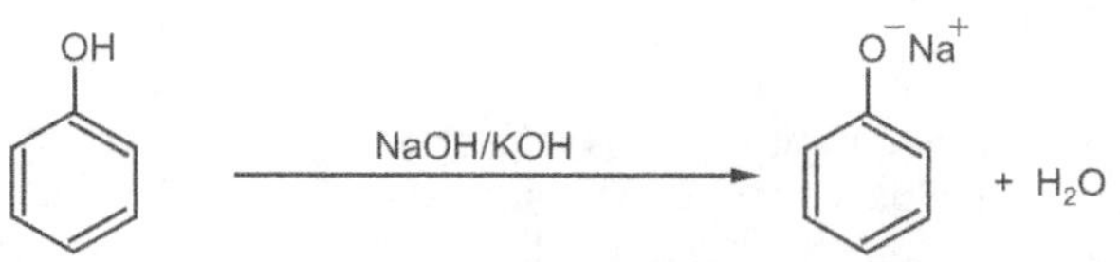

PhOH $\xrightarrow{NaOH/KOH}$ PhO$^-$Na$^+$ + H$_2$O

2. Ester formation:

Phenols can be converted to esters by reaction with acids, acid chlorides or acid anhydrides.

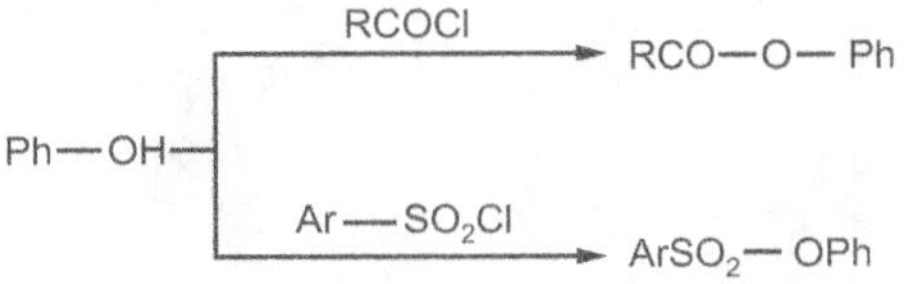

Ph—OH → (RCOCl) → RCO—O—Ph
Ph—OH → (Ar—SO$_2$Cl) → ArSO$_2$—OPh

The reaction of phenol (or alcohol) with acid chlorides is called as **Schotten-Baumann** reaction. In this reaction, the acid chloride is added to a mixture of phenol and base (aqueous sodium hydroxide or pyridine) in small quantities followed by vigorous shaking after each addition. The base is used as a catalyst and it also neutralizes the free acid formed during the reaction.

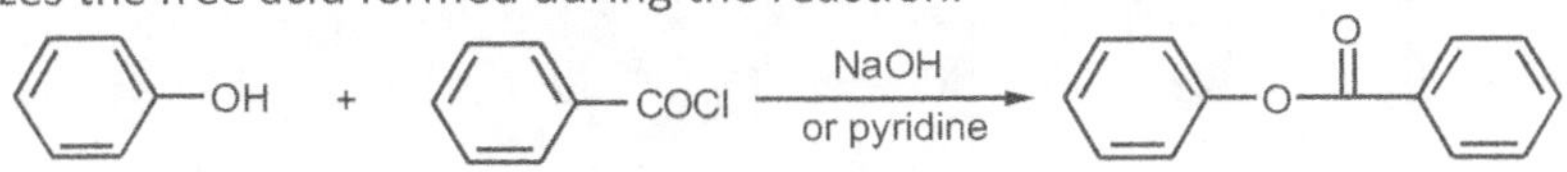

Phenol + Benzoyl chloride —(NaOH or pyridine)→ Phenyl benzoate

3. Substitution at the benzene/arene ring of phenol:

The **electrophilic substitution** on the benzene ring of the phenol takes place preferentially at the *ortho* or *para* positions because of the activation of the ring by the –OH group. Polysubstitution often takes place in phenols. Hence, special precautions must be taken to avoid undesirable polysubstitution or oxidation.

(i) Nitration:

Phenol reacts with dilute nitric acid at low temperature to yield a mixture of *o*-nitrophenol and *p*-nitrophenol. The yield is very low because of the oxidation of the ring as nitric acid is good oxidizing agent. The *ortho* and *para* isomers can be separated by steam distillation. The *ortho* isomer is more volatile (because of intramolecular hydrogen bonding) than *para* isomer (it has intermolecular hydrogen bonding) and distills out.

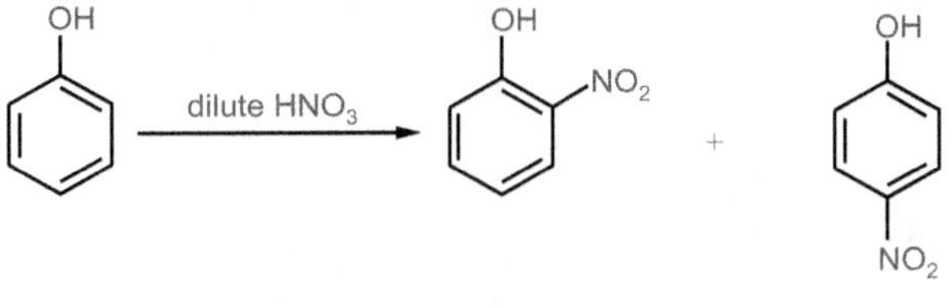

Phenol —(dilute HNO$_3$)→ *o*-Nitrophenol (30-40%) + *p*-Nitrophenol (15%)

With concentrated nitric acid polynitration occurs and the product formed is 2,4,6-trinitrophenol (picric acid). The product is yellow in color and the three electron withdrawing nitro groups make it very acidic. That is why even though it has no COOH group, it is called as acid.

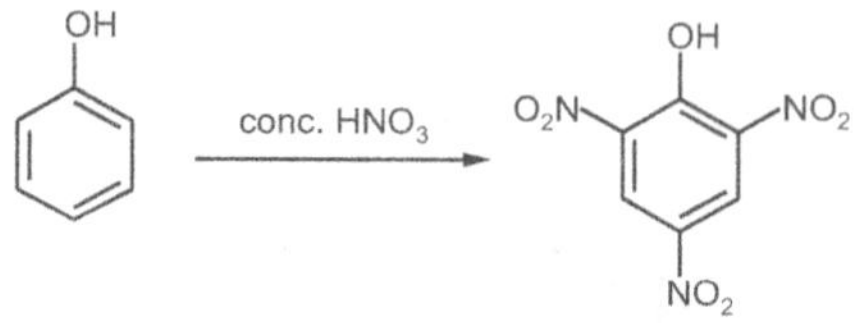

Phenol → (conc. HNO₃) → 2,4,6-Trinitrophenol (Picric acid)

(ii) Sulphonation

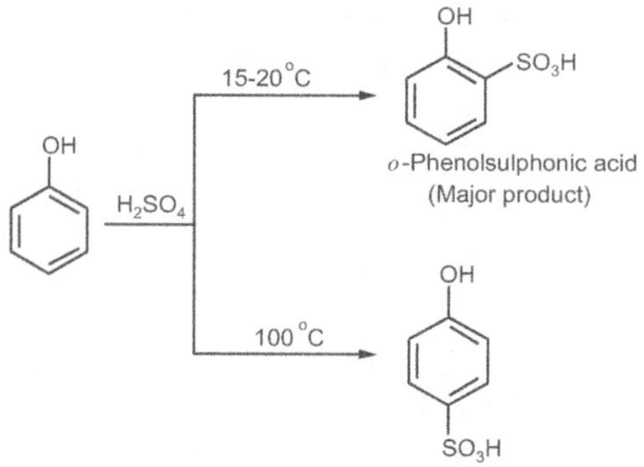

Phenol + H_2SO_4:
- at 15-20°C → o-Phenolsulphonic acid (Major product)
- at 100°C → p-Phenolsulphonic acid (Minor product)

Phenol reacts with concentrated sulphuric acid to form phenolsulphonic acid. At high temperatures *para* isomer is formed while, at low temperatures *ortho* isomer is formed. Oleum (H_2SO_4 + SO_3) is used as a better sulfonating agent in industry.

(iii) Halogenation:

When phenol is treated with aqueous bromine all the hydrogens *ortho* or *para* to the –OH group are replaced by the bromine atom to form 2,4,6-tribromophenol.

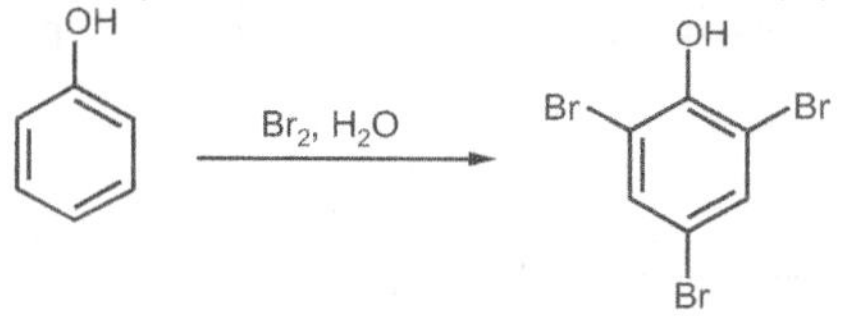

Phenol → (Br_2, H_2O) → 2,4,6-Tribromophenol

Monobromo derivative can be obtained by carrying out the reaction in carbon disulphide at low temperature, thus lowering the electrophilic reactivity of the bromine.

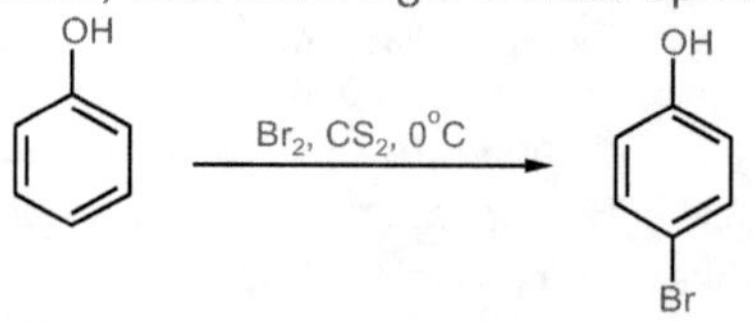

Phenol → (Br_2, CS_2, 0°C) → p-Bromophenol

(iv) Friedel Craft's alkylation:

Phenol + CH₃Cl →(HF) p-Methylphenol (p-Cresol)

Phenols undergo Friedel Crafts alkylation to form alkylphenols. Hydrofluoric acid is the catalyst. One can also use $AlCl_3$ as a lewis acid.

(v) Friedel Craft's acylation:

m-Cresol + CH_3COOH →($ZnCl_2$) m-Cresol methyl ketone

Phenolic ketones can be prepared by Friedel Crafts acylation of phenols but, the yield is very low. Hence, Fries rearrangement is the preferred method for preparation of phenolic ketones. The acylium breaks out from the ester and migrates to the *ortho* position.

m-Cresol →($(CH_3CO)_2O$) m-Cresyl acetate →($AlCl_3$)
- 25 °C → 2-Methyl-4-hydroxyacetophenone
- 160 °C → 4-Methyl-2-hydroxyacetophenone

(vi) Nitrosation:

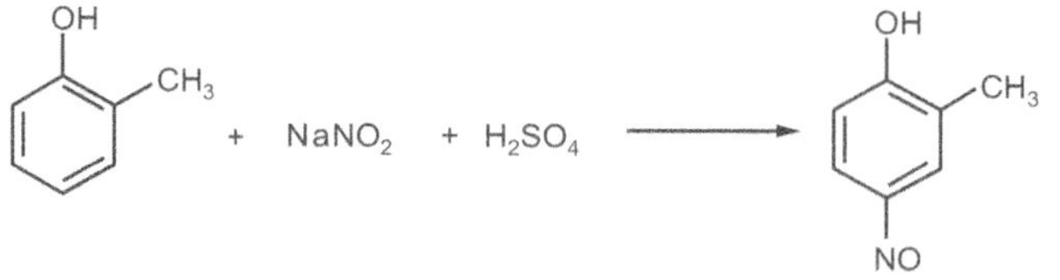

o-Cresol + NaNO$_2$ + H$_2$SO$_4$ → 4-Nitroso-2-methylphenol

Phenols undergo substitution reaction by weak electrophiles like nitrosonium ion ($^+$NO) to give nitrosophenol. NaNO$_2$ and H$_2$SO$_4$ on reaction generate HNO$_2$ *in situ*.

(vii) Coupling with diazonium salts:

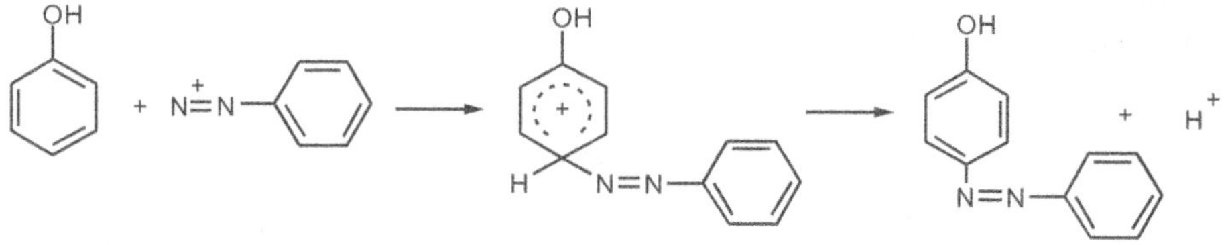

Phenols react with diazonium salts to form azo compounds. This is also an electrophilic aromatic substitution reaction. The –OH group is electron-releasing and therefore activating. Hence, the substitiution takes place at the *para* position. The reaction is carried out in slightly alkaline medium. In alkaline medium phenol exists as phenoxide ion. The negatively charged oxygen is highly electron releasing than the undissociated phenol. Hence, the reaction proceeds faster in alkaline medium. But the solution must not be too alkaline so that the concentration of the diazonium ion is very low and which could slower the rate of reaction as well as decrease the yield. Hence, the pH of the medium should be suitably adjusted.

4. Kolbe reaction:

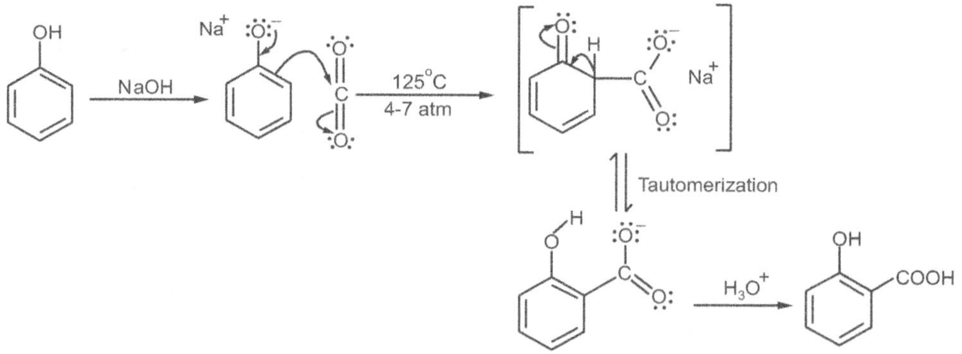

Phenol → (NaOH) → Sodium phenoxide → (CO$_2$, 125°C, 4-7 atm) → intermediate → Tautomerization → → (H$_3$O$^+$) → Salicylic acid

The salts of phenol react with carbon dioxide to introduce a carboxyl group at the *ortho* position. This reaction is called as **Kolbe reaction**. Its most important application is for the preparation of *o*-hydroxybenzoic acid (salicylic acid) from phenol. Some quantity of *p*-hydroxybenzoic acid is also formed. But both the isomers can be separated easily by steam distillation.

5. **Reimer-Tiemann reaction (Aldehyde formation):**

When phenols are treated with chloroform and aqueous sodium hydroxide an aldehyde group is introduced onto the aromatic ring at the *ortho* position. This reaction is called as **Reimer-Tiemann reaction**.

Phenol + CHCl$_3$ $\xrightarrow{\text{aqueous NaOH}}$ Salicylaldehyde

This is an electrophilic substitution reaction. Chloroform reacts with aqueous base to form the dichlorocarbene which acts as an electrophile.

$OH^- + CHCl_3 \rightleftharpoons H_2O + {}^-:CCl_3 \longrightarrow Cl^- + :CCl_2$ (Dichlorocarbene)

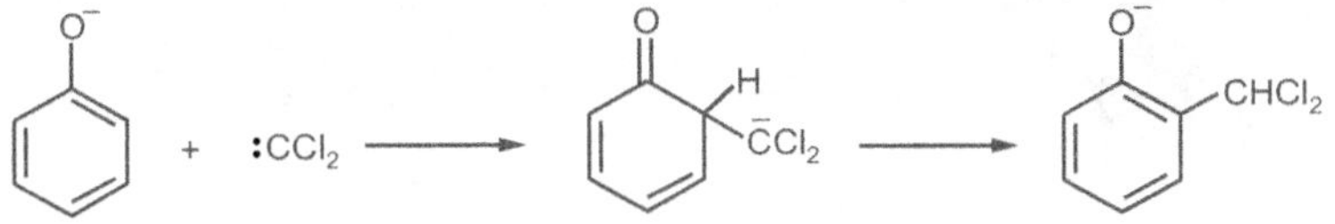

6. **Reaction with formaldehyde:**

This is initial formation of phenol to its *o*-methyl alcohol derivative which is further esterified with another phenol molecule.

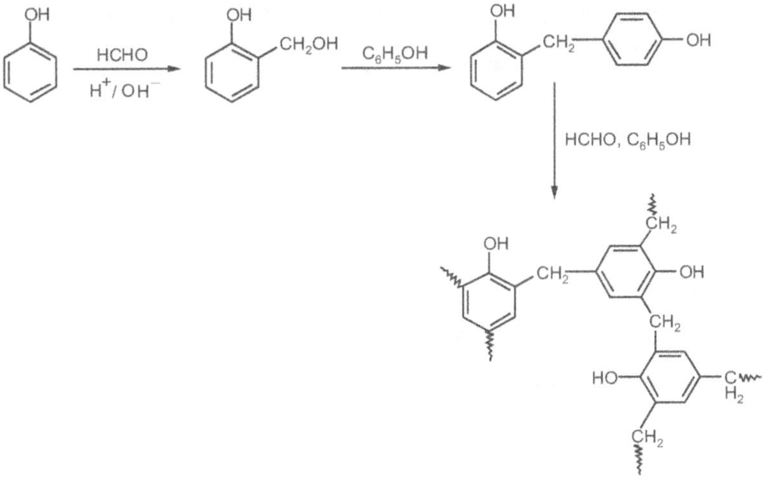

When phenols are treated with formaldehyde in the presence of alkali or acid they polymerize to form high-molecular-weight polymers in which many phenol rings are held together by $-CH_2$ groups.

7. Ether formation (Williamson synthesis):

Phenols react with alkyl halides in alkaline solution to form alkyl aryl ethers. This method is called as **Williamson synthesis.** For preparation of methylphenylethers, methyl sulphate is used instead of methyl halides.

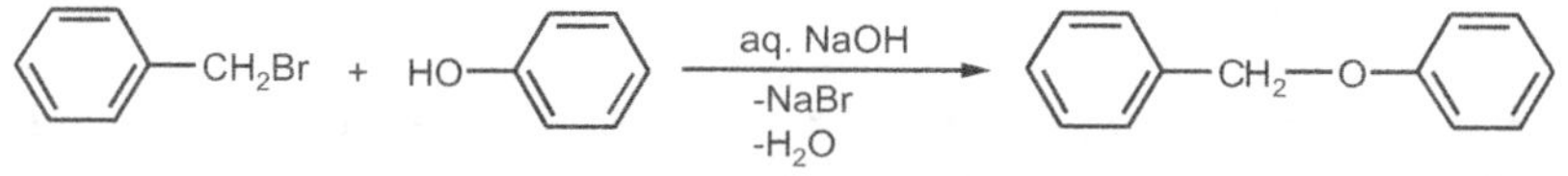

$$Ph-CH_2Br + HO-Ph \xrightarrow[\text{-NaBr, -H}_2\text{O}]{\text{aq. NaOH}} Ph-CH_2-O-Ph$$

In alkaline solution phenol exists as phenoxide ion which acts as nucleophile and attacks the halide (or sulphate) and displaces the halide ion (or sulphate ion).

$$Ph-O^- + R-X \xrightarrow{\text{alkali}} ArO-R + X^-$$

$$ArO^- + H_3C-OSO_3CH_3 \xrightarrow{\text{alkali}} ArO-CH_3 + {}^-OSO_3CH_3$$

Alkyl aryl ethers can be prepared by two methods, either by reacting alkyl halides with phenols or by reacting aryl halides with alcohol. But the second type of reaction is not carried out because of the low reactivity of aryl halides.

8. Mannich Reaction:

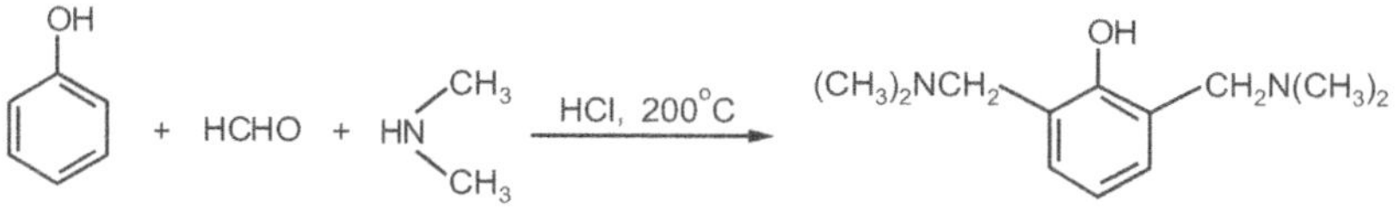

$$\text{PhOH} + HCHO + HN(CH_3)_2 \xrightarrow{\text{HCl, 200°C}} (CH_3)_2NCH_2-C_6H_3(OH)-CH_2N(CH_3)_2$$

Phenols react with formaldehyde and a secondary amine in presence of an acid to form Mannich bases. Substitution takes place at the *ortho* and *para* positions since these positions are most active.

SUMMARY OF THE PREPARATION AND REACTIONS OF PHENOL

QUESTION BANK

1. What are phenols? Discuss their nomenclature and physical properties
2. Discuss why phenols are acidic but alcohols are neutral.
3. Enumerate various methods for the preparation of phenols?
4. Discuss various reactions of phenols with mechanisms, wherever required?
5. Short notes on:
    (a) Kolbe's Synthesis
    (b) Reimer Tiemann Reaction
    (c) Mannich Reaction.
6. Discuss how will you synthesise various phenol derivatives
    (a) *p*-Nitrophenol and *o*-nitrophenol
    (b) *m*-nitrophenol
    (c) Salicylic acid
    (d) Salicylaldehyde
    (e) Nerolin
    (f) Cresol
    (g) Resorcinol
    (h) Catechol
7. Arrange in order of increasing acidity with proper justification
    (a) Phenol
    (b) Alcohols
    (c) Carboxylic acids.
8. Write the structures of:
    (a) β-Napthol
    (b) Salicylaldehyde
    (c) Hydroquinone
9. What is H-bonding and its influence on physical properties of phenols?
10. What type of reaction is involved in Dow process? Why it is difficult?

11. Give mechanisms of:
    (a) Friedel Craft alkylation of phenols
    (b) Fries rearrangement
    (c) Riemmer-Tiemann reaction
12. What is the structure of Picric acid? Why is it called an acid?
13. How will you separate a mixture of two solids in a simple and single step? One is carboxylic acid, another is phenol?

Chapter 3 ...

SULPHONIC ACIDS

CONTENTS
Nomenclature, properties, methods of preparation and general reactions.

Introduction:

Compounds that have a –SO₃H (sulphonic acid) group attached to an alkyl or aryl or aralkyl substrate are called **sulphonic acids**. e.g.,

$$R-\underset{\underset{O}{\|}}{\overset{\overset{O}{\|}}{S}}-OH, \quad R = \text{alkyl, aryl or aralkyl}$$

Nomenclature of sulphonic acids:

For the nomenclature of sulphonic acids the parent alkane is selected corresponding to the longest chain and the suffix "sulphonic acid" is added to it.

E.g.,

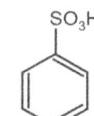

p-Toluenesulphonic acid   Benzenesulphonic acid   CH₃SO₃H Methanesulphonic acid

PROPERTIES

Physical Properties:

Sulphonic acids are deliquescent, irritant thick liquids or solids. They are highly polar substances and ionize completely in water.

$$R-SO_3H \xrightarrow{H_2O} R-SO_3^- + H_3O^+$$

$$Ar-SO_3H \xrightarrow{H_2O} Ar-SO_3^- + H_3O^+$$

Acidity of sulphonic acids:

Sulphonic acids are stronger than carboxylic acids. The sulphur atom of the sulphonic acid group is bonded to the C atom and to –OH group by single bond while, it is bonded to the two oxygen atoms by two double bonds. The SO_3H group has –I and –R effects. The central S atom bears a partial positive charge (δ^{++}) charge while the two doubly bonded oxygen atoms attached to the sulphur have partial negative charge (δ^-). Hence, the S-O-H has the tendency to donate the proton and thus, sulphonic acids are acidic in nature.

$$R-S(=O)_2-OH \longrightarrow R-S(=O)_2-O^- + H^+$$

METHODS OF PREPARATION

Various synthetic methods for the preparation of sulphonic acids are discussed below:

1. **Sulphonation of arene ring:**

$$ArH \xrightarrow[\text{or } H_2SO_4 + SO_3 \text{ (Oleum)}]{\text{conc. } H_2SO_4} ArSO_3H$$

When arenes are treated with concentrated sulphuric acid or oleum they form arenesulphonic acids. This is electrophilic aromatic substitution, where $\overset{+}{SO_3}$ is the electrophile.

2. **By action of chlorosulphonic acid on arenes:**

$$Ar-H \xrightarrow[-H_2O]{ClSO_3H} Ar-SO_2Cl \xrightarrow[-HCl]{NH_3} Ar-SO_2NH_2 \xrightarrow{HCl/H_2O} ArSO_3H$$

Arene   Arenesulphonyl chloride   Sulphonamides   Arenesulphonic acid

When arenes are treated with chlorosulphonic acids they form arenesulphonyl chlorides. These, on treatment with water give the corresponding sulphonic acids. Arenesulphonyl chlorides are important intermediates for well known sulphonamides.

3. **Oxidation of thiols or thiophenols:**

$$\begin{array}{c} R-SH \\ \text{or} \\ Ar-SH \end{array} \xrightarrow[HNO_3]{KMnO_4 \text{ or}} \begin{array}{c} R-SO_3H \\ \text{or} \\ Ar-SO_3H \end{array}$$

When alkanethiols or thiophenols are treated with $KMnO_4$ or HNO_3, they undergo oxidation to form the corresponding sulphonic acids. This is of course economically expensive route to sulphonic acids.

4. Oxidation of disulphides:

$$R-S-S-H \xrightarrow[\text{or HNO}_3]{\text{KMnO}_4} R-SO_3H$$

Disulphides when treated with $KMnO_4$ or HNO_3, undergo oxidation to form the corresponding sulphonic acids. This is economically attractive route, widely used.

Dialkyl disulphides also yield sulphonic acids, similarly.

$$R-S-S-R \xrightarrow[\text{or HNO}_3]{\text{KMnO}_4/H^+} 2\ R\ SO_3H$$

5. Action of sulphites on alkyl halides:

$$RX \xrightarrow[H_2O]{K_2SO_3/H^+} R-SO_3H \quad X = \text{halides}$$

When alkyl halides are treated with potassium sulphite in acidic medium, they form the corresponding sulphonic acids.

6. Addition of bisulphite to double bonds of alkenes:

Alkylsulphonic acids can be prepared by reaction of alkene with sodium bisulphite in acidic medium. The reaction takes place in the presence of oxygen or nitrous oxide, which abstract a proton in the final step.

$$RCH=CH_2 \xrightarrow[H_3O^+]{NaHSO_3} R-CH_2CH_2SO_3H$$

$$NaHSO_3 \rightleftharpoons Na^+ + {}^-OSO_2H$$

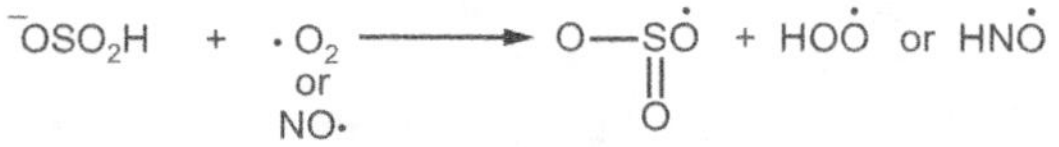

$$^-OSO_2H + \cdot O_2 \text{ or } NO\cdot \longrightarrow {}^-O-\overset{\cdot}{S}(=O)-O + HO\dot{O} \text{ or } HN\dot{O}$$

The proton is abstracted to generate free radicals.

$$RCH=CH_2 + {}^-O-S(=O)-O\cdot \longrightarrow R-\overset{\cdot}{C}H\cdot CH_2-O-S(=O)-O^-$$

The SO_3 adds across the double bond of the alkene.

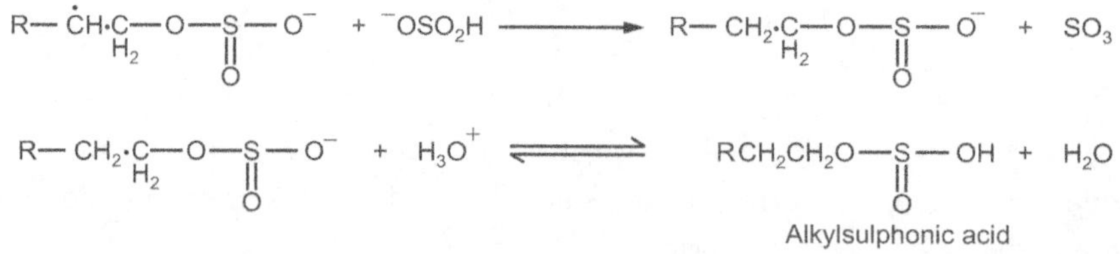

$$R-\overset{\cdot}{C}H\cdot CH_2-O-S(=O)-O^- + {}^-OSO_2H \longrightarrow R-CH_2\cdot CH_2-O-S(=O)-O^- + SO_3$$

$$R-CH_2\cdot CH_2-O-S(=O)-O^- + H_3O^+ \rightleftharpoons RCH_2CH_2O-S(=O)-OH + H_2O$$

Alkylsulphonic acid

7. **Addition of bisulphite across C=O bond of carbonyl compounds:**

   Sodium bisulphite adds across the C=O bond of the carbonyl groups to form the sulphonic acids.

$$R-\underset{\underset{O}{\|}}{C}-R' \xrightarrow[H_3O^+]{NaHSO_3} R-\underset{\underset{OH}{|}}{\overset{\overset{R'}{|}}{C}}-SO_3H$$

   Mechanism:

$$NaHSO_3 \rightleftharpoons Na^+ + {}^-OSO_2H$$

$${}^-OSO_2H + \cdot O_2 \text{ or } NO \longrightarrow O-\overset{\cdot}{\underset{\underset{O}{\|}}{S}}-O + HO\dot{O} \text{ or } HN\dot{O}$$

$$R-\underset{R'}{\overset{\|}{C}}=O + \cdot O-\underset{\underset{O}{\|}}{S}-O^- \longrightarrow R-\overset{\overset{R'}{|}}{\underset{O-\underset{\underset{O}{\|}}{S}-O^-}{C}}=O$$

$$\underset{R'}{\overset{R}{\rangle}}\underset{O \cdot}{\overset{O-\underset{\underset{O}{\|}}{S}-O^-}{C}} + O-\underset{\underset{O}{\|}}{S}-OH \longrightarrow \underset{R'}{\overset{R}{\rangle}}\underset{O-\underset{\underset{O}{\|}}{S}-O^-}{\overset{OH}{C}} + SO_3$$

$$\underset{R'}{\overset{R}{\rangle}}\underset{O-\underset{\underset{O}{\|}}{S}-O^-}{\overset{OH}{C}} + H_3O^+ \longrightarrow \underset{R'}{\overset{R}{\rangle}}\underset{OSO_2H}{\overset{OH}{C}}$$

REACTIONS OF SULPHONIC ACIDS

Various reactions undergone by sulphonic acids are attributed to the SO_3H group as well as the influence of the aryl /alkyl moiety and substituents attached to it.

1. **Acidity of sulphonic acids:**

   Sulphonic acids are strong acids. They dissociate in water as follows:

$$R-SO_3H \longrightarrow R-SO_3^- + H^+$$

   Sulphonic acids react with sodium bicarbonate to form sodium sulphonate (salt) and water along with effervescence of carbon dioxide.

$$R-SO_3H + NaHCO_3 \longrightarrow R-SO_3^-Na^+ + CO_2 + H_2O$$

2. Reaction with concentrated hydrochloric acid:

$$ArSO_3H + HCl \xrightarrow[\text{pressure}]{150\,^\circ C} ArH + ClSO_3H$$

Sulphonic acids get desulphonated when treated with concentrated hydrochloric acid at 150°C under pressure.

3. Reaction with alkali:

$$ArSO_3H + NaOH \longrightarrow ArSO_3Na + H_2O$$

Sulphonic acids react with aqueous alkali to form salt and water. But when sulphonic acids are fused with solid NaOH of high temperatures desulphonation takes place and the product formed is sodium phenoxide which is used in synthesis of phenols.

$$ArSO_3H + \underset{\text{(solid)}}{NaOH} \xrightarrow{\Delta} ArO^- Na^+$$

4. Reaction with alkaline KSH:

$$ArSO_3H \xrightarrow[KSH_{(s)}]{aq.\ KOH} ArSH$$

Sulphonic acids react with solid potassium thiol in presence of aqueous potassium hydroxide to give benzenethiol.

5. Reaction with aqueous alkali:

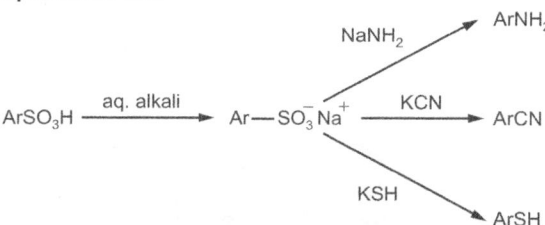

Aromatic sulphonic acids when treated with aqueous alkali give the corresponding salt. This salt can be treated with various reagents like sodamide, potassium cyanide and potassium thiol to give the corresponding amine, nitrile and thiol, respectively.

6. Reaction with PCl₅

$$ArSO_3H \xrightarrow{PCl_5} ArSO_2Cl \xrightarrow{NH_3} ArNH_2$$

Aromatic sulphonic acids react with PCl_5 to form arenesulphonyl chloride. This on further treatment with ammonia gives the corresponding amine. PCl_3 and $POCl_3$ can also be used instead of PCl_5.

SUMMARY OF THE PREPARATION AND REACTIONS OF SULPHONIC ACIDS

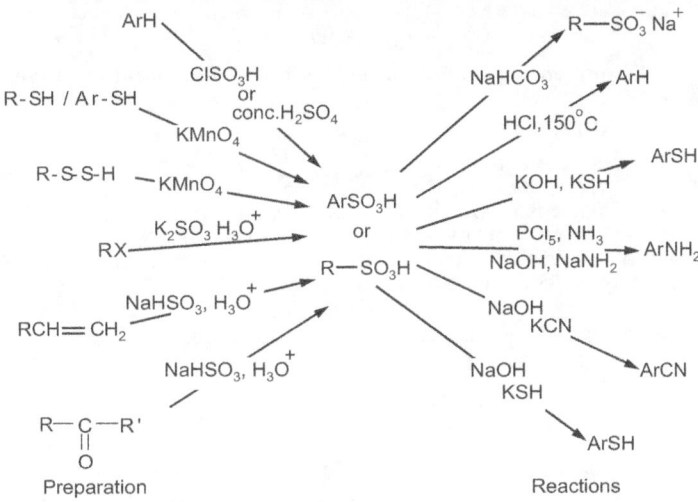

Preparation — Reactions

QUESTION BANK

1. What are sulphonic acids? Discuss their nomenclature and physical properties.
2. Discuss the physical properties and in particular the acidity of sulphonic acids.
3. Discuss the various methods of synthesis/preparation of sulphonic acids.
4. Discuss various chemical reactions undergone by sulphonic acids.
5. Discuss various reactions of sulphonic acids with mechanisms wherever required?
6. How will you prepare from benzene the following?
   (Give only reaction equations and conditions)
   (a) Benzene sulphonamide
   (b) Sulphanilamide
   (c) Methane (N-methyl) sulphonamide

Chapter 4 …

ALCOHOLS AND ETHERS

CONTENTS
Common and IUPAC nomenclature, Properties, Methods of preparation, Types and general reactions.

ALCOHOLS

Alcohols are compounds in which a hydroxyl (-OH) group is attached to a saturated carbon atom or alkyl carbon atom. Alcohols containing one hydroxyl group are called **monohydric alcohols.** Alcohols with two, three or more hydroxyl groups are known as **dihydric alcohols, trihydric alcohols** and **polyhydric alcohols**, respectively.

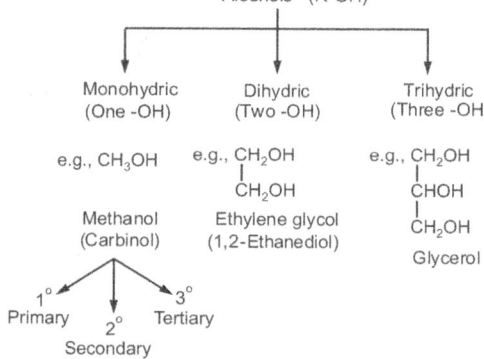

Primary (1°), secondary (2°), and tertiary (3°) alcohols

Monohydric alcohols are classified as primary (1°), secondary (2°), or tertiary (3°), depending upon whether the – OH group is attached to a primary, a secondary, or a tertiary carbon.

Example:

1°	2°	3°
R—CH₂—OH	R—CHR'—OH	R—CR'R"—OH
CH₃OH	H₃C—CH(CH₃)—OH	H₃C—C(CH₃)₂—OH
1. Methanol (Carbinol)	1. *Isopropylalcohol*	1. *tert*-Butylalcohol

NOMENCLATURE

Alcohols are named by three systems:

1. **Common System**:

In this system, alcohols (R-OH) are named as alkyl alcohols. The alkyl group attached to the – OH group is named and 'alcohol' is added as a separate word.

Example:

CH_3OH	CH_3CH_2OH	$CH_3CH_2CH_2OH$	$H_3C-\underset{H}{\underset{|}{\overset{CH_3}{\overset{|}{C}}}}-OH$
Methyl alcohol	Ethyl alcohol	n-Propyl alcohol	Isopropyl alcohol

As we go higher in the series, it becomes necessary to indicate whether a particular alcohol is Primary (1°), Secondary (2°), or Tertiary (3°). The prefix secondary is abbreviated as *Sec-*. The prefix tertiary is abbreviated as *tert-* or *t-*.

Example:

$CH_3CH_2CH_2CH_2OH$	$H_3CH_2C-\underset{H}{\underset{|}{\overset{CH_3}{\overset{|}{C}}}}-OH$	$H_3C-\underset{CH_3}{\underset{|}{\overset{CH_3}{\overset{|}{C}}}}-OH$
n-Butyl alcohol	sec-Butyl alcohol	tert-Butyl alcohol

2. **Carbinol System:**

In this system, alcohols are considered as derivatives of methyl alcohol which is called *carbinol*. The alkyl group attached to the carbon carrying the –OH group are named in alphabetic order. Then the suffix – carbinol is added.

Example:

$H-\underset{H}{\underset{|}{\overset{H}{\overset{|}{C}}}}-OH$	$H_3C-\underset{H}{\underset{|}{\overset{CH_3}{\overset{|}{C}}}}-OH$	$H_3CH_2C-\underset{H}{\underset{|}{\overset{CH_3}{\overset{|}{C}}}}-OH$
Carbinol (Methyl alcohol)	Dimethyl carbinol (Isopropyl alcohol)	Ethyl methyl carbinol (Ethyl methyl alcohol)

3. **IUPAC System:**

In this system, alcohols are named as *Alkanols*. The IUPAC rules are:

(a) Select the longest continuous carbon chain containing the –OH group.

(b) Change the name of the alkane corresponding to this chain by dropping the ending –*e* and adding the suffix –*ol*.

e.g. $CH_3 CH_2 \underset{|}{\overset{OH}{CH}} - CH_3$ Butan-2-ol or 2-Butanol.

(c) Number the chain so as to give the carbon carrying the –OH group, the lowest possible number. The position of the –OH group is indicated by this number.

(d) Indicate the position of other substituents or multiple bonds by numbers.

Example:

CH_3OH	CH_3CH_2OH	$CH_3CH_2CH_2OH$	$\overset{5}{H_3C}-\overset{4}{\underset{NH_2}{CH}}-\overset{3}{CH_2}\overset{2}{CH_2}\overset{1}{CH_2}OH$
Methanol	Ethanol	1-Propanol	4-Aminopentan-1-ol

PHYSICAL PROPERTIES

The O-H bond of alcohols is highly polar because of oxygen. The oxygen carries a partial negative charge (δ^-) and the hydrogen carries a partial positive charge (δ^+). The polarity of the O-H bond gives rise to forces of attraction between partially positive hydrogen in one alcohol molecule and partially negative oxygen in another alcohol molecule. These forces of attraction are referred to as **Hydrogen Bonding**. The reason that alcohols have higher boiling points is that a great deal of energy (in the form of heat) is required to overcome these attractive forces. Alkanes which have no –OH group, do not undergo hydrogen bonding. Therefore, their boiling points are low.

A compound that forms hydrogen bonds between its own molecules can also form hydrogen bonds with water. These alcohol-water hydrogen bonds are the cause of high solubility of lower alcohols in water. In higher alcohols, the non-polar alkyl group becomes more important. They have lesser tendencies to form hydrogen bonds with water and hence, are less soluble.

METHODS OF PREPARATION OF ALCOHOLS

1. **Hydrolysis of Alkyl Halides:**

    Alkyl halides react with aqueous sodium hydroxide to form alcohols. This is a simple nucleophilic substitution reaction.

    $$R-X + NaOH \xrightarrow[\Delta]{H_2O} R-OH + NaX$$
    Alkyl Halide → Alcohol

    $$CH_3CH_2-Br + NaOH \xrightarrow[\Delta]{H_2O} CH_3CH_2-OH + NaBr$$
    Ethyl bromide → Ethyl alcohol

2. **Hydration of Alkenes:**

    Alkenes react with sulphuric acid to produce alkyl hydrogen sulphates, which upon hydrolysis give alcohols.

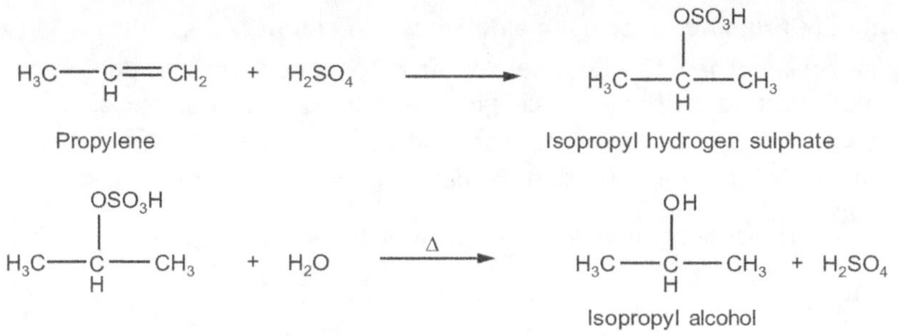

$$H_3C-\underset{H}{C}=CH_2 + H_2SO_4 \longrightarrow H_3C-\underset{H}{\overset{OSO_3H}{C}}-CH_3$$

Propylene → Isopropyl hydrogen sulphate

$$H_3C-\underset{H}{\overset{OSO_3H}{C}}-CH_3 + H_2O \xrightarrow{\Delta} H_3C-\underset{H}{\overset{OH}{C}}-CH_3 + H_2SO_4$$

Isopropyl alcohol

3. Hydroboration-Oxidation of alkenes:

Alkenes react with diborane B_2H_6 to form trialkylboranes. Diborane adds as borane, BH_3. The positive part of BH_3 is the BH_2 the negative part is hydrogen. The addition can take place upto three alkane molecules, followed by hydrolysis.

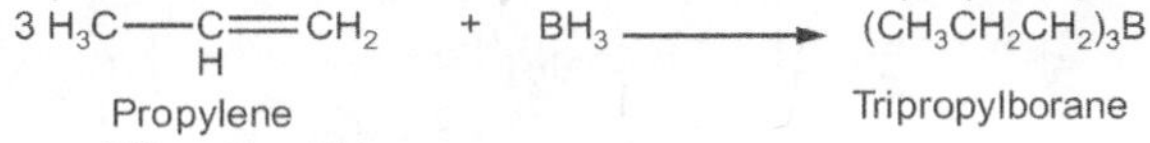

$$3\ H_3C-\underset{H}{C}=CH_2 + BH_3 \longrightarrow (CH_3CH_2CH_2)_3B$$

Propylene → Tripropylborane

$$BH_3 = \underset{\delta-}{H}-\underset{\delta+}{BH_2}$$

Trialkylboranes are used for making primary alcohols by reaction with alkaline aqueous solution of hydrogen peroxide.

$$(CH_3CH_2CH_2)_3B + H_2O_2 \xrightarrow{^-OH} 3CH_3CH_2CH_2OH + H_3BO_3$$

Tripropylborane → 1-Propanol

4. Hydrolysis of esters:

Alcohols may be prepared by base or acid catalyzed hydrolysis of esters.

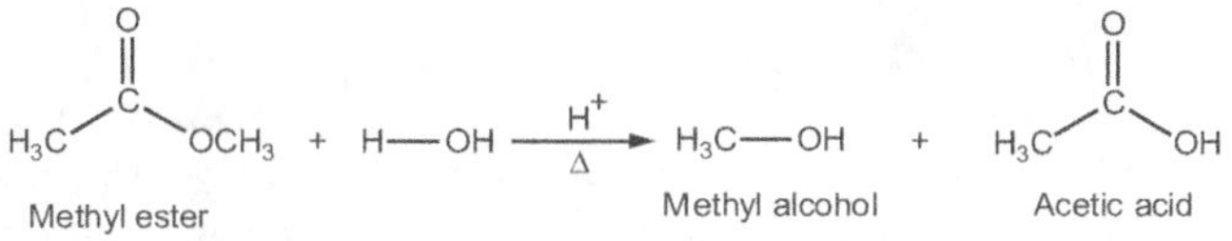

$$H_3C-\overset{O}{\underset{\|}{C}}-OCH_3 + H-OH \xrightarrow[\Delta]{H^+} H_3C-OH + H_3C-\overset{O}{\underset{\|}{C}}-OH$$

Methyl ester — Methyl alcohol — Acetic acid

5. Reduction of aldehydes and ketones:

Aldehydes and ketones can be reduced with H_2/Ni or lithium aluminium hydride to form the corresponding alcohols. Aldehydes give primary alcohols. Ketones give secondary alcohols.

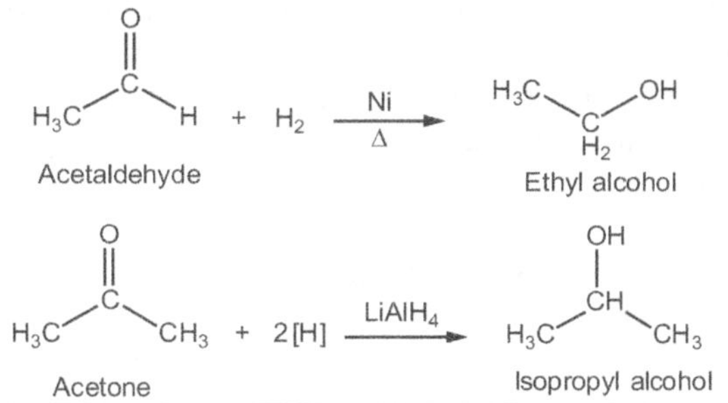

$$H_3C-\overset{O}{\underset{\|}{C}}-H + H_2 \xrightarrow[\Delta]{Ni} H_3C-\underset{H_2}{\overset{OH}{C}}$$

Acetaldehyde → Ethyl alcohol

$$H_3C-\overset{O}{\underset{\|}{C}}-CH_3 + 2[H] \xrightarrow{LiAlH_4} H_3C-\overset{OH}{\underset{}{CH}}-CH_3$$

Acetone → Isopropyl alcohol

6. Addition of Grignard reagents to aldehydes and ketones:

Grignard reagent reacts with aldehyde or ketones to form an addition compound, which on hydrolysis with dilute acid gives the corresponding alcohols.

The alkyl part R of the reagent is δ^- and gets added to electropositive carbonyl carbon, while the MgX portion being δ^+ gets added to the carbonyl oxygen. $\begin{bmatrix} R - MgX \\ \delta^- \quad \delta^+ \end{bmatrix}$. The adduct on hydrolysis yields the alcohol.

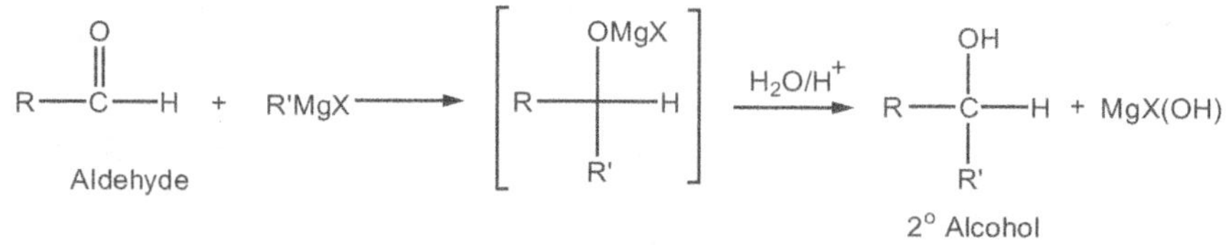

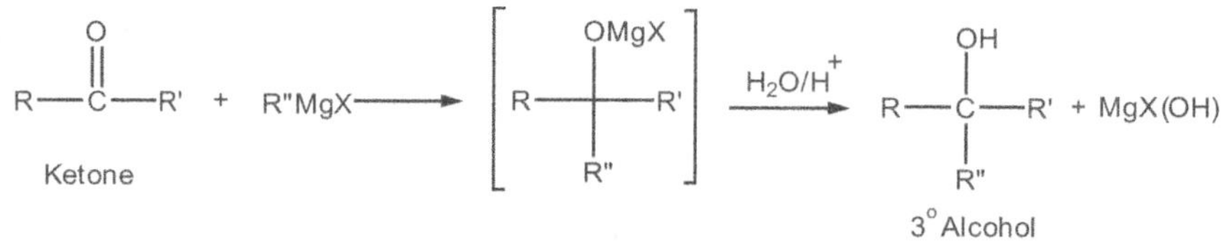

$$R-\underset{\text{Aldehyde}}{\overset{O}{\underset{\|}{C}}}-H + R'MgX \longrightarrow \begin{bmatrix} R-\underset{R'}{\overset{OMgX}{\underset{|}{C}}}-H \end{bmatrix} \xrightarrow{H_2O/H^+} R-\underset{R'}{\overset{OH}{\underset{|}{C}}}-H + MgX(OH)$$
$$\text{2° Alcohol}$$

$$R-\underset{\text{Ketone}}{\overset{O}{\underset{\|}{C}}}-R' + R''MgX \longrightarrow \begin{bmatrix} R-\underset{R''}{\overset{OMgX}{\underset{|}{C}}}-R' \end{bmatrix} \xrightarrow{H_2O/H^+} R-\underset{R''}{\overset{OH}{\underset{|}{C}}}-R' + MgX(OH)$$
$$\text{3° Alcohol}$$

REACTIONS OF ALCOHOLS

1. Reactions with metals:

Alcohols react with sodium or potassium to form alkoxides with the liberation of hydrogen gas.

$$2\ CH_3CH_2OH + 2\ Na \longrightarrow 2\ C_2H_5 + H_2 \uparrow$$
$$\text{Ethyl alcohol} \qquad\qquad \text{Sodium ethoxide}$$

The above reaction shows that alcohols are acidic in nature. The reason for this is that the O – H bond in alcohols is polar and allows the release of the hydrogen atom as proton (H$^+$). However, alcohols are weaker acids (Ka = 10^{-16} to 10^{-18}) than water. This is because the alkyl groups in alcohols exert a, +I effect. They release electrons towards the oxygen atom so that it becomes negatively charged. This negative charge on oxygen makes the release of the positive proton more difficult.

Tertiary alcohols are less acidic than secondary alcohols. Whereas, the secondary alcohols are less acidic than primary alcohols. This is because the +I effect would be maximum in tertiary alcohols, as they contain three alkyl groups attached to the carbon bearing the –OH group.

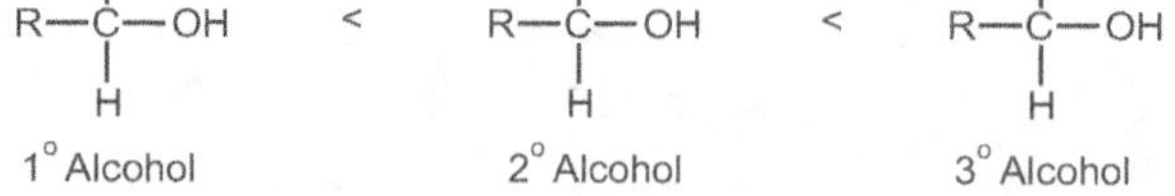

$$R-\underset{H}{\overset{H}{\underset{|}{\overset{|}{C}}}}-OH \quad < \quad R-\underset{H}{\overset{H}{\underset{|}{\overset{|}{C}}}}-OH \quad < \quad R-\underset{H}{\overset{H}{\underset{|}{\overset{|}{C}}}}-OH$$
$$\text{1° Alcohol} \qquad\qquad \text{2° Alcohol} \qquad\qquad \text{3° Alcohol}$$

Alcohols are not acidic enough to react with aqueous NaOH or KOH.

$$ROH + NaOH \longrightarrow \text{No reaction}$$

2. **Reaction with phosphorus halides:**

    Alcohols react with phosphorus pentahalides (PX_5)/phosphorus trihalides (PX_3) to form alkyl halides and phosphorus oxyhalides. The later are also good halogenating agents.

    $$CH_3CH_2\text{—}OH + PBr_5 \longrightarrow CH_3CH_2\text{—}Br + POBr_3 + HBr$$
    Ethyl alcohol   Phosphrous pentabromide   Ethyl bromide   Phosphrous oxybromides

3. **Reaction with thionyl chloride:**

    Alcohols react with thionyl chloride ($SOCl_2$) to form alkyl chlorides.

    $$CH_3CH_2\text{—}OH + SOCl_2 \longrightarrow CH_3CH_2\text{—}Cl + SO_2\uparrow + HCl\uparrow$$
    Ethyl alcohol   Thionyl chloride   Ethyl chloride

4. **Reaction with hydrogen halides:**

    Alcohols react with hydrogen halides (HX) to form the corresponding alkyl halides.

    $$CH_3CH_2\text{—}OH + HBr \longrightarrow CH_3CH_2\text{—}Br + H_2O$$
    Ethyl alcohol   Hydrogen bromide   Ethyl bromide

    The order of reactivity of hydrogen halides is HI > HBr > HCl. No catalyst is required in the case of HBr or HI. HCl reacts only in the presence of a catalyst (anhydrous $ZnCl_2$).

    Mechanism: Primary alcohols react with hydrogen halides by SN_2 mechanism.

    Step 1: Protonation of ethyl alcohol

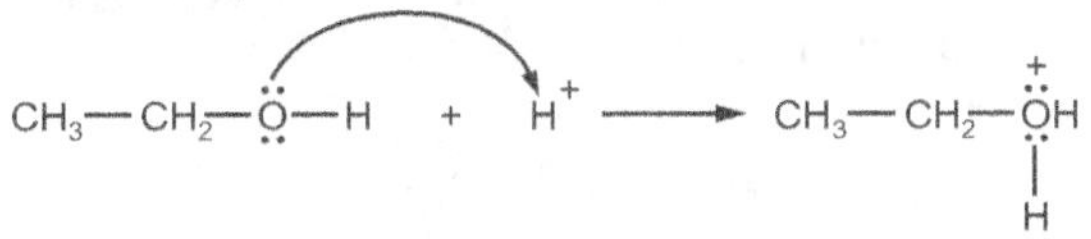

    $$CH_3\text{—}CH_2\text{—}\ddot{O}\text{—}H + H^+ \longrightarrow CH_3\text{—}CH_2\text{—}\overset{+}{\ddot{O}}H\text{—}H$$

    Step 2: Nucleophile (Br^-) attacks the carbon holding the protonated hydroxyl group to form ethyl bromide.

    $$Br^- + CH_3\text{—}CH_2\text{—}\overset{+}{\ddot{O}}H\text{—}H \longrightarrow CH_3CH_2\text{—}Br + H_2O$$

    Tertiary and secondary alcohols react with hydrogen halides by SN_1 mechanism.

5. **Reaction with nitric acid:**

    Alcohols react with nitric acid to form alkyl nitrates.

    $$CH_3CH_2\text{—}OH + HNO_3 \longrightarrow CH_3\text{—}CH_2\text{—}O\text{—}NO_2 + H_2O$$
    Ethyl alcohol   Ethyl nitrate

6. **Reaction with sulphuric acid:**

   The reaction of alcohols with sulphuric acid is very sensitive to reaction conditions.

   (i) When ethyl alcohol is treated with concentrated sulphuric acid at room temperature, ethyl hydrogen sulphate is produced.

   $$CH_3CH_2-OH + HO-SO_2OH \xrightarrow{R.T.} C_2H_5-O-SO_2OH + H_2O$$
   Ethyl alcohol   Sulphuric acid   Ethyl hydrogen sulphate

   (ii) **Dehydration of alcohols to alkenes:** When ethyl alcohol is treated with concentrated sulphuric acid at 170°C, ethylene is formed. Notice that only one alcohol molecule is involved in the reaction.

   $$CH_3CH_2-OH \xrightarrow[170\,°C]{Conc.\ H_2SO_4} CH_2=CH_2 + H_2O$$
   Ethyl alcohol   Ethylene

   The ease of dehydration of alcohols follows the order 3° > 2° > 1° which is also the order of stability of the carbonium ions. Dehydration of secondary and tertiary alcohols containing four or more carbon atoms gives a mixture of two alkenes. **The alkene produced in greater abundance is indicated by Saytzeff's Rule. It states that the alkene formed preferentially is the one containing the higher number of alkyl groups.**

   Example:

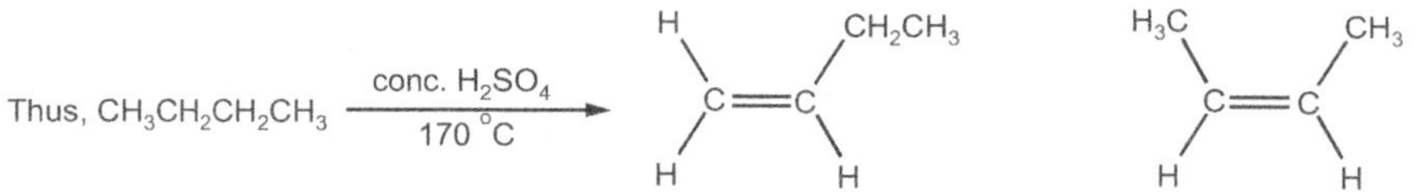

   Thus, $CH_3CH_2CH_2CH_3 \xrightarrow[170\,°C]{conc.\ H_2SO_4}$

   1-Butene (Minor product)   2-Butene (Major product)

   (iii) **Dehydration of alcohols to form ethers:** When excess of ethyl alcohol is treated with concentrated sulphuric acid at 140°C, diethyl ether is formed. Notice that two alcohol molecules are involved in the reaction.

   $$CH_3CH_2-OH + CH_3CH_2-OH \xrightarrow[140\,°C]{Conc.\ H_2SO_4} CH_3CH_2-O-CH_2CH_3$$
   Ethyl alcohol   Diethyl ether

   Dehydration of alcohols to ethers or alkenes can also be brought about by passing the vapours of the alcohol over heated alumina catalyst.

7. **Reaction with carboxylic acids:**

   Alcohols react with carboxylic acids to form esters. Concentrated sulphuric acid is used as a catalyst. The reaction is reversible and can be shifted in the forward direction by removing water as soon as it is formed.

   $$CH_3CH_2-OH + CH_3COOH \underset{-H_2O}{\overset{H^+}{\rightleftharpoons}} CH_3CH_2-O-\overset{O}{\underset{\|}{C}}-CH_3$$
   Ethyl alcohol   Acetic acid   Ethyl acetate

   The reaction between an alcohol and a carboxylic acid to form an ester is called **Esterification**.

8. Reaction with Grignard reagents:

Alcohols react with Grignard reagents (RMgX) to form alkanes.

$$CH_3CH_2-OH + CH_3MgBr \longrightarrow CH_4 + CH_3CH_2OMgBr$$

Ethyl alcohol   Grignard reagent   Methane

9. Reduction:

Alcohols undergo reduction with concentrated hydroiodic acid and red phosphorus to produce alkanes.

$$CH_3CH_2-OH + 2HI \xrightarrow[\Delta]{P} CH_3CH_3 + I_2 + H_2O$$

Ethyl alcohol   Ethane

10. Oxidation:

Alcohols can be oxidized. The nature of the product depends on the types of alcohol and the conditions of the reaction. Most widely used oxidizing agents are $KMnO_4 + H_2SO_4$ or $Na_2Cr_2O_7 + H_2SO_4$. **Oxidation of alcohols can be used to distinguish between primary, secondary, and tertiary alcohols.**

Primary alcohols are first oxidized to aldehydes and then to acids.

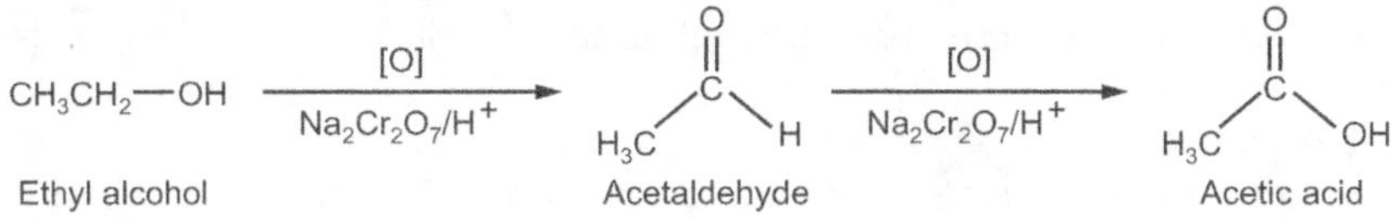

$$CH_3CH_2-OH \xrightarrow[Na_2Cr_2O_7/H^+]{[O]} CH_3CHO \xrightarrow[Na_2Cr_2O_7/H^+]{[O]} CH_3COOH$$

Ethyl alcohol   Acetaldehyde   Acetic acid

Notice that the acid and the alcohol contain the same number of carbon atoms. The reaction can be stopped at the aldehyde stage by removing it from the oxidizing medium as it is formed (e.g., by distillation).

Secondary alcohols are oxidized to the corresponding ketones.

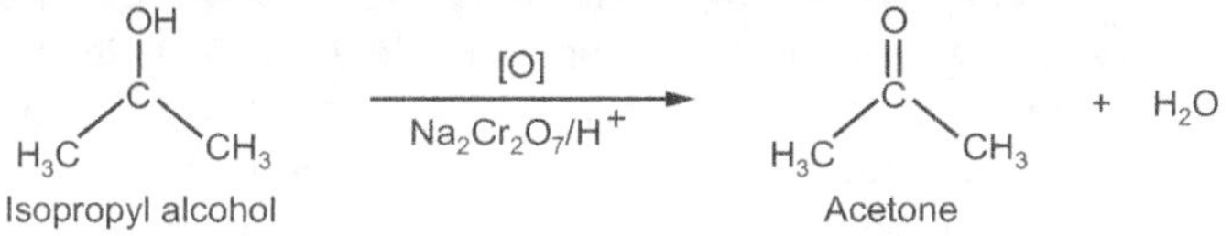

$$(CH_3)_2CHOH \xrightarrow[Na_2Cr_2O_7/H^+]{[O]} (CH_3)_2C=O + H_2O$$

Isopropyl alcohol   Acetone

Tertiary alcohols are stable to oxidation under normal conditions.

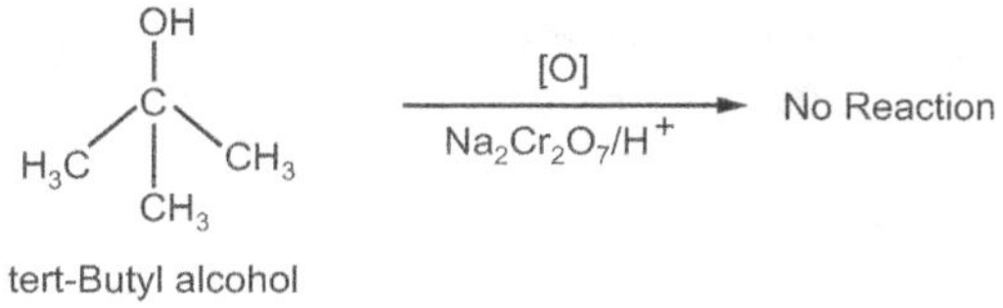

$$(CH_3)_3COH \xrightarrow[Na_2Cr_2O_7/H^+]{[O]} \text{No Reaction}$$

tert-Butyl alcohol

11. Dehydrogenation:

Different types of alcohols give different products when their vapours are passed over copper gauze at 300°C.

Primary alcohols lose hydrogen and give an aldehyde.

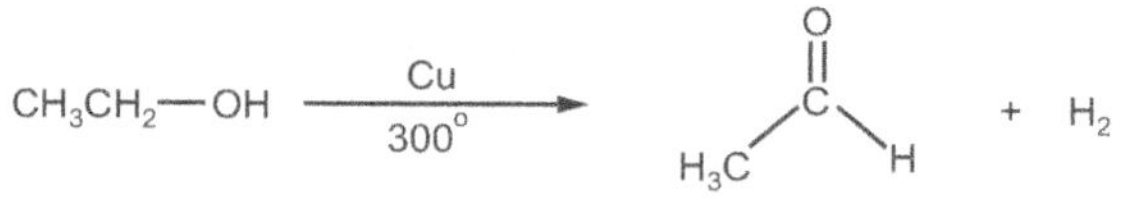

$$CH_3CH_2-OH \xrightarrow[300°]{Cu} CH_3CHO + H_2$$

Ethyl alcohol → Acetaldehyde

Secondary alcohols lose hydrogen and yield a ketone.

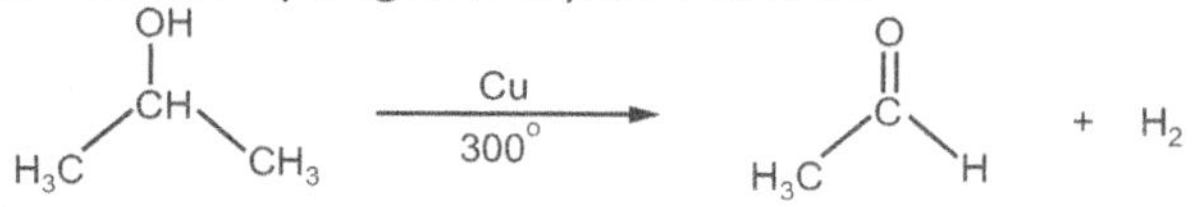

$$(CH_3)_2CHOH \xrightarrow[300°]{Cu} (CH_3)_2C=O + H_2$$

Isopropyl alcohol → Acetone

Tertiary alcohols are not dehydrogenated but lose a molecule of water to give alkenes.

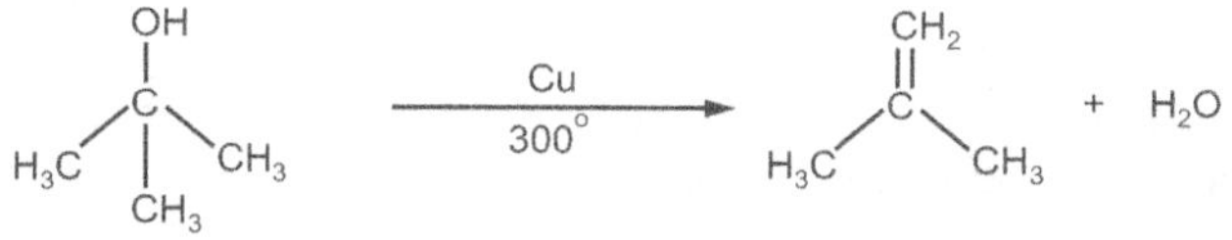

$$(CH_3)_3C-OH \xrightarrow[300°]{Cu} CH_2=C(CH_3)_2 + H_2O$$

tert-Butyl alcohol → 2-Methylpropene

The following tests are used to distinguish between primary, secondary, and tertiary alcohols.

1. **Lucas Test:**

   In this test, alcohols are treated with a solution of HCl and Zinc chloride (*Lucas reagent*) to form alkyl halides. Zinc chloride serves as a catalyst.

   $$R-OH + HCl \xrightarrow{ZnCl_2} R-Cl + H_2O$$

   Alcohol → Alkyl halide

   The three types of alcohols undergo this reaction at different rates. Tertiary alcohols react with *Lucas reagent* very rapidly. Secondary alcohols react somewhat slower. Primary alcohols react with *Lucas reagent* even more slowly only at high temperatures.

   Lucas test is carried out as follows: alcohol is mixed with concentrated HCl and $ZnCl_2$. The alkyl chloride, which is formed, is insoluble in the medium. It causes the solution to become cloudy before it separates as a distinct layer.

   (a) With **Tertiary alcohols** cloudiness appears immediately.
   (b) With **secondary alcohols** cloudiness appears in 5 minutes
   (c) With **primary alcohols** the solution remains clear. This is because primary alcohols do not react with *Lucas reagent* at room temperature. High temperatures are needed.

2. **Dichromate Test:**

   This test is based on the fact that different types of alcohols give different products on oxidation. The alcohol is treated at room temperature with sodium dichromate in sulphuric acid (orange solution). Identification of the products gives information regarding the types of the alcohol.

(a) **Primary alcohols** give a carboxylic acid containing the same number of carbons. These will be change in colour of the solution from orange to green.

(b) **Secondary alcohols** give a ketone containing the same number of carbons. There will be a change in colour of the solution from orange to green.

(c) **Tertiary alcohols** don not react under these conditions. Solution will remain orange.

ETHERS

Ethers are the compounds having general formula $C_nH_{2n+2}O$ which is the same as that of monohydric alcohols. They possess a bivalent oxygen function (-O-) and are represented by the general structures, R – O – R, R – O – Ar or Ar – O – Ar.

(I) Ethers: R-O-R'; R' = Alkyl or aryl

CH_3-O-CH_3 $CH_3-CH_2-O-CH_3$ $CH_3-CH_2-O-CH_2-CH_3$ $CH_3O-C_6H_5$

1. Methylether   2. Ethyl methyl ether   3. Ethylether   4. Methyl phenyl ether (Anisole)

(II) Cyclic Ethers (Epoxides):

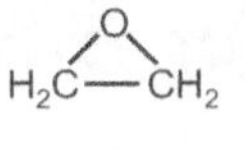

Ethylenepoxide 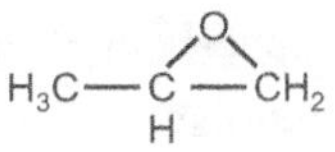   2-Methylethyleneoxide

(III) Crown Ethers:

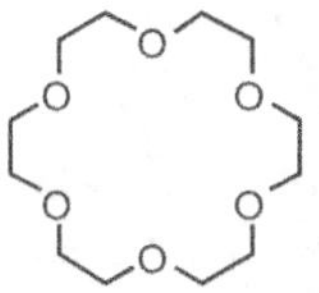

[18] Crown-6

The numbers 18 and 6 indicate the total number of atoms in the cyclic ether molecule and total number of oxygen atoms in it, respectively, the word crown is used as they are highly symmetrical crown shaped molecules.

NOMENCLATURE

Ethers are named by two systems:

1. Common System:

When two alkyl groups are attached to oxygen, the alkyl groups are named alphabetically and the word ether is added.

CH_3-O-CH_3 $CH_3-CH_2-O-CH_3$ $CH_3-CH_2-O-CH_2-CH_3$

1. Methylether   2. Ethyl methyl ether   3. Ethylether

2. **IUPAC System**:

In this system, ethers are named as **Alkoxyalkanes.** The larger alkyl group is considered to be alkane. The name of the alkane is prefixed by the name of alkoxy group and position number.

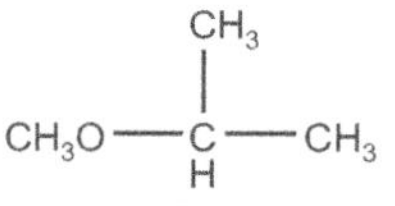

$$CH_3O-\underset{H}{\underset{|}{\overset{CH_3}{\overset{|}{C}}}}-CH_3 \qquad H_3C-\underset{H}{\underset{|}{\overset{OCH_2CH_3}{\overset{|}{C}}}}-CH_3$$

2-Methoxyisopropane 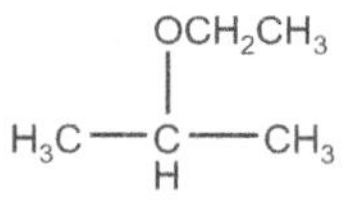   2-Ethoxyisopropane

PHYSICAL PROPERTIES

These are mostly colorless liquids, immiscible with water (exception; dioxane), but readily misable with alcohols and benzene. The lower ethers like diethyl ether are very volatile. These are highly inflammable liquids. Aryl ethers (diphenyl ether) have high b.p. and used as high boiling solvents in many reactions. Ethers are neutral and non-acidic in nature. Therefore, used as solubilizing agent or solvents, routinely in chemical industry. The oxygen of ethers is sp^3 hybridized and bond angle is 107°.

METHOD OF PREPARATION OF ETHERS

1. **Dehydration of alcohols:**

   Ethers are usually prepared by heating the corresponding alcohols with conc. H_2SO_4.

   $$2\ CH_3CH_2-OH \xrightarrow[140\ °C]{Conc.\ H_2SO_4} CH_3CH_2-O-CH_2CH_3 + H_2O$$

   Ethyl alcohol   Diethyl ether

2. **Williamson's synthesis:**

   This method is very popular in the laboratory preparation of ethers. It consists of treating appropriate alkyl halide with an alkoxide (produced by the action of sodium on alcohol) or a phenoxide (prepared by the action of sodium hydroxide on the corresponding phenol).

   $$R-ONa + R'-X \longrightarrow R-O-R' + NaX$$

   Sodium alkoxide   Alkyl halide   Ether

   $$H_3CH_2C-ONa + H_3CH_2C-Cl \longrightarrow H_3CH_2C-O-CH_2CH_3 + NaCl$$

   Sodium ethoxide   Ethyl chloride   Diethyl ether

   Mechanism: Willimason's synthesis follows SN_2 mechanism.

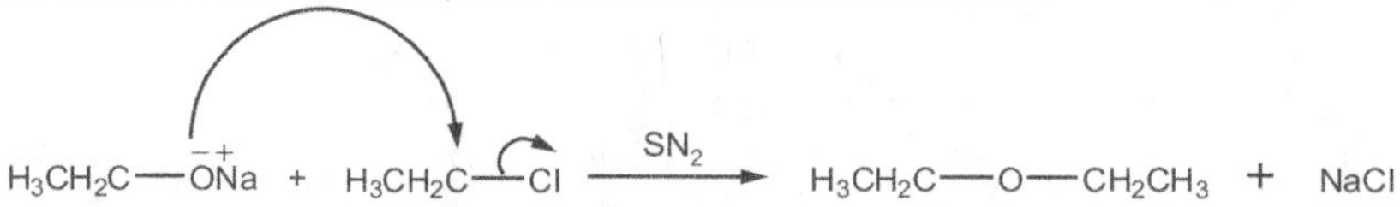

   $$H_3CH_2C-\overset{-}{O}\overset{+}{Na} + H_3CH_2C-Cl \xrightarrow{SN_2} H_3CH_2C-O-CH_2CH_3 + NaCl$$

   Sodium ethoxide   Ethyl chloride   Diethyl ether

3. Action of diazomethane on alcohols:

Ethers can be obtained by action of diazomethane on alcohols in presence of HBF_4.

$$H_3CH_2C-OH + CH_2N_2 \xrightarrow{HBF_4} H_3CH_2C-O-CH_3 + N_2$$
Ethyl alcohol   Diazomethane   Ethyl methyl ether

Diazomethane is used as a good, selective *o*-methylation reagent.

REACTIONS OF ETHERS

Since the C – O bond does not cleave readily, the ethers are relatively less reactive (neutral) compounds and hence quite useful as solvents in organic reactions. Unlike alcohols, the ethers are not acidic under ordinary conditions. However, they undergo some unusual cleavage reactions (β-elimination) with very strong carbanionic bases such as methyllithium. Due to the presence of lone pair of electrons on sp^3 orbitals, ethers behave as weak bases reacting with strong acids to form unstable oxonium salts.

1. Halogenation:

The ethers are readily halogenated upon treatment with halogens in absence of sunlight.

$$CH_3CH_2-O-CH_2CH_3 \xrightarrow{Cl_2} CH_3\underset{Cl}{C}H-O-\underset{Cl}{C}HCH_3$$
Diethyl ether   Dichlorodiethyl ether

2. Reaction with PCl_5:

Alkyl chlorides are obtained by treatment of PCl_5 on ethers.

$$CH_3CH_2-O-CH_2CH_3 + PCl_5 \xrightarrow{\Delta} 2\ CH_3CH_2Cl + POCl_3$$
Diethyl ether   Ethyl chloride

3. Autooxidation:

Peroxides are formed when ethers combine with atmospheric oxygen. These are quite reactive. Therefore, ethers are tested for peroxide before their use, if they are stored for a prolonged time.

$$CH_3CH_2-O-CH_2CH_3 + O_2 \xrightarrow{Longer\ Time} CH_3\underset{OOH}{C}H-O-CH_2CH_3$$
Diethyl ether   Peroxide of diethyl ether

4. Cleavage by acids:

Alcohols and alkyl halides are formed by treatment of hot concentrated HBr or HI on ethers.

$$CH_3CH_2-O-CH_2CH_3 + HBr \xrightarrow{\Delta} CH_3CH_2OH + CH_3CH_2Br$$
Diethyl ether   Ethyl alcohol   Ethyl bromide

5. Reaction with acetyl chloride:

Ethyl chloride and ethyl acetate are formed by treatment of acetyl chloride in presence of anhydrous $ZnCl_2$ on ethers.

$$H_3CH_2C-O-CH_2CH_3 + H_3C-\underset{\underset{Acetyl\ chloride}{}}{\overset{\overset{O}{\|}}{C}}-Cl \xrightarrow{ZnCl_2,\ \Delta} CH_3CH_2Cl + H_3C-\underset{\underset{Ethyl\ acetate}{}}{\overset{\overset{O}{\|}}{C}}-OCH_2CH_3$$

(Diethyl ether) (Ethyl chloride)

6. Hydrolysis:

Alcohols are obtained by hydrolyzing ethers using dilute H_2SO_4.

$$H_3CH_2C-O-CH_2CH_3 + H_2O \xrightarrow{H^+,\ \Delta} 2\ CH_3CH_2OH$$

(Diethyl ether) (Ethyl alcohol)

QUESTION BANK

1. Define and classify alcohols with examples.
2. Explain different synthetic methods for the preparation of alcohols.
3. Explain why boiling points of alcohols are much higher than those of the corresponding alkanes.
4. Why water solubility of alcohols falls rapidly as we go to higher alcohols?
5. How will you distinguish between 1°, 2°, and 3° alcohols?
6. Explain different synthetic methods for the preparation of ethers.
7. How are alcohols prepared? Describe their important reactions.
8. How is methyl alcohol manufactured?
9. How do primary, secondary, and tertiary alcohols differ in their behavior towards oxidation?
10. What will be the products when methyl magnesium bromide is reacted with
    (a) Propanol
    (b) Acetophenone
    (c) Acetone
11. Why are crown ethers called 'crown' ether? Explain the nomenclature of 12 crown 4, with its structure.
12. What will be the major product of reaction of concentrated sulphuric acid and n-hexane at 180°C? Explain the reason.
13. Draw the structures of following:
    (a) Anisole
    (b) 1, 4-Dioxane
    (c) Diglyme
    (d) Diphenyl ether.

14. What happens when ethyl alcohol is treated with conc. sulphuric acid under different conditions?
15. What happens when ethyl alcohol is treated with alkaline solution of iodine?
16. What happens when tert–butyl alcohol is passed over heated copper at 300°C?
17. How will you distinguish among primary, secondary and tertiary alcohols?
18. How will you distinguish between 1-propanol and 2-propanol?
10. How will you distinguish between methyl alcohol and ethyl alcohol?
20. Explain why alcohols have higher boiling point than alkanes of comparable molecular weights?
21. Explain why ethyl alcohol has higher boiling point than diethyl ether?
22. Explain different synthetic methods of preparation of ethers.
23. Comment on Williamson's ether synthesis.
24. Predict the product:

$$H_3C-\overset{O}{\underset{\|}{C}}-OCH_3 + H-OH \xrightarrow[\Delta]{H^+}$$

Methyl Ester

25. Can you draw the structure of quaternary alcohol?
26. Which will have higher boiling C_2H_5OH or C_2H_5SH? Why?
27. Name the compound, $CH_3\ CH\ (Br)\ CH = CH\ CH_2\ OH$.
28. Using Grignards reagent, CH_3MgX, how will you prepare the following (Give only reaction equations).
    (a) Ethanol
    (b) Isopropyl alcohol
    (c) t-Butyalcohol.

Chapter 5 ...

AMINES

CONTENTS
Common and IUPAC nomenclature, Chemistry of amines, Separation of amines, Methods of preparation, Types, General reactions, Preparation and use of diazonium salts.

INTRODUCTION

Hydrocarbon derivatives of ammonia are called as "Amines". When the hydrocarbon group of amine is alkyl, allyl or cycloalkyl it is said to be an aliphatic amine; while if the hydrocarbon group is aryl, the amine is called an aromatic amine.

There are three kinds of amines.

$R-NH_2$ or $Ar-NH_2$ = 1° or Primary amine

$R-NH-R'$ or $Ar-NH-R'$ = 2° or Secondary amine

$R-N-R'-R''$ or $Ar-N-R'-R''$ = 3° or Tertiary amine

$-\overset{|}{\underset{|}{N}}^{\oplus}-$ = 4° or Quaternary ammonium compounds.

Example:

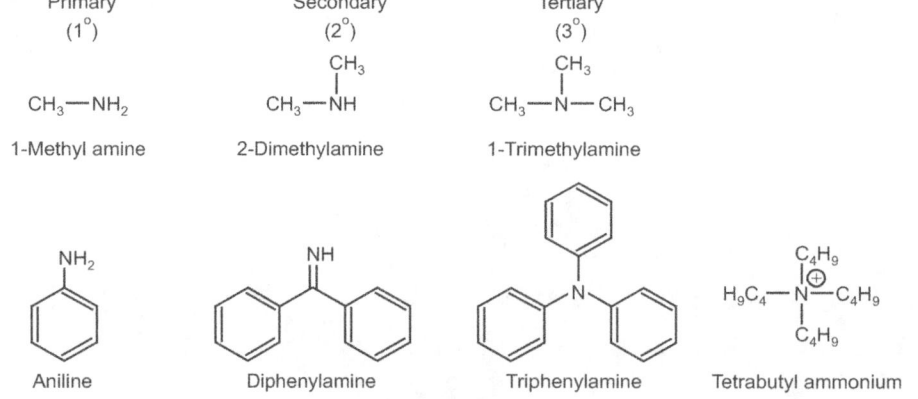

Primary (1°)	Secondary (2°)	Tertiary (3°)	
CH₃—NH₂	CH₃—NH—CH₃ (with CH₃)	CH₃—N(CH₃)—CH₃	
1-Methyl amine	2-Dimethylamine	1-Trimethylamine	
Aniline	Diphenylamine	Triphenylamine	Tetrabutyl ammonium

IUPAC Nomenclature:
1. The name ending with suffix **amine**.
2. Longest carbon chain selected as parent chain and its name given.
3. The ending name of **alkane** is replaced with **amine**. e.g. alkanamine.
4. Numbering of chain is done such that carbon bearing amino group gets least number.
5. The name of substituents and their respective locants are prefixed with base name.

Example:

$$CH_3-CH_2CH_2\underset{\underset{NH_2}{|}}{CH}-CH_3$$
2-Pentanamine

2-Methylaniline

Structure of amines: The nitrogen in amines like in ammonia in sp^3 hybridized. The three alkyl groups/hydrogen occupy corners of a regular tetrahedron and the remaining sp^3 orbital containing the unshared electron pair is directed towards the remaining 4th corner. Amines have a pyramidal structure with a bond angle of 108°. Amines are polar liquids/semisolids/solids with fishy order, high b.p. and brown-black colour.

METHODS FOR PREPARATION OF AMINES

1. **Reduction of nitro compounds:**
   This method can not be used when the molecule also contains some other easily hydrogenated groups, such as C = C double bond. The *in situ* generation of H_2 through reaction of metal and mineral acid is commonly employed for the purpose.

Example:

$$Ar-NO_2 / R-NO_2 \xrightarrow{Metal, H^{\oplus} or\ H_2\ catalyst} Ar-NH_2 / R-NH_2$$
$$1°\ Amine$$

o-Nitroacetanilide $\xrightarrow{H_2/Pt}$ o-Aminoacetanilide

2. **Reductive amination:**
   Many aldehydes (RCHO) and ketones (R_2CO) are converted into amines by reductive amination in presence of ammonia.

Benzaldehyde $\xrightarrow{NH_3}$ Benzylimine $\xrightarrow{H_2/Ni}$ Benzylamine

3. Ammonolysis of halides:

$$R\text{—}X + NH_3 \longrightarrow R\text{—}\overset{\oplus}{N}H_3\overset{\ominus}{X}$$

$$R\text{—}\overset{\oplus}{N}H_3\overset{\ominus}{X} + \overset{\ominus}{O}H \longrightarrow R\text{—}NH_2 + H_2O + X^\ominus$$

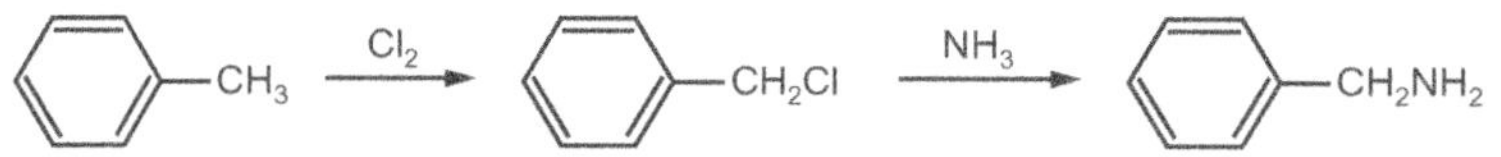

Toluene $\xrightarrow{Cl_2}$ Benzylchloride $\xrightarrow{NH_3}$ Benzylamine

4. Hoffmann degradation of amides:

Hoffmann degradation of amides has the special feature of yielding a product containing one less carbon than the starting material. This involves a rearrangement reaction of an N-haloamide into an isocyanate which, hydrolyses rapidly to an amine.

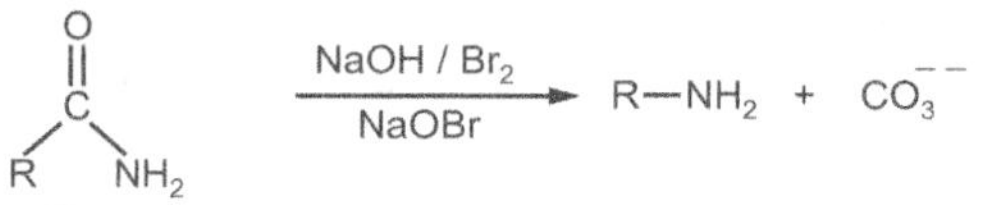

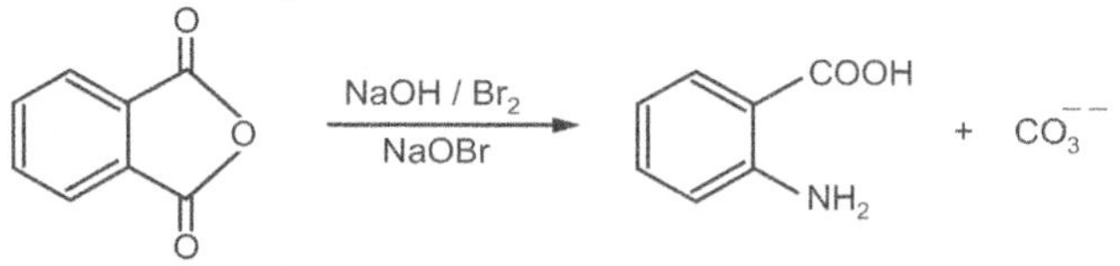

$$R\text{—}\underset{NH_2}{\overset{O}{\overset{\|}{C}}} \xrightarrow[NaOBr]{NaOH \,/\, Br_2} R\text{—}NH_2 + CO_3^{--}$$

Phthalic anhydride $\xrightarrow[NaOBr]{NaOH \,/\, Br_2}$ Anthranilic acid (COOH, NH_2) + CO_3^{--}

Mechanism:

Step 1: Electrophilic substitution reaction occurs at the N atom of an amide, here a positive halogen atom attaches the N atom and a proton is abstracted by the OH⁻ to form N–haloamide.

$$2\,NaOH + Br_2 \longrightarrow Na\overset{\oplus}{O}\overset{\ominus}{Br}$$

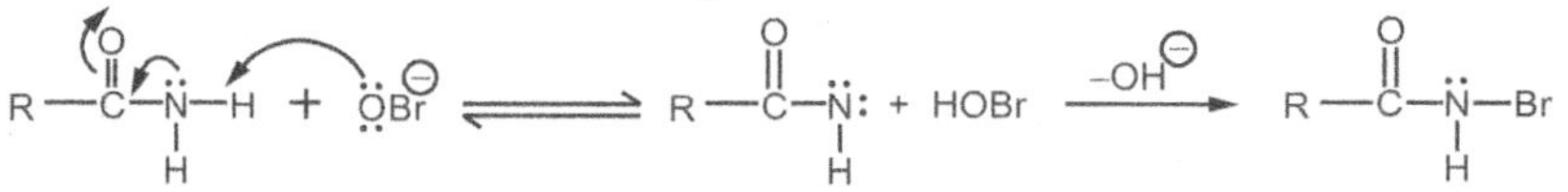

$$R\text{—}\underset{H}{\overset{O}{\overset{\|}{C}}}\text{—}\ddot{N}\text{—}H + \overset{..}{\overset{..}{O}}\overset{\ominus}{Br} \rightleftharpoons R\text{—}\underset{H}{\overset{O}{\overset{\|}{C}}}\text{—}\ddot{N}: + HOBr \xrightarrow{-OH^\ominus} R\text{—}\underset{H}{\overset{O}{\overset{\|}{C}}}\text{—}\ddot{N}\text{—}Br$$

Step 2: The H atom on the N atom is abstracted by OH⁻; the electron withdrawing effect of the carbonyl and bromo group makes H highly acidic.

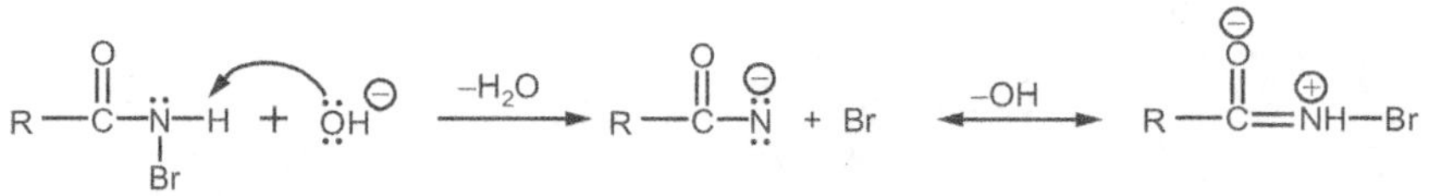

$$R\text{—}\underset{Br}{\overset{O}{\overset{\|}{C}}}\text{—}\ddot{N}\text{—}H + \overset{..}{\overset{..}{O}}H^\ominus \xrightarrow{-H_2O} R\text{—}\overset{O}{\overset{\|}{C}}\text{—}\ddot{N}^\ominus + Br \xleftarrow{-OH} R\text{—}\overset{\overset{\ominus}{O}}{\overset{\|}{C}}\text{=}\overset{\oplus}{N}H\text{—}Br$$

Step 3: Elimination of the halide ion and migration of R occurs in a concerted step to form isocyanate. Probably this is the rate determining step.

$$R-\overset{O}{\underset{||}{C}}-\overset{\ominus}{N}-Br \longrightarrow \underset{\underset{R\quad Br}{}}{C\cdots N} \xrightarrow{-Br} R-N=C=O \text{ Isocyanate}$$

Step 4: Isocyanate hydrolyses to 1° amine and carbonate ion by the aqueous alkali.

$$R-N=C=O \longleftrightarrow R-\overset{\ominus}{\underset{..}{N}}-\overset{\oplus}{C}=O \underset{H\quad H}{\overset{-Br}{\rightleftharpoons}} R-\overset{\ominus}{\underset{..}{N}}-\overset{\oplus}{C}=O$$

$$R-\underset{H}{\overset{H}{\underset{|}{N}}}-\overset{O}{\underset{||}{C}}-O^{\ominus} \xleftarrow{OH^{\ominus}} R-NH-\overset{O}{\underset{||}{C}}-O^{\ominus} \xleftarrow{OH^{\ominus}} R-NH-\overset{O}{\underset{||}{C}}-OH$$

$$\downarrow$$

$$R-NH_2 + CO_3^{--}$$

Example:

$$\text{>C=O} + NH_3 \xrightarrow{H_2/Ni} \text{>CH-NH}_2$$
1° amine

$$\text{>C=O} + RNH_2 \xrightarrow{H_2/Ni} \text{>CH-NHR}$$
2° amine

$$\text{>C=O} + R_2NH \xrightarrow{H_2/Ni} \text{>CH-NR}_2$$
3° amine

SEPARATION OF MIXTURES OF AMINES

(A) By Hinsberg method (With benzenesulphonyl chloride)
(B) By Hoffmann method (With diethyl oxalate)

(A) Hinsberg Method:

This is very important method for distinguishing and separation of 1°, 2°, 3° amines.

Amine + 1 ml pyridine + dil. NaOH + 1-2 drops of benzenesulphonyl chloride

Yellow colour after shaking = 1° amine
Orange colour = 2° amine
Violet colour = 3° amine

1° amine gives N – alkyl benzenesulphonamide

$$C_6H_5-SO_2Cl + RNH_2 \xrightarrow{OH^-} C_6H_5-SO_2NR(H) + HCl$$

Benzenesulphonyl chloride → N-alkyl benzenesulphonamide (Insoluble) [Acidic hydrogen]

$$\xrightarrow{NaOH} C_6H_5-SO_2NR^- \ Na^+$$

Soluble salt

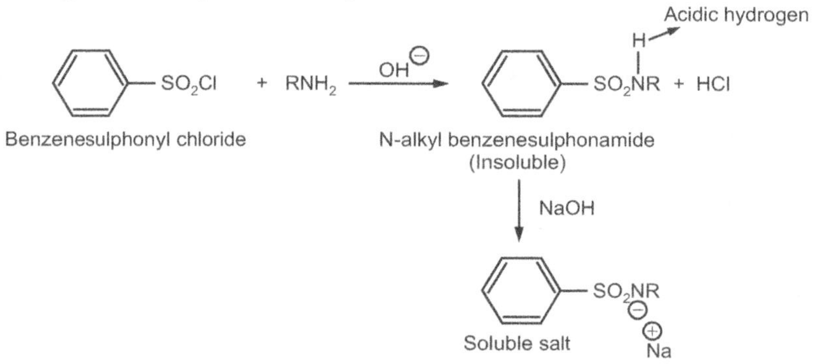

2° amine gives N, N – dialkyl benzenesulphonamide

$$C_6H_5-SO_2Cl + RNHR' \xrightarrow{OH^-} C_6H_5-SO_2NRR' + HCl$$

Benzenesulphonyl chloride → N,N-dialkylbenzenesulphonamide (Insoluble) [No acidic hydrogen present]

↓ NaOH

No reaction because no acidic hydrogen present

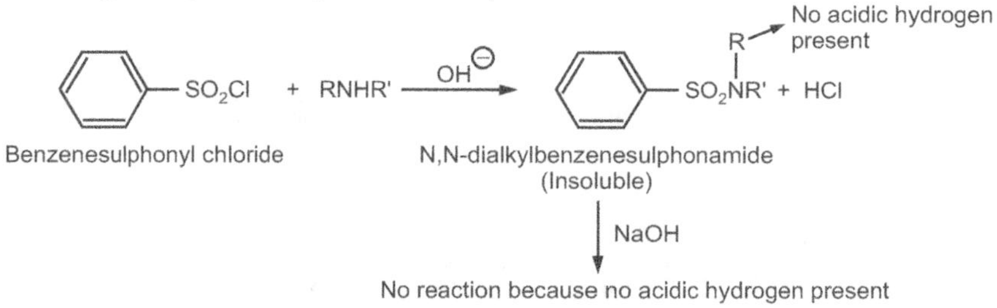

3° amine does not react because no hydrogens at all.

Now-a-days, benzenesulphonyl chloride has been replaced by *p*-toluenesulphonyl chloride, ($CH_3-C_6H_5-SO_2Cl$), since the substituted sulphonamides thus formed are stable solids which can be easily recrystallized. Also *p*-toluenesulphonyl chloride is safe and easy to handle.

(B) Hoffmann's Method:

The process utilizes the fact that, 1° amine contains two active hydrogen atoms, 2° amine contains one active H atom and 3° amine contains none.

So when a mixture of three types of amines is treated with ethyl oxalate, 1° amine forms a solid oxamide, 2° amines forms a liquid oxamic ester while, 3° amine remains unreacted. So the 3° amine is distilled out after treating the mixture with ethyl oxalate.

Oxamide and the oxamic ester being solid and liquid respectively, are separated by the process of filtration.

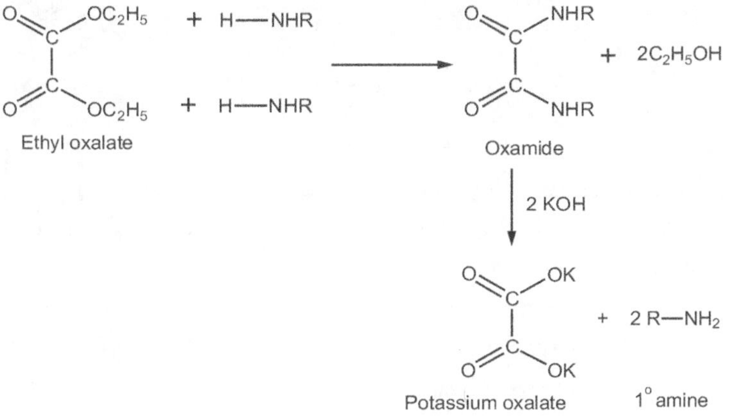

Ethyl oxalate + H—NHR → Oxamide + $2C_2H_5OH$

Oxamide + 2 KOH → Potassium oxalate + $2R-NH_2$ (1° amine)

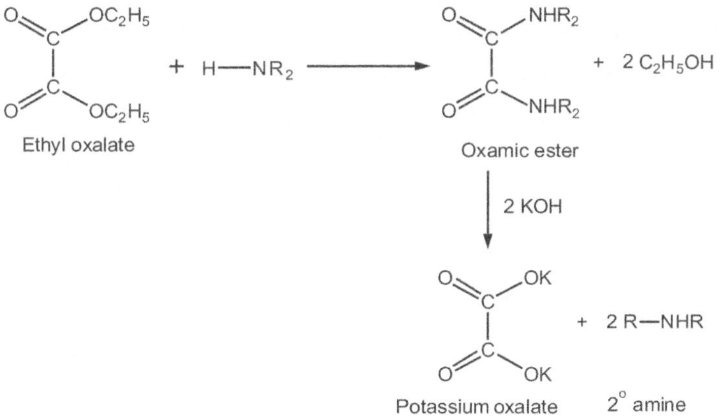

Ethyl oxalate + H—NR_2 → Oxamic ester + $2C_2H_5OH$

Oxamic ester + 2 KOH → Potassium oxalate + $2R-NHR$ (2° amine)

REACTION OF AMINES

1. Basicity:

Owing to the presence of a one pair of electrons on the N atom of amines, they are basic in nature.

E.g., The conjugate acid of guanidine is very stable since it is a resonance hybrid of three equivalent resonating structures. Being very stable, the conjugate acid is a weak acid and consequently the parent base is very strong.

Because the electron releasing alkyl groups tend to disperse the positive charge of the substituted ammonium ion and therefore stabilize it in a way that is not possible for the unsubstituted ammonium ion.

It will be seen that the introduction of an alkyl group into ammonia increases the basic strength markedly, because positive Inductive effect of alkyl group.

pKa of CH_3NH_2 = 10.64, pKa of aniline = 4.62 and pKa of NH_3 = 9.25

More the pKa more is the basicity.

In aniline, the nitrogen atom is again bonded to sp^2 hybridized carbon atom but, more significantly, the unused electron pair on nitrogen can interact with the delocalized π (pi) orbitals of the aromatic ring.

Aniline molecule is thus, stabilized w.r.t. the anilinium cation and it is therefore "energetically unprofitable" for aniline to take up a proton. Hence, methylamine is more basic than ammonia and aniline is a weak base than ammonia.

2. Reaction with nitrous acid (HNO₂):

This reaction is a good means for differentiating three types of amines.

1° aliphatic amines give alcohol and evolve molecular N_2 with several other side products.

$$CH_3CH_2CH_2-NH_2 + HNO_2 \longrightarrow CH_3CH_2CH_2-OH + N_2\uparrow + H_2O$$

HNO₂ being unstable, it can not be kept in the laboratory and is always generated *in-situ* by the reaction of mineral acids on nitrites.

$$NaNO_2 + HCl \longrightarrow NaCl + HNO_2$$

1° aromatic amines react with nitrous acid to yield "diazonium salt" is one of the most important reactions in organic chemistry.

$$Ar-NH_2 + NaNO_2 + 2HCl \xrightarrow[0-5\,°C]{Cold} Ar-\overset{\oplus}{N}\equiv\overset{\ominus}{N}\,Cl + NaCl + 2H_2O$$

1° amine → Diazonium salt

2° amines, (both aliphatic and aromatic) reacts with HNO₂, to yield N-nitrosamine (*Libermann's Nitrosamine test*).

2° amine → N-nitroso-N-methylaniline

A 3° aliphatic amine forms a salt with nitrous acid.

$$R_3N + HNO_2 \longrightarrow R_3\overset{\oplus}{N}H-\overset{\ominus}{N}O_2 \equiv R_3NH\cdot HNO_2$$

Whereas, N,N-dimethylaniline (aromatic) gives N,N-dimethyl – p-nitrosoaniline on treatment with nitrous acid.

3° amine

So, the three types of aliphatic amines give different products with nitrous acid.

(i) 1° amine evolves molecular N_2
(ii) 2° amine forms nitrosoamine
(iii) 3° amine forms nitrite salt

3. Acetylation and Benzoylation:

The replacement of active H atoms of amines by CH_3CO or PhCO groups is called acetylation or benzoylation, respectively. The benzoylation is analogous to Schotton Baumen reaction of alcohols.

$$RNH_2 \xrightarrow[(CH_3CO)_2O]{CH_3COCl \text{ or}} RNHCOCH_3 \xrightarrow[(CH_3CO)_2O]{CH_3COCl \text{ or}} RN(COCH_3)_2$$

Monoacetyl Diacetyl

$$RNH_2 \xrightarrow{PhCOCl} RNHCOPh \xrightarrow{PhCOCl} RN(COPh)_2$$

Monobenzoyl derivative Dibenzoyl/derivative

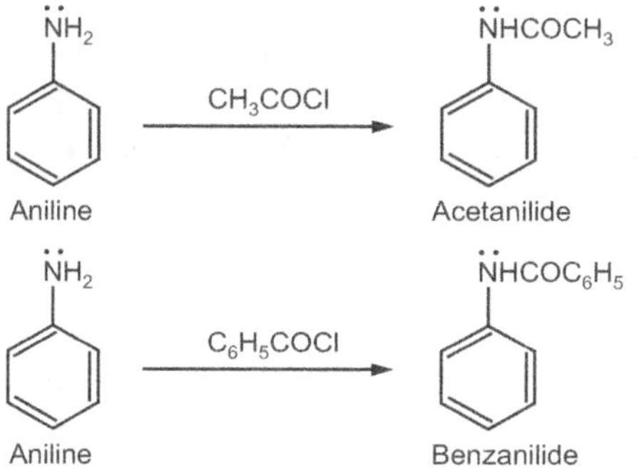
NH2
CH3COCl
NHCOCH3
Aniline
Acetanilide
NH2
C6H5COCl
NHCOC6H5
Aniline
Benzanilide

Mechanism:

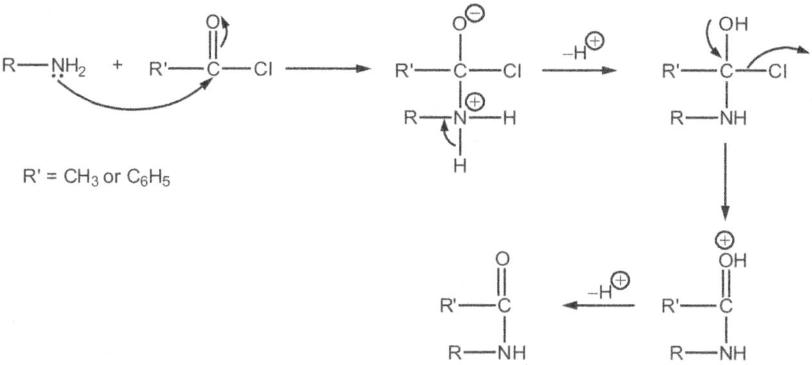
R—NH2 + R'—C—Cl
O
R' = CH3 or C6H5
R'—C—Cl
R—N—H
H
-H
OH
R'—C—Cl
R—NH
R'—C
R—NH

Acetylation and benzoylation processes have analytical as well as synthetic values. When activating groups (e.g. $-NH_2$, OH) are acetylated or benzoylated, the activity of group decreases owing to the –I and –R effects of the carbonyl group, because of low activity. Monosubstituted products are usually obtained when they are subjected to electrophilic substitution reaction.

Acetylated and benzoylated groups have –o/p directing effect; but such groups being very bulky, para products are obtained predominantly. Thus, acetylation and benzoylation are used to protect the activating group in order to introduce substituent's in aromatic amines and phenols.

The acetyl or benzoyl groups can be removed by hydrolysis after the introduction of substituents at proper positions. Also, to prepare solid derivatives of amines to identify them.

Example:

Synthesis of p-bromoaniline:

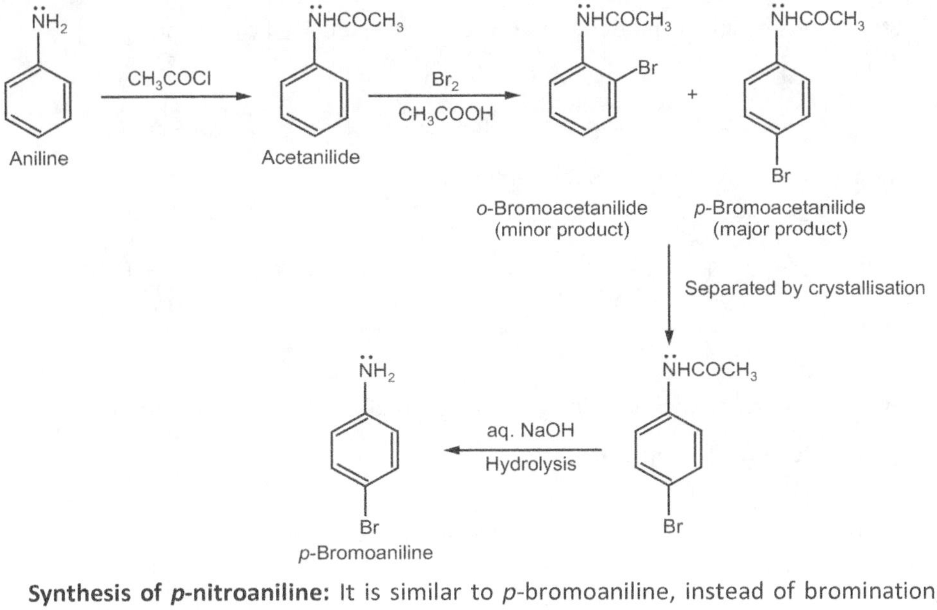

Aniline $\xrightarrow{CH_3COCl}$ Acetanilide $\xrightarrow[CH_3COOH]{Br_2}$ o-Bromoacetanilide (minor product) + p-Bromoacetanilide (major product)

p-Bromoacetanilide $\xrightarrow[\text{Hydrolysis}]{\text{aq. NaOH}}$ p-Bromoaniline

Separated by crystallisation

Synthesis of p-nitroaniline: It is similar to p-bromoaniline, instead of bromination; nitration is carried out in second step.

The acetyl amino group is less activating and mild o-director as compared to free amino group. Also its steric bulk, hinders in the bromination or nitration to occur at o-position as compared to the p-position. Thus, p-isomer is the major product.

4. **Mannich Reaction:**

The acid or base catalyzed reaction of aldehyde/ketone, ammonia/primary/ secondary amines and a compound containing at least one active hydrogen to yield amino or amino substituted derivative of the compound is called '**Mannich Reaction**'. The product is called '**Mannich Base**' (Compounds containing active hydrogen may be aldehyde, ketone, β-ketoester, β-cyano ester, nitroalkane, monoalkyl or aryl acetylene, alcohol, phenol etc.)

$$\text{Acetophenone} + \text{HCHO} + \text{Diethylamine} \xrightarrow{HCl} \text{β-aminoketone}$$

$$C_6H_5\text{-CO-CH}_3 + HCHO + HN(C_2H_5)_2 \xrightarrow{HCl} C_6H_5\text{-CO-CH}_2\text{CH}_2\text{N}(C_2H_5)_2$$

Mechanism: Base catalysed – 3 step.

Step 1: Reversible formation of the resonance – stabilized carbanion.

$$R-\underset{\parallel}{\overset{O}{C}}-CH_2-H \xrightarrow{OH^-} R-\underset{\parallel}{\overset{O}{C}}-\ddot{C}H_2 \longleftrightarrow R-\underset{\mid}{\overset{O^{\ominus}}{C}}=CH_2$$

Step 2: Addition of amine to formaldehyde.

$$H-\underset{\underset{R_2}{\overset{\mid}{HN}}}{\overset{O}{\overset{\parallel}{C}}}-H \rightleftharpoons H-\underset{\underset{\oplus}{\overset{\mid}{N}}-R_2}{\overset{O^{\ominus}}{\underset{\mid}{C}}}-H \rightleftharpoons H-\underset{\underset{R_2}{\overset{\mid}{N}}}{\overset{OH}{\underset{\mid}{C}}}-H$$

Step 3: The resonance stabilized carbanion replacess the –OH group and reaction follows SN$_2$ pathway.

$$H-\underset{\underset{R_2}{\overset{\mid}{N}}}{\overset{OH}{\underset{\mid}{C}}}-H + R-\underset{\parallel}{\overset{O}{C}}-\ddot{C}H_2 \rightleftharpoons R-\underset{\parallel}{\overset{O}{C}}-\underset{H_2}{C}\cdots\underset{\underset{R_2}{\overset{\mid}{N}}}{\overset{H \ H}{\underset{\mid}{C}}}\cdots OH$$

$$\downarrow$$

$$\overline{O}H + R-\underset{\parallel}{\overset{O}{C}}-CH_2CH_2N(R_1)(R_2)$$

PHARMACEUTICAL ORGANIC CHEMISTRY - I AMINES

5. Sandmeyer Reaction:

Replacement of the diazonium group of an aromatic diazonium salt by a chloro or bromo group by the action of cuprous chloride (Cu_2Cl_2) in HCl or (Cu_2Br_2) cuprous bromide in HBr, respectively, in an aqueous solution of the diazonium salt is known as "Sandmeyer Reaction". CuCN is used for cyanation and KI/H^+ used for iodination.

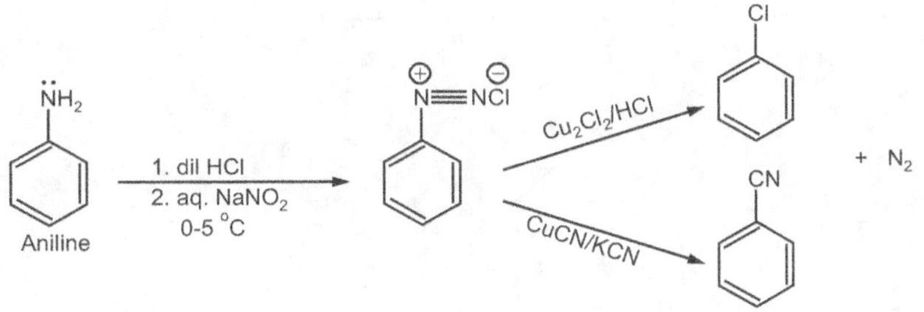

The Gattermann reaction is the modification of the Sandmeyer reaction. In this reaction copper powder and halo acids are used instead of cuprous halide.

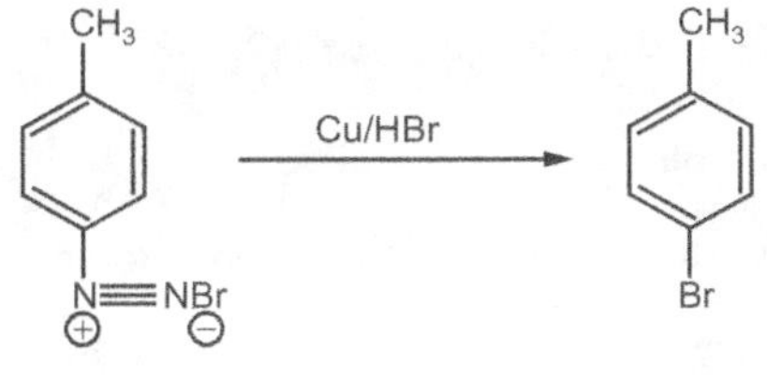

Example:

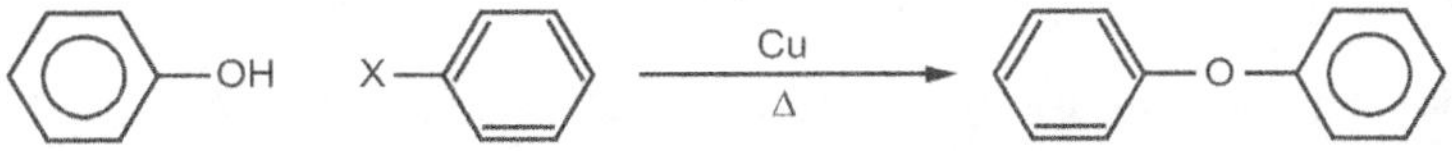

Mechanism:

Step 1: Complexation between the diazonium ion and the cuprous halide and the transfer of one electron from $CuCl_2$ to the diazonium ion through a chloride bridge T.S.

$$ArN_2Cl + CuCl \longrightarrow [Ar-N\equiv N\cdots Cl-Cu-Cl]$$

$$\downarrow$$

$$Ar\cdot + N_2\uparrow + CuCl$$

There are more examples of Sandmeyer reactions.

Step 2: Radical abstraction of chlorine atom of the cupric chloride by the aryl radical.

$$Ar\cdot + Cl-Cu-Cl \xrightarrow{Fast} ArCl + CuCl$$

However, aryl fluorides can be prepared by HBF_4 and aryl iodide by KI.

QUESTION BANK

1. Define and classify amines with examples.
2. Explain different synthetic methods for preparation of amines.
3. Explain Hoffmann degradation of amides with mechanism?
4. How will you prepare 1°, 2° and 3° amines?
5. Explain methods of distinguishing among 1°, 2° and 3° amines?
6. Why aliphatic amines are more basic than ammonia?
7. Explain methylamine (CH_3NH_2) is stronger base than ammonia and aniline is weaker than ammonia?
8. Which is more basic, N, N-dimethylaniline or 2, 6-dimethyl aniline?

9. Explain acetylation and benzoylation of amines with examples?

10. Write a short note on Mannich reaction.

11. Write a short note on Sandmeyer reaction.

12. What are amines? How are they prepared?

13. Discuss the basicity of amines.

14. Comment on guanidine is the strongest base among organic compounds.

15. Explain why amines are more basic than amides?

16. Explain acetylation and benzoylation of amine with suitable example?

17. How will you prepare anthranilic acid?

18. Explain the Hinsbergs test for distinguishing among amines.

Chapter 6 ...

CYANIDES AND ISOCYANIDES

CONTENTS
Structure, Nomenclature, Preparation, Physical properties and Chemical reactions.

CYANIDES AND ISOCYANIDES

Two types of organic derivatives of hydrocyanic acid (HCN) are known as *cyanides (RCN)* and *isocyanides (RNC)*. The alkyl cyanide is commonly called as *nitrile*, whereas alkyl isocyanides are isomers of cyanides and referred as *isonitriles* or *carbylamines*.

Example:

$R-C\equiv N$ $R-\overset{+}{N}\equiv \overset{-}{C}$
Cyanide   Isocyanide
Or   Or
Nitrile   Isonitrile

R = Alkyl or Aryl group

The nitrile group C ≡ N is highly polar and low molecular weight nitrites are good solvents for polar compounds.

NOMENCLATURE

Cyanides and isocyanides are usually named as cyanides or isocyanides of corresponding acid. The name of corresponding alkyl group is prefixed to the cyanide or isocyanide. Alternatively, the name of nitrile is constructed by replacing the *'propanoic acid'* of the carboxylic acid with *'propionitrile'*.

Example:

$CH_3-C\equiv N$ Methyl cyanide Or Acetonitrile
$CH_3CH_2-C\equiv N$ Ethyl cyanide Or Propionitrile
$H_2C=\underset{H}{C}-C\equiv N$ Vinyl cyanide Or Acrylonitrile
$CH_3-\overset{+}{N}\equiv \overset{-}{C}$ Methyl isocyanide Or Methyl isocyanide
$CH_3CH_2-\overset{+}{N}\equiv \overset{-}{C}$ Ethyl isocyanide Or Ethyl isocyanide

METHODS FOR THE PREPARATION OF CYANIDES AND ISOCYANIDES

1. Methyl cyanide from carboxylic acid:

Alkyl cyanides are prepared commercially from mixture of carboxylic acid and ammonia which is passed over alumina at 500°C. The overall reaction involves the amidation of the carboxylic acid and subsequent dehydration by alumina.

$$CH_3-COOH + NH_3 \xrightarrow[500\,°C]{Al_2O_3} CH_3-CONH_2 + H_2O \xrightarrow[500\,°C]{Al_2O_3} CH_3-C{\equiv}N$$

Acetic acid, Ammonia → Acetamide → Methyl cyanide Or Acetonitrile

Alumina acts as an acidic catalyst in both steps.

2. **Methyl cyanide from grignard reagent:**

$$CH_3MgCl + ClCN \longrightarrow H_3C-C{\equiv}N + MgCl_2$$

Methyl magnesium chloride, Cyanogen chloride, Methyl cyanide Or Acetonitrile

Mechanism:

$$Cl-C{\equiv}N + CH_3-MgCl \longrightarrow Cl-\underset{CH_3}{\underset{|}{C}}{=}NMgCl \xrightarrow{-MgCl_2} CH_3C{\equiv}N$$

3. **Methyl cyanide from alkyl halide:**
The most convenient way to prepare cyanides is to heat the alkyl halides with ethanolic solution of KCN. This is a simple nucleophilic displacement reaction.

$$R-X + KCN \longrightarrow R-C{\equiv}N + K-X$$

Alkyl halide, Potassium Cyanide, Alkyl/aryl cyanide, Potassium halide

$$CH_3-Cl + KCN \longrightarrow CH_3-C{\equiv}N + K-Cl$$

Methyl chloride, Potassium cyanide, Methyl cyanide Or Acetonitrile, Potassium chloride

4. **Methyl cyanide from amides and aldoximes:**
The dehydration of amides or aldoximes in presence of P_2O_5 at high temperatures gives cyanides.

$$CH_3-\underset{}{\overset{O}{\overset{\|}{C}}}-NH_2 \xrightarrow[\Delta]{P_2O_5} CH_3-C{\equiv}N + H_2O$$

Acetamide → Methyl cyanide Or Acetonitrile

Similarly, oximes can also be dehydrated with phosphorus pentoxide at high temperatures.

$$H_3C-\overset{H}{\underset{}{C}}{=}N-OH \xrightarrow[\Delta]{P_2O_5} H_3C-C{\equiv}N + H_2O$$

Acetaldoxime → Methyl cyanide Or Acetonitrile

5. **Methyl isocyanide from amines *(Carbylamine reaction)*:**
The reaction of primary amine with $CHCl_3$ in presence of alkali yields isocyanide.

$$CH_3NH_2 + CHCl_3 + 3NaOH \longrightarrow CH_3-\overset{+}{N}{\equiv}\overset{..}{C} + 3NaCl$$

Methyl amine, Chloroform, Methyl isocyanide

6. **Methyl isocyanide from alkyl iodide and silver cyanide:**

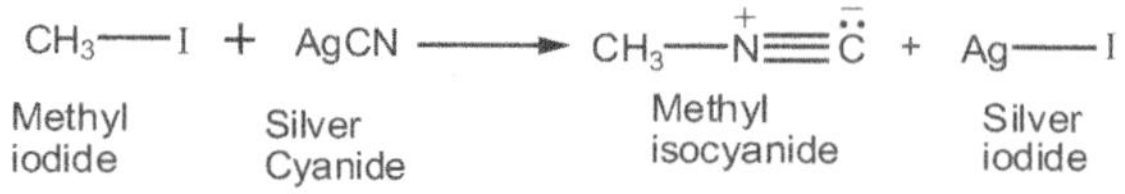

$$CH_3-I + AgCN \longrightarrow CH_3-\overset{+}{N}\equiv\overset{..}{C}^{-} + Ag-I$$

Methyl iodide + Silver Cyanide → Methyl isocyanide + Silver iodide

7. **Methyl isocyanide from N-alkyl formamide (dehydration):**

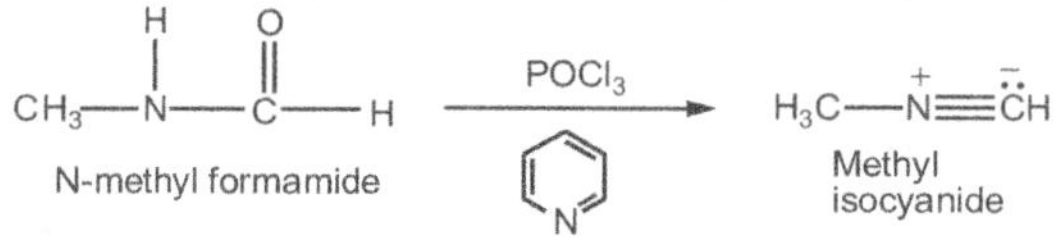

$$CH_3-\underset{H}{\overset{H}{N}}-\overset{O}{\underset{}{C}}-H \xrightarrow[\text{pyridine}]{POCl_3} H_3C-\overset{+}{N}\equiv\overset{..}{C}H^{-}$$

N-methyl formamide → Methyl isocyanide

PHYSICAL PROPERTIES

Alkyl cyanides are pleasant in smell, water soluble, colourless liquids and not poisonous as HCN. Whereas alkyl isocyanides are non-pleasant in smell, water insoluble and poisonous.

REACTIONS OF CYANIDES AND ISOCYANIDES

1. **Hydrolysis:**

Alkyl cyanides are hydrolyzed by acids or alkalis to the corresponding carboxylic acids *via* amide formation.

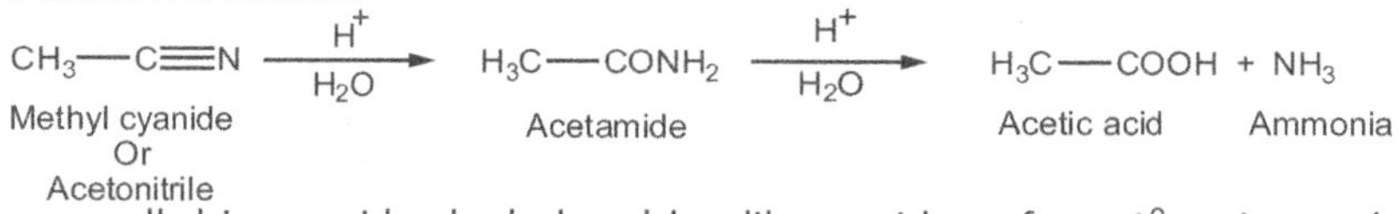

$$CH_3-C\equiv N \xrightarrow[H_2O]{H^+} H_3C-CONH_2 \xrightarrow[H_2O]{H^+} H_3C-COOH + NH_3$$

Methyl cyanide Or Acetonitrile → Acetamide → Acetic acid + Ammonia

Whereas alkyl isocyanides hydrolyzed by dilute acids to form 1° amine and formic acid.

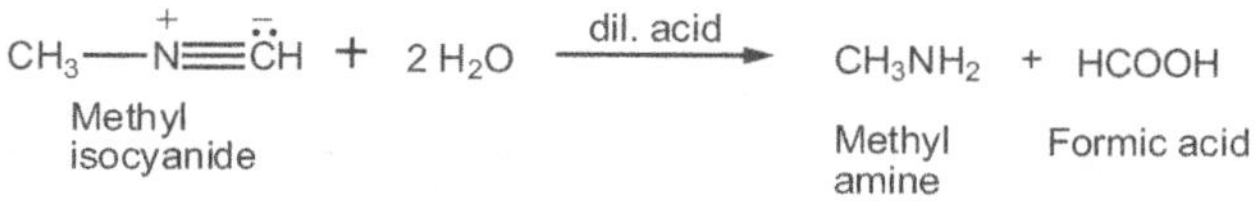

$$CH_3-\overset{+}{N}\equiv\overset{..}{C}H^{-} + 2H_2O \xrightarrow{\text{dil. acid}} CH_3NH_2 + HCOOH$$

Methyl isocyanide → Methyl amine + Formic acid

2. **Reduction:**

Alkyl cyanides are reduced by H_2/Pt or $LiAlH_4$ to yield 1° amine.

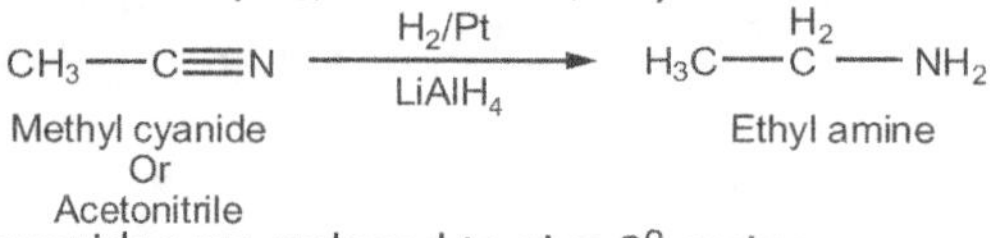

$$CH_3-C\equiv N \xrightarrow[LiAlH_4]{H_2/Pt} H_3C-\overset{H_2}{\underset{}{C}}-NH_2$$

Methyl cyanide Or Acetonitrile → Ethyl amine

Whereas alkyl isocyanides are reduced to give 2° amine.

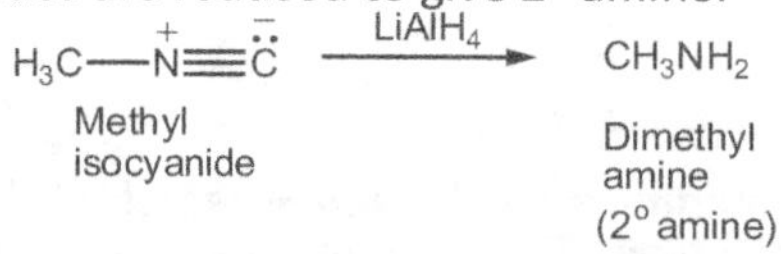

$$H_3C-\overset{+}{N}\equiv\overset{..}{C}^{-} \xrightarrow{LiAlH_4} CH_3NH_2$$

Methyl isocyanide → Dimethyl amine (2° amine)

3. **Thorpe Nitrile condensation:**

Two moles of alkyl cyanides are condensed in presence of a base (NaOEt) to yield iminonitriles. The carbon of one molecule involved, the reaction is known as *"Thorpe Nitrile Condensation."*

[Reaction scheme:]

CH₃—CH₂CN →(NaOEt) CH₃—C̈HCN⁻ Na⁺ →(H₃C—CH₂CN) CH₃—CH₂C(=N⁻Na⁺)—C(H)(CH₃)—CN →(EtOH) CH₃—CH₂C(=NH)—C(H)(CH₃)—CN

4. **Addition of ammonia**:
   Alkyl cyanides combine with ammonia to form amidines in dry state.

   R—C≡N + N̈H₃ → R—C(=N̈)—N̈H₂⁺—H → R—C(=NH)—NH₂

5. **Reaction with acid anhydrides**:
   Alkyl cyanides when heated with acid anhydrides, tertiary acid amides are formed.

   R—C≡N + (RCO)₂O → (RCO)₃N

6. **Addition of sulphur to isocyanide**:
   Alkyl isocyanide reacts with sulphur to form alkyl isothiocyanates.

   R—N⁺≡C̈⁻ + S → R—N=C=S
   Alkyl isocyanide   Alkyl isothiocyanates

7. **Action of heat on Isocyanide**:
   Upon prolonged heating isocyanides rearrange to more stable cyanides.

   R—N⁺≡C̈⁻ → R—C≡N
   Alkylisocyanide   Alkylcyanide

QUESTION BANK

1. Explain different synthetic methods for the preparation of cyanides and isocyanides.
2. How will you distinguish between cyanide (nitrile) and isocyanide (isonitrile)?
3. Comment on Thorpe nitrile synthesis.
4. How will you prepare isothiocyanate from isocyanide?
5. Who is more reactive cyanide or isocyanide?
6. How will you prepare acetamidine from acetonitrile (methyl cyanide).
7. Prepare the following from suitable reagents (only reaction equations).
   (a) Methylcyanide (acetonitrile)
   (b) Benzonitrile (phenylcyanide)
   (c) Phenylacetonitrile (benzylcyanide).

■■■

Chapter 7 ...

ESTERS AND AMIDES

CONTENTS
Mechanism of Claisen and Dieckmann reactions, use of acetoacetic ester and malonic ester in synthesis. Unsaturated compounds: Michael addition and addition of Grignard reagents. Ammonolysis of esters.

MECHANISM OF CLAISEN AND DIECKMANN REACTIONS

Claisen Condensation Reaction:

Esters like aldehydes and ketones are weakly acidic. When an ester with an α-hydrogen is treated with 1 equivalent of a base such as sodium ethoxide, a reversible carbonyl condensation reaction occurs to yield a β-ketoester. For example, ethyl acetate yields ethyl acetoacetate on base treatment. This base catalysed reaction between two ester molecules is known as the **Claisen condensation reaction**.

Reaction:

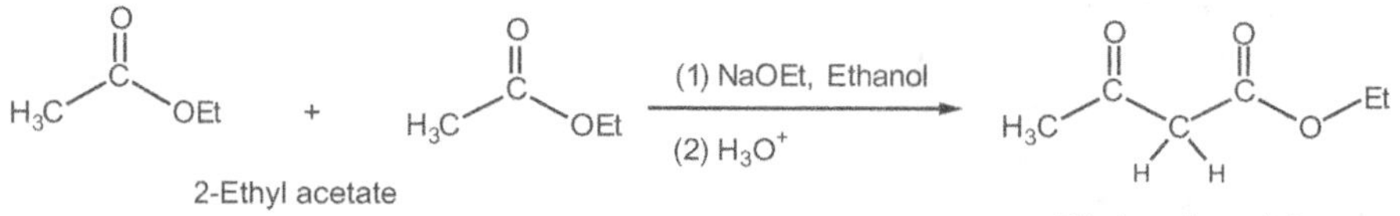

$$H_3C-C(=O)-OEt \; + \; H_3C-C(=O)-OEt \xrightarrow[(2) H_3O^+]{(1) NaOEt, Ethanol} H_3C-C(=O)-CH_2-C(=O)-OEt$$

2-Ethyl acetate

Ethyl acetoacetate
(a β-ketoester (75%))

Mechanism:

The mechanism of the Claisen condensation is similar to that of aldol condensation and involves the nucleophilic addition of an ester enolate ion to the carbonyl group of a second ester molecule. The starting ester must contain two α-hydrogen atoms.

- **Step 1:** An alkoxide ion (base) abstracts an acidic alpha hydrogen atom from the active methylene carbon of an ester molecule, yielding an ester enolate ion (I). The alkoxide base should correspond to the ester group to avoid transesterificatin.
- **Step 2:** The enolate ion adds as nucleophilic addition to the carbonyl carbon of a second ester molecule, giving a tetrahedral alkoxide intermediate (II).
- **Step 3:** The tetrahedral intermediate expels ethoxide ion (-OEt⁻) to yield a new carbonyl compound, ethyl acetoacetate (III).

Step 4: Ethoxide ion (formed in step 3) acts as strong base and again deprotonates ethyl acetoacetate (III) forming enolate ion (IV), by abstracting a proton from the active methylene group.

Step 5: Reprotonation of the enolate ion (IV), by an acid yields the final product (β-ketoester) (III) again.

Mixed or Crossed Claisen Condensation: Reaction between two different ester molecules of which one must contain no α-hydrogen. e.g. ethylformate and ethylacetate in presence of ethoxide base. The product is a β-aldoester.

2. Dieckmann reaction (Intramolecular Claisen Condensation):

The Dieckmann Cyclization: Intermolecular condensation with diesters (1,6 and 1,7-diesters).

The intermolecular condensation of a 1,6-diester gives a five membered cyclic β-ketoester and cylclization of a 1,7-diester gives a six membered cyclic β-ketoester. Highest yields are obtained when 1, 6- and 1, 7-diesters are used as starting materials.

Reaction:

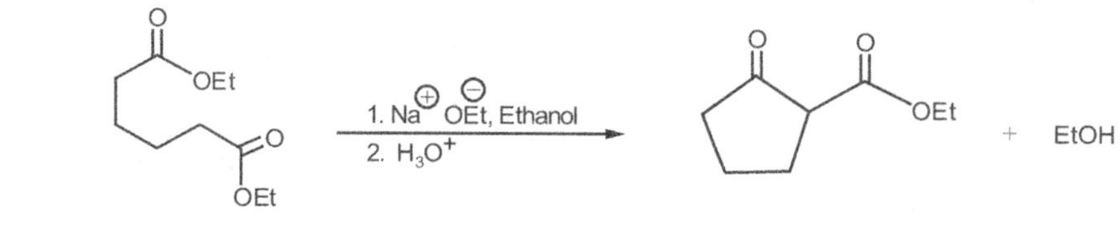

Diethyl hexanedioate (a 1,6-diketone) → [1. Na⁺ ⁻OEt, Ethanol; 2. H₃O⁺] → Ethyl 2-oxocyclopentanecarboxylate (a cyclic β-ketoester) + EtOH

Mechanism:

The mechanism of the Diekcmann cyclization is similar to Claisen condensation here one of the two ester groups is converted into an enolate ion, which then carries out a nucleophilic acyl substitution on the second ester group at the other end of the molecule. A cyclic β-ketoester is the final product.

Step 1: Base abstracts an acidic α-proton from the carbon atom next to one of the ester groups, yielding an enolate ion (I).

Step 2: Intramolecular nucleophilic addition of the ester enolate ion to the carbonyl carbon of the second ester at the other end of the chain then gives a cyclic tetrahedral intermediate (II).

Step 3: Loss of alkoxide ion from tetradedral intermediate (II) forms a cyclic β-ketoester (III).

Steps 4 and 5: Deprotonation of the acidic β-keto ester gives an enolate ion (IV) which is protonated by addition of aqueous acid to generate the neutral cyclic β-ketoester (V).

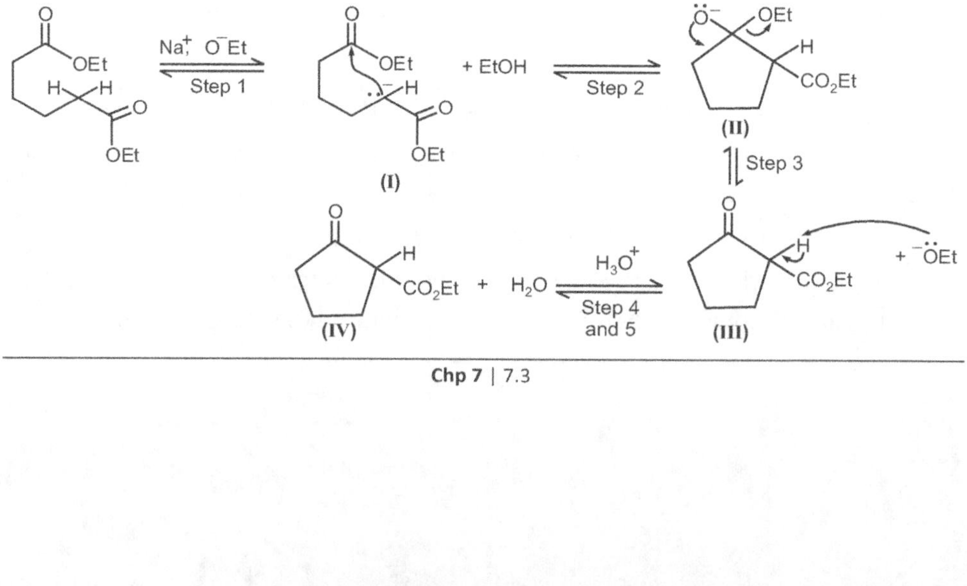

USES OF ETHYL ACETOACETATE (ACETOACETIC ESTER) AND KETONES

1. **Preparation of succinic acid:**
   Succinic acid is prepared by reaction of sodium ethyl acetoacetate with ethyl chloroacetate followed by acid hydrolysis.

   Example:

   $$CH_3-CO-CH_2-COOC_2H_5 \xrightarrow{C_2H_5O^-Na^+} CH_3-CO-CHNa-COOC_2H_5$$
   (Ethyl acetoacetate) → (Sodium salt)

   $$\xrightarrow[-NaCl]{ClCH_2COOC_2H_5} CH_3-CO-CH(CH_2COOC_2H_5)-COOC_2H_5$$

   $$\xrightarrow[+H^+, -CH_3COOH]{aq.\ NaOH,\ H_2O/H^+} \begin{array}{c} CH_2COOH \\ | \\ CH_2COOH \end{array}$$
   (Succinic acid)

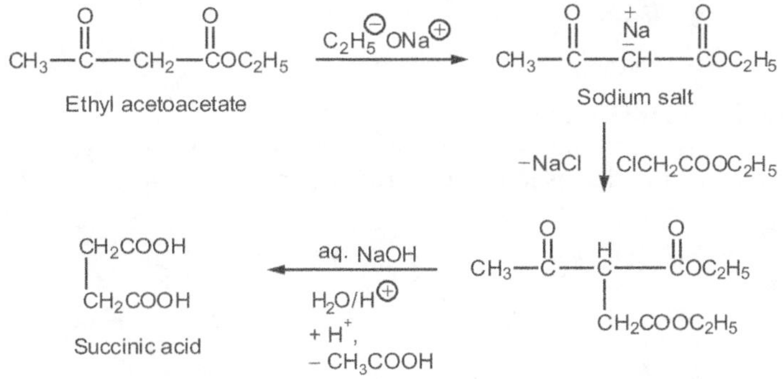

2. **Preparation of adipic acid:**
   Adipic acid is prepared by reaction of sodium ethyl acetoacetate with a methylene diiodide followed by acid hydrolysis.

   Example:

   $$2CH_3-CO-CH_2-COOC_2H_5 \xrightarrow{C_2H_5O^-Na^+} 2CH_3-CO-CHNa-COOC_2H_5$$
   (Ethyl acetoacetate) → (Sodium salt)

   $$\xrightarrow[-2NaI]{CH_2I_2} CH_3-CO-CH(COOC_2H_5)-CH_2-CH_2-CH(COOC_2H_5)-CO-CH_3$$

   $$\xrightarrow[-2CH_3COOH]{conc.\ NaOH,\ H_2O/H^+} \begin{array}{c} H_2C-COOH \\ | \\ CH_2 \\ | \\ CH_2 \\ | \\ H_2C-COOH \end{array}$$
   (Adipic acid)

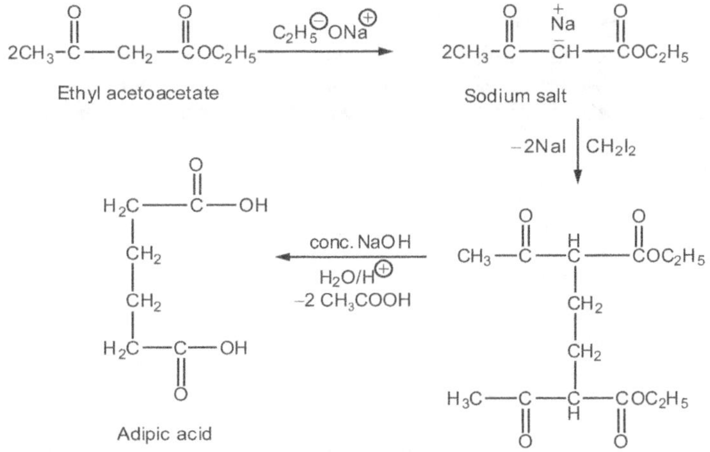

3. **Preparation of crotonic acid (α, β unsaturated acid):**
   Crotonic acid is formed when base catalyzed reaction of ethyl acetoacetate with an acetaldehyde molecule is followed by acid hydrolysis.

Example:

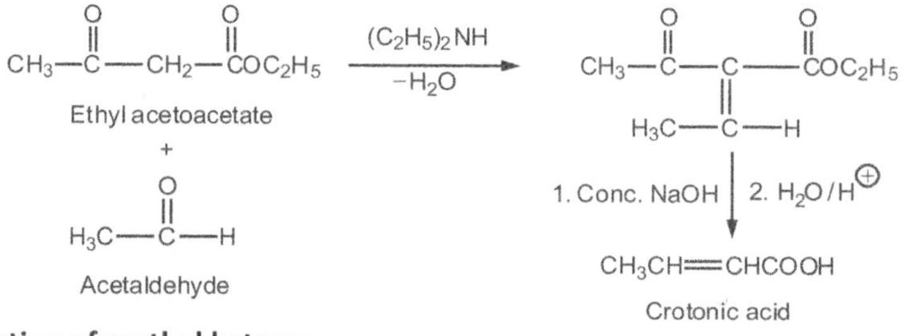

$$CH_3-\underset{O}{\overset{\|}{C}}-CH_2-\underset{O}{\overset{\|}{C}}OC_2H_5 \;+\; H_3C-\underset{O}{\overset{\|}{C}}-H \xrightarrow[-H_2O]{(C_2H_5)_2NH} CH_3-\underset{O}{\overset{\|}{C}}-\underset{\underset{H}{\overset{\|}{C}}}{C}-\underset{O}{\overset{\|}{C}}OC_2H_5$$

Ethyl acetoacetate + Acetaldehyde

$$\xrightarrow{\text{1. Conc. NaOH} \quad \text{2. } H_2O/H^{\oplus}} CH_3CH=CHCOOH$$

Crotonic acid

4. Preparation of methyl ketone:

The reaction of sodium ethyl acetoacetate with an alkyl halide (RX) followed by the hydrolysis of the ester and subsequent decarboxylation gives methyl ketone.

Example:

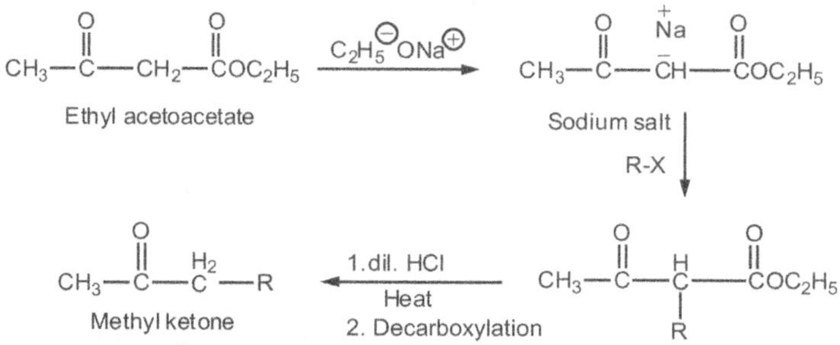

$$CH_3-\underset{O}{\overset{\|}{C}}-CH_2-\underset{O}{\overset{\|}{C}}OC_2H_5 \xrightarrow{C_2H_5^{\ominus}ONa^{\oplus}} CH_3-\underset{O}{\overset{\|}{C}}-\overset{\overset{+}{Na}}{\underset{}{\overline{C}H}}-\underset{O}{\overset{\|}{C}}OC_2H_5$$

Ethyl acetoacetate → Sodium salt

↓ R-X

$$CH_3-\underset{O}{\overset{\|}{C}}-\overset{H_2}{\underset{}{C}}-R \xleftarrow[\text{Heat, 2. Decarboxylation}]{\text{1. dil. HCl}} CH_3-\underset{O}{\overset{\|}{C}}-\underset{R}{\overset{H}{\underset{|}{C}}}-\underset{O}{\overset{\|}{C}}OC_2H_5$$

Methyl ketone

5. Preparation of acetylacetone (1,3-Diketones):

Acetylacetone (2,4-pentadione) is obtained by the reaction of sodium ethyl acetoacetate with acetyl chloride followed by hydrolysis and decarboxylation.

Example:

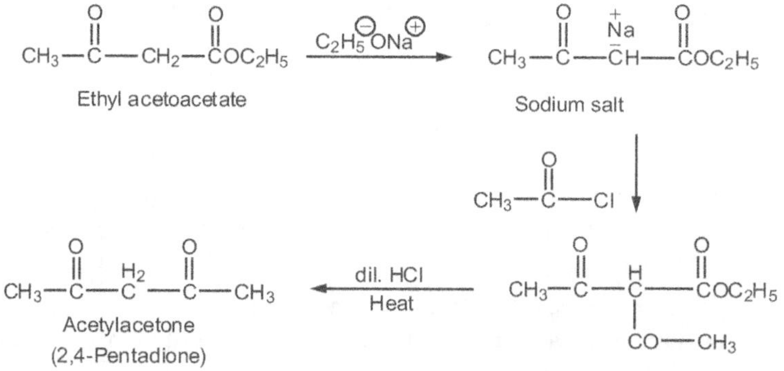

$$CH_3-\underset{O}{\overset{\|}{C}}-CH_2-\underset{O}{\overset{\|}{C}}OC_2H_5 \xrightarrow{C_2H_5^{\ominus}ONa^{\oplus}} CH_3-\underset{O}{\overset{\|}{C}}-\overset{\overset{+}{Na}}{\underset{}{\overline{C}H}}-\underset{O}{\overset{\|}{C}}OC_2H_5$$

Ethyl acetoacetate → Sodium salt

↓ $CH_3-\underset{O}{\overset{\|}{C}}-Cl$

$$CH_3-\underset{O}{\overset{\|}{C}}-\overset{H_2}{\underset{}{C}}-\underset{O}{\overset{\|}{C}}-CH_3 \xleftarrow[\text{Heat}]{\text{dil. HCl}} CH_3-\underset{O}{\overset{\|}{C}}-\underset{CO-CH_3}{\overset{H}{\underset{|}{C}}}-\underset{O}{\overset{\|}{C}}OC_2H_5$$

Acetylacetone (2,4-Pentadione)

6. Preparation of 4-methyl uracil:

Ethyl acetoacetate (enol form) reacts with urea in the presence of phosphoryl chloride to give 4-methyl uracil. Such a cyclocondensation of an N-C-N unit with a β-dicarbonyl compound (ethyl acetoacetate) is referred as the "Principal Synthesis" of pyramidine.

Example:

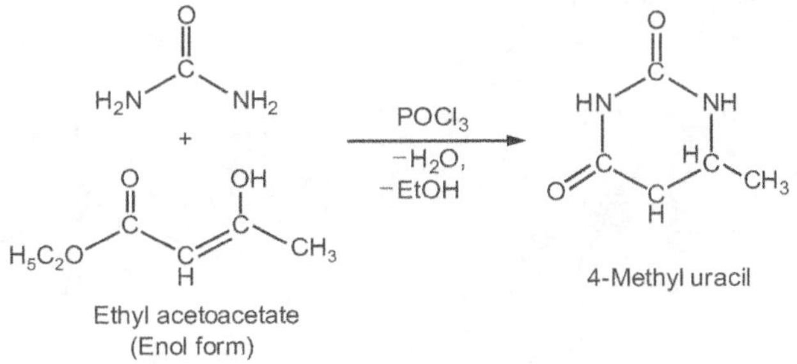

$$H_2N-CO-NH_2 + H_5C_2O-CO-CH=C(OH)-CH_3 \xrightarrow[-EtOH]{POCl_3, -H_2O} \text{4-Methyl uracil}$$

Ethyl acetoacetate (Enol form)

7. Preparation of antipyrine:

Ethyl acetoacetate reacts with phenylhydrazine to give antipyrine.

Example:

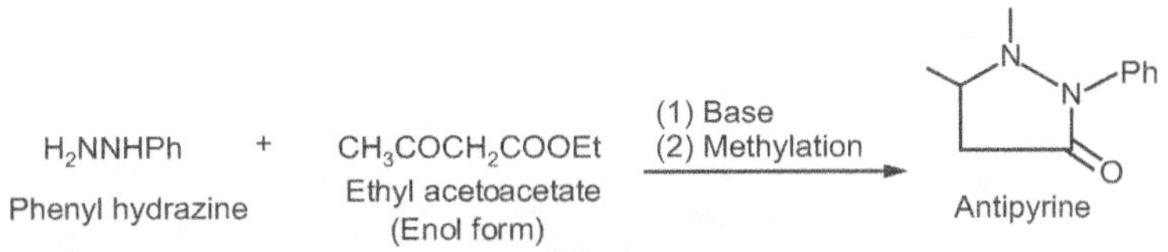

$$H_2NNHPh + CH_3COCH_2COOEt \xrightarrow[(2)\ \text{Methylation}]{(1)\ \text{Base}} \text{Antipyrine}$$

Phenyl hydrazine   Ethyl acetoacetate (Enol form)

MICHAEL ADDITION

The Michael reaction or Michael addition is the nucleophilic addition of a carbanion or another nucleophile to an α, β-unsaturated carbonyl compound. It belongs to the larger class of conjugate additions. This is one of the most useful methods for the formation of C–C bonds. Many asymmetric variants exist.

Reaction:

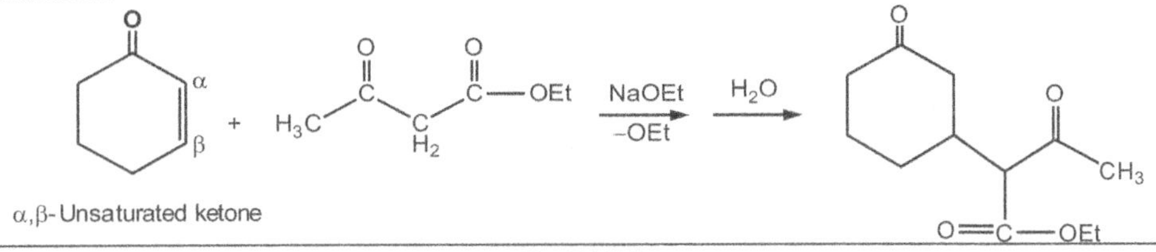

α,β-Unsaturated ketone + $H_3C-CO-CH_2-CO-OEt$ $\xrightarrow[-OEt]{NaOEt,\ H_2O}$ product

Mechanism:

Step I: Formation of enolate: The base (EtO⁻) abstracts an acidic alpha hydrogen from the β-ketoester to generate a resonance stabilized enolate ion (I) (which acts as a nucleophile).

Step II: The nucleophile (enolate I) adds to the α, β-unsaturated ketone (II) to generate a new enolate (III) as product.

Step III: The enolate (III) abstracts an acidic proton from the solvent (EtOH) to yield the final addition product (IV).

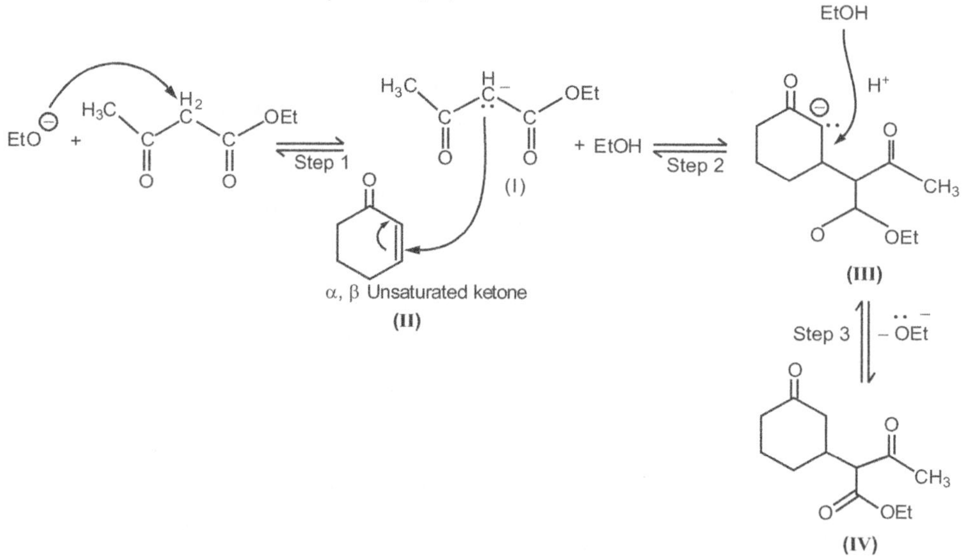

ADDITION OF GRIGNARD REAGENT

Esters react with Grignard reagent to afford 3° alcohols.

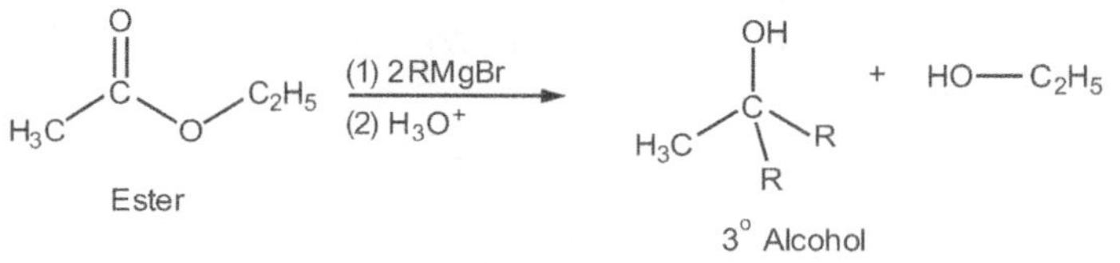

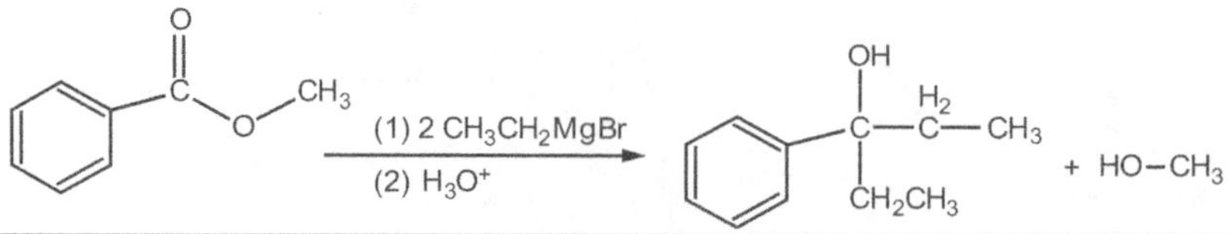

Mechanism:

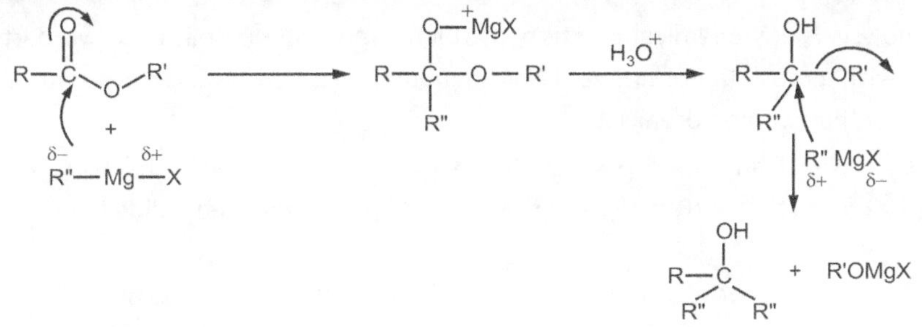

$$R-\underset{O}{\overset{O}{\underset{\|}{C}}}-O-R' + \underset{\delta-}{R''}-\underset{\delta+}{Mg}-X \longrightarrow R-\underset{R''}{\overset{O-\overset{+}{M}gX}{\underset{|}{C}}}-O-R' \xrightarrow{H_3O^+} R-\underset{R''}{\overset{OH}{\underset{|}{C}}}-OR'$$

$$\xrightarrow[\delta+ \quad \delta-]{R''\,MgX} R-\underset{R''}{\overset{OH}{\underset{|}{C}}}-R'' \quad + \quad R'OMgX$$

The reaction involves two moles of Grignards reagent against one mole of the ester.

A step wise explanation is as follows:

Step I: Nucleophilic attack by Grignard reagent (**I**) at (electron deficient) carbonyl carbon of ester (**II**) to form a tetrahedral intermediate (**III**).

Step II: The unstable intermediate (**III**) stabilizes to form a ketone (**IV**) and bromomagnesium ethoxide (**V**).

Step III: The resulting ketone (**IV**) rapidly reacts with a second molecule of Grignard reagent, giving rise to the tertiary alkoxide (**VI**).

Step IV: Protonation of alkoxide (**VI**) gives the final product tertiary alcohol (**VI**).

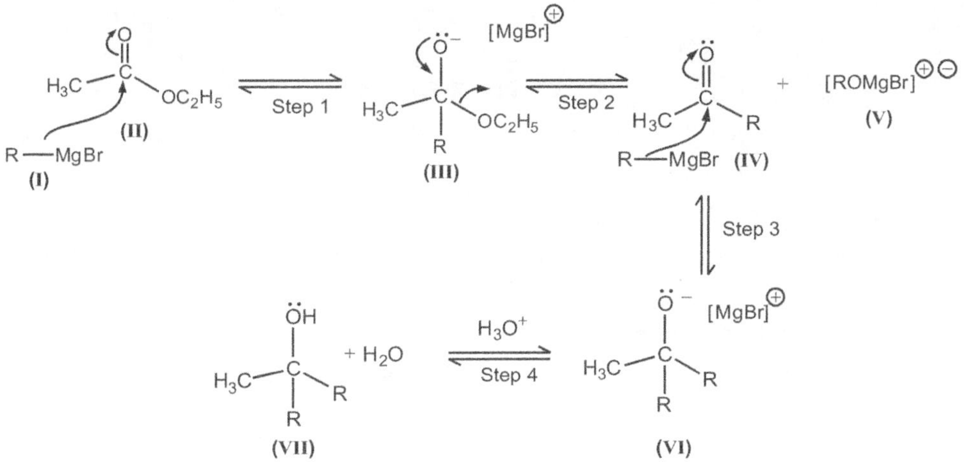

$$H_3C-\underset{(II)}{\overset{O}{\underset{\|}{C}}}-OC_2H_5 \quad \underset{R-MgBr}{\xrightarrow{\text{Step 1}}} \quad H_3C-\underset{R}{\overset{\overset{\ddot{O}^-\,[MgBr]^+}{|}}{\underset{|}{C}}}-OC_2H_5 \quad \xrightarrow{\text{Step 2}} \quad H_3C-\underset{R-MgBr\;(IV)}{\overset{\overset{\ddot{O}}{\|}}{C}}-R \quad + \quad [ROMgBr]^{\ominus} \;(V)$$

(I)   (III)

↕ Step 3

$$H_3C-\underset{R}{\overset{\overset{\ddot{O}H}{|}}{\underset{|}{C}}}-R \quad \underset{\text{Step 4}}{\overset{H_3O^+}{\rightleftharpoons}} \quad H_3C-\underset{R}{\overset{\overset{\ddot{O}^-\,[MgBr]^+}{|}}{\underset{|}{C}}}-R$$

(VII)   + H₂O   (VI)

AMINOLYSIS OF ESTERS

Aminolysis is any chemical reaction in which a molecule is split into two parts by its reaction with a molecule of ammonia or an amine. (like hydrolysis, where water breaks a molecular, here amine breaks it).

An example of an aminolysis reaction is the replacement of a halogen in an alkyl halide (R-X) by an amine (R'-NH$_2$) and the elimination of hydrogen halide (HX).

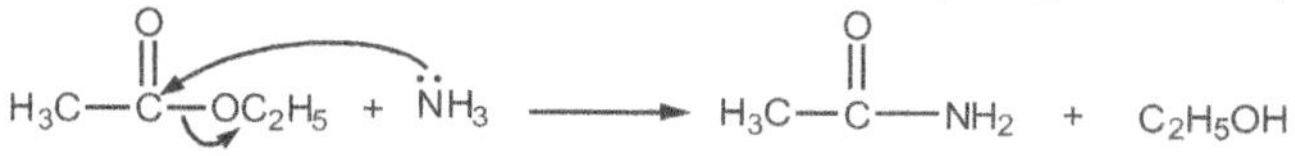

$$H_3C-\overset{O}{\underset{}{C}}-OC_2H_5 + NH_3 \longrightarrow H_3C-\overset{O}{\underset{}{C}}-NH_2 + C_2H_5OH$$

Mechanism:

Step I: Nucleophilic attack by ammonia (I) on electron deficient carbonyl carbon of ester (II) to give intermediate (III).

Step II: Internal proton shift in intermediate (III) to give (IV).

Step III: Stabilization of (IV) to give the product (V) which is an amide.

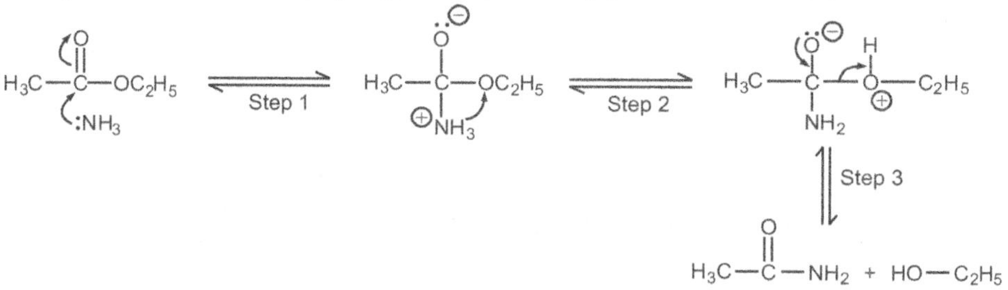

QUESTION BANK

1. Write down reaction mechanisms of the following reactions:
   (a) Claisen condensation
   (b) Dieckmann condensation
2. Explain the detailed mechanism for the formation of ethylacetoacetate from ethyl acetate.
3. Write a note on uses of ethylacetoacetate.
4. What is adipic acid? How it is prepared from ethylacetoacetate?
5. Write a note on Michael addition.
6. Write a note on addition of Grignard Reagent to esters.

7. What do you mean by amonolysis of esters? Explain with mechanism.
8. What is the Claisen condensation product of ethylpropionate under catalysis of ethoxide base.
9. What will be the product of Dieckmann reaction of 1,6-hexane dioate?
10. What is the Michael addition product for the base catalysed reaction between:
    (a) 2, 4-Pentadione and ethyl propionate?
    (b) 2, 4-Pentadione and ethyl vinyl ketone.

Chapter 8 …

ALKYL HALIDES

CONTENTS
Methods of preparation, general reactions, kinetics, mechanism and stereochemistry of SN_1, SN_2 and SN_i reactions, factors affecting nucleophilic substitution reactions, Substitution *vs* Elimination.

Alkyl Halides:

Alkyl halides are also known as haloalkanes. These are classes of compounds which are derived from alkanes (including cylcoalkanes) by replacing one or more *hydrogens* with a *halogen* atom (fluorine, chlorine, bromine, iodine). They are represented by general formula R-X ('R' represents an alkyl group and 'X' represents one of the four halogen atoms).

Example:

Two simple members of this class are methyl chloride (CH_3Cl) and ethyl chloride (C_2H_5Cl).

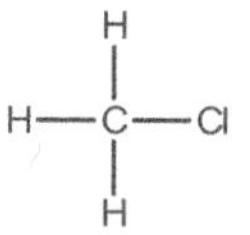

Chloromethane (Methyl chloride)

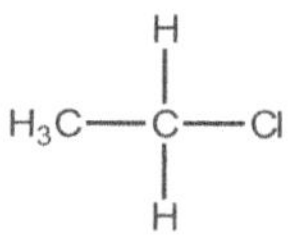

Chloroethane (Ethyl chloride)

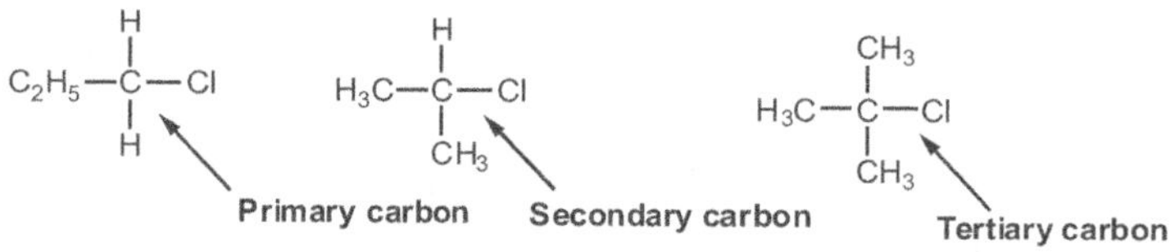

Chloropropane (Propylchloride) 1° Halides — Primary carbon

2-Chloropropane (Isopropylchloride) 2° Halides — Secondary carbon

2-Chloro-2-methylpropane (tert-Butyl chloride) 3° Halides — Tertiary carbon

Based on the number of alkyl groups attached to the C-X unit, alkyl halides are classified as **Primary (1°), Secondary (2°) or tertiary (3°).**

A *geminal* (gem)-dihalide is one which possesses two halogen atoms on the same carbon, and a vicinal (*vic*)-dihalide is one which possesses halogen atoms on adjacent carbon atoms.

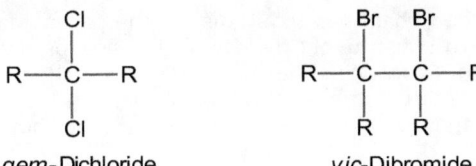

gem-Dichloride   vic-Dibromide

Nomenclature of Alkyl Halides:

According to the IUPAC system, alkyl halides are treated as alkanes with halogen substituents. The halogen prefixes are fluoro, chloro, bromo and iodo. An alkyl halide is named as an haloalkane with an alkane as the parent structure. The position of each halogen is indicated by a number.

Example:

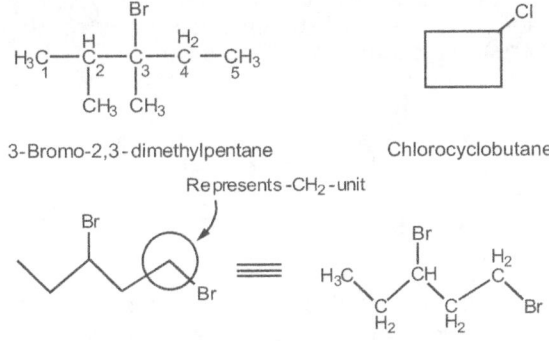

3-Bromo-2,3-dimethylpentane   Chlorocyclobutane

1,3-Dibromopentane = 1,3-Dibromopentane

(a) The compound has four carbons, so the parent name is **butane.** Fluorine is the only substituent, and hence the carbon chain is being numbered so that fluorine substituent number is coming minimum.

$$H_3C-\underset{1}{\overset{H}{C}}-\underset{2}{\overset{|}{\underset{F}{C}}}-\underset{3}{\overset{H_2}{C}}-\underset{4}{CH_3}$$

2-Fluorobutane

(b) The parent name is **cyclopentane**. Since *bromo* comes before *methyl* (alphabetically), the lower number is given to the bromine's position (i.e., 1-bromo) and higher number to methyl (*2-methyl*).

1-Bromo-2-methylcyclopentane

(c) The longest carbon chain has six atoms, so the parent name is **hexane**. In this example, the two substituents (i.e., two iodo groups and one methyl groups) appear on 3 and 4 carbons either we number the chain from right or left. But number the chain from the side where iodo groups are coming at minimum substituent number (3rd) is preferred. Hence, correct numbering and name will be:

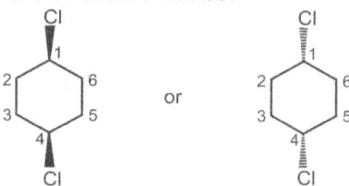

3,3-Diiodo-4-methylhexane

Structures of alkyl halides from IUPAC names

(a) **As the name ends with cyclohexane:** The structure should possess a six membered unsaturated (without any double bond) cyclic ring. Also at position 1 and 4 there are two 'chloro' substituents which are 'cis' (in the same plane) to each other therefore the structure will be:

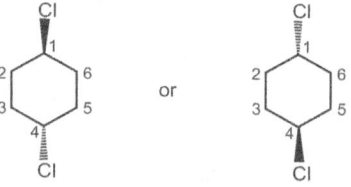

cis 1,4-Dichlorocyclohexane

(b) Parent nucleus is again a cyclohexane but the alignment of chloro substituents are different i.e 'trans' (in opposite plane) to each other. Therefore, the structure will be:

trans 1,4-Dichlorocyclohexane

(c) IUPAC name ends with 'butane' the parent structure will be a four carbon containing alkane. Also the name consists of two substituents (2,2-difluoro) both are fluorine and at position 2 (second carbon). Therefore, structure will be:

2,2-Difluorobutane

(d) IUPAC name suggests the parent structure as cyclobutane (four carbon containing cycle) containing two substituents (*chloro* at second position, and *bromo* at first position). Also both substituents are trans to each other. Therefore, structure will be:

trans-1-Bromo-2-chlorocyclobutane

METHODS FOR PREPARATION OF ALKYL HALIDES

Alkyl halides may be prepared in the laboratory by the following general methods.

```
                    Methods for Preparation of Alkyl Halides
                                    |
   ┌──────────────┬──────────────┬──────────────┬──────────────┬──────────────┐
(A) From Alkanes (B) From Alkenes (C) From Alcohols (D) From Silver salts of  (E) By Halide Exchange
                                                   Carboxylic acids           (Finkelstein Reaction)
```

(A) From alkanes:

Simple alkyl halides can be prepared by reaction of an alkane with Cl_2 or Br_2 in the presence of light through a radical chain-reaction pathway,
The mechanism for chlorination:

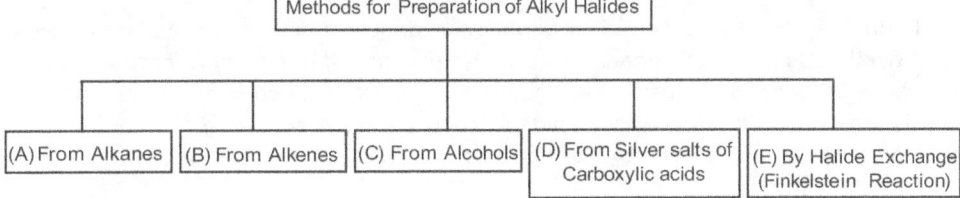

Mechanism: It is free radical substitution reaction which completes in three of steps: initiation, propagation and termination. **Initiation step** involves production of radicals, the reaction continues in a self-sustaining cycle. The cycle requires two repeating **propagation steps** in which a radical, the halogen, and the alkane yield alkyl halide product plus more radicals to carry on the chain. The chain is occasionally **terminated** by the combination of two radicals (**termination**).

Preparation of alkyl halides by halogenation method is of poor synthetic utility, because mixtures of products are formed. For example, chlorination of methane does not stop cleanly at the monochlorinated stage, but continues to give a mixture of dichloro, trichloro and even, tetrachloro products.

$$CH_4 + Cl_2 \xrightarrow{h\nu} CH_3Cl + HCl$$
$$\xrightarrow{Cl_2} CH_2Cl_2 + HCl$$
$$\xrightarrow{Cl_2} CHCl_3 + HCl$$
$$\xrightarrow{Cl_2} CCl_4 + HCl$$

(B) From alkenes:

Hydrogen halides add across carbon-carbon double bonds. These additions follow **Markovnikov's rule**, which states that *"the positive part of a reagent (a hydrogen atom, for example) adds to the carbon of the double bond that already has more hydrogen atoms attached to it. The negative part adds to the other carbon of the double bond. Such an arrangement leads to the formation of the more stable carbocation."*

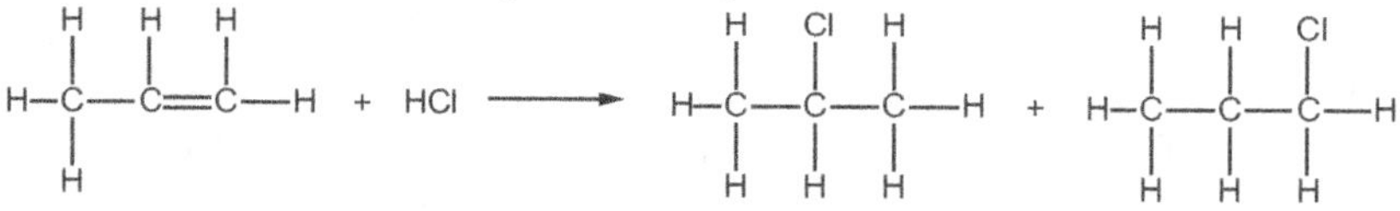

Propene → 2-Chloropropane (Major product) + 1-Chloropropane (Minor product)

Another method for preparing alkyl halides from alkenes is by reaction with *N*-bromosuccinimide (abbreviated NBS) in the presence of light to give products resulting from substitution of hydrogen by bromine at the position next to the double bond (the allylic position). Cyclohexene, for example, gives 3-bromocyclohexene.

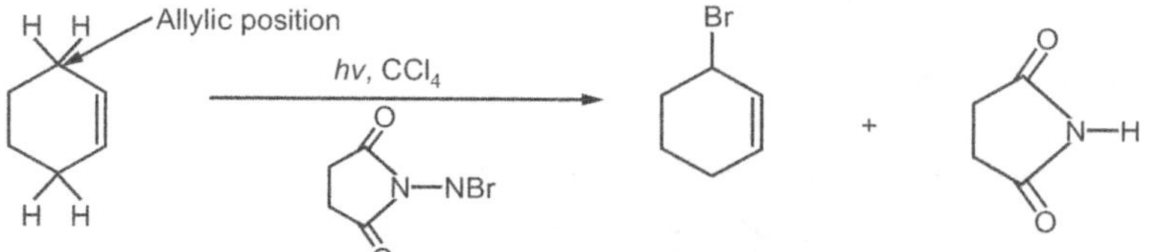

Cyclohexane   N-Bromosuccinimide   3-Bromocyclohexane (85%)

(The mechanism of allylic bromination with NBS is analogous to the alkane chlorination reaction discussed in the previous section i.e., it occurs by a radical chain reaction pathway-*Initiation, propagation and termination*).

(C) From Alcohols:

(i) Using hydrogen halides: The general reaction takes place as below:

$$R\text{—}OH + HX \longrightarrow R\text{—}X + H_2O$$
$$X = Cl, Br, I$$

(Reactivity of ROH: Tertiary > Secondary > Primary > Methyl)

(a) Making chloroalkanes: Tertiary chloroalkanes (alkylhalides) can be successfully prepared from the corresponding alcohols and concentrated hydrochloric acid, but to make the primary or secondary, one needs to modify this method as the reaction rates are too slow.

A tertiary chloroalkane can be made by shaking the corresponding alcohol with concentrated hydrochloric acid at room temperature.

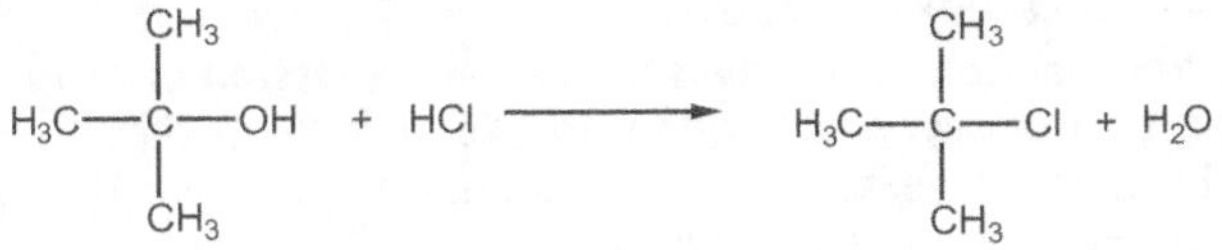

$$(CH_3)_3C\text{—}OH + HCl \longrightarrow (CH_3)_3C\text{—}Cl + H_2O$$

(b) Making bromoalkanes: Bromoalkanes can be prepared by reacting alcohol with a mixture of sodium or potassium bromide and concentrated sulphuric acid. This produces hydrogen bromide *in situ* which reacts with the alcohol. The mixture is warmed to distil off the bromoalkane.

$$H_3C\text{—}CH_2\text{—}OH + HBr \longrightarrow H_3C\text{—}CH_2\text{—}Br + H_2O$$

(c) Making iodoalkanes: In this case, the alcohol is reacted with a mixture of sodium or potassium iodide and concentrated phosphoric acid (H_3PO_4). The iodoalkane obtained is distilled off. The mixture of the iodide and phosphoric acid produces hydrogen iodide which reacts with the alcohol.

$$H_3C\text{—}CH_2\text{—}OH + HI \longrightarrow H_3C\text{—}CH_2\text{—}I + H_2O$$

Phosphoric acid is used instead of concentrated sulphuric acid because, sulphuric acid oxidises iodide ions to iodine and hardly any hydrogen iodide is produced. A similar thing happens to some extent with bromide ions in the preparation of bromoalkanes, but not enough to get in the way of the main reaction.

(ii) Using phosphorus halides:

(a) Making chloroalkanes: Chloroalkanes can be made by reacting an alcohol with liquid phosphorus (III) chloride, PCl_3.

$$3\,H_3C\text{—}CH_2\text{—}CH_2\text{—}OH + PCl_3 \longrightarrow 3\,H_3C\text{—}CH_2\text{—}CH_2\text{—}Cl + H_3PO_3$$

They can also be made by adding solid phosphorus (V) chloride, PCl_5 to an alcohol. (This reaction is violent at room temperature, producing clouds of hydrogen chloride gas).

$$H_3C-\underset{H_2}{C}-\underset{H_2}{C}-OH + PCl_5 \longrightarrow H_3C-\underset{H_2}{C}-\underset{H_2}{C}-Cl + HCl$$

Instead of PCl_3, use of $POCl_3$ can also be made. However it leads to side products.

(b) **Making bromoalkanes and iodoalkanes:** These are both prepared in the same general way. Instead of using phosphorus (III) bromide or iodide, the alcohol is heated under reflux with a mixture of red phosphorus and either bromine or iodine.

$$2P + 3Br_2 \longrightarrow 2PBr_3$$
$$2P + 3I_2 \longrightarrow 2PI_3$$

The phosphorus first reacts with the bromine or iodine to give the phosphorus (III) halide.

These then react with the alcohol to give the corresponding halogenoalkane which can be distilled off.

(D) From silver salts of carboxylic acids:

The **Hunsdiecker reaction** (also called the **Borodin reaction** after Alexander Borodin) is the organic reaction of silver salts of carboxylic acids with halogens to give organic halides (alkyl halides). It is an example of a halogenation reaction. The reaction is named after Heinz Hunsdiecker and Cläre Hunsdiecker.

$$R-\overset{O}{\underset{\|}{C}}-\bar{O}\ Ag^+ \xrightarrow[CCl_4]{Br_2} R-Br$$

Reaction mechanism:

The reaction mechanism of the Hunsdiecker reaction involves organic radical intermediates. The silver salt of the carboxylic acid **1** reacts with bromine to form intermediate **2**. Formation of the diradical pair **3** allows for radical decarboxylation to form the diradical pair **4**, which quickly recombines to form the desired organic halide **5** (alkyl halide).

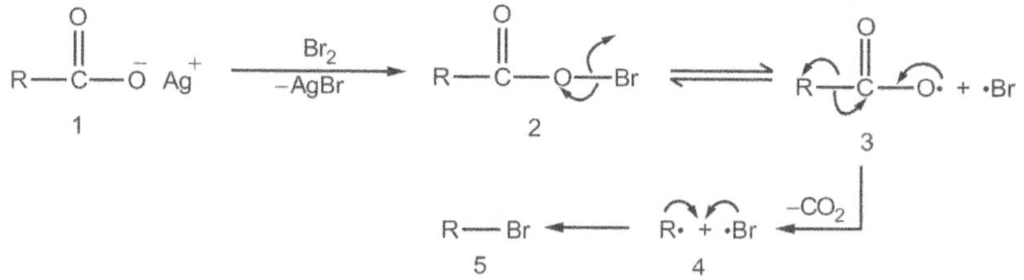

$$\underset{1}{R-\overset{O}{\underset{\|}{C}}-\bar{O}\ Ag^+} \xrightarrow[-AgBr]{Br_2} \underset{2}{R-\overset{O}{\underset{\|}{C}}-O-Br} \rightleftharpoons \underset{3}{R-\overset{O}{\underset{\|}{C}}-O\cdot + \cdot Br}$$

$$\underset{5}{R-Br} \longleftarrow \underset{4}{R\cdot + \cdot Br} \xleftarrow{-CO_2}$$

(E) By halide exchange (Finkelstein Reaction):

$$R-X + X' \rightleftharpoons R-X' + X$$

The Finkelstein reaction, named for the German chemist Hans Finkelstein, involves the exchange of one halogen atom for another (by SN_2 mechanism). Halide exchange is an equilibrium reaction, but the reaction can be completed by using a large excess of the halide salt. This is also popularly known as the **Halex Reaction**.

$$R-X + X' \rightleftharpoons R-X' + X$$

Example:

$$H_3C-CH_2Br + NaI \longrightarrow H_3C-CH_2I + NaBr$$
(acetone) (acetone) (acetone) (s)

The conversion of an alkyl chloride or an alkyl bromide to an alkyl iodide by treatment with a solution of sodium iodide in acetone. Sodium iodide is soluble in acetone while, sodium chloride and sodium bromide are not. For example, bromoethane can be converted to iodoethane.

GENERAL REACTIONS OF ALKYL HALIDES

Organohalides are valuable starting materials for many synthetic reactions. They react with certain metals to give very valuable reagents, e.g. with Mg, they give R MgX alkyl magnesium halides (**Grignards reagent**); with Li they form alkyl lithium, which when react with Cu(I), Iodide gives Lithium dialkyl copper called as **Gilman reagent**, which when reacts with alkyl halide gives corresponding coupling compound.

$$RX + Li \longrightarrow RLi \xrightarrow{CuI} R_2Cu\,Li \xrightarrow{R'X} R-R' + R\,Cu + LiX$$

| R MgX + Carbonyl $\longrightarrow$ Alcohol |
| R_2 CuX + R'X $\longrightarrow$ R – R' |

The functional group of alkyl halides is a carbon-halogen bond, the halogens attached are fluorine, chlorine, bromine and iodine. With the exception of iodine, other halogens have electronegativities significantly greater than carbon. Therefore, this functional group (carbon-halogen bond) is polarized (recall inductive effect) so that the carbon is electrophilic (electron deficient) and the halogen is nucleophilic (electron rich), as shown below.

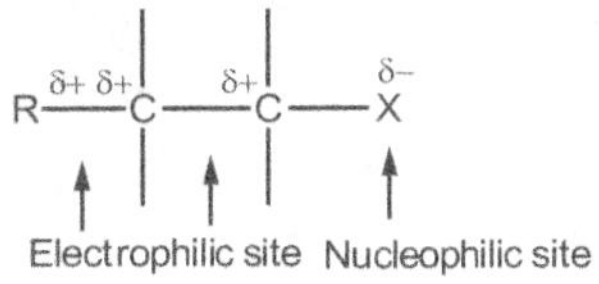

$$R \overset{\delta+}{-} \overset{\delta+}{C} \overset{\delta+}{-} \overset{}{C} \overset{\delta-}{-} X$$

Electrophilic site Nucleophilic site

The C-X bonds in alkyl halides are highly polar due to the higher electronegativity and polarizability of the halogen atoms. Halogens (Cl, Br and I) are good leaving groups in the neucleophilic substitution reactions. The electronegativity of halides decreases and the polarizability increases in the order of: F < Cl < Br < I.

Alkyl halides undergo two basic types of reactions:

(1) **Substitution reactions:** Which involve reactions occurring at sp^3 carbon directly attached to halogen. E.g., Nucleophilic substitution reactions: SN_1, SN_2, SN_i.

(2) **Elimination reactions:** Which involve the β-carbons of alkylhalides.

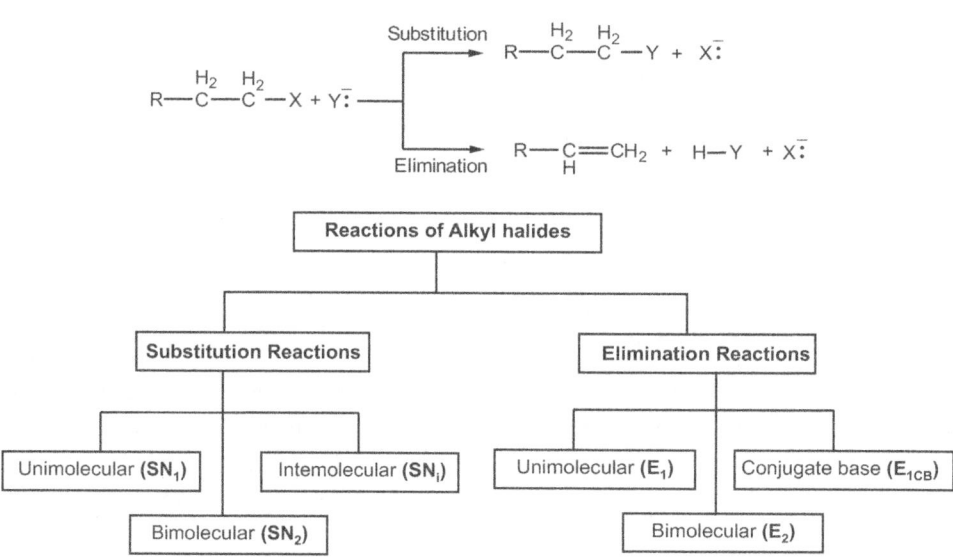

Nucleophilic substitution reactions:

In haloalkanes (alkyl halides), the C-X bond is polarized due to high electronegativity of halogen and thus, carbon is electrophilic (electron deficient). The substitution reactions in alkyl halides involve the replacement of halogen (as leaving group) by a nucleophile (incoming group) and are called nucleophilic substitution reactions.

Halides ions (being weak bases) are easily displaced by nucleophiles and thus, behave as good leaving groups (Recall weak bases are good leaving groups).

$$R-X + :Nu^- \longrightarrow R-Nu + :X^-$$

An alkyl halide ; Nucleophile (Incoming group) ; Nucleophilic substituted product ; Leaving group (Halide ion)

Depending upon the nature of substrate and also the nature of reagent and reaction conditions, the nucleophilic substitution reactions are of the following sub-classes:

(a) Substitution nucleophilic Unimolecular reaction (referred as SN_1)

(b) Substitution nucleophilic Bimolecular reaction (referred as SN_2)

(c) Substitution nucleophilic Intermolecular reaction (referred as SN_i)

Nucleophilic substitution unimolecular reactions (SN$_1$):

Mechanism: The nucleophilic substitution in a Unimolecular mechanism, that is, SN$_1$ mechanism is favoured in presence of weak bases or poor nucleophiles. It takes place in two steps. The first step involves heterolytic cleavage of C-X bond resulting in the formation of a carbocation (positively charged carbon).

$$R_3C-X \xrightarrow{:X^-} R_3C^+ \xrightarrow{:Nu^-} R_3C-Nu$$

Step I   Carbocation   Step II

Reaction Mechanism:

Step 1: Heterolytic cleavage in C-X bond: formation of carbocation: In alkyl halides the C-X carbon in sp^3 hybridized and heterolytic cleavage results in the formation of carbocation (which is sp^2 hybridized).

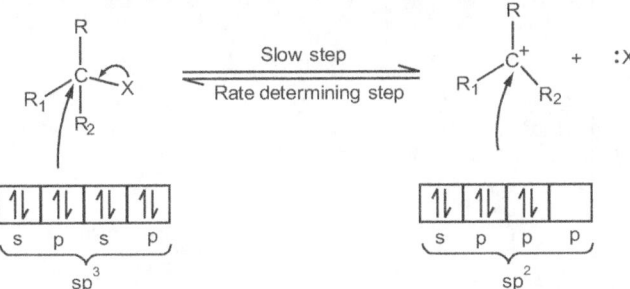

1. The formation of carbocation is a slow step and is thus, rate determining step. The rate of reaction (formation of carbocation) is dependant only on the concentration of alkyl halides. The rate of reaction is first order (the reaction which depends on the concentration of one reactant only). Once the carbocation is formed the attack of :Nu$^-$ (incoming nucleophile) is very fast.

2. Since only one molecule (or reactant) interacts in the rate determining step and also the rate of the reaction is dependant on the concentration of alkyl halides (reactant), the reaction is unimolecular (that's why it is called SN$_1$).

Step 2: Attack of nucleophile (:Nu$^-$) on carbocation (fast step): The carbocation (sp^2 hybridized) has a planar structure and can undergo attack by the nucleophile (incoming nucleophile) from front side or rear side resulting in the formation of a substituted product.

Reaction order and Kinetics of SN$_1$ mechanism: As the rate determining step (slow step, or step 1) involves formation of carbocation, which is generated from alkyl halide (reactant only), only one reactant (species) is involved in rate determining step. Hence the rate of reaction will depend upon the concentration of reactant only (and not on the concentration the nucleophile which is involved in step II, which is not rate determining step).

Hence, SN$_1$ reaction mechanism follows **first order kinetics** (Recall: first order reactions are the reactions in which the rate of **reaction depends on concentration of only one species**) i.e., the substrate.

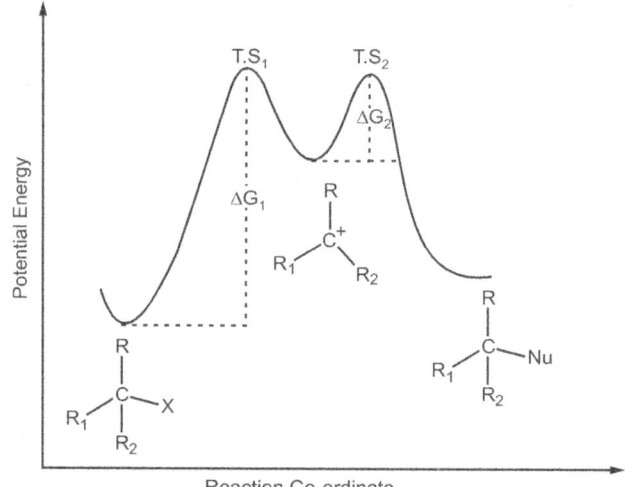

Fig. 8.1

Stereochemistry:

Since the carbocation formed in step I is planar and can be attacked by the nucleophile (incoming nucleophile) from either side resulting in the formation of a stereo product mixture.

An attack from the front results in the formation of product having same configuration (known as retention of configuration) as compared to the reactant (alkyl halide). (Recall: configuration means arrangement of different atoms or groups in the molecule).

When the nucleophile attacks from the back side (rear side), results in the formation of a product having a configuration opposite (inversion of configuration) as compared to the reactant (alkyl halide).

Therefore, SN$_1$ mechanism results in the formation of product with 50% retention and 50% inversion of configuration.

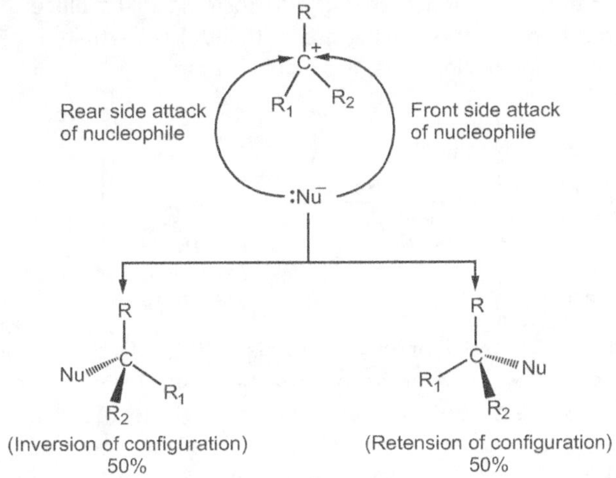

Fig. 8.2

As both the products (with retention and inversion of configurations) are mirror images of each other (in the ratio of 50 : 50) i.e. the racemic mixture.

Evidence for racemisation by SN$_1$ reaction mechanism:

The hydrolysis of S-3-bromo-3-mehylhexane with aqueous NaOH follows SN$_1$ pathway as below:

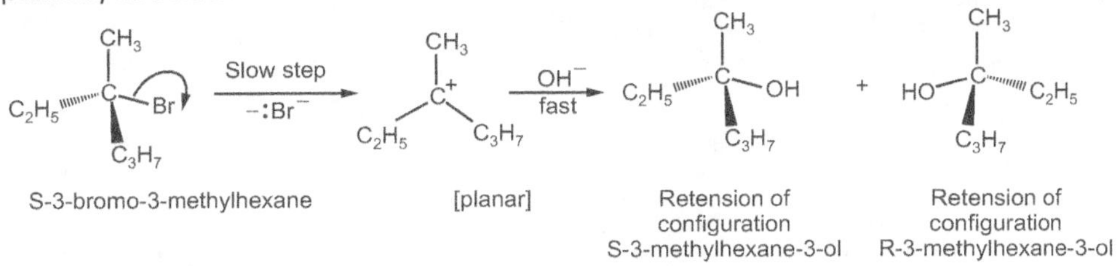

S-3-bromo-3-methylhexane → [planar] → Retension of configuration S-3-methylhexane-3-ol + Retension of configuration R-3-methylhexane-3-ol

Nucleophilic substitution bimolecular reactions (SN$_2$):

Mechanism: In a bimolecular mechanism, the attack of nucleophile on sp^3 hybridized carbon of alkyl halide and removal of halide ion (or the leaving group) occurs simultaneously in a single step. Here the attack of nucleophile (incoming nucleophile) takes place in the presence of leaving group (halide ion) the incoming nucleophile can attack from a side *opposite* to the leaving group (or halide ion).

The reaction proceeds in a single step (also known as single concerted step), in which the transition step consists of a partial attachment of nucleophiles (incoming and outgoing) i.e. Nu⁻ and :X⁻. Bond breaking and forming takes place at same time. In transition state the bond to the leaving group (halide) is partially broken and bond to the nucleophile (incoming nucleophile) is partially formed.

Reaction order and Kinetics of SN₂ mechanism: The rate determining step involves interaction of two species, i.e. alkyl halide (reactant) and the nucleophile. Thus, rate is dependent on the concentration of these two species and the reaction is referred as bimolecular which follows second order kinetics (Recall: second order reactions are the reactions in which the rate of reaction depends on concentration of two species/reactants).

$$\text{Rate of reaction} \propto [\text{Subtrate}] [\text{Nucleophile}]$$

Both the substrate and the nucleophile are reactants.

Energy profile diagram for SN₂ reaction mechanism / Energy consideration of SN₂ reaction mechanism:

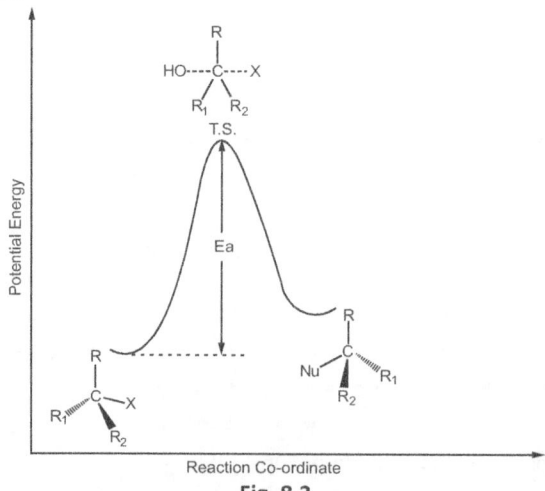

Fig. 8.3

Evidence for stereospecificity by SN₂ reaction mechanism:

The reaction SN_2 mechanism is stereospecific in nature as it leads to the formation of substituted product with a configuration opposite to that of the initial alkyl halide. In other words SN_2 mechanism involves the inversion of configuration (known as **Walden inversion**).

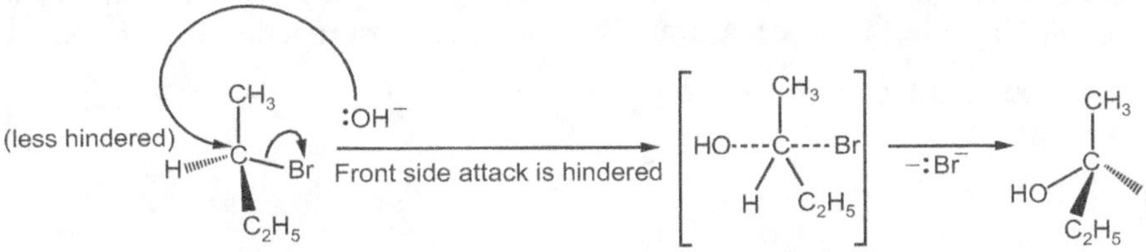

R-2-Bromobutane (with inverted configuration) → Transition state → S-Butane-2-ol (with inverted configuration)

Nucleophilic substitution intermolecular reactions (SN_i):

Mechanism: It is nucleophilic substitution reaction where a part of leaving group is acting as a nucleophile, resulting into an internal substitution. The reaction takes place in two steps. Step 1 involves the generation of carbonium ion (carbocation) due to ionisation of the substrate to release the leaving group. The reaction is known as SN_i since the attacking nucleophile has already been present on the substrate (alkyl halide) and the attack takes place internally.

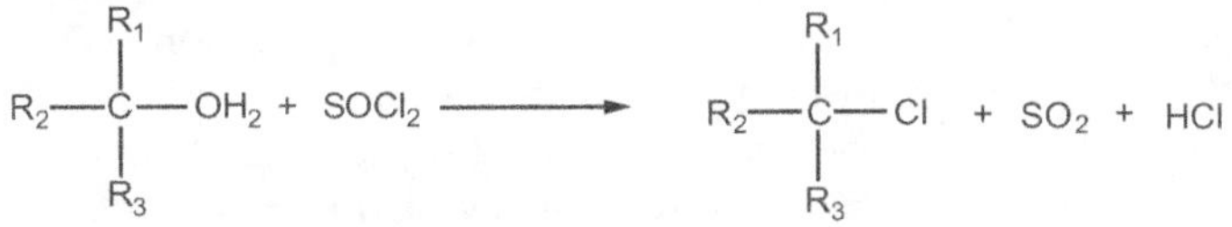

$$R_2-\underset{R_3}{\overset{R_1}{C}}-OH_2 + SOCl_2 \longrightarrow R_2-\underset{R_3}{\overset{R_1}{C}}-Cl + SO_2 + HCl$$

The reaction takes place in three steps:

Step 1: Formation of an intermediate (alkyl chlorosulphite)

$$R_2-\underset{R_3}{\overset{R_1}{C}}-OH + \underset{Cl}{\overset{Cl}{>}}S=O \longrightarrow R_2-\underset{R_3}{\overset{R_1}{C}}-O-\underset{Cl}{\overset{}{S}}=OH + HCl$$

Alkyl chlorosulphite intermediate

Step 2: Alkyl chlorosuphite then dissociates slowly into an intimate ion pair, i.e. a carbenium ion and $-OSOCl$:

$$R_2-\underset{R_3}{\overset{R_1}{C}}-OH + \underset{Cl}{\overset{Cl}{>}}S=O \longrightarrow R_2-\underset{R_3}{\overset{R_1}{C}}-O-\underset{Cl}{\overset{}{S}}=O + HCl$$

Alkyl chlorosulphite intermediate

FACTORS AFFECTING SN₁, SN₂ REACTION MECHANISMS

1. **Effect of substrate structure:**

   (a) On SN₁ reaction: The substrate which forms the most stable ion will develop the most stable transition state and ΔG for the substrate will be lowest. The reaction will take minimum time to overcome the transition state. Hence, the reaction rate will be highest i.e. the substrate is found to be most reactive, therefore:

   $Ph_3C-G \gg Ph_2HC-G \gg PhH_2C-G \approx H_2C=C\underset{H}{\overset{H_2}{-}}C-G > H_3C-G \gg H_2C=\underset{H}{C}-G > HC\equiv C-G$

   $Ph_3C-G \gg Ph_2HC-G \gg PhH_2C-G$

   $3° \gg 2° > 1°$

   If the substrate bears more strain (i.e., bulky groups) than the other (i.e., less bulky groups/ less strain), its ground state energy will be more as compared to the substrate having less strain. The substrate having more strain will try more than the latter (with less bulky groups) to get the relief of strain. By considering the carbocationic transition state, the more strained substrate gets the relief leading to lower energy of transition state. Therefore, the ΔG for reaction with less strained species. Therefore, the more strained will react faster than the less strained.

   Also, as the rate determining step involves the formation of carbocation, the substrate which forms the most stable carbonium ion (carbocation) will develop most stable transition state and ΔG for the substrate will be lowest. The reaction will take minimum time to overcome the energy of transition state (T.S). Hence, the reaction rate will be highest i.e., the substrate is found to be most reactive. Therefore,

Substrate	$H_3C-\underset{CH_3}{\overset{Br}{\underset{|}{\overset{|}{C}}}}-CH_3$	$H_3C-\underset{CH_3}{\overset{Br}{\underset{|}{\overset{|}{C}}}}-H$	$H_3C-\underset{H}{\overset{Br}{\underset{|}{\overset{|}{C}}}}-H$	$H-\underset{H}{\overset{Br}{\underset{|}{\overset{|}{C}}}}-H$
Reactivity	More reactive in SN₁ →			Methyl less reactive in SN₁
Stability of carbocation in step 1 →	$H_3C-\underset{CH_3}{\overset{\oplus}{\underset{|}{C}}}-CH_3$	$H_3C-\underset{CH_3}{\overset{\oplus}{\underset{|}{C}}}-H$	$H_3C-\underset{H}{\overset{\oplus}{\underset{|}{C}}}-H$	$H-\underset{H}{\overset{\oplus}{\underset{|}{C}}}-H$
	More stable			Less stable

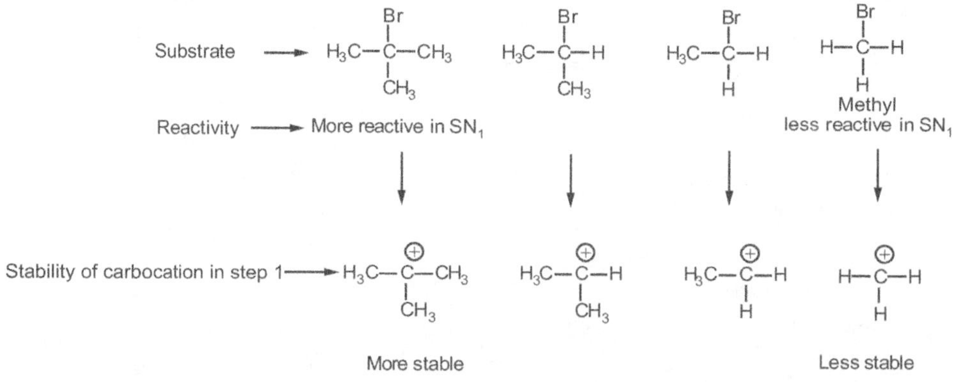

If the substrate bears more strain (bulky groups/ alkyl groups) than the other, its ground state energy will be more as compared to the substrate having less strain. By considering the carbocationic transition state, the more strained substrates gets relief by losing the leaving group to get the low energy transition state. Therefore, the ΔG for the reaction with the more strained substrates will be less than the ΔG for more strained substrate. Hence, more strained (containing more substitutions on substrate carbon) will react faster.

(b) On SN₂ reaction: During the conversion of substrate from ground state to transition state (in SN₂), the bond angle of methyl systems H-C-H increases from 109° to about 120° at the same time, angle H-C-G (where G is leaving group) and H-C-Nu (where Nu is incoming nucleophile) decreases to 90°.

When 'H' are replaced by much larger methyl groups, the interference between 'G' and 'Nu' and methyl groups increases (because the angle between them decreases). Due to this the covalent bond compresses between H-C-H and Nu-C-G in the transition state, which leads to increase in potential energy. Therefore, the order of potential energy of the T.S. involving alkyl systems is:

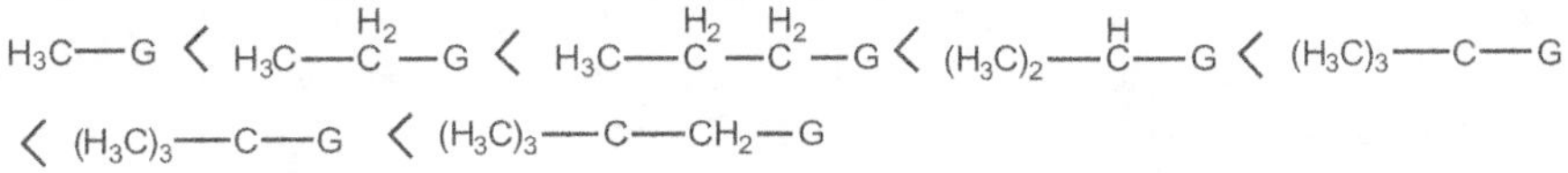

$$H_3C-G < H_3C-CH_2-G < H_3C-CH_2-CH_2-G < (H_3C)_2-CH-G < (H_3C)_3-C-G$$

$$< (H_3C)_3-C-G < (H_3C)_3-C-CH_2-G$$

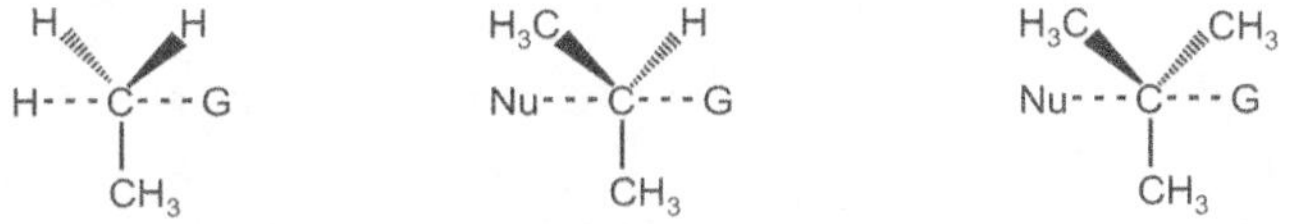

Less strained   Strained   More strained

Tertiary alkyl halide groups are less likely to react by SN₂ mechanism than primary or secondary halides since, the presence of three alkyl groups linked to the reaction centre (substrate) lower the electrophilicity of alkyl halide by inductive effects.

Tertiary alkyl halides have three bulky groups attached to the reaction centre which act as steric shields and hinder the approach of incoming nucleophiles. Primary alkyl halides have only one carbon (alkyl group) attached to the reaction centre and so approach of nucleophile is easy.

2. **Effect of nucleophile:**

   (a) On SN₁ reaction: The strength of the nucleophile does not affect the reaction rate of SN₁ because, as stated above, the nucleophile is not involved in the rate-determining step. However, if more than one nucleophile are competing to bind to the carbocation, the strengths and concentrations of those nucleophiles affect the distribution of products. For example, if (CH$_3$)$_3$CCl is reacting in water and formic acid where the water and formic acid are competing nucleophiles, two different products: (CH$_3$)$_3$COH and (CH$_3$)$_3$COCOH will be formed. The relative yields of these products depend on the concentrations and relative reactivities of the nucleophiles.

3. **Effect of leaving group:**
   (a) **On SN$_1$ Reaction:** Good leaving groups are essential for SN$_1$ reactions. The leaving group should be **highly polarisable and least basic**. The leaving group should be stable after it has left with the bonding electrons. This is possible with a weak base. The leaving group starts to take a partial negative charge as the cation starts to form. The rate of leaving group reactivity is:

   $$H_2O > ROH > Ac\overline{O} > \overline{OH}$$

   The more polarisable a group, the more will be its reactivity. Thus, reactivity order among halogens is:

   $$I > Br > Cl > F$$

   The better the leaving group's ability to leave, the higher the ionic character of the transition state.

   (b) **On SN$_2$ reaction:** The relative nucleophilic strength of incoming nucleophiles affects the rate of SN$_2$ reaction. Strong nucleophiles react faster. A charged nucleophile is a stronger nucleophile than corresponding uncharged nucleophile.

   $$R\overline{O} > \overline{O}H > RCO\overline{O} > ROH > H_2O$$

4. **Effect of Solvent:**
   (a) **On SN$_1$ Reaction:** A solvent with **high dielectric constant** and **ion-solvating ability** enhances the rate of SN$_1$ reaction. Polar hydroxylic solvents like water, methyl alcohol, formic acid have high dielectric constant as well as ion-solvating ability so they are the good solvents for SN$_1$ reaction and they increase the rate. Polar hydroxylic solvents solvate both cations and anions and hence they are capable of stabilizing the carbocationic transition state (of SN$_1$). These solvents stabilize the substrates of SN$_1$ reactions as well as the transition state.

E.g., water being a polar hydroxylic solvent can solvate the positively charged carbocation (C⁺) by its negative pole and negatively charged leaving group (Br⁻) by its positive pole ($\overset{+}{H}$—O—$\overset{+}{H}$).

(b) **On SN$_2$ Reaction:** Polar aprotic solvents are used for SN$_2$ reactions since, they solvate cations but not anions. As a result nucleophiles are naked.

Examples: Polar aprotic solvents : Acetonitrile (CH$_3$CN) or Dimethylformamide (DMF).

These solvents are polar enough to dissolve the ionic reagents required for nucleophilic substitution. They solvate the metal cations rather than anions. Anions are solvated by hydrogen bonding and since (aprotic) solvent is incapable of hydrogen bonding, the anions remain unsolvated. Such nacked 'anions' retain their nucleophilicity and react more strongly with electrophiles.

SUBSTITUTION VS ELIMINATION

Elimination *versus* Substitution in Alkylhalides:

1. **The reactions:**

    Both reactions involve heating the halogenoalkane (alkylhalide) under reflux with sodium or potassium hydroxide solution.

    Nucleophilic substitution: The hydroxide ions present are good nucleophiles, and one possibility is a replacement of the halogen atom by an -OH group to give an alcohol *via* a nucleophilic substitution reaction.

    $$H_3C-\underset{H}{\overset{Br}{C}}-CH_3 + NaOH \longrightarrow H_3C-\underset{H}{\overset{OH}{C}}-CH_3 + NaBr$$

    In the above example, 2-bromopropane is converted into propan-2-ol.

    Elimination: Halogenoalkanes also undergo elimination reactions in the presence of sodium or potassium hydroxide, but the base should be in higher concentrations.

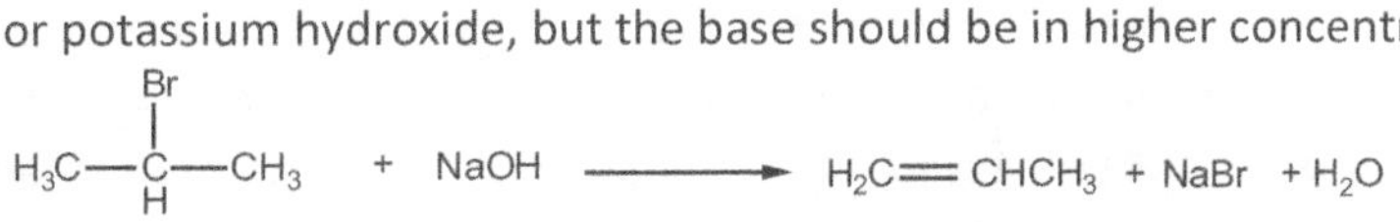

    $$H_3C-\underset{H}{\overset{Br}{C}}-CH_3 + NaOH \longrightarrow H_2C=CHCH_3 + NaBr + H_2O$$

    2-Bromopropane undergoes elimination of HBr to give an alkene; 1-propene.

2. **Factors affecting substitution or elimination:**

    The reagents used are the same for both substitution or elimination reactions. i.e., the halogenoalkane and either sodium or potassium hydroxide solution. In all cases, a mixture of both reactions takes place simultaneously - some substitution and some elimination. Factors, that govern substitution or elimination reactions include:

(a) **The type of halogenoalkane:** This is the most important factor.

Type of halogenoalkane	Substitution or elimination?
Primary	Mainly substitution
Secondary	Both substitution and elimination
Tertiary	Mainly elimination

(b) **The solvent:** The proportion of water to ethanol in the solvent matters.
- Water encourages substitution.
- Ethanol encourages elimination.

(c) **The temperature:** Higher temperatures encourage elimination.

(d) **Concentration of the sodium or potassium hydroxide solution:** Higher concentrations favour elimination.

(e) **The role of the hydroxide ions:**

  (i) **The role of the hydroxide ion in a substitution reaction:** In the substitution reaction between a halogenoalkane and OH⁻ ions, the hydroxide ions are acting as nucleophiles. For example, one of the lone pairs of electrons on the oxygen can attack the slightly positive carbon. This leads to the loss of the bromine as a bromide ion and the -OH group gets attached in its place.

$$H_3C-\underset{Br}{\overset{H^{\delta+}}{C}}-CH_3 \quad \overset{:\bar{O}H}{\curvearrowleft}$$

  (ii) **The role of the hydroxide ion in an elimination reaction:** Hydroxide ions have a very strong tendency to combine with hydrogen ions to make water in other words, the OH⁻ ion is a very strong base. In an elimination reaction, the hydroxide ion hits one of the hydrogen atoms in the CH₃ group and pulls it off. This leads to a cascade of electron pair movements resulting in the formation of a carbon-carbon double bond, and the loss of the bromine as Br⁻.

$$H-\underset{H}{\overset{H}{C}}-\underset{Br}{\overset{H}{C}}-CH_3 \quad \overset{:\bar{O}H}{\curvearrowleft}$$

E_1 vs SN_1:

Point	E_1	SN_1
Number of Steps	Reaction takes place in two steps	Reaction takes place in two steps
Example	*(reaction scheme showing two-step E1 mechanism: carbocation formation followed by elimination to form alkene)*	*(reaction scheme showing two-step SN1 mechanism: carbocation formation followed by nucleophilic attack)*
Reagent	Solvent plays role of reagent	Solvents and weekly basic reagents of low concentrations are used.
Solvent	Polar hydroxylic solvents of low dielectric constant are used.	Polar hydroxylic solvents of high dielectric constant are used.
Substrate (Order of reactivity)	Tertiary > Secondary > Primary	Tertiary > Secondary > Primary
Kinetics	First order reaction	First order reaction
Transition state	*(transition state structure with $\delta+$ and $\delta-$)*	*(transition state structure with $\delta+$ and $\delta-$)*
Stereochemistry	Not Stereospecific	Retention and inversion of configuration takes place leading to Racemization
Temperature	High temperature favour elimination.	Low temperature favour substitution.

E_2 vs SN_2:

Point	E_2	SN_2
No. of Steps	Reaction takes place in one step	Reaction takes place in one step
Example	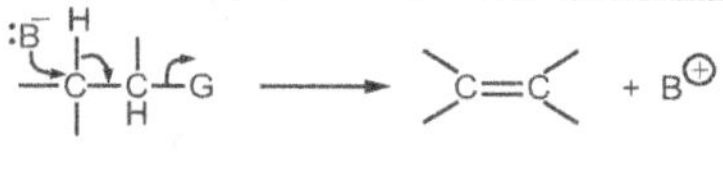 [reaction scheme showing base abstracting H, leaving group G departing, forming C=C + BH]	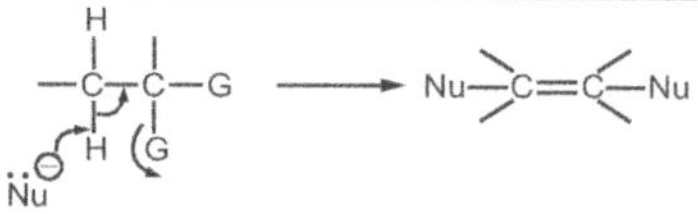 [reaction scheme showing Nu attacking C, G leaving, forming Nu-C=C-Nu]
Reagent	Strong base	Strong nucleophile
Solvent	Non-hydroxylic solvents of low polarity increases the rate of reaction	Non-hydroxylic solvent of high polarity increase the rate.
Substrate (Order of reactivity)	Tertiary > Secondary > Primary	Primary > Secondary > Tertiary
Kinetics	Rate = K [substrate] [base]	Rate = K [substrate] [Nucleophile]
Transition state	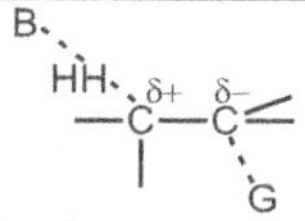 [transition state diagram with B, H, δ+, δ−, C-C, G]	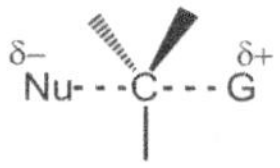 [transition state diagram with Nu---C---G, δ−, δ+]
Stereochemistry	Stereospecific	Stereospecific (Walden inversion)
Temperature	Favoured by high temperature.	Favoured by low temperature.

QUESTION BANK

1. What are alkylhalides? Classify with examples.

2. Give IUPAC names to following structures.

    (a) 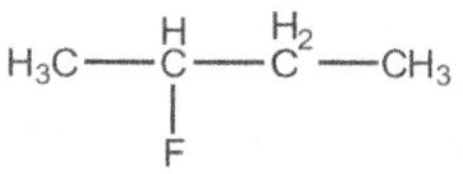 $H_3C-\underset{F}{\underset{|}{\overset{H}{\overset{|}{C}}}}-\overset{H_2}{C}-CH_3$ (b) [cyclopentane with CH₃ and Br substituents]   (c) [branched structure with two I atoms]

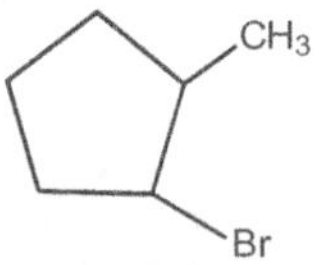

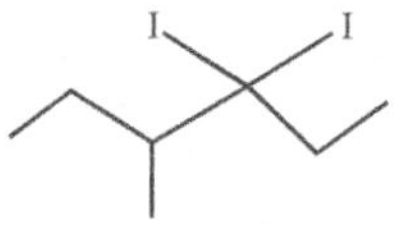

3. Draw the structures of the following alkyl halides from following names:

    (a) Vinylbromide, (b) Alkyl chloride, (c) Benzyleodide (d) 3-Chloroheptane (e) Cyclohexyl methyl bromide

4. Write down the methods for the preparation of alkyl halides.
5. Discuss general reactions of alkyl halides.
6. SN_1 reaction results in racemisation. Explain Energy profile diagram for SN_1 reaction mechanism / Energy consideration of SN_1 reaction mechanism:
7. SN_2 reaction mechanism is stereo specific. Please explain.
8. Explain Walden Inversion? Write a note on stereochemistry of SN_2 reaction mechanism.
9. Discuss various factors affecting SN_1/SN_2 reactions.
10. Distinguish between substitution and elimination reactions? Or Compare substitution with elimination.
11. How will you prepare propylbromide using a suitable alkane?
12. How will you prepare ethylchloride using a suitable alkene?
13. Complete the following reaction and explain it.

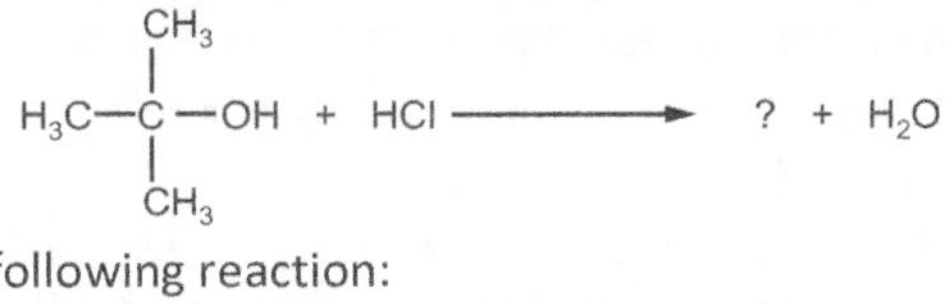

$$H_3C-\underset{\underset{CH_3}{|}}{\overset{\overset{CH_3}{|}}{C}}-OH + HCl \longrightarrow ? + H_2O$$

14. Complete the following reaction:

$$? + PCl_5 \longrightarrow H_3C-\overset{H_2}{C}-\overset{H_2}{C}-Cl + HCl + POCl_3$$

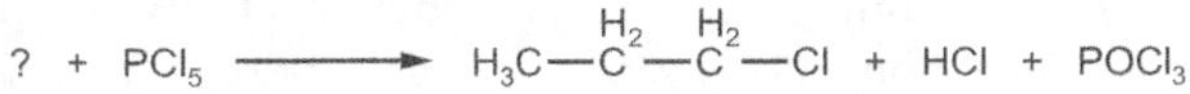

15. How alkyl halides are prepared using a silver salt of carboxylic acid.
16. Write a note on mechanism, stereochemistry and kinetics of SN_1 reactions.
17. Discuss reaction mechanism and stereochemistry of SN_2 reactions.
18. Discuss factors affecting on the following reaction mechanisms.
    (a) SN_1 (b) SN_2 (c) SN_i
19. Which alkyl halide has most polar alkyl-halogen bond? Explain.
    (a) RF (b) RCl (c) R-Br (d) R-I
20. Which alkyl halide has strongest alkyl-halogen bond? Explain.
    (a) RF (b) RCl (c) R-Br (d) R-I

Chapter 9 ...

CARBOXYLIC ACIDS (AROMATIC AND ALIPHATIC)

CONTENTS

Common and IUPAC nomenclature, properties, methods of preparation and reactions. Functional derivatives of carboxylic acids, acid chlorides, anhydrides, esters and amides, their IUPAC nomenclature, general methods of preparation and reactions (along with mechanism), dicarboxylic acids.

INTRODUCTION

The organic compounds having carboxyl functional group are called carboxylic acids. The carboxyl group carries a **carbo**nyl group CO attached to hydro**xyl** OH group therefore, name **carboxyl**. The simplest series of carboxylic acids are the alkanoic acids, R-COOH, where R is a hydrogen or an alkyl or an aryl group. Compounds may also have two or more carboxylic acid groups per molecule and are called dicarboxylic acids.

Classification of Carboxylic acids:

The carboxylic acids are classified into monocarboxylic acids, dicarboxylic acids, tricarboxylic acids etc., depending upon the number of COOH groups present in the organic compound. The monocarboxylic acids are further classified as aliphatic carboxylic acids and aromatic carboxylic acids.

Example:

Monocarboxylic acids:

HCOOH
Formic acid

CH_3COOH
Acetic acid

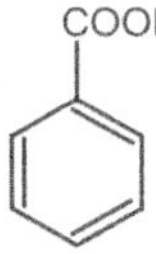

C_6H_5COOH (Benzoic acid)
Bezoic acid

Dicarboxylic acids:

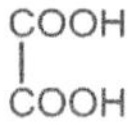

COOH
|
COOH

Oxalic acid

CH_2COOH
|
CH_2COOH

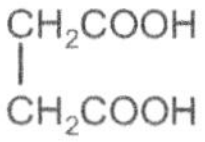

Succinic acid

Polycarboxylic acid:

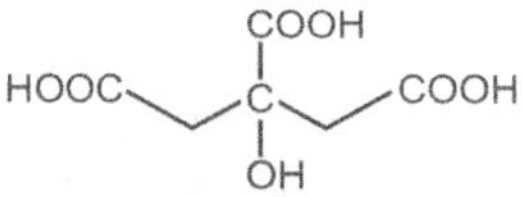

HOOC—C(COOH)(OH)—COOH

Citric acid

Structure of carboxylate ion:

The carboxylate ion has two canonical structures, both equally stable. The carbon atom is joined to two oxygen atoms, one by a single bond and the other by a double bond. But due to the resonance the bonds continuously shift from one oxygen atom to the other. So neither of the bonds can be called as a single or a double bond. Hence, the bond between carbon atom and each oxygen atom is said to be "one-and-a half" bond.

$$R-C(=O)-O^- \longleftrightarrow R-C(-O^-)=O$$

The carbon atom of the carboxyl group is sp^2 hybridized and the three orbitals form the sigma bonds. The remaining p-orbitals of the carbon overlap very well with the p-orbitals of the oxygen atom. Hence, the electrons are bound to three nuclei and thus held very strongly. Thus, the carboxylate anion is more stable. All the bond angles around the carboxyl carbon are 120°.

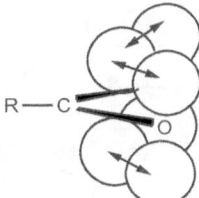

Fig. 9.1: Overlap of *p*-orbitals

PROPERTIES AND NOMENCLATURE

Physical properties:

Carboxylic acids are polar molecules. They can form hydrogen bonds with each other and with other kinds of molecules. Carboxylic acids are soluble in less polar solvents such as ether, alcohol, benzene etc. Some carboxylic acids have higher boiling points than alcohol because, they are held together by two hydrogen bonds. Carboxylic acids have unpleasant odour. Higher carboxylic acids are odourless.

Nomenclature:

The carboxylate anion R-COO⁻ is usually named with the suffix *-ate*, so acetic acid, for example, becomes acetate ion. In IUPAC nomenclature, carboxylic acids have an *-oic acid* suffix (e.g., butanoic acid). In common nomenclature, the suffix is usually *-ic acid* (e.g., butyric acid). Butanoic acid (IUPAC) while butyric acid (common name). (*Please refer to chapter 2 for more details*).

Table 9.1: Nomenclature of some monocarboxylic acids

Carbon atoms	Common name	IUPAC name	Chemical formula
1.	Formic acid	Methanoic acid	HCOOH
2.	Acetic acid	Ethanoic acid	CH_3COOH
3.	Propionic acid	Propanoic acid	CH_3CH_2COOH
4.	Butyric acid	Butanoic acid	$CH_3(CH_2)_2COOH$
5.	Valeric acid	Pentanoic acid	$CH_3(CH_2)_3COOH$
6.	Caproic acid	Hexanoic acid	$CH_3(CH_2)_4COOH$
7.	Enanthic acid	Heptanoic acid	$CH_3(CH_2)_5COOH$
8.	Caprylic acid	Octanoic acid	$CH_3(CH_2)_6COOH$
9.	Pelargonic acid	Nonanoic acid	$CH_3(CH_2)_7COOH$
10.	Capric acid	Decanoic acid	$CH_3(CH_2)_8COOH$
11.	Lauric acid	Dodecanoic acid	$CH_3(CH_2)_{10}COOH$
12.	Palmitic acid	Hexadecanoic acid	$CH_3(CH_2)_{14}COOH$
13.	Stearic acid	Octadecanoic acid	$CH_3(CH_2)_{16}COOH$

Table 9.2: Nomenclature of some dicarboxylic acids

Common name	IUPAC name	Chemical formula
Oxalic acid	Ethanedioic acid	COOH-COOH
Malonic acid	Propanedioic acid	$COOHCH_2COOH$
Succinic acid	Butanedioic acid	$COOH(CH_2)_2COOH$
Glutaric acid	Pentanedioic acid	$COOH(CH_2)_3COOH$
Adipic acid	Hexandioic acid	$COOH(CH_2)_4COOH$
Maleic acid	*cis*-Butenedioic acid	*cis*-COOHCH=CHCOOH
Fumaric acid	*trans*-Butenedioic acid	*trans*-COOHCH=CHCOOH

METHODS OF PREPARATION OF CARBOXYLIC ACIDS

Various synthetic methods for the preparation of carboxylic acid are discussed below

1. **Oxidation of alkenes:**

Alkenes can be oxidized using hot alkaline $KMnO_4$ to give carboxylic acids. Other strong oxidizing agents which can be used are CrO_3, $K_2Cr_2O_7$ etc.

$$RCH=CHR' \xrightarrow[H_3O^+]{KMnO_4, OH^-, \text{heat}} R-COOH + R'-COOH$$

2. Oxidation of primary alcohols and aldehydes:

Primary alcohols can be oxidized with $KMnO_4$ to give carboxylic acids. Aldehydes can also be oxidized to carboxylic acids using mild oxidizing agents such as $Ag(NH_3)_2^+OH^-$.

Aldehydes and primary alcohols are oxidized to carboxylic acids with chromic acid (H_2CrO_4) in aqueous acetone (Jones oxidation). Other reagents like potassium dichromate, potassium permanganate or sodium chlorite also can be used.

$$R-CHO \xrightarrow[H_3O^+]{Ag_2O} R-COOH$$

$$R-CH_2OH \xrightarrow[H_3O^+]{KMnO_4,\, OH^-,\, heat} R-COOH$$

The direct oxidation of primary alcohols to carboxylic acids normally proceeds *via* the corresponding aldehyde, which is transformed *via* an aldehyde hydrate (R-CH(OH)$_2$) by reaction with water before it can be further oxidized to the carboxylic acid.

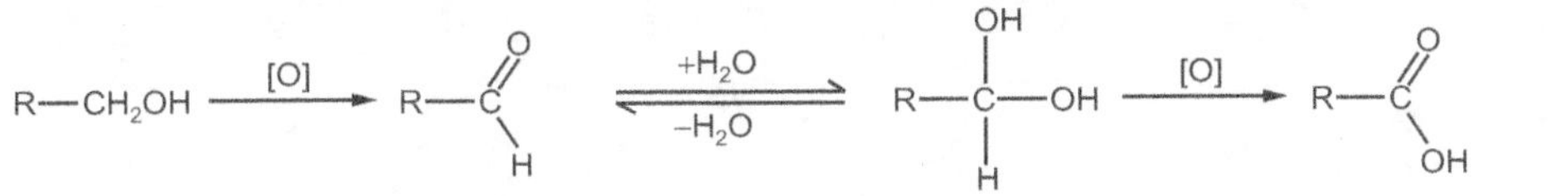

$$R-CH_2OH \xrightarrow{[O]} R-C(=O)H \underset{-H_2O}{\overset{+H_2O}{\rightleftharpoons}} R-CH(OH)_2 \xrightarrow{[O]} R-COOH$$

Primary alcohol   Aldehyde   Aldehyde hydrate   Carboxylic acid

3. Oxidation of alkylbenzenes:

Primary and secondary alkyl groups directly attached to the benzene ring can be oxidized to carboxylic acid. Tertiary groups do not undergo this reaction. The oxidizing agents used are strong ones and ensure complete oxidation to the carboxylic acids.

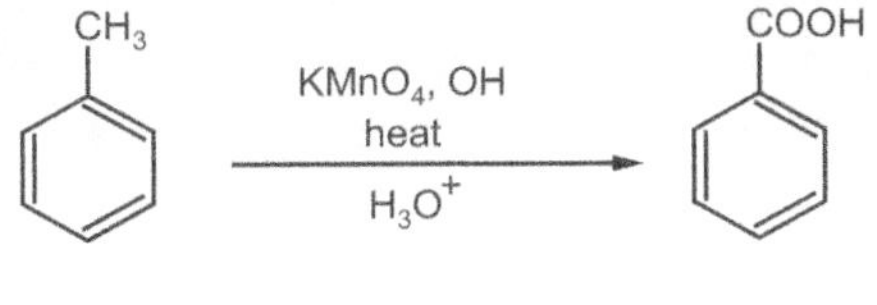

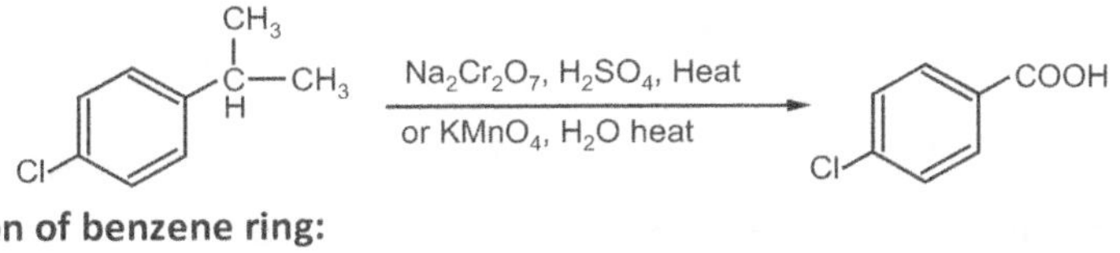

$$C_6H_5-CH_3 \xrightarrow[H_3O^+]{KMnO_4,\, OH^-,\, heat} C_6H_5-COOH$$

$$\text{4-Cl-C}_6H_4\text{-CH(CH}_3)_2 \xrightarrow{Na_2Cr_2O_7,\, H_2SO_4,\, Heat \text{ or } KMnO_4,\, H_2O\, heat} \text{4-Cl-C}_6H_4\text{-COOH}$$

4. Oxidation of benzene ring:

The benzene ring of an alkylbenzene can be converted to carboxylic acid by ozonolysis followed by treatment with hydrogen peroxide. This requires very strong oxidizing reagents and conditions, as benzene is stable towards weaker reagents.

$$R-C_6H_5 \xrightarrow[H_2O_2]{O_3,\, CH_3COOH} R-COOH$$

5. Oxidation of methyl ketones:

Methyl ketones can be converted to carboxylic acids *via* haloform reaction. Iodoform is preferred haloform and the reaction is called as Haloform reaction.

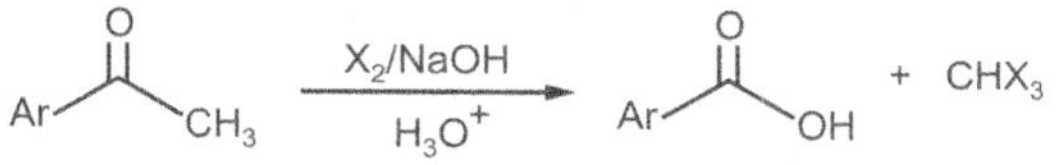

$$Ar-CO-CH_3 \xrightarrow[H_3O^+]{X_2/NaOH} Ar-COOH + CHX_3$$

6. Carbonation of Grignard reagent:

Grignard reagent adds to the carbon-oxygen double bond of carbon dioxide to form magnesium salt of the carboxylic acid. This magnesium carboxylate on acidification produces carboxylic acid.

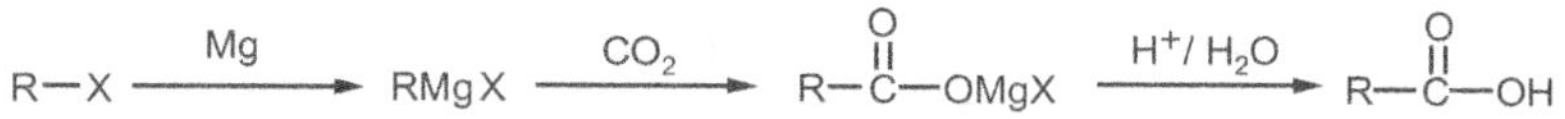

$$R-X \xrightarrow{Mg} RMgX \xrightarrow{CO_2} R-\underset{\underset{O}{\|}}{C}-OMgX \xrightarrow{H^+/H_2O} R-\underset{\underset{O}{\|}}{C}-OH$$

Mechanism:

$$R-MgX + CO_2 \longrightarrow R-\underset{\underset{O}{\|}}{C}-OMgX \xrightarrow{H^+} R-\underset{\underset{O}{\|}}{C}-OH + Mg^{2+} X^-$$

[Reaction scheme: 2-bromo-1,3,5-trimethylbenzene → (Mg) → Grignard reagent → (CO₂) → COOMgBr derivative → (H⁺) → 2,4,6-trimethylbenzoic acid]

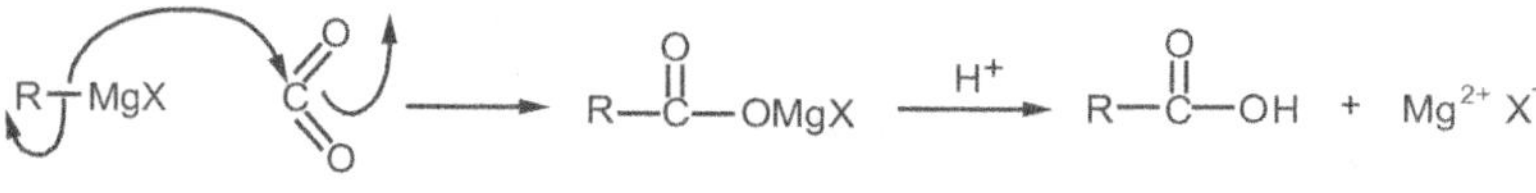

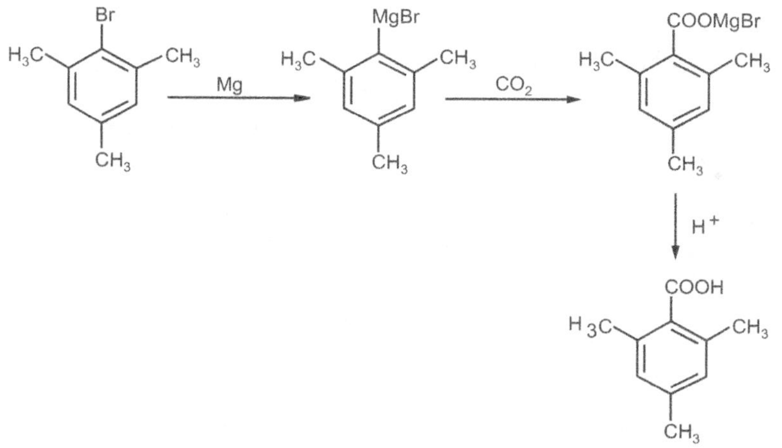

7. Hydrolysis of nitriles and cyanohydrins:

Hydrolysis of nitriles yield carboxylic acid. Aliphatic nitriles are prepared from corresponding alkyl halides using sodium cyanide while, aromatic nitriles are prepared from diazonium salts since, aryl halides are less reactive. These nitriles are hydrolysed to give carboxylic acid with one carbon atom more than the alkyl halide.

$$R-C\equiv N + 2H_2O \xrightarrow{H^+} R-COOH + NH_4^+$$

$$\xrightarrow{^-OH} R-COO^- + NH_3$$

e.g.,

[o-methylbenzonitrile] ⟶ [o-methylbenzoic acid] + NH$_3$↑

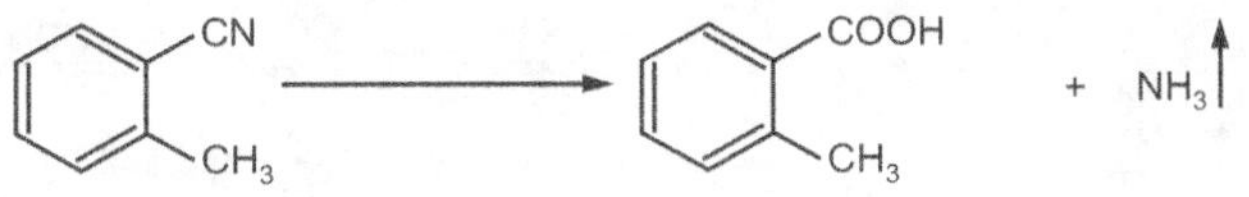

Acidic hydrolysis of nitriles give carboxylic acids. In acidic hydrolysis the first step is the protonation of the nitrogen atom. This protonation increases the polarization of the nitrile group and makes the carbon atom more susceptible to nucleophilic attack. The loss of a proton from the oxygen atom produces tautomeric form of amide. The nitrogen gains a proton to form a protonated amide which follows the same sequence of hydrolysis of amide to form carboxylic acid.

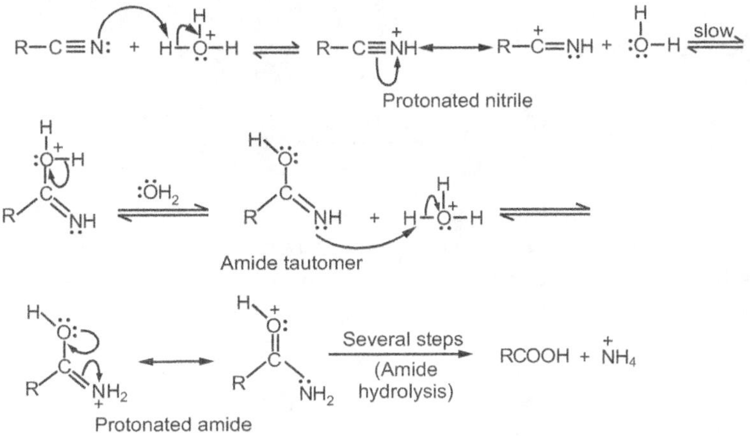

$$R-C\equiv N: + H-\overset{+}{O}-H \rightleftharpoons R-C\equiv \overset{+}{N}H \longleftrightarrow R-\overset{+}{C}=NH + :O-H \xrightarrow{slow} $$

Protonated nitrile

[Amide tautomer intermediate structures]

Amide tautomer

[Protonated amide structures] $\xrightarrow[\text{(Amide hydrolysis)}]{\text{Several steps}}$ RCOOH + $\overset{+}{N}H_4$

Protonated amide

Basic hydrolysis of nitriles yield carboxylate ion. In basic hydrolysis, a hydroxide ion attacks the nitrile carbon atom, and subsequent protonation leads to the amide tautomer. Further attack by the hydroxide ion leads to hydrolysis similar to that of amides.

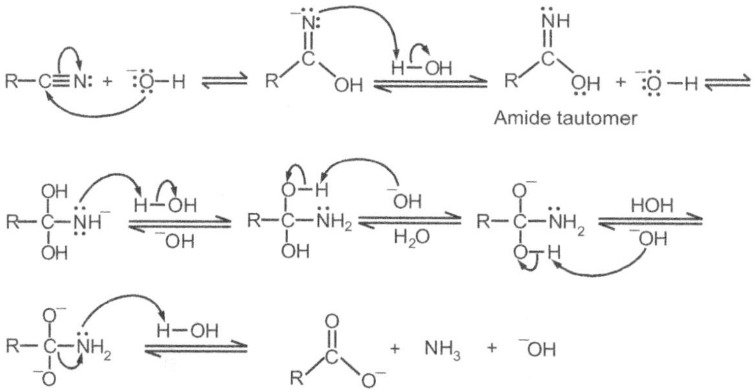

$$R-C\equiv N: + \ddot{\underset{..}{O}}-H \rightleftharpoons R-\overset{\overset{\ddot{N}:}{\|}}{\underset{OH}{C}} \xrightarrow{H-OH} R-\overset{\overset{\ddot{N}H}{\|}}{\underset{OH}{C}} + \ddot{\underset{..}{O}}-H \rightleftharpoons$$

Amide tautomer

$$R-\overset{OH}{\underset{OH}{\overset{|}{\underset{|}{C}}}}-\ddot{N}H \xrightarrow{H-OH} R-\overset{O-H}{\underset{OH}{\overset{|}{\underset{|}{C}}}}-\ddot{N}H_2 \rightleftharpoons R-\overset{OH}{\underset{OH}{\overset{|}{\underset{|}{C}}}}-\ddot{N}H_2 \xrightarrow{H_2O} R-\overset{O^-}{\underset{OH}{\overset{|}{\underset{|}{C}}}}-\ddot{N}H_2 \xrightarrow{HOH} $$

$$R-\overset{O^-}{\underset{O^-}{\overset{|}{\underset{|}{C}}}}-\ddot{N}H_2 \xrightarrow{H-OH} \underset{R'}{\overset{O}{\underset{\|}{C}}}\underset{O^-}{} + NH_3 + {}^-OH$$

The amide tautomer is the key intermediate in both types of hydrolysis.

Aldehydes and ketones can be converted to cyanohydrins which on hydrolysis give α-hydroxy acids.

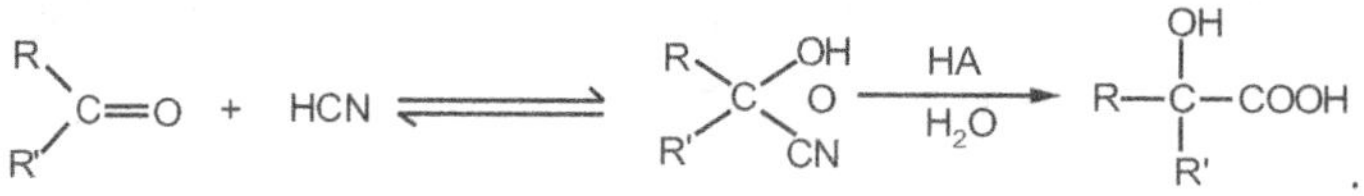

$$\underset{R'}{\overset{R}{\diagdown}}C=O + HCN \rightleftharpoons \underset{R'}{\overset{R}{\diagdown}}C\underset{CN}{\overset{OH}{\diagup}} \xrightarrow[H_2O]{HA} R-\underset{R'}{\overset{OH}{\underset{|}{\overset{|}{C}}}}-COOH$$

8. Malonic Ester Synthesis:

Step 1:

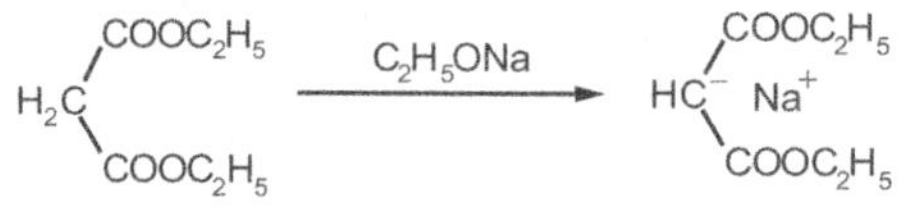

$$H_2C\underset{COOC_2H_5}{\overset{COOC_2H_5}{\diagup}} \xrightarrow{C_2H_5ONa} H\overset{-}{C}\underset{COOC_2H_5}{\overset{COOC_2H_5}{\diagup}} Na^+$$

Diethyl malonate

Malonic ester contains two acidic hydrogens α to the two carbonyl groups. When malonic ester is treated with sodium ethoxide in presence of absolute alcohol it gets converted to sodiomalonic ester.

Step 2:

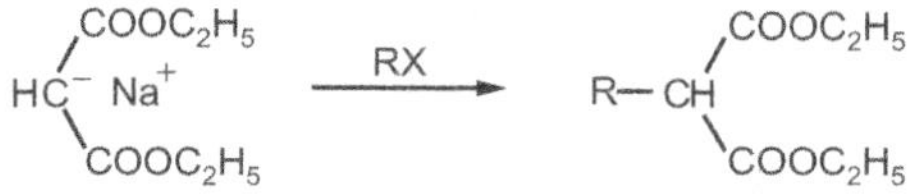

$$H\overset{-}{C}\underset{COOC_2H_5}{\overset{COOC_2H_5}{\diagup}} Na^+ \xrightarrow{RX} R-CH\underset{COOC_2H_5}{\overset{COOC_2H_5}{\diagup}}$$

When sodium malonate is treated with an alkylhalide it yields alkylmalonic ester. This reaction involves nucleophilic attack on the alkyl halide by the carbanion, $CH(COOC_2H_5)_2$. The yield is highest when treated with primary alkyl halides and lower with secondary alkyl halides. Tertiary alkyl halides do not give appreciable yield.

The alkylmalonic ester has one more α hydrogen atom so on treatment with sodium ethoxide it can also be converted to salt. This salt, when reacted with an alkyl halide yields a dialkylmalonic ester.

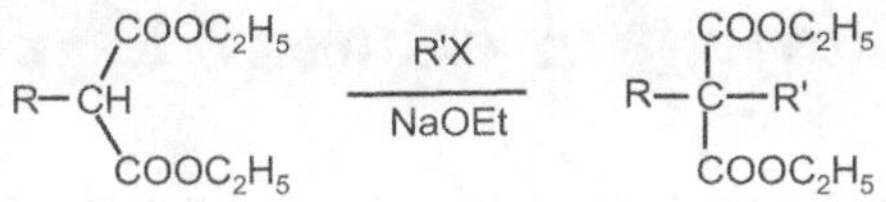

$$R-\underset{\underset{COOC_2H_5}{|}}{\overset{\overset{COOC_2H_5}{|}}{CH}} \xrightarrow[NaOEt]{R'X} R-\underset{\underset{COOC_2H_5}{|}}{\overset{\overset{COOC_2H_5}{|}}{C}}-R'$$

Step 3:

$$R-\underset{\underset{COOC_2H_5}{|}}{\overset{\overset{COOC_2H_5}{|}}{CH}} \xrightarrow{^-OH/H_2O} R-\underset{\underset{COO^-}{|}}{\overset{\overset{COO^-}{|}}{CH}} \xrightarrow{H^+} R-\underset{\underset{COOH}{|}}{\overset{\overset{COOH}{|}}{CH}}$$

$$R-\underset{\underset{COOC_2H_5}{|}}{\overset{\overset{COOC_2H_5}{|}}{C}}-R' \xrightarrow{^-OH/H_2O} R-\underset{\underset{COO^-}{|}}{\overset{\overset{COO^-}{|}}{C}}-R' \xrightarrow{H^+} \underset{R'}{\overset{R}{>}}C\underset{COOH}{\overset{COOH}{<}}$$

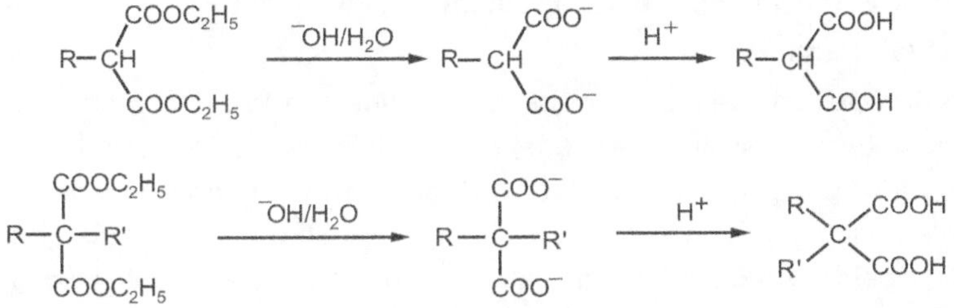

The monoalkyl and dialkylmalonic esters when hydrolysed and acidified form dicarboxylic acids.

Step 4:

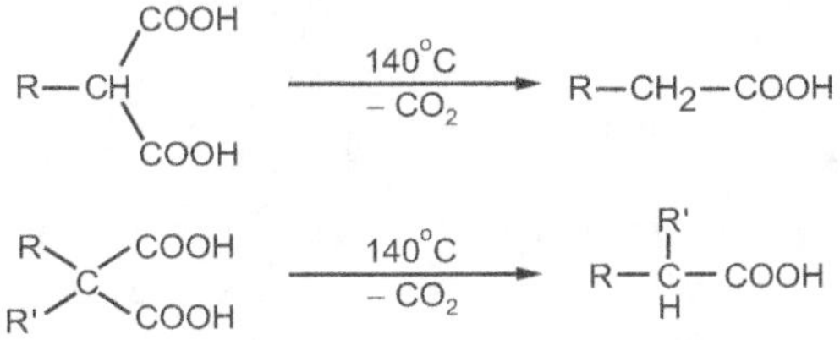

$$R-CH\underset{COOH}{\overset{COOH}{<}} \xrightarrow[-CO_2]{140°C} R-CH_2-COOH$$

$$\underset{R'}{\overset{R}{>}}C\underset{COOH}{\overset{COOH}{<}} \xrightarrow[-CO_2]{140°C} R-\underset{H}{\overset{R'}{\underset{|}{\overset{|}{C}}}}-COOH$$

The dicarboxylic acid when heated readily loses a carbon dioxide molecule to give substituted acetic acid.

9. **Special methods for phenolic acids:**

Example:

Kolbe Schmidt reaction (refer the chapter on phenols).

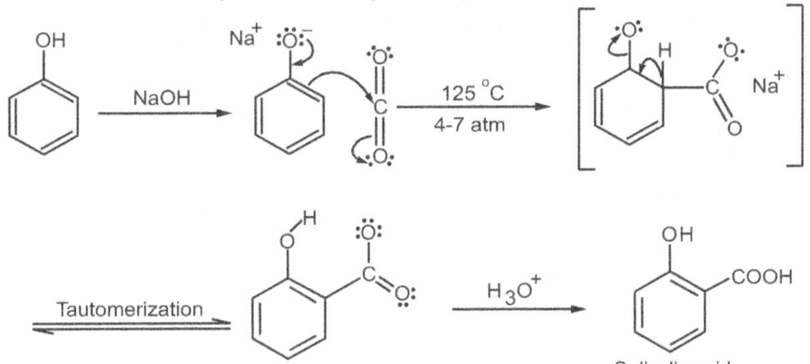

Salicylic acid

REACTIONS OF CARBOXYLIC ACIDS

Reactions:

Various reactions undergone by carboxylic acids are attributed to the carboxylic acid group, as well as, the influence of the group (R/Ar) attached to it.

1. **Acidity: salt formation:**

Carboxylic acids are weaker than the strong mineral acids. In comparison with other organic acids like alcohols and acetylene; carboxylic acids are very strong. Also they are stronger than water. They readily react with aqueous hydroxides and weak bases like sodium bicarbonate to form salt. The salts are crystalline, non-volatile and have very high melting points. The alkali metal salts are soluble in water but, insoluble in non-polar solvents.

$$R-COOH \rightleftharpoons R-COO^- + H^+$$

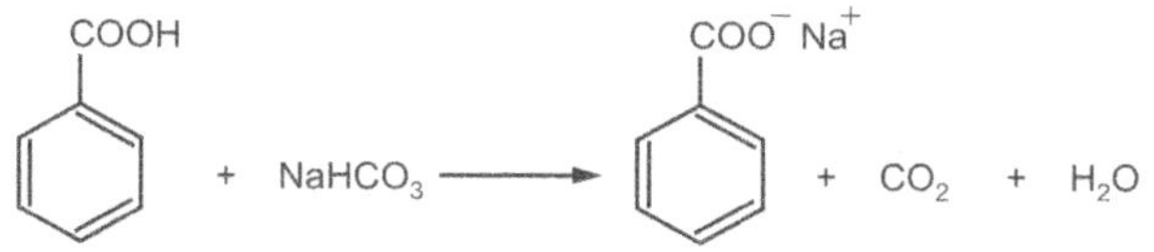

$$C_6H_5COOH + NaHCO_3 \longrightarrow C_6H_5COO^-Na^+ + CO_2 + H_2O$$

Substituted carboxylic acids can be either stronger or weaker acids, as compared to the parent acid. This depends on the nature of the substituents. If the substituent stabilizes the carboxylate anion then it increases the acidity of the acid. Similarly, if the substituent decreases the stability of the carboxylate anion, then it decreases the acidity of the acid. Electron-withdrawing substituents have the tendency to disperse the negative charge thus, stabilizing the carboxylate ion and hence increase the acidity whereas electron-releasing substituents destabilize the carboxylate ion and hence decrease the acidity. Higher value of Ka, stronger the acid.

Table 9.3: Acidity Constants of Aliphatic Carboxylic acids

Acid	Ka
HCOOH	17.7×10^{-5}
CH_3COOH	1.75×10^{-5}
$ClCH_2COOH$	136×10^{-5}
$CH_3CH_2CH_2COOH$	1.52×10^{-5}
$CH_3CH_2CHClCOOH$	139×10^{-5}
$CH_3CHClCH_2COOH$	8.9×10^{-5}
$ClCH_2CH_2CH_2COOH$	2.96×10^{-5}

Table 9.4: Acidity Constants of Substituted Benzoic Acids
Ka of benzoic acid = 6.3×10^{-5}

Substituent	Ka
p-NO$_2$	36×10^{-5}
p-Cl	10.3×10^{-5}
p-CH$_3$	4.2×10^{-5}
p-NH$_2$	1.4×10^{-5}
m-NO$_2$	32×10^{-5}
m-Cl	15.1×10^{-5}
m-CH$_3$	5.4×10^{-5}
m-NH$_2$	1.9×10^{-5}
o-NO$_2$	670×10^{-5}
o-Cl	120×10^{-5}
o-CH$_3$	12.4×10^{-5}
o-NH$_2$	1.6×10^{-5}

2. Conversion to functional derivatives

$$R-COOH \longrightarrow R-CO-Z$$

Z = X (acid halide), OR' (ester), NH$_2$ (amides)

(a) Conversion to acid chlorides:

$$R-COOH \xrightarrow[\text{Reflux}]{SOCl_2 / POCl_3} R-COCl$$

Carboxylic acids can be easily converted to acid chlorides using thionyl chloride (SOCl$_2$), phosphorous trichloride (PCl$_3$) or phosphorous pentachloride (PCl$_5$). Thionyl chloride is preferably used for this conversion since, the byproducts formed are gaseous and hence can easily be separated from the acid chloride. Any excess of thionyl chloride can be removed by distillation since it is low boiling.

Acid chlorides are highly reactive and can be readily converted to many other types of compounds including esters and amides.

Benzoic acid + SOCl$_2$ or POCl$_3$ $\xrightarrow{\text{Reflux}}$ Benzoyl chloride + SO$_2$ + HCl

(b) Conversion to esters: Carboxylic acids react with alcohols to form esters.

$$R-COOH + R'OH \underset{\Delta}{\overset{H^+ \text{(Mineral acid)}}{\rightleftharpoons}} R-COOR' + H_2O$$

Acid — Alcohol — Ester

Acids can also be converted to esters *via* their acid chlorides.

$$R-COOH \xrightarrow{SOCl_2} R-COCl \xrightarrow{R'OH} R-COOR'$$

Acid — Acid chloride — Ester

Carboxylic acids can be directly converted to ester when heated with an alcohol in the presence of a little mineral acid; usually concentrated sulphuric acid is used. This is called as **Fischer esterification**. This is a reversible reaction and reaches equilibrium when there are appreciable quantities of reactants and products. Hence, there is no complete conversion of the reactants to products. Thus, the yield is low. In order to increase the yield the equilibrium must be shifted towards the product. This can be done either by increasing the concentration of the reactants or by decreasing the concentration of the product by simultaneously removing the product. The choice of increasing the concentration of one of the reactant depends upon the cost and availability of the reactant.

Preparation of ester *via* acid chloride is preferred since both the steps (conversion to acid chloride and then conversion to ester) are irreversible and reach completion. Also, acyl chlorides are more reactive than carboxylic acid toward nucleophilic addition-elimination. The reaction of an acyl chloride and alcohol occurs rapidly and does not require any catalyst. Pyridine is used in this reaction to react and trap with the HCl that is formed. Pyridine can also react with acyl chloride to form acylpyridinium ion which is more reactive than acyl chloride. The only advantage of direct esterification is that it is a single step reaction.

(c) Conversion to amides:

$$R-COOH \xrightarrow{SOCl_2} R-COCl \xrightarrow{R'-NH_2} R-CONH-R'$$

R, R' = H, alkyl or aryl

Amides are prepared by treating the acid chlorides with ammonia. Acid chlorides react with ammonia to form the corresponding amide. If ammonia is used then a primary amide is formed. If a secondary amine is used then *N*-monosubstituted amide is formed and if a tertiary amine is used then *N,N*-disubstituted amide is formed.

3. Conversion to alcohol:

$$4 \text{ R—COOH} + 3 \text{ LiAlH}_4 \longrightarrow 4 \text{ H}_2 + 2 \text{ LiAlO}_2 + (RCH_2O)_4 \text{AlLi}$$

$$\downarrow H_2O$$

$$4 \text{ R—CH}_2\text{OH}$$

Carboxylic acids can be reduced using lithium aluminium hydride to form the corresponding alcohol. An alkoxide intermediate is formed and the alcohol is liberated by hydrolysis.

LiAlH$_4$ is a good reducing agent and gives excellent yields. But it is very costly and hence can be used only for the reduction of small quantities of compounds. Hence, as an alternative to direct reduction, acids can be converted to alcohols by first converting them to esters and then reducing these esters using various other reagents.

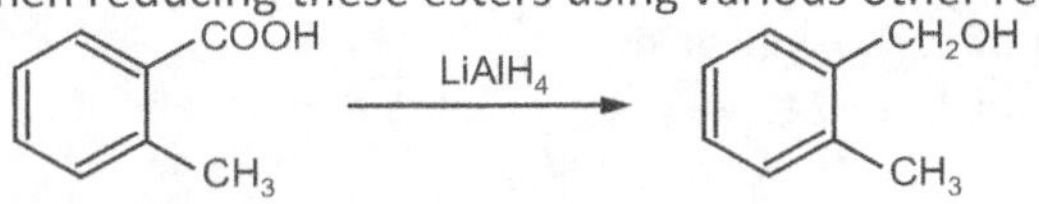

o-CH₃-C₆H₄-COOH $\xrightarrow{\text{LiAlH}_4}$ o-CH₃-C₆H₄-CH₂OH

4. Substitution of R- of R-COOH:

α-Halogenation of aliphatic acids: Hell-Volhard-Zelinsky reaction

$$R\text{—CH}_2\text{COOH} + X_2 \xrightarrow{Cl_2, [P]} R\text{—CHXCOOH} + HX$$

X = Cl, Br

Aliphatic acids react easily with chlorine or bromine to yield a compound in which the α-hydrogen is replaced by halogen. This substitution takes place only at the α position.

$$CH_3COOH \xrightarrow{Cl_2, [P]} ClCH_2COOH \xrightarrow{Cl_2, [P]} Cl_2CHCOOH \xrightarrow{Cl_2, [P]} Cl_3CCOOH$$

The function of phosphorous is to convert a small quantity of acid to acid halide.

Mechanism of α-halogenation of R-CH$_2$COOH

$$2P + 3X_2 \longrightarrow 2PX_3$$

$$RCH_2COOH + PX_3 \longrightarrow RCH_2COX$$

$$RCH_2COX + X_2 \longrightarrow R\text{—CHX—COX} + HX$$

$$R\text{—CHX—COX} + RCH_2COOH \rightleftharpoons R\text{—CHX—COOH} + RCH_2COX$$

This reaction has considerable synthetic importance. The halogen of the halogenated acid undergoes nucleophilic displacement and elimination. Hence, this reaction forms the first step in conversion of carboxylic acid to many important substituted carboxylic acids.

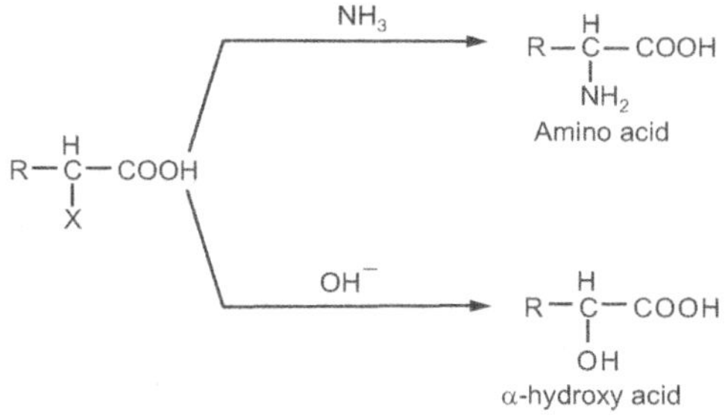

$$R-\underset{X}{\underset{|}{\overset{H}{\overset{|}{C}}}}-COOH \xrightarrow{NH_3} R-\underset{NH_2}{\underset{|}{\overset{H}{\overset{|}{C}}}}-COOH$$

Amino acid

$$\xrightarrow{OH^-} R-\underset{OH}{\underset{|}{\overset{H}{\overset{|}{C}}}}-COOH$$

α-hydroxy acid

$$RCH_2CHCOOH + KOH \longrightarrow RCH=CHCOO^- \xrightarrow{H^+} RCH=CHCOOH$$
$$|$$
$$Br \phantom{+ KOH \longrightarrow RCH=CHCOO^- \xrightarrow{H^+}} \text{α, β-unsaturated acid}$$

5. Decarboxylation of carboxylic acids

The reaction in which the carboxylic acid loses a molecule of carbon dioxide is called as **decarboxylation**.

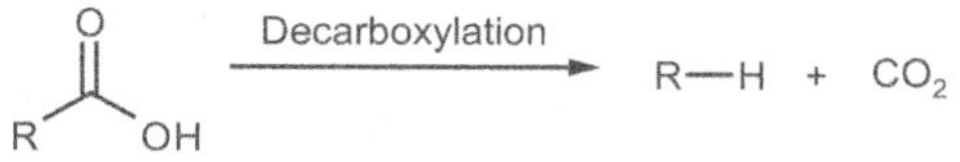

$$R-\overset{O}{\overset{||}{C}}-OH \xrightarrow{\text{Decarboxylation}} R-H + CO_2$$

Decarboxylation of most carboxylic acids is an exothermic process and not always easy to carry out. Special groups have to be present on the acid for decarboxylation to be rapid. **β-keto acids** decarboxylate easily when heated to 100-150°C. Often higher temperatures than these along with metal catalysts like Cu, Zn etc. are also required.

$$R\overset{O}{\overset{||}{C}}CH_2\overset{O}{\overset{||}{C}}OH \xrightarrow[\Delta]{100-150°C} R\overset{O}{\overset{||}{C}}CH_3 + CO_2$$

6. Nucleophilic addition-elimination of acyl carbon

The reactions of carboxylic acids and their derivatives are characterized by nucleophilic addition-elimination at the acyl carbon atom. The derivatives of carboxylic acids contain the carbonyl group which is retained in the products of most reactions. The carbonyl group performs two functions: (i) it provides a site for nucleophilic attack, and (ii) it increases the acidity of hydrogens attached to the *alpha* carbon. The mechanism for the reaction is as follows:

Acyl transfer by nucleophilic addition-elimination:

Acyl compound	Tetrahedral intermediate	Another acyl compound
Nucleophilic Addition		Elimination

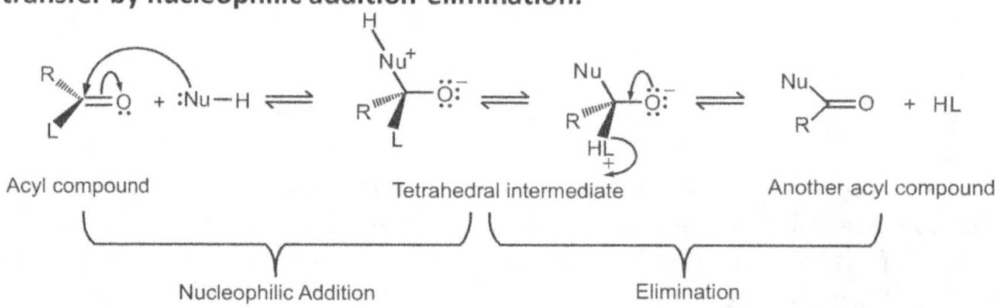

The first step of the reaction involves nucleophilc addition at the carbonyl carbon atom to form a tetrahedral intermediate. If the tetrahedral intermediate is formed from an aldehyde or ketone, it accepts a proton to form a stable addition product.

If the tetrahedral intermediate is formed from an acyl compound it usually eliminates a leaving group. This elimination leads to regeneration of the carbon-oxygen double bond and hence the trigonal geometry of the molecule. Thus, a substitution product is formed. Hence, the overall process in case of acyl substitution occurs by a nucleophilic addition-elimination mechanism. The ease with which the leaving group leaves depends upon its basicity i.e., the weaker the base the better the leaving group.

An *acyl chloride* reacts by losing a *chloride ion*; a very weak base and hence, a very good leaving group.

An *acid anhydride* reacts by losing a *carboxylate anion* or a molecule of a *carboxylic acid*, both are moderately weak bases.

Esters react by losing a molecule of *alcohol*, *acids* by losing a *water* molecule and *amides* by losing *ammonia or amine*.

For an aldehyde or ketone to react by nucleophilic addition-elimination the tetrahedral intermediate will need to lose a hydride ion (:H⁻) or an alkide ion (:R⁻) which are very strong bases. Hence, aldehydes and ketones always react *via* addition mechanism.

PREPARATION AND REACTIONS OF CARBOXYLIC ACIDS

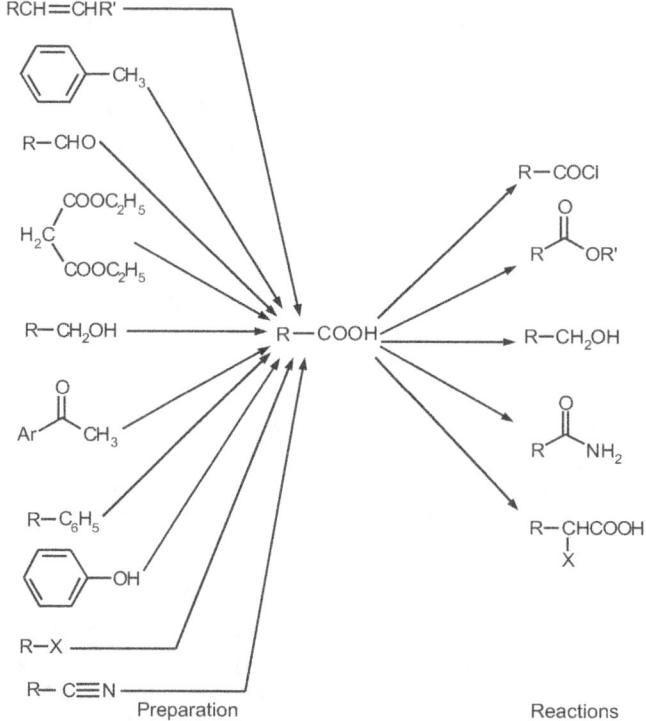

DERIVATIVES OF CARBOXYLIC ACIDS

1. ACYL CHLORIDES

Preparation of acyl chlorides: Acyl chlorides are highly reactive derivatives of acids. They are prepared by reaction of the carboxylic acids with phosphorous trichloride, phosphorous pentachloride or thionyl chloride, as discussed in earlier section.

$$R-COOH \xrightarrow{POCl_3 / SOCl_2 / PCl_3 / PCl_5} R-COCl$$

These reactions involve nucleophilic addition-elimination by a chloride ion on a highly reactive intermediate, a protonated acyl chlorophosphite, a protonated acyl chlorophosphate and a protonated acyl chlorosulfite with the respective reagents.

Mechanism:

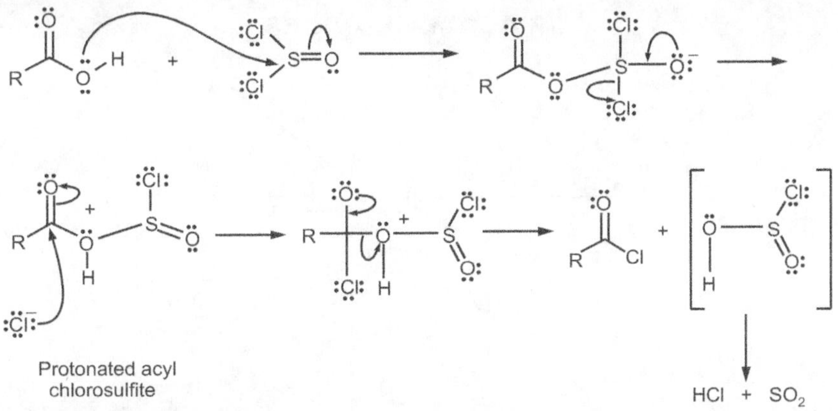

[Mechanism scheme showing reaction of carboxylic acid with SOCl₂ through protonated acyl chlorosulfite intermediate, yielding acyl chloride + HCl + SO₂]

Protonated acyl chlorosulfite

HCl + SO₂

Reactions of acyl chlorides:

Acid chlorides are the most reactive derivatives of carboxylic acids. They undergo nucleophilic substitution reactions. The nucleophile displaces the chloride ion since, chloride is a good leaving group. The carbonyl group makes the compound more reactive and the substitution takes place more rapidly than the corresponding nucleophilic substitution reactions of the alkyl halides.

Conversion to acids:

$$R-COCl + H_2O \longrightarrow R-COOH + HCl$$

In this reaction, water molecule acts as a nucleophile and substitutes the –Cl by –OH thus, forming the corresponding acid.

Conversion to amides:

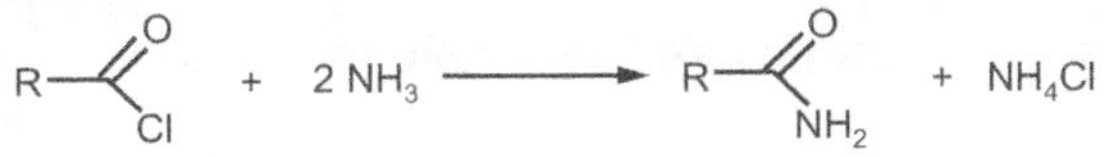

$$R-COCl + 2\ NH_3 \longrightarrow R-CONH_2 + NH_4Cl$$

Conversion to esters:

$$R-COCl + R'OH \longrightarrow R-COOR' + HCl$$

Conversion to anhydrides:

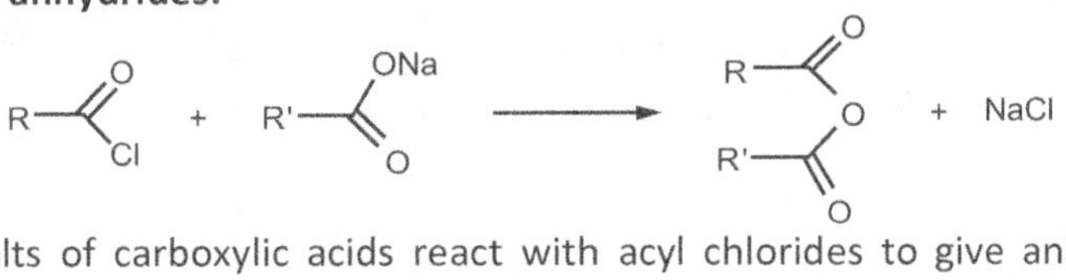

$$R-COCl + R'-COONa \longrightarrow R-CO-O-CO-R' + NaCl$$

Sodium salts of carboxylic acids react with acyl chlorides to give anhydrides. The carboxylate ion acts as a nucleophile and brings about the nucleophilic substitution reaction at the acyl carbon of the acyl chloride.

IN SUMMARY PREPARATION AND REACTIONS OF ACID CHLORIDES

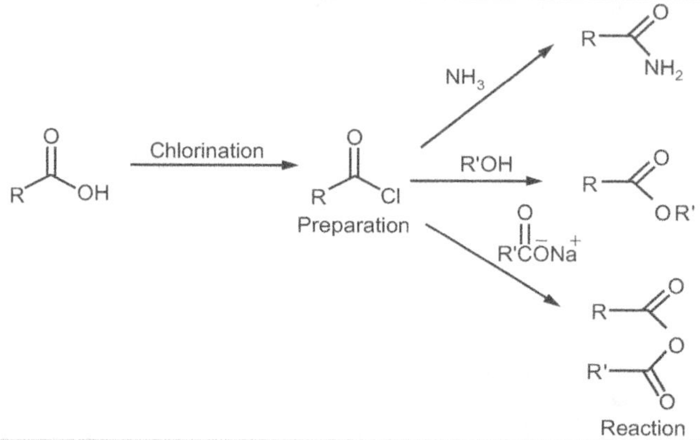

[Scheme: R-COOH → (Chlorination) → R-COCl (Preparation); R-COCl reacts with NH₃ → R-CONH₂; with R'OH → R-COOR'; with R'COO⁻Na⁺ → R-CO-O-CO-R' (Reaction)]

2. ACID ANHYDRIDES

Preparation of acid anhydrides from acids and acid chloride:

Carboxylic acid anhydrides are prepared by reacting carboxylic acids with acid chlorides in the presence of pyridine.

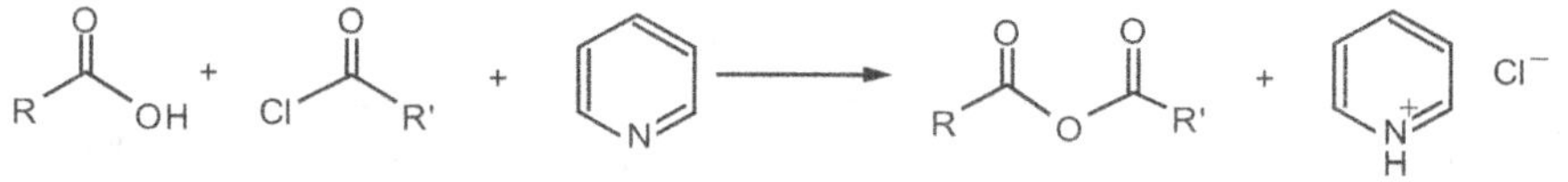

R-COOH + Cl-CO-R' + pyridine ⟶ R-CO-O-CO-R' + pyridinium·Cl⁻

This method is used for the synthesis of symmetrical (R=R') and mixed (R≠R') anhydrides.

From acid chlorides and sodium salts of carboxylic acid:

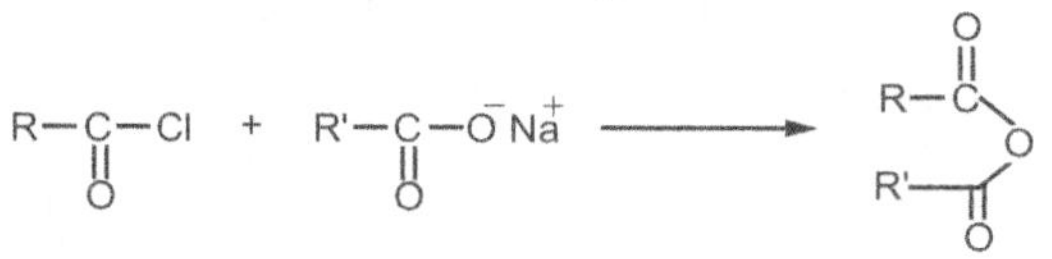

$$R-\underset{O}{\underset{\|}{C}}-Cl + R'-\underset{O}{\underset{\|}{C}}-O^-Na^+ \longrightarrow R-CO-O-CO-R'$$

From dicarboxylic acids:

Anhydrides of dicarboxylic acids can be prepared by simple heating of the acid. This method is useful only when five or six membered ring is formed.

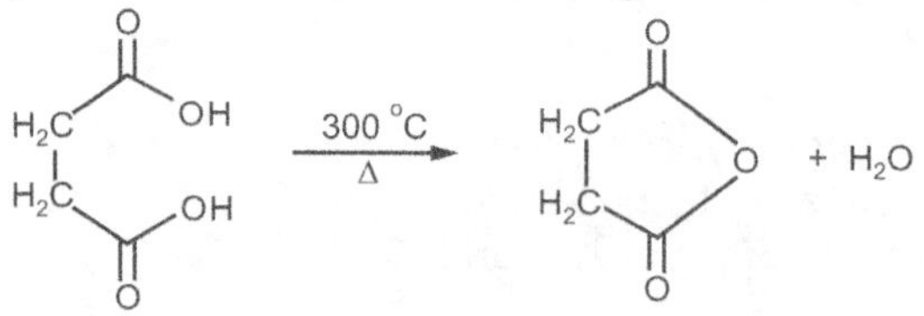

HOOC-CH₂-CH₂-COOH $\xrightarrow{300\,°C,\,\Delta}$ cyclic anhydride + H₂O

Acetic anhydride is prepared by heating acetic acid with ketene, $CH_2=C=O$. Ketene is prepared by high temperature degradation of acetic acid.

$$CH_3COOH \xrightarrow[700°C]{AlPO_4} H_2O + CH_2=C=O \text{ (Ketene)} \xrightarrow{CH_3COOH} (CH_3CO)_2O \text{ (Acetic anhydride)}$$

Reactions of acid anhydrides:
Conversion into acids:

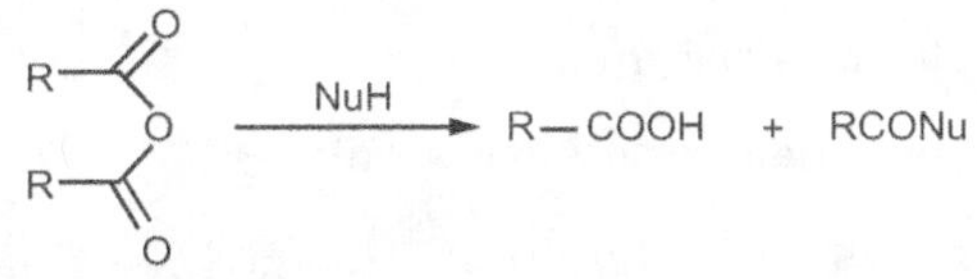

$$(RCO)_2O \xrightarrow{NuH} R-COOH + RCONu$$

Nu = OH, OR'

Acid anhydrides on hydrolysis give the acid.

$$(CH_3CO)_2O + H-OH \longrightarrow 2\ CH_3COOH$$

If water is used as nucleophile the product fomed is only acid.

$$(CH_3CO)_2O + CH_3-O-H \longrightarrow CH_3COOH + H_3C-C(=O)-O-CH_3$$

If alcohol is used as nucleophile then, acid and ester are formed.

Conversion into amides (ammonolysis):

Acid anhydrides when treated with ammonia give amides. Ammonolysis is the use of a nitrogen containing compound as the nucleophile which displaces the carboxylate ion. The product is an amide. The reaction goes relatively well because of the strong leaving group, the carboxylate ion. If ammonia is used the amide formed is a simple amide. If a primary amine is used as the nucleophile then a mono-substituted amide is formed. If a secondary amine is used then the product is a disubstituted amide.

$$(CH_3CO)_2O + 2\ NH_3 \longrightarrow CH_3CONH_2 + CH_3COO^- NH_4^+$$

Acetic anhydride → Acetamide + Ammonium acetate

Succinic anhydride + $2\ NH_3 \longrightarrow$ $\begin{array}{c}CH_2CONH_2\\|\\CH_2CONH_4\end{array}$ (Ammonium succinamate) $\xrightarrow{H^+}$ $\begin{array}{c}CH_2CONH_2\\|\\CH_2COOH\end{array}$ (Succinamic acid)

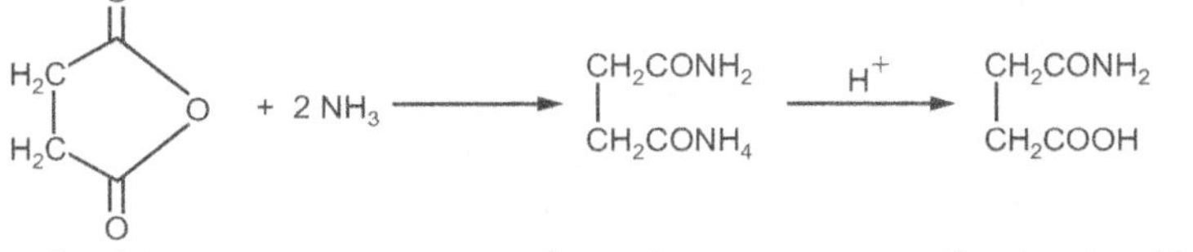

Conversion into esters (alcoholysis)

$$(RCO)_2O + R'OH \longrightarrow RCOOR' + RCOOH$$

Acid anhydrides on treatment with alcohol form the esters. This is a better method for synthesizing esters since it does not involve use of a strong acid, which may cause side reactions. The reaction is relatively fast and does not require any catalyst because the leaving group in this substitution is a carboxylate ion, which is a relatively weak base and therefore an excellent leaving group.

Conversion into ketones (Friedel Crafts acylation):

$$(RCO)_2O + Ar-H \xrightarrow{AlCl_3} R-\overset{O}{C}-Ar + RCOOH$$

Phthalic anhydride + benzene $\xrightarrow{AlCl_3, 0°C}$ o-Benzoylbenzoic acid

This is Friedel-Crafts acylation. In this reaction, the anhydride reacts with an aromatic compound in presence of Lewis acids ($AlCl_3$, $SnCl_4$ etc.) to form a ketone.

SUMMARY OF PREPARATION AND REACTIONS OF ACID ANHYDRIDES

3. ESTERS

Esters have the general formula RCOOR' where a carbonyl group is bonded to an alkoxyl group.

Preparation of esters:

From acids and alcohols:

$$CH_3COOH + C_2H_5OH \underset{}{\overset{H^+ \text{ (mineral acid)}}{\rightleftharpoons}} CH_3COOC_2H_5$$

Acetic acid → Ethyl acetate

Mechanism:

[Reaction mechanism showing protonation of carboxylic acid, nucleophilic attack by alcohol, formation of tetrahedral intermediate, loss of water, and deprotonation to give the ester]

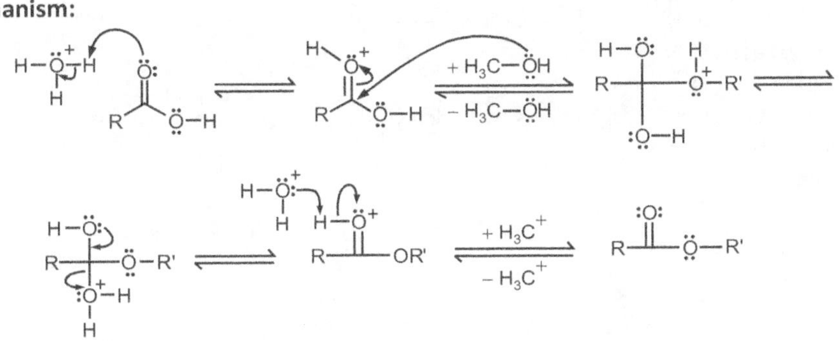

The carboxylic acid accepts a proton from the strong acid catalyst. The alcohol (acting as nucleophile) now attacks the protonated carbonyl group to form the tetrahedral intermediate. This intermediate loses a water molecule (leaving group) to form the protonated ester. This protonated ester donates the proton to a base to give the ester.

The forward reaction gives the formation of ester from the acid while the backward reaction gives the mechanism for acid catalyzed hydrolysis of ester to form acid.

Steric factors strongly affect the rate of reaction. If bulky groups are present near the reaction site either in alcohol or acid then the reaction rate is slowed. Hence, tertiary alcohols react slowly by this mechanism. Esters of tertiary alcohol are, therefore, prepared by the use of acyl chlorides and anhydrides as given below.

From acid chlorides and anhydrides by reaction with alcohols:

$$R-COCl + R'OH \longrightarrow R-COOR' + HCl$$

$$(RCO)_2O + R'OH \longrightarrow RCOOR' + RCOOH$$

From esters (Transesterification):

Transesterification: Esters often react with metal alkoxides to undergo exchange of the alkoxide group attached to the carbonyl carbon with the metal alkoxide. If the alkoxide of the metal alkoxide is different (R" ≠ R') than the alkoxide group of the parent ester, the resulting product after their exchange in a different ester. This reaction is called as ' Transesterification'. In many cases, to avoid such reactions, selection of the alkoxide catalyst is very important. Transesterification often is a side reaction.

$$R-\underset{O}{\overset{O}{\|}}C-OR' + Na^+ OR" \longrightarrow R-\underset{O}{\overset{O}{\|}}C-OR" + NaOR'$$

$$CH_3C(=O)-OC_2H_5 + NaOCH_3 \longrightarrow CH_3COOCH_3 + NaOC_2H_5$$

Reactions of esters:
Conversion to acids:

Esters can be converted to acids by hydrolysis. Hydrolysis can be carried out by using either an acid or a base.

Acidic hydrolysis:

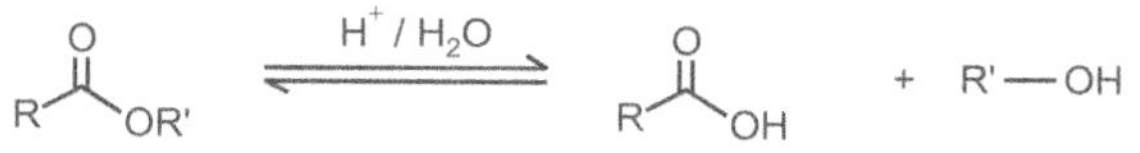

$$R-C(=O)-OR' \xrightleftharpoons{H^+/H_2O} R-C(=O)-OH + R'-OH$$

Mechanism:

[Mechanism showing stepwise protonation of carbonyl oxygen, nucleophilic attack by water, proton transfers, and loss of R'OH to give the carboxylic acid.]

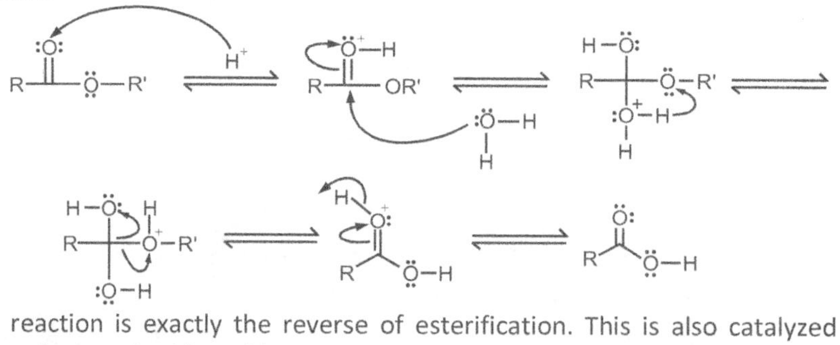

This reaction is exactly the reverse of esterification. This is also catalyzed by the presence of mineral acid. In this reaction, water molecule is a nucleophile while alcohol is the leaving group.

Alkaline hydrolysis:

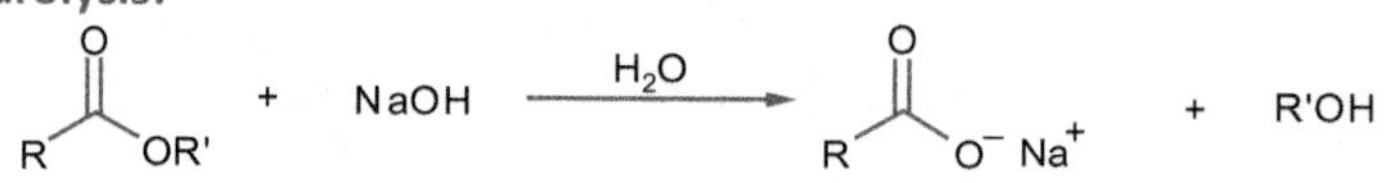

$$R-C(=O)-OR' + NaOH \xrightarrow{H_2O} R-C(=O)-O^-Na^+ + R'OH$$

Ester   Sodium carboxylate

A carboxylic ester can also be hydrolyzed using an alkali. When alkali is used the product obtained is in the salt form. Acid can be liberated from the salt by addition of mineral acid. The alkaline hydrolysis of ester is also called as **saponification**. This reaction is irreversible since the carboxylate ion is very unreactive towards nucleophilic substitution.

Mechanism:

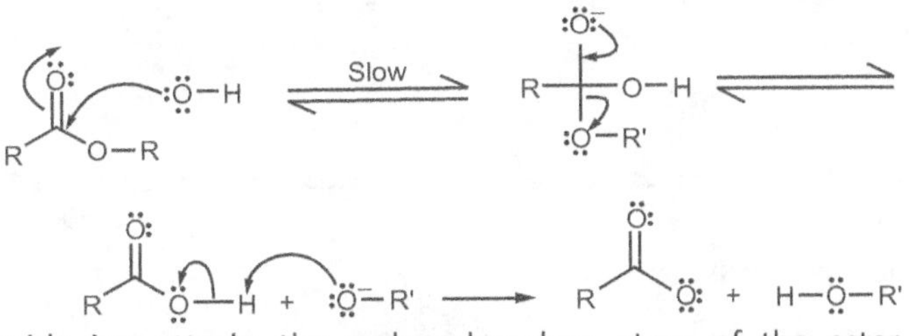

The hydroxide ion attacks the carbonyl carbon atom of the ester to form the tetrahedral intermediate. This intermediate loses an alkoxide ion to form the acid. Since, the medium is alkaline the acid abstracts a proton from the acid to form the carboxylate ion which exists in salt form. The acid can be isolated by acidification of the medium using mineral acid.

Conversion to amides:

When esters are treated with ammonia (or with primary or secondary amines) they undergo nucleophilic addition-elimination at their acyl carbon atom to form amides. This is called as *ammonolysis*.

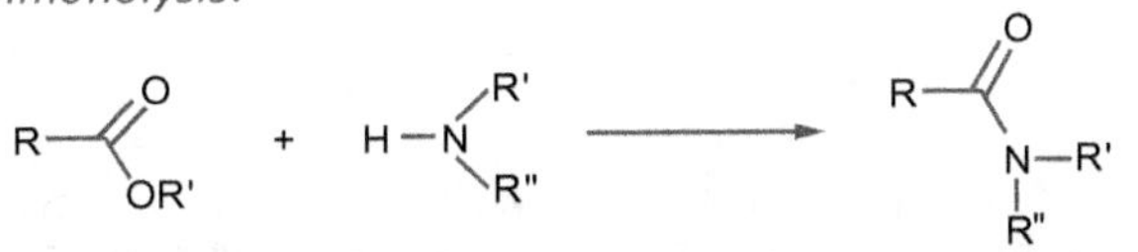

This reaction involves nucleophilic attack by a base, ammonia, on the electron-deficient carbon, the alkoxy group is then replaced by the $-NH_2$ group.

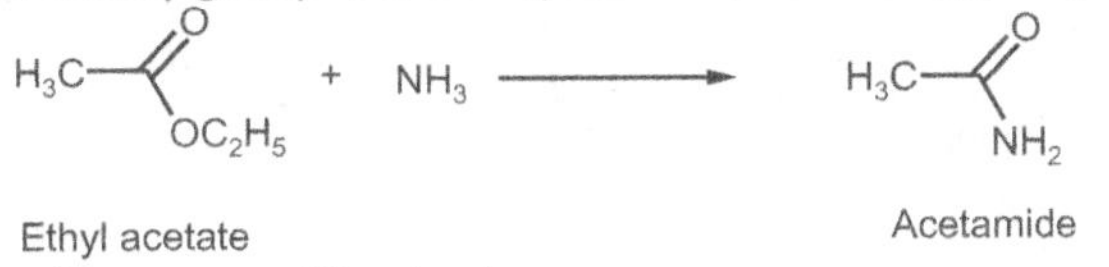

Ethyl acetate → Acetamide

Conversion to esters (Transesterification):

In the esterification of an acid, an alcohol acts as a nucleophile while in hydrolysis of ester; alcohol is a leaving group and is displaced by a nucleophilic reagent. This dual property of alcohol to act as nucleophile in one reaction and as leaving group in another is used in transesterification.

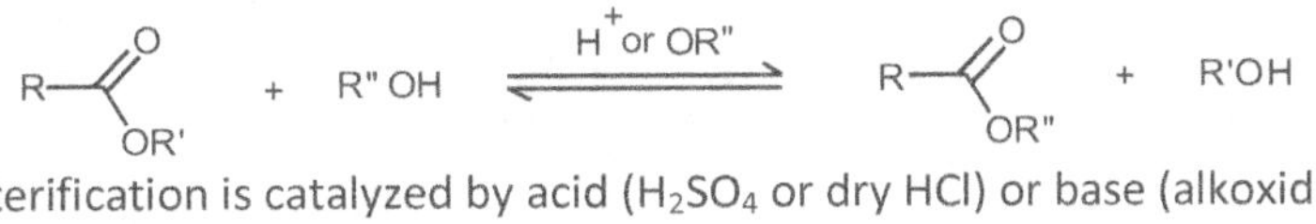

Transesterification is catalyzed by acid (H_2SO_4 or dry HCl) or base (alkoxide ion).

Mechanism (acid catalyzed):

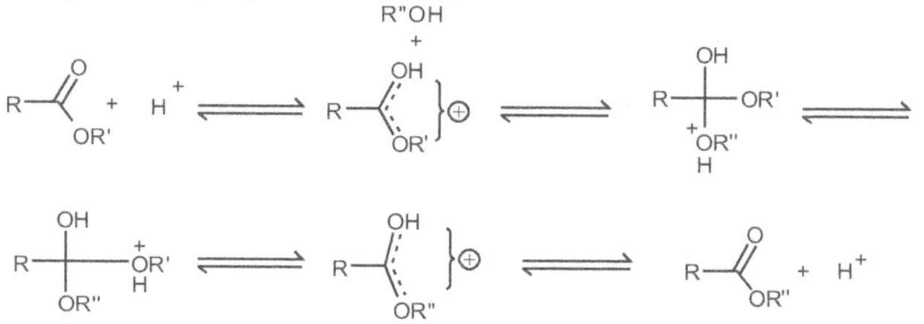

[Reaction scheme showing acid-catalyzed transesterification mechanism with protonation of the ester carbonyl, nucleophilic attack by R"OH, proton transfers, and loss of R'OH to give the new ester.]

Mechanism (base catalyzed)

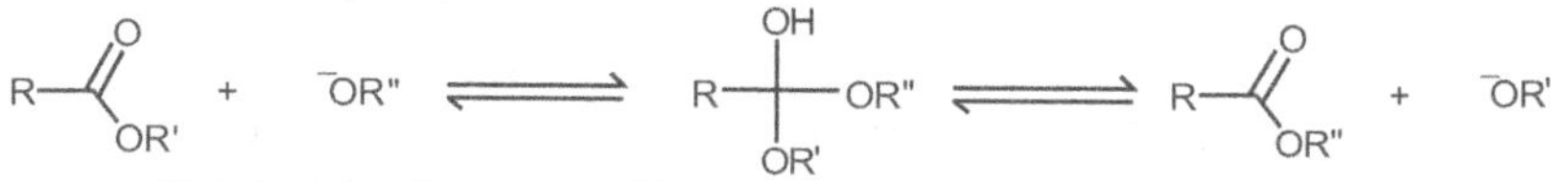

[Reaction scheme showing base-catalyzed transesterification: alkoxide $^-OR''$ attacks the ester carbonyl to form a tetrahedral intermediate, which collapses to give the new ester and $^-OR'$.]

Transesterification is also reversible reaction. To drive the reaction to completion the equilibrium must be shifted to right. This can be done by either increasing the concentration of the reactants or by decreasing the concentration of the product by simultaneously removing the product.

Reaction with Grignard reagent:

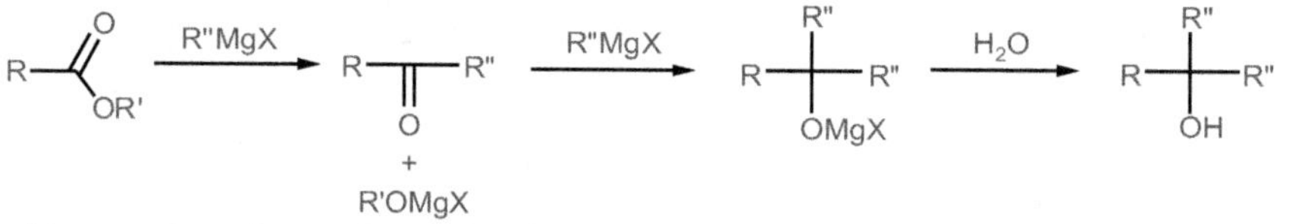

[Reaction scheme: ester R-CO-OR' + R"MgX → ketone R-CO-R" + R'OMgX; then R"MgX adds to the ketone to give R-C(R")(R")-OMgX, which on hydrolysis with H₂O gives the tertiary alcohol R-C(R")(R")-OH.]

In this reaction, the nucleophilic alkyl (or aryl) group of Grignard reagent attaches to the carbonyl carbon and an alkoxide group is removed. This results in the formation of ketones. In some cases, this ketone can be isolated. But the ketones, being highly reactive, react with Grignard reagent to give tertiary alcohol.

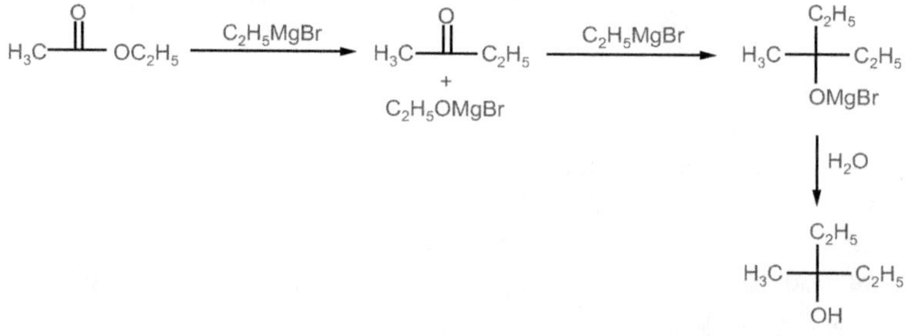

[Specific example: $H_3C-CO-OC_2H_5$ + C_2H_5MgBr → $H_3C-CO-C_2H_5$ + C_2H_5OMgBr; then + C_2H_5MgBr → $H_3C-C(C_2H_5)(C_2H_5)-OMgBr$; then H_2O → $H_3C-C(C_2H_5)(C_2H_5)-OH$

2-Ethyl-2-butanol]

As we can see from the reaction, two of the three alkyl groups attached to the carbon atom come from the Grignard reagent. Hence, the alcohol formed will have two identical groups attached to the carbon. This poses limitation upon the alcohols synthesized using this method.

Reduction of esters:

Esters can be reduced in two ways:
  (i) by catalytic hydrogenation using molecular hydrogen or
  (ii) by chemical reduction

In the both the cases, ester is reduced to a primary alcohol corresponding to the acid portion of the ester.

$$R-COOR' \longrightarrow R-CH_2OH + R'OH$$
$$\text{1° alcohol}$$

Hydrogenolysis (cleavage by hydrogen) requires more severe conditions than simple hydrogenation (addition of hydrogen) to a carbon-carbon double bond. High pressure and elevated temperatures are used. The catalyst most often used is a mixture of oxides known as copper chromite.

$$CH_3(CH_2)_{10}COOCH_3 \xrightarrow[150°C,\ 5000\ psi]{H_2,\ CuO.CuCr_2O_4} CH_3(CH_2)_{10}CH_2OH + CH_3OH$$

Methyl laurate (Methyl dodecanoate) → Lauryl alcohol (1-Dodecanol)

Chemical reduction (*in-situ* hydrogenation) is carried out by use of sodium metal and alcohol or lithium aluminium hydride in non-polar solvents.

$$CH_3(CH_2)_{14}COOC_2H_5 \xrightarrow[H^+]{LiAlH_4} CH_3(CH_2)_{14}CH_2OH$$

1-Hexadecanol

SUMMARY OF PREPARATION AND REACTIONS OF ESTERS

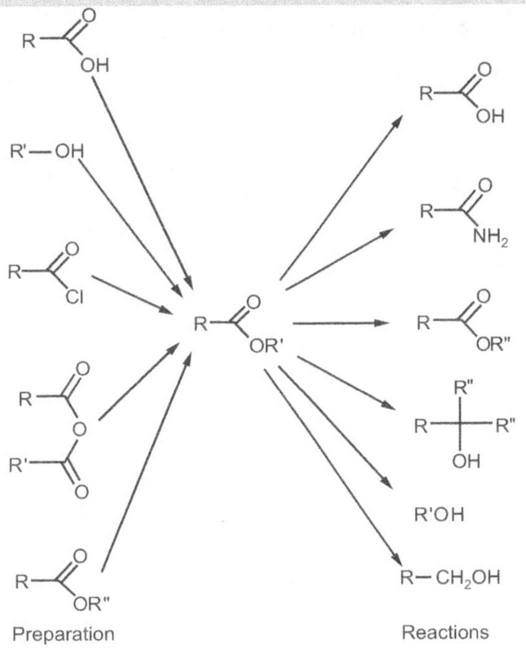

Preparation | Reactions

4. AMIDES

Amides have formulae $RCONH_2$, $RCONHR'$, $RCONR'R''$ in which a carbonyl group is bonded to a nitrogen atom bearing hydrogen and/or alkyl groups.

Preparation of amides:

From acyl chlorides:

$$R-COCl + 2\,NH_3 \longrightarrow R-CONH_2 + NH_4Cl$$

From carboxylic anhydrides:

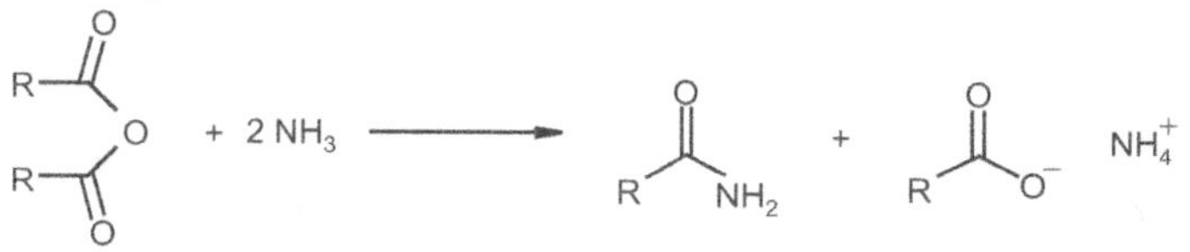

$$(RCO)_2O + 2\,NH_3 \longrightarrow RCONH_2 + RCOO^-\,NH_4^+$$

From esters:

$$R-COOR' + NH_3 \longrightarrow R-CONH_2$$

From carboxylic acids and ammonium salts/ammonia:

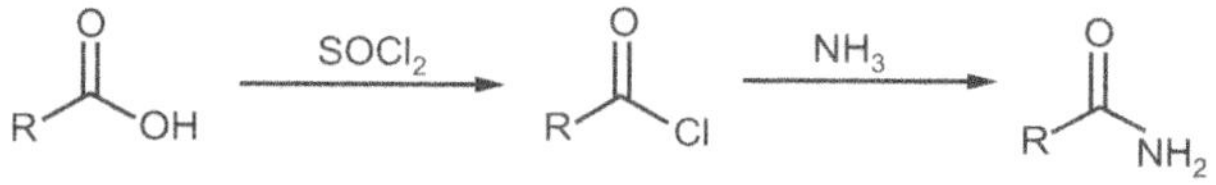

$$R-COOH \xrightarrow{SOCl_2} R-COCl \xrightarrow{NH_3} R-CONH_2$$

Carboxylic acids on treatment with aqueous ammonia form ammonium salts. The reaction stops here because of the low reactivity of the carboxylate ion towards nucleophilic addition-elimination. This salt can be isolated by evaporating water. If this dry ammonium salt is heated it produces amide.

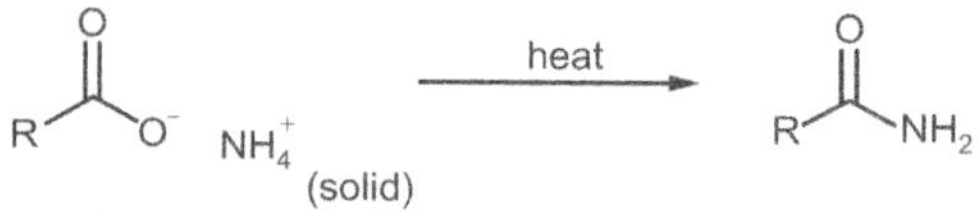

$$R-COO^-\,NH_4^+ \text{ (solid)} \xrightarrow{heat} R-CONH_2$$

Reactions of amide:

Hydrolysis:

Amides undergo hydrolysis when heated with aqueous acid (acidic hydrolysis) or aqueous base (basic hydrolysis). Hydrolysis of amides is slower than the hydrolysis of corresponding ester. Thus, hydrolysis of amide requires rigorous conditions of heat and strong acid or base. Acidic hydrolysis yields carboxylic acid while alkaline hydrolysis forms salt.

Acidic hydrolysis:

$$R-C(=O)-NH_2 + H_3O^+ \xrightarrow[\text{heat}]{H_2O} R-C(=O)-OH + NH_4^+$$

In acidic hydrolysis the amide accepts a proton from the aqueous acid to form a proronated carbonyl group. This is further attacked by water molecule (nucleophile) to form a tetrahedral intermediate. A proton is lost from the oxygen and gained at the nitrogen. Further the molecule loses ammonia to form protonated carboxylic acid. The proton is transferred to ammonia to give carboxylic acid.

Basic hydrolysis

$$R-C(=O)-NH_2 + Na^+OH^- \xrightarrow[\text{heat}]{H_2O} R-C(=O)-O^-Na^+ + NH_3$$

In basic hydrolysis, the hydroxide ion attacks the carbonyl carbon of the amide to form an anion. Another hydroxide ion takes up the proton to form a dianion. The dianion loses a molecule of ammonia (or an amine) to form the carboxylate ion.

Dehydration:

$$R-C(=O)-NH_2 \xrightarrow{P_2O_5} R-C\equiv N + H_3PO_4$$

Amides when reacted with dehydrating agents like P_2O_5 or thionyl chloride ($SOCl_2$) lose a water molecule to form the corresponding nitrile. This method is widely used for preparation of nitriles which cannot be prepared by nucleophilic substitution reactions between alkyl halides and cyanide ion.

5. NITRILES

Preparation of Nitriles:

From amides:

Nitriles from amides through dehydration is a standard procedure of preparation. The dehydrating agent used are phosphorus pentoxide, phosphorus pentachloride, phosphorous oxychloride, acidic anhydride and/or silica, alumina. Very high temperatures are required.

Example:

$$R-\underset{O}{\underset{\|}{C}}-NH_2 \xrightarrow[\Delta]{P_2O_5} R-C\equiv N + H_3PO_4$$

$$Cl-CH_2-\underset{O}{\underset{\|}{C}}-NH_2 \xrightarrow[\Delta]{P_2O_5} ClCH_2C\equiv N + H_3PO_4$$

Chloroacetamide   Chloroacetonitrile

From alkyl halides:

Aliphatic nitriles can be prepared from the corresponding alkyl halide by reacting it with sodium cyanide in a solvent that dissolves both. The reaction occurs rapidly and exothemically in dimethylsulfoxide (DMSO) at room temperature.

$$R-X + CN^- \longrightarrow R-C\equiv N$$

From diazonium salts:

$$R-X + CN^- \longrightarrow R-C\equiv N$$

Aryl halides are very unreactive. Hence, aromatic nitriles cannot be prepared by above method. Aromatic nitriles are prepared from the diazonium salts (prepared from aromatic amines). Diazonium salts are treated with cuprous cyanide to give the corresponding nitrile.

Reactions of Nitriles:

Hydrolysis of nitriles:

Nitriles are hydrolysed to carboxylicacids or their salts via amides under both acidic and basic conditions.

Acidic hydrolysis:

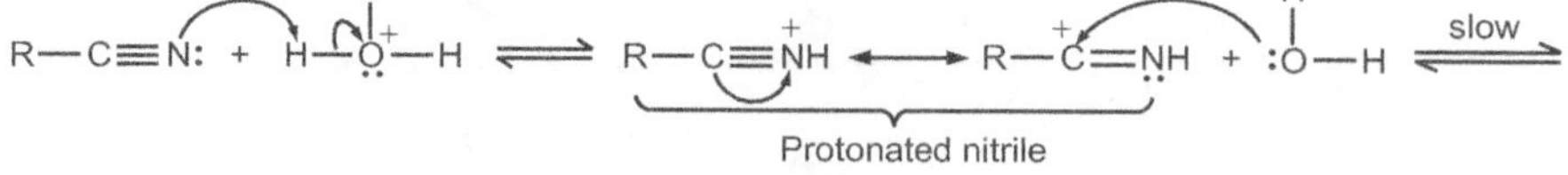

$$R-C\equiv N: + H-\overset{H}{\underset{..}{\overset{|+}{O}}}-H \rightleftharpoons \underbrace{R-C\equiv\overset{+}{N}H \longleftrightarrow R-\overset{+}{C}=NH}_{\text{Protonated nitrile}} + :\overset{H}{\underset{..}{O}}-H \xrightleftharpoons{\text{slow}}$$

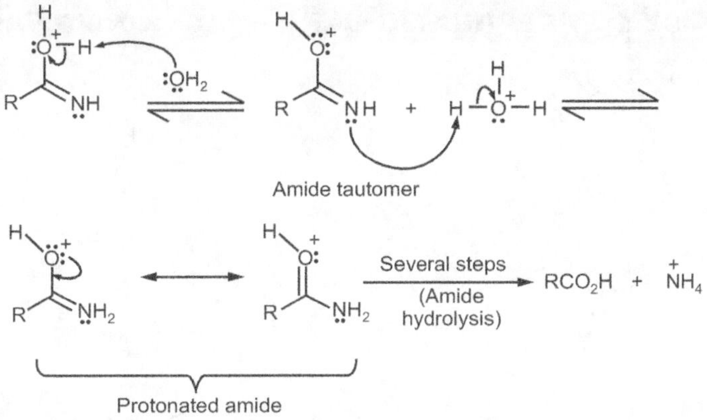

[Reaction schemes showing amide tautomer and protonated amide intermediates leading to $RCO_2H + NH_4^+$ via several steps of amide hydrolysis.]

In acidic hydrolysis, the nitrile, in the first step, is protonated. This protonation increases the polarity of the nitrile group and makes the carbon atom more susceptible to nucleophilic attack by weak nucleophile like water. The loss of proton from the oxygen atom then produces a tautomeric form of the amide. Gain of a proton at the nitrogen atom gives a protonated amide. Then the reaction follows same mechanism as that of acidic hydrolysis of amides.

Basic hydrolysis:

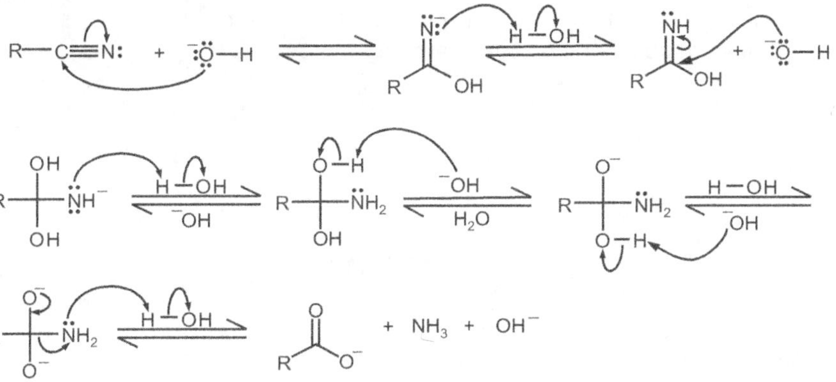

[Reaction scheme showing hydroxide attack on nitrile, progressing through intermediates to give $RCO_2^- + NH_3 + OH^-$.]

In basic hydrolysis, a hydroxide ion attacks the nitrile carbon atom, and subsequent protonation leads to the amide tautomer. Further attack by the hydroxide ion leads to hydrolysis in a manner similar to that of basic hydrolysis of amides.

SUMMARY OF PREPARATION AND REACTIONS OF AMIDES

Preparation   Reaction

6. IMIDES

Cyclic anhydrides react with ammonia to form a product that contains both –CONH$_2$ and –COOH groups. When this acid-amide is heated it loses a water molecule and the product cyclizes such that two carbonyl groups attached to nitrogen. This is called as an **imide**, as it has a double bond α-to the carbonyl carbon.

Pthalimide

7. LACTAMS

When the amide group is completely the part of cyclic system i.e., both the carbonyl carbon as well as the amine nitrogen are members of the cyclic ring. The nomenclature β, γ, δ - lactans indicated the position of the carbonyl group from the amide nitrogen.

β-lactam   γ-lactam   δ-lactam

Dicarboxylic acids:

If the substituent on a carboxylic acid is a second carboxylic acid group, the compound is a dicarboxylic acid.

$HOOCCH_2COOH$ $HOOCCH_2CH_2COOH$ $HOOC(CH_2)_4COOH$

Malonic acid   Succinic acid   Adipic acid

Dicarboxylic acids have two ionizable hydrogens. Ionization of the second carboxyl group occurs less readily than first carboxyl group. More energy is required to separate a positively charged hydrogen from the carboxylate anion.

$$\begin{array}{c}COOH\\|\\(CH_2)_n\\|\\COOH\end{array} \underset{}{\overset{K_1}{\rightleftharpoons}} H^+ + \begin{array}{c}COO^-\\|\\(CH_2)_n\\|\\COOH\end{array} \underset{}{\overset{K_2}{\rightleftharpoons}} H^+ + \begin{array}{c}COO^-\\|\\(CH_2)_n\\|\\COO^-\end{array} \quad K_1 > K_2$$

Dicarboxylic acids show same chemical behaviour as monocarboxylic acids. They can be prepared by same methods as used for monocarboxylic acids.

$$\begin{array}{c}CN\\|\\(CH_2)_n\\|\\CN\end{array} \xrightarrow{\text{Hydrolysis}} \begin{array}{c}COOH\\|\\(CH_2)_n\\|\\COOH\end{array}$$

Hydrolysis of a dinitrile yields a dicarboxylic acid.

p-xylene $\xrightarrow{KMnO_4}$ terephthalic acid (COOH on each end of benzene ring)

Oxidation of dimethylbenzenes yield dicarboxylic acid.

$$Cl-CH_2COO^-Na^+ \xrightarrow{CN^-} \begin{array}{c}COO^-Na^+\\|\\CH_2\\|\\CN\end{array}$$

Sodium chloroacetate → Sodium cynoacetate

$\xrightarrow{H_2O, H^+}$ $\begin{array}{c}COOH\\|\\CH_2\\|\\COOH\end{array}$ Malonic acid

$\xrightarrow{C_2H_5OH, H^+}$ $\begin{array}{c}COOC_2H_5\\|\\CH_2\\|\\COOC_2H_5\end{array}$ Ethyl malonate

Reactivity of carboxylic acid derivatives:

QUESTION BANK

1. What are carboxylic acids? Discuss the structure of carboxylate ion.
2. Discuss the nomenclature and classification of carboxylic acids.
3. Enumerate various methods of preparation of carboxylic acids.
4. Discuss various reactions of carboxylic acids with mechanisms.
5. Short note on dicarboxylic acids.
6. Discuss the methods of preparations and reactions of various carboxylic acid derivatives:
   (a) Amides
   (b) Anhydrides
   (c) Esters
   (d) Nitriles
   (e) Imides
   (f) Acyl chlorides
7. Discuss the physical properties as well as common and IUPAC nomenclature of carboxylic acids in brief.
8. Discuss the various chemical reactions undergone by carboxylic acids.
9. Summarize schematically the preparation and reactions of carboxylic acids.
10. Discuss the various derivatives of carboxylic acids their preparations and reactions.
11. Which is more soluble in water and why?
    $CH_3(CH_2)_8COOH$ or $HOOC(CH_2)_8COOH$
12. Which has higher b.p. and why? CH_3CH_2COOH or $CH_3CH_2CH_2COOH$.
13. Will $CH_3C(O)CH_2CH_3$ and oxidation yield an acid? Why?
14. If maliec acid is heated at 200°C, what will be the product? Give the structures.

15. What will be the product of reaction between succinic anhydride and ethanol? Give the reaction.
16. What is the name of ester formed between formic acid and ethanol?
17. If ethyl acetate is reduced with LiAlH$_4$, what will be the product?
18. Give the structures of:
    (a) N, N-dimethyl acetamide
    (b) N, N-dimethyl formamide
    (c) Phthalimide
    (d) Phthalamide
19. Which is acidic and why, phthalamide or phthalimide?
20. How will you prepare bezonitrile (phenyl cyanide) from benzamide?
21. Arrange in order of increased reactivity:
    esters, acid halides, anhydride, amides.
22. Draw the products that results from reaction of malonic ester with a base and ethyl chloride.

Index

SEMESTER I

Acidity, 6.1
Acyl Halides, 2.9
Addition – Elimination, 9.19
Addition Reactions of Alkenes, 8.3
Alcohols, 2.3
Aldehydes, 2.5
Aldoximes, 2.10
Alkanes, 2.1
Alkenes, 2.2, 2.18
Alkenes: Preparation and Reactions, 8.1, 8.3
Alkyl Halides, 2.8
Alkynes, 2.2, 2.18
Alkynes, 8.16
Allylic substitution (using NBS), 8.19
Amides, 2.9
Amines, 2,7
Anhydrides, 2.6, 2.19
Application of Inductive, 6.10
Aromatic Hydrocarbons, 2.2
Aryl Halides, 2.9
Atomic orbitals, 1.1
Basicity, 6.9
Bond energy, 1.18
Bond fission, 1.17
Carbanions, 5.7
Carbenes, 5.16
Carbocations, 5.2
Carbonyl compounds, 2.4
Carboxylic acids, 2.6, 2.18
Classes of Reactions, 4.1
Classes of reagents, 4.9
Conjugated Dienes, 8.13
Covalent bond, 1.12
Cycloalkanes, 2.2
Diels–Alder Reaction, 8.15
Dipole moment, 3.1
Distereomer, 3.10
E_1, E_2 and E_{1cB} Elimination, 8.10
Electromeric effect, 1.20
Electronegativity 1.14,
Electrophiles, 4.9
Electrophilic aromatic substitution, 9.8
Enantiomers, 3.9
Epoxides, 2.4

Ethers, 2.4
Free radicals, 5.10
Friedel Crafts reaction, 9.13
Geometric isomerism, 3.8
Halogen Halide, 8.7
Halogenation, 9.10
Halohydrin Formation, 8.8
Hukel's Rule, 9.5
Hybridization of atomic orbitals of carbon, 1.6
Hydrazines, 2.8
Hydroboration – Oxidation, 8.9
Hydrogen bonding, 1.15
Hydrogen bonding, 3.5
Hydroxylation, 8.9
Hyperconjugation, 1.24
Hyperconjugation, 6.13
Imides, 2,10
Imines, 2.7
Inductive effect, 1.19
Intermolecular forces, 3.2
Isomerism, 3.7
Ketones, 2.5
Ketoximes, 2.10
Mechanism of nucleophilic aromatic substitution, 9.18
Meso-compounds, 3.10
Mesomeric effect, 1.21
Molecular orbitals, 1.4
Net result, 4.3
Nitration, 9.9
Nitrene 5.14
Nitrenium ions, 5.15
Nitriles, 2.7
Nitro compounds, 2.10
Nucleophiles, 4.10
Orientation and reactivity in monosubstituted benzene, 9.15
Oxymercuration–Demercuration, 8.8
Ozonolysis, 8.10
Phenols, 2.4
Polarity of molecules, 3.1
Reactions of Alkanes, 7.1
Regioselectivity, 8.4

Resonance effects, 6.13
Resonance in benzene and derivatives, 9.4
Saytzeff and Hoffman rules, 8.12
Stereoisomerism, 3.7
Steric effect, 6.14
Sulphonamides, 2.11

Sulphonation, 9.12
Sulphonic acids, 2.10
Sulphonylhalides, 2.11
Tautomerism, 1.26
Theory of reaction mechanism, 1.19

SEMESTER II

Acetal, 1.13
Acid chloride, 9.17
Acidity of Phenols, 2.2
Acyl chlorides, 9.15
Alcohols, 4.1
Aldehydes, 1.7
Aldol condensation, 1.23
Alkyl halides, 8.1
Amides, 9.25
Amines, 5.1
Ammonolysis of esters, 7.9
Anhydrides, 9.17
Borodin reaction, 8.7
Cannizarro's reaction, 1.23
Carbinol system, 4.2
Carboxyl, 9.1
Carboxylic acid, 9.1
Claisen reactions, 7.1
Cyanides, 6.1
Dicarboxylic acids, 9.1, 9.30
Dichrome test, 4.9
Dieckmann reactions, 7.2
Dow process, 2.3
Elimination, 8.18
Enamine, 1.21
Esters, 9.20
Ethers, 4.10
Fischer esterification, 9.11
Grignard Reagents and Hydrides, 1.22
Haloform reaction, 1.25
Hinsberg method, 5.5
Hoffmann's method, 5.5
Hydrazones, 1.18
Hydrogen bonding, 4.3

Imides, 9.29
Imine, 1.17
Initiation, 8.4
Isocyanides, 6.1
Ketones, 1.9
Kinetics, 8.11
Knoevenagel reaction, 1.25
Kolbe reaction, 2.9
Lactams, 9.29
Libermann's Nitrosamine test, 5.8
Lucas test, 4.9
Mannich reaction, 1.26
Michael addition, 7.6
MPV reduction, 1.22
Nitriles, 9.27
Oximes, 1.16
Perkin reaction, 1.25
Phenol, 2.1
Propagation, 8.4
Reactions of Amines, 5.6
Reformatsky reaction, 1.24
Sandmeyer reactions, 5.11
Semicarbazones, 1.19
Separation of amines, 5.4
SN_1, 8.10
SN_2, 8.12
SN_i, 8.14
Substitution, 8.18
Sulphonic acid, 3.1
Termination, 8.4
Thorpe nuitrile condensation, 6.3
Williamson synthesis, 2.11, 4.11

■■■

www.ingramcontent.com/pod-product-compliance
Lightning Source LLC
Chambersburg PA
CBHW080422230426
43662CB00015B/2181